Edinburgh Jazz Enlightenment

The Story of Edinburgh Traditional Jazz

– GRAHAM BLAMIRE –

An environmentally friendly book printed and bound in England by
www.printondemand-worldwide.com

Mixed Sources
Product group from well-managed
forests, and other controlled sources
www.fsc.org Cert no. TT-COC-002641
© 1996 Forest Stewardship Council
FSC

PEFC Certified
This product is
from sustainably
managed forests
and controlled
sources
PEFC
PEFC/16-33-415
www.pefc.org

This book is made entirely of chain-of-custody materials

www.fast-print.net/store.php

Edinburgh Jazz Enlightenment –
The Story of Edinburgh Traditional Jazz
Copyright © Graham Blamire 2012

ISBN 978-178035-290-9

First published 2012 by
FASTPRINT PUBLISHING
Peterborough, England.

About The Author

Graham Blamire

(from the collection of the author, photographer unknown)

The author is a double bass player who began playing traditional jazz in Edinburgh in the late 1950s, starting before he had left school. Over the course of more than 50 years, he has played with many of the local bands and has had many opportunities to play with well-known visiting jazz musicians. A habitual keeper of notes and scrap books, he accumulated a wealth of information and anecdotes about his own playing experiences and about those with whom he played. After the advent of home computers, he began compiling and organising a data bank about the individual jazz musicians and bands during his time in Edinburgh. He also began collecting information from others involved, including some who remembered jazz in Edinburgh well before his time. A member at one time or another of the well-known Edinburgh bands 'Old Bailey and his Jazz Advocates', 'The Scottish Jazz Advocates', 'The Louisiana Ragtime Band' and 'The Spirits of Rhythm', he played innumerable gigs and festivals and made a number of recordings, broadcasts and television appearances. For over 25 years, he has led the four-piece 'Maid of the Forth Stompers', entertaining passengers on the cruise boat 'The Maid of the Forth', sailing from South Queensferry on the Firth of Forth.

Dedication

This book about Edinburgh traditional jazz is dedicated to the 'punters', those loyal, enthusiastic and much-valued followers of local jazz who, over the years and decades, turned up in support at the pubs, clubs and jazz events. Without them there would have been no real local jazz scene at all and nothing for me to write about.

JGB 2011

Lino cut by and with the permission of Ian Boyter

Author's Foreword and Acknowledgements

In writing this book, I had the support and assistance of many people. Many of my jazz colleagues willingly (as far as I knew) gave of their time as I ransacked their memories, sometimes of events that had taken place anything up to 60 years ago. I am particularly grateful to those who were able to tell me about pre-1960s Edinburgh jazz, which largely pre-dated my personal experience. They included: Billy Alison, Jim Baikie, Dougie Campbell, Ron Carruthers, Roger Craik, Peter Davenport, Jim Douglas, Fionna Duncan, Iain Forde, Fraser Gauld, Jimmy Gavin, George Hewitt, Dizzy Jackson, Dave Keir, Pete Kerr, Ralph Laing, Andrew Lauder, Jake McMahon, Kenny and Violet Milne, Fred Murray, Jim Petrie, Mike Pollett, Ronnie Rae, Ken Ramage, Bill Salmond, Bobby Stewart, Norrie Thomson, Jim Walker, Jack Weddell, Brian Weld and Jim Young.

A great deal of information was made freely available to me by John Latham of the Sandy Brown Society, Ian Maund who runs the Sandy Brown Jazz website and Jim Keppie of the Edinburgh Jazz Archive Group. I also received support and help from writers who have published material about Edinburgh jazz, including Alastair Clark, John Gibson, Kenny Mathieson and Tony Troon, and the local newspapers, the Scotsman and Edinburgh Evening News. I also wish to acknowledge the help and encouragement that I received from Mike Hart, Founding Director of the Edinburgh International Jazz and Blues Festival. I wish to acknowledge the power of meticulous work put in by Norrie

Thomson in compiling the discography appendix. I must also mention Donald 'Chick' Murray, school pal and so often rhythm section comrade-in-arms, without whose prompting (ie nagging) I might never have got started.

This is not a critical account but is intended as an affectionate look at the story of traditional jazz in a City that bred so many fine jazz musicians and supported the music over so many decades. The book traces a chronological sequence from about 1920 until the first decade of the 21st Century. Throughout the book are profiles of many of the personalities who made Edinburgh traditional jazz what it was and is; the profiles are usually placed chronologically, either at the point where an individual first appeared on the jazz scene or when he or she made their greatest impact. The profiles vary greatly in length. This should not be taken as a measure of an individual's significance but merely as the product of how much information was available and the extent to which his story reflects a particular period. The sharp-eyed will undoubtedly spot a few anomalies and contradictions and, in an account that has relied on memories stretching back over many decades, who could wonder at that?

I have made no attempt to cover the development in Edinburgh of modern jazz, by which I mean jazz which stems from the harmonic and rhythmic advances of bebop and post-bebop jazz. Although I have included a number of jazz musicians who were able to play in both the traditional and more modern forms, I am simply not qualified, either by playing or listening experience, to do justice to the development of these important and more modern forms. It is my hope that someone else will write the story of Edinburgh modern jazz, perhaps as a companion to this volume.

Every effort has been made to identify and acknowledge copyright holders of material referred to or reproduced in this book, and I apologise for any omissions. To my regret, all efforts to trace the current holders of copyright in respect of two books by James Lincoln Collier, 'The Making of Jazz' and 'Louis Armstrong – a biography', have been unsuccessful. In addition, it has also proved impossible to trace the current copyright holders of Sinclair Traill's book

'Concerning Jazz', published in 1957 by Faber and Faber. A number of the photographs date from many years ago and, in many cases, the identity of the photographer has long been forgotten. Never-the-less, the efforts of these photographers in ensuring that the Edinburgh jazz scene of their time was put on the record is acknowledged and I apologise for the lack of individual acknowledgement.

I also wish to acknowledge the support and forbearance of my wife, Liz, and the rest of my family who, for over two years, became accustomed to my normal (or perhaps I should say usual) behaviour being replaced by a sort of mental and physical limbo, while I researched and struggled to write this account.

To all of these I am grateful for their patience, kindness, interest and support. So many people told me that the story of Edinburgh traditional jazz had to be written sometime. I hope I have done it justice.

Graham Blamire, December 2011.

Foreword by Mike Hart MBE

Founding Director, Edinburgh International Jazz and Blues Festival

There can be no doubt that the story of Edinburgh traditional jazz deserved to be written down. The City has had a long link with the music which, although it began as a purely American phenomenon, has become, over the last hundred years or so, perhaps the most significant musical development of the 20th century. Jazz now straddles the whole world but, like any worthwhile art form, continues to operate at all levels: from international to local, from amateur to professional, from high art to playing for personal pleasure, from the great concert halls to the local pub. Edinburgh traditional jazz has all of these and a jazz history that has now lasted for almost a hundred years. It is that story that this book is all about. It traces the major developments, the notable events, the memorable bands and, most of all, the personalities that made the story. It is sometimes assumed that jazz in Edinburgh began in the 1940s. However, this is not so and it is interesting and surprising to be able to read something of the Edinburgh jazz world of the 1920s and 30s. That this early period is covered is one indication of just how much work has gone into the writing of this book.

There have been, of course, a number of well-known high points in the history of Edinburgh traditional jazz. These include the pioneering days of the 1940s and early 1950s, which produced an astonishing number of fine players, such as Sandy Brown, Al Fairweather, Stan Greig, Archie Semple and Alex Welsh, who were to make their mark in both UK and world terms. There was also the spell during the 1980s, when the Edinburgh International Jazz Festival was graced by the presence of some of the legends of middle period jazz, including players of the stature of Harry 'Sweets' Edison, Buddy Tate, Teddy Wilson, Jay McShann, George Chisholm, Earle Warren, Dick Hyman, Al Grey, Milt Hinton and Doc Cheatham.

However, this book is about much more than the great names and great times. Notable as these were, it is good to have the emphasis on the jazz musicians and bands which made the jazz scene of Edinburgh surely one of the most active and buoyant in the UK, if not in the whole of Europe. Jazz is a music that demands character in both the music itself and the people who play it and Edinburgh jazz has had plenty of both. Who could forget the drive and excitement of the playing of Tello (Ian Telford), Dave Paxton, Jim Petrie or John McGuff? What about the sheer musicality of Alex Shaw's piano playing? Or the rumbustious humour and energy of Charlie McNair? Or, for that matter, the commitment and dedication of those, including all the above, who played jazz in their chosen style, because they believed it to be a music of great worth, with a tradition that should be kept alive?

Edinburgh has been fortunate in having so many jazz musicians, so many jazz bands and so much jazz. However, none of it would have meant much without the support it received from the public and it is good to see that this book is dedicated to the jazz followers. I said that the story of Edinburgh traditional jazz deserved to be written down. Now it has been and Graham Blamire has done the Edinburgh jazz world a service. I wish the book well.

Mike Hart, Edinburgh, December 2011

Contents

Chapter I

Prelude to a Tidal Wave

This book is primarily concerned with the story of traditional jazz in Edinburgh since the mid-nineteen forties; that is, traditional jazz played in and around Edinburgh by local jazz musicians and bands. It is not much concerned with jazz played in and around Edinburgh by visiting bands, professional or otherwise, except in passing and when such bands have had a marked effect on local jazz, this being especially the case in the early years. Similarly, the significant number of local jazz musicians who went on to become distinguished or even famous professional players at a UK or international level, will primarily be discussed in respect of their careers when playing in Edinburgh in local bands, rather than their contributions in a wider and better known context. In some cases, the wider reputations will be covered more than adequately in more resounding publications than this.

Jazz, as a recognisable form of music, appears to have emerged in the USA sometime during the last decade of the 19th century and the first decade of the 20th century. Over the years since, the music, in the first place a product of many cultures, developed in a number of ways and in a number of places. The result was that different styles of jazz became recognisable. These included, for example, the classic New Orleans styles of the 1920s as played by Joe 'King' Oliver, Louis Armstrong, Sydney Bechet and Jelly Roll Morton, although not necessarily played exclusively in New Orleans. There was a style that developed in Kansas City

1

and was typified by the bands of Benny Moten and later, Count Basie. In Harlem, jazz was played by stride piano players such as James P Johnston, Willie 'The Lion' Smith and Fats Waller and the band of Duke Ellington in the 1920s and 1930s. A group of white youngsters in Chicago, inspired by the great black bands and a white trumpet player called Bix Beiderbecke, founded what came to be known as Chicago jazz. Another predominately white style, which came to be called Swing in the mid-1930s and early 1940s, was exemplified by the music of Benny Goodman, Tommy Dorsey, Artie Shaw and their big bands. By then, jazz had spread to many countries, particularly to France and the UK, and had become recognised as an artistic phenomenon which was to be the major influence in 20th century popular music.

Of course, jazz in the early days (or 'jass' as it was apparently then spelt) had not been welcomed with open arms by everybody. It was a new and, to many, an alarmingly aggressive sound. In addition, it was no longer safely obscure but, because of the new-fangled radio and phonograph machines, suddenly in everybody's ears. Established standards of music and taste were being challenged and swept aside; musical mayhem and anarchy had arrived. Even in New Orleans, its apparent birthplace, it was hardly surprising that a music that had close associations with the Red Light district was going to upset the city fathers. Jim Godbolt, the jazz writer and historian, in his book 'The World of Jazz - in printed ephemera and collectibles'[1], reports that a 1918 edition of the New Orleans 'Times-Picayune' referred to jazz as a *'form of musical vice'* and said *'Its musical value is nil, and its possibilities of harm are great'*. Jim also adds that, as early as 1921, the Ladies Home Journal posed the question *'Does jazz put the sin in syncopation?'* and reports that *'...children of all ages, removed the 'J' from posters'* when bands were advertised as 'jass bands'. There are other accounts of such unflattering terms as 'unspeakable jazz' and 'filthy jazz', which, in all probability, simply acted as a major motivator towards jazz

---

[1] Godbolt J,, 'The World of Jazz in Printed Ephemera and Collectibles', Studio Editions Ltd, 1990, by permission of Jim Godbolt

for the rebellious youth of the time. However, these Blimpish reactions were hardly a new phenomenon in society and were to be repeated at intervals throughout the history of 20th Century music even, perhaps more surprisingly, within jazz itself, whenever the more radical developments took place.

Sometime around the late 1930s or early 1940s, there began two dramatic and opposite developments, one looking forward to the future and one looking back to the past. These were firstly, the advent of new concepts of rhythm and harmony which led to the development of bebop and the later variations of modern jazz. Secondly, there arose what the distinguished American musicologist and critic, James Lincoln Collier, called *'a tidal wave of traditional jazz'*[2] – a world-wide movement back towards earlier forms of jazz and a rejection of Swing and the modern developments of bebop. This 'tidal wave' came to be called the Revival. It is principally what took place in Edinburgh in the wake of the Revival, from the mid-1940s on, with which this book is concerned. However, before exploring that, what had been Edinburgh's jazz history up to that point?

It seems perfectly clear that there was jazz activity in Edinburgh before the mid-1940s, although not a great deal is known about it. At the time of writing in 2011, it seems unlikely that there are many people alive who will remember much about those now distant days. There are however, a few sources of information.

In particular, there was one jazz musician who was active in Edinburgh in the 1950s and who, as a professional journalist, occasionally produced articles about jazz. One or two of these give a brief account of the pre-war period. He was the late George Crockett, a drummer who played in Edinburgh in the 1940s and 50s and who later moved to work and live in the west of Scotland. Much of the information in this chapter is taken from his published work. Although George had left Edinburgh by the time I

[2] Collier J L, 'The Making of Jazz – a Comprehensive History' Granada Publishing 1978. Every effort has been made to trace the current holder of copyright for this work but without success.

was making my way into the Edinburgh jazz scene in about 1959, I met him several times and played in a band with him on at least one occasion. In particular, I remember meeting him in 1988 when he turned up at a gig at which I played with Bill Salmond's Louisiana Ragtime Band in the Harbour Arts Centre in Irvine, on the Ayrshire coast. George did not play on that occasion but, in his capacity as a journalist, he wrote a review of the gig in a local paper. It seemed to me that he was a jazz enthusiast whose interest extended beyond listening and playing into the historical and sociological background of the music.

According to George in an article[3] published in the Edinburgh Weekly in 1966, there had been an interest in jazz in Edinburgh since the end of the Great War in 1918. With the possible exception of the days of the so-called 'trad boom' in the early 1960s, jazz generally has been a minority interest since the World War II. However, George considered that the time when jazz enjoyed its greatest local popularity was as a new and novel form of dance in the early 1920s. He says that the first person to bring jazz to Edinburgh was a piano player called **Symon Stungo**. Stungo formed a five-piece band inspired by the Original Dixieland Jazz Band (ODJB), the white American band which had an enormous impact when they came from the USA to take London by storm at the Hammersmith Palais in 1919. Stungo's band, like the ODJB, had trumpet, clarinet, trombone, piano and drums. It is not clear from George's writing where the Stungo band was based and they may have come from elsewhere to play in Edinburgh. It appears that the band was called **Symon Stungo and his Jazz-maniacs** and George speculates that Edinburgh must have taken to jazz much as London had taken to the ODJB.

Reports of the time tell us that the ODJB had come as something of a shock to polite London society of 1919. They had opened at Albert de Courville's 'Joy Bells' at the Hippodrome but these self styled 'musical anarchists' did

---

[3] Crockett G, Edinburgh Weekly, 22 December 1966, 'From the Twenties to the Sixties – All That Jazz in Edinburgh'. All efforts to trace the copyright holder of this article have failed but the author wishes to acknowledge the valuable record that this article represents. Information used by kind permission of Eileen Mack, closest living relative of George Crockett.

not last long there.   The comedian George Robey was apparently on the bill and it was at his instigation that the ODJB were hastily removed from the programme.   Robey, who is said to have regarded them as an abomination, seems just as likely to have been highly miffed at being upstaged by these brash newcomers.   Whatever, the ODJB went on to a very successful nine month run at the Hammersmith Palais and twentieth century music was never to be the same again.   I have no doubt that the impact of Stungo's outfit on staid Edinburgh society would be similar - the punk rockers of their day, upsetting those you would expect and delighting the returning survivors of the war who would, no doubt, take all the cathartic, social amusement they could get, after the tensions and repressions of 'the war to end all wars'.   The so-called Jazz Age of the 1920s had begun, even in staid old Edinburgh. George Crockett goes on to tell us that, in Edinburgh, a friend of Stungo's converted an old drill-hall into the Wemyss Ballroom, where he intended to feature jazz.   This was apparently at a time when other Edinburgh dance halls still had notices instructing that there was *'No jazzing allowed'*, no doubt to the relief of local George Robeys and stately Edinburgh matrons with their knickers in a twist.

Stungo had been asked by this friend to bring his band to play in Edinburgh.   This suggests that he was based elsewhere but it does sound fairly likely that they were a Scottish band and, indeed, it seems that Stungo may well have run more than one band.   Apparently, the popularity of the Stungo band or bands was not confined to Edinburgh and George Crockett says that they *'...opened the Tay Street Palais in Dundee and the Aberdeen Music Hall dances'*. They also played at the Bobby Jones Ballroom in Ayr.   In Edinburgh, Stungo had bands at the North British Hotel (now the New Balmoral but still the NB), the Oak Room Cafe in the New Picture House (apparently where Marks and Spencers shop was situated in Princes Street in 1966) and at the Havana night club, which by 1966 had become the Pibroch Restaurant.   These venues, particularly the North British Hotel, were prestigious places and it seems reasonable to assume that Stungo ran bands of some quality and reputation.   Al Stewart, an Edinburgh dance band and jazz musician who was playing in Edinburgh in the 1920s and still active in the 1990s, gives a slightly different account. Al, in an article published in an Edinburgh jazz magazine, The Scottish Jazz News, in the early 1990s, says *'The first jazz band imported from London in 1926 was Symon Stungo's Jazz Maniacs which contained Nick Ivanoff* (an Edinburgh musician). *They played in the Marine Gardens for wages of, believe it or not, £25 a week each. I'll leave you to work out what that would be at today's values'*[4].

Apparently, it was from the Havana Club that Stungo's band was included in a list of bands for some early broadcasting which George Crockett says presented *'...a form of jazz or let's settle for jazz-oriented dance music'*. Stungo managed to attract show business stars from the old Empire Theatre or the King's Theatre to drop in at the club after their shows, when he gave them a champagne supper and would persuade them to do a spot. Some, at least, appear to have been jazz musicians as, on one occasion, Symon Stungo persuaded Coleman Hawkins, the great American tenor sax player, to visit the club. George estimates that this must have been in the early 1930s, when Hawkins was touring Britain with the Jack Hylton band. Thanks to the work of Jim Keppie and the Edinburgh Jazz Archive Group, we know that Symon Stungo had attended the Royal High School of Edinburgh. This was the school which was later to gain considerable renown in the jazz world as the producer of an almost incredible number of jazz musicians, some of them of international stature. In particular, the 1940s and 1950s would see the school produce so many jazz musicians that they became known collectively as the 'Royal High School Gang', of whom we will hear a great deal more later in this book. Jim Keppie, himself a former pupil of the school, also tells us that Symon Stungo, in his eighties at the time, played ragtime piano at a concert at the Old Royal High School on 30th November 1974, accompanied by two rather younger alumni of his old school, Dizzy Jackson (bs) and John

---

[4] Stewart A, Scottish Jazz News, Volume 2, issue 5 , July/August 1990

Nicholson (drms)[5]. It looks as if Symon Stungo was the very first of the Royal High School jazz musicians that we know about, the first of what was to be a long and distinguished line.

George Crockett goes on to comment that the depression years of the early thirties *'put jazz in the doldrums'*. However, when the Swing craze swept the USA in the mid to late 1930s, *'Britain was unmoved in the mass but collectors of jazz recordings were multiplying and most large cities had rhythm clubs'*. George had access to some copies from 1935 of a magazine called Swing Music which, even when he was writing in 1966, was long defunct. These magazines carried reports from the rhythm clubs and, although there were such clubs in Glasgow and a thriving one in Dundee, there was no mention of a rhythm club in Edinburgh at that time. George's own introduction to live jazz, rather than on gramophone records or the meagre ration provided by BBC radio, was when he heard the great Fats Waller in early 1939, at the old Empire Theatre. Fats shared the bill with a programme of variety troupers including comedians and acrobats. George reports that the theatre was half empty and that two elderly ladies sitting near him read out *'Fats Waller, rhythm pianist'* in the programme and wondered *'Who's he?'* When Fats made his appearance, he apparently made little impression on the elderly ladies but certainly impressed George.

Fats Waller was, of course, already a legend in jazz by that time and was renowned for working hard, living hard and playing hard. Fats' manager at the time, Ed Kirby, recalled an incident during this 1939 visit to Edinburgh when, after his show was over, Fats paid a visit to the Havana Club, where he consumed a generous quantity of his favourite brand of gin. Ed and Fats had later left the club in the 'wee sma' hours', got into a taxi and headed for wherever they were staying. As the taxi was heading up the Mound, a steep and winding street leading off Princes Street, Fats somehow contrived to fall out of the taxi. Ed Kirby is reported as saying *'I shouted to the taxi driver to*

---

[5] Later known as the actor, John McGlynn

stop the damn cab. I was glad to see Fats pick himself up and catch up with the cab as if nothing had happened.'

Also early in 1939, Coleman Hawkins made another visit to Edinburgh, this time on a private tour sponsored by the Selmer saxophone company, and a private show for the local trade took place at the Kintore Rooms. George comments that he considered this to be *'more like it'* and that Hawkins blew in front of a local rhythm section which, he reports, *'acquitted themselves very well'*. As far as he was able to recall, the rhythm section included Bill Stark, who was later to play with the Vic Lewis band, on bass, Eddie Canelli on guitar, George Buchanan on piano and a *'very fine Edinburgh drummer'* called Jackie McHardie. Jackie McHardie was later to pursue his musical career in the south and George reports that, in about 1965, he was playing with George Chisholm's Jazzers in the Black and White Minstrel Show (how non-PC can you get?) at London's Victoria Palace Theatre. Apparently there was a *'hip audience'* present for the show at the Kintore Rooms and this inspired Hawkins to an excellent performance. George Crockett commented that he was always glad to have heard this performance, because Coleman Hawkins was at the peak of his creative ability during this period.

Another journalistic source of information about the 1930s is an article written by the Scotsman newspaper jazz writer and critic Tony Troon, in the programme notes for the Edinburgh International Jazz Festival in 1986. In this article, Tony reports that *'Edinburgh has a strong jazz and dance-band tradition and in the thirties supported no fewer than 36 dance halls. Visiting American musicians, like Fats Waller, Coleman Hawkins and Benny Carter, played one-night stands here during that decade'*[6].

Al Stewart, whom we have already met, was born in about 1909. We know this because he wrote to the local 'Scottish Jazz News' in January 1990, to thank everyone who had helped make his surprise eightieth birthday party, at the Blue Lagoon pub, such a success. Al played both double bass and alto saxophone and was still active as a

---

[6] Troon A, 'The Second Chorus Factor', McEwen's Edinburgh International Jazz Festival programme, 1986

regular 'sitter in' on the Edinburgh jazz scene in the 1990s. He also contributed three brief articles to the Scottish Jazz News[7], recording his memories of jazz and dance music in pre-WWII Edinburgh. By the mid-1920s, Al was already on the road to becoming an active musician and, when he was around fifteen years old, he had already tried *'putting some beat'* into tunes like 'Alexanders', 'Who's Sorry Now?' and 'Dinah' on his mouth organ. While at Boroughmuir High School, he had received a few lessons on double bass, which he said was *'very rare in those days'*, presumably meaning the lessons rather than the double bass. Sometime during the next couple of years, he managed to buy a clarinet for 7/6d (about 35 pence in today's money) and started to play at socials and Boys Brigade dances the next week. He also tells us that music had started to change around that time, with bands like the Harlem Foot Warmers, 'Henderson', 'Lunceford' and 'Armstrong' heralding what was to become 'swing music', and adds that *'...jazz as we know it today really took off'*. In Edinburgh, Al reports, the people responsible were *'...Frankie Smith (trumpet), Nick Ivanoff (tenor sax), Bill Landles (alto sax) and at least half a dozen more, really good jazz men'*. He adds that probably the best of them all was Jimmy Miller (violin) who was *'as good as Venuti'* (Joe Venuti, the great American jazz violinist) and suggests that George Chisholm would verify this, having played a few gigs with Miller in Edinburgh in the early 1930s. The piano and accordion wizard was apparently Chrissie Colette and the guitar ace was Eddie Canale. Al goes on tell us that the place to be was the New Dunedin, which was half way down the steps off the Lawnmarket. After the war, this venue became known as the Anchor Palais and was owned by Billy Fawcet. Fawcet was a bass player for whom Al sometimes deputised ('depped' in jazz parlance), as he could not play and run the ballroom at the same time. Others whom Al remembers as having played at this venue were Derick McLean (alto), Bobby Stewart senior (drums), Archie McLean, brother of Derick (piano), Jimmy Miller (violin), Eddie Canale (guitar), Bobby Jack (sax), Allan Thompson (sax) and a trumpet

---

[7] Stewart A, Scottish Jazz News, Volume 2 issues 5 and 7, Volume 3 issue 3, 1990

player whose name Al could not recall.   Apparently, everyone in town who could play jazz went along to this place to sit in, including Chrissie Colette (piano), Chick Knox (trumpet), Alfie Bell (drums), Tom, Reg and Jack Rutherford who were all drummers, Al Wilson (piano), Nick Ivanoff (ten sax), Bill Landles (alto sax), Bertie Roy (alto sax) and many others.

Another venue of the time was the Star Cafe, which was at the bottom of Easter Road *'in one of the tunnels on the left'.* Al remembers that, in the early days, the bandstand at this place was high up on the wall, with an old tram spiral stair to climb up! Later, the bandstand was shifted to the floor, as the previous arrangement had only been safe for piano, drums and four musicians, although Al recalls *'...seeing eight up there and, Dagostino, who was the owner couldn't do much about it. On a bottle of whisky a day, he couldn't see that far'!* The personnel at the Star Cafe were Nick Ivanoff (tenor-fiddle, leader), Alfie Bell (drums), Al Weston (piano) and Al Stewart himself on bass and alto sax. Many other musicians also played there, including Angus Mailland and Chick Know (trumpets), someone called 'Melville' instrument unknown, Chrissie Colette (piano and accordion), Bill Landles, Bertie Roy, Andy 'Choo' Richardson and Jock Wright (reeds).   Al Stewart finished his 1990 memoir by saying *'All these people, and many more, beyond my memory now, played a lot of jazz there in the early thirties'.*

As already stated, by the 1940s, jazz had already developed a number of quite recognisable styles, not surprising in a music that had, by then, had the best part of half a century in which to develop.   The jazz history books tell us that it was the re-discovery of a number of almost forgotten New Orleans based veterans that sparked off the Revival.   However, as time was to demonstrate, the Revival would itself both reflect and, to some extent at least, replicate some of the stylistic changes that had appeared in the first forty to fifty years of jazz history.   Of course, the question arises as to what style (or styles) of jazz was to appear in Edinburgh in the mid 1940s, when the Revival, James Lincoln Collier's *'tidal wave of traditional jazz',* first arrived in town. That and what followed it, is what the rest of this book will be about.

Another question that is worth asking is what was the attitude to jazz at the time of the Revival? In art, there is often a tension between a very earnest, 'art for art's sake' approach on the one hand and a populist, usually more commercially slanted, showmanship on the other, with all degrees in between. Jazz was and is certainly no different. A glance at jazz writings around the time of the Revival, such as those of Rudi Blesh in the USA and Rex Harris in the UK, will quickly demonstrate that it was a time of earnest research and romantic, nostalgic reflection.

Further information about Edinburgh jazz at that time comes from the recollections of the redoubtable Jackie MacFarlane, a remarkable and resilient character who had a career in the City Cleansing Department and had fought in the Spanish Civil War. Jackie was around the Edinburgh jazz scene and sang with many bands in Edinburgh, from the 1940s through to his death in 1993. Happily for us, Jackie recorded many of his memories when he was interviewed for a feature in the programme of the 1980 Edinburgh International Jazz Festival[8]. It appears that he had kept a *voluminous scrapbook* about his jazz experiences in Edinburgh and, with the help of this, was able to recall events back to *about 1940 when he went to see Fats Waller in the Empire Theatre*. It seems likely that this was, in fact, the visit of Fats Waller in 1939, as described above in George Crockett's recollections. Jackie remembered an advertisement for the Edinburgh Rhythm Club, which was to meet in the studios at Methven Simpson's music shop in Princes Street. As this was after Jackie returned from war time service in the forces, it was probably around the middle 1940s. At this club, he met a young man called David Mylne, later to become a noted collector of and authority on recorded jazz, especially the work of Sydney Bechet. The meetings of the Edinburgh Rhythm Club, according to Jackie, were at first sessions which featured only recordings of jazz, which contrasts with

---

[8] The Edinburgh International Jazz Festival 1980 programme, page 23 'Jackie looks back'

11

George Crockett's account above. He goes on to say that live jazz first appeared after the war, at the YWCA in Reigo Street and that this involved such names as Sandy Brown, Al Fairweather, Stan Grieg and Archie Semple. Jackie, who was a life-long teetotaller, reports sardonically that tea and lemonade were served and that 'the really bad boys had to go across the road to the pub for stronger stuff'. As the next few decades were to demonstrate more than adequately, Jackie's 'really bad boys' must have rapidly achieved a dominant role, which was soon to establish the pub as the natural habitat of local jazz activity.

Yet another good source of information about the late 1940s and early 1950s is George Hewitt, one of the remarkably large group of Royal High School of Edinburgh pupils, who were at the heart of the traditional jazz Revival in Edinburgh. George Hewitt, a trombone player is, at the time of writing in 2011, still playing and putting on a monthly jazz concert in the Harbour Arts Centre in Irvine, Ayrshire. George, in a memoire written in 2008, like George Crockett and Jackie MacFarlane, gives information about the Edinburgh Rhythm Club in which he says:

"According to Stu Eaton (and who would want to disagree with him?), the Edinburgh Rhythm Club had its first meetings in the mid-1940s in a room above Methven Simpson's in Princes Street (SBSoc, NL, 58)[9]. The next location seems to have been at 20 Hill Street (SBSoc, NL,117&118). Thereafter there were the David Mylne sessions, already described (see later), followed, it would appear, by a similar set up at the Lidop Hotel at Douglas Crescent (SBSoc, NL, 135). By 1952-53 the Crown Bar known as the 'Stud Club' in Lothian Street, was one jazz centre while another was the India Buildings in Victoria Street where Dave Milne operated on Sundays. I can recall playing there at least a couple of times in 1955-56 with the Eagle Jazzmen – I think that great character and ubiquitous figure Jackie MacFarlane insisted on singing with us – but other 'survivors' e.g. Dizzy Jackson and Mike Hart are much better sources for both these venues than myself."

John Latham, who was to be instrumental in establishing the Sandy Brown Society (SBS) in 1996, told

[9] Sandy Brown Society (SBS), Newsletter 58

me that he seems to remember Stuart Crockett[10] saying that the room used by the Rhythm Club in 20 Hill Street was also used by Orkney and Shetland islanders as a social club.

Jackie MacFarlane also says that in 1950, the Archie Semple Band was formed and played regularly at monthly Jazz Band Balls in the Oddfellows Hall in Forrest Road. Jackie was what he called a *'purveyor of peace'* or bouncer at these events. On occasions he shared this task with an ex-art college male model called 'Big Tam' Connery, later to achieve world-wide fame as the film actor Sean Connery. The next venue for live jazz was the Escom Jazz Club, named by Archie Semple after a well known building in Johannnesburgh (why is not recorded), and located in the Tolbooth Hall in the High Street. Jackie reports that, during these years, there was a Musician's Union ban on foreign bands and it was the early 1950s before the first of the touring bands appeared in the form of Graeme Bell's Australian Jazz Band. This was an event which took place in the West End Cafe in Shandwick Place, near the west end of Princes Street. Another band to appear was Mick Mulligan's Magnolia Jazz Band, with a very young singer called George Melly. Freddie Randall, the 'Deb's Delight', and his band regularly appeared alongside the Sandy Brown Band, as did Joe Daniels and his Hot Shots, with whom Jackie made several guest appearances. Jackie also recalled a period when the Edinburgh Jazz Club had difficulty finding premises, having been thrown out of one venue after another (see also Chapter VII). At one point, the only home available to them was the basement of a pet shop in London Road where they were surrounded by the pet shop stock including flying foxes, snakes, rabbits and budgies. The banjo and guitar player, Mike Hart, also recalled playing there while being watched by a large flying fox, a type of bat, hanging upside down from a nearby shelf.

The MacFarlane scrapbook is said to have included some *'rather embarrassing photos'* said to have shown a fifteen year old Mike Hart (later founder and Director of the Edinburgh International Jazz Festival) *'playing drums with*

---

[10] See chapter IV

Sandy Brown, Charlie McNair, Dizzy Jackson et al on a tram returning from a gig in Musselburgh'.

Apparently the drums kept rolling off the driver's platform onto the road and the tram had to be stopped about three times, much to the annoyance of the 'clippie'.

The Oddfellows Hall in 2010 – scene of many an early Jazz Band Ball (photograph by the author)

It is unclear whether the above implies that the various musicians were actually playing jazz on the tram or simply travelling on it with their instruments but it would not surprise me if they had been playing. Concerts around that time in the Usher Hall featured big names such as Billy Eckstine, Frankie Laine, Big Bill Broonzy, Josh White and Sarah Vaughan and it was Jackie's habit to go back stage to meet the stars. On the dance band side, The Palais de Dance featured bands such as those of Harry Roy, Bert

Ambrose, Lew Stone and *'the excellent resident band led by Basil Kirchin'*.

It seems clear from the memories referred to above that, although there had been some interest in jazz before that time, there was a major increase in jazz activity in the years just following the second World War. By the mid-1940s local interest in jazz and, more significantly, interest in playing jazz, was really on the move and accelerating, but would it last and would it lead to anything? As it turned out, James Lincoln Collier's *'tidal wave of traditional jazz'*, the Revival, had unleashed a flood tide in Edinburgh. The result was to be a burgeoning local traditional jazz scene, which would produce many fine jazz musicians and bands and, as it happens, quite a bit of mayhem and general falling about as well, very much in the tradition already established by Fats Waller. Traditional jazz in Edinburgh was to continue to flourish for many decades to come.

Chapter II

The Revival

Edinburgh, in the latter half of the twentieth century, was to gain a well-deserved reputation as a major centre of traditional jazz. The world-wide renewal of interest in earlier forms of jazz that arose in the 1940s, which came to be known as the **Revival**, had a particularly notable impact in Edinburgh. This resulted in, not only a lively and active coterie of local, amateur jazz players, but the emergence of a number of musicians who went on to make a career in jazz, some with reputations at an international level. Local traditional jazz was to thrive and continue for many decades (as did more modern forms of jazz) and was to receive added impetus from a second (and more populist) resurgence of interest in the early 1960s, the so-called 'Trad Boom'. Yet another boost came with the creation, in the late 1970s, of the Edinburgh International Jazz Festival. The foundations for what was to come later were laid down by a remarkable group of local jazz musicians, together with their followers and supporters, that arose in the late 1940s and early 1950s.

At the heart of this group were a surprisingly large number of individuals who were pupils at the City's Royal High School. Jazz history already had its Austin High School Gang, a group of enthusiastic youngsters with an interest in jazz in 1920s Chicago, which included Bud Freeman (ten), Jim Lannigan (bs), Jimmy McPartland (tpt), Dick McPartland (bjo), Frank Teschemacher (clt) and others. They all attended the Austin High School, most of them started in music on the violin before switching to something more suited to jazz and several of them became notable jazz musicians. The precedent was there in the jazz books and it was natural that the Edinburgh group became known as the **Royal High School Gang**. Two prominent individuals in the Royal High School Gang were an aspiring clarinet player called Sandy Brown and a trombone player, later to switch to trumpet, Al Fairweather.

The members of the Royal High School Gang were not the only ones involved however, and there was another, equally significant group, not associated with any one school, which was just as active. They were grouped around a pair of brothers who played clarinet and trumpet, Archie and John Semple respectively, and a trumpet player called Alex Welsh. Both groups were engaged in playing traditional jazz but, from accounts of the time, it appears that even then, they were reckoned to play different forms of the music.

The singer and writer, George Melly, in his vastly entertaining autobiographical book 'Owning Up'[11], makes a clear distinction between two separate forms of jazz which emerged at the time of the Revival, both of which he says claimed the name **New Orleans Jazz**. Melly allocates separate names to each, in the interests of clarity. The renewal of interest in early jazz as played by the top New Orleans professional musicians, such as Louis Armstrong, Jelly Roll Morton and Joe 'King' Oliver, although in fact mostly played and recorded in Chicago and elsewhere, he calls **revivalist jazz**. The other form, based on the music of rediscovered veterans such as Bunk Johnson and George Lewis who had, for the most part, remained in New Orleans, he calls **traditional jazz**. I can understand Melly's reasoning on this but, for me, his terms are unsatisfactory, mainly because both forms arose from the Revival and it is therefore confusing to call one of them 'revivalist jazz'. For myself and for greater clarity, I would prefer to replace Melly's terms with classic jazz and fundamentalist jazz respectively. However, although I consider 'fundamentalist'

---

[11] 'Owning Up' by George Melly (Copyright © George Melly, 1965) Reprinted by permission of A. M. Heath and Co ltd

to be the term that best expresses the 'back to the source' principle of this kind of jazz, the term does seem to carry a politically negative flavour nowadays. As I do not wish to use the term in this negative way, I am going to use instead 'purist jazz', a term that was in common usage for this type of jazz in the 1950/60s, reflecting the desire to play the music in its pure form, unsullied by commercialism. I will therefore use the terms **classic jazz** (deriving from Armstrong, Oliver, Morton et al) and **purist jazz** (deriving from Johnson, Lewis et al), when referring to the two forms of New Orleans jazz that emerged within the Revival.

As we will see later, as time went on, the purist style won the battle of names and claimed the term **New Orleans jazz** for itself. This came about, I believe, because so much post-Revival jazz in the UK followed the purist style, rather than the classic style, and this trend was apparent even by the late 1950s and early 1960s. This is reinforced by the excellent Phillip Larkin who, writing in 1962, gave the credit to Ken Colyer, saying *'That British traditional jazz turned from the Armstrong-Oliver pattern to that offered by George Lewis and the modern New Orleans bands was largely the work of Ken Colyer, who visited the Crescent City as a seaman and brought back the inspiration that is the foundation of Barber and Bilk today'*[12]. At the time of writing in 2010, I believe that it is this purist style that is in the best health of any of the traditional forms. There are still hundreds of bands across the UK and on the Continent playing in this style and there are whole jazz festivals devoted to presenting it.

In addition, I will use the term **traditional jazz** to mean all jazz music, including Swing and other big band jazz, that sprang from the older harmonic and rhythmic tradition that pre-dated the advent of the new harmonic and rhythmic directions of bebop in the 1940s, the greatest and most dramatic change of direction in jazz history. Of course, Edinburgh had its bebop developments too but this seems to me to have had a separate life of its own. For this reason, plus the fact that I am by no means qualified to do so, this book will not attempt to cover Edinburgh's bebop

---

[12] Larkin P, 'All What Jazz?', pages 55-56, published by Faber and Faber, 1970

and other modern jazz developments. When required, I will use the collective term **modern jazz** to cover all of bebop and the post-bebop jazz developments.

Inevitably, the term **contemporary jazz** will crop up but it is a term fraught with peril. I remember Humphrey Lyttelton once, on his radio show 'The Best of Jazz', saying that he had received a letter criticising him for the lack of contemporary jazz in his weekly selections of recordings. Humph then announced that the next record would put that right. The next record turned out to be by the Ken Colyer Band playing, as always, jazz of an uncompromising purist variety. After the record had finished, Humph pointed out that it had been recorded just three weeks previously and '*...you can't get much more contemporary than that*'!

Happily, the George Crockett article from 1966, referred to in the last chapter, also gives a little information about the Edinburgh jazz scene during the 1939-1945 war years and just after. It seems that, in contrast to the situation in 1935, there was a thriving Rhythm Club in Edinburgh during the war years. In the nature of things at that troubled time, both the members and the players involved were mostly itinerant and it was apparently 1945 and the end of the war, before the local jazz scene assumed a more settled state. George Crockett reports that the Rhythm Club did not just function on a diet of recorded jazz but also featured a live band. He describes the band as '*enthusiastic amateurs playing the traddiest of trad*' and recalls that there was one individual who played the tuba until the mouth piece went missing! This band contained some local jazz talent which would make a substantial mark in a wider context in the not so distant future. Beyond '*traddiest of trad*' George Crockett does not give any further information about the style of this band. However, George Melly writes of visits to Edinburgh in the early 1950s and says that the Edinburgh jazz scene was divided into two separate cliques. Describing one of these, he goes on: '*There were the purists led by a clarinet player called Sandy Brown and a trumpet player called Al Fairweather. They played at that time Ken Colyer music at its most uncompromising and they listened to our* (ie The Mick Mulligan Band's) *brand of Dixieland with glowering disapproval'.* Ken Colyer was, of course, the English trumpeter who remained faithful, throughout his entire career, to the early traditions of New Orleans jazz, that is, purist jazz. In many ways, he was one of the prime movers in the surge of traditional jazz that developed in the UK in the 1940s, 50s and 60s. Melly even goes so far as to say that Ken Colyer '...*invented British traditional jazz'*, which may sound like an exaggeration but seems to me, at least in terms of purist jazz, to be not all that far from the truth.

Melly's view that Brown and Fairweather '...*played Ken Colyer music at its most uncompromising'* I find hard to believe. It may be that Al and Sandy did start off playing music inspired by the rediscovered veterans but the evidence seems to me to make that very unlikely. I played a few of times with Sandy, with Al on a greater number of occasions and I have listened to their recordings throughout most of my life. In my experience, most jazz musicians retain in their playing at least a little of their original inspiration. I was never aware of the slightest discernable George Lewis influence in Sandy's playing and heard not the remotest trace of a Bunk Johnson sound in Al's. Jim Godbolt, who acted as agent for Sandy and Al in the 1950s, and who therefore should have known what he was talking about, wrote *'Clarinettist Sandy Brown and trumpeter Al Fairweather first played together in Edinburgh, their band based entirely on the classic Louis Armstrong Hot Five and Hot Seven records'*[13]. Brian Lemmon, who played piano with Sandy for many years, said of him *'To me the only obvious influence was Johnny Dodds, in sound and phrasing.'* Stu Eaton, an Edinburgh trumpet player and early associate of both Sandy and Al, says *'The early standards were Dodds for Sandy and Louis for Al'*[14]. Further evidence comes from Sandy Currie who was one of the Royal High School Gang. He says, on the sleeves notes to a CD issued around 1998[15], that it was not until the time that this recording was made

[13] Godbolt J, 'All This and Many a Dog', page 75, Northway Publications revised edition 2007 and by permission of Jim Godbolt
[14] Eaton S, Sandy Brown Society Newsletter No 99, March 2005
[15] Sleeve note by Sandy Currie, 'Sandy Brown – The Historic Usher Hall Concert 1952', Lake Records LACD94

in 1952, that the purist revival was underway, with '...*people trying to play like the recently discovered and recorded Bunk Johnson, George Lewis and many others who had never left New Orleans.*' Currie goes on to say that Sandy Brown's band remained true to their original ideal of King Oliver's Creole Jazz Band and Louis Armstrong's Hot Five. All this seems to me to be spot on. Certainly, judging by the recordings of Sandy and Al, especially those made in the early 1950s, there can be no doubt that Sandy's early inspiration was Johnny Dodds, the clarinettist on most of Louis Armstrong's seminal 1920s 'Hot Five' and 'Hot Seven' recordings. Similarly, Al's playing clearly arises directly from early Louis Armstrong with perhaps a bit of Tommy Ladnier, who recorded with Sydney Bechet, in there as well.

All this evidence is in accord with the accounts of Dave Paxton, another great Edinburgh clarinettist, and a contemporary of Sandy and Al. I played with Dave for a number of years in the Edinburgh bands the New Society Syncopators and Bill Salmond's Louisiana Ragtime Band. Dave Paxton was closely associated with the Sandy and Al group in their early days and he was absolutely clear that both he and Sandy had their early roots in the playing of Dodds. Dave Paxton seemed to me to be little interested in the clarinet playing of George Lewis and, on several occasions, made it clear that he considered the influence of the purist school to have arrived considerably later than his own formative years in Edinburgh. In fact, he seemed to consider it primarily a 1950s influence in the UK and I remember him, on at least one occasion referring, without much warmth, to the British purist influence as '*That 1950s stuff*'. In addition, when Dave and I played with the Louisiana Ragtime Band in Holland in 1987, I brought home a review of the band from a local newspaper. I later had it translated and well remember Dave's indignant reaction when he discovered that he had been accredited with playing in the style of George Lewis, whom he certainly did not rate as highly as Johnny Dodds.

Regarding George Melly's comment, it seems to me to be much more likely that the '*glowering disapproval*' of the Brown band was directed at the performance of the

Mulligan band, rather than that they failed to play *'Ken Colyer music'*.

The other, equally important, Edinburgh jazz grouping of the time, that centred around **Alex Welsh and the Semple brothers**, was clearly considered to play in a different style to that of the Brown/Fairweather crowd. Although George Melly says that *'The Brown-Fairweather axis and the Welsh-Semple clique hardly communicated'*, it is clear from early, locally made recordings, that there was in fact quite a bit of mixing between the two groups. Pete Davenport, a trumpet player later to form and lead a jazz band at the Edinburgh Art College, told me in 2010 that, although there was quite marked intolerance between advocates of the two styles, this was much more prevalent amongst the followers than amongst the musicians themselves.

Melly says of the Welsh/Semple clique that they *'played Condon music'*, by which he means that they followed the path of the white Chicagoans around the guitar player Eddie Condon. Jim Young, a fine New Orleans style bass player who played a leading role in Edinburgh jazz from the mid-1950s, recognised this in conversation with me in 2010, but said that he considered that the Revival had quickly divided into <u>three</u> separate styles. Jim identified the three as classic jazz, purist jazz and the Chicagoan/Condon style of the Welsh/Semple groups. However, having thought hard about this, I feel that in fact there was basically a division into only <u>two</u> styles. The bands led by Eddie Condon (born 1905) had themselves followed in the footsteps of Oliver, Armstrong and the white cornet player Bix Beiderbecke (born 1903). They were barely a generation younger than Oliver (born 1885) and Morton (born 1890), not all that much younger than Armstrong himself (born 1900 or 1901), and their music pre-dated by many years the re-discovery of the New Orleans veterans. Their music seems to me to have derived directly from the classic jazz tradition and they were, therefore, themselves part of that tradition. Applying this theory to the Edinburgh jazz scene of the 1940s, it seems to me that, in spite of the clear differences between the Brown/Fairweather group and the Semple/Welsh group, they both belonged squarely within the classic jazz part of the Revival. I suppose, by the judgemental standards of the time, the Welsh/Semple clique were seen to be moving off down an off-shoot of the classic style and perhaps they were even considered to be compromising it.

As in the case of Sandy Brown and Al Fairweather, I certainly never detected the slightest trace of a purist influence in the playing of Alex Welsh, who seemed to me to have modelled his playing on that of Bix Beiderbecke and Wild Bill Davison. A lack of purist influence was also true of Archie Semple, whose playing reflected that of both Ed Hall and Pee Wee Russell, both frequent associates of the so-called Chicagoans. The recordings made years later, when Welsh and Semple had long-since moved to a London base, certainly confirm their Chicago style, with no trace of a purist influence. However, even in the early days, they were clearly off down a path that was different from that of Brown and Fairweather. It seems that, as early as the late 1940s, the classic jazz tradition of the Revival was already sub-dividing.

Further confirmation that the Edinburgh jazz of the late 1940s and early 1950s was inspired by classic jazz and not the purist school, comes from trombonist Mike Pollett who was active in Edinburgh jazz between 1951 and 1958, during which time he was a member of the Climax Jazz Band. I met with him in 2010 when working on this book and, with no prompting from me, Mike volunteered the information that he had belonged to '...the New Orleans school, as inspired by Bunk Johnston and George Lewis'. He also made a point of saying that the purist influence had not been felt in Edinburgh until the 1950s, the formation of the Climax Jazz Band being a result of this. Although Mike Pollett was clearly familiar with the music of Sandy Brown and Al Fairweather and Alex Welsh, he had not been part of the groups around them and was clear that his involvement in Edinburgh jazz was both different and later than theirs. Illustrating this he said that he had never, to his knowledge, met Archie Semple.

So what was it that really separated the classic and purist categories and had seemed so important in the early days of the Revival? It certainly was not simply the race or colour of the originals, as Afro-Americans, white Americans and Creoles of French or Spanish ancestry had all played prominent roles in New Orleans. It seems to have been perceived as a divide between the music of those who had stayed on in New Orleans and those who had moved away to find success elsewhere, such as Chicago or New York. This suggests a divide between those who saw commercial opportunities for themselves elsewhere and did something about it and those who stayed behind in New Orleans. The purist concept seems to have been that, by moving away for commercial reasons, the music was contaminated by the need to be commercial. The very use of the term purist jazz implies an adherence to an early form of jazz, uncontaminated by commerce or non-New Orleans influences. There is no doubt whatsoever that the followers of this style sincerely believed that this was so and believed that this older, unspoiled and 'pure' form represented something of particular artistic merit, a far from unreasonable perception.

Looking back now, it seems to me that the main musical difference was that the purist school used a lot of ensemble playing (ie simultaneous improvising) and virtually no arranged passages, whereas the classic style increasingly moved towards a music dominated by soloists and a tendency towards sometimes quite elaborate arrangements. Whether this represented contamination by commercialism or simply an increasing sophistication of the music is a matter for the individual to consider. In addition, many recordings give the clear impression that the technical abilities of the classic jazz musicians were of a considerably higher standard overall, than those of the purist persuasion. However, this is a technical rather than an artistic distinction and does not, in my view, diminish the artistic value of the less technically accomplished playing. In any case, it has to be recognised that some of the re-discovered veterans were getting on a bit in years by the time they were rediscovered and given the chance to record. In addition, some of them had played little in their immediate past. We should simply be thankful that their playing was put on record before it was too late. Their important influence in Edinburgh will be the subject of Chapter VII – The Jazz Purists.

It must be remembered that, when George Melly spoke of two forms of jazz within the Revival, he was speaking only about two forms of <u>New Orleans</u> jazz and not all of jazz. The path of jazz during the first half of the 20th Century had already demonstrated the organic development that would be expected of any living art form. These changes came about as individuals, groups of individuals and even the geographical spread of the music, exerted their influence. It seems likely to me that, if an art form failed to grow organically in this way, failed to develop and change, it would rapidly stagnate and die.

Although the original inspiration behind the Revival seems to have been a turning back to the origins and a rejection of many of the organic developments that had taken place, it does not seem to me that the Revival, in the end, can be said to have achieved this. What really seems to have happened was that the organic changes simply started all over again, demonstrating once again that change was inevitable. By the time I became actively involved in the Edinburgh traditional jazz scene, some fifteen years or so after the mid-1940s Revival, there were plenty of local jazz musicians whose styles reflected influences well outside the classic and purist models. These included musicians whose inspiration arose, for example, from such as Jack Teagarden and Dickie Wells (tbn), Bobby Hackett and Muggsy Spannier (tpt), Coleman Hawkins and Lester Young (ten) and the Ellington musicians. Few of these could be said to belong to either of the Revival categories and most were not New Orleans musicians at all but came from various other centres of jazz, including Kansas City, Chicago, New York and even Texas. The local jazz musicians they inspired, however, were active <u>within</u> the Revival movement and inevitably, had an effect upon it. These musicians had simply discovered that jazz had a wider stylistic base than New Orleans alone, even if they themselves had been originally attracted by the jazz of the Revival. The 1940s Revival was itself no more capable of freezing jazz at a point in time than the first half of the twentieth century had been. Having started out as a New Orleans concept, the Revival itself was changing (degenerating some would have said) and other stylistic variations of traditional jazz re-appeared, to an extent reflecting and replicating the developments of the first half century of jazz.

Later on, terms descriptive of these changes, some of which had been in use in jazz long before the Revival, became commonplace. These included the already mentioned **Chicago style**, which was said by French writer Jean Pierre Lion to be '...*an energetic and fierce adaptation of the New Orleans style*'[16]. The term Chicago style was often replaced by the term **Condon music**, a tribute to the key role played by Eddie Condon, who, for so long, had kept the flame of small band traditional jazz alive in his bands and clubs.

A term which became closely allied to this style was **dixieland**. This rather awkward term, which in the USA was often used to denote any small group traditional jazz, in the UK was used to describe traditional jazz of the white school. Unfortunately, it was also sometimes used, especially by those who believed that only Afro-Americans could play jazz, as a derogatory term implying an inferior, superficial type of jazz. This is illustrated by the 'Guinness Jazz A – Z' which said of dixieland '...*to many it still suggests white jazz, and the revivals of the 1940s tended to perpetuate the error (if it may be termed an error – or is it just another case of usage dictating?). The revival of traditional jazz idioms, complete with banjos, pumping tubas and four-square rhythms, was often done under the name of Dixieland, frequently by white bands in such places as Nick's in New York, where it was inevitably referred to as Nicksieland jazz. In the widest possible sense, it now embraces all traditional styles, but there is a clear need for clarification of what one intends by using the name*'[17]. These are wise words and, in this book, I will use the term in a purely descriptive, non-derogatory way, meaning jazz inspired by the Chicagoan tradition, exemplified by the

---

[16] Lion J P, 'Bix - The Definitive Biography of a Jazz Legend', pub 2007, Reproduced by permission of the Continuum International Publishing Group Ltd

[17] Clayton P, Hammond P, 'The Guinness Jazz A – Z', Guinness Superlatives 1986, by kind permission of Guinness World Records Ltd

predominately white group of musicians of the 1920s, gathered around the organizing figure of Eddie Condon.

Another term was the **European tradition**, usually relating to music derived from the music of Django Reinhardt and the 'Hot Club of France', the first truly original European contribution to the development of jazz. **Rhythm and blues** or **R & B** referred to a predominantly black, blues based music that was to become one of the most important building blocks of rock music. The music of small, extrovert and very 'jumping' bands was sometimes called **jump** or **jump jive**. The term **trad**, which was really just an abbreviation of traditional jazz, came to be used, rather slightingly, for the music of British traditional jazz bands during the 'Trad boom' of the late 1950s and early 1960s. An even more derogatory term, **traddy pop** was used to describe recordings by trad bands with the aim of selling vast number of records and getting into the Top Twenty, which they sometimes did.

There was also an interesting, middle-of-the-road term, which was **mainstream**. This was apparently invented in the 1950s by the jazz writer and critic, Stanley Dance. According to the 'Guinness Jazz A – Z'[18], Dance described this as *'a kind of jazz which, while neither 'traditional' nor 'modern', is better than both'*. However, it must be remembered that Dance's definition belongs to the 1950s and relates to jazz of that time. The 'Guinness Jazz A – Z' goes on to say that mainstream was employed to describe *'...the music of jazz musicians who were by no means past their prime but who had formed their styles and made their reputations before or during the Swing era and found themselves short of work when the jazz audience divided itself into modern and traditional, paying scant attention to what lay in between'*. Another term, **small band swing**, was almost synonymous with mainstream, and was used to describe the music of bands of around six to eight musicians who had spent most of their time playing in the big Swing bands. Certainly, by the 1980s, when I was involved in a band that styled itself mainstream, I thought

---

[18] Clayton P, Hammond P, 'The Guinness Jazz A – Z', Guinness Superlatives 1986, by kind permission of Guinness World Records Ltd

of it as meaning the kind of small group music played by middle period jazz musicians such as Buck Clayton, Dickie Wells, Teddy Wilson, Benny Goodman and Johnny Hodges, many of whom had made their names in big bands during the 1930s and 1940s.

The term **Swing** itself, of course, referred to the music of the big, predominately white bands of the period between about 1935 and the late 1940s, such as those of Benny Goodman, Artie Shaw and the Dorsey brothers. There was one band, however, that seems to me to deserve a term of its own and that is the band of Duke Ellington, which has always seemed to me best described as a **jazz orchestra**.

Finally, in this explanation of terms, I should add that, throughout this book, I have used the term **'jazzer'** to embrace all those who populate the jazz scene, including all enthusiasts, supporters, listeners, organisers and writers, as well as those who play the music; in other words the whole jazz crowd. The term **'punter'** will also crop up. The term is not in any way derogatory but is widely and affectionately used by the players to identify those who turn out to support bands, act as volunteers at festivals, run events, distribute publicity and produce newsletters, articles, magazines and websites: all those, in fact, without whom the jazz scene would be a sad and empty place. All these terms and others, imprecise and over-lapping as they undoubtedly are, will be of use as we follow the course of Edinburgh traditional jazz over the second half of the twentieth century.

Reading some of the above, it may seem that the Revival had been a bit of a waste of time and that everything simply returned to how it had been before the Revival, but this was not so. The Revival was a major, world-wide renewal of interest in the earlier forms of jazz and perhaps the most important part of it was the large number of these new enthusiasts who actually started playing the music. Another important factor was that many of the early generations of jazz musicians were still alive and still playing and suddenly found themselves back in demand. In addition there were some, like Bunk Johnson (tpt) and Kid Ory (tbn), who were no longer playing but were located, given help to resume playing (including the provision of new false teeth!) and found themselves with a new career in jazz. The Revival, in spite of petty squabbles, parochialism and some fairly dire music along the way, re-invigorated traditional jazz. It brought back great and almost forgotten figures from the past and it provided the music with, literally, fresh blood. A great deal of notable music resulted, some of it locally in Edinburgh, where gifted musicians played originally and eloquently, not slavishly copying, but producing inspired music within their chosen idiom. Because of the Revival, traditional jazz, instead of just fizzling out, was able to continue as a vital, vigorous music, not really in competition with modern jazz but alongside and in parallel with it. I doubt that this would have been possible without the Revival.

Chapter III

The Classic Jazz Pioneers

Most accounts of traditional jazz in the UK credit the Red Barn, a pub in Barnehurst, Kent, as the birth place of the Revival in the UK. Presumably, this means the birth place of the *active playing* of traditional jazz, as there were clearly plenty of Rhythm Clubs around before this, where listening to recorded jazz was the norm. The Red Barn sessions featured a band called the George Webb Dixielanders. During the early years of WWII, while working in the Vickers-Armstrong munitions factory, the leader of this band, pianist George Webb, had founded the Bexleyheath Rhythm Club. Sometime after this, and after taking piano lessons, he began rehearsing with a like-minded trumpeter called Owen Bryce. Together they formed the George Webb Dixielanders and fixed up a regular gig in the basement of the Red Barn pub. The band went on to make some recordings, broadcast on the radio and play concerts in various cities in the UK but disbanded in early 1948. Several members of the band went on to make names for themselves in years to come, in particular the trumpeter Humphrey Lyttelton and clarinettist Wally Fawkes.

George Webb, who was sometimes called the 'father of British jazz', was born on 8th October 1917 and died on 10th March 2010, at the age of 92. There is no doubt of the importance in British jazz of this band, but whether it was in fact the first to start playing Revival jazz in the UK is not clear and does not really matter much. What does matter is that, in a number of centres around the country, similar efforts to form bands to play traditional jazz were gathering pace. It seems very unlikely that these well-scattered efforts were inspired by the George Webb Dixielanders, given that there would be few recordings of British traditional bands at that time. In addition, there would be little jazz communication across the country in these days, before much in the way of a jazz press existed. In fact, all around the country, interest in early jazz was burgeoning and, following the example of revivalist bands such as that of Lu Waters and Turk Murphy et al in the USA, people were learning to play instruments and bands were being formed. The jazz writer Sinclair Traill, in his book 'Concerning Jazz'[19], says that *The band which first took up cudgels on behalf of traditional jazz in this country was George Webb's Dixielanders'* but goes on to name other early bands. Traill lists them as the bands of Chris Barber and Ken Colyer in London, The Saints Jazz Band in Manchester, The Merseysippi band in Liverpool and significantly, Sandy Brown and Alex Welsh who were pioneering traditional jazz in Edinburgh.

As we have already seen, the early revivalists in Edinburgh in the early to late 1940s were organised into two groups, one centred on clarinettist Sandy Brown and the other on fellow clarinettist Archie Semple with his brother John Semple and Alex Welsh, both of whom played trumpet. As we have already heard, the group associated with Sandy Brown had come to be identified as the **Royal High School Gang (RHS Gang)**, because so many of the group had attended the city's Royal High School. It is hard to be precise about just how many Royal High scholars were actively involved in jazz in Edinburgh in the 1940s but it is clear that there were quite a few. It seems likely that there were somewhere between twenty and thirty of them actively playing or attempting to play the music, ranging from a few who would become internationally famous in jazz, through a good number who would establish lengthy local careers, to others who were only active briefly, before dropping out.

---

[19] Traill S, 'Concerning Jazz', page 136, Faber and Faber 1957. All attempts to trace the current copyright holder of this book have been unsuccessful.

There was clearly a central group of talented musicians, who led the way, but it is equally clear that there were many others who also played an important part. Amongst the latter, there would be some who were less committed, perhaps less able, musicians and certainly many who were non-playing enthusiasts. However, there can be no doubt that they, collectively, comprised a self-sustaining jazz movement, both within and beyond the school, the effects of which are around to this day. This jazz movement at the Royal High School may even have had something of a crusade about it, a sense of pursuing and supporting an earlier and more worthwhile form of jazz, something that added up to a cause worthy of commitment. Jazz, like any other organic entity, needs a suitable environment in which to grow and the doings of the whole group collectively – musical, organisational or just turning up to listen – seems to have provided just that environment. It did not end there either and, in the following decades, there would be many other jazzers, younger but just as committed, from the Royal High School jazz production line.

Just when the appellation, the Royal High School gang, first came to be used is uncertain but I think it must have been fairly early on. Certainly, I was aware of the term shortly after I came into the Edinburgh jazz scene around 1960 and the drummer, Kenny Milne and trumpeter Andrew Lauder, whose Edinburgh jazz histories go back beyond mine, also remember the term from early in their careers. I can remember established jazzers with whom I played, such as Archie Sinclair and Jack Duff, not only using the term but relishing its links to the music of the Austin High School Gang, a form of jazz with which each had much in common. Going still further back, the drummer Bill Strachan, who was a school contemporary of the group associated with Sandy Brown, has also confirmed that he remembers the collective term RHS crowd or gang being used quite early on in his jazz career, as early as the late 1940s or early 1950s. I have also heard the term used in a variety of ways, from the quite specific, meaning only the early Sandy Brown band, to a more generic inclusion of the entire Royal High School jazz crowd of the 1940s and 50s. It is worth noting that there were even some who, like

Dave Mylne and Ian Arnott whom we shall meet shortly, did not actually attend the Royal High School but were so closely involved with the Gang that they were often assumed to be a part of it. The most common usage, in my early experience, was to use it as a collective tag for the jazz musicians from the school, although at that time, we would not have thought of putting a capital G on gang, often just saying the Royal High gang or crowd. In my view, the term is such an obvious one, given the jazz precedent of the Austin High School Gang in Chicago, that I think that it is extremely likely that it was 'invented' on a number of occasions, by different people, at different times and in different places. The first published use of the term of which I am aware, was by jazz critic Tony Troon, writing in The Scotsman after Al Fairweather's death in 1993, when he referred to Al as '...one of the Royal High School 'gang' of musicians of the early Fifties...'[20].

The term was also used by John Latham, about whom we will hear more shortly, in an article headed 'The Royal High School Gang' which appeared in the May 1996 edition of Jazz Journal'[21]. The article pointed out that, in the New Orleans jazz revival of the 1940s, jazz bands were springing up all over the UK and not just in London. Latham explains that Sandy Brown's band, then playing in the West End Cafe and including Sandy's old school mates Al Fairweather and Stan Grieg, could be described as the Royal High School Gang. The article goes on to describe the early recording activities of Sandy and the others and finishes by reiterating that '...very important music was being created in Scotland and that far from being centred in London, the British jazz movement sprang to life simultaneously at several independent locations, of which one of the most important was Edinburgh'. In this book, it will be in its widest and most general sense that I shall use the term. The Royal High School Gang (the RHS Gang) seems to me a term that embraces the whole spectrum of components that make jazz on any scale a communicative art form – players,

[20] Troon Anthony, 'Al Fairweather: jazz trumpeter', The Scotsman, 22nd June 1993
[21] Latham J, 'The Royal High School Gang', Jazz Journal May 1996, by permission of Jazz Journal www.jazzjournal.co.uk

organisers, listeners, recorders of sounds and images and, no doubt, critics as well – and they all seem to me to have played their part and earned their place.

Amongst the RHS Gang who were already playing instruments in the mid-1940s, were Sandy Brown (clt and pno), Al Fairweather (tbn), Stu Eaton (tpt), Neil Pringle (pno) and Ronnie Geddes (drms). An RHS pupil, who was not an active player but a keen jazz follower, was Jim Walker. Jim, who came to Edinburgh from Peterculter near Aberdeen at the age of seven, was a contemporary of several of the musicians, including Al Fairweather, Stu Eaton and Bob Craig who were in his year, and Sandy Brown who was in the year below. Dave Paxton was a couple of years ahead and Stan Greig was about three years behind him. In about 1990, Jim Walker wrote a memoire about these early days in which he said *'Jazz must have oozed out of the walls in the old Royal High School building during the war years because it seemed that just about everybody in my year and the year below was a jazz fan'*. Jim put much of this enthusiasm down to the influence of Sandy Brown and adds that there may have been a touch of a *'one in the eye for authority'* gesture about it. Jim's introduction to jazz came through a talk given by Sandy at the literary and debating society, which was illustrated with a selection of recordings. His interest was furthered by his pal, Stu Eaton, who was more knowledgeable than Jim was about jazz and encouraged him. A group of these young jazz followers would invade Clifton's Record Shop in Princes Street on Saturday mornings to hear the latest jazz releases, mostly on the rhythm series from Parlophone. Apparently, each 78 rpm record cost five shillings and four pence half-penny, which is only about twenty seven pence in today's money, but was considered a fortune at the time. The secret was to attach yourself to someone who had a bit of cash and could buy a record. Jim recalls how impressed he was by Sandy Brown's ability to hear a boogie woogie record only a couple of times, before he was able to play it in full on the RHS gym piano. A jazz band of variable membership would practice in the school gym, including a few who were not RHS pupils. Even at that time, Sandy seemed to have *'been born note perfect'* on the clarinet, never playing anything less than fluently, although he tended to impose his own high standards on others. When novices showed some promise and a willingness to take advice, Sandy could be encouraging and tolerant but Jim remembers him once telling an aspiring trombone player *'I could make a better sound with my arse'!* The drummer Bill Strachan has also said that, at times, Sandy could be quite brutal in his criticism of others and remembers the banjo player, Norrie Anderson, being reduced to a quivering wreck by Sandy's complaints about the chords he was playing, saying despairingly *'I suppose I must be playing the wrong chords but I am playing them properly'!* The front-line of the school gym band was often Stu Eaton on trumpet, Sandy on clarinet and Al Fairweather on trombone while Bob Craig, modest and still very unsure of himself, would try out his trombone quietly in the background.

The RHS gym band, however, was not the only active traditional jazz band around and Jim Walker remembers a group of rather older musicians who, around 1945, played at the Edinburgh Rhythm Club, located in the rehearsal room above Methven Simpson's music shop in Princes Street. This group included Bob Fairley (tpt), Drew Bruce (ten and sometimes, sop sax), Drew's mother Ma Bruce (pno) and Bill McGregor (bjo) and we will meet some of them, in a little more detail, in the next chapter. George Crockett was also associated with this group, playing drums both at Methven Simpsons and a few years later, when the band reconstituted itself in new premises at the YWCA in Riego Street. Sandy and Al Fairweather were quickly drawn into the group at the Rhythm Club, although the main business was listening to a record recital, with the live music almost an impromptu afterthought at the end of the session. Around this time, another band was formed by Archie Semple (clt) and his brother John who, Jim Walker says, played a strong if not very original lead on trumpet, with George Crockett on drums. Their main interest was in the white Chicago jazz of the Eddie Condon type and we will hear much more about them in Chapter V.

In UK terms, **Sandy Brown (clarinet, piano, vocals)** was clearly into early revivalist action, his profile on the Sandy Brown Jazz website saying that he formed his first band in

1943[22].   Many years later in the mid-1990s, long after
Sandy's death and mainly through the sterling work of Dr
John Latham, a Senior Lecturer in International Economic
History at the University of Wales in Swansea, a Sandy
Brown Society (SBS) was formed to celebrate his life.   In
about 1996 the SBS began publishing regular newsletters
and the special 99th Edition newsletter, published in March
2005, the 30th anniversary of Sandy's death, gives some
indication of dates.   In John Latham's summary of Sandy's
career, he states *It is said that Sandy Brown formed his first
band as early as 1943, and the latest Sandy Brown
Discography shows him to have been recording in 1946'*[23].
These early activities also involved Sandy's near
contemporaries Stu Eaton (tpt), Alastair (Al) Fairweather
(tbn and later, tpt), Bob Craig (tbn), Dave Paxton (clt) and
Stan Grieg (drms and pno).   They, like Sandy, attended the
Royal High School, Stan the year behind Sandy and Al and
Bob a couple of years ahead, John Latham telling us that
both Stan and Al were members of Sandy's early bands.

Stu Eaton has said[24] that he, Al and Bob all started
school together in October 1932 and that the three of them,
when they were about 12 years old, had started *fooling
around with music'* in his mother's basement.   He adds that
Sandy, whom he says was *'the catalyst'*, joined them about
two or three years later.   Eaton also tells us that Sandy
played an Albert system clarinet, as he then considered that
the more modern Boehm system was only for *'classical
stuff, wimps and Benny Goodman'*.   However, it seems that
he may not have stuck with his original model of clarinet.
Jim Walker has recalled that Sandy, at some point, had
said goodbye to *'...his old Albert clarinet (all held together
with insulating tape and bits of string with a decided droop
in the middle) and had acquired a new Boehm'*.   Sandy used
a very hard reed, in an attempt to sound as much like
Johnny Dodds as possible, and there is a story that Wally
Fawkes, having inspected one of Sandy's reeds, asked him
what he used, suggesting that it might be floor boards!

[22] http://sandybrownjazz.co.uk
[23] SBS Newsletter No. 99, March 2005
[24] SBS Newsletter No. 7, June 1997

Eaton throws some light on the issue of Sandy's teeth, telling us that they were *'less than dazzling'* and, before starting to play, he would smoothly convey them to his pocket with one sweep of his handkerchief, without his audience being much the wiser.   Stu Eaton also says that Sandy's clarinet mouth piece was *'very marked'*[25], by which he presumably means that the surface was pitted by tooth marks.   Just how this came about is something of a mystery, in the light of Sandy being known to remove his false teeth before playing – unless he had gums like iron! The answer may lie in information from the sax player, Tony Coe, who revealed in a SBS Newsletter[26] that it was only Sandy's upper teeth that were missing and confirmed that it was these that he removed to play clarinet.   Like so many jazz musicians, Sandy was self taught on his instrument and John Latham, in Sandy's biography in the Oxford Dictionary of National Biography, says that the absence of formal training was crucial to his unique approach to the clarinet[27].

John Latham also gives details about Sandy's place of birth and his arrival in Edinburgh.   Jazz reference books consistently give Sandy's date and place of birth as 25 February 1929 in Izatnagar in India.   He was the second son of John Brown, a railway engineer and his wife, Minnie Henderson.   In recent years, doubts have been raised by some of Sandy's contemporaries about his place of birth. However, Latham's research into the matriculation registers for the Royal High School of Edinburgh shows that Sandy entered the school on 2 October 1933 at the age of four and that his previous school was the infant school, Garahkpur. Latham quotes Sandy's book, 'The McJazz Manuscripts: A Collection of the Writings of Sandy Brown' (Ed. David Binns, Faber and Faber, London and Boston, 1979), as giving his place of birth as Izatnagar near Bareilly in India, where his father had been an engineer on the railway network. Latham also refutes the tale that Sandy's mother was

---

[25] SBS Newsletter No. 7, June 1997

[26] SBS Newsletter No 90, June 2004

[27] Oxford Dictionary of National Biography: Oxford Dictionary of National Biography Index of Contributors by Colin Matthew and Brian Harrison (2004) p4-5 Volume 8 (not verbatim), by permission of Oxford University Press, www.oup.com

Indian and quotes Sandy's cousin Elsie, who told Stan Grieg that Sandy's mother (Elsie's Auntie Minnie) was as Scottish as she was. This is given further weight as the Royal High School records indicate that he was staying with his maternal grandmother, Mrs Henderson, which does not sound much like an Indian surname to me! Apparently, Sandy did sometimes say that his mother was Indian and, indeed, in the 'McJazz Manuscripts', he claims that she was Muslim and had turned Christian on her marriage. Certainly, judging by his looks, Sandy could have had Indian blood in him. However, it looks as though this story has to be put down to the idiosyncratic Brown sense of humour. On the family's return to Scotland in the early 1930s, they lived at first in Wishaw before moving to Edinburgh. It appears that Sandy's father had been unwell and that he died in about 1936, when Sandy was still very young. Latham also confirms that Sandy spent all his school days at the Royal High School and had lived at 4 Abercorn Crescent, which is off Willowbrae Road, in the Jock's Lodge area of Edinburgh.

Drawing by Patricia Davenport of Sandy Brown in the Crown Bar in 1954 (by kind permission of Peter and Patricia Davenport)

Sinclair Traill, in his 1957 'Concerning Jazz' already quoted, gives an interesting verbatim statement of Sandy's which gives us a good idea of his views early in his jazz career:

'I've always tried to have a <u>hot</u> band because that is what jazz has to offer. It means playing real blues with a beat – and I don't mean just 12 bar themes; the blues is part of all jazz that I like. For that reason I don't like British jazz much. For another reason too: most British players can't play very well technically, so they never attempt what they don't feel they can do. The result is light music, which I hate, and they ought to. Fairweather and I compose a lot of the band's repertoire – it makes us think what we're doing, and creation is always apt to be better than emulation. I don't agree with the theory that jazz shouldn't be <u>sung</u>. The dearth of jazz singers here is no argument. It means only that there is a dearth of jazz singers! I like the vocal blues harmonies, and generally oppose the "Brass Band" theory that seems to have the traditionalist world by the throat today.'[28]

Small wonder then that the music produced over the years by Sandy Brown and Al Fairweather was to be some of the most original and hottest traditional jazz ever heard in Britain. Small wonder either that John Latham, in a May 1996 article in the magazine 'Jazz Journal'[29], emphasises this early activity in Edinburgh when he says *'We have to realise that very important music was being created in Scotland and that far from being centred on London, the British jazz movement sprang to life simultaneously at several independent locations, of which one of the most important was Edinburgh.'*

This book will not presume to attempt a fully detailed biography of any of the jazz musicians mentioned, but it is interesting to consider what sort of people they were, especially in the early days of the Revival. For a glimpse of Sandy Brown as a young man, we are again indebted to the SBS. In the SBS Newsletter No 99 already alluded to, some

---

[28] Traill S, 'Concerning Jazz', page 140, Faber and Faber 1957. All attempts to trace the current copyright holder of this book have been unsuccessful.
[29] Latham J, 'Jazz Journal' 'The Royal High School Gang', May 1996, www.jazzjournal.co.uk

of Stu Eaton's recollections are recorded and he describes Sandy as *'a standout at school'*. He goes on to say that Sandy was *'highly visible and audible'* and was the leading light of a group who broke the rules and indulged in jokes *'practical and impractical'*! He also says that Sandy and Al Fairweather were seen as a pair, not just because they played jazz together, but because they were considered to be equally good. Eaton considered Al to be the hotter player while Sandy was the bluer player, meaning of course, that Sandy's playing was suffused by the influence of the blues. The blues influence was certainly apparent in all of Sandy's playing and 'The McJazz Manuscripts' lists an early recording by Sandy (made privately in 1948) of a tune called 'Emigratin' Blues'. On this recording, Sandy plays piano, accompanying the blues singing of Drew Bruce. Drew Bruce was a clarinet and sax player and was described by Stan Grieg as *'a blues singer of great talent'*[30]. His mother, known as 'Ma' Bruce, played piano around the Edinburgh jazz scene in the 1940/50s, although said by Stu Eaton to *'...read all her music'*[31].

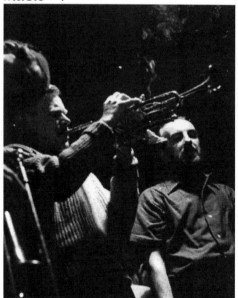

Al Fairweather and Sandy Brown
(by kind permission of Peter Davenport)

---

[30] SBS Newsletter No. 56, August 2001
[31] SBS Newsletter No 91, July 2004

After leaving school, Sandy did his National Service with the Royal Army Ordnance Corps in the years 1948/49 and then went on to the Edinburgh College of Art, where he trained as an architect, eventually specialising in acoustic architecture. His jazz activities continued while he was a student and in 1952, his band played a famous concert at the Usher Hall, when they supported the Mississippi blues singer, Big Bill Broonzy, an occasion we shall look at in more detail in the next chapter. There was a second Usher Hall appearance the next year, supporting the Freddy Randall band and, also in 1953, the band travelled to London to take part in a National Jazz Federation concert at the Royal Festival Hall.

Amongst the jazz memorabilia in the possession of Jim Walker was one particularly unexpected and delightful relic. This was a 78 rpm record, on the Wildcat label, with 'Oh, Didn't he Ramble' printed on one side and just the name Sandy Brown on the other. The labels are quite simply printed although not, I would say, home-made, there is no serial number and the titles on the labels are typed, as by an ordinary, old-fashioned type writer. This seems to have been quite a usual practice at the time, when recordings were often made privately by some local recording firm. The labels on the Swarbrick and Mossman recordings made by the early Sandy Brown band, about which we will hear later, are also typed in this way. On one side of the disc, the recording of 'Oh, Didn't he Ramble' is hot and driving, with a band apparently consisting of trumpet, clarinet, trombone, banjo, bass and drums. The trumpet is clearly Al Fairweather and the clarinet is obviously Sandy, still in his early Doddsian mode. The trombonist sounds like Bob Craig and it seems likely that the banjoist is Norrie Anderson. Dizzy Jackson, in 2012, told me that he had no recollection of being on this particular recording. The track has the usual 'Oh, Didn't He Ramble' out of tempo introduction, complete with the 'Ashes to Ashes, Dust to Dust' spiel, spoken by Sandy I think, followed by some quite convincing howls of grief and mourning from the rest of the band. The drums pick up the tempo and are followed by two ensemble choruses, a chorus each from clarinet, trombone and trumpet, then two closing ensemble choruses.   It is a good spirited stuff but it is the other side of the record that is really fascinating.

Jim Walker says that this reverse side is a recording of Sandy being interviewed on the radio programme 'In Town Tonight', an occasion which he remembers, and says that Sandy's interview followed one with Boris Karlof!   Jim reports that he found the record in a charity shop somewhere and, as it is precious and fragile, he had copied it onto tape, a copy of which he gave me.   Because the interview gives such a good account of what Sandy and his band were up to at the time, it is well worth giving the whole story.   There is a brief single chorus of a blues played by the band and then the BBC interviewer (I) begins:

I   *That music was by Sandy Brown and his band from Edinburgh* (actually, what he says is 'That was Sendy Brown and his Bend from Aidinburgh').   *The band is paying its first visit to London and here's its leader, architect and clarinet player Sandy Brown. Well, what are you doing in London apart from playing jazz Mr Brown?*

SB   *Well, we came down to take part in the National Jazz Federation annual concert at the Festival Hall the other day.*

I   *Uhhu*

SB   *That was particularly interesting to me musically and architecturally.*

I   *I can well imagine it.   All the eight members of your band – do they all have different jobs?*

SB   *Oh yes.   The drummer's a surveyor, the bass player's a law student, the trumpet player's an artist and so on.*

I   *A very versatile bunch.   When did you first get together?*

SB   *It really started at school then we did our time in the services and when we came out, three years ago, we decided to learn our instruments seriously.*

I   *Where have you played?*

SB   *In Scotland of course and several times in Paris. Every summer we play there.   The first year when we were there the boys gave me a nasty shock.*

42

I *Really? What did they do?*

SB *We were booked to play in a cafe but they all got lost except the trombone player and myself. So we decided we couldn't carry on by ourselves so we had to run round the streets of Paris frantically searching for unemployed French musicians. As a report for duty, it was the strangest assortment of instrumentalists ever assembled.*

I *Well, what did you do? How long did you play?*

SB *We played all the night there and the people in the cafe were delighted with what they thought an all Scottish band.*

I *Where as it was French with just a dash of Scotch, eh? What are you going to play for us?*

SB *Well, we've been celebrating Louis Armstrong's birthday today and appropriately, we'd like to play a number of his he recorded twenty years ago and it's still popular today - When You're Smiling.*

(The band plays)

I *Well, hot music from hot Scotland eh? Thank you very much Sandy Brown and your band.*

The band then plays a couple of choruses of ensemble on 'When you're Smiling', and the interviewer, for all his awful BBC accent, was quite right – it is hot. As to the line-up of the band on this side of the record, in the interview Sandy refers to the drummer as 'a surveyor' and Ralph Laing, a near contemporary of the RHS Gang and later to be a fine jazz piano player, confirms that this description would fit Farrie Forsyth. The bass player is said by Sandy on the recording to be law student, which puzzled me at first, until I was tipped off by John Latham. John told me that it was Dizzy Jackson, who had been a law student before changing course and becoming a teacher and a quick phone call to Dizzy confirmed this. He added that, in addition to Boris Karloff, the black pianist 'Hutch' had also made an appearance on the show. Hutch was a Grenadian who had been one the biggest cabaret stars of the 1920/30s and whose full name was Leslie Arthur Julien Hutchinson.

Just why the interviewer refers to *'all the eight members of your band'* is not at all clear, unless he simply miscounted. Dizzy recalls that the line-up for the recording was Al Fairweather (tpt), Bob Craig (tbn), Sandy (clt), Norrie Anderson (bjo), Dizzy (bs) Dru Paterson (pno) and Farrie Forsyth (drms). Apparently, Stan Greig, who would have otherwise played piano, was on National Service at the time and could not always get away to play. It sounds like only a six-piece band on the recording and, although there may well be a piano as well, I cannot convince myself that I can hear one. This recording is certainly a fascinating peep into the distant past but how on earth did it come to be on a 78 rpm record? Perhaps the BBC gave them a recording of their efforts as a memento and, of course, there would be few readily available recordings on tape then, but who knows what its origins were? The mention in Sandy's interview of Louis Armstrong's birthday, at that time believed to be 4th July, would seem to fix the day and Sandy's reference to coming out of the services three years ago should make it 1952/53, so it seemed likely that the BBC recording was made on the 1953 trip mentioned above. Dizzy has confirmed that it was 1953, although he also said that the recording was made on his birthday, which would make it the 14th of July rather than on Louis' birthday on the 4th.

There is other information that relates very closely to the above and further confirms the line-up of Sandy's band on the broadcast. Dizzy has confirmed it was on this same trip that Sandy's band made some other recordings. These were made for the Esquire label and are listed in Sandy's discography[32] as having been recorded on 11th July 1953. The tunes recorded were 'Dr Jazz' (two takes), 'Four or Five Times' (two takes) and 'Wild Man Blues' (single take). The band line-up is given as Al Fairweather (tpt), Sandy Brown (clt), Bob Craig (tbn), Dru Paterson (pno), Norrie Anderson (bjo), Dizzy Jackson (bs) and Farrie Forsyth (drms). There is an additional recording[33], made for Esquire on 11th July 1953, this being two takes of 'King Porter Stomp', which

---

[32] Bielderman G et al, Sandy Brown Discography, Eurojazz Discos No. 5
[33] Bielderman G et al, Stan Greig Discography, Eurojazz Discos No. 45, Nov 1995, Sandy Brown's Jazz Band, Esquire 20-022, EP28,333, recorded London, 11th July 1953. A footnote says that Stan Greig does not appear on five other titles from this session, presumably the other Esquire tracks discussed above.

were made by the same line-up but with Stan Greig on drums, to the exclusion of Farrie Forsyth.

Al Fairweather stayed on in London about this time, with Alex Welsh taking his place in the Brown band back in Edinburgh. A year or so later in 1954, Sandy joined the lengthening list of Edinburgh jazz musicians who had moved to London. There he joined up again with Al Fairweather and went on to further great success in jazz and in his professional career, but these London based happenings are beyond the scope of this book. On 29th September 1954, Sandy married Flo' Armstrong, a legal secretary. Happily Sandy's later career is well covered in recordings and jazz publications, including his own 'The McJazz Manuscripts'. Both the recordings and the 'Manuscripts' are amongst the very best and most original ever produced in British jazz and are highly recommended to everyone who likes their jazz (and their reading) original, hot and exciting.

I played with Sandy Brown on a few occasions, probably not more than half a dozen in all, when he sat in with our band, Old Bailey and his Jazz Advocates. This was when he was visiting Edinburgh back in the 1960s, but I cannot say that I knew him as a person. My impression was of a strong-minded individual with a formidable intellect and the most ferocious musical attack of any jazz musician I ever played with. The only other with an attack comparable to Sandy's was the American trumpeter, Wild Bill Davison, with whom I played a couple of times in the mid-1970s. As Bill Davison was elderly by the time I played with him, perhaps I should declare it a draw between the two most open, honest and expressive musicians I ever heard live. Both clearly played straight from the heart and both set about the music with a fierce, emotional drive that was utterly gripping. I once heard Sandy give an opinion on an up and coming young jazz musician and the main thrust of his view was that the youngster's playing 'had no balls'. No one could have ever accused Sandy's playing of lacking balls; it was one of the most forth-right and vigorous sounds in all of jazz.

Another story which gives a good picture of Sandy's character, according to John Latham, originated with the jazz critic and writer Alun Morgan. He had been at a concert in Canterbury, Kent, which featured a number of jazz reed players, including Sandy. Morgan was compering the show, and after announcing a young modern jazzer who played unaccompanied soprano sax, he retired to the bar. Sandy was there, a glass of whisky in one hand and a glass of water in the other. The sound of far-out, unaccompanied soprano sax came over the PA. Sandy took a sip from each of his glasses in turn then remarked *'While I respect the courage and determination of young men who push the boundaries of music further out, I retain the right to not f- - king well listen'*[34].

Later, the Fairweather-Brown band moved towards a more mainstream style, a move perhaps not meeting with everyone's approval, but it remained exciting and original music, even if it had shed some of the rough magic of their earlier approach.

It has been reported that Sandy once calculated that the average life span of a jazz musician was somewhere in the mid forties. His prediction was to be horribly accurate in his own case, for Sandy was to die of malignant hypertension at the tragically young age of 46, on 15 March 1975, while watching on TV, Scotland lose to England in a rugby Calcutta Cup match. His death was a huge loss to jazz, to his professional field of architecture and, of course, to his family and friends. He was truly a great clarinet player, perhaps the most distinguished and original jazz musician Britain has ever produced, certainly in the traditional field. What he might have gone on to achieve if his health had held up, we shall never know, but it seems unlikely that he would ever have been willing to rest on the laurels of his past.

Although I hardly knew Sandy as a person, I was fortunate enough to get to know **Al Fairweather (trumpet)** quite well, after he had returned to Edinburgh in the late 1980s. Al was born in Edinburgh on 12 June 1927 and brought up in the Portobello area of the city. Like Sandy Brown, he attended the RHS and discovered jazz while in secondary school. With Sandy and others of the RHS Gang,

---

[34] Sleeve note by Alun Morgan on HEP LP 2017

he was already actively involved in playing jazz by the mid-1940s, starting out, not on the trumpet on which he would make his name, but on the trombone. Another one of the Gang, Sandy Currie, says that Al was stuck with trombone *'having lost on the toss of a coin'* to Stu Eaton, when they both wanted to play trumpet[35]. Al's original trombone is still around. It was made in Czechoslovakia, probably before WWI, and has a shamrock on the bell. It has been in the possession of yet another, but rather younger, RHS pupil, trombonist George Hewitt, since he bought it from Al in the early 1950s. George had had to return the 'Boosey and Hawkes' trombone, on which he started out, when he left school in 1952 and he raised the £7 that Al wanted for his instrument by working at a harvest camp near Coldstream. Al's former trombone has been resident in George Hewitt's attic in Irvine for many years. George got it with a battered wooden case which had replaced the oilskin wrapping that Al had originally used. Al's old trombone was brought to Edinburgh in 2010 to be an exhibit in an exhibition celebrating Edinburgh jazz.

George Hewitt says that it was Sandy Brown who persuaded Al to switch to the trumpet. Al's initial attempts on trumpet did not immediately impress Jim Walker, who wondered if a horrible mistake had been made. Jim remembers that at first, Al hardly ever moved out of the lower register, had a coarse, unattractive tone and every one missed his trombone playing. However, Jim also says that, although his early lack of technique was obvious, Al had retained his superb phrasing, the total cohesion of his solos and his drive in the ensembles. Jim highlighted Al's joined-up playing beautifully by saying *'When other soloists often play unrelated phrases, Al played in sentences, which made up a paragraph which in turn contributed to the whole story of the tune'*. Jim recalled that the band had made its first recording only about six weeks after Al had started on trumpet and, although his comparative lack of technique was apparent, his imagination and jazz feeling shone through.

---

[35] Sleeve note by Sandy Currie, 'Sandy Brown – The Historic Usher Hall Concert 1952', Lake Records LACD94

Like Sandy, Al went on to Edinburgh College of Art, where he gained a diploma in painting and drawing. He was clearly a talented artist, as well as an outstanding jazz musician, and a portrait by Al of Sean Connery, retained in the Art College collection, appeared in the centenary show at the Edinburgh College of Art in 2007 and got a mention in the Times. This dated from a time, long before his 007 days, when the then Big Tam Connery acted as a 'bouncer' at the Jazz Band Balls held at the Oddfellows Hall in the evenings and posed as a model at the Art College during the day.

In late 1953, a year before Sandy had finished his course at Art College, Al went to live in London. There he joined the band of Cy Laurie, another Johnny Dodds inspired clarinet player, with whom he made some excellent recordings. A year or so later, when Sandy too moved south, the two great Edinburgh players teamed up again and went on to produce a series of wonderful, original recordings, mostly featuring compositions and arrangements by Al and Sandy. In my view, these recordings were the absolute zenith of British traditional jazz, never bettered to this day. Later, while Sandy concentrated on his architectural affairs, Al spent a number of years with Acker Bilk's band, where he joined up with another great British original, the alto sax and clarinet player, Bruce Turner, in what many would consider to have been the best band that Bilk ever had. Later still, in the late 1980s, when Al's health was causing serious problems, he returned to Edinburgh where he teamed up with his contemporaries Bob Craig and Dave Paxton and others, with whom he continued to produce terrific music.

I liked Al Fairweather a lot. He was friendly, totally modest, indeed incredibly self deprecating considering his achievements, and encouraging to me personally. In the late 1980s, I was involved in a five piece band, which we called the Jazz Masters, playing a mainstream form of jazz. Al, as well as sitting in with us quite frequently, was also happy to dep with us when we were short handed, and was endlessly encouraging about what we were trying to do musically.

Al Fairweather's original trombone and other memorabilia in a showcase at an exhibition at the Central Library to mark the setting up of an Edinburgh Jazz Archive, in 2010 (photograph by the author)

He was also kind enough to give me arrangements of two tunes that he had written. The band folded before we got these numbers into our repertoire and, as these were numbers that Al told me he had never done anything with himself, I believe they remain to this day two originals by a great jazz musician that have never been played or heard. Writing this has prompted me to do something about this and they may yet make their belated appearance on the Edinburgh jazz scene[36].

I was always struck by how genuinely modest and self-deprecating Al was about his own abilities and achievements. In addition to being a great trumpet player, he had written and arranged some of the most original and exiting material ever played by British jazz bands - and yet he told me what a struggle it had been. He said that he was a poor and slow reader and writer of music and everything he had done had cost him a huge amount of time and effort.

---

[36] One of them, 'Bonzo Bounce', we brought into our repertoire in 2011

Al wrote in a letter to Stuart Carter '...*I have been doing some arranging. I don't know if you have ever tried it (I suspect you have) but it is one of the most difficult things to attempt. I've been doing it for some years now and it doesn't get any easier – it seems that the mind seizes up when you are faced with a blank manuscript and ideas don't come very readily. The funny thing is, the ideas come quickly enough if you were playing!'*[37]

You would never have guessed his difficulty with reading and writing music from the results. Even in the early days in Edinburgh, it is clear that Al was a friendly, encouraging and laid back sort of person. George Hewitt tells of how Al, already an established name in local jazz, was none-the-less willing to go along and fill-in at rehearsals with the schoolboy band in which George was playing at the time, when their young trumpeter Kenny Jack was unable to make it. Many years later, Al was to return to Edinburgh and to playing jazz on the local jazz scene, where we will catch up with him in a later chapter. Al Fairweather died in Edinburgh on 21st June 1993.

Stan Greig (piano and drums) was born in Edinburgh on 12th August 1930. His father, Artie, was a piano tuner, a trade that Stan would also follow later, and had a piano shop in the Jock's Lodge part of Edinburgh. Artie Greig also played drums and Stan's mother taught English and played piano. Stan was educated at the RHS and, according to 'The Rough Guide to Jazz'[38], he joined Sandy Brown's band in 1945. Like others of the RHS Gang, he lived in the Joppa/Portobello district of Edinburgh. Dizzy Jackson, who was later to play bass in the Brown band, tells us[39] that Sandy always had a problem because Stan was both the best piano player and the best drummer available but, of course, could not play both at once. Stan made his first recordings with the Brown band in 1949 and 1950, recording for the Swarbrick and Mossman (S & M) label.

---

[37] SBS Newsletter No. 66, June 2002
[38] Carr, Fairweather and Priestly 'The Rough Guide to Jazz', 3rd Edition May 2004, Rough Guides Ltd, distributed by the Penguin Group
[39] SBS Newsletter No. 11, November 1997

Stan was not only a versatile musician but was clearly an effective proselytiser on behalf of jazz. George Hewitt recollects that he and Kenny Jack, both slightly younger RHS pupils, had become acquainted with Stan and he was to be a major musical influence on them. Stan had left the RHS some years before this and was serving an apprenticeship at Henry Robb's Shipyard in Leith, intent on becoming a ship's engineer. More relevantly to Hewitt and Jack, he was the piano player in the Sandy Brown band with whom he played at jazz dances at the Oddfellows Hall, regular spots at the West End Cafe and at gigs in the Crown Bar, which was host to the 'Stud Club'. They used to meet him on Sundays in an Italian cafe on the Portobello seafront, where Stan would enthuse volubly about jazz and let them borrow some of the records that he brought along with him.

After completing his apprenticeship, Stan was called up for National Service, joining the Royal Engineers (Inland Water Transport) and found himself in charge of a floating crane at Marchwood Camp, near Southampton. John Latham tells the story of Stan being discovered to be a 'crack shot' and being chosen to compete in the Royal Engineers rifle team. Happily Stan, realising what the outcome of this would be, brought his potential career as a sniper to an abrupt end by deliberately aiming off target![40] On his return to Edinburgh in 1952 after being de-mobbed, he rejoined the Brown band, playing at a famous Usher Hall concert in 1952 supporting Big Bill Broonzy, making further recordings with them for S and M, and broadcasting with the band on BBC Scotland in 1952.

Stan went to London in 1954 where he worked with Ken Colyer (on drums), Humphrey Lyttelton, the Fairweather–Brown band, Bruce Turner's band, Acker Bilk and the John Chilton Footwarmers with George Melly, before returning for another eight years with the Lyttelton band. Between about 1966 and 1968, when Stan was with Acker Bilk's band, his Edinburgh colleague Al Fairweather was on trumpet. I remember Bruce Turner, back in the 1960s, telling me how

[40] Latham J, Lee R and Bielderman G, 'Stan Greig Discography', Eurojazz Discos No. 42, 2nd Edition April 2001

highly he rated Stan's drumming, emphasising his formidable ability to swing a band, and expressing a wish that he could persuade him back into his own band. Ralph Laing, himself a fine piano player, once told me that he felt that Stan was very much under-rated as a piano player. He pointed out that Stan's playing had an authentic blues feel, which was quickly recognised by American musicians who were always keen to have Stan backing them. An example of this was Stan's inclusion as the only non-American in several tours of Europe in the 1980s with the stellar Harlem Jazz and Blues. Ralph considered Stan's playing to be endlessly thoughtful, never playing two choruses the same way and constantly responding to the playing of those whom he was accompanying.

Stan remained a major player in the British jazz world over the next four or five decades, continuing to put in time and recording with most of the prominent British jazz bands. He also led bands of various sizes, ranging from a trio to the 1975 London Jazz Big Band which included, amongst others, Al Fairweather. As well as playing trumpet, Al was the main arranger for the band. In fact, this band was of considerable stature, playing every week at the 100 Club and was a formidable aggregation, including many of the top players of the day. In the 1980s and 90s, after a four year spell with George Melly and a return to Humphrey Lyttelton's band, Stan played mostly as a solo pianist in clubs, pubs and jazz festivals. Sadly, Stan was affected by Parkinson's disease in later life and it was the disabilities associated with this debilitating condition, although he tried to hide it, which brought an end to his second spell with the Lyttelton band. Ralph Laing, who knew him well, has said that, in spite of his difficulties, Stan never stopped trying and late in his career, kept stoically working with Laurie Chescoe's band, while he still had reasonable movement in his hands. In addition, it was during this difficult period in his life that Stan helped Jools Holland to develop the bluesy piano playing, for which he would become famous.

For readers who wish to follow Stan's later career, there is an excellent biography, written by John Latham, in the 'Stan Greig Discography' published by 'Eurojazz Discos', which gives a detailed account of his career as a professional jazz musician[41]. A further mark of Stan's major impact on jazz is the fact that, by Ralph Laing's calculations, he has no fewer than one hundred and five LP recording sessions listed. Stan Greig was made President of the Sandy Brown Society from its inception in 1996 and in 2010, still held that office.

Bob Craig (trombone) was, for a period spanning six decades, one of the great stalwarts of the Edinburgh traditional jazz scene. He was born in Edinburgh in 1927, the son of a publican who ran a pub on Nicholson Street in the Southside of the town. Bob's schooling was at the RHS, where he was in the same class as Stu Eaton and Al Fairweather. A profile of Bob on the Sandy Brown Jazz website[42] tells us that the three of them became friends and, during the years of WWII when they were in their teens, they began both to listen to jazz and to learn to play the music. They also got together with Sandy Brown, who was in the year below them. Bob, who had for some reason acquired the nickname of 'Bugs', had taken up the trombone and, when Al Fairweather switched to trumpet, became the trombone player in the Brown band. After school, there were the usual interruptions of those days when National Service affected all of them at one time or another and Bob, who was in the RAF, grew what was to become his trademark handlebar moustache. Trumpeter and band leader Charlie McNair, reminiscing years later, recalled how in the 1960s, after Bob had appeared on STV, presenter Bill Tennant had remarked on the moustache and said that Bob was the Jimmy Edwards of the music business.

In the early 1950s, when Fairweather and Brown left for London, Bob stayed on in Edinburgh, where he had completed his BSc in engineering at Edinburgh University.

---

[41] Latham J, Lee R and Bielderman G, 'Stan Greig Discography', Eurojazz Discos No. 42, 2nd edition 2001

[42] www.sandybrownjazz.co.uk/profilebobcraig.html

SANDY BROWN (Clt.), AL FAIRWEATHER (Tpt.), BOB CRAIG (Tbn.), JIMMY FORSYTH (Drs.), NORRIE ANDERSON (Bjo.), CHARLIE JACKSON (Bass).

(from the collection of Peter Davenport, photographer unknown)

The trumpeter and journalist, Alastair Clark, who wrote Bob's obituary[43] when he died in 1998 at the age of 71, referred to him as *'the most modest of men'* and said that Bob *'never reckoned that he could compete at the highest level'* in jazz. It may have been for that reason that he did not move to London with his band colleagues but London's loss was to be very much Edinburgh's gain.

A story about Bob that went the rounds at one time, was that he had gone with others of the Gang to hear the Louis Armstrong All Stars, on one of their infrequent visits to the UK. Bob and the others had inveigled themselves by some means into the band room and had even managed to have a word or two with Louis himself. The clarinettist with the band was the great Barney Bigard, who had made his name as one of Duke Ellington's star sidemen throughout the 1930s. I suppose as much to have something to say to Louis as anything else, Bob mentioned what many jazz followers in those days were saying, which was that Bigard, great player though he was, was not the ideal clarinettist for the Armstrong band. Apparently, Louis was not greatly taken with this view and the story went that he continued publically to castigate Bob, whom he apparently referred to

---

[43] Clark A, 'Bob Craig', The Scotsman obituaries, 5 August 1998

as 'Bops' Craig, whenever he introduced Bigard during the rest of their tour.

After Sandy's and Al's departure, Bob continued to be very active around the local jazz scene and at various times, led bands of his own and played in many of the other Edinburgh bands, including those of Charlie McNair and Mike Hart. He later became part of an outstanding front line, comprising Ian 'Tello' Telford (trumpet), Dave Paxton (clarinet) with Bob himself on trombone, in the band that got together when Paxton returned to Edinburgh in the mid-1960s. This band later metamorphosed into 'Mike Hart's Society Syncopators' and I played with them for a couple of years in the 1970s, when the original bass player, Donald McDonald, went off to play saxophone. What made this front line so good was the unerring instinct the three of them had for their respective roles in a traditional jazz band. All three of them played a style that came direct from the music of King Oliver and early Louis Armstrong, each was master of that style and that frontline gelled magnificently. I consider that, of all the front lines with whom I played over a fifty year career in local jazz, none played together so naturally and convincingly as this one and the ensemble passages, when all three horns played together, were a joy to hear. As Alastair Clark said years later, Bob's trombone playing consisted of, *'nothing flashy, just the hot, punchy, chordal fundamentals that provided a marvellous platform for other horn players to take off on'*[44]. His playing always reminded me of that of the great Kid Ory, the trombonist on many of the classic Louis Armstrong 'Hot Five' and 'Hot Seven' recordings, recordings which Bob and his colleagues certainly considered to be the pinnacle of traditional jazz.

In the early recordings of the Sandy Brown Band, made before Sandy, Al and Stan Greig departed for the south, Bob's playing stands up well alongside that of the others, playing the traditional role of the trombone to perfection, just as he was to do across six decades in Edinburgh jazz. He was also to make much memorable music in the 1980s with his old pals Dave Paxton and Al Fairweather, both

---

[44] Clark A, 'Bob Craig', The Scotsman obituaries, 5 August 1998

home again after many years away, and bass player Dizzy Jackson, who like Bob had remained in Edinburgh. Bob was also to put in a lengthy spell in the 1980s with Bill Salmond's Louisiana Ragtime Band and he remained an active player right up to his death in 1998.

Another of the Gang, and another who was to be an important Edinburgh musician into the 1990s, was **Dave Paxton (clarinet)**. With a date of birth of 16 April 1926, he was fairly close to Al and Bob Craig in age and had attended Portobello High School, before joining the others at the RHS. A SBS Newsletter[45], with information courtesy of Edinburgh's Jim Keppie, tells us that Dave left school at fifteen and completed a course at the Leith Nautical College. This enabled him to join the RAF in 1942, as an apprentice. Eyesight problems prevented him from making air crew but he served for four years before returning to Edinburgh in 1948. Dave was self taught on clarinet and, like Sandy, was an ardent follower of the great Johnny Dodds. He also admired the playing of two other great American clarinetists, Omar Simeon and Jimmy Noone. I remember Dave telling me that he also had a lot of time for the great Swing clarinetists, Benny Goodman and Artie Shaw, although he said he could never decide which of these two he preferred. Dave often played with Sandy and Al at the Edinburgh Jazz Club in Riego Street, which had previously been known as the Rhythm Club, a period Jim Walker recalls as a golden age. The Jazz Band Balls in the Oddfellow's Hall had also started around this time and, although plenty came to dance, many came along just to listen. Jim recalls that the music seemed to get better and better. One night, Sandy's band took a break which seemed to go on and on and then a clarinettist, unknown to Jim Walker, got up on the band stand and played one lyrical solo after another, accompanied only by piano. This was Dave Paxton and Jim remembers the occasion as *'pure magic'*.

After working as an insurance clerk in Edinburgh, Dave went out to the Persian Gulf in about 1951, to work in the oil industry, and did not return to Edinburgh permanently

---

[45] SBS. Newsletter 150, June 2009

until the mid-1960s. He then rapidly re-established himself as a major player in the local jazz scene. I remember Al Fairweather telling me that Dave, a hard working and conscientious musician himself, had constantly urged Sandy Brown to practice hard at his clarinet playing. I had also been aware for many years of the famous story, a legend of Edinburgh jazz, about the weekend spent by Sandy and Dave in a wooden hut in the Pentland Hills. Bill Strachan says that the hut was at Ravelrigg junction, on the railway line just to the west of Balerno, and was one of a group of holiday huts, all of them made from old, wooden, railway goods wagons. Apparently, the two clarinetists had taken themselves off to this remote spot and there they had spent an entire weekend (Jimmy Keppie reports that it was a whole week) practicing together. Their programme had followed a pattern: practice scales all morning; then practice blues choruses all afternoon, providing criticism of each other, before moving on to playing call and response phrases in the evening. They were said to have survived for the entire duration on nothing but eggs!

Sandy, of course, would go on to become an internationally renowned jazz musician, a player whose abilities and originality saw him acclaimed as a genius, but he was not the only outstanding player amongst these pioneers. Dave Paxton, in my view, was a talent comparable to Al Fairweather's. Both were very good indeed, both were under rated; Al because of his constant association with Sandy, and Dave, both because of association with Sandy and by the fact that he never played full time or made anything like the number of recordings that his ability deserved. In addition, and unlike Al, Dave had fewer opportunities to play with musicians whose talents matched his own. I knew, admired and played with Dave for many years and we will hear much more about him later in this book, after his return from the Middle East.

These then, were amongst the more prominent of the Royal High School Gang but they were by no means all of them. There were many more who were contemporary with those mentioned above and then a whole line of others over the years to come. We will meet many of them in the next chapter.

Chapter IV

The RHS Jazz Production Line

Another in the same school year at the RHS as Al Fairweather and Bob Craig was **trumpeter Stu Eaton** who was a significant figure on the early jazz scene. As a clue to Stu Eaton's style, John Latham tells us that Eaton, responding to the comment that his playing was too 'white', retorted *'Well, I am white.'* As John Latham goes on to say, this was an interesting comment from someone who believed that only Negroes, Jews and Scots could play jazz, and who personally qualified on two counts![46] Stu Eaton emigrated to Canada in 1954 where he still lives at the time of writing in 2010. Eaton had played initially with a band that included fellow trumpeter Bob Fairley, Bill McGregor (bjo), Drew Bruce (rds) and Drew's mother, 'Ma' Bruce (pno). It is not clear just how early this band was, although we know from Jim Walker that it was already playing in 1945. As a group, they were older than the RHS Gang. There was however, another early RHS jazzer around at this time as well. He was Edward 'Teddy' Gage, who played the soprano sax and was later to become an art teacher at Fettes School, a senior lecturer at Napier University and a distinguished art critic with The Scotsman. By 1946/47, Eaton was playing trumpet in one of Sandy's earliest bands, with Al

---

[46] SBS Newsletter No. 2, August 1996

Fairweather (tbn), George Crockett (drms), Ma Bruce (pno) and Drew Bruce who played sax and sang[47].

Jim Walker says that **Drew Bruce (reeds, vocals)**, while not impressing him as a sax player, made up for it with his infectious enthusiasm for the music and was also a good vocalist with a very earthy sound. Jim thinks that Drew would have been about ten years older than most of the RHS crowd. According to Bill Strachan, Drew Bruce's father had a market garden in York Road in the Trinity area of Edinburgh (others have said it was near Orchard Brae) where, during the years of WWII, they grew vegetables as part of the war effort. A further benefit of the market garden was that it put Drew in a reserved occupation, thus allowing him to avoid being called up. Bill Strachan says that Drew was something of an opportunist, putting him in mind of Private Walker in 'Dad's Army', the TV series about the Home Guard. Apparently, Drew was a gifted wheeler dealer, using the Three Tuns pub in Hanover Street, then sometimes known ironically as the Exchange, as his personal market place. There he did very well, bartering vegetables for fags and clothes from members of the American forces. Bill recalls that some of the RHS Gang would occasionally work at the Bruce market garden to earn a bit of extra pocket money. Another enterprising venture of Drew's was an attempt to make some illicit hooch, trying to create alcohol by fermenting some of his vegetable products with invert sugar. Someone produced an equally illicit, small still affair and a quantity of very rough spirit was obtained. When tasted by Bob Craig, it almost slew him on the spot and the experiment was not repeated. Ma Bruce is said to have owned copies of the sheet music of all Jelly Roll Morton's compositions but her collection was lost when their house was sold.

Bill McGregor (banjo), who was born on 2nd September 1910 and educated at George Watson's College, was a generation older than any of the RHS Gang. Bill had a grocer's shop in the Marchmont area of Edinburgh, a shop which his son Kenny, continued to run as a grocers until

---

[47] SBS Newsletters Nos. 7 Jun 1997, 31 Jul 1999, 54 Jun 2001, 58 Oct 2001, 144 Dec 2008, 145 Jan 2009

2006. Clearly a man of parts, Bill was also involved with a water polo club at Warrender Baths, not far from his shop. Jim Walker remembers him as being a very solid banjo player. As an interesting historical aside, Bill Strachan reports that Bill McGregor owned, not only a wax cylinder of Caruso singing, but also the requisite machine on which to play it. This is confirmed from an unexpected source. I had known Kenny McGregor since he was a school boy, and when I met with him in 2011 to talk about his father's career in jazz, he lent me a letter received by his father, dated 12th December 1946. This letter is signed by Gerald Lascelles and is almost completely about their mutual interest in jazz. The letter makes it clear that they had already corresponded a lot but gives no hint as to how the two came to know each other.

The Honourable Gerald Lascelles (1924 - 1998) was the younger son of the 6th Earl of Harewood and Mary, the Princess Royal and daughter of King George V. The Princess Royal was thus sister to both Edward XIII and George VI and her son, Gerald Lacelles, first cousin of our present Queen. More pertinently to us, Lascelles was well known as a passionate jazz enthusiast and supporter in his day and his name turns up quite regularly in jazz writings of the time. He was certainly a significant figure in British jazz, particularly in the 1940/50s and, like his fellow aristocratic jazz buff, the Marquis of Donegal, was greatly valued as an opener of jazz clubs and festivals, when his name was a guarantee of copious press coverage.

In the letter, Lascelles congratulates Bill on his recent acquisition of an Edison cylinder gramophone, which he describes as 'a bit primitive, but very amusing', and goes on to say that his brother once had some cylinders lent to him '...but they were all opera and sounded grim'. He also says that he did not know of anyone who had any cylinders at that time but '...will enquire in case I can chance upon one of the fabulous Bolden ones on Blue Ambriol'[48]. It seems that

---

[48] Lascelles probably meant Blue Amberol Records, a trademarked name for cylinder recordings made by the Eddison Co of the USA between1912 and 1929. They originally produced 2 minute wax cylinders, then changed to 4 minute black wax 'Amberol' cylinders from 1908. They then changed again to 'indestructible'

Lascelles knew his jazz history and, interestingly, this is the only reference, of which I am aware, in which the legendary, and still untraced, Buddy Bolden recordings are said to be on a named recording label. Bill had apparently been filling up his record collection with '... *some choice Bix and Bessie, not to mention Morton'*, which gives us a fairly clear picture of his tastes in jazz. Lascelles goes on to say that, while he saw (Jelly Roll) Morton recordings as '...*very much an acquired taste'*, he had liked all he had heard to date. However, he did not approve of the Yerba Buena Band, although he had never heard them, and found it '...*hard to accept their instrumentation'*. In spite of never having heard them, and only had them *'preached at me'*, he speculated that they had a somewhat coarse tone or, at least, '...*I found this to be the case on hearing the Webb Dixielanders who I think have much the same instrumentation'*.

Lascelles then goes on to write about his ongoing career in the 2nd Battalion, the Rifle Brigade, British Army of the Rhine, in which he was serving. He had been made Education Officer for the battalion and part of this role was to run what he calls a 'Rhythm Club'. He explains that this was mostly about dishing out a certain amount of jazz and jive on records, to anyone who wished to hear it. The most popular records are reported to be the Muggsy Spaniers followed by the (Benny) Goodman Sextet and his other small groups. He also *'lashes out a little piano music on wax – Hines and Waller mostly'*. Lascelles reports that he had attended a live broadcast at BFN (British Forces Network), as a member of the audience, and had bumped into a sergeant who ran the Swing Club. In the true spirit of the Revival, he says that the Swing Club was '...*not as bad as its name implies as they play Mezz/Ladnier and Muggsy and Bix on occasions'*. The meeting with the sergeant had provided an opportunity for Lascelles to bring back some records, when he returned from leave, followed by the chance to participate in a broadcast, which he hoped '...*might be a good chance to put over a line of really first-*

'Blue Amberol' cylinders, which lasted approx 4 minutes and were made of celluloid with a Plaster of Paris core and were blue in colour (Wikipedia)

class jazz to those who want it'. The crusading spirit of the Revival!

Lascelles own record buying had been fairly extensive and he had acquired records '*...ranging from the Mary Lou Williams Sextet on Asch to some real gems of piano and blues singing on early and I think unheard-of labels from the USA, which I got through the MM* (presumably, the Melody Maker) *and a charming man who is selling out his collection of almost entirely piano jazz, mostly solos which I think you disapprove of!'* On British labels he had contented himself with Bechet's 'Texas Moaner' and *'the Bunk'*, which he had not as yet heard, as it was at home. He had also got hold of some Josh White on Brunswick and (Wingy) Manone's 'Ain't Got Nobody', which was not as good as he had hoped. He had liked Mel Powell's piano playing on the Goodman Sextet's 'Ain't Misbehavin'' and the *'classic Stardust by Waller on BB, which is now one of my favourite discs'*. He goes on to report that *'The wax my brother brought back from the States is really terrific, especially some of the Commodore sides, and that beautiful* (Art) *Hodes 'Selections from the Gutter'*. Finally with regard to his record collection, he says that he had had the great misfortune to lose the entire catalogue of his collection and was having to make a new one, '*...more or less on a card index principle, as it is the best way of sorting out all the information in the most get-attable form!'* Lascelles final paragraph in the letter gives a marvellous insight to the thinking in jazz circles of the time and is worth quoting in full. He writes:

'The revival of jazz is in sight – so you say – but I wonder just how much of it is revival and where the decline comes in. Frankly with this Rebop around the corner, and name bands breaking up all over the States, it is hard to say where one stands. Certainly swing has had it in no mean manner, but whether jazz or some bastard music will replace it is a risky thing to bet on right now. People like jazz in large numbers – but they don't really appreciate it in the full sense of the word, and regard it as just another phenomenon of the popular music world, which is never a good thing in my opinion. The ban on foreign musicians is another serious deterrent to any serious attempt to revise our views and

standards of jazz in GB. This will no doubt be lifted in time, but it may be too late then.'

Gerald Lascelles' letter is a wonderful time capsule of the jazz world of the mid-1940s. It is a microcosm of the times, expressing many of the hopes and fears of a music, in the dying days of Swing, in the process of splitting itself in two – the two parallel channels of the future: Revivalist jazz and the bebop revolution. It certainly demonstrates that the fabled feuds of the 1940s were very real at the time and gives life to the stories of the two camps haranguing each other in bitter and fierce rivalry. This battle royal between the beboppers and the 'Mouldy Fygges', as they called the traditionalists, was to an extent still around when I came on the jazz scene of the late 1950s but had diminished to an occasional irritable lack of tolerance.

Kenny McGregor, to whom I am especially grateful for allowing me access to Lascelles letter, remembered nothing of his father's jazz playing. It seems that Bill McGregor had stopped playing, either before Kenny was born or early in his life. He had kept his banjo though, which Kenny still has, and I remember Bill McGregor letting me see the instrument back in the 1960s, when I told him that I was involved in jazz. Kenny does however, remember his Dad listening to recordings of the bands of Duke Ellington, Count Basie and Louis Armstrong and going with him to hear the Ellington band in concert in Newcastle in 1969, a concert that I too managed to attend. Kenny also remembers his Dad complaining that none of the jazz greats seemed to come to play in Edinburgh. Bill McGregor, one of the earliest Edinburgh jazzers that we know about, died in 1970, in his sixty first year.

Bob Fairley (trumpet) seems to have had a weak lip for trumpet and could only manage a few numbers before his embouchure failed him. Jim Walker recalls that Bob had a lovely tone and imaginative phrasing, rather reminiscent of Bix Beiderbecke.

An Edinburgh jazz band, location unknown but probably in the 1940s.
Drew Bruce (clarinet), Bob Fairley (trumpet), Bill McGregor (banjo), Ma Bruce (piano) Drummer unknown but it could be a young Bob Craig on trombone (photo from the collection of Kenny McGregor, photographer unknown)

Stu Eaton would sometimes take over from Bob Fairley when his lip gave out and gradually Drew Bruce took more of a back seat. Ma Bruce, however, continued for a while and was renowned for hammering out chords on the key board, to the extent that Jim Walker felt with her around, there was hardly a need for a drummer.

A sign of Revival activity elsewhere was a visit, by Stu Eaton, Drew Bruce, Bill McGregor and Bob Fairley, to Hawick on 4th April 1946 to hear the George Webb Dixielanders with their new addition, Humphrey Lyttelton on trumpet, and Wally Fawkes on clarinet. This was apparently Humph's first gig with the Webb band and the event was further distinguished by Drew Bruce joining the band to sing a couple of numbers, including 'Winin' Boy'[49].

---

[49] SBS Newsletter No 141, Sept 2008

Apparently, Wally Fawkes was required to judge the Belle of the Ball and Pretty Ankle competitions! An even more adventurous visit by Eaton and others of the RHS Gang, was to Paris in the following year, when they met the great New Orleans clarinet and soprano sax player, Sydney Bechet[50]. This and a second visit to Paris, is vividly described in Sandy Brown's 'The McJazz Manuscripts'[51]. There seems to have been a surprising amount of travelling around by the Edinburgh jazz crowd in the early days. Jim Walker tells the tale of one trip by an early Edinburgh band to Manchester, where they were warned against setting foot in a certain area because there was a wild and dangerous gang around. Inevitably, the band found its way to the danger area and, sure enough, the dreaded gang hove into view. The band immediately started singing 'I Belong to Glasgow' and the wild and dangerous gang quietly melted away!

The earliest drummer with Sandy Brown's bands is believed to have been journalist **George Crockett (drums)**, into whose published information on pre-WWII jazz in Edinburgh we have already delved in Chapter I. It is clear that he had an interest in jazz before 1940 and, having been born in Galashiels on 16th July 1920, he was about half a generation older than most of the RHS Gang. Crockett seems to have been one of the earliest musicians to be involved in the Revival in Edinburgh and he played and recorded with Sandy Brown in his earliest period. According to Derek Copland, in a memoire published on the Sandy Brown Jazz website[52], the earliest recordings by the Brown band, were made in 1946/47. They were made privately and recorded on acetate and George Crockett was the drummer on these recordings. A Sandy Brown Society Newsletter[53] gives the line-up on these early recordings as Stu Eaton (tpt), Sandy Brown (clt), Ma Bruce (pno), Billy Neill (gtr), Bruce (in fact, Bill) McGregor (bjo) and Gerald (in fact, George) Crockett (drms). The first of these Glasgow

[50] SBS Newsletter No. 141, Sept 2008

[51] Binns D (editor), 'The McJazz Manuscripts – A Collection of the Writings of Sandy Brown', Faber and Faber, 1979, by kind permission of David Binns

[52] Copland D, http://sandybrownjazz.co.uk/profilegeorgecrockett.html

[53] SBS Newsletters No 54, June 2001 and No 58, October 2001

recording dates is given in October 1946 and the tunes were 'Yellow Dog Blues', 'untitled', 'Doctor Jazz' and 'Shoe Shiner's Drag'. The same line-up is said to have made further recordings, again in Glasgow, on 3rd January 1947, when the tunes were 'Careless Love' with Div (presumably Drew) Bruce (voc) and 'Bill Bailey'. Then, on 25th January 1947, they recorded 'Buddy Bolden's Blues', 'Jazz Me Blues', 'Sad Ole Blues', 'Royal Garden Blues' (on which Bob Fairley was added on trumpet) and 'Joe Turner's Blues' with Drew Bruce on vocal. Finally, a session on 4th July 1947 produced 'I Ain't Gonna give Nobody None of my Jellyroll' and 'Careless Love'. Apparently, a copy of these old acetate recordings was taken by discographer and Sandy's old commanding officer, Horace Meunier Harris, to the National Sound Archive to find out if they could be cleaned up but, unfortunately, they were beyond restoration.

Although he had played and recorded with Sandy Brown, George Crockett seems to have been drawn to the more Dixieland oriented music of the group around Alex Welsh and Archie Semple. Certainly, his later playing was to be mostly with Welsh, Semple and others of the *'more Dixieland'* persuasion, and we will hear more of him in Chapter V.

Another by the name of Crockett, **Stuart 'Stu' Crockett (tbn)**, had played trombone with trumpeter Stu Eaton in his earliest days. Although I had been told that they were not related, it has also been reported that Stu and George Crockett were cousins. The bass player, Dizzy Jackson, tells us that Stu Crockett was at one time band manager for the Sandy Brown band and, amongst other duties, organized a two week tour around gigs in London in 1953, including one at the Royal Festival Hall and one at Wood Green. Many years later, Stu Crockett was to be a member of the committee which was responsible for organizing a memorial plaque to Sandy Brown and Al Fairweather[54]. Stu Crockett, one of the RHS Gang, died in the Edinburgh area on the sixteenth of February 2012 at the age of 87.

Sandy Currie, also an RHS scholar, has already been mentioned and seems to have been one of those invaluable

---

[54] SBS Newsletter No 4

enthusiasts around the jazz scene who contribute a great deal through their willingness to organize, keep notes and even make recordings. It appears that Sandy also got actively involved in playing as the Edinburgh drummer, Kenny Milne, says that he can remember him playing bass with one of Charlie McNair's bands in the 1950s. Sandy Currie had been secretary and treasurer of the Edinburgh Jazz Club when it was run by another notable enthusiast, Dave Mylne. It is to Sandy Currie's heroic efforts that we owe the recording of a historic and important concert at the Usher Hall in February 1952, involving the Sandy Brown band and the great Mississippi Blues singer, Big Bill Broonzy, of which more later. Sandy Currie too, in the 1990s, was on the various committees responsible for memorial plaques to Sandy Brown and Al Fairweather at the Royal High School, the Usher Hall and London's 100 Club. I met him when I was playing with Old Bailey and his Jazz Advocates in the 1960s and, after a gig, he insisted on me and several others accompanying him back to his flat in the Morningside district of town. There, we listened to jazz records and much reminiscing from Sandy, until I made my escape to stagger home, bleary eyed and shivering from cold and lack of sleep, as the dawn broke over the early morning milk carts and paper boys delivering the day's news. I only wish now, that I had been better prepared to listen and take note of what Sandy Currie had to say; it would have been extremely interesting and a valuable source of information for this book.

It may be that Sandy Currie's boundless enthusiasm was a bit much for at least one jazz musician. There was a story around that someone Sandy knew was to make a trip to Paris. Sandy insisted that he should look up a famous American jazz musician, then resident in the French capital. *'I know him well'* Sandy Currie had said *'I spent a lot of time with him when I was in Paris recently myself. Just say you know me.'* His friend duly made his way to the house of the famous American, said he had been recommended to call by his friend, Sandy Currie - and promptly had the door slammed in his face and was told to f- - k off in no uncertain terms! I have no idea if this was true or not, but it is a good story. Sandy Currie died in Edinburgh on 15th January 2011.

Dave Mylne was associated with the RHS Gang, although not a pupil of the school. He was a great enthusiast for classic jazz, an enthusiastic collector of jazz records and something of an entrepreneur. He was to become an architect, based, I understand, in Duns in the Scottish Borders. In the 1940s, his father was headmaster of a private school then located in Dalhousie Castle, now a posh hotel, out on the south side of Edinburgh near Bonnyrigg. Apparently, the Brown band played quite regularly for weekend dances at the school and the band members were also allowed access to a collection of jazz records and books, presumably belonging to either Mylne senior or junior. This information comes from another Sandy Brown Jazz website profile of another member of the Brown band, Willie Burns[55], who replaced George Crockett on drums in the later 1940s. Malcolm Burns, son of Willie, told me that his Dad used to talk about how they had to travel to Dalhousie Castle, complete with drum kit, by public transport.

Dave Mylne himself clearly had aspirations to get involved in the playing side of jazz and tried his hand at drumming. A photograph, sent in by Drew Landles and shown in an SBS Newsletter[56], shows him playing drums in a band at the Oddfellows Hall, with Bob Craig, Stu Eaton, Drew Bruce and Drew Landles himself on piano. Dave Mylne was much involved in promoting jazz in Edinburgh during the Revival, had presented many record sessions and, by 1950, was running the Edinburgh Rhythm Club. He later became known as an authority on classic jazz, particularly the playing of Sydney Bechet. Unfortunately, the impressive and extensive record collection which he had built up was auctioned off and broken up after his death. As this collection apparently included a lot of Edinburgh based jazz, it is a great pity that there was no Edinburgh jazz archive at that time, into which it could have been placed.

---

[55] http://sandybrownjazz.co.uk/profilewillieburns.html
[56] SBS Newsletter No. 88, April 2004

Willie Burns (drums) did not attend the RHS but had arrived in Edinburgh with his parents, who had come originally from Stornoway, on the Isle of Lewis in the Hebrides. The profile of Willie on the Sandy Brown Jazz website alluded to above (which is packed with interesting information and is highly recommended to all readers of this book), tells us that his parents had emigrated to Australia, where Willie was born on 5th November 1932. They then returned to Scotland and eventually ended up in Edinburgh, sometime in the later 1930s. On arrival in Edinburgh, Willie was enrolled at George Watson's College but by good fortune, his family put down their roots in Joppa, not far from several members of the RHS Gang, including Stan Grieg and Johnny Twiss (banjo and guitar), both of whom played with the early Brown band. Stan and Johnny Twiss were pals of Willie's older brother Malcolm, known as Mal, and through this connection Willie also got to know them.

Willie was keen on music and had learned to play drums with a local pipe band. He was apparently an extroverted character and he may well have volunteered himself as a drummer, when he found himself in contact with the members of the Brown band. It is reported that these youngsters were able to rehearse in the Burns family home in Esplanade Terrace, in Joppa, and even give impromptu public performances. When the weather was good, the big bay windows of the upstairs room would be wide open and holiday makers from the beach would find themselves being treated to an unofficial jazz concert. Willie's son, Malcolm Burns, told me that there was a story in his family, which he remembers hearing when he was young, that Willie was already playing with the band in Rose Street pubs when he was only 14 years old. If this was so, then it would have been in about 1947, which would certainly tie in nicely with the time scale of the early Sandy Brown band. It would also, of course, fit in with the future development of the Edinburgh jazz scene, which came to rely on the pubs for regular playing venues.

The Sandy Brown Band
Johnny Twiss (bjo), Stan Greig (pno), Sandy Brown (clt),
Al Fairweather (tpt), Willie Burns (drms)
(from the collection of Malcolm Burns, photographer
unknown)

A record from the time tells us that the band on 29th October 1949 was Al Fairweather, Sandy Brown, Stan Greig, Johnny Twiss on banjo, Will Redpath on bass and Willie Burns on drums. This was also the line up for the band's first studio recording session, the results of which were issued in 1950 on S & M (Swarbrick and Mossman) Records, with the serial numbers S&M 1001 and 1002. The tunes were *Melancholy Blues*, *Irish Black Bottom*, *Alexander* and *Of All the Wrongs You You've Done to Me*. These recordings are now very rare and if anyone has a copy, they are very fortunate. Willie's son Malcolm has a copy of one of the old 78 rpm records but unfortunately it is in two pieces and has been for a long time, the breakage dating from before Malcolm's mother handed it on to him!

Willie became a teenage engineering apprentice, serving his time in Henry Robb's yard in Leith. Willie's family returned to Stornoway in 1950, when his father (yet another Malcolm) 'retired' to run a small Harris Tweed business, and

Willie completed his engineering apprenticeship there before, in the 1950s, becoming a ship's engineer. George Hewitt says that Willie was eventually replaced in the Brown band, at different times, by Farrie Forsyth and Bill Strachan. Malcolm Burns believes that his father never played again with the Brown band after his return to Stornoway. However, he remembers his mother saying that they used to meet up and hang out with Sandy and the band, when they played in Glasgow in the late 1950s, by which time Willie and his wife were living there. Malcolm also remembers a story about Sandy showing off his false teeth, which were apparently split in two to help his blowing technique or something of the sort. Given Sandy's later reputation and the many stories about his teeth, it seems a shame that no enterprising salesman has tried to market special Sandy Brown dentures, already split in two, to help clarinet disciples play like Sandy!

Willie Burns died, at the age of 60, on 5th May 1993, having suffered a heart attack. After he died, Stan Greig got in touch with his wife Barbara and Willie's son Malcolm, visited Stan in London. Several members of Willie's family had an interest in music, including his son who took up guitar in the 1970s, and several grandchildren who sing, play guitar or bagpipes. One granddaughter won a prize for her singing and has a saxophone playing grandfather on her mother's side of the family. His name is Jim Galloway but this is not the Jim Galloway from Ayrshire, who was to be great success in the Edinburgh International Jazz Festivals of the 1980/90s, but another reeds player of the same name who came from Kirkcaldy. He attended Edinburgh College of Art and played jazz on the sax and clarinet, sometimes leading bands, from the late 1950s on, playing in the bebop style. Later, he lived in London and Manchester, where he became involved in playing with big bands. He now, in 2011, lives near Glenrothes, where he has continued to play, and has appeared in Glasgow with the Michael Deans band.

Rather endearingly, **Will Redpath (bass)**, who played bass on the S&M recordings, described himself, as *'the*

World's worst bass player'[57]. In the profile on Dizzy Jackson on the Sandy Brown Jazz website[58] (another profile well worth reading), there is another good story about Will Redpath, who clearly did not mind telling stories against himself. Firstly, Dizzy Jackson tells us *'Someone once told me that Will used to play with a pair of leather gloves on. I don't know if that's true.'* Will then goes on to explain *'The story about me wearing gloves (or rather one on my right hand) – or Elastoplast - is true. I had taken up the bass because I was desperate to participate in this music I loved, but I quickly found out that I was no musician and had to do feverish mental calculations when the boys decided to change key, which they did instinctively. I had bought the double bass from a pawn shop for £5. It leaked, so that I had to pull the strings very hard. This resulted in shredding my fingers and producing a noise dominated by the string hitting the wood. The whole episode was one that I would rather have forgotten'.* (Note: Will was not alone in his suffering, or his solutions. When I first got into skiffle music in the late 1950s, I started on the washboard and found that (a) I could not keep the thimbles on my fingers and that (b) when the thimbles flew off, I was left scrubbing away with my bare fingers. This had an effect like a cheese grater and clearly could not be allowed to continue as I was beginning to have visions of being left fingerless. I too wore gloves, with thimbles riveted on, which partly solved the problem (the rivets hurt my fingers inside the gloves) but left me looking a bit of a prat).

Jim Walker remembers what he describes as a tremendous party at Will Redpath's house in Morningside Place. This took place at the time when Graeme Bell's Australian Jazz Band was in town and the pianist from that band turned up at the party. Jim recalls that the pianist *'played until his fingers must have been raw'* and that Sandy Brown, who was *'...incredibly drunk, was propped up against the door post with his clarinet and played some of the most marvellous music I have ever heard'.* However poorly he rated his own bass playing, Will was clearly an

---

[57] SBS Newsletter No. 95, November 2004
[58] http://www.sandybrownjazz.co.uk/profiledizzyjackson.html

enthusiastic jazzer and we know that he came from a creative family, Jim Walker telling us that he was the nephew of the famous Scottish painter, Anne Redpath. Jim also says that Will had taken up bass after a *'valiant struggle with the sousaphone'*. I would like to have met Will Redpath. I think I would have liked him and, after all, whatever he might say about his own contribution, he did record with several of the legendary figures of British traditional jazz, something that not everyone can claim.

Charles 'Dizzy' Jackson (bass), who was born in Edinburgh on 14th July 1932 and attended the RHS, replaced Will Redpath in the Brown band. He had acquired his nickname because he could waggle his ears in imitation of a 'B' movie actor of the time, who was called Dizzy. He was a little younger than Sandy, Al and Bob, who were already active with their earliest jazz band, and Dizzy recalled that he heard them play in the school playground during a mock election project. Dizzy noted that Sandy was *'the dominant figure in the band – as ever!'* Later, Dizzy and some friends started going regularly to listen to jazz at the West End Cafe in Shandwick Place, the street that is a continuation of the west end of Princes Street. This establishment crops up constantly in tales of the Revival in Edinburgh and Dizzy's memory of the place is recorded in his profile on the Sandy Brown Jazz website mentioned above[59]. He says *'It had an ornate entrance and you would go down a long corridor where you could get coffee, to a huge room at the back. The room was about twenty feet high with a stage at the back. There was no alcohol served, just coffee with waitress service at the tables. I can remember hearing the Graeme Bell Band and many others there.'*

Again we are indebted to the profile of Dizzy on the Sandy Brown Jazz website for the tale of how he came to replace Will Redpath. Jimmy Gavin, a close associate of the RHS Gang, apparently told Dizzy that the band was looking for a bass player, as Will Redpath had left. Jimmy apparently informed Dizzy that as he, Dizzy, had played violin at school, he ought to be able to handle a double bass! Having given this some thought, Dizzy bought himself

---

[59] http://www.sandybrownjazz.co.uk/profiledizzyjackson.html

a bass for £20 at Gordon Simpson's music shop, which was in Stafford Street, just round the corner from the West End Café. Like so many in jazz history, Dizzy commenced to teach himself how to play and went along to practice with the band. Help from Stan Greig, regarding chord structure and musical intervals, enabled Dizzy to make progress and he soon became a regular member of the band, playing with them in the West End Café and at other gigs. Incidentally, he bought well and in 2011 he is still playing the same double bass. It would be interesting to know its value now.

Dizzy has recalled how astounded he was (gobsmacked is the word he used) by the trumpet playing of Al Fairweather and says that he was moved to tears by the quality of Al's playing, particularly his hot tone and musical ideas. Al, Dizzy reported, always had something to say and the numbers would get increasingly hotter and hotter, as the ensemble playing developed. He also tells of playing at the Art Revels, an annual dance of incredible wildness run by the students at the Edinburgh College of Art. It was at this gig that Al Fairweather once removed an irritating invader of the band stand by shifting his trumpet to his left hand and belting the invading nuisance with his right. I can also vouch for the wildness of the Art Revels, having played at the event on many occasions in the 1960s. It was a fancy dress dance and once, just as I was arriving, a reveller turned up dressed in a large cardboard tube with balloons at his feet. Asked by the doorman what he was supposed to be, he responded that he was an erect penis and was most indignant to be refused entry on the grounds of obscenity. Nothing if not resourceful, he stamped on his balloons and was allowed in as a rocket.

Dizzy is listed as a member of the Brown band that played at the Big Bill Broonzy concert at the Usher Hall in 1952, mentioned above and recorded by Sandy Currie. Many years later, in 1998, a transcription from Sandy Currie's recording of the concert was released by Lake Records (LAKE CD94). This recording reveals just how good the Brown band was at this early point in its history. The band line-up is given on the CD sleeve as Sandy Brown, Al Fairweather, Bob Craig, Stan Greig (who played both piano and drums during the concert), Norrie Anderson (banjo),

Dizzy Jackson (bass) and Farrie Forsyth (drums). Although Sandy Currie's original recording tape had deteriorated, the recording had at some time been copied onto acetate, and it was possible to clean this up to a condition suitable for general release. Sandy's profile on the Sandy Brown Jazz website says that the band played the first half of the concert and Broonzy the second half[60]. However, this is not what the printed programme for the concert says. The programme gives the running order as:

1. Sandy Brown's Jazz Band set the pace for tonight (list of tunes)
2. Big Bill Broonzy and his guitar ramble through a selection of Folk songs, guitar solos and spirituals (list of tunes)

Intermission

3. The Jazz Band returns to the fray (list of tunes)
4. Big Bill's Skiffle Party ends the evening during which he and the band will play a completely unpredictable choice of blues (list of tunes)

As indicated in the above extract, the programme lists the tunes that the band would play and the tunes from which Broonzy would select his songs for the evening. Of course, on the night either Broonzy or the band or both may well have deviated from this plan and, given the improvisatory nature of jazz and the blues, this seems not unlikely.

Dizzy Jackson's place in the band at this concert has been questioned by some who believe that it was a bass player called John Rae who played. This includes a contemporary, Bill Strachan, who also says that it was he who played drums at this concert and not Farrie Forsyth. Jazz enthusiast the late Janol Scott also believed that Bill Strachan and John Rae were the drummer and bass player respectively. In addition, John Rae's widow, Jacqueline Rae, wrote about this to the SBS in October 2000[61], making a convincing case that it had been her late husband who

---

[60] http://sandybrownjazz.co.uk/sandybrown.html
[61] SBS Newsletter No. 16 April 1998, 46 October 2000

played bass. John Rae, who died in 1976, was a medical student who played with Al and Sandy in about 1951-52. George Hewitt, however, believes it was Dizzy he heard that night and Dizzy himself is adamant that it was he who played. Dizzy has said[62] *'I played the '52 concert on bass. I had already been with the band for a year when the concert took place. I actually still have a visual memory of being on the stand in the hall and playing and got particularly excited at Sandy's solo in High Society. I can even remember signing the visitor's book in the Shakespeare Bar next to the Usher Hall as visiting artists did and getting a free drink. What musician would forget that? Bob and Stan are quite certain it was me playing. Farrie was already the regular drummer when I joined the band'.* Jim Young, another long serving Edinburgh bass player whom we will meet later, was also at the concert and confirms that he remembers Dizzy Jackson playing bass that night and this is also the view of trombonist Mike Pollett, who was another attending the concert.

I thought that I might have been able to throw some light on the situation when I managed to get hold of a copy of the printed programme for the concert from trumpeter Peter Davenport, but no such luck. The programme, although detailed in other respects, does not give the line-up of the band. On the back of the programme, there are several advertisements, including one for a Jazz Band Ball, featuring Sandy's band, at the Oddfellows Hall the following Friday. This does list the band line-up but, frustratingly, shows Stan Grieg as 'piano and drums' but does not list any other drummer and lists no bass player at all! We already know that Stan played both piano and drums at the Broonzy concert because, clearly audible on the CD, Sandy announces, rather condescendingly in my view, that Stan is going to have *'an attempt'* on the drums. Stan had been playing piano up to this point and there is clearly another drummer playing at the same time. The advert for the Jazz Band Ball also lists Hoss Ross on washboard but there is no trace of a washboard on the CD recording of the concert. All very mysterious!

---

[62] SBS Newsletter No. 16, April 1998

The sleeve notes for the CD of the concert, issued by Lake Records, were written by Sandy Currie himself and he certainly lists Dizzy as the bass player. However, Sandy Currie himself later contributed to the uncertainty, when he sent to the SBS, a photograph of the band setting up prior to the concert and identifies a figure in the photo as John Rae[63]. This certainly reinforces the doubt about the identity of the bass player. Further to this, Sandy Currie pointed out that there were in fact, not one but two concerts at the Usher Hall, involving the Sandy Brown Band. The second concert took place in January 1953, a year after the Big Bill Broonzy concert, with the Brown Band supporting, on this occasion, the Freddy Randall Band. Perhaps the source of the confusion lies here and, remembering that these two concerts took place a very long time ago in the early 1950s, memories of who played at which concert may well have become hazy. As anyone who has tried interviewing people about times in the past will know, it is quite amazing how memories, with absolutely no ulterior motive, will differ in accounts of the same events. It seems to me totally understandable that memories vary, sometimes quite substantially, about events of more than fifty years ago. I played with the Old Bailey band in the Usher Hall on 1st April 1966 (45 years ago at the time of writing) when we played as support band to the touring Alex Welsh band with Earl Hines. This was our equivalent to the Brown band Usher Hall concerts in 1952 and 1953, and yet, incredibly, I can remember almost nothing about it. This seems utterly ridiculous but it is absolutely true. Furthermore, one member of our band who played that night remembered it as Earl Hines actually playing with us, which he certainly did not, playing only with the Welsh band. As Stu Eaton apparently once said 'Time has a way of distorting the past'!!

In a final effort to resolve the question of who played at the Usher Hall concerts of 1952 and 1953, in 2011 I went to the Shakespeare Bar, still next to the Usher Hall as described by Dizzy, and asked if they still had visitor's books from the 1950s. The manager said that she had no knowledge of any such books but suggested they may have

---

[63] SBS Newsletter No. 20, Aug 1998

been handed over to the Usher Hall itself or to the City Central Library. Both would have been suitable depositories for what were, after all, interesting local historical documents but there was record of them at either location. It remains to be resolved but for the moment at least, it must remain a mystery.

Dizzy also took part in the London tour in 1953, mentioned above, and recalls that *'Sandy and Al were now colossal and Bob Craig was at his prime'*. He also says that Wood Green was a marvelous gig. Trombonist Archie Sinclair, of whom we will hear much more later in this book, was down from Edinburgh and he, Dizzy and Ken Colyer went home by tube *'more than a little drunk'*. Ken tried to demonstrate the single-handed way to roll a cigarette and covered the floor in tobacco and fag paper. Archie was sick, then fell asleep in a toilet cubicle and had to be rescued by Al Fairweather, who had appeared from somewhere, and who climbed over the cubicle door and released him.

After Dizzy had completed his National Service, in about 1956, he was invited by Sandy and Al to move to London to join up with them again. However, Dizzy was in the throes of completing his degree at Edinburgh University and did not feel like moving to London in any case, so he turned down the offer and stayed where he was. Dizzy Jackson, in his 'day job', was a school teacher and later a Headmaster and, like Bob Craig, he remained for decades a much valued and active player of jazz in Edinburgh. He will appear again later in this book, when he played with important Edinburgh bands such as 'Charlie McNair's Jazz Band', the 'Spirits of Rhythm' and 'Dave Keir's Hot Five' and eventually on into the twenty first century.

Jimmy Gavin (trumpet), who had been instrumental in encouraging Dizzy Jackson to take up the double bass, was born in Duns in the Borders in 1928 but moved with his family to Edinburgh when he was only three weeks old. Although he was to be closely involved with the RHS Gang and the rest of the Edinburgh jazz crowd of the 1940/50s, he did not attend the Royal High School but was educated at James Clark's School. On leaving school, Jimmy worked as a draughtsman surveyor with the Ordnance Survey and then, when he was twenty seven, he entered the Edinburgh

79

College of Art. He was later to become an artist and lecturer in art at the Carlisle College of Art, now part of the University of Cumbria. He had heard jazz on the radio from an early age and had been captivated by it right away. By the age of sixteen or seventeen, Jimmy had acquired a trumpet and proceeded to teach himself how to play it, commenting to me in 2011 that, while he thought that he had a good tone, he considered his technical skills to have been fairly limited. His first model on trumpet was Bix Beiderbecke, soon to be followed by Louis Armstrong. Technically limited or not, he was soon associating with other like-minded jazzers, including Mike Hart (then playing drums), the trombone player Jimmy Hilson, clarinettists Norrie Sinclair and Ian 'Daz' Arnott and pianist Drew Landles, some of whom will feature later in this book. In time, he formed a band of his own, **Gavin's Gloryland Jazz Band**, which, at one time or another, had Mike Hart on drums, Jimmy Hilson on trombone and Daz Arnott on clarinet. Jimmy remembers the band playing gigs in Musselburgh Town Hall and at a church hall in Liberton.

Gavin's Gloryland Jazz Band playing at the 1950 or '51 student's rag week parade. Jimmy Gavin (tpt), Jimmy Hilson (tbn), Norrie Sinclair (clt) and Mike Hart (drms). Jazz band leader-to-be Archie Sinclair gazes out from the foreground. (from the collection of Jimmy Gavin, photographer unknown)

80

Amongst Jimmy's other jazz related memories is one which concerns a visit to Paris in the 1950s. Jimmy and Dizzy Jackson were in a Paris pub when Dizzy said that he thought that a man standing at the end of the bar looked like Albert Nicholas, the great Creole clarinettist. Nicholas, born in New Orleans in 1900, was an almost exact contemporary of Louis Armstrong and one of the finest and most mellow clarinet players in all of jazz. Like his childhood friend Sydney Bechet, he had found his star on the rise again in the context of the post-WWII traditional jazz revival and had settled in France in 1953. Greatly daring, Jimmy Gavin approached the chap at the bar who confirmed that he was indeed Albert Nicholas and, after a few drinks together, invited Dizzy and Jimmy back to his flat where he cooked them the famous New Orleans dish of red beans and rice. What an experience for two young Edinburgh jazzers who must have felt that one of their Gods was walking the Earth. Although Jimmy Gavin's career as an active jazz musician was to be fairly brief, his interest in jazz was to be life-long and in 2011, now in his eighties, he was still turning up at Edinburgh jazz gigs, his enthusiasm for the music undimmed.

Jim 'Farrie' Forsyth (drums), according to George Hewitt, played drums with just about every band there was in Edinburgh and Glasgow in the 1950s and 60s. George describes him as an *excellent Baby Dodds style drummer with an infectious brand of humour'*. Lenny Herd, a fine trumpet player from Paisley, has a photo of Farrie playing with Glasgow's George Penman's Jazzmen in 1961 and he also played with George Hewitt and Ralph Laing (then playing trumpet but later a well-known piano player and writer) in the Eagle Jazz Band, which was west coast based, in 1955/56. This band also included the banjo player Brian Weld, who is still (in 2011) playing regularly in Edinburgh. George Hewitt also says that Farrie played on some of the sides made with the S&M recording people. Farrie eventually departed to London, where he played with jazz musicians of the calibre of Ken Sims, a top trumpet player who put in time with Acker Bilk's famous band. Farrie Forsyth died in December 1999.

Two other close associates of the Gang, although not RHS scholars, were **Norrie Anderson (banjo)** and Ian 'Daz' Arnott, yet another of the long list of good Edinburgh clarinet players. Norrie Anderson, tall and red haired, was a contemporary of Sandy Brown and Al Fairweather at Art College and replaced Johnny Twiss in the Brown band in about 1951. He continued to play on a regular basis through 1951/52 and played with the band at the famous Big Bill Broonzy Usher Hall concert in 1952. He also, according to George Hewitt, appeared with the band on various recordings issued by Swarbrick and Mossman, Lake and Esquire. Norrie Anderson died in December 2009. Unfortunately, I have been unable to unearth any information about the earlier banjo player, Johnny Twiss.

Ian 'Daz' Arnott (clarinet), although not RHS educated, was closely associated with the RHS Gang and played in 1951/52 with a 'second line' RHS band, **Kenny Jack's Jazzmen**. This band was run by Kenny Jack while still a schoolboy and its membership included Kenny Jack (tpt), George Hewitt (tbn), Ian 'Daz' Arnott (clt), George Patterson (pno), Alec Wilson (bjo) and Fraser Bowman (drms/washboard). Apparently this band actually made a recording. The tunes were 'Muskrat Ramble' and 'Buddy's Habit' and the recording took place at Graham's Recording Studios in Haddington Place, Edinburgh. Ian Arnott failed to turn up and George Hewitt describes the recordings as probably sounding like the Buddy Bolden Band on a very bad day.

Later, Ian played with Mike Hart and also various short-lived bands formed by George Hewitt and Ralph Laing in about 1953/54. He was a great admirer of the playing of Sandy Brown, trying determinedly to emulate Sandy's Doddsian tone and even striving to imitate Sandy's way of holding his clarinet and his characteristic 'bull neck' when playing. Allegedly, he and Sandy Brown once went up Arthur's Seat (non-Edinburgh readers will be relieved to hear that this refers to a hill and not to a person) for an alfresco duet. Ian also played occasional duets with Sandy at the West End Café, before he emigrated to Canada in about 1954. There is story that he and Sandy Brown were supposed to record some duets in London but Ian failed to turn up (was this becoming a habit?), as he had burned his fingers trying to repair a faulty car exhaust. Ian occasionally re-appeared in Edinburgh thereafter, but spent most of his life in Toronto, where both Stu Eaton and Ralph Laing played with him and were impressed.

In Canada, Ian played with many great jazz names including Buck Clayton, Ruby Braff, Vic Dickenson, Edmund Hall, Jimmy Rushing, Pee Wee Russell, Cootie Williams, Rex Stewart, Dickie Wells, Lil Hardin, Paul Barbarin, George Lewis, Willie 'The Lion' Smith, Wingy Manone and Ben Webster. He was a member of the Imperial Jazz Band in Toronto and Dr McJazz, led by expatriate Glasgow trumpeter Charlie Gall, and also played with a Canadian Climax Jazz Band. Ian was invited to join Turk Murphy's band but was unable to do so, because of union rules. He also played classical music. George Hewitt describes him as a fine Johnny Dodds styled player and likens his playing to that of Dave Paxton. Ian Arnott came over as a soloist to play at the 1981 Edinburgh Jazz Festival and played with the Scottish Jazz Advocates, in a venue in Hanover Street called Refreshers. I played at this session but, for reasons I would now rather draw a veil over, I can remember next to nothing about it and regrettably, nothing about Ian's playing. Not his fault but mine, but I can remember others in our band talking about what a good player he was. Late in life, Ian Arnott suffered heart problems and he died in Canada in May 2006.

Another drummer with the Brown band was the aforementioned **Bill Strachan (drums)**, who was born in Edinburgh in 1928 and attended the RHS, a year or two after Sandy Brown. Although not attending the same school, during his school days Bill was friendly with John and Archie Semple. Bill began playing drums in the local Boys Brigade Band and was with them from the age of 15 until he was 18. He was introduced to jazz on record and began buying one record each month, an early favourite being Muggsy Spanier. A friend, Bill Roberts, worked on Salveson's whaling ships and was able to bring back many records which were not then available locally. Another source of good listening was a school friend called Janol Scott, who had managed to get hold of a lot of Jelly Roll

Morton recordings. Bill soon started going along to the Edinburgh Rhythm Club, then in Methven Simpson's music shop, where he met and heard some of the early jazzers, including Drew Bruce and Bill McGregor. These were clearly interesting times and Bill remembers some of the jazz crowd going to Edinburgh's only Indian restaurant, near the Crown Bar, where they could only afford the cheapest item on the menu, a cup full of rice tipped onto a plate with a hard-boiled egg covered in curry sauce.

National Service followed in 1948/49, during which time he never left the UK because he was in the army rugby team! Back in Edinburgh, when Willie Burns dropped out of the Sandy Brown Band in about 1950, Bill became the drummer, the line up at that time being Sandy Brown (clt), Al Fairweather (tpt), Bob Craig (tbn), Norrie Anderson (bjo), Johnnie Rae (bs), and Stan Grieg, who played both piano and drums with the band. Soon after this, business and rugby dominated Bill's life and he moved to live in the west of Scotland, not returning to Edinburgh until 1977.

Interested in reviving his jazz career, a vacancy in Bill Salmond's Louisiana Ragtime Band, created by the departure of drummer Iain Forde, led to Bill joining this band, with whom he stayed for about a year. Later he was to play in Jim Petrie's band in Basin Street, a popular and busy jazz lounge in the Haymarket Station Bar. Later still, in the late 1980s, he played with his fellow RHS Gangsters Bob Craig and Dizzy Jackson together with Al Fairweather, who had also returned to town by then. These veterans of the early days were joined by Jack Graham (clt), Graham Scott (pno) and Jock Westwater (bjo), all of whom we will meet in later chapters. Bill says that, for a spell, Kenny Milne, better known as a drummer, played second trumpet in this band, which had a regular spot at the Glen Elg Hotel, at the foot of Leamington Terrace. He also played another regular, although short-lived, spot with Jim Petrie's band, which at that time include the clarinet player Dick Lee, at a pub in Auchendinny, a village near Penicuik. Other gigs that were regular for a while were with a band in the Nelson Hotel in Nelson Street and in the Royal Hotel in Royal Terrace but then, sometime in the early 1990s, Bill retired from playing. At the time of writing in 2011, he continues to meet up regularly with other veteran jazzers involved in the Edinburgh Jazz Archive Group and with them, he played a part in the successful setting up of an archive of Edinburgh jazz in the Central Library.

St Andrew's Rag Day 1954
Ian Arnott (clt), unknown (pno), Ralph Laing (tpt),
George Hewitt (tbn), Jim Goudie (bjo)
(from the collection of George Hewitt, photographer
unknown)

Kenny Jack (trumpet) attended the RHS from 1946-52 and, with contemporary **George Hewitt (trombone)**, formed the school boy band Kenny Jack's Jazzmen, with the line-up given above. Later, Farrie Forsyth played drums with the band and Dizzy Jackson sometimes played bass. Kenny Jack's health was to break down in later life and he died in the 1980s. George Hewitt, whose recollections of the 1940s and 50s have contributed so much to this account already, had started to play trombone in his third year at the RHS, when both he and Kenny Jack had lessons from an elderly brass band conductor, John Faulds. The tuition took place in the Brass Band Hall in Hanover Street. Here Mr Faulds demonstrated his abhorrence of girls wearing any form of makeup, the lessons being punctuated by abrasive comments on 'painted women' observed from the Hall window. George and Kenny were given welcome encouragement by Stan Greig and they were invited to rehearsals of the Brown band at Stan's parent's house in Morton Street, Portobello. They also went along to the West End Café and to Dave Mylne's record sessions, when Mylne would deliver talks on various aspects of jazz, illustrated with recordings from his extensive collection.

George Hewitt recalls that the Kenny Jack Jazzmen were rehearsing in the Brass Band Hall by 1952 and a whole afternoon spent trying to get a single tune right was not at all unusual. They eventually began to get a few gigs, including an interval spot at the RHS summer dance, probably the first time jazz had been heard in the hallowed precincts of the RHS preparatory school. Occasionally they hit the big time and played as second band to the Sandy Brown band at Jazz Band Balls, held at the Oddfellow's Hall. George later moved to live in Ayrshire where, after continuing to make the long journey to and from Edinburgh for band rehearsals for a time, he joined up with Ralph Laing, who played trumpet at that time, and they formed first the Ayrshire Jazz band and, later, the Eagle Jazz Band. At the time of writing in 2011, George Hewitt continues to play trombone with his 'New Orleans Joymakers' at monthly jazz concerts at the Harbour Arts Centre in Irvine, a band that includes Lenny Herd (tpt), Tom Taylor (clt), Tony Lang (bjo) and Hamish Hendry (drms), all from the west of Scotland, and Graham Blamire (bs), who travels through from Edinburgh. In spite of the generally parlous state of traditional jazz in 2011, it is good to be able to report that these sessions are consistently well supported, with many regulars making sure of their tickets by booking well in advance.

Now come two names who will make much more major appearances later in this book, **Mike Hart (drums, banjo later)** and Charlie McNair (trumpet), both of whom were RHS schoolboys, although a year or two younger than the original Gang.

The Sandy Brown Band playing at Pete Davenport's 21st Birthday party. Bob Craig, Al Fairweather, a youthful Mike Hart, Sandy Brown, Farrie Forsyth (by kind permission of Peter Davenport)

Mike, who was born in Inverness on 23 March 1934, originally appeared as a drummer and first played with a band led by Jimmy Gavin, Gavin's Gloryland Band in 1949, when only in his mid-teens. He then went on to play drums with the Sandy Brown band between 1950 and 1952.

One night in the West End Café, Sandy had come up to Mike and asked him if he would like to sit in with the band. Mike recalls that he *'nearly fell over but immediately accepted and I did a number of gigs with Sandy over the years'*. Mike also says of Sandy that *'He was not an easy person to play with, in that his musical direction was conveyed to me via Al Fairweather and Stan Greig. He never spoke to me at all. His standards were so high that I used to feel extremely nervous. He was virtually a God to us young chaps'[64]*. Mike has also said how much he was influenced in his jazz career by his early association with Sandy, Al Fairweather and Stan Greig. With the Brown band, Mike made a trip to London in 1952 when they played several gigs including the 'Big Jazz Show', run by Maurice Kinn at the Royal Albert Hall. The band that made the trip was Al

---

[64] SBS Newsletter No. 68, August 2002

Fairweather (tpt), Sandy Brown (clt), Bob Craig (tbn), Stan Greig (pno), Norrie Anderson (bjo), Dizzy Jackson (bs) and Mike on drums. Stan Greig played a couple of numbers on drums at the Albert Hall but was probably a bit handicapped, as the bass drum pedal had broken while Mike was playing. (NB This story will be of particular interest to the many drummers whom Mike castigated for banging the bass drum too hard, later in his career!) Among the other bands taking part were the Mick Mulligan band with George Melly, the Sid Phillips band and the Yorkshire Jazz Band. Mike later, of course, switched to banjo and guitar and went on to play a very major part in Edinburgh jazz for the next six decades. The frequent appearance of his name throughout this book will be a tribute to his work and influence.

Charlie McNair (trumpet), who was a couple of years older than Mike Hart, started playing in the early 1950s and rapidly established himself as a band leader. It was Charlie's band that Dizzy Jackson joined when he turned down the chance to go to London to rejoin Sandy and Al. Later in this book, we will pick up Charlie's long and successful career as an Edinburgh band leader.

We now come to a unique and ubiquitous figure, not RHS but another associate of the Gang, and one who was to be a constant presence in the local jazz scene from the mid-1940s until his death in 1993. His name was **Jackie MacFarlane (vocals)**, into whose early recollections we have already dipped in Chapter I. Jackie was around the jazz scene in the early days of the Brown band and, unable to play an instrument, clearly decided that his way into active participation was by becoming a singer. In addition to his habit of popping up at gigs volunteering a song or two, a habit he would maintain across six decades, Jackie also served as 'bouncer' at various locations at which jazz was presented. He is particularly remembered for his 'bouncer' duties at the Oddfellow's Hall, duties shared with Tam (later Sean) Connery, when he was reckoned to be a much more effective bouncer than Connery. Sandy Brown attributed Jackie's 'bouncering' effectiveness to his experiences when he fought in the Spanish Civil war[65]. By 1954 Jackie was acting as master of ceremonies at the Sunday evening gigs at the Condon Club in India Buildings. In spite of his success as a bouncer, Jackie was a good natured and kind hearted chap. There was at least one occasion when an Edinburgh jazzer had had to put one of his musical instruments into hock and Jackie, who could not have been all that well-off for cash himself, immediately offered to pay to retrieve the instrument, allowing the jazzer to continue to play his gigs. I can also remember Bob Craig habitually introducing Jackie, who was of generous girth, as '..*our resident globe...*', with Jackie chortling away, enjoying the joke as much as anyone.

The Edinburgh Jazz Club's Christmas Jubilee

JAZZ BAND BALL

is at the Oddfellows Hall, Forrest Road, on 30th December 1949, from 8 p.m. to 1 a.m.

With Sandy Brown's Jazz Band

Special Buffet   Late Buses

THREE SHILLINGS TO BE PAID AT THE DOOR

(From the collection of George Hewitt)

There were a number of locations where all this jazz activity took place. According to George Hewitt, the Edinburgh Rhythm Club had its first meetings, in the mid-1940s, above Methven Simpson's music shop, which was then in Princes Street. Later, the club moved to 20 Hill Street followed by a similar set up at the Lido Hotel in Douglas Crescent. By 1952/53, the Crown Bar in Lothian

---

[65] Binns D (editor), 'The McJazz Manuscripts - A collection of the writings of Sandy Brown', Faber and Faber 1979, by kind permission of David Binns

Street was functioning as 'The Stud Club' and another jazz centre was 'The Condon Club', meeting on the top floor of India Buildings in Victoria Street. The bass player, Jim Young, recalls that it was mostly the Archie Semple/Alex Welsh band that played there and their Dixieland/Chicagoan style certainly ties in with the name 'Condon Club'. Rather disappointingly, the name 'The Stud Club' did not make any reference to the general virility of the jazz crowd but was just an abbreviation of 'The Student Club', and was initially run by Sandy Brown.

Lothian Street, where the Crown Bar was situated, is now long gone, swept away during the development of the area around the McEwan Hall. The Crown Bar was still going strong as a jazz venue in the 1960s when I first appeared around the jazz scene and I remember gigs there with a band led by the trumpeter Jim Petrie and also with the band put together in the mid-1060s for the return from abroad of Dave Paxton. In addition to these, as we have already seen, jazz had been featured in the West End Café (later to become the 'New Yorker') in Shandwick Place and, as we have already heard, there were the 'Jazz Band Balls' in the Oddfellow's Hall in Forrest Road. The West End Café seems, at least for a while, to have thrived on jazz events. As we have already noted, quite a number of touring bands appeared there including the Freddie Randall Band, Mick Mulligan's Band with George Melly and Graeme Bell's Jazz Band from Australia.

The very fact that so many, and so many good, jazz musicians were produced by a single High School in such a short period of time of course begs the question 'Why?' That the school itself encouraged jazz seems at least uncertain and there are some indications that it may have displayed a disapproving attitude. However, accounts vary, even amongst those who were involved at the time. Dizzy Jackson says *'jazz was not generally encouraged at the school*[66]. Dickie Alexander, an Edinburgh town councillor who was involved in the work to set up the memorial plaque to Sandy Brown and Al Fairweather, in a letter to the Scotsman in 1996, subsequently included in a Sandy

---

[66] www.sandybrownjazz.co.uk/profiledizzyjackson.html

Brown Society Newsletter, said *'The thrawn resistance to flair and innovation goes back a long way. At the old Royal High School, Edinburgh, pupils were forbidden to play jazz, so Sandy Brown and his pals played in the school lavatories out of earshot of the music master'.* Dickie, who was writing in support of the plan to create a memorial to Sandy Brown and Al Fairweather, then goes on to propose *'Let's put a plaque outside the old school lavatories at the Calton Hill building. That's where it all began!'*[67]

On the other hand, George Hewitt who, along with Kenny Jack, had been invited by Bill Bowie, the head of music at the school, to learn to play the trombone and trumpet respectively, with a view to joining the school orchestra, gives a rather different slant. George says *'...Bill Bowie had never objected to Kenny and myself being involved in jazz since he reckoned it improved our playing for the classical stuff.'* Another Royal High pupil from the 1940s, Jim Walker, is also very much of the view that the school, if not quite giving jazz an official blessing, at least did nothing to put obstacles in its way. Jim felt that one speaker at the ceremony when the memorial plaque was put in place had given a clear impression that the school had been highly discouraging towards jazz. Jim rejects this view and points out that, as no one stepped in to stop the use of the gym for jazz band practices and a jazz band in full cry is not the easiest of things to keep dark, there was at least a degree of tacit approval from within the school.

It seems to me that the most likely thing is that the world-wide awakening of interest in traditional jazz had impacted on some of the youngsters at the school, just as things new and probably a bit rebellious, would always intrigue the young. What perhaps was different, was that one or two of the youngsters, Sandy Brown particularly but also Al Fairweather, Stu Eaton, Dave Paxton, Bob Craig and Stan Greig, were not only sufficiently strong characters to influence their peers but were quickly good and successful enough to encourage others and keep the movement going. What remains surprising is the sheer number of

---

[67] SBS Newsletter No 1, July 1996, from letter by Dickie Alexander to 'The Scotsman', 14th June 1996

youngsters, RHS and associated others, who got involved, the astonishing quality of the best of the music they produced and just how long their influence was to last. The supply of jazz musicians from the RHS (and increasingly from other sources in Edinburgh) did not finish with the RHS Gang of the 1940s and early 1950s. Several more from the RHS were to come along over the next decade or so, including Jack Duff, Bill Salmond and John Nicholson, later well known as the actor John McGlynn, who starred in the famous TV series 'All Creatures Great and Small'.

As we have already noted, there was a second group of pioneers around who, even in the 1940s, had started to go down a different musical track. This was the group which formed around the trumpeter Alex Welsh and the clarinetist Archie Semple. They were almost exact contemporaries of the RHS Gang and although Alex, Archie and the trombone player Dave Keir played at various times with the RHS Gang, their loyalties and music belonged to a slightly different version of the classic jazz tradition, as described in Chapter II. They were to become known as the Dixielanders and they too were to make a major impact on the world of traditional jazz. It is to them that we will turn our attention next.

Chapter V

The Dixieland Pioneers

I t is an astonishing fact that Edinburgh produced, not only the RHS Gang which was to provide several high quality British jazz musicians but, more or less simultaneously, a second group which was to have a similar impact. Although this group could not claim a handy label arising from a common scholastic background, they did come to be distinguished from the RHS Gang by being referred to as the **Dixielanders**. This term, used in the descriptive, non-derogatory manner described in Chapter II, seems to me a reasonable title for them, as their principle inspiration was the music played by the so-called Chicagoans associated with Eddie Condon. The Edinburgh Dixielanders of the late 1940s and early 1950s were centred on a pair of brothers, Archie (clt) and John Semple (tpt) and another trumpeter, Alex Welsh. The Semple/Welsh grouping, the Dixielanders, has a place in Edinburgh's jazz history just as significant and long lasting, as that of Sandy, Al and the RHS Gang.

Chronologically, the first of the Dixielanders around the Edinburgh jazz scene was the journalist **George Crockett (drums)**, born in 1920, whom we have already met through his published works and his involvement with the RHS Gang. We know from George Hewitt and others that Crockett seemed more interested in the *'more dixieland'* style of jazz, and this seems to me to make chronological sense. George Crockett's writings demonstrate that he was already interested in jazz by the middle to late 1930s, when he heard both Fats Waller and Coleman Hawkins play in

Edinburgh. In other words, Crockett's interest pre-dated the Revival and it is clear that he was listening to both the live and the recorded jazz of the 1930s. In the 1930s, George would have been an impressionable teenager and, like most of us, it is likely that the music he heard in his teenage years would tend to establish his musical leanings. As this was an era when the cutting edge of jazz was in the hands of people such as Benny Goodman, Artie Shaw, Teddy Wilson and others of their generation, in addition to the slightly older musicians such as Louis Armstrong and Duke Ellington, it would seem logical that Crockett's tastes in jazz were already well formed before the Revival really took hold. In addition to the great Swing Bands, he would almost certainly have been aware of the smaller group music of the Chicago musicians and others, many of whom would have made their living playing in the sections of the big Swing bands.

Although George Crockett was involved, to the extent of making recordings, with the Sandy Brown Band, when the time was ripe, he seems to have been a key factor in the formation of the first Edinburgh band that played in the Dixieland style. This was the band which was to function under Archie Semple's leadership and usually called **Archie Semple's Dixielanders**. This band was later to metamorphose into the **Nova Scotia Jazz Band**, often called simply the Nova Scotians. Both George Hewitt and trumpeter Pete Davenport believe that George Crockett was instrumental in ensuring that a band in the Dixieland style continued after the point when Archie Semple departed Edinburgh for the south. This view is endorsed by Edinburgh trumpeter Andrew Lauder, who joined the Nova Scotians in the mid-1950s, when George Crockett was still active in Edinburgh and still playing in the band. It appears that John Semple also dropped out at about the time his brother left for the south, to be replaced on trumpet by Alex Welsh. It also seems likely that George Crockett, having been instrumental in founding the new band, did not actually lead it but left this duty to someone better suited to leading, even if only because of playing one of the front-line instruments. Later, George was to move to live in Ayrshire, where he continued his career in journalism, and where, in the late 1980s or early 1990s, he hosted a regular jazz programme on West Sound radio. He used the broadcasts to play his favourite records and to interview local musicians and jazz followers. Derek Copland, who knew him well all the years he was in Ayrshire, told me that George continued to play drums and in his final years was playing with Jimmy McCullough and his Scottish Country Dance Band. George Crockett died in Ayr, on 5th January 1996.

Trombonist Dave Keir had moved from the Sandy Brown band to join the Archie Semple led band, reporting that its membership when he joined was John Semple (cnt), Archie Semple (clt and ldr), Dave Keir (tbn), Percy Pegg (pno), Jimmy Mooney (gtr), Mike Samuels (bs) and George Crockett (drms). It was to be Dave Keir who assumed the leadership of the band after Archie's departure and he also reports that he named it the Nova Scotia Jazz Band. The reason for using a band name not based on the name of an individual was because the new trumpeter, Alex Welsh, felt that, if it was to continue but under a new leader's name, it would lose any reputation it had built up. Apparently this had happened previously. Dave Keir says that the original membership of the Nova Scotians was Alex Welsh (tpt), Dave Keir (tbn, ldr), Jack Graham (clt), Drew Landles (pno), Jimmy Mooney (gtr), Dickie Alexander (bs) and George Crockett (drms). When Dave Keir, in his turn, set off to join the Mick Mulligan band in London in early 1953, Alex Welsh became leader of the Nova Scotians, thus continuing Edinburgh's Dixieland alternative to the fairly strict classicism of the Sandy Brown band.

Amongst the hundreds of papers that I read when writing this book, there was a copy of a part of a letter that had been published in a newspaper or magazine. Unfortunately, there was no clue to the publication, no date given and the name of the writer was missing from the copy. However, the same letter is quoted in a SBS Newsletter[68] and it is clear that it was written by the Edinburgh piano player Ronnie Carruthers. The letter says that students of the jazz scene in Edinburgh would be interested in what it

---

[68] SBS Newsletter No. 31, July 1999

calls '...*the seminal events that occurred in the city's Braid Crescent.*' This street is in the Morningside area of Edinburgh and number 1 Braid Crescent was the home of the Semple family. Ronnie goes on to say that a corporate decision was taken by the family that a band be formed to further the jazz interests of the two boys, John and Archie. A band was duly formed and the line-up is given as Ian Brown (instrument unspecified), Jack McDonald (t – presumably trumpet), John Semple (bugle), Archie Semple and Sandy Brown (clts), Archie Deacon (d – presumably drums) and letter writer, Ronnie Carruthers himself, on piano. Whether this is the Ian Brown, who later played bass around Edinburgh, is uncertain and just how John was going to play jazz on a bugle is not explained. However, this is very early evidence of collaboration involving Sandy Brown and the Semple brothers. Ronnie tells us that, at the start, the combined knowledge of those involved was two tunes and that he could '...*still see the sad twittering of the those Morningsider's curtains as they realized that another day of rest was not to be once the band began to strut their stuff*'. The hostile stirrings from the neighbours unfortunately seem to have alarmed the previously supportive Semple parents, and Ronnie records that, after many happy Sundays, the sessions were suddenly abandoned. He goes on to note however, that '...*the seeds of jazz were truly sown as a result of those unfettered sessions*'. This seems to signal the start of the Semple brothers jazz playing careers and it seems likely that this episode was in the early to mid-1940s, when John would have been in his later teens and Archie and Sandy Brown in their early teens.

John Semple (cornet, piano, drums) was born in Edinburgh around 1925. He and his younger brother Archie developed an early interest in jazz and both brothers took up instruments, John, cornet (he may later have also played trumpet) and piano, and Archie, both trumpet and clarinet. The Semple family moved to South Africa for a while but, before long, returned to Edinburgh. John Semple followed a career as a photographer, working for a firm called Edinburgh Cameras, having served his apprenticeship with Yerburys, the famous Edinburgh photographers, for many years based up on Churchill, in the Morningside area of the town. However, the Semple brothers interest in jazz continued and, away from the day job, John played in a variety of bands, organised and led by Archie or John himself. There was a degree of friendly rivalry but also cooperation, with the other contemporary group of Edinburgh jazzers which included Sandy Brown, Al Fairweather, Stan Greig and others of the RHS Gang. The friendship and cooperation between the two groups is demonstrated by the personnel listings for the recording sessions shown below. Later, when Alex Welsh came along to play trumpet, John Semple switched to piano.

Unlike Alex Welsh and his brother Archie, John was not interested in pursuing a career in full time music. He seems to have been unwilling, for a number of reasons, to consider a move to London, a move which appears to have been considered a pre-requisite for full-time, professional jazz. In addition, it seems that he was modest about his playing abilities, Dave Keir telling me that John was aware of what he saw as his own limitations and had told his brother that, if he found better, he would step down from the trumpet chair. Around the time in the early 1950s when Archie and Alex Welsh departed for the south, John gave up regular playing and concentrated on his career in photography. His interest in jazz continued however, attending concerts and taking a great interest in his brother's and Alex Welsh's successful professional jazz activities in the south. Later on, he played in sessions involving friends, usually playing keyboard or drums. However, it is clear that John Semple had been a significant figure in the early days of Revival jazz in Edinburgh, playing an important part in building the foundations of the traditional jazz hotspot that Edinburgh was to become. John Semple died in Edinburgh, in his late sixties, in 1993.

Archie Semple (clarinet), brother of John, was born in Edinburgh on 31st March 1928. According to John Chilton's 'Who's Who of British Jazz', when he was in his teens, Archie played trumpet as well as clarinet. This would explain why Archie, who was to make a great name for himself as a clarinet player, is listed on trumpet on one of the recordings listed below. Chilton says that Semple served in the Royal Navy in 1946-48 and, by Autumn 1949, was leading a band in Edinburgh called the **Escom Jazz Band**, which later became known as the **Capitol Stompers** and then the **Capitol Jazzmen**. There were clearly several band names in use as there are also accounts of Archie's band being called **Archie Semple's Dixielanders** and **Archie Semple's Capital Jazzmen**.

The Castle Jazz Band, probably at Dalhousie Castle Believed to be Stu Crockett (tbn), John Semple (tpt), Archie Semple (clt), Willie Burns (drms), Johnny Twiss (gtr) and Stan Greig (pno) (from the collection of Malcolm Burns, photographer unknown)

In Spring 1952, Archie moved to London to take up an invitation to join Mick Mulligan's Jazz Band. Later, he was to move to the Freddy Randall band, with whom he played from January 1953 until August 1954. This was followed by a spell in pianist/trombone player Norman Cave's jazz band in late 1954. After that, Archie teamed up again with his Edinburgh colleague Alex Welsh, who had followed him to London, and he remained in this, the first great Alex Welsh band, from February 1955 until March 1963. With that band, Archie made many memorable recordings, in which he beautifully complements the Welsh trumpet, and features on many wonderful tracks. Unhappily, the various pressures of playing jazz for a living started to take their toll on an already less than robust personality, otherwise he might have gone on for very much longer as a member of what was by then, the finest Dixieland band that the UK had ever produced. John Latham, writing in 1993[69], says that when he heard this early version of the Alex Welsh band, Archie was the outstanding player. He describes his tone as having a sweeter and truer edge than that of Pee Wee Russell, noting how effectively Archie could use the bottom register of the clarinet, especially when playing ballads.

Archie Semple seems to have been a vulnerable sort of chap and, to help us understand something of his personality, we are fortunate to have the recollections of Roy Crimmins, a fine trombone player from Perth, recorded in a 1998 article written by John Latham[70]. Roy Crimmins first met Archie in 1951, when Archie's Capitol Jazzmen were support band to the Mick Mulligan band, in which Crimmins was playing. He records that the whole Mulligan band was *'knocked out'* by Archie's playing and that Mulligan asked his bandsmen to take a cut in their already meagre pay, so that Archie could join them. Later, after Alex Welsh came down to London in 1954, both Crimmins and Archie became members of the Alex Welsh band, thus reversing the leader/sideman relationship that Archie and Alex had in Edinburgh. Roy Crimmins says that it soon became obvious that Archie was far from well and, during a strenuous month-long spell at the New Orleans Bierbar in Dusseldorf, his health broke down and he had to return to the UK. Archie's playing at that time, according to Crimmins, was based on that of the great Ed Hall, with a bit of Pee Wee Russell's influence in there as well. However, as Archie became less well, his style became pure Pee Wee Russell. Crimmins recounts that it was not only Pee Wee's musical style that appeared but also some other

---

[69] Latham J, 'Archie Semple', Foot Tappers News (Cardiff), March/April 19930
[70] Latham J, 'Archie Semple (1928-1974) - Roy Crimmins remembers', Jazz Rag, March/April 1998

mannerisms.   Archie, when striving for the right words, would sometimes stammer and tap his teeth with his right forefinger. Years later when Crimmins was touring with Pee Wee Russell, he found to his amazement that Pee Wee did exactly the same thing. What made this extraordinary was that Archie could not have known about this habit of Pee Wee's until that tour, as they had never previously met.

Sadly, Crimmins says that *'slowly Archie cracked up again'* and his playing got more and more like that of Pee Wee Russell. The 'Rough Guide to Jazz'[71] describes Archie as *'a spiritual son of Ed Hall, then Pee Wee Russell'.* This change in Archie's style did not please Alex Welsh, who would make pointed comments that Ed Hall was his favourite clarinet player. Understandably, this made Archie more and more uncomfortable. He had spent most of his life following Ed Hall, whose playing he adored, but as Crimmins said, he just could not help playing like Pee Wee. In the end, there was a shockingly unhappy experience during a BBC broadcast, that left Archie devastated. During the run-through, the producer came into the studio to say that the clarinet player was not, under any circumstances, to play any solos. If ever there was a statement that indicated a complete ignorance of what jazz was about, this was surely it. Archie was then in his Pee Wee Russell phase and Pee Wee's style was one of the most idiosyncratic in all of jazz, full of unexpected twist and turns, bent notes, croaks, wheezy inflections and growls. He has been described by Gunther Schuller[72], a great admirer of Russell's playing and one of the USA's most distinguished musicologists, as *'...a unique, wondrously self-contained musical personality'* and *'...also one of the most touching and human players that jazz has ever known'.* However, Schuller also admits that *'At first hearing, one of those Russell solos tended to give the impression of a somewhat inept musician, awkward and shy, stumbling and muttering along in a rather directionless fashion'.*   To an

---

[71] Carr, Fairweather and Priestly, 'The Rough Guide to Jazz', 3rd Edition May 2004, Rough Guides Ltd, distributed by the Penguin Group

[72] 'The Swing Era: The Development of Jazz, 1930-1945 (History of Jazz)': by Gunther Schuller (1992) 49 words p610, by permission of Oxford University Press, www.oup.com

uninitiated listener, such as this hapless BBC producer, there is little doubt that the playing of Archie Semple in his Pee Wee mode, would sound strange and even alien. Unfortunately, the BBC producer that day was not only unfamiliar with jazz, and therefore unsuitable to be involved with this broadcast, but seems also to have been an extremely insensitive individual. In Archie's hearing, he added to his first comment that the clarinet player was not to solo, saying '...not on my programme, he just can't play'. A much more robust personality than Archie would have been severely shaken by this crass statement. Roy Crimmins, describing Archie's reaction, says 'He was broken. He started shaking with nerves and embarrassment, and he couldn't move or talk. I walked over and took him to the gents where we both had a very large Scotch....He was now a very frightened man in the band'.

Whether this horrible incident caused it or not, Archie's fragile nervous health deteriorated and he started missing gigs with the band. Eventually, he was unable to return to the band, although Alex Welsh continued to pay him. In 1964 he returned briefly to lead his own quartet, but his health broke down once again and he was forced to retire from playing. The 'Rough Guide' says of him 'A charming man but with a deeply nervous disposition, Semple suffered a breakdown on stage at the 1964 Richmond jazz festival and never really played again'. Archie Semple, yet another great Edinburgh jazz man to die young, died in London on 26 January 1974, at the age of only forty five.

Alex Welsh (cornet and trumpet/cornet) was born in Leith on 9th July 1929, the eldest child of Alexander Welsh, a coal merchant, and his wife, Ann Livingstone Plank. The family lived at 2 Lorne Square, just off Leith Walk. John Chilton's 'Who's Who of British Jazz'[73] tells us that Alex played accordion while at Broughton Secondary School and, after leaving school, took up a position of clerk with the Ministry of Works. Alex's girlfriend during his years in Edinburgh was Frances Maxwell, who later married and became the mother of a fine Edinburgh jazz musician of a

---

[73] John Chilton 'Who's Who of British Jazz', second edition 2004, reproduced by permission of Continuum International Publishing Group

later generation, John Burgess. Speaking in 2011, Frances could not recall Alex working with the Ministry of Works but does remember him working for the Scottish Widows, the major life insurance company, in St Andrew's Square. Later, he had lessons on the cornet from one Bill Taverner and started playing with the Leith Silver Band. He seems to have developed an early interest in jazz, modeling his style on that of Bix Beiderbecke, and by 1951, Alex was playing cornet with Archie Semple's Dixielanders. Again, there seems to be some doubt about the name of this band, the internet Wikipedia naming the band as Archie Semple's Capital Jazz Band. The band included Dave Keir on trombone who, like Archie Semple, played in the Chicago style associated with Eddie Condon, a style which would have been entirely compatible with Alex's Bix Beiderbecke inspired trumpet playing. Some recordings were made by this band on the Glasgow based S & M (Swarbrick and Mossman) label.

At some point in 1952, at the time when Archie Semple left go to London, the band that was to be called the Nova Scotians was formed, and Alex played cornet with them for a while. The Nova Scotians seem to have been built originally from the remnants of the Archie Semple band. Dave Keir, who played trombone in this band, tells us that Alex had come in on trumpet to replace John Semple and they also had Dickie Alexander on bass, who was later replaced by Pat Malloy. Sometime after this, Alex Welsh joined Sandy Brown's Blue Five, replacing Al Fairweather, who had moved to London in late 1953. In retrospect, it all sounds a bit like a game of musical chairs.

There was clearly quite a bit of movement generally amongst the Edinburgh jazz musicians at this time and it is hard to be certain about who played in which band and when. However, it is probably correct to assume that there was a pool of jazz musicians who got together in various combinations at various times. Documentation that was with a collection of early acetate recordings, presumably made privately and now in the ownership of Ishbel Semple, includes 'tentative' personnel listings. The tracks are shown as having been recorded between 1945 and 1952 and the personnel listings give an idea of those involved.

They also demonstrate that there were many different combinations of musicians, but give no indication about the permanency or otherwise of these groupings. It seems likely that some of the aggregations were simply set up for the purpose of a recording session, rather than representing permanent bands. Those involved are listed as:

Trumpet/cornet	John Semple, Alex Welsh, Stu Eaton, Archie Semple
Clarinet	Archie Semple, Sandy Brown
Trombone	Stuart Crockett, Dave Keir
Piano	Stan Greig, Drew Landles
Guitar	Ken Duncan, Jimmy Mooney
Bass	Pat Malloy
Drums	Willie Burns, George Crockett
Vocals	Jackie MacFarlane, Jack Thomson

Some of the above recordings were apparently taken from a broadcast, introduced by Steve Race, who gives the line up as John Semple (tpt), Archie Semple (clt), Dave Keir (tbn), Percy Pegg (pno), Jimmy Mooney (gtr or bjo), Mike Samuels (bs) and George Crockett (drms).

Alex Welsh is described in the Oxford Dictionary of National Biography as *'short and dapper, with a perky demeanor'*[74]. He walked with a pronounced limp, the result, I have always believed, of polio when he was young although others have suggested it was caused by an injury. Like Sandy Brown and Al Fairweather, a single hearing left little doubt as to where Alex's musical roots lay. The music that Alex loved beyond all others was clearly the free-wheeling, driving music of the so-called Chicagoans. In fact, this might be better termed 'Condon music', meaning the jazz played by the group of American musicians who, in the 1930s and 1940s, grouped themselves around the guitar player Eddie Condon, as many of them were not from Chicago at all. In particular, as his playing developed, Alex's trumpet style seemed to have common roots with the

---

[74] Oxford Dictionary of National Biography: Oxford Dictionary of National Biography Index of Contributors by Colin Matthew and Brian Harrison (2004) 7 words p84 Volume 58, by permission of Oxford University Press, www.oup.com

group of trumpeters associated with Condon - Wild Bill Davison, Muggsy Spannier and Jimmy McPartland. Like their playing, Alex's was a wonderful mix of the lyricism of Bix Biederbecke, spiced up with the aggressive attack and rough edges that Davison especially, liked to add to his sound. This style, of course, was itself derived from the classic jazz laid down in the 1920s, by Louis Armstrong and King Oliver, strongly enhanced by the influence of Beiderbecke. Like Sandy Brown and Al Fairweather, Alex was aided and abetted by other Edinburgh musicians of a like mind, creating wonderful music locally, but also forging the skills that enabled him, and his colleagues Archie Semple and Dave Keir, to pursue professional careers in jazz, from a London base.

Alex moved to London in May 1954, to join the band of Dave Keir who had already moved south. However, Alex left Dave's band after only three weeks, to form a band under his own name, which first appeared in June 1954. Sinclair Traill, in his 'Concerning Jazz'[75], published in 1957, comments on how many Scottish jazz musicians there were in British traditional bands and goes on to say *'The Scots, it would seem, take to jazz music'*. Traill gives the personnel of the first London based **Alex Welsh Jazz Band** as including two other Scots, trombonist Roy Crimmins (from Perth) and Archie Semple on clarinet. He goes on to say *'The brand of jazz the Alex Welsh band play is strictly from Dixie. Bright, clean and well rehearsed, the band portray the music of the white musician, as opposed to the coloured man's music from New Orleans. This policy has resulted in some quite undeservedly harsh criticism from those purists who can only see one facet of jazz, namely New Orleans music. The band play Dixieland music, a type of jazz which has its followers the world over. As long as they play it well, let's be fair and give credit where credit is due.'* This last sentence seems to me just a little bit patronizing and perhaps reveals something of his own preferences. It certainly sounds a bit dismissive now, in the light of the

---

[75] Traill S, 'Concerning Jazz', pages 143-144, Faber and Faber 1957. All attempts to trace the current copyright holder of this book have been unsuccessful.

great music the Welsh band was to play over the coming years.

Alex Welsh went on to run an extremely successful band over the next twenty five years. They were frequently selected to accompany famous visiting Americans, including Ruby Braff (cnt), Red Allen and Wild Bill Davison (tpt), Bud Freeman (ten) and Earl Hines (pno). All of these regarded the band, which had steadily moved towards embracing a more mainstream style of playing, as world class. In addition, Alex led his band to America in 1968, when they were invited to play at the prestigious Newport Jazz Festival, to considerable critical acclaim. Later, in the 1970s and early 1980s when his health began to give way, Alex was forced to disband for a while but was able to resume playing in September 1981. However, by the middle of the next year, his health was once again failing and he played what was to be his final gig on 10 June 1982. The Alex Welsh band was revered as the best in its style, a reputation that remains to this day. At one time or another, it featured top class musicians such as Roy Crimmins and Roy Williams (tbn), Archie Semple, Al Gay and Johnny Barnes (rds), Fred Hunt (pno), Jim Douglas (gtr), Ronnie Ray and Ron Mathewson (bs) and Lenny Hastings (drms). Alex was offered but declined, a place in the band of the great American trombonist Jack Teagarden. Bud Freeman, the famous tenor sax playing Chicagoan, said of the Welsh band that they were *'the best small band of their kind in the world'*[76]. George Melly, who knew all the London based bands well, also praised the Welsh band saying *'...one of the most grown up bands, musically speaking, that this country has yet produced – hot yet controlled, exciting yet intelligent, professional yet uncompromising, unswayed by fashion but the opposite of obscurantist'*[77].

Throughout his career, Alex Welsh remained faithful to the music of the Chicagoans, veering at times into a mainstream style. In addition to Alex's trumpet playing, his

---

[76] Carr, Fairweather and Priestly, 'The Rough Guide to Jazz', 3rd Edition May 2004, Rough Guides Ltd, distributed by the Penguin Group

[77] Simpson N, Bielderman G, 'Alex Welsh Discography', Eurojazz Discos No.20, September 2007 edition

band always included musicians of the highest class and the band's style, captured on many recordings, remains a model of its kind. If at times his sidemen stole the solo honours, Alex unfailingly played a great lead and created several great bands in succession, all of which were regarded with great esteem and affection by several generations of jazz followers in the UK and abroad. Like the Fairweather – Brown band, the Welsh band were never really part of the populist 'Trad Boom' of the late 1950s and early 1960s, eschewing fancy uniforms and a showy presentation in favour of straight-ahead Dixieland jazz and great playing. As John Latham says of Alex in the Oxford Dictionary of National Biography, '...*his real contribution was in holding together for more than twenty years, a band of the highest professional quality, and providing a platform for other more creative but volatile personalities'*[78]. Unfortunately, Alex Welsh was to be yet another of Edinburgh's Revival jazz musicians to die young. After what the 'Rough Guide to Jazz' refers to as a long, debilitating illness, he died in London at the age of 52, on 25th June 1982, and is buried in Ruislip Cemetery.

Alex's near contemporary, **Dave Keir (tbn, tpt, euphonium, rds and pno)**, was a remarkably versatile musician and, once again, we are indebted to the Sandy Brown Jazz website[79] for a great deal of relevant information. Dave was born on 9th April 1928 in Townhill, a small mining village two miles north of Dunfermline in Fife. His father worked in the dockyard at Rosyth, about four miles from their home. Dave's first exposure to music was to the playing of his mother who, through her own determination, had taught herself to play hymns and light classics on an old harmonium. At the age of about ten, Dave started to learn to play the cornet, receiving free tuition from a miner who played with the local miners' brass band. After this, he began to improvise to his mother's playing, something that he considers good training for the

---

[78] Oxford Dictionary of National Biography: Oxford Dictionary of National Biography Index of Contributors by Colin Matthew and Brian Harrison (2004) 30 words p84 Volume 58, by permission of Oxford University Press, www.oup.com
[79] http://sandybrownjazz.co.uk/profiledavekeir.html

jazz sounds to which he would later turn. Dave attended secondary school in Dunfermline where the music teacher, 'Pop' Gardiner, being short of trombone players, provided him with a bass trombone pitched in the key of G, together with a 'teach yourself' manual. Dave taught himself to play the instrument in six weeks and was able to take his place in the school orchestra. As Dave found it easy to 'busk' (ie improvise) everything, he never found the time to become a good reader of music. Later, he managed to procure a trombone of his own and began to play with a local dance band in the evenings.

Later still in the 1940s, inspired by seeing the Bing Crosby film 'Birth of the Blues', he developed a fancy for leading a jazz band on clarinet. As a result of this, he bought himself an old Albert system clarinet and, once again, taught himself how to play it. During National Service in the RAF, whilst posted in Yorkshire, he played in a dance band which gave him the opportunity to play alto saxophone and clarinet and he also had the chance to play euphonium in the station band. Unfortunately he missed out on an opportunity to get together with Monty Sunshine, later to gain fame as clarinetist in the Chris Barber Band who, unknown to Dave, was stationed in the same camp.

On returning to Dunfermline, Dave started a course of study at Edinburgh University and played with two local bands, the Creole Belles Jazz Band and Jock Turner's Jazz Band, with whom he went to London to play some jazz club gigs. Moving to lodgings in Edinburgh, he soon discovered the Sandy Brown band, with whom he was allowed to sit in on clarinet, which must have been an unnerving experience alongside the highly competitive Sandy. Later, this association brought him the chance to join the Brown band, although on trumpet, replacing Stu Eaton. At this stage, Al Fairweather was away on National Service and was, in any case, still playing trombone. Al's return brought about a switch of roles, with Al becoming the band's trumpeter and Dave moving to the trombone chair. Dave relates how Sandy had heard Al play someone's trumpet and was so impressed by the sound he made, considering Al to be a 'natural' on trumpet, that he persuaded Al to make a permanent change to trumpet.

Sandy's aim of achieving the sound of the Louis Armstrong Hot Five resulted in him bringing in Bob Craig to play trombone in the required Kid Ory style, and Dave moved over to join Archie Semple's Dixielanders. He found their Chicago style much more to his taste and, when Archie Semple moved south to join Mick Mulligan's band in London, as we have heard, Dave took over leadership of the band and gave it a new name, the Nova Scotians[80]. Alex Welsh had just replaced John Semple on trumpet, Pat Malloy soon took over from Dickie Alexander on bass and Jack Graham, who was to become an important Edinburgh jazz musician over the next five decades, was recruited to take Archie Semple's place on clarinet. It should be pointed out that this Dickie Alexander is not the same Dickie Alexander who was a Town Councillor and who was to be a member of the committee which organized a memorial plaque to Sandy Brown and Al Fairweather in the 1990s. After about a year, Dave Keir himself departed south to join Archie Semple in the Mulligan band and Alex Welsh became leader of the Nova Scotians.

Dave Keir went on to have a successful career as a professional jazz musician, mostly playing trombone, in a number of good bands, including those of Freddy Randall and Bruce Turner, in addition to leading a number of bands of his own. In 1957, he went to Moscow with Bruce Turner's band. He also played a variety of instruments when gigging with other bands, including those of Sid Phillips, Bobby Mickleburgh, Johnny Parker and Ken Colyer's Omega Brass Band, before joining a band led by clarinetist Dick Charlesworth and again, setting up bands of his own. When the popularity of 'trad bands' began to wane around 1964, Dave returned to Edinburgh to complete his degree, became a teacher of mathematics and physics and then, for the next twenty years or so, hardly played at all. However, he was to return to playing jazz many years later and we shall catch up with Dave Keir again, later in this book, when we reach the 1980s.

---

[80] http://sandybrownjazz.co.uk/profiledavekeir.html

NOVA SCOTIA JAZZ BAND
ALEC WELSH (Cor. or Tpt.), JACKIE GRAHAM (Clt.), DAVE KEIR (Tbn.), JIMMY MOONEY (Gtr. and Bjo.)
DICK ALEXANDER (Bass), GEORGE CROCKETT (Drs. and leader), DREW LANDLES (Pno.)
DAVE KEIR has since left the band to join Mick Mulligan's Magnolias. His place has been taken by IAN ANDERSON.
Trumpet spot is now occupied by STU EATON.

Nova Scotia Jazz Band business card, probably around 1953 (from the collection of Peter Davenport, photographer unknown)

The departure of Alex Welsh, Archie Semple and Dave Keir, like that of Sandy Brown, Al Fairweather and Stan Greig, left the band more than a bit short handed. However, they did not all disappear at the same time and replacements were found as required. The band, now known as the Nova Scotians, soldiered on and the Dixieland tradition remained alive and well in Edinburgh. George Crockett was still around playing drums with the band and it may well have been his efforts again that kept the band going.

Dave Keir tells us[81], in his profile on the Sandy Brown Jazz website that, when Archie Semple moved away to London, **Jack Graham (clarinet, alto sax, vocals)** took over his place in the Nova Scotians. Frances Burgess (nee Maxwell), Alex Welsh's girlfriend in the 1950s, speaking in 2011, says that she remembers Jack being there at the

---

[81] http://www.sandybrownjazz.co.uk/profiledavekeir.html

meeting at which the band was formed. The line-up of the band now included Alex Welsh (tpt), Dave Keir (tbn), Jack Graham (clt), George Crockett (drms) and Pat Malloy from Dunfermline, who had replaced Dickie Alexander on bass. I remember Dave Keir telling me that Jack Graham just seemed to appear at the right time and no one was really very sure where he had come from. Jack was born in 1929 and, like Dizzy Jackson and Bob Craig, was to remain a major player in the Edinburgh jazz scene for a very long time. I was fortunate enough to play in several bands with Jack over many years and got to know him well. He was a gifted musician with a remarkable musical ear and he had the ability to fit smoothly into bands, from New Orleans to Swing, which played in widely differing styles. In many ways, it was this versatility and ability to fit in so readily, that was to make him made him such a well-loved and respected player.

After his spell with the Nova Scotians, Jack put in lengthy service with Charlie McNair's Jazz Band, Old Bailey and his Jazz Advocates, Mike Hart's Society Syncopators, The Scottish Jazz Advocates and The Scottish Society Syncopators, all major local bands, all of which made their mark on Edinburgh jazz. Jack also occasionally ran bands under his own name. We will hear more about these bands later, as well as the fine four piece band, The Diplomats of Jazz, led by trumpeter Jim Petrie, in which Jack played through most of the 1990s. He also played a great deal of dance music over the years and was never short of gigs. Jack was an accomplished clarinet player, a fact that always made me wonder how he, a man renowned for his liking for a quiet life, ever raised enough energy to learn to play such a difficult instrument so fluently. In fact, I suspect that he may well have learned to play the clarinet while doing his National Service.

Jack was one of the most laid back individuals I ever met and, at times, he gave every indication of complete lethargy. He had a career as a telephone engineer but always seemed to be suffering from a chronic shortage of cash, a state which seemed to give him an air of gentle bewilderment. His sinuous and graceful playing was much admired, not only around the Scottish jazz scene, but also in a wider context when, in the 1980s, he played at many jazz festivals in the UK, the USA and in Europe. His style was sometimes likened to that of the great Ed Hall but, in fact, his sound and style were very much his own. He did, however, share with Ed Hall a raspy, agile approach that was instantly recognisable, his supple and responsive playing nicely complementing the trumpet lead and enhancing the ensemble. I was aware, from early in our acquaintance, that Jack had once been voted the best clarinet player in Scotland. This was at some competitive jazz event in the 1950s, and I knew about it because Archie Sinclair, the trombonist who led the Old Bailey band when both Jack and I were members, often made reference to this achievement when introducing him.

In addition to his general air of somnolence, Jack was also very fond of his food and there were many legends about his capacity to stuff himself, particularly when there was access to free food. On one occasion, when playing with the Old Bailey band at a barbecue event on the harbour side at Dunbar, the band was supplied with a filled roll apiece. A single roll was never going to be enough for Jack, although he was very pleased to discover that the filling was a whole kipper, a favourite of his. Brian Sinclair, a young bass player from Dunfermline (and now an extremely able bass player based in the USA), was depping for me on this gig, and was much less chuffed to find a kipper in his roll. With a grunt of disgust, Brian threw his kipper to the flock of gulls circling about the harbour. Andrew Lauder was on this gig and said that the kipper only just escaped Jack's clutching hands as it flew through the air. Jack then turned in wrath on the astounded Brian, whom he subjected to many bitter recriminations about wasting good food that would have been a lot better disappearing down Jack's gullet than a gull's. Andrew, not to mention Brian, was absolutely amazed. *'I thought he was going to have a seizure.'* Andrew said afterwards, *'I never thought he could move that fast. He damn nearly caught the kipper before the gull got to it'.*

In character, Jack was a friendly, quiet man and the type around whom many affectionate anecdotes, such as those above, tended to gather. He was a much valued member of every band he adorned, even if he drove every band leader for whom he ever worked half demented with his skill, indeed genius, for arriving at the very last minute for every gig. He made quite a number of recordings with the various bands with which he played including Charlie McNair's band, Old Bailey's Jazz Advocates, Mike Hart's Scottish Society Syncopators, the Scottish Jazz Advocates and the Diplomats of Jazz[82]. These recordings, many of which will be found listed in the discography appendix, remain to remind us of his talent and musicianship. Later in life, Jack had serious health problems requiring major surgery. Happily, he made a good recovery and was able to resume playing. Jack Graham eventually retired to Spain where he died, on 26th of January 2005, at the age of 77.

There were, of course, many others who played with the bands led by Archie Semple and the Nova Scotians, in the late 1940s and early 1950s. Some we have already met in earlier chapters in association with the RHS Gang, including Sandy Brown himself, Stu Eaton, Stan Grieg, Willlie Burns and Jackie MacFarlane, again emphasising that there was some mixing between the two groupings. Others who played and even recorded, were pianists Ronnie Carruthers and Drew Landles, bass player Pat Malloy, vocalist Jack Thomson and guitarists Ken Duncan and Jimmy Mooney.

Drew Landles (piano) was born in 1928 in Hawick, where he spent his early years, and was introduced to piano by his mother, an accomplished player herself. Drew went on to gain the Advanced Preparatory Certificate with Honours from the Trinity College of Music. After National Service in the Royal Navy, he arrived in Edinburgh in 1948 to attend Art College, where he studied architecture. In town, he lived with Will Redpath, and Stu Eaton, both jazzers we have already met, and someone he describes as *'an eccentric American Forces jazz enthusiast'* called Lee Cross. Bill Strachan also knew this character and tells the tale of an attempt to go to Paris on a jazz seeking trip, the transport being Lee Cross' motor bike. Apparently, they got only as far as Dunbar before the motor bike packed in,

---

[82] See discography appendix

Cross having never put any oil in it. They did make it to Paris however, although only by hitching lifts the whole way. Bill also tells the story of an episode which started with a pie eating contest in Paddy's Bar in Rose Street. Lee Cross had the motor bike with him and they decided to head for the West End Café. According to Bill, about seven of them somehow got onto the bike and went roaring off down Rose Street. Hardly surprisingly, they were stopped when they reached a police box and were escorted to the police station in the High Street, where a police doctor was called to check their alcohol content. When the doctor got to Lee Cross, he immediately declared his American citizenship and stated that he was in Scotland to learn to play the bagpipes. This was apparently partly true and the incident came to an end with Lee Cross being invited to go along to a rehearsal with the Edinburgh Police Pipe Band and the rest of them allowed to make their way home, with no charges laid.

Around this time, while he was an Art College student, Drew Landles also met Sandy Brown, Al Fairweather, Stan Greig and Bob Craig and was invited to go along to their practice sessions. He also became friendly with John and Archie Semple and Alex Welsh around the same time, and began to play gigs with them. One of the high-lights of this musical association was an appearance on the second of three BBC jazz concerts, this one being devoted to Chicago style jazz. A short while after this, the band was paired with the Mick Mulligan band from London and, with them, they toured in Scotland and the north of England. Drew apparently played piano rather in the manner of Swing pianists, such as the great Teddy Wilson who had made his name with the Benny Goodman small groups in the 1930s. It was this fluent style that made him a popular choice on piano in bands involving both the Brown/Fairweather gang and the Semple brothers. After qualifying as an architect in 1953, Drew was transferred to London by the company with whom he had secured a job. There, he gradually lost touch with the active music scene and his playing career ended in about 1956, as he concentrated on developing his architectural practice.

Much later in 2010, long retired and back in Edinburgh, Drew was one of the Edinburgh Jazz Archive Group (EJAG)[83], which planned and organized an exhibition and the establishment of an archive of Edinburgh jazz, in the Edinburgh Central Library. The contribution which Drew brought to the work of the EJAG was largely the story of his involvement with the Alex Welsh and Archie Semple group and, to an extent, the Sandy Brown and Al Fairweather group, back in the 1940s and 50s. Drew Landles saw the successful fulfillment of the Archive Group's projects in 2010 but, sadly, died in Edinburgh just a few weeks later, on September 21st 2010. Drew's contribution, late in his life, to the work of the EJAG must have given him a great deal of satisfaction. It was good too that Drew's personal contribution, as an active and influential player in Edinburgh jazz, was recorded and preserved by the work of EJAG, from which much of the above information about Drew has been taken.

Pat Molloy (bass) came from Dunfermline where, according to George Melly in 'Owning Up', he had been an insurance agent. Melly describes him as of Irish origin and very small with '*...a classic Irish face with black curly hair and a complicated mouth full of teeth*'[84]. Pat had joined the Archie Semple Dixielanders, at the suggestion of Dave Keir who shared his Dunfermline background, replacing Mike Samuels whose lecturing duties at the University were causing him to miss gigs. Later, Pat Malloy and Archie Semple went off south to join the Mick Mulligan band at about the same time as another Edinburgh jazzer, the **guitarist Jimmy Currie**, who was later to become well known as solo guitarist in the 'Lonnie Donegan Skiffle Group'. Jimmy Currie seems to have been something of an all-rounder. In addition to his jazz and skiffle playing, George Melly describes him as a convinced modernist but also says that he had worked out a cabaret act which

---

[83] Edinburgh Jazz Archive Group 2010 - Jim Keppie, Bll Strachan, Donald 'Chick' Murray, Drew Landles
[84] 'Owning Up' by George Melly, (Copyright © George Melly, 1965) Reprinted by permission of A. M. Heath & Co Ltd

required him to dress up as a Mexican and deliver what Melly describes as *'abysmal patter'*!

Another Edinburgh jazzer who appeared around the late 1940s and early 1950s was **pianist Ronnie Carruthers**. Ronnie came from a musical family, his Granny having been the pianist who played for silent movies in the building in Shandwick Place which became the West End Café. Although most of Ronnie's musical career was to be with the dance bands of Edinburgh, he was involved in the earliest activities of the Revivalists in Edinburgh and, as we have heard, he was one of the group that gathered at the Semple household at 1 Braid Crescent when the Semples, Sandy Brown and others were just beginning to make their way in jazz[85]. There is a photograph, sent in by Ronnie, and shown in a SBS Newsletter, which shows Archie Semple accompanied by Archie Deacon on drums and Ronnie on piano[86].

Before the end of the war, Ronnie was a visitor at 4 Hillside Crescent, where a number of like-minded musicians gathered to play, including Jimmy Walker, Duncan Campbell, Stan Reynolds and others from the Palais Dance Band. Later on, in common with many musicians involved in dance music, Ronnie's interest in jazz moved towards the mainstream and modern forms, rather than more traditional jazz. He was a founding member of the Modern Jazz Club, which functioned between 1945 and 1954 on Sunday afternoons on the top floor of 1 India Buildings, after the New Orleans practice session earlier in the day had finished. Ronnie describes this as *'...a proper club with a membership register and membership cards, which was just as well as it was frequently raided by police who were looking for drink and drugs'*. Apparently the police harassment became quite serious, until Dr Selby Wright, the well-known and much respected minister of the Canongate Church, remonstrated with them on behalf of the club. Ronnie seemed to have a knack of settling into residencies that were to last. For example, he was with Tony Fusco's band in Tony's Ballroom in Picardy Place from

---

[85] SBS Newsletter No. 31, July 1999
[86] SBS Newsletter No. 35, November 1999

1949 to 1953 and with Alex Ferguson's band at the Leith Assembly Rooms from 1955 to 1959. However, his longest residency was to be his weekly solo piano spot at Henderson's vegetarian restaurant in Hanover Street, which began in 1990 and was still going strong more than twenty years later. Another long term and successful gig for Ronnie was his place in the resident rhythm section at monthly jam sessions run by the drummer, Roger Craik. At these sessions, which took place at the Starbank Hotel in Newhaven, guest horn players were invited by Roger to feature with the rhythm section and they regularly drew a good and enthusiastic crowd. A decade into the twenty-first century, Ronnie Carruthers, now in his eighties, was still playing regularly around town, and played wonderfully well in a piano, guitar and drums trio, later joined by John Burgess on tenor sax, which graced the opening of the exhibition on Edinburgh jazz in the Central Library on 31st July 2010.

Chapter VI

Moves towards Mainstream in the 1950s

The departure southwards in 1954 of Alex Welsh, left the 'Nova Scotians' short of a trumpet player and, as far as I have been able to find out, Stu Eaton, whom we have already met with the RHS Gang, and then **Bob Harley (cornet)** were the replacements. Eaton's name appears on a Nova Scotians photographic band card, which actually shows Alex Welsh, but has a foot note which says *'Trumpet spot now occupied by Stu Eaton'*. The same foot note also states that *'Dave Keir has since left the band to join Mick Mulligan's Magnolias. His place has been taken by Ian Anderson'*. Bob Harley seems to have originated from Kirkcaldy in Fife and Andrew Lauder, who would eventually replace him in the Nova Scotians, remembers him as *'...a fine Dixieland styled player. He didn't play in the manner of Bobby Hackett or Wild Bill Davison but was perhaps a bit like Jimmy McPartland in his sound and style'*. Andrew thinks that, when Bob left the band, it was to go to London to seek a career in jazz.

At some point, a second reeds player joined the Nova Scotians. This was **Johnny Winters (tenor sax and clarinet)** who came from Stenhousemuir, near Stirling, to attend Edinburgh University, where he studied economics as a mature student. Both the drummer Roger Craik and trumpeter Andrew Lauder have said that Winters was really a tenor sax player, rather than clarinet, and Roger described him as playing in the manner of Eddie Miller, a fine American tenor player who made his name with the

Bob Crosby Band. Winters played tenor sax with band until Jack Graham left, when he switched to clarinet and, for a time, led the band. Roger Craik and Andrew Lauder both remarked that Johnny Winters had an interest in the more modern forms of jazz. Andrew, who also described him as a good player, added that Winters, while initially keen on the Eddie Condon or Chicagoan style of jazz, later became interested in the clarinet playing of Jimmy Giuffre, although he never actually seemed to play in this style himself.

Johnny Winters was active on the Edinburgh traditional jazz scene while he remained at University but, after he had graduated, he moved away from Edinburgh. He did, however, take part in a private recording session arranged by Roger Craik in June 1969. I was involved in this session, playing bass, along with Andrew Lauder (tpt), Graeme Robertson (tbn), Alan Anderson (pno) and Roger Craik himself on drums. The recording quality is not great but, from what can be heard through the rather jumbled sound, it is clear that Johnny Winters was indeed a fine player. I can remember him complaining at this session that he was badly out of practice. He said, after we had been playing for a while, that his lips felt so tired and jelly-like that he was afraid to blow hard, as it felt as if his lips were going to go flying right down the outside of the barrel of the clarinet! Johnny Winters died in the mid-1990s.

In 1956, the afore-mentioned **Andrew Lauder (trumpet)** came in to replace Bob Harley. Andrew had been introduced to jazz by his brother, who had a number of New Orleans recordings, and Andrew says that he can remember being puzzled by the music he was hearing, recalling that he could not hear the tune. He reports that it was hearing a Sid Phillips record that enabled him to make sense of what was going on and how the various instruments played their part. He found himself homing in on what the trumpeter was playing and, around his eighteenth birthday in 1955, he bought himself an old trumpet. He discovered that there was a jazz club, called the Condon Club, which operated in India Buildings in Victoria Street. This was a function hall high up in the building, with a caretaker who lived on the top floor. A drummer called Alan Hastie, who worked with Andrew in the organ building trade, introduced him and he became a member, later becoming a member of the club committee. Andrew started to go the regular Sunday evening sessions and got to know the band and their arrangements.

India Buildings in Victoria Street the home of much early Edinburgh jazz activity (photo by the author)

The band was the Nova Scotians whose line up by this time was: Bob Harley (tpt), Ian Anderson (tbn), Johnny Winters (ten sax and co-leader), Jack Graham (clt), Bert Murray, who was from Fife (pno), Jim Baikie (gtr), someone who Andrew thinks was called Bert Paterson (bs) and George Crockett (drms and co-leader). The band also used the services of a couple of vocalists, the already mentioned drummer Alan Hastie and Brenda New, whose real name was Brenda Tosh. Sometimes, Alan Hastie would bring his drum kit along and there would be a number featuring two drummers. Changes in the band brought in Norman Skinner on piano and a black Grenadian, Len Barclay, who replaced Ian Anderson. Ian Anderson was apparently 'something in the City' and he could be seen on occasions during the day wearing a bowler hat and carrying a brolly! He later moved to London. Andrew Lauder described Len Barclay as a nice smooth trombonist but not really a Dixieland player. Jack Graham eventually left the band but was not replaced, Johnny Winters, as we have already heard, switching to clarinet. The Condon Club also featured interval bands at these sessions, including more modern players such as Dougie Campbell (gtr), Johnny Smith (tpt) and Ronnie Carruthers (pno).

Andrew, as a member of the committee, would arrive early at the club, to set up the lighting and get the place ready, and this led to opportunities for him to sit in. When Bob Harley took the road to London in 1956, Andrew, just ten months after starting on trumpet, was invited to take his place in this well established band. Around this time, in about 1956, Andrew started to meet other jazzers around town, including trumpeters Charlie McNair and Jim Petrie and trombonist Archie Sinclair, whom he first came across in the West End Café and with whom he was later to have a lengthy musical partnership. He also became aware of the Climax Jazz Band, of whom we will hear much more in the next chapter, and remembers other bands led by Mike Hart and Bob Craig, although he thinks that Mike may have been playing with the Climax band at this time. Eventually, Andrew says, the Nova Scotians sadly just faded out, a common enough fate for local jazz bands, but a shame in the case of a band which had started out under Archie Semple's leadership and carried the local Dixieland banner for a decade or more.

At this point, as with so many of the jazzers in the 1940 and 50s, Andrew was called up to do his National Service which he spent in the RAF, serving in, amongst other places, the Middle East. Here he bumped into another Edinburgh musician, Bill Marshall, later to make a local reputation in folk and country music, before still later re-inventing himself as a clarinet player on the jazz scene. On his return from the Forces, Andrew was approached to play with a new band being organized by **Pete Kerr (clarinet)**, who was from Haddington, where he had previously run a band. The new band was called **Pete Kerr's Capital Jazz Band** and the purpose of forming it was a bid to play full time. The band that Kerr got together was: Andrew Lauder (tpt), Johnny McGuff (tbn). Pete Kerr (clt and leader), Alex Shaw (pno), Jim Douglas (bjo and gtr), Ian Brown (bs) and George Crockett (drms) and it was clearly another band in the Dixieland tradition. This band went off to Germany on a tour that lasted from November 1960 to early 1961, as we will hear shortly, and then the band folded, bringing to an end Andrew's short-lived professional career.

Pete Kerr's Capital Jazz Band, like Pete himself, had its origins, not actually in Edinburgh itself but in Haddington, the county town of East Lothian, about twenty miles east of the capital, and we can follow the band's history from the recollections of their **banjo and guitar player, Jim Douglas**. Jim was born near Gifford, a small East Lothian town not far from Haddington, on 13th May 1942. His father was a drummer in the Royal Army Medical Corps pipe band and his mother a shepherd's daughter who was in service at Newton Hall, where his father's regiment was billeted. Jim's education took place mostly at Yester Primary School and then at the famous Knox Academy at Haddington, which was where he met a fellow pupil, Pete Kerr. Jim had become interested in the current craze for skiffle and, after successfully pestering his mother into buying him a guitar, he had got down to some serious practice which, he claims, bored both his immediate family and his uncle, who became his severest critic. Jim then became a member of the local 'Tynesiders Skiffle Group', which took its name from the East Lothian River Tyne and not the Newcastle one, until he heard the Chris Barber Jazz Band, an experience which promptly changed his musical allegiance. Soon afterwards, in his own words, he was 'completely wrapped up in traditional jazz'.

It was not long before he was finding his way into the Edinburgh jazz scene of the late 1950s, where he began visiting the Royal Mile Cafe in the High Street to listen to the Royal Mile Jazz Band, led by trumpeter Eric Rinaldi. This band included drummer Sandy Malcolm who, like Jim himself, would later put in some time with the famous Clyde Valley Stompers. Another member of the band was guitarist Alex Marshall, at whose house Jim would sometimes stay after the jazz sessions. It was Alex who introduced Jim to the music of Django Reinhardt and to whom Jim gives considerable credit for laying the foundations of his whole future career in jazz. His enthusiasm for jazz well and truly established, Jim then found himself helping school pal Pete Kerr to form the 'Hidden Town Dixielanders', the 'Hidden Town' being Haddington. They soon had a band together which included, in addition to Pete on clarinet and Jim on guitar, Jack Blair (tbn), Kimber Buglass (tpt), John Logan (bs) and Bob Sandie (drms).

The Hidden Town Dixielanders was clearly quite a talented outfit and, after winning the local heat of the 'Carroll Levis Discoveries Show', they were rewarded with a trip to London to take part in a broadcast. However, with success came change and, within a few months, Ken Ramage came in on trombone, Alastair Clark on trumpet, George Crockett on drums and a piano player, Bob McDonald, was recruited. In addition, the band's name was changed to Pete Kerr's Dixielanders. A couple of recordings were issued (about which we will hear more shortly, when we meet Alastair Clark) and, as the band grew in popularity, they were approached by an impresario based in Germany. He was John Martin, who owned the Storyville Club in Cologne and, having heard the band on the recordings, he offered them a chance of a couple of months playing, with the possibility of other work in Germany to follow. This, however, meant the band becoming a professional outfit and, inevitably, this brought more changes in personnel, most of them bringing in names which would become well known in jazz circles. The talented trombonist Ken Ramage had already turned professional, heading south to join the Charlie Gall band, and his replacement had been Johnny McGuff. Trumpeter Alastair Clark's burgeoning journalistic career precluded any professional ambitions in jazz and it was this that brought Andrew Lauder into the band. Bob McDonald was studying medicine in Edinburgh and vacated the piano chair in favour of Alex Shaw and Ian Brown came in on bass to replace John Logan, who worked in the printing trade. Jim Douglas himself had just been taken on as an apprentice potter with Castle Wynd Potteries and, although somewhat reluctant to give up a promising career,

122

in the end, with the brave encouragement of his disappointed mother, he took the plunge and moved into the world of professional jazz.

The German adventure brought a month in Cologne's 'Storyville', followed by a further month in Mannheim's 'Schwabinger Kunstler Keller'. However, the work was hard, Pete Kerr recalling that they were required to play from 8.00pm to 2.00am all seven nights of the week, with additional matinees on Saturdays and Sundays. Unfortunately, further work in Germany did not materialize, Pete commenting that beat groups from the UK were beginning to move in on the German clubs, and the band returned to the UK after their original two months were completed. None-the-less, in spite of the hard work and the lack of further work, the time in Germany had allowed them to enjoy some wonderful musical experiences. Amongst these were gigs when they accompanied bongo/conga player and vocalist Frank Holder, who had played and sung with the Johnny Dankworth band, and some gigs accompanying the fine veteran American reeds man, Benny Waters. There was also, to the astonished delight of drummer George Crockett, the chance to meet the great modern jazz drummer, Art Blakey. When the band returned to the UK in February 1961, it was to find that the Trad Boom was in full swing and they expected this to bring them a lot of work. However, several Scottish bands had already been making forays into England and the London agents approached by Pete did not deem an invasion by yet another one as necessary. Sadly, they decided to disband and returned northwards and homewards, to pick up the pieces.

However, for some of the band at least, all was far from lost. Forrie Cairns, star clarinetist with the Scotland's famous Clyde Valley Stompers, had decided – like others before him – to leave and form his own band. Pete Kerr was invited to replace him, his recruitment coinciding with the band moving its permanent base from Glasgow to London. Shortly afterwards, the Scottish nature of the band was further maintained by the recruitment of Jim Douglas.

**Pete Kerr's Dixielanders in Germany 1960/61
In checked shirts from the left – Pete Kerr, Alex Shaw,
Andrew Lauder, Ian Brown, George Crockett
(Photo by permission of Jim Douglas)**

As it turned out, this new version of the Stompers was also to have an unsettled time, with the leader, trombone player Ian Menzies, sadly having to stop playing because of health issues. What, in fact, happened was that, although Ian Menzies retired to Jersey and later to Canada, he retained a controlling interest in the band by forming a company called Clyde Valley Stompers Ltd with London agent Lyn Dutton, whose office acted both as the band's booking agent and as business managers of the limited company. Pete Kerr took over leadership of the band and brought in Johnny McGuff to replace Menzies and added pianist Bert Murray. When the re-jigged Stompers took the road under Pete's leadership, the line-up was Malky Higgins and later Joe McIntyre (tpt), Pete Kerr (clt), Johnny McGuff (tbn), Bert Murray (pno), Jim Douglas (bjo/gtr), Bill Bain (bs) and Robbie Winter (drms). This edition of the Stompers, through its constant touring all over the UK, set about extending the loyal fan base that earlier line-ups had established in the band's west of Scotland heartland. In 1962, the Stompers recorded their biggest-selling single recording, featuring an arrangement, largely by Bert Murray, of Prokopiev's 'Peter and the Wolf', with ex-Syd

Phillip's sideman Joe McIntyre on trumpet. This recording, made for the Parlophone company under the direction of one George Martin, later to become famous for his work with the Beatles, made it to the very edge of the revered Top Twenty pop charts. The popularity of this record led to the Stompers becoming, for a time, the most televised jazz band in Britain, with regular spots on such top network programmes as 'Thank Your Lucky Stars', 'Cool for Cats' and 'The Morecambe and Wise Show'. Film work also beckoned, with an appearance in Tommy Steele's 'It's All Happening' followed by an invitation to provide the title music for Norman Wisdom's 'On the Beat'. The band's contribution to the soundtracks of these movies was taped, like their Parlophone records, at EMI's famous Abbey Road Studios and again produced by George Martin. However, despite such unprecedented success, this version of the Clyde Valley Stompers, in its time Scotland's most successful traditional jazz band, did not last much longer. The choice of band personnel lay with the business managers, giving rise to concerns being raised by Pete about how this might reflect on musical policy. The resulting discord ultimately led to Ian Menzies withdrawing use of the Clyde Valley Stompers name, ownership of which he had retained, and the Pete Kerr led version of the band came to an end.

The Clyde Valley Stompers phase of their jazz careers over, Pete Kerr and Jim Douglas returned to Edinburgh and the formation of the last of Pete's bands, this time under the name Pete Kerr's Scottish All Stars. The personnel of this band had an average age of less than twenty one and included the exceptional young bass player from Shetland, Ron Mathewson, and an excellent young Edinburgh drummer, Billy Law. However, with the decreasing demand for live jazz, the band was obliged to travel, quite literally, the length and breadth of Britain to stay in business, once trekking overnight from an engagement in Southampton to Glasgow for a radio broadcast, followed immediately by a dance in Hawick and another overnight drive to a gig in Thurso! They also made a couple of extended play recordings[87] at the Craighall Studios in Edinburgh, 'Jazz at the Capital' in 1963 and 'More Jazz at the Capital' in 1964. These were released on Waverley Records, the company with which Pete Kerr had made his recording debut some five years previously. The full line-up of the band on these recordings was Mike Scott (tpt), Pete Kerr (clt), Eddie Lorkin (tbn), Mike Oliver (pno), Jim Douglas (bjo/gtr), Ron Mathewson (bs) and Billy Law (drms).

Sadly, this band too had a short life, coming to an end when Pete Kerr took up an offer from EMI to become a record producer. Pete's career in record production was a successful one, most of his two hundred or so recordings being of music with a Scottish flavour but also including three albums by the Alex Welsh band, recorded at the Craighall Studios, 'Alex Welsh at Home', 'Alex Welsh Vintage 1969' and 'The Alex Welsh Dixieland Party'. However, the biggest selling record produced by Pete was that of 'Amazing Grace' by the Royal Scots Dragoon Guards, recorded at Redford Barracks, Edinburgh, which became an international number one hit, going on to sell some thirteen million copies still, in 2012, the highest selling instrumental single of all time. Years later, the talented and versatile Pete Kerr was to embark on yet another successful career, this time as an author, publishing a number of books, both travel writing and fiction, including 'Snowball Oranges', 'Thistle Soup' and 'The Gannet Has Landed'[88].

While Pete was developing his career away from playing jazz, Jim Douglas and Billy Law headed south and eventually, after a fairly lean time, Billy joined the band led by clarinet player Terry Lightfoot and Jim, at first covering for Diz Disley, went on to become a permanent member of the Alex Welsh band. Jim and Billy moved into a famous jazz house at Fawley Road, West Hampstead, sharing the accommodation with well known jazzers Brian Lemon, Colin Purbrook, Keith Ingham and Tony Bayliss, with the added attraction of having Sandy Brown living just round the corner. Jim recalls having the great good fortune to be

---

[87] See discography appendix
[88] www.peter-kerr.co.uk

asked by Sandy to play at his Christmas parties where, he says, '...*the measures became legendary*'!

Jim Douglas remained with the Alex Welsh band for all of eighteen years, all of course well documented and all delightfully happy years for Jim, playing with some of the finest jazz musicians ever produced in this country. The band played at the famed Newport Jazz Festival in the USA in 1968, made many notable recordings and accompanied some of the great names of jazz on tour. It is well worth listing some of these great players as they give some idea of the stature of the Welsh band of that time – Henry 'Red' Allen, Wild Bill Davison, Earl Hines, Ruby Braff, Willie 'The Lion' Smith, Pee Wee Russell, Eddie 'Lockjaw' Davies, Eddie Miller, Ben Webster, Dickie Wells, Rex Stewart, Peanuts Hucko, Bob Wilbur, Dick Wellstood, Billy Butterfield, Pee Wee Erwin, Sammy Price, Johnnie Mince, Yank Lawson, Vic Dickenson and others – a roll call of some of the finest players of the middle period of jazz.

Since the untimely death of Alex Welsh in 1982, Jim Douglas' career has taken many twists and turns, involving bands led by Digby Fairweather, Keith Smith, Val Wiseman, Pete Strange and Dave Shepherd. He also played a number of concerts with Stephane Grapelli, played a gig with the South Rampart Street Paraders, which included the great drummer Nick Fatool, and toured Europe with Bob Haggard, Bob Barnard and an Alex Welsh tribute band, which Jim was instrumental in putting together. Jim married Alex Welsh's widow, Margaret in 1983 and, when their son Will was young and '...*when the road got too long*', he also pursued a career as a chef. He retired from playing in 2009 but in 2011, with his family responsibilities nicely under control, he was able to return to playing, when the drummer Laurie Chescoe asked him to join his re-union band. With Laurie's band, Jim Douglas appeared at the 2011 Edinburgh International Jazz and Blues Festival. I was lucky enough to play in the band that alternated with them at the Mardi Gras in the Grassmarket, and it was great to hear Jim playing as well as ever, a tower of strength both in the rhythm section and in his solo playing.

However, we must return to the 1950s and again pick up the story of what was happening in the Edinburgh jazz world of the time. After his brief professional career, Andrew Lauder was to join another Edinburgh band, one which was to have a long and successful run. This was Old Bailey and his Jazz Advocates, a band of which we will later hear much more. I played more with Andrew than I did with any other musician: from 1964 to 1970 and 1975 to January 1981 with the Old Bailey band, from January 1981 to 1984 with the Scottish Jazz Advocates and then, from 1987 to date (ie 2011), in a four piece band, The Maid of the Forth Stompers, which played on a cruise ship. Over this long period, I reckon I got to know his playing almost as well as he knew it himself. Andrew did not play in the hot, driving style aspired to by most traditional jazz trumpeters. His style was cooler, lyrical and thoughtful, his roots drawing on the model laid down by Bix Biederbecke and continued by trumpeters such as Bobby Hackett, Jimmy McPartland, Ruby Braff and even Chet Baker.

In particular, it was always said that Andrew had modeled himself on the playing of the white American Bobby Hackett, whose playing Andrew revered above all others. Andrew himself credited the Glasgow based trumpet player, George Ogilvie (still playing in Glasgow in 2011), for turning his attention towards Hackett. However, I believe that, in fact, his approach to improvisation was rather different to that of Hackett. Leonard Feather, the distinguished jazz musician and writer, in his 'The Book of Jazz'[89], defines three approaches to melodic improvisation used by jazz musicians. The first and simplest is where *'...the original melody is respected completely; the only change lies in the lengthening or shortening of some notes, repetition of others, use of tonal variations and dynamics to bring out its in conformity with the personality of the interpreter.'*

The second is where *'...the melody remains completely recognizable but its phrases are subject to slight additions and changes; here and there a note is added or subtracted and perhaps a whole phrase is transmuted, but to the layman listener the original melody remains perceptible*

---

[89] Feather, L 'The Book of Jazz', pub. 1957 by Arthur Barker Ltd, an imprint of The Orion Publishing Group, London

throughout either in the actual statement or by indirection.'
Gunther Schuller, in his scholarly book 'Early Jazz - its
roots and development' gives a similar view from the veteran
clarinet player, Buster Bailey. Bailey, commenting on his
own clarinet playing around 1917, said *'I...was embellishing
around the melody. At that time, I wouldn't have known
what they meant by improvising. But embellishing was a
phrase I understood'*[90]. In the same book, Schuller also
adopts a term previously applied to this form of improvising
by the French jazz writer Andre Hodier, which is
'paraphrase improvisations'. He explains that this is a type
of improvisation *'...based primarily on embellishment or
ornamentation of the original melodic line'*[91].

Feather's third category is where *'...the soloist departs
entirely from the melody; in fact rather than using it as a
point of departure, he uses instead the chord pattern of the
tune.'* This is given further strength by James Lincoln
Collier who, after pointing out Louis Armstrong's advances
in technical ability and confidence in the mid-1920s, goes
on to say *'Third – and this is extremely significant – he uses
the written melody less and less as a guide and embarks
more and more on wholly original voyages, navigating only
on the chord changes – the song's underlying harmonies.
Where in the Oliver solos he followed a preset line and in the
Henderson solos frequently paraphrased the melody, he is
now, as the Hot Five series progresses, throwing the
frequently pedestrian melodies the scornful glance they
deserve and inventing entirely new melodies'*[92]. Schuller
also comments on this where he says *'In all the early New
Orleans performances the original composition played a
predominant role in "improvisation". The younger men like
Armstrong, Sidney Bechet and Johnny Dodds gradually*

---

[90] 'Early Jazz: Its Roots and Musical Development (The History of Jazz)', by Gunther
Schuller (1968) 25 words p66, by permission of Oxford University Press,
www.oup.com

[91] 'Early Jazz: Its Roots and Musical Development (The History of Jazz)', by Gunther
Schuller (1968) 13 words p323, by permission of Oxford University Press
www.oup.com

[92] Collier J L, 'Louis Armstrong – a Biography', Pub. Michael Joseph Ltd, 1984. Every
effort has been made to trace the current holder of copyright of this work but
without success.

broke away from the theme improvisation concept, and, after the mid-twenties solo improvisation, with few exceptions, came to mean extemporizing on chords rather than melodies'[93].

While I do not think that jazz improvisers necessarily fall neatly into a single one of these three categories, but may well fit in somewhere between them or even move between them, they none-the-less help us understand how improvisation may be approached.

Bobby Hackett was not only a trumpet player but also an able, professional guitarist, the significance of which is recognized by James Lincoln Collier when he points out *'As a guitarist, Hackett was more familiar than many horn players with how chords fit together.'* He then goes on to contrast Hackett's playing with that of Max Kaminsky and says *'Where Kaminsky was a minimalist, playing perhaps only one of the notes of a chord, Hackett very frequently played all of them.'*[94] Hackett certainly frequently plays tumbling, graceful lines through the chord changes, with an ease that indicates a comprehensive familiarity with their makeup and relationship to each other. To that extent, he seems to me to be a player who improvised on the chord pattern of the tunes, albeit constructing wondrously melodic choruses, in the manner of Leonard Feather's third category of improvising. Andrew does not seem to me to improvise that way. He has a terrific ear for harmony and seemed to me always to work from the melody, his gifted ear enabling him to find notes that altered and enhanced the melody line. Andrew himself always maintained that he did not know the theory of chord construction or the musical relationship between different chords. However, whatever were the differences in their approaches, like Bobby Hackett, Andrew was a graceful, lyrical player who always sounded musicianly and controlled. He was probably the

---

[93] 'Early Jazz – Its Roots and Musical Development (The History of Jazz)' by Gunther Schuller (1968) 52 words p80, by permission of Oxford University Press, www.oup.com

[94] Collier, J L, 'The Making of Jazz – a Comprehensive History', Granada Publishing Ltd, 1978 Every effort has been made to trace the current holder of copyright of this work but without success.

best player of melody with whom I ever played, with a great ability to expose the real beauty of a melody, particularly when the tune was a ballad. He was to remain an important player in Edinburgh for over fifty years.

Jim Baikie (guitar) was born in India and came to Edinburgh in 1944, where he was educated at George Watsons College. While at school, he took up the ukelele and met Roger Craik, later to be a well-known local jazz drummer. It was while at University between 1949 and 1952, that Jim developed an interest in jazz. Hearing about jazz sessions at India Buildings, he went along and, outside the venue, bumped into George Crockett and helped him in with his drum kit. This was to be Jim's first experience of live jazz and it seems likely to have been the band led by Archie Semple, prior to his departure for London. Later, of course, the band became the Nova Scotians and, by now playing guitar, Jim got the chance to sit in with the band and, as he puts it, other variations of the group. He remembers playing at this time with Alex Welsh, Johnny McGuff (tbn), Archie Semple, Dicky Alexander (bs), Jimmy Mooney (gtr) and George Crockett (drms). Jim later played 'on the boats', the term used by musicians to denote work in bands which were employed to provide music on trans-Atlantic liners.

Jim became a very able guitar player and this, plus his good singing voice and easy empathy with audiences, made him a natural band leader. He set up and led a dance band which worked steadily in town for over thirty years, a band which included musicians such as Ronnie Carruthers (pno), Alfie Seely (accordion), Derek Lawton or Eric Rinaldi (tpt), Ronnie Dunn (bs) and Ian Gillan (drms). Many of them, including Jim himself, were interested in jazz and played in jazz combos as well as dance bands. Jim's love for and interest in jazz continued and, much later, beginning in the 1990s and continuing until 2010, he was to be a regular in the resident rhythm section organized by Roger Craik, which hosted monthly jazz sessions at the 'Starbank Inn' in Newhaven and featured invited guest horn players.

After the demise of the Nova Scotians, the Dixieland tradition was to be kept alive in Edinburgh by **The Royal Mile Jazz Band**, which played in the Chicagoan tradition.

This band, according to Andrew Lauder, played at the Royal Mile Café, which was owned by the mother of the band's trumpet player, Eric Rinaldi. Others who played in this band included Jack Duff and Joe Smith on reeds, David 'Eed' Smith who played both trombone and banjo (although presumably not at the same time), Tom Finlay on piano and Sandy Malcolm on drums.

'Boosey and Hawkes', the musical instrument makers, sponsored a 'National Trad Band Contest' in 1962 and the local heat took place in the Edinburgh Palais de Dance, in December of that year. This competition was very much a sign of the times, as the infamous 'Trad Boom' was upon us and trad jazz records were featuring in the Pop charts. The Contest Rules included the statement *'Any musical instrument may be used but each group must contain at least one trombone, one trumpet, one banjo and one clarinet'* – a sign of the times indeed! I took part in this contest, playing with a schoolboy band, the **Mound City Jazz Band** and, at that stage of our collective development, we were really just there to make up the numbers. However, the Royal Mile Jazz Band also took part and, hardly surprisingly considering their line-up, were serious contenders, eventually finishing as runners up to Old Bailey and his Jazz Advocates. The local heat was reviewed in the Edinburgh Evening News and the reviewer, John Gibson, reported that the Royal Mile band sounded well rehearsed and seemed engrossed in a Condon-type sound. They played *'I've Found a New Baby'*, *'Mood Indigo'* and *'My Gal Sal'*. Gibson also noted that *'...clarinetist Jack Duff and drummer Sandy Malcolm emerged as two of the evening's outstanding musicians'*[95]. This was not surprising as these two went on to have full time careers in jazz, in Jack Duff's case, a lengthy and distinguished one.

Another journalist and a colleague of John Gibson, was **Alastair Clark (trumpet)**, who had become interested in jazz through hearing the Sid Phillips band on the wireless in the mid-1950s. In Alastair's case, his interest in jazz was very much a personal thing. He was not involved in any jazz gang, nor was he taken to jazz sessions or persuaded to

---

[95] Gibson J, Edinburgh Evening News, 4th December 1962.

132

buy jazz records by already committed friends. He simply got into jazz on his own, without even wondering if there were others around with the same interests. He was not even aware that Edinburgh was already considered something of a hot spot for jazz. He had been educated at Daniel Stewart's College and, while at school, saved up £6 with which he bought a trumpet from Mev Taylor's shop at Haymarket. He then persuaded the school to allow him to have trumpet lessons from the brass teacher, who played trumpet in the Empire Theatre pit band. Alastair was taught the rudiments but was finally caught out by his tutor who said *'You're faking'* as he battled his way through 'Baa Baa Black Sheep'. The tutor was correct, Alastair was playing by ear, not reading the music, and that is the way it was to stay.

Alastair's interest, at this time, was in black music, much influenced by the writings of the Frenchman Hugues Panassie, and Alastair strove to achieve a sound like that of Louis Armstrong – a laudable aim if ever there was one! After practice at home, when he played into a cupboard full of clothes to muffle the sound, he went to his first live gig after being told by a pal that there were jazz sessions in the Crown Bar in Lothian Street. Here he not only heard Sandy Brown but discovered that were others who shared his interest in hot music. Alastair was knocked out by Sandy's playing, considering him to be better than any clarinetist that he had ever heard on record. Attending the Crown sessions also brought him into contact with the bass player Jim Young, who arranged for him try out for a band he was forming. This was followed by several makeshift bands and then came what Alastair has called his *'big break'*. Al Fairweather followed by Sandy Brown had departed for London and trombonist Bob Craig, intent on filling in the gaps to keep the band playing, offered Alastair the trumpet slot. Alastair describes this as a fabulous experience and recalls that Dougie Campbell, whom he describes as a great guitarist, was in the band. Even without Al and Sandy, the band under Bob Craig's leadership continued to be successful and played some important gigs, including one in the Usher Hall when they were the warm up band for the Chris Barber band. This gig was sold out and Pat Halcox,

Barber's fine trumpeter, afterwards complimented Alastair on his playing.

Later, Alastair was to play trumpet with **Pete Kerr's Dixielanders**, a band with whom he made a couple of singles records. I have a copy of one of these recordings and the lineup is Alastair Clark (tpt), Pete Kerr (clt and leader), Ken Ramage (tbn), Bob McDonald (pno), Jim Douglas (bjo), Johnny Logan (bs) and George Crockett (drms). The tunes are *'Stars and Stripes for Ever'* on one side and *'Ice Cream'* on the other and it is was on Waverley Records, No. SPL 505[96]. The band sounds quite fiery and Alastair, playing well himself, was clearly in good company. Later, he had to leave the band to concentrate on his career in journalism, when Pete Kerr had a stab at playing full time, taking the band to Germany under the name Pete Kerr's Capital Jazz Band, as described earlier. As we have already heard, Andrew Lauder was the replacement for Alastair. Later still, after National Service, Alastair returned to Edinburgh, switched to alto saxophone, and formed a band with Ian 'Tello' Telford on trumpet, Donald McDonald on bass and Dennis Morton on drums. This band played *'mainstreamy, swingy stuff'*, according to Alastair, and had a fortnightly gig at the Art College, where they attracted a good following.

Alastair went on to have a successful career in journalism, becoming a senior journalist with the 'Scotsman' newspaper and, although the pressures of his work put an end to his jazz career, he looks back on his playing days as the happiest of his life. He is of the view that jazz is the most creative form of art because it is instant and *'you live or die by what you come up with in the next 30 seconds'*. He also points out how many jazzers were creative in other ways, in addition to their music, and considers that jazz is the ultimate platform for creativity. He tempers this, however, in terms of more recent developments in jazz, believing that some of the heart has gone out of the music, feeling that attempts to be more ludicrously virtuosic than the next guy have taken over. Alastair Clark stopped playing far too soon and his

---

[96] See Discography Appendix

Armstrong inspired trumpet (and his alto sax playing, although I never heard this) was a serious loss to Edinburgh traditional jazz.

The trombonist who recorded the *'Stars and Stripes/ Ice Cream'* single with the Pete Kerr band was **Ken Ramage (trombone and later, drums)**. He was born in 1937 and educated at Leith Academy, where he learned to play violin in the school orchestra. A viewing of the 'bio-pic' 'The Glen Miller Story' in 1953 awakened in him an ambition to play jazz trombone and he was quickly into action, one of his first gigs being at the Stud Club, then located on St John's Hill off the Pleasance. At this gig he met local jazzers Peter Davenport, Jim Petrie and Jim Young. In 1959, Ken played with Johnny Keating's Big Band, which played regularly in a venue called the Harmony Inn in the Canongate. Keating, who was also involved in the running of the famous Ted Heath Band, had suggested that Ken be recruited for this band. However, in the end, although Ken's jazz playing was well up to the standard required, Keating came to the conclusion that his music reading was not and reluctantly felt that he could not put Ken's name forward.

Not long after this, Ken decided that he wanted to pursue a professional career in jazz and joined Charlie Gall's band, touring Germany with them in 1959. On the return of the band to London, it was to find that the so-called Trad Boom was underway and everything in the traditional jazz world had moved towards a more commercial approach. Ken, by now a player with a formidable technique, found himself fired *'...for playing too many notes'*! Ken interpreted this as a conflict between Dixieland, which was his preferred style, and New Orleans jazz, which was very much in fashion, and, as Ken put it, *'...trombone players were expected to sound like Jim Robinson again'*! Jim Robinson, who played very much in the early tailgate manner, was of course the trombone player in the George Lewis band whose style was followed by many of the successful British traditional bands. The few British bands which played outside this model, such as Alex Welsh's band and the Sandy Brown and Al Fairweather band, were never really a part of the Trad Boom and had something of a struggle to find gigs while the boom lasted. I should add, for the sake of accuracy, that the Kenny Ball band, which followed a white dixieland model rather than a New Orleans one, was also extremely successful during the boom. However, this was mostly because they followed a notably commercial policy of producing jazzed-up versions of catchy, well-known tunes, many of them from shows and films, such as 'Samantha', 'The Green Leaves of Summer' and '88 Days in Peking'.

After his exit from the Charlie Gall band, Ken joined the band of Eggy Ley and stayed with them for about a year. Eggy Ley, whose real name was Derek William Ley, was a London born reeds player who ran a number of bands, which worked mainly on the Continent, and who later became a radio producer. With the Eggy Ley band in 1961, Ken toured and recorded with Benny Waters, a legendary reeds player from the USA who had played and recorded with Joe 'King' Oliver in the 1930s.

Ken himself then organized a band, the Ken Ramage Dixielanders, to tour in Germany in 1962, and this he regards as the best of all the many bands with which he played. This is not a surprising view given the quality of the line-up which included Per Hansen on trumpet, Edinburgh's own Jack Duff and Alec Shaw on reeds and piano respectively, George Cole on drums and an outstanding bass player, Ron Mathewson from Shetland. The band was not only good but also successful, making a number of live broadcasts on BFN (British Forces Network) and AFN (American Forces Network) while they were in Germany. Ken remembers that this band was, at the time, the only professional jazz band which was playing the terrific material written by Sandy Brown and Al Fairweather other than, of course, the Fairweather-Brown band itself. The young bass player, Ron Mathewson, was to go on to have a major jazz career, firstly with the Alex Welsh band and then into more modern forms of jazz with Ronnie Scott, amongst many others. I remember Ron Mathewson arriving in Edinburgh from Shetland in the very early 1960s and, even then, his playing scared me to death. He was to become an awesome player, with an amazing technique, who seemed to be able to play at the speed of light. His brother Matt Mathewson was a fine pianist who played in Edinburgh for a while in the 1950s.

The Ken Ramage Dixielanders later broke up while still based in Germany and Ken was briefly stranded there. However, out of the blue came a chance to join an American band, which was playing the Storyville Club in Frankfurt. This band was called the Route Two Tooters and they had won the American Inter-Collegiate Band National Contest, a win which had led to a tour in Europe. Illness had resulted in the departure of their trombone player and Ken was on the spot at just the right time to be offered his place in the band, an offer he was only too pleased to accept. He then sailed with the band as they headed back to the USA, fulfilling the next part of their contract by playing on the liner as it sailed across the Atlantic. A final perk of his spell with the Rout Two Tooters was the chance to record with them for the famous Riverside Records in New York, although sadly the recordings were never released. It was during this recording session that Ken became aware that the great modern jazz trumpeter, Dizzy Gillespie, was in the next studio. Later, when most of the Route Two Tooters had departed back to college, Ken, with help from an American trumpet playing friend, made his way to Albany, in up-state New York, where he played part-time with the local Dixieland band. He also worked in the golf course business for a while, where his Scots accent came in handy, many of the green keepers in those days being Scots! The trumpet player who had assisted Ken was Superintendent of the Albany Country Club and it turned out that Dizzy Gillespie, who was apparently keen on horses, went there quite regularly to do some riding when he was in the area. A happy outcome of this was that Ken got to know the famous bebopper quite well.

Ken returned to Edinburgh in 1967 to take over the family shop, his father having gone into local politics. He set about forming various jazz groups, sometimes four-piece sometimes a sextet, and held down regular gigs at The White Cockade in Rose Street and The Yellow Carvel in Hunter's Square, behind the Tron Church. Both of these were good and popular jazz venues, supporting many bands over the years, including that of Charlie McNair. Ken Ramage also did a lot of work with dance bands and in the clubs. This latter term tends to mean the likes of Working

Men's Clubs, Miner's Clubs and so on, there being a lot of them scattered around Fife and in the Borders.

Ken also played a series on STV with piano player Alec Shaw, a fine guitarist called Bill Mulholland, Ronnie Rae on bass and on drums Davie Dunn, who was to emigrate to Australia. The series was called 'A Touch of Jazz' and it was shortly after this TV work that he went back on the boats, cruising to the Bahamas and the Caribbean area generally. When working on the boats, each musician was expected to play two instruments, presumably to increase the versatility of the bands. The Edinburgh drummer Kenny Duff was in the boat band and Ken Ramage would take over on the drum kit whenever Kenny Duff was taking his breaks. Because of this, Ken nominated drums as his second instrument, a portent of the future because, as we will see later in this book, Ken Ramage was later to suffer dental problems that would result in him having to stop playing trombone and to switch to drums. He would also later return to the Edinburgh jazz scene.

The reeds player in the band nominated by Ken Ramage as the best he ever ran, was **Jack Duff (reeds, piano)**. Jack was born in Edinburgh on 13th August 1940 and was educated at the Royal High School. He started on piano at the age of seven and took up clarinet at fifteen, later adding all the various saxes to his musical armoury. Although ten years or so younger than the original RHS Gang, he was much influenced by them, particularly by the playing of Sandy Brown. Jack was also influenced by the great tenor saxist Coleman Hawkins and was certainly more oriented towards middle period jazz and Swing than New Orleans jazz. He first appeared on the Edinburgh jazz scene in the late 1950s and, as a teenager, played with the Charlie McNair band and the Royal Mile Jazzmen. He then went on to play full time with the local dance band leader, Cam Robbie, and then in 1959, with the Geraldo Orchestra.

Jack was and remained throughout his career, a great enthusiast and was an inveterate sitter-in whenever the chance came up. Often the first sign that he was around would be a hopeful face smiling round the edge of the door and you knew that Jack had arrived and was looking for a sit-in. This happened so often when I was playing with the

Old Bailey band in the early 1960s, that band leader Archie Sinclair gave him the nickname 'Face'! He was a terrific musician and was always welcome. When I first met him in the early 1960s, he was particularly enthused by the playing of Paul Gonzalves, the tenor sax player with the Duke Ellington band, and I remember going to Newcastle with Jack and several others to hear the Ellington band in concert, still with all the great names playing as wonderfully well as ever.

Jack joined the band that Ken Ramage put together to tour Germany in 1962, the band Ken said was his best ever. At the end of this tour, he returned to London and then moved to Jersey in 1964, where he worked with another Edinburgh exile, the bass player Gerry Rossi, and led his own band. Jack became the leading jazz player on Jersey and his band accompanied many international stars including Johnny Griffiths, Sonny Stitt, Harry Edison, Kenny Davern, Kay Starr, Jimmy Witherspoon, Roy Eldridge, Benny Waters and Joe Harriot. During this period of his career, he recorded three albums, including one with trumpeter Kenny Wheeler as guest. Jack's yearly programme, when based on Jersey, was to remain there during the six-month long summer seasons, then play full time on the ocean liners, including the Queen Elizabeth and the Canberra, in the winters. His ability as a more than competent jazz pianist was a great asset during the work on the boats. He maintained this pattern for more than twenty years, visiting many exotic destinations in the USA, Australia and the Caribbean. At various other times, Jack also put in time with the Sid Lawrence Orchestra, played with the fine American clarinet player Peanuts Hucko at the Jersey Jazz Festival in the late 1970s and with Humphrey Lyttelton at the 1982 Edinburgh Jazz Festival.

Jack eventually returned to Edinburgh in 1990, when he quickly slotted in as if he had never been away, working both as a soloist and setting up bands under his own leadership. He was a featured soloist with Hamish McGregor's Fat Sam's Band (see chapter XIV) and became the reeds player with Mike Hart's Scottish Society Syncopators, making many festival appearances with these bands, both in the UK and abroad. He was a consummate and extremely versatile musician for whom music was his whole life. He was completely at home in most jazz styles and this enabled him to sustain a full time career in the music over a long period. One of the many admirable things about Jack was, whatever his own actual preferences may have been in jazz, he never gave less than his enthusiastic best, whoever he was playing with. In addition to his musicianship, Jack had a full, rounded tone on all the reed instruments that he played and he enhanced the sound of every band with whom he played. Sadly, after only ten years back in his home city, his health began to give problems and Jack Duff died in Edinburgh at the age of only sixty, on 30th September 2000. There was however, to be an odd little tail piece to Jack's story.

In the Edinburgh Evening News of 11th December 2000[97], there appeared an article by John Gibson which described the unique way in which Jack's widow, Erika, had managed to scatter his ashes just where he would have wished. Jersey, in the Channel Islands, had been a special place in Jack's life and he had a tremendous affection for the island that had been his home and provided his living, for so many years. Erika decided that it was from the coast of Jersey that Jack's ashes should be scattered into sea. There was however, a problem; the Jersey authorities were very much against the ashes of anyone but current residents being scattered there. Nothing daunted, it did not take long for the ever-resourceful Erika to come up with a scheme to get round the problem and, in the process, share a last laugh with Jack. Erika had been invited to Jersey to attend a memorial concert to Jack and decided this was the time to smuggle his ashes back to the island. She accomplished this by adding the ashes to the content of a bottle of Jack Daniels whisky, a favourite tipple that the two of them had shared on many an occasion! It was this, of course, that gave rise to John Gibson's witty heading of 'My fond farewell with a bottle of Jack...'! The memorial concert, which featured the Jersey Big Band and the playing of two fine London jazzers, Kathy Stobart and Digby Fairweather,

---

[97] Gibson J, 'My fond farewell with a bottle of Jack...', Edinburgh Evening News, December 11 2000

was presented in the Grand Hotel in St Helier and was a great success, with the proceeds going to charity. On the morning following the concert (although probably not all that early!), Erika quietly made her way down to the shore in front of the hotel and scattered the contents of the bottle into the bay. Erika had reported that, although she had shed the odd tear, she did so with a smile, knowing how much Jack would have appreciated the memorial event, the location and, perhaps most of all, the sheer audacity and humour of this final act of his long and successful jazz career.

Roger Craik (drums) was born in 1940 and was introduced to pipe band drumming while at George Watson's College. He was also introduced to jazz when at school and played in the George Watson's Jazz Babies, with fellow pupils Hamish Hay (clt) whom Roger describes as talented, 'Vally' Valentine (tpt), Chick Mooney (bjo), Bobby Kidd (bs) and Roger himself, by now playing a full drum kit. Roger reports that the Headmaster eventually put a stop to the jazz activities, a far from unfamiliar story!

Roger's older brother, Gus, played guitar and through him, Roger came into contact with a group of Edinburgh University musicians, which included Jim Baikie (gtr) and Johnny Winters (rds). As Roger remembers it, many of the jazz musicians who were around the Edinburgh scene at this time played a great deal of dance music but took every chance they could to play jazz. Apparently, there was a division between the University players and the Edinburgh players, the two groups tending to keep apart. Roger found himself more involved with the University group and was a frequent dep with the band that Jim Baikie put together. He also did a season up in the Trossachs with a trio which included his brother Gus and a pianist called Bob McDonald, who was a medical student. This trio played what Roger describes as Swing oriented dance music.

Roger was also involved in a residency at the Student's Union, near the McEwan Hall, where he played with a band which included Charlie McNair. This band featured Charlie on trumpet, Bill Skinner on clarinet, Laurie Gardner, another medical student, on piano, Norrie Gray on guitar, Charlie McCourt, whom Roger remembers as a postman, on bass and Roger himself on drums. Many years later, in the 1980s, Roger was a member of the band called The Festival City Jazz Band, which played at the Clarenden Hotel and included Ian Scott, who was the band leader, on piano, Jimmy Shortreed (clt), Andrew Lauder (tpt), Bill Smith (tbn) and Jim Baikie (gtr). Later still, in July 1996, Roger was to set up the very successful monthly jazz sessions at the Starbank Inn in Newhaven, where he had a resident rhythm section which backed invited horn players.

Although there were occasional temporary changes, the resident rhythm section at the **'Starbank' sessions** was Roger (drms), Jim Baikie (gtr and vocals), and the 'two Ronnies' – Ronnie Caruthers (pno) and Ronnie Dunn (bs). These sessions were popular with both audience and musicians, always well attended, and provided a showcase for top Edinburgh horn players including Jack Duff, Jack Graham, Hamish McGregor, Tom Chalmers, Jimmy Woods Keith Edwards and Dick Lee (rds), John McGuff (tbn), Andrew Lauder and Colin Steele (tpt), Dougie Campbell (gtr) and also the popular singer, Jean Mundell. Also deserving of a mention is the owner of the 'Starbank Inn', Scott Brown, a long time supporter of jazz, whose goodwill and on-going support was crucial to the success of these Sunday afternoon sessions.

Roger Craik modestly described himself to me as a having been a *'sort of permanent dep'* during his early days, when he often helped out the bands of the time when they were short of a drummer. Saying this, he gave the impression that he did not consider himself good enough to hold down a regular place in a band. In fact, he was a skillful drummer who was extremely knowledgeable about jazz and who always did a fine job when he was called on to play. Roger had a high-flying career in the legal profession, becoming a Queen's Counsel and a Sheriff, and I suspect that his jazz playing was restricted by his studies when he was at University and then later, by a busy and demanding career.

An early enthusiast of tape recordings, not the least of his many contributions to the Edinburgh jazz scene were the many recordings he made, carefully catalogued and stored, of many of the Edinburgh bands. Sometimes he would bring together a selected band for a recording session and these recordings too, are part of Roger's extensive collection. It would be good to think that, sometime in the future, these recordings will become part of an archive of Edinburgh jazz[98]. Roger Craik has also written articles on jazz for various jazz publications, including one published in the September 2010 edition of the Journal of the International Association of Jazz Record Collectors[99], entitled 'The Legacy of Alex Welsh', for which he got an award from the Association.

Ronnie Dunn (bass), who played bass for many years at Roger Craik's Starbank sessions, became interested in jazz around 1954 when he was thirteen years old, largely because his two elder brothers were interested and had an extensive record collection. Most of the material he heard was the music of Art Tatum, Louis Armstrong and, eventually, Charlie Parker and Dizzy Gillespie. Around the same time, Ronnie began playing cornet in his local Boys Brigade band and then, in 1957, he went to the Usher Hall to hear the Gerry Mulligan Quartet with Bob Brookmeyer, Joe Benjamin and Dave Bailey. After that, as he has said, he was totally hooked on jazz.

Local jazz also attracted his attention and he started going to the West End Cafe on Sunday nights to hear the Dickie McPherson Quintet with McPherson (tpt), Robbie Richardson (ten sax), Alex Shaw (pno), Gerry Rossi (bs) and Billy Allison (drms). Ronnie first played the double bass when, at Leith Academy, a show was to be put on and they had everything they needed except a bass player. He volunteered and borrowed the school bass and, as he put it, *'started mucking around with it'*! Trombone player Ken Ramage was a fellow pupil at the school and, when he heard that Ron was playing bass, he invited him to join his band which was playing at the Condon Club in India Buildings. At these sessions, Ron met Jack Duff (rds) for

---

[98] An archive of Edinburgh jazz was launched at the Edinburgh Central Library on 30th July 2010, largely thanks to the sterling work of Jim Keppie, Donald Murray, Bill Strachan and Drew Landles. The evening also featured a small exhibition about the history of jazz in Edinburgh and a quartet led by pianist Ron Carruthers

[99] IAJRC Journal – Journal of the International Association of Jazz Record Collectors, published quarterly

the first time and remembers that Ken McCullough was the guitar player.

Things started to move rapidly after that and, over the next year or so, Ron made contact with a host of jazzers who were involved in the more modern reaches of local jazz, including Jim Baikie, Roger and Gus Craik, Tom Finlay (pno) who had just appeared from Cowdenbeath, Dougie Campbell (gtr), Norman Skinner (pno), Alan Hastie (drms) and the vocalist Jimmy Gilmore, who at that time was playing clarinet and tenor sax. However, there was obviously a strong local traditional jazz scene around as well and Ron found himself going to the Royal Mile Cafe on Sunday evenings. There he heard jazzers such as Eric Rinaldi, (tpt) Jack Duff, Johnny McGuff (tbn), Forbes Laing (bs) and Sandy Malcolm (drms) amongst others. When the Finlay-Gentleman Quintet was formed in 1960, Ron was the bass player with Alec Gentleman (ten sax), Tom Finlay, Johnny Smith (tpt) and Ian McDonald (drms). This band was to become popular and played at a number of venues around town, as well as playing at the likes of the Art College Revels. At this event, the Quintet played as the opening band before the big name bands came on. These included the Johnny Dankworth Big band and the Tubby Hayes Quintet and it was at an Art Revels that Ron met, for the first time, the fine Scottish trumpeter, Jimmy Deuchar.

In 1961 or 1962, the London based modern sax player Ronnie Scott opened a jazz venue in Edinburgh, located behind John Knox's house in the High Street. Here the Finlay-Gentleman band played as openers for a succession of London bands including those of Joe Harriot, Ronnie Scott himself, Les Condon, Tubby Hayes and Phil Seaman. Then, at the end of 1963 , Ronnie together with Tom Finlay and drummer Billy Allison signed up for 'Geraldo's Navy', the bands run by the Geraldo organisation to play on cruise liners, and the three of them spent six months playing on the Empress of Canada, cruising between New York and the West Indies. This brought them the wonderful experience of three nights every two weeks in New York, when they were able to hear Miles Davis, Wes Montgomery, Al Cohn, Zoot Sims, John Bunch, Woody Herman, Lionel Hampton, Dizzy

Gillspie, the Gerry Mulligan Concert jazz band and a host of others.

After returning to Edinburgh, Ron gigged around town with the Finlay-Gentleman and Jim Baikie bands and with the brothers from Shetland, pianist Matt and bass player Ron Mathewson. In 1967, Ron left Edinburgh for Scone in Perthshire and there was a gap in his playing career. He did, however, cover the trip to the Sacramento Jazz Festival with the Scottish Jazz Advocates in 1981, when I was unable to get away from the day job to make the trip. Then, in 1987 the guitarist Dougie Campbell persuaded him out of retirement and they got together in a duo which, as late as 2010, still made occasional appearances. In addition to this, Jimmy Deuchar, also based in the Perth area, brought Ron into his Quintet with which Ron played until Deuchar's death in 1993. Since then Ron has stayed in action, mostly playing gigs as a dep, but also putting in time with bands backing Edinburgh singers Edith Budge and Jean Mundell. Ron also played with bands put together to back visiting jazzers such as Martin Taylor, Eddie Thompson, Benny Waters, Joe Temperley, trombonist Joe Wilson from the Woody Herman band and a good number of others, visiting from a London base.

From the above account, it will be clear that Ronnie Dunn's interest and playing was mostly in the sphere of more modern styles of jazz rather than the jazz styles with which this book is principally concerned. However, he is typical of a group of able and versatile Edinburgh jazzers, such as Jack Duff, Tom and Jack Finlay, Dougie Campbell and Jim Baikie who, to a significant degree, were active across the spectrum of local jazz. Not the least of Ronnie's contributions to Edinburgh jazz, was the part he played in the Starbank sessions. These sessions were almost unique in Edinburgh jazz, providing a forum for local jazzers to get together in the time honoured jam session setting and proved to be an extremely popular Sunday afternoon gig for many years. Sadly, while I was engaged in writing this piece about him, Ronnie Dunn died suddenly, in Perth at the age of 69, on 17th October 2010.

Now we come to two particularly distinguished Edinburgh figures, both of whom were amongst the best of their generation on any instrument. Both favoured middle period jazz and both were highly respected professional musicians with formidable reputations. Both had long and successful careers and, simply because they made their first mark in Edinburgh jazz in the late 1950s and early 1960s, I have included them in this chapter.

The first is **Ronnie Rae (bass)**, who was born 1938 in Edinburgh and was brought up in the Musselburgh area. Ronnie started playing tuba when he was eleven years old and was encouraged by a school friend to join the Musselburgh and Fisherrow Brass Band. It was during his spell with this band that he won a prize as the best tuba player in Scotland. Later, health problems interfered with his tuba playing and he switched to the double bass, attending Johnnie Keating's School of Music from 1957-1958, where he learned the basics of the instrument under the tutelage of another great Edinburgh bass player, Jimmy Luke. Ronnie played his first gig on bass in the Crown Hotel in Hawick with Edwin Holland's band and remained with this band for a number of months. A fellow member of the band was trombonist Johnnie McGuff, who would also go on to a notable career in jazz. Later, Ronnie worked with the Palais bands in Edinburgh and Glasgow. He also worked with another fine trombone player Ken Ramage, and as a member of the Alex Shaw trio, in gigs around Edinburgh during the 1960s.

In the 1960s, Ronnie began his professional career as a jazz musician, moving south to play with the Alex Welsh Band, then in its great years, and completing two spells with this band, one in 1963 and the other in 1965. During his time with the Welsh band, Ronnie played, broadcast and made recordings with some of the great jazz names who toured with the band. These included Ruby Braff, Ben Webster, Bill Coleman, Eddie Miller, Eddie 'Lockjaw' Davis, Bud Freeman, Wild Bill Davison and Earl Hines.

On his return to Edinburgh, Ronnie played seven nights a week with pianist Alex Shaw in the Mount Royal Hotel. It was during the course of this work that Ronnie again backed the great piano player Earl Hines, in the Chimes Casino in Edinburgh. Although now back in Scotland, Ronnie remained a bass player with an international reputation and, from his Edinburgh and later Glasgow bases, he worked as a 'free lance', touring and playing gigs with a host of great jazz men. Their names read like a 'Who's Who' of middle period jazz – Ray Bryant, George Chisholm, Al Cohn, Georgie Fame, Art Farmer, Tal Farlow, Buddy de Franco, John Griffin, Barney Kessel, Lee Konitz, Humphrey Lyttelton, Red Norvo, Shorty Rogers, Buddy Tate, Scott Hamilton, Warren Vache, Teddy Wilson, Louis Stewart, Spike Robinson and many more – the list just goes on and on. He played all over the world, including many of the most famous jazz festivals, at Sacramento, San Diego, Los Angeles, Palm Springs, Toronto, Calgary, Vancouver, Switzerland, Jakarta in Indonesia, Bali and Bangkok, Germany, China, Russia and, nearer home, Cork, Glasgow and Edinburgh.

Added to all that, Ronnie was bass player in residence at the Fife Summer Jazz School for ten years and for six years taught and played at the Scottish Arts Council and Lottery funded 'Fionna Duncan Vocal Jazz Workshops', which took place across Scotland. A Scottish Arts Council grant in 1999 enabled him to take sufficient time out from playing to write and arrange eleven of his own compositions. This led to him forming a band called Scotia Nostra, to perform his compositions on a concert tour around Scotland.

A great double bassist, Ronnie has had an illustrious career in jazz, much of it in what would now be seen as the mainstream of jazz, and he played, toured and recorded on numerous occasions with some of the finest jazz musicians that ever played. Those wishing to trace Ronnie's playing should turn to the professional jazz catalogues which contain many fine recordings featuring his playing in stellar company. Ronnie was, and is, such an accomplished player that he was perfectly capable of playing any form of jazz and, a true professional, he never gave anything other than a great performance, whoever he played with and wherever he played. He was even willing to deputise for me with the Old Bailey band and the Scottish Jazz Advocates, going on tour with them to the Sacramento Jazz Jubilee in 1982 and 1983, when I was unable to make the trips, something that makes me feel very humble to this day. Perhaps my only claim to any sort of note in the jazz world is that, according to Fionna Duncan, it was my calling off from a trip to Sacramento that brought Ronnie and Fionna together, a partnership still going strong almost thirty years on.

I can remember very clearly the awe with which I and the other local bass players, always regarded him and this remains true even in 2011, with Ronnie now in his seventies. Throughout his long career in jazz, Ronnie has remained Scotland's number one bass player and is also Scotland's most experienced and most in demand bassist. The huge repertoire he has built up over the years made him the ideal choice to lead the all-star trio that has hosted the official Late Night Jam Sessions at the Glasgow International Jazz Festival.

Not the least of Ronnie's many contributions to Scottish jazz was his founding of a jazz dynasty, all of his family of two sons and four daughters making their mark in the contemporary jazz world. Their interest in music was hardly surprising given Ronnie's stature as a bass player and the fact that their mother, Margaret, was a music teacher. Between them, the young Raes, who chose which instruments they wished to study at about the age of eight, played piano, cornet, guitar, drums, violin, French horn and oboe. All four daughters are accomplished singers, elder son Ronnie junior is a fine jazz pianist and younger son John a highly rated jazz drummer and composer. Three of the girls, Cathie, Gina and Sylvia, perform together as The Rae Sisters, as well as appearing individually, and youngest sister Gillian is also a fine singer, although seldom heard in public. The achievements and stature of the younger Rae's are reflected in their high reputations in contemporary jazz and jazz promotion and administration and are a great credit to Ronnie. However, their jazz styles and activities are well beyond the scope of this book and this is not the place to explore their careers. Readers who wish to know more about Scotland's biggest and best known contemporary jazz family should refer to their family website[100] and seek opportunities, live and recorded, to enjoy the astonishing talents of this gifted family.

---

[100] http://raefamilyjazz.com

The second of these two great Edinburgh players is **Alex Shaw (piano)**, and he, like Ronnie Rae, he was one of finest and most versatile Edinburgh jazz musicians of his generation. Indeed, Alex was another of the Edinburgh jazzers who could hold his own with anyone and he should have been a much better known figure on the UK jazz scene than is the case. Alex's interest in jazz began in the early 1940s when he heard a 78 rpm recording of the great pianist Art Tatum and from then on, jazz was to be his music. It is strange and not a little sad that Alex does not feature in the standard British jazz references book and left very few recordings to remind us of his brilliance. He did however, along with Ronnie Rae, record with the brilliant, modern American clarinet player Buddy de Franco, the recording including, rather unexpectedly, an almost straight version of the Scottish tune 'The Dark Island'.

On the few occasions when Alex moved away from Edinburgh to play, for example when he went to play in Germany with Pete Kerr's Capital Jazz Band in 1960, he found it difficult to cope with life on the road. Well aware of this, he was to settle for a life playing jazz at home in Edinburgh. Although this deprived the wider world of Alex's scintillating playing, it was greatly to Edinburgh's benefit and, although he had plenty of offers to play elsewhere, including invitations to play in the USA, he turned them all down. He was once approached to record for the prestigious Hep Records but, when it transpired that he would have to undertake a tour to promote the recording, he again said no. Similarly, although he occasionally appeared on a more formal stage, particularly at the Queen's Hall when the Scottish jazz organization Platform was at its most active in the 1980s, Alex was most at home playing in more informal settings, such as his long-running residencies at the George Hotel and in the Platform One bar, in the Caledonian Hotel.

In Edinburgh, Alex was a jazz institution and a by-word for quality jazz. His forte was the standard repertoire of quality popular tunes and an Alex Shaw residency was a Mecca for local followers of top-notch piano playing and visiting jazz musicians alike. His knowledge of the twentieth century song book was vast and his sensitive and always swinging interpretations a joy to hear. His Platform One residency was followed by others at the Drum and Monkey and then the Dome in George Street, where he played until shortly before his death. He usually played with a trio, adding bass and drums to his piano, and over the years his frequent companions were musicians of the caliber of bass players Ronnie Rae and Brian Shiels and drummers Mike Travis and Dave Swanston.

He was to be a fixture on the Edinburgh International Jazz Festival (EIJF) programme, even in its earliest days, being included in the second Festival in 1980 when it was said that his trio was as far as the then very traditional programme would go towards modern jazz. The performance of the Alex Shaw trio was hailed the following year as '...a popular and refreshing break from the hot music which made up the main part of the programme'[101]. From then on, Alex and his trio would become the accompanists of choice for scores of distinguished visiting jazzers and they were often the house trio for the late night jam sessions during the EIJF. When jazz journalist Kenny Mathieson wrote Alex's obituary in the Scotsman he said 'If Shaw knew the tunes, he knew how to play them. His command of jazz phrasing and rhythm was complete, his melodic invention never flagged, and he sailed through the most fearsome tempo with unruffled assurance'[102]. Mathieson also recounted how, when Alex suffered a broken arm in the late 1980s, and was unable to play for a while, a benefit evening held at Calton Studios attracted a large proportion of the Edinburgh jazz crowd and a substantial number from elsewhere.

Alex was held in the highest respect and affection by everyone and, as Ronnie Rae reminded me recently, was affectionately known as 'Faither', a tribute to his pre-eminent position on the Edinburgh jazz scene. In the early post-WWII decades, both he and Ronnie Rae would without a doubt, have been regarded as modern jazz musicians. Now, in 2011, it is easy to understand that they were in fact right in the mainstream of jazz: versatile, thoroughly

---

[101] The Edinburgh International Jazz Festival 1980 programme
[102] Mathieson K, 'Alex Shaw', The Scotsman, April 2000

capable and creative. Both made wonderful music, as Ronnie still does, both gave enormous encouragement to other jazzers and Edinburgh jazz was greatly enriched by their playing. By a happy chance, Alex lived in the flat above the young Gordon Cruikshank, later to be one of Edinburgh's best mainstream tenor sax players. Gordon could hear Alex practicing in the room above and eventually, when he was about twelve years old, he approached Alex to ask what this music was that he could hear. Alex explained and played the youngster some recordings by the likes of Cannonball and Nat Adderley. The rest, as they say, is history. Gordon could not get enough of the music after this and was destined for a notable career in jazz. Alex, in a town that had more than its fair share of fine jazz piano players, was a revered figure who should have been better known nationally and was one of Edinburgh's finest ever. Alex Shaw, pianist and gentleman and one of the most modest and likeable of all Edinburgh jazzers, died at home in Edinburgh, on 2nd April 2000.

It will have become clear in the chapters on the Royal High Gang and the Semple/Welsh Dixielanders and from the accounts of others like Alex Shaw and Ronnie Rae, just how many of the early post-WWII generation of Edinburgh jazzers had a go at a full time career in jazz. George Melly, in 'Owning Up', speculates on just why there were so many Scottish jazzers when he says *'Why are there so many Scots jazz musicians and, come to that, why so many good ones? Sandy Brown, a convinced Scottish Nationalist, has a theory that it's to do with the fact that Scottish folk music is still a reality'*[103]. Bruce Turner also ruminated on this very point when he stayed with us, during a playing visit to Edinburgh with his Jump Band back in the 1960s. It does seem to me that there is some kind of affinity between Scots and jazz but just why, I do not know. I suppose some sort of link could be found between the deprived, down-trodden nature of the early jazzers, especially the black musicians in the southern states of the USA, and the Scots' perceptions of

---

[103] 'Owning Up' by George Melly, (Copyright © George Melly, 1965) Reprinted by permission of A. M. Heath & Co Ltd

their own history of subjugation and disadvantage (and an inferiority complex!) compared to a stronger southern neighbour, but it sounds a tenuous link to me. Perhaps it's a rhythmic thing, with Scottish country dance and ceilidh music a lively and top-tapping tradition. However, what I do know is, and it will probably bring down derision on my head, I sometimes detected in Sandy Brown's impassioned clarinet playing something of the unbuttoned wildness of the bagpipes.

Chapter VII

The Jazz Purists

Although there were many fine players left in Edinburgh, the departure of musicians of the calibre of Sandy Brown, Al Fairweather, Stan Greig, Alex Welsh, Archie Semple, Dave Paxton and Dave Keir would have left a large hole in any local jazz scene. However, hardly had these great players disappeared down the A1, or in Dave Paxton's case, the road to Bahrain, than belatedly and quite surprisingly, there was another jazz renewal. Out of the blue and almost a decade later than the classic jazz part of the Revival, the missing purist element arrived in Edinburgh. What follows in this chapter is a series of profiles of some of the major jazzers involved, with their accounts of the bands and venues of the time. Inevitably and hardly surprisingly, with more than sixty years having gone by, there are a few contradictions in these accounts but these hardly matter. What does matter is the picture they paint of a lively jazz scene, still with that pioneering, almost crusading spirit that was such a big part of the Revival.

Perhaps the first sign of purist jazz activity in Edinburgh came with a band formed by someone who was not from Edinburgh at all. **Peter Davenport (trumpet)**, who was born in 1931, came from Staffordshire in the English Midlands. Peter, towards the end of the war, had been listening to recordings of the Sid Phillips band, which he says he found quite exciting and then, because he was intrigued by the name, he bought a recording of Bunk

153

Johnston playing 'When the Saints go Marching In'. Bunk Johnson, an elderly trumpeter who had been rediscovered after years out of music was, of course, an iconic figure in purist jazz and his rediscovery was perhaps the key to the whole purist jazz movement. Peter was to be much influenced by this kind of jazz but this was to come later, after his National Service.

His National Service was with the North Staffordshire regiment and he found himself posted to Trieste. There he discovered that his Education Sergeant was one Diz Disley, later to become a noted guitar player with several British jazz bands, including some particularly fine recordings with Sandy Brown and Al Fairweather. Eventually Disley, a mercurial character, was to become a member of Stephane Grappelli's band. This gives some indication of Disley's stature as a guitarist, as he was following in the footsteps of one of Europe's most resounding jazz names, the great Django Reinhardt. However, at the time of their encounter in the army, Diz Disley was to have no impact on the future jazz career of Peter Davenport, who had not, at this time, begun to play an instrument. Disley did, however, contrive to create a lasting impression. Later in his jazz career, he was to establish a reputation as something of wanderer, whose habit seemed to be to create or join bands and then disappear.

His wandering tendencies were certainly to the fore while he was stationed in Trieste. Apparently, he went walk about and succeeded in crossing a border into Yugoslavia, then under the stern communist rule of Marshall Tito. Here he was promptly arrested and clapped in jail, no doubt with the intention of subjecting him to close and severe interrogation. Diz Disley, a man of pronounced left wing views, was more than a match for the situation. Deftly turning the tables on his captors, he lectured them on their luke-warm brand of communism, pointing out that they were not running it at all properly and proffering enthusiastic advice on how to mend their ways. It was all too much for his bemused captors who hastily dispatched him back to Trieste, clearly greatly relieved to be shot of him and, no doubt, well and truly chastened by the experience.

154

After his National Service was completed, Peter Davenport arrived in Edinburgh in 1949 to attend Art College. There he studied drawing and painting, the same course undertaken by Al Fairweather, but a year or so after Al, joining the 1949 intake a term late in January 1950. This meant that Peter was at Art College around the same time as Sandy Brown, who was studying architecture. Peter's future wife, Patricia, was also at college and, like Peter, was studying painting and drawing. He discovered that there were dances every month, which everybody tried to attend. Cam Robbie, for many years a successful Edinburgh dance band leader, had his band in the downstairs hall, while there was jazz in the upstairs hall. Through this and later visits to the Crown Bar, Peter became aware of what he describes as the great music of Sandy Brown and Al Fairweather.

He and a group of fellow students were greatly enthused by this and went, as a group, to Rosenblume's shop at the top of Victoria Street, where there was a plentiful supply of second-hand musical instruments for sale. Eventually, each became the proud owner of an instrument: Peter had acquired a trumpet, Andrew Gilmour a clarinet, both Ian Gordon and Mike Duncan had bought banjos, Baxter Cooper had a drum kit, Jimmy Lane a trombone and, in addition, there was Colin Bennett who played piano and who later took up the double bass. Together they formed the **Art College Jazz Band** and their first gig was at a hall near Blackhall, on the west side of Edinburgh. Just how soon it was after the band was formed that this gig took place is not clear but it was probably quite soon, enthusiasm likely to have been more vital than musical expertise. On a personal note on this topic, in the late fifties, when I was starting, I played my first gig on double bass before I had really found out how to tune the instrument properly and well before I had ventured above the Bb note on the first string or attempted to use the fourth string at all. This was the result of pressure from other band members who were well ahead of me and had no intention of waiting until I caught up, if I ever would.

Things then began to conspire to encourage the young, aspiring trumpet playing Davenport in finding his way around the jazz world. Sandy Brown soon became aware of the Art College band and Peter has said how kind and encouraging he found both Sandy and Al Fairweather. Friendly and welcoming though Al was, Peter was completely intimidated by his ability as a trumpeter, to the extent that he never once dared to play on a band stand alongside him. Perhaps because of this, Peter came to know Sandy better than Al. Once, Sandy dragooned Peter into driving him and the visiting Wally Fawkes, already a famous name with the Humphrey Lyttelton band and a cartoonist of renown, around Glasgow, so that Wally could view some buildings of which he required to draw cartoons.

Peter's mother was French and this led to visits to relatives in France. A cousin there was the girlfriend of the trumpeter with Claude Luter's famous jazz band and she was able to sneak Peter in free to hear the great Sidney Bechet guesting with the band. By this time, the Art College band had starting listening with great interest to recordings arriving from the USA of the George Lewis band. When talking about this, Peter pointed out that this was the time of what he called *'the Ken Colyer thing'* in the UK. Colyer, of course, was the Norfolk born trumpet player who was to dedicate his entire playing career to the music of the rediscovered veterans like Lewis and Bunk Johnson. His influence in the UK was to be very considerable. At the time of writing 60 years on, there remains in Britain an extremely healthy purist jazz movement with many bands, festivals, recordings and publications, largely inspired by Colyer's efforts. There were also, for many years after Colyer's death in 1988, a Ken Colyer Trust and a Ken Colyer Trust Jazz Band, still delivering Colyer's message – a fine tribute to a sincere and dedicated jazzer.

Their interest in the Lewis band recordings and the 'Colyer thing' was to take the Art College band down a very different jazz track compared to that of Sandy and Al or for that matter, Alex Welsh and Archie Semple. The Art College band became what was to become known as 'purist' jazz musicians, a label denoting those who were inspired by the music of George Lewis and his New Orleans veterans, the music of early New Orleans.

Pete Davenport's Jazz Band
L to R: Mike Pollett (tbn), Pete Davenport (tpt), Baxter
Cooper (drms*), Ian Arnott (clt), Mike Duncan (bjo),
Colin Bennett (pno) (*Cooper is playing Farrie Forsyth's
drums) (From the collection of Peter Davenport,
photographer unknown)

In due course, Peter and the others completed their
courses and left Art College but the band continued in
Edinburgh, now known as **Pete Davenport's Jazz Band**.
The membership of the band had inevitably changed over
time and the post-Art College band included at times Chris
Cook or 'Squire' Hartley on clarinet, Mike Pollett and later
Jack Weddell on trombone, Farrie Forsyth, Baxter Cooper
and later Kenny Milne on drums, Colin Bennett and later
Jim Young on bass. Baxter Cooper now, in 2011, lives in
Glenfarg but has been inactive in jazz for many years.
There was also a piano player around, whom Peter only
remembered as Paterson but who I think, on the basis of
information from Mike Hart, was probably Johnny Paterson.

Peter stayed on in Edinburgh until around 1956/57,
during which time the band made a visit to play in London,
which seemed to have been an irresistible attraction to
aspiring jazzers in those days. The trip was arranged by

either Jim Young or Farrie Forsyth and they played three gigs there: one at Woodgreen, one at the Ken Colyer Club and one other, the location of which is lost in the mists of time. At one of the gigs *'dozens of chaps clutching washboards'* arrived and asked to sit in with the band. The band, which had at this time never heard of skiffle, were fairly taken aback by this and also by the arrival of the sax player Dick Heckstall-Smith, who also sat in. Heckstall-Smith, a musician with modernist tendencies, had already played with Sandy Brown and A Fairweather, who were by now London based, and he was also a bit taken aback by the purist style of the Davenport band. He had assumed that all Edinburgh bands would play like Sandy and Al and the pronounced difference in style must have been quite a shock.

In the late 1950s, Peter took himself off to Argyllshire to pursue a career as a painter of abstracts but, when this provided less than boundless riches, he got himself into farming as well. This period had about zero jazz content but, after a return to Edinburgh in 1960, he began again, sitting in with various Edinburgh bands. He then found the delightful Tullybannocher in Comrie, Perthshire and moved there, farming about 250 acres with a further investment in 1972 in a restaurant. As before, local jazz activity was practically nil but Peter continued to make visits to Edinburgh, where he was again welcomed as a sitter-in with bands, including those of Archie Sinclair, Charlie McNair and Mike Hart. Peter remembers that Archie Sinclair in particular, was always pleasant and made him very welcome. Later, from 1980 to 1990, the restaurant was let out to Crawfords but, in 1990, Peter took it back under his own management, which enabled him to start the Tullybannocher jazz evenings. These went on to become very successful over the next twenty years or so, and were a favourite annual gig for many bands from Edinburgh and elsewhere. About once a year, Peter would put together a band of invited veterans and featured them as his 'Re-union Jazz Band'. The monthly Tullybannocher jazz nights ran on a Friday evening and were a nicely balanced combination of jazz and a buffet supper, with the option of dancing if people were so inclined. They continued on after Peter had retired from the business and, although reduced in number, they continued to feature Peter's re-union band.

The Pete Davenport Art College band, purist in style, had disappeared from the Edinburgh scene by 1957 but that, by no means, meant the end of purist jazz in town. Other bands in the same tradition were to appear and these were to include some of the jazzers who had played in Peter Davenport's bands. The purist tradition was to remain in good hands and some of the musicians were to make big reputations for themselves in their field.

Mike Hart (banjo/guitar), whom we last met playing drums with the Sandy Brown band when little more than a school boy, had gone off to do his National Service in the RAF between 1952 and 1954 and had continued to play drums when in the services. It is all too easy to forget nowadays what an impact National Service had in the 1950s. I was only about half a generation younger than jazzers who played in the 1940s and 50s and National Service had ceased by the time I left school, but people only a year or two older than me had had to do their bit. Many of the earlier jazzers have commented on how the early bands were constantly being disrupted by people being called up, replacements being sought and returning people fitted back into bands. It was clearly a time not only of post-war austerity and rationing but also of major disruption to people's lives.

When Mike returned to Edinburgh in 1954, it was to discover that Charlie McNair had formed a jazz band. Mike had by this time taken up the banjo and he joined the McNair band as banjoist and also played any one-off gigs that were around. However, Mike was then, as ever, a man of some ambition and energy, not to mention being of an entrepreneurial bent, and it was inevitable that he would lead bands of his own. Around this time, he set up the first of his **Blue Blowers**, a band name he would continue to use over many years. This first version was a proper 'jug band', as befitted the name, no doubt in the tradition of the Mound City Blue Blowers, led in Chicago by Red McKenzie and Eddie Condon. This kind of band, in addition to the odd legitimate instrument, used kazoos, paper and comb, washboards and jugs, which could be blown into to produce convincing tuba-like bass notes. Mike's Blue Blowers had jug, washboard, guitar, banjo and trumpet, which was played by Ian 'Tello' Telford. Mike played several of these instruments, sometimes playing washboard and jug or banjo and jug simultaneously, the jug held on a special stand to leave his hands free. The Blue Blowers played in the Shoestring Café, which was in the High Street opposite the Canongate Church, and had been set up by the minister of that church, the Rev Dr Selby Wright. Around the same time, Mike also ran a skiffle group. This was called 'The Ravers' and included in its number was Dougie Campbell, later to become one of Edinburgh's best jazz guitarists.

Starting in jazz about the same time as Mike, was a young piano player called Johnny Paterson who, as we have heard, had played with the Pete Davenport band. He apparently played in the stride piano tradition and later emigrated to New York. Mike Hart was studying to go to engineering college at this time and his father, knowing that Paterson was a gifted engineer, employed him to give Mike some extra tutoring. This noble effort by Hart senior to build a respectable career in engineering for his son sadly came to nothing. Mike and Johnny Paterson used the money Mike's father had paid for tutoring to go drinking instead! Mike was clearly already very active around the local jazz scene but soon another band came along, the Climax Jazz Band, in which he was to play a founding role, along with several other jazzers who were to have long and important careers in Edinburgh jazz.

Mike Pollett (trombone) was born in Bombay on 23rd August 1934 and later moved with his family back to Scotland, settling in Edinburgh. He was educated at George Watson's Boy's College where there was no jazz influence whatsoever but he believes that singing bass in the school choir may well have created an affinity for trombone parts in traditional jazz bands. Attracted to jazz, he became a frequent visitor to the West End Café and the Stud Club and found himself, in his own words, completely captivated by the jazz of Sandy Brown and Al Fairweather. Having taken up trombone, he joined Pete Davenport's band in 1955, making a front line with Pete (tpt), Squire Hartley (clt) and with a rhythm section of Mike Duncan (bjo), Colin

Bennett (pno) and Farrie Forsyth or Baxter Cooper (drms). He also played with an early Charlie McNair band, which included Joe Smith on clarinet, with which band he played a winter of Sunday nights at the jazz club in India Buildings. The band also played on stage in a cinema in Rodney Street, during the interval of a public showing of a film, which may have been 'The Five Pennies', a bio-pic of the life of cornetist Red Nichols. With the McNair band, Mike appeared on a Beltona recording of two numbers made at a Scottish Jazz Band championship held in Glasgow, the two tracks being Hiawatha Rag and Meadow Lane Stomp[104] about which we will hear more in chapter XIII.

An early version of the Climax Jazz Band playing in the Moir Hall
Jim Young (bs), Al Hanney (clt), Kenny Milne (drms), Jim Petrie (tpt), Mike Hart (bjo), Mike Pollett (tbn) (from the collection of Jim Petrie, photographer unknown)

---

[104] See discography appendix

Mike Pollett, like Mike Hart, then became a founder member of the Climax Jazz Band in 1956. The band played at the Stud Club, which was variously located in a number of venues including the Roman Eagle Hall at 1 Johnstone Terrace, the Moir Hall on St John's Hill in the Pleasance, a venue in York Place, the Dofos Pet Shop on the corner of Leith Walk and London Road and in the basement of bass player Jim Young's house in Viewforth. The early Climax line-up with which Mike Pollett played was Jim Petrie (tpt), Stewart Pitkethly and later Alistair Hanney (clt), Mike himself on trombone, Jim Young (bs), Mike Hart (bjo) and Kenny Milne (drms). This early Climax band practiced in the Pollett parents' house and played Climax Rag as its signature tune. Mike says that this was the inspiration for the name of the band but there are at least two other versions of this, to which we will come shortly.

Later, Jake McMahon also came into the band on clarinet and Mike recalls that Jim Young was stage leader of the band, an arrangement that seems to indicate that, while Jim was the front man, the band was run on a cooperative basis. Apparently Jim Young was also the owner of a large motor car which was big enough to transport the band to gigs, with the double bass strapped to the roof - or not, as the case may be. On one particularly memorable occasion, the bass was left unstrapped and, at the first corner, the car turned but the bass went straight on and was smashed to fragments on the road! I remember once, in the 1960s, sitting in on a bass that Jim Young was playing and noticed that it was an unorthodox shape and size. I am sure that this was the unfortunate fragmented bass, lovingly restored to playing condition, if not its original shape and size, by the ever resourceful Jim Young. Many years later, while I was writing this book, I was reminiscing with Jim and the topic of this reconstructed instrument came up and I told Jim that I remembered thinking that it was the Quasimodo of the double bass!

Another memorable occasion for Mike Pollett was when he played with one of the Edinburgh bands, not the Climax band but probably either that of Charlie McNair or Pete Davenport, at a concert at the St Andrew's Hall in Glasgow, where they were the support band for the Dave Brubeck

162

Quartet. In 1958, after Mike completed his training as a Chartered Accountant, he went into the army for National Service, which included a spell in Portsmouth when he played with trumpeter Cuff Billet, a fine player later to be a prominent name in jazz. After demob, Mike departed to Singapore where he briefly played with a local cosmopolitan band, including a trumpet player from the USA embassy, at up-market functions.

Looking back in 2011, Mike thought that he probably had quite a significant impact on the development of interest in the purist variety of Revivalist jazz in Edinburgh. He had discovered a shop in the West Bow which sold records and remembers that it had broken 78 rpm records pinned up on the wall, by way of advertising. There he bought a number of recordings on the HMV label by the Bunk Johnson band, including a recording of the tune I Wish I Could Shimmy Like My Sister Kate. With these records in his possession, Mike was able to let others hear what we now know were seminal recordings in the development of purist jazz in the UK and he believes that this played an important part in the rise of interest in this type of jazz in Edinburgh. This is corroborated by drummer Kenny Milne who told me that the fact that they were able to listen to Mike Pollett's collection of recordings in the purist style was crucial in the formation of the Climax band's style. Mike's first important individual contact in Edinburgh jazz had been with Mike Hart and, soon after this, he was in touch with others including trumpeter Jim Petrie and, a bit later, the bass player, Jim Young. Although Mike was very much attracted to purist jazz for its own sake, an interest that remains intact in 2011, he also speculated that a part of the attraction at the time, in terms of trying to play jazz, was the fact that there seemed to be fewer technical demands than in what was perceived as the more advanced music of the likes of Louis Armstrong and Jelly Roll Morton. In particular, there seemed no need to be able to read written music and this was a major help in encouraging these enthusiastic youngsters in making a start in jazz. Although Mike Pollett is, at the time of writing, back living in Scotland near Kinross, he no longer plays.

Kenny Milne (drums and later trumpet) was born on 1st May 1937 and educated at Broughton High School, where he was one of a group of school pupils who got together to listen to jazz records in the school gym. Apparently Sandy Brown, who was already an active jazz musician, turned up in the gym one day, having heard the sound of the records as he was passing the school. In about 1951, at the instigation of one of the group, Graeme Robertson, they decided to form a jazz band which they called the Broughton School Jazz Band. The band included Graeme Robertson, who was later to play both trombone and bass, Karl Ekeval (clt), Stewart Sangster (washboard), Andy Cockburn (bjo) and Kenny Milne (drms). Graeme Robertson once brought to school the sheet music for the famous jazz tune Hello Central, Give Me Dr Jazz which they proceeded to hand over to their music teacher, with a request that he play it. Thinking back on this after about sixty years, Kenny Milne said that he seemed to remember that the music teacher had been unable to play it. However, Graeme Robertson remembers it differently and assures me that he could handle it without any bother, having been much involved in the dance band world when he was a student. Graeme remarked that he had been pleasantly surprised to find that his music teacher was a lot more 'hip' than he had expected and this is partly mirrored in a similar experience I and my fellow jazz followers had while at school. A former pupil of the school had returned to teach music and, having been known as a serious student of music even as a schoolboy, the expectation was that he would be little interested in our awakening jazz enthusiasms. However, we were wrong. He not only took an interest but, when he heard that we were going to hear the Humphrey Lyttelton band in the Place Jazz Club, he arranged with us to get hold of a ticket for him. He duly came along to the Place, taking a keen interest in the music and even prepared to ask us about the way a jazz band could maintain an organized sound when there was clearly a great deal of improvisation goingon. We were fairly green ourselves, at that point in our jazz education, but he seemed genuinely interest and said nothing to make us feel that we were being in any way patronized. It was a particularly impressive version of Humph's band that we heard that night, including both Danny Moss (ten) and Joe Temperley (bar) in its line-up.

However, we need to get back to Broughton High School in the early 1950s and its group of budding jazzers. From Sandy Brown, the group had discovered that he and others played at the West End Café and the Crown Bar in Lothian Street. Kenny Milne ventured along to the Crown one night and heard **Bob Craig's Jazz Band**, which had Bob on trombone, with Ian 'Daz' Arnott on clarinet, Farrie Forsyth on drums, Kenny Wheatley on bass and, as far as Kenny can remember, Al Clark on trumpet. Another band that Kenny remembers from this time played in the Crown Bar on Monday evenings and had a two-trumpet line up, the two being Ian 'Tello' Telford and Kenny Jack, whom Kenny describes as sounding like Joe 'King' Oliver. The two trumpeters apparently had fights about the music, something that is confirmed by Pete Davenport, who remembers them arguing heatedly over which notes they should each be playing! Iain Forde, whom we will meet shortly, also remembers traumas involving Tello and Kenny Jack, whom he remembers as 'Jacko'. In a later band, in which Iain Forde played trombone and Karl Ekeval clarinet, they discovered that their two trumpeters had learned all the famous two-trumpet breaks from the 1920s 'King' Oliver records. Unfortunately, they had copied them from old recordings which did not play in accurate pitch, resulting in them learning them in ridiculous and totally unreasonable keys such as B natural and Gb. This, not surprisingly, completely foxed Iain and Karl Ekeval, rendering all Tello's and Jacko's hard work unusable!

By the time of his visits to the Crown Bar, Kenny Milne had become aware of a style of New Orleans jazz in which much of the music played consisted of ensemble passages, with all the front line instruments playing simultaneously. This was in contrast to other jazz he had heard on recordings of Louis Armstrong and Jelly Roll Morton, which included a lot of solo playing.

In the meantime, Kenny Milne had discovered for himself that Revival jazz was split into the two different ways of playing, classic and purist jazz. He bought some records which included one by George Lewis and his New Orleans Stompers on the Vogue label, and describes how, on hearing it, the hairs stood up on the back of his neck. From that point on, Kenny's main jazz interest was to be the purist style.

Visits to the West End Café made him aware of others who turned up regularly, among them was one called Jack Weddell and a tall, thin individual with a mop of black hair, who turned out to be called Jim Petrie. Later, Kenny attended a party for Sandy Brown, who was leaving for London, and met Mike Hart, who introduced him to Weddell and Petrie. This was to be a fruitful meeting as it led to a decision to get a band together. Andy Cockburn, who had played banjo with the Broughton School Jazz Band, had disappeared by this time, so the band formed included Mike Hart. The band they put together was to be called the **West Richmond Street Stompers**, the original line up including Jim Petrie (tpt), Jack Weddell (tbn), Kenny Milne (drms) and a piano player whom Kenny only remembers as 'Walter'. Later, Joe Smith, who was already playing clarinet with Charlie McNair's band, came in on bass. Just how long the West Richmond Street Stompers were in existence is not clear, but around 1956, much the same group of jazzers was to be involved in the formation of a band that was to have a long and distinguished history in Edinburgh. This was the Climax Jazz Band.

Kenny Milne moved to London in 1960, to further his career in pharmacy, and there he played with many of the best UK New Orleans jazzers including Cuff Billett (tpt), Pete Dyer (tbn) and Bill Greenow (rds). He also replaced the famous band leader and drummer, Barry 'Kid' Martyn, in the Kid Martyn Band, when Barry Martyn went off to New Orleans. Kenny Milne was to return to Edinburgh in 1977, where we will meet him again later, taking up trumpet as well as continuing as one of the finest New Orleans style drummers in the UK.

Jack Weddell (trombone and vocals), who was born in Edinburgh in 1937, had sung as a boy soprano in his school choir. His interest in jazz was sparked off by hearing a recording, quite a well known and commercially successful recording in fact, of the Pee Wee Hunt band

166

playing 'Twelfth Street Rag'. This was quite a corny record by any standards and may seem an unfortunate early exposure for a budding jazzer. However, Jack survived this to become a key and long-term member of the decidedly purist Climax Jazz Band. He had received trombone lessons while at school and was in an early jazz band with trumpeter Jim Petrie by the time he was fourteen, making this about 1951. Later, he played in a band with Petrie, Kenny Milne (drms), and Karl Ekeval (clt), playing in a variety of clubs, many of which he remembers as being run by Jim Young. He was already one of the group that was later to form the core of the Climax band, but he also put in time as trombonist with the bands of the two trumpet playing band leaders, Pete Davenport and Charlie McNair.

As with all his contemporaries, Jack was called up for National Service when he was about nineteen and played bass trombone while in the RAF band. Here he experienced great trouble reading the parts and blithely busked his way through most of the music. Loss of his teeth caused a temporary hiatus in his trombone playing, resulting in a switch to bass drum and cymbal in the military band. Happily for Edinburgh jazz, the problem with his teeth was overcome and he returned to Edinburgh at the age of twenty one, where he replaced Mike Pollett with the Climax band. A move to London in 1962 brought the opportunity to play with various bands and to make some recordings with the legendary Kid Sheik Colar in a band which also included top rank players such as Sammy Rimmington (clt), Paul Sealley (bjo), Barry Richardson (bs) and Barry Martyn (drms).

After a spell back in Edinburgh from 1967, when he re-joined the Climax band, Jack was again in London from 1977 to 1982, and then returned once more to both Edinburgh and the Climax band. He later also joined a new Edinburgh band of which we will hear much more, the Spirits of Rhythm and he continued to play with these bands for many years. Throughout Jack's career, there were also many gigs with parade bands. These were marching bands in the New Orleans tradition and amongst those with whom Jack played were the Excelsior band in London and the Auld Reekie and Criterion parade bands in

Edinburgh. Jack also toured in Holland, Germany and Switzerland with the Climax band and, much later, was on the Australian tour with the Climax Re-union Band in 1992.

Jack was a fine player in the early New Orleans school of trombone playing and an able and appealing singer. It so happened that many of the songs he sang were of a melancholy and quite sentimental nature and I can remember depping with the Spirits of Rhythm when Kenny Milne referred to them as *'Jack's weepies'*! Later on, for some personal reason, Jack stopped playing earlier than most of his contemporaries, and his playing and singing were a real loss around the Edinburgh jazz scene.

Jim Petrie (trumpet and vocals), born on 14th April 1937, was a player who was to be a mainstay of Edinburgh jazz for decades and was to make a big name for himself in New Orleans jazz. Jim was educated at Tynecastle School, where a fellow pupil was Jack Weddell, and where they both were offered a chance to join the school band. While Jack chose the trombone, Jim went for the cornet. The instrument he was allocated was an Eb Cornet, which Jim still maintains ruined his lip for the rest of his life! Jim had lessons from a Jimmy Pennel, a tutor who visited the school and who played in Alexander's Dance Band, at the Leith Assembly Rooms. Jim and Jack were lent records by Jack's brother in law, including some by the trombone playing band leader, Pee Wee Hunt.

Jim left school in 1952 and, with his interest in jazz like Weddell's stimulated by the recorded music, the two of them began going along to the West End Café where the first band that Jim heard was Graeme Bell's Australian Jazz Band. Many years later, Jim was to play a session in the Bruntsfield Links Hotel with Bell, when the Australian was on a visit with Preacher Hood's band. Jim also found his way to the Jazz Club functioning in India Buildings, where he heard the Sandy Brown band playing the first hour and a band including Alex Welsh playing the second. The Crown Bar soon drew their attention too and it was there in 1954, at the farewell party for Sandy Brown who was leaving for London, that Mike Hart introduced Jim and Jack to Kenny Milne and clarinetist Karl Eckvall. More or less immediately, plans were put in place to get a jazz band together and, as we already know, it was this group that was to be the core of the West Richmond Street Stompers. This band with Jim, Jack, Kenny Milne on drums and Jim Young on bass, was soon into action with jazz club gigs at the Dofos Pet Shop in London Road, in premises in York Place and the Eagle Lodge, as the club moved about, seeking a reliable home.

Sometime during these years, Jim was given a record by his brother John who told him that, although he did not much care for the music himself, Jim might like it. The record was of the Bunk Johnson band playing Tishomingo Blues and Jim was an instant convert to what was becoming known as purist jazz. Like others who experienced similar immediate conversions to jazz or a specific style of jazz, he still describes his reaction to hearing the Bunk record vividly and says he can remember the reaction he felt as clearly today as he did all those years ago. From then on, he was to model his style on the playing of the re-discovered early New Orleans trumpeters, including Bunk Johnson of course and also Avery 'Kid' Howard, who played with the George Lewis band.

In 1955, when plans to form the Climax Jazz band came along, Jim was to be a founder member and he remembers the original band as himself on trumpet, Mike Pollett (tbn), Chris Cook (clt), Mike Hart (bjo), Jim Goudie (bs) and Kenny Milne (drms), although Mike Pollett is certain that Jim Goudie never played bass in the Climax band when he was a member. Although in and out of the band several times, including a gap in 1957-59 when he was away on National Service, Jim was to put in a lot of time with the Climax band in the late 1950s and early 1960s. Amongst the many venues at which Jim remembers the band playing were the Moir Hall, Jim Young's jazz club in the cellar of his home in St Peter's Place and the Crown Bar. Jim also played with the band in the Scottish Jazz Band Championship in Glasgow in 1957. In the 1960s, with the departure to London of many of the original members, the Climax band continued to be as active as ever under Jim's leadership with Alan Quinn (tbn), George Gilmour (clt), Bill Salmond (bjo), Willie Mack (bs) and Jimmy Elliott (drms).

Jim Young (double bass/brass bass) was born in Edinburgh on 7th June 1933 but was to spend much of his school years in Canada. He had been brought up on classical music, meaning in his case, music up to 1790, but learned to play sousaphone in his school brass band in Canada. Jim says that he was to become aware of a similarity between jazz and baroque, especially in the up and down movements of fugues. He later returned to the UK and, in the Grand Cinema in Stock Bridge in 1945, he saw a short film about the revival of interest in early jazz. He can remember how the rhythm affected him and, like Kenny Milne, he felt the hairs on the back of his neck rise. From that point on, it was to be rhythm and swing that mattered to Jim. In the film, there was a clip of the Original Dixieland Jazz Band making a recording, in which each member of the band played into a very large, white trunk or funnel affair, about five or six feet long and shaped like a trumpet bell. This apparently was to ensure proper separation of the sound of each instrument as it was transmitted to the mechanical recording device. Jim also went to the West End Café, where he heard Graeme Bell's Australian Jazz Band and made his way to hear the Sandy Brown band in the Oddfellow's Hall. He was also at the Usher Hall concert when the Brown band supported Big Bill Broonzy and is sure that Dizzy Jackson played bass and Farrie Forsyth drums on that famous occasion. Another jazz venue he visited was in India Buildings, where it was mostly the bands involving Alex Welsh that he heard.

Jim was called up for National Service in the RAF and Bomber Command, where he played brass bass in the military band and with this band, he played at the Queen's coronation in 1953. While still in the RAF, Jim started to learn to play the trumpet. By way of recruiting musicians into the RAF band, they were allowed a brief chance to ask new comers if they played an instrument as they got off the bus. Amongst these new comers was one called Mike Hart, who reported that he had played drums in Edinburgh. Jim remembered having seen the band on a student Charities Parade and got out a photograph he had taken and there was Mike in the photo. After National Service was over in 1954 and they were back in Edinburgh, Mike Hart contacted Jim who was now playing trumpet but, he says, very badly. Mike had by then made his switch to banjo and they put a band together with Jim on trumpet and Mike on banjo. Also included was one Richard Robertson, known as Big Richard, who was supposed to play drums but, according to Jim, could actually only play on wood blocks. Alastair 'Shorty' Gauld, brother of the trumpet playing Fraser who would later make his mark in Edinburgh jazz, was another who played banjo with the band, presumably with Mike also on banjo. The impression is that bands at that time tended to recruit who they could from the limited number around, even if it meant that two people played the same instrument.

At some point, Jim also had a go at playing trombone, playing in a band which had Al Clark on trumpet and Chris Cook on clarinet, and which played interval spots to Pete Davenport's Art College Jazz Band. The Stud Club had been initiated by Sandy Brown at the Crown Bar in Lothian Street some time before and Jim, an energetic organizer, became involved in running this in a number of other locations. It was based successively at the Orkney Rooms, the Dofos Pet Shop at the top of London Road, then the Caithness Rooms, the Roman Eagle Hall at 1 Johnston Terrace and the Moir Hall, which was in the Pleasance. Jim remembers great trouble when trying to run the various jazz clubs, as the police were very wary of them and kept trying to have them closed down. I can remember this problem clearly and, when I first ventured into the jazz clubs around 1960, many of them were run on a membership basis, with membership cards that had to be shown to gain entry, in an attempt to satisfy the police that the club was legitimate.

The question of just why the police were so against any attempt to run a jazz venue is an interesting one. Jim reports that the Stud Club, then on Wednesday evenings in the 'Crown Bar', was shut down by the police, after a policeman's daughter told her father that she had paid to get in and he ordered it closed. Apparently, only sixpence was charged so that the band could be given something at the end of the session.

171

(By permission of Jim Young)

Jim and Bob Craig then tried to run it as proper club with rushed-out membership cards, but again the police took action, telling the publican that he might lose his license the next year if they did not stop. The publican was unhappy about the club closing but, as if in compensation, allowed the band to buy the piano at a very low cost.

Peter Davenport then found a venue for the Stud Club at the Orkney Rooms in Hill Street where jazz flourished for a few months. This was followed by the move to the cellar of the pet shop, where several different bands played. However, once again it was not to last and the pet shop owner's license was threatened by the police. This initiated a move to the cellar of the Blenheim Café next door, where they again lasted a few months before yet another visit from the police. The café owner was told that she would have a visit from the Health Inspector if the jazz club was not closed down. As banjo player Brian Weld recalls it *'An officious police inspector from Gayfield Square police station forced the jazz cellar to quit. We never knew why and he wouldn't say, because there was absolutely no alcohol or drugs, the young musicians and audience being perfectly well behaved. No drunks ever came in that I remember – revival New Orleans jazz in those days was very much a young person's peccadillo'.*

Jim Young
(by permission of the late Alan Quinn)

Jim Young made a trip to Gayfield Square police station and saw a superintendent who told him that he would shut down any premises he opened on his patch. Another venue tried, in York Place, was followed by short spells at the Roman Eagle Hall and then two years at the Moir Hall in the Pleasance. Jim then moved the Stud Club to the cellar of his home in St Peter's Place. This ran for two years until, in July 1960, they got notice to quit, this time not from the police but from the Town Council, in a document signed by the Town Clerk, no less. The document stated that Jim was running an illegal club in a private house and that he could be fined £20 for every day the notice to quit was ignored. The actual offence was described as '...*the partial change of use of a dwelling house at 19 St Peter's Place, Edinburgh, to a club has been carried out without the grant of planning permission...*'.

173

Jim later discovered from a jazz follower who had been a trainee policeman, that the police thought that he was running a house of ill repute! They had set up a watch in the house opposite and watched for two weeks but saw nothing, which was hardly surprising. The Edinburgh jazzers were nothing if not determined and even the loss of Jim Young's cellar venue did not stop them. An undated newspaper cutting reported that *'Members of the Stud Jazz Club, Edinburgh – closed by order – jived again last night...in the middle of the Firth of Forth. The club hired the M.V. Second Snark, took along a band and for two hours they rocked the boat. The club met in the basement of band leader Jim Young's Edinburgh home until banned by the Corporation'.*

Dofos Pet Shop in London Road
Once home to the Stud Club and still flourishing in 2010 (Photo by the author)

Presumably the police had the laws of the time on their side but what on earth was all the paranoia about? Was it a fear that there was illegal drinking going on? Or drugs? What nameless health threats did a jazz band carry that would require the Health Inspector to be called in? Suspecting the existence of a brothel seems fairly bizarre but they were obviously very suspicious. Surely they could have simply checked to see if there was any illegal drinking or drugs or prostitution? If paying at the door was the issue, why not just sort that out? But no, they seemed to have been determined to close down any attempt to put on jazz that was open to the public. Nowadays, I am sure it would be seen as harassment. It certainly seems to have had the flavour of an official kill-joy attitude about it. Perhaps it was in tune with stern Scottish Presbyterianism; a glowering, authoritarian disapproval of anyone having the temerity to enjoy themselves. It must have seemed as if the Ten Commandments had been specially abbreviated until there was only one left reading 'THOU SHALT NOT!!!!'

Of course, this was only the 1950s and the war years, with their aura of strict control of everything, were not that long gone. Perhaps the shades of grim war time restrictions remained in the attitudes of the authorities of the day, with a belief that society, unless rigidly controlled, would go on the rampage. Perhaps we should be grateful that the 1960s, with new attitudes and a willingness to cock a snoot at authority, especially by the younger generation, were just around the corner.

Jim Young had taken up double bass by accident. He had been at the jazz club one evening when the Pete Davenport band was playing. The band had someone who was learning to play double bass but he had not turned up that night. By good fortune however, the bass was there. Pete Davenport spotted Jim and called over to him *'You know about music, pick up that bass and play it. It has the notes marked on it so you should have no problem!'* Jim did as instructed and that was the start of his career as a double bassist. Later, in 1955, a lack of bass players led him to acquire a double bass of his own and he played for while with a band led by Jim Petrie, the Crescent City Jazz Band, which included, besides Jim Petrie on trumpet, Jack Weddell on trombone and Kenny Milne on drums.

After a spell in London, Jim returned to Edinburgh, where the early versions of the **Climax Jazz Band** began to appear. These early versions of this important Edinburgh band involved a number of musicians including Jim Petrie on trumpet, Mike Pollett on trombone, Chris Cook, Stewart

175

Pitkethly or Alistair Hanney on clarinet, Mike Hart on banjo, Jim Goudie or Jim Young on double bass and Kenny Milne on drums. The music the band played was strictly in the purist style and most of these players were to remain with the band for a number of years. Jim Young stayed with the Climax band, playing a leading part, until 1963 when he went abroad, returning in 1967 to re-join the band, and remaining active with them throughout the 1970s.

Kenny Milne reports that the early rehearsals of the Climax Jazz Band took place in Mike Pollett's house in Craigmillar or at Mike Hart's garage, which was near the Meadows. Mike Pollett was well supplied with recordings of the Bunk Johnson and George Lewis bands, and these formed the basis of the band's style. I had always assumed that Climax band acquired its name because of the famous Climax sessions recorded by the George Lewis band, but apparently this may not have been so. Mike Pollett's version, as we have heard, was that the name came from the tune 'Climax Rag'. However, at least one later member of the band claims that the name came about because, when the band was rehearsing in its early days, someone noticed that there was work to remove tram lines going on outside which involved a 'Climax' compressor! You pays your money and you takes your choice!

As with all the bands at this time, there were to be changes brought about by National Service and other factors, and Jim Goudie, who had played bass for a while, took the well-worn road to London, where later he could be found playing with the Mike Peters band. Kenny's brother, Jimmy Milne, was for a time manager of the Climax band and they played at jazz clubs at Ayr, Glenrothes, and Dundee but, in the early days, they did not have a residency in Edinburgh. At some point around 1956, Mike Hart left and was replaced by Brian Weld on banjo. Later changes brought in Dougie Boyter on banjo, Tom Wood on piano, Dougie Goodall on clarinet and Jack Weddell on trombone, as National Service continued to be an issue. Tom Wood was later to emigrate to Australia and was to play an important part in the re-union tour of Australia, made by the specially re-formed Climax band, in the early 1990s.

When Jim Petrie went off to complete his stint in the army, Charlie Malley who was from Falkirk or Jake Simpson from Glasgow, played trumpet in his place. Inevitably, there were some band politics as well and, for a while, Kenny Milne and Stewart Pitkethly left the band. Stewart Pitkethly was replaced on clarinet by Alastair Hanney, who was later to become an eminent academic in Norway, and Kenny Milne was replaced on drums by Colin Cant. When Jim Petrie returned from National Service, he also returned to the band and this paved the way for the return of both Stewart Pitkethly and Kenny Milne.

When Mike Hart left the Climax band, he had been replaced for a time by **Brian Weld (banjo and tenor guitar)**. Brian's day job was civil engineering and he had taken up banjo in about 1952, after being introduced to jazz by the drummer Farrie Forsyth. Farrie had played a Bunk Johnson recording to him in a record shop booth and Brian reports that he was totally captivated by the sound and swing of the band and, in particular, by the playing of the banjo player Lawrence Marrero. As a result, he bought a banjo from Gordon Simpson's Music Shop in Stafford Street, where he was allowed to pay it up with no written agreement and no interest charged. Incidentally, this is by no means the only story of Gordon Simpson's kindness to budding musicians, several others commenting on various small favours done by a decent man who seemed genuinely concerned to help musicians. I remember once when, before a gig, our band met in a pub in William Street and found Gordon Simpson there. When our banjo player discovered he had forgotten to bring his spare banjo strings with him, Gordon Simpson was good enough to return to his shop and open it up to supply him with strings.

Another in the same vein was **Pete Seaton (accordion)** who at one time worked in Gordon Simpson's music shop but, later, set up on his own music shop, over on the south-side of town. Pete had taken up accordion in 1942 and, after taking lessons from a Miss Sutherland, had become a highly proficient player. Although he played Scottish country dance music, it was not the sort of music that appealed to him, having a preference for a wider repertoire. He worked in the music shop during the day and played accordion in the evenings, making a big name for himself as a top class dance band musician. He was resident in the Palais when the BBC came to film heats for the television programme 'Come Dancing' and then went on to a six nights a week residency at the George Hotel, playing for dinner dances. He remained there from 1950 until 1960 and, during this time, he performed on radio with the Swedish Royal Concert Orchestra in 1960.

Pete was always interested in jazz and it showed in his playing, of which he said *'You couldn't play the same tune a hundred times without exploring alternative themes'*. Pete also played in the West End Café and was the arranger for the third one of a series of BBC jazz concerts, the third being devoted to modern jazz. He was also a member of the band for that concert, the line-up of which was Jim Walker (rds), Pete Seaton (accordion), Dave Simpson (pno), Dickie Alexander (bs) and Kenny Duff (drms). Later, Pete played piano in the bar of the Caledonian Hotel. Like Gordon Simpson, Pete was a greatly respected figure around the Edinburgh dance and jazz scene and there are many examples of his willingness to assist musicians. When my double bass was burned in a fire at the Manhattan Jazz Club in the mid-1960s, Pete allowed me a new instrument from his shop, not only before I could pay for it, but before I had any idea of how I was going to raise the money.

The trombonist, Bill Munro, also paid tribute to Pete Seaton. Bill found himself without an instrument, when he had to return a trombone to the works silver band with whom he had been playing. Having failed to pick up anything suitable on the second hand market, he found what he wanted in Pete's music shop, a nice Selmer instrument priced at £26. It turned out that Pete was supplier to the afore-mentioned silver band and, not only did he knock the price down to £21, he would not take a deposit saying *'Ach well, you can pay it up out of any gig money you get'*. Bill was not even in a band at this point but did eventually manage to pay it off, with Pete charging him no interest whatsoever. A fine musician with a real interest in jazz, Pete Seaton was always willing to extend a helping hand, as well as endless encouragement, to his fellow musicians. Pete's son, Murray Seaton, was later to open a music shop specializing in drums in the Newington area of town.

Meanwhile, Brian Weld, whom we left the proud owner of his first banjo, fixed up some lessons from someone he described as an elderly banjo player in Edinburgh, and got started in jazz, playing in one of Charlie McNair's practice bands. This was followed by a spell with a band led by Bob Craig at the Crown Bar and some gigs with Pete Davenport's band, including some private recordings. As Brian tells it, Bob had taken over the Sandy Brown band when Sandy went off to London. Al Fairweather had also departed for the south and Al Clark had replaced him on trumpet, with Brian taking over from Norrie Anderson on banjo. The Crown Bar gig closed when new owners put up the rent, making it financially no longer viable, and the Bob Craig band moved to what Brian calls *'the fabulous jazz cellar in Blenheim Place'*. Apparently the cellar was beautifully decorated with murals of some of the jazz greats, including Louis Armstrong, Fats Waller, and Bessie Smith. The murals had been painted by Farrie Forsyth whom Brian says had turned out to be a very talented mural painter as well as a great New Orleans drummer. The rent for the cellar was covered by a very small entrance fee, similar to that charged at the Crown Bar. Brian played there quite a bit, mostly with pick-up bands involving well known jazzers such as Ian 'Tello' Telford and Charlie McNair, but does not remember ever being paid more than a few shillings.

When, as we have already heard, the jazz cellar was forced to close by the police, the Bob Craig band moved to a church hall in High School Yards, a street just off and parallel to the Canongate, where they played every week for a year or two, the band including Bob, Brian, Jim Young, Farrie Forsyth and Pete Davenport. Later still, Brian was to play with Charlie McNair's band at the 1957 Scottish Jazz Band Championships in Glasgow. The later 1950s must have been a particularly busy period for him as he played simultaneously with a couple of Glasgow based bands and the Climax band in Edinburgh. However, it sounds as if this all got too much for him as he retired from playing in 1959 and was not to re-appear as an active jazzer until the early 1980s, where we will catch up with him later.

The Climax Jazz Band
Violet Milne (voc), Jim Young (bs), Dougie Boyter (bjo),
Jim Petrie (tpt), Kenny Milne (drms), Jack Weddell (tn),
Jake McMahon (clt), Tom Wood (pno)
(From the collection of Jim Petrie, photographer
unknown)

More changes in the Climax band occurred in about 1958/59, when the excellent clarinet player, Jake McMahon and Allan Ritchie, who played the banjo left-handed, came into the band. A further change came about when Kenny Milne, who had qualified as a pharmacist in July 1960, went to London to work, and he was replaced by Allan Ritchie's brother, Pete Ritchie. Further changes, as the band moved on into the 1960s, were to bring in, for a varying lengths of time, Brian Smith on trumpet, Alan Quinn on trombone, Bill Salmond on banjo and Jimmy Elliott or George Hutchinson on drums.

It seems clear that, by this time, there was an increased number of jazz musicians available locally and, of course, when National Service was abandoned in 1960, this further eased the pressure on bands. There was another band around in the mid-1950s which played in approximately the same style as the Climax band. This band was led by **Iain Forde (drums, trombone, piano)** who played trombone at this time. A photograph of the time confirms that the band was called the Excelsior Ragtime Band, at least at one point in its history. Notes about recordings made by this band show a changing line-up which included at one time or another:

Trumpet:	M Underwood or Fraser Gauld
Trombone:	Iain Forde
Clarinet:	Graham 'Willie' Cairns or Sandy Gracie or Jake McMahon
Banjo:	Fraser Gauld or A Davidson or Allan Ritchie
Bass:	Graham 'Willie' Cairns
Drums:	Graham Orr or Pete Ritchie

The recordings were made between 1956 and 1960, the period when Iain was at art College studying architecture, and in a variety of locations including Coatbridge Terrace, an Ann Street cellar and Victoria Buildings. It is tedious to keep listing band personnel in this manner, but what the list above illustrates is that there was a certain amount of switching between instruments going on. It has to be assumed that the musicians were trying out various instruments until they found one on which they could settle. Iain Forde himself, on trombone on all the above recordings, was later to become a successful drummer. The Ritchie brothers and Jake McMahon were all to be lured away from the Iain Forde band by the chance to play in the already well established Climax band.

Iain Forde had started in a skiffle group in 1956 with, among others, the future trumpet player Fraser Gauld, and was to become something of a multi-instrumentalist in his search for his best niche in traditional jazz, playing, at various times, tuba, banjo, trombone, drums and piano. He also played bagpipes.

Iain Forde's 'Excelsior Ragtime Band' in the 1950s
Back row: Willie Cairns (bass), Graham Orr (drums),
Alan Davidson (banjo)
Front row: Sandy Gracie (clarinet), Fraser Gauld
(trumpet), and Iain Forde (trombone)
(from the collection of Fraser Gauld, photographer
unknown)

I never heard of him trying bagpipes in a jazz context, although I would not have put it past him! Iain claims to have converted to purist beliefs on the advice of Stewart Pitkethly and, as a result, threw away all his 'modernist' records of people like Louis Armstrong and Kid Ory!

In 1965 Iain heard that there was a band playing in the Woolpack pub in Bristo Place. He went along to hear them and, within a few weeks, found himself playing trombone in a band that included Fraser Gauld, Bill Salmond and Jim Young. However, it was not to be all that long before Jack Weddell returned from the south and the band decided that Jack would come in on trombone and Iain would play drums. As he recalls, the drum kit at first consisted of a snare drum and a cardboard box but he was later to inherit a proper drum kit that had belonged to Colin Cant. It was to be on drums in fact, that Iain was to make a considerable impact and he was later to put in time as drummer with a number of quality Edinburgh bands, including bands led by banjoist Bill Salmond and the Climax band. A man with a subtle and delightful sense of humour, Iain Forde could be very funny. Clarinetist Gerard Dott tells the story of a jazz gig in an Edinburgh pub when Iain was on drums and Simon Carlyle on sousaphone. A punter who was a regular drinker in the place but who usually left before there was any danger of the band starting to play, was still there one night when the band was setting up. He looked on in incredulous disbelief as Simon Carlyle assembled the enormous brass complexities of his sousaphone. Clearly unable to believe his eyes, the punter asked *'Is that thing heavy?'* Before Simon could respond, Iain Forde replied *'Well you see, it is hollow inside so that makes it a bit lighter'*!

The account above, describing the many changes in the composition of the Edinburgh jazz bands, is undoubtedly more than a bit confusing and rather resembles tales of the Swing era in the USA, when bands competed ferociously for musicians, when better known bands raided lesser bands for recruits and there was a never-ending movement of musicians from one band to another. However, in the 1950s jazz world of Edinburgh, there would not have been very much of a financial reward on offer, if any, and most of the changes would no doubt have been on the basis of perceived prestige, band politics and who happened to be on good terms with whom, at the time. George Melly, in 'Owning Up', writes about how there are always changing loyalties and friendships in touring bands and says *'...a musician who is a friend can become an enemy, someone to be avoided at all costs, and then, a week later, become a friend again. As in medieval Europe the pattern of alliances is always changing.'*[105] I have no doubt that this was true but, in my experience it can happen just as readily in a local, amateur or semi-pro band. Melly is correct too, I am

---

[105] 'Owning Up' by George Melly, (Copyright © George Melly, 1965) Reprinted by permission of A. M. Heath & Co Ltd

sure, in pointing out that it is often the most trivial of things that can count, for or against.

**The power of advertising in the 1950s!
(by permission of Jim Young)**

Jim Young tells the story of one Hogmany (New Year's Eve, for any uncivilized people reading this) when he had been playing with the Climax band at the Tempo Club, situated next to John Knox's house in the High Street. Sharing the bill with them was Barry 'Kid' Martyn's Jazz Band from London and, at the end of the gig, they got the two bands together and went to the nearby Tron Kirk, where they marched round and round, playing as a marching band. There was a huge crowd already gathered there, the Tron being a traditional meeting place at Hogmany. Jim recalls that the police were remarkably cooperative, this being quite surprising at a time when jazz seemed to be ranked about equal with gun running or worse in police circles. After a bit, the joint bands marched off round the town, gathering a bigger and bigger crowd as they went. Jim reckoned that, with this resounding success to their credit, the Climax band had a good claim to be the originators of the famous Edinburgh Hogmany parties of later years!

At one point in the early 1960s, so many members and ex-members of the Climax band had moved to London that the band re-formed as a London based Edinburgh Climax Jazz Band and played in the White Hart pub in Drury Lane. This pub is reputed to be the oldest licensed premises in London. Included in the London version of the band were Jim Young, Kenny Milne, Jake McMahon, Jack Weddell and Allan Ritchie – Edinburgh must have seemed quite empty of 'purist' jazzers for a while. Happily, a recording of the London band was made during a rehearsal in 1965 and this was preserved. The Edinburgh jazzers on the recording were the above, but without Allan Ritchie. They were joined by Christer Fellows, a French trumpet player, and Lars Edregran, a piano player from Sweden. As is typical of jazz band rehearsals in my experience, some of the musicians arrived late, after the recording had begun, and both Jack Weddell and Kenny Milne only appear on some of the 16 sides recorded[106].

While Jim Young was London based, he soon established himself as a much-in- demand bass player and played with the bands of Mike Peters and Bill Brunskill. Jim can remember a gig in Bristol with the Mike Peters band when the interval band was that of Acker Bilk. Amongst his many other gigs, there was an occasion when he was called in by the famous band leader, Chris Barber, to play brass bass on a recording of New Orleans style parade band jazz.

Jake McMahon (clarinet and tenor sax), born in Edinburgh on 21st January 1941, was several years younger than the group which had founded the Climax Jazz Band. He was educated at Tynecastle School and went on to have a very successful career as an accountant before retiring when he was 52, as Finance Director of a multinational company. He was to become yet another in the long line of outstanding clarinet players that Edinburgh produced. His interest in jazz was sparked off by a visit to India Buildings, where he heard a band led by Bob Craig. This band included, in addition to Bob, Alastair Clark (tpt), Johnny Winters (clt) and Eed Smith and Brian Weld, both on banjos. This was followed by another visit to the same

---

[106] See Discography Appendix

venue when he heard Charlie McNair's band, with Joe Smith on clarinet and Jimmy Hilson on trombone. Jake then discovered the Stud Club, at that time located at the Moir Hall, and it was through this that he fell under the spell of George Lewis.

It seems likely that it was the Climax Jazz Band, playing in their customary George Lewis style, that Jake heard at the Stud Club. Jake describes the Climax band of that time as a 'moveable feast', on account of constant changes in band membership, mostly because of National Service. Inspired by the jazz he had heard, Jake started on clarinet. He took a few lessons from someone who played with the Post Office band, but he considers himself largely self-taught. By 1958, at the age of 17, he was playing sufficiently well to join a band led by Iain Forde, then on trombone, with Fraser Gauld on trumpet, Allan Ritchie on banjo and Donald Macdonald on bass. After serving an apprenticeship with this band, Jake then graduated to the Climax band, replacing Dougie Goodall who had gone to South Africa, and joining trumpeter Jim Petrie and trombonist Jack Weddell in a strong front-line.

A great high-light for Jake was the chance to play, on his 18th birthday, with the George Lewis band on their visit to Edinburgh in 1959. Jake stayed with the Climax band until 1963, when he moved to London to further his career in accountancy. There he met up with other Climax expatriates and played in the London version of the band, before joining the band of trumpeter Bob Wallis. This band is notable in retrospect, as it had on drums Ginger Baker, later to be a major star as a rock drummer with the supergroup 'Cream'. Later, Jake was to play with Pete Dyer's band with Cuff Billett on trumpet and then had a long spell with Keith Smith's band. With this band he toured the continent, accompanying famous musicians such as Memphis Slim, Sammy Price and Champion Jack Dupree.

Kenny Milne once told me about the Climax band taking part in the 1957 Scottish Jazz Band Championship, when they had been heavily marked down by the judges on 'presentation'. In addition, when an East of Scotland heat of the 1962 'Boosey and Hawkes' sponsored 'National Trad Band Contest' was reviewed by John Gibson of the Edinburgh Evening News, he said that the Climax Jazz Band was *'purist and too idealist for this type of competition'*[107]. In retrospect, I consider that both of these comments should be interpreted, not negatively, but as a positive reflection on a band which was serious about its music and preferred a degree of dignity to some of the embarrassing excesses of presentation and material that were around at the time of the so-called 'Trad Boom'. I played in the latter contest and can remember some of what passed for band uniforms. Of one band, which will remain nameless, John Gibson said *'...had it sunk to a vote on band uniforms, they would have lost any poll'*. As I recall, they were dressed in white laboratory coats.

So Edinburgh, in addition to being a hot-house for jazzers of the classic jazz persuasion had, in the mid-1950s, become a nursery for a formidable purist tradition as well. As time has gone on, it seems the purist style of traditional jazz has won the battle for ownership of the term 'New Orleans jazz'. At the time of writing this in 2011, New Orleans jazz in this sense, has perhaps the largest following of any form of traditional jazz. This seems to be especially so in Europe, where a number of jazz festivals are devoted to this style. As with the earlier crowd around Sandy Brown, Al Fairweather, Alex Welsh and the Semple brothers, Edinburgh had again produced players of considerable calibre in their field, including some such as Jim Young, Jim Petrie, Kenny Milne, Jack Weddell and Jake McMahon who made big reputations for themselves and were and are highly rated. Their status is confirmed by their many invitations to back and record with touring New Orleans veterans and to play at New Orleans styled jazz festivals in the UK and abroad. Again, like the earlier jazzers, the tradition did not stop with the originators but was to march

---

[107] Edinburgh Evening News, 5th December 1962.

on, with younger musicians and new bands coming along to play in the same style. We will meet many of them in the next chapter.

Chapter VIII

The Great Communicators

The late 1950s and early 1960s were a very odd time for traditional jazz generally in the UK and Edinburgh was no different. By one of these inexplicable changes in the public taste, traditional jazz suddenly became popular. In fact jazz (or a certain kind of jazz) was probably more popular with the general public in the UK than it had ever been, with the possible exception of the great Swing craze of the 1930/40s. This seems to have been a peculiarly British phenomenon because, although traditional jazz continued to have a large following on the continent, there it seemed to be more a music for the committed jazz fan, rather than the general public.

Just why this UK upsurge in interest happened is hard to say. George Melly, in his perceptive book 'Revolt into Style'[108], points out that the Trad Boom was both unexpected and untypical (in terms of general popularity) because its practitioners were '...*far older than the norm and had been around much longer; the emphasis was instrumental rather than vocal and the sexual aspect was almost non-existent*' (presumably this latter comment refers to Trad's appeal, rather the behaviour of its practitioners!) Melly credits Chris Barber as being the great populariser and it is certainly true that the Barber band had an enormous following, playing to packed houses everywhere it

---

[108] 'Revolt into Style – The Pop Arts in Britain' by George Melly, (Copyright © George Melly, 1970) Reprinted by permission of A M Heath & Co Ltd.

went. Also, the Barber band recording of Sydney Bechet's 'Petite Fleur', featuring clarinettist Monty Sunshine, made its way into the Pop charts in April 1959. However, two other bands, in the end, were to have a much greater Pop following than Barber. These were the bands of Kenny Ball, who played a strong, Dixieland style and the inimitable Acker Bilk who, with his folksy, rustic approach, brilliantly enhanced by a contrasting Edwardian presentation, became the central figure of the 'Trad Boom'.

In fact, the first significant UK post-war traditional jazz hit was Humphrey Lyttelton's recording of a blues piece, 'Bad Penny Blues', with Stan Grieg on piano, which was recorded in April 1956 and entered the Pop charts later that year. However this recording, in retrospect, seems a genuinely accidental 'one-off'. Certainly, Humph never seems to have made any attempt to flirt with Pop success again, nor does it seem to have provoked any sudden, general increase in the popularity of traditional jazz. In contrast, the success of Barber, Bilk and Ball was to spark off a remarkable movement across the country, with bands springing to prominence at both local and national level. Bands were already in place of course, because of the Revival, but what had changed was the sudden demand from what seemed to be the general public. For local bands, there was suddenly the opportunity to get out of the pubs and into the local limelight.

What Melly does not say much about, is the relationship between 'Trad' and skiffle. Melly does give an outline description of what skiffle was and says *'Originally the word had been used, during the 20s, to describe a sort of jazz in which some or all the legitimate instruments were replaced by kazoos, washboards or broom-handle bass fiddles. Later there was, in British skiffle, a resurrection of the music within the traditional meaning of the term, but at first the word was deliberately misapplied to mean a folk-spot within the context of an evening of traditional jazz'*[109]. Skiffle in the UK, in the first place, was indeed an off-shoot of traditional jazz. Ken Colyer once again had led the way, featuring a

[109] 'Revolt into Style – The Pop Arts in Britain', by George Melly, (Copyright © George Melly 1970) Reprinted by permission of A.M. Heath & Co Ltd.

skiffle session in the middle of his jazz sessions, the skiffle group made up from within his band. The music was fairly simple, drawing mostly on the folk-blues of the southern states of the USA, especially the songs of Huddie Ledbetter, better known as 'Leadbelly'.

Chris Barber had been a member of Colyer's band and, after he left and formed a band of his own, he retained the idea of skiffle sessions. Barber's skiffle sessions were centred on the singing of his Glasgow born banjo player, Lonnie Donegan, who had also been with Colyer. Out of the blue, a track originally on a Chris Barber LP then issued as a single, became a hit, climbing to Number 1 in the Pop charts in May 1956. This was a version of an old American railroad song, associated with Leadbelly, called 'Rock Island Line'. Why this recording should have taken off as a major seller is unclear but its success led to Donegan going off on his own. He went on to have a string of popular hits in the late 1950s, although gradually moving away from the American inspired original material and becoming more and more like an old time music hall act.

Part of the appeal of skiffle was certainly the ease with which enthusiasts could get in on the act. As George Melly said in 'Revolt into Style': *There was the 'Anyone can do it' side to it; a few chords on the guitar and you were away'*. This was certainly the attraction for me and, at the age of about fifteen, I was soon making a start as a skiffler, my initial instrument being the washboard. I was not alone. There were many other local skifflers and, across the whole UK, many thousands, all scrubbing away earnestly on washboards, guitars, banjos, tea-chest basses and any other article with the capacity to make a reasonably rhythmic noise.

Several of my local contemporaries, who started in skiffle, went on to establish themselves in the Edinburgh jazz scene. Among them were Mike Travis, later a top modern jazz drummer, and clarinettist Gerard Dott. Bill Salmond, who was to become a long-serving Edinburgh band leader, was a Lonnie Donegan follower and started a skiffle group in about 1957. For us and, I am sure, for hundreds like us, the next step after skiffle had been almost inevitable; we got increasingly interested in the music of the bands from which skiffle had sprung. Gradually, proper instruments were acquired, rudimentary skills put in place and a batch of new jazzers was added to the Edinburgh jazz pool. In addition, a number of skifflers moved the other way, towards folk music, and were to be a factor in the burgeoning folk music movement of the next couple of decades.

The move into traditional jazz was logical – skiffle had not only sprung from the bosom of the traditional jazz bands but also shared much of its cultural roots and, above all, the same rhythmic base. Skiffle, like traditional jazz, was at its best when it was played with a swinging beat. In addition, of course, traditional jazz was carrying a high profile with the younger generation, because of the success of Barber, Bilk and Ball, and there is no denying that this was attractive to many of us. I have always believed that the easy start that skiffle provided was a key factor in enabling a healthy number of new jazz musicians to come flooding into local jazz around 1960. It was hardly on the scale of the Revival but the 'Trad Boom', for all its absurdities, with its influx of new blood, was another shot in the arm for traditional jazz. It was certainly right up the street of two Edinburgh band leaders in particular – Charlie McNair and Archie Sinclair. Both were serious jazzers who cared about the music, both understood the history of jazz but, above all, they were both born communicators and both thrived on having an audience.

Charlie McNair (trumpet and vocals), who was born in 1932, had been around the Edinburgh jazz scene for some time. Charlie worked in the grocery business and was at one time manager of a Lipton's shop at Tolcross but, later in his career, he ran a Delicatessen of his own in Forrest Road. Charlie was educated at the Royal High School and was thus a fully-paid-up member of the RHS Gang, although a year or two younger than the Sandy Brown and Al Fairweather crowd. Probably through school contacts, he found out about jazz sessions in Riego Street, near Tolcross, went along and heard Sandy and Al playing. His interest in jazz blossomed and he took up trumpet, being self taught like so many of his generation. There was a story around at one time, that Mike Hart had found an old trumpet on a rubbish heap somewhere and had sold it to Charlie for 7/6d, but this is unsubstantiated.

Apparently, his early practice attempts at home were not much appreciated by at least one neighbour, who pushed anonymous letters objecting to the noise through the letterbox, greatly upsetting Charlie's mother who interpreted these as death threats! Another Charlie story from a bit later, concerns his role in Big Bill Bronnzy's appearance in Edinburgh. Charlie was in Shrewsbury when on National Service and had made a habit of visiting Liverpool on a regular basis. There he had met up with Broonzy at a club which was almost certainly the Cavern, later to be famous as the early home of the Beatles, and had had a chance to speak with the great blues singer. Big Bill, finding out that Charlie was from Edinburgh, told him he was coming up to play at the Usher Hall, but was much bothered by the prospect of being harassed on his arrival by hordes of newspaper men.

Charlie was already in regular touch with Sandy Currie, who was still in Edinburgh, and between them they hatched a plot to kidnap Big Bill off his train at Haymarket Station. This was the stop before Big Bill's destination of Waverley Station, where the paparazzi would be lying in wait. The plan is said to have worked perfectly and the two of them whisked a grateful Big Bill off his train at Haymarket and off to the Shakespeare Bar, next door to the Usher Hall, where they no doubt celebrated in a suitable manner. As I know of no other appearance by Big Bill Broonzy in Edinburgh in the 1950s, if the story is true, this must have been before the famous concert in 1952, when the Sandy Brown band was also on the bill.

It was not long before Charlie, a man of indomitable enthusiasm and optimism, was into the business of putting a band together and he was to become one of the longest serving of all Edinburgh jazz band leaders. As we have already heard, trombonist Mike Pollett played in a band led by Charlie in the mid-1950s and, with that band, made a couple of recordings on the 'Beltona' label[110]. This was a 78 rpm record (BL2670), with Hiawatha on one side and

---

[110] See Discography appendix

Meadow Lane Stomp on the other[111]. Apparently, the name of the second of the titles arose from the location of Mike Hart's father's garage in Meadow Lane, where the band held its practice sessions. Inexplicably, the name of the band on the 78 single is 'Charlie McNair's Skiffle Group', inexplicable because it is clearly a straight ahead traditional jazz band! At the time of writing, the recording of Hiawatha is available on the internet site, You Tube. When I met with Mike Pollett in 2011, I asked him to cast his mind back over sixty years to this recording and who had been in the band. Mike was certain that, in addition to Charlie McNair trumpet and Mike himself on trombone, the band also included Joe Smith on clarinet and probably Mike Hart on banjo. He was less certain about the identity of the drummer but thought that it was likely to have been Sandy Malcolm. He was unable to recall who, if anyone, had played bass. The two tracks had been recorded at a Scottish Jazz Band Championship at the St Andrew's Hall in Glasgow and it seems that the McNair band competed in this event at least four times, in 1955, '56, '57 and '58. By a process of elimination, we were able to fix the year of the recording as 1955, as there is other information about this same competition in the years 1956 and 1957 which precludes Mike Pollett's involvement in these years.

On 30th June 1956, at the next Championship, again in the St Andrew's Hall in Glasgow, Charlie's band again competed. This time they were again recorded, contributing a single track, 'Oh, Didn't He Ramble', to a Beltona 10" LP (ABL 519) featuring the bands that took part. The LP was called 'Scots Traditional Jazz Concert' and was apparently the first live recording of a jazz concert in Scotland. The sleeve notes are by Sandy Brown and the other tracks are by Alan Mason's Jazzmen and an early version of the famous Clyde Valley Stompers who, with vocalist Mary McGowan, are said on the sleeve to have won the 1955 Scottish Traditional Jazz Band Championship a year previously. The line-up of the McNair band is given on the LP cover as Charlie (tpt), Jimmy Hilson (tbn), Joe Smith

---

[111] See Discography appendix

(clt), Mike Hart and Eed Smith (bjos), and Sandy Malcolm (drms). There is no mention of a bass player.

In the Edinburgh Jazz Archive, there is a printed programme for the third Scottish Jazz Band Championship in which the McNair band competed. This was again held in the St Andrew's Hall and was on Sunday, 31st March 1957. This event was under the aegis of the Evening Times and the Glasgow Jazz Club and, on this occasion, the McNair band had Charlie (tpt), Joe Smith (clt), Archie Sinclair (tbn), Brian Weld (bjo), Gerry Rossi (bs) and Arthur Ferguson (drms). As far as I have been able to find out, there was no recording made that year.

Charlie's band competed in the Championship yet again the next year, 1958, and was listed among the twelve competing bands in a special edition of the Glasgow Evening Times on Friday, 5th September 1958. The Evening Times and the Glasgow Jazz Club were, once again, joint sponsors of the event. This special edition of the newspaper was apparently not on general sale but only available at the jazz championship venue, the St Andrew's Halls. The covering article[112] gives a comprehensive preview of the event, firstly announcing that the twelve bands comprised no fewer than eighty-four musicians. Several of the competing bands were from Edinburgh, the full list being: Chic Chisholm's Jazz Men (Castlemilk), Bob Craig's Jazz Band (Edinburgh – Stud Club), Jack Duff's Jazz Men (Edinburgh – Stud Club), Charlie Gall and his Modern Dixieland Band (Glasgow – Woodend Club), Charlie McNair's Jazz Band (Edinburgh – West End Cafe Club), Bill Miller's Jazz Men (Glasgow), George O'Donnell and his Dixieland All-Stars (Cupar, Fife), The Omega Jazz Men (Dundee – Dundee Jazz Club), the Stateside Jazz Men (Paisley – Delta Jazz Club), the Storyville Jazz Band (Glasgow – Pan Club), the Vernon Jazz Band (Glasgow – Pan Club, Low Roof Jazz Club) and the Royal Mile Jazz Band (Edinburgh – Royal Mile Cafe Club).

Charlie McNair's resident spot at the West End Cafe was said to be '...one of Edinburgh's busiest clubs where they

---

[112] Reproduced with permission of Herald and Times Group, Glasgow Evening Times, 'The boys are rarin' to go', MacDougall J, 5th September 1958

regularly pull in 600' and Bob Craig's band is described as *'One of the longest established Edinburgh groups, some of whose past members have made the big time'.* The Royal Mile band is described as *'...one of the pioneer groups'* while Jack Duff's band unfortunately gets short shrift, being hailed only as *'Another Edinburgh group'*! Charlie McNair's band played 'Hot Lips', Big House Blues' and 'Yama Yama Man', Bob Craig's band played 'Atlanta Blues', Ain't Misbehavin'' and 'Monday Date', while the Jack Duff band played 'Pennies from Heaven', 'Tin Roof Blues' and 'At the Jazz Band Ball'. The Royal Mile band is listed as playing 'Clarinet Marmalade' but their other selections are illegible in the rather battered available copy of the newspaper.

A review article from the Evening Times[113], published after the championship, announced that the Vernon Jazz Band, led by trombonist Mark Bradley, had been the winners for 1958, with three bands tying for second – Bob Craig's band, George O'Donnell's band and a band that was not even listed in the preview article, Laurie Dunlop's Esquire Band, from Glasgow. This presumably accounts for the increased participation figures quoted, which are given as thirteen bands and ninety musicians. The winning band got £40 and the three runners-up shared £60. In the individual awards, the best performance of the evening went to banjoist Mike Hart of Charlie McNair's band. The individual instrumental awards went to trombonist George O'Donnell, clarinettist Jack Graham and trumpeter Bob Harley, both of Bob Craig's band, and the Vernon band's rhythm section was judged best rhythm section. Best performance was rewarded with £5, donated by the Glasgow Record Shop, and the best individual instrumentalists each got £5, donated variously by McCormacks, Ken-dals Shirts and the Clydesdale (presumably the bank, rather than a horse). The best rhythm section got a £6 voucher, donor unspecified. The judges were listed as 'jazz authority' Lord Donegal, Decca's manager Dick Rowe and London bandleader Mickey Ashman. The judges had agreed that the jazz standard was higher than they had expected and

---

[113] Reproduced with permission of Herald and Times Group, Glasgow Evening Times, 'Vernon Band are the jazz champions', 6th September 1958

they were also surprised at the strength of the jazz movement in Scotland! Three of the Edinburgh bands had phoned the venue at the starting time to say that they were fog-bound and unlikely to make the contest, however they had eventually arrived just in time to compete. All of which, I think you will agree, adds up to a fascinating glimpse of Scottish jazz, circa 1958.

As Irene McNair, Charlie's wife, remembers it, Charlie had a band in about 1956/57, which was similar in line-up to those shown above and it included Charlie (tpt), Joe Smith (clt), Archie Sinclair (tbn) and Mike Hart (bjo). As Irene recalls, David 'Eed' Smith was later added on a second banjo and Bob Craig came in to replace Archie Sinclair. It is clear from the above that Charlie's band was already extremely active by the middle 1950s and that there were many changes in the band personnel along the way.

Charlie McNair's Jazz Band sometime in the 1950s
Dizzy Jackson, Al McPake, Bill Skinner, Sandy Malcolm,
Charlie McNair, Mike Hart, Archie Sinclair
(From the collection of Mike Hart, photographer
unknown)

By 1958, Charlie had established himself as Master of Ceremonies at the West End Cafe Sunday evening sessions. At this gig, the band included Charlie, Bob Craig, Jack

Graham (clt), Mike Hart (bjo), Al McPake (gtr), Dizzy Jackson (bss) and either Sandy Malcolm or Bobby Stewart (drms). This seems to have continued as a regular gig through 1959 and 1960. At that time, as throughout his long career in jazz, Charlie was able to attract well known personalities from the British jazz scene and the West End Cafe was usually full of young, Coke swilling, coffee drinking jazz fans hoping to see the likes of Sandy Brown, Al Fairweather and George Chisholm (tbn), as a free bonus. I should perhaps explain that the word 'Coke' above refers to the fizzy drink Coca Cola and not, in those innocent days, anything of a more potent nature!

Another feature of the West End Cafe sessions was a cabaret spot starring the ever enterprising Mike Hart. Apparently, Mike did a spot in the cafe programme which he called 'Dr Strabismus, whom God preserve, of Utrecht', this act consisting of Mike touring around the punter's tables delivering a performance involving a tuba, a violin and vocal. This continued every week, to the great enjoyment of the band but not, it is feared, the punters, until the manager promised to fire the band unless it stopped forthwith. It is perhaps too much to hope for, but it would be wonderful if the Edinburgh Jazz Festival board could prevail on Mike to reprise this cultural gem in the next year or two, before it is lost forever.

Sometime in the late 1950s (possibly the early 1960s), Charlie's band recorded again, this time on the Edinburgh based label 'Waverley Records'. There were two records, a single which had 'Colonel Bogey March' on one side and 'My Journey to the Sky' on the other, and a second single with 'The Fish Man' and 'Big House Blues' (Waverley Records SLP 502 & 504)[114]. The line up for this recording was Charlie, Bob Craig (tbn), Jack Graham (clt), Mike Hart (bjo), Dizzy Jackson (bss) and Bobby Stewart (drms).

In 1961, the Charlie McNair band, now known as **Charlie McNair's Confederate Jazzmen**, complete with appropriate uniforms, made an appearance at a Jazz Band Ball at Anchor Close. Other bands on same the bill were the Finlay Gentleman Quintet and the Bill Stronach Four,

---

[114] See discography appendix

both of which played in a modern jazz style. The Finlay Gents, as they were often called, featured Tom Finlay on piano and Alec Gentleman, a sax player from Falkirk, while the vibes player, Bill Stronach, led the other band. Bill Stronach used to adopt an exaggerated, hunched posture as he applied himself to his vibes keyboard, with the result that we christened him 'The Praying Mantis'. The ever enterprising Charlie had meanwhile initiated away fixtures for which he ran buses taking band followers to venues far enough away from Edinburgh to qualify as Bona-fide travellers. This was to get round the Sunday drinking laws of the time which insisted that only bona-fide travellers could be served alcohol on a Sunday. Still in the early 1960s, there was a National Trad Band Contest late in 1961 and Charlie's band competed in the local heat. The band included clarinettist Bill Skinner who, John Gibson in the Evening News reported, *caught the ear*[115] and Dougie Campbell, who at this time was playing both guitar and banjo with the band.

Dougie Campbell (guitar), who was born in Fife on 26th May 1925, had established himself as a fine musician and guitarist by the 1950s. He was a versatile player who was capable of playing in a wide range of styles in both jazz and dance music. He had been influenced early in his career by the playing of Charlie Christian, the great American guitarist who made his name with Benny Goodman in the late 1930s and early 1940s, before his early death from TB. Dougie also played sax and was to develop into a notable and greatly respected arranger, even early in his career providing several local bands with well-crafted and thoughtful arrangements. Dougie, as an extremely able and flexible player, knew and had played with all the Edinburgh jazz musicians and, even when they moved south, many would stay in touch with him. This included Sandy Brown and, between the 1950s and the 1970s, Dougie produced a number of arrangements for the Sandy Brown band, now of course London based.

His musical interest was wide and certainly tended towards the more modern and progressive forms of jazz.

---

[115] Gibson J, Edinburgh Evening News, December 1961

His first public performances had been in a venue which he describes as *'up a close off the Grassmarket'* with Ron Gilbertson (tenor sax), Ian Brown (bass) and Sandy Malcolm (drums). He later moved on to the 88 Club, which was then *'up a close off the High Street'*, by which time Dizzy Jackson was on bass. Dougie joined the Charlie McNair band in 1957 and, at the same time, was playing a regular Art College gig with Gilbertson, Jackson and Bobby Stewart, who had replaced Sandy Malcolm on drums. By the early 1960s, Dougie had become more involved with club and dance work and had developed his arranging skills to the point where as well-known a band as that of Humphrey Lyttleton was using his arrangements. Examples of his work can be found on Humph's LP 'I Play as I Please', which includes a number of Dougie's arrangements.

The piano player Ralph Laing recalls Stan Greig telling him that, when he was playing in the Humphrey Lyttelton band, he had spoken with Lyttelton about bringing Dougie into the band, which at that time had no guitarist. Lyttelton made the offer of a place in his band but, not wishing to move to London, Dougie turned down the offer and stayed on in Edinburgh. Speaking with Dougie in 2010, he said that this was something that he had later come to regret, recalling that, had he joined the Lyttelton band, the first tour would have been around Europe in the company of the great Sydney Bechet. As his reputation as an arranger spread, Dougie was commissioned to arrange material for other well-known band leaders including Johnny Dankworth and Kenny McIntosh, who ran a big band in the Wimbledon area, and for whom Dougie wrote a number of commercial arrangements.

As his career progressed, Dougie remained as adaptable as ever and featured with a number of R and B groups in the late 1960s. In the 1970s and 1980s, he was invited to play with Jimmy Deuchar, the famous Dundee born trumpeter who had made his name with the bands of Johnny Dankworth, Oscar Rabin, Geraldo, Ronnie Scott, Tubby Hayes and Jack Parnell, amongst many others. Deuchar had moved back to Scotland in the later part of his career and Dougie would sometimes cover for Deuchar's piano player, playing with Deuchar's small group that also included Edinburgh's Ronnie Dunn on bass. The association with Deuchar also brought Dougie the opportunity to play with the band at a number of jazz festivals in the west of Scotland, including those at Rothesay and Dunoon. The work with the Deuchar band had been an experience that Dougie had greatly enjoyed, saying how much he had admired Jimmy Deuchar's playing. In the 1980 and early 1990s, much of Dougie's playing was in a guitar/bass duo, again working with Ronnie Dunn, a lot of the gigs being in pubs, restaurants and lounges. He also worked for a time in a trio setting with Al Fairweather, recently back in Edinburgh, and the former professional bass player, Lindsay Cooper. In addition, he continued to enjoy guitar and bass duo work, often with the fine bass player, Kenny Ellis.

Dougie remained a highly respected Edinburgh jazzer throughout his lengthy playing career, always welcome as a guest or sitter-in with both traditional and more modern Edinburgh bands. He had, and I am sure has, a pawky and dry sense of humour with a nice line in sending up the hip language of the day, referring to his fellow jazz musicians, in a broad, vernacular Edinburgh accent, as 'they caats'. At the time of writing in 2011, Dougie Campbell is still active in local music after a career that has already spanned seven decades, from the 1940s to the 2000s. His current musical activity he describes as 'odd gigs' as and when they arise. In 2010, he was working with the small, modern styled band of the pianist Roger Cull. He played with this group, together with guest trumpeter Colin Steele, at the Balerno Music Festival in September 2010 attracting, as always, a great deal of praise that had everything to do with the quality of his playing and nothing to do with his age. At the age of 84, Dougie Campbell can look back on a career as one of the most capable and flexible jazz musicians that Edinburgh has ever produced, a true elder statesman of Edinburgh jazz.

Before looking at the career of Dougie Campbell, we had left the Charlie McNair band just entering the hectic 1960s. Over the next few years, Charlie continued to run his band with his customary enthusiasm, with changes in personnel along the way. I can remember playing in support of his band, with a band called **Fred Terry's Capital Jazz Band,** on Friday evenings at the Jazz Gallery Club which was located in a bakers shop and restaurant in Hanover Street. As I recall, the McNair band at this time had Bob Craig or sometimes Graeme Robertson (tbn), Bill Skinner (clt), Frank Gifford (bjo), Kenny Wheatley (bss) and Bobby Stewart (drms) and was playing very much in the traditional mode. The Jazz Gallery was run by a promoter called Noel McNally and was quite an ambitious project. The bill often had two Edinburgh bands, usually the bands of Charlie McNair and Fred Terry, and sometimes featured a guest band, such as the West Nile Jazz Band from Glasgow.

The drummer Mike Travis and I had graduated, in early 1962, from our school boy band, the **Mound City Jazz Band** to Fred Terry's band, which had Fred (tpt), Grant Liddell (clt), Alan Quinn (tbn) and John Yuill (bjo). The band was short lived, breaking up later the same year when Fred went south to further his day job career, but was quite a busy band during its short life span. The promoter, Noel McNally, had further ambitions and ran a Jazz Gallery Promotions event at the Eldorado Ballroom in Leith on 16th April 1962. This show had an extensive bill and was billed as an 'All Night Rave'. The bill included the Al Fairweather – Sandy Brown All Stars, now of course a London based band, Alex Harvey's Big Soul Band, and the Charlie McNair and Fred Terry bands. The Al and Sandy band was by then in its mainstream phase and the line up was Al, Sandy, Tony Milliner (tbn), Brian Lemon (pno), Brain Prudence (bs) and Jackie Dougan (drms). Later, McNally relocated his Jazz Gallery Club to the Lotus Club in Musselburgh, where he combined jazz bands with Pop groups including the Dean Hamilton Combo and the Roadsters.

It was at a Jazz Gallery gig that Charlie McNair's band had a contretemps with the Lothians and Borders Constabulary. The police staged a raid on the club one Friday evening, although what they thought they might find was not clear. The place was not licensed and the most they might have found was a hip flask or the odd screw top of pale ale, which we were perfectly entitled to carry. In any case, Charlie's band, which was in full cry when the police arrived, was required to stop playing while the police prowled about looking suspiciously into every corner. When at last the police departed, Charlie's sense of humour got the better of him and the band broke into a version of the 'Z Cars Theme', the signature tune of a then current cops and robbers TV series. The police were clearly not amused and got their revenge on Charlie and some of the band by hanging about until the gig had finished and then catching them drinking after hours in some pub.

Charlie McNair, at some point in the mid-1960s, also made changes in his band in pursuit of a more mainstream sound. Graeme Robertson, whom we last met as a jazz crazy schoolboy at Broughton High School in the company of Kenny Milne et al, came in on trombone, with Dougie Campbell now on guitar and Bill Skinner on clarinet. Bill Skinner was a fine reeds player who later emigrated to South Africa, a sad loss to the Edinburgh scene. Charlie replaced him with a sax player with modernist tendencies, Ron Gilbertson and then further enhanced the mainstream sound by starting to play flugelhorn himself.

At the end of the 1960s, Charlie made a move in the direction of populist appeal, this being the era of Pop culture, flower power and psychedelic happenings, and re-named the band **The Purple Eyes Jazz Noise**! The line-up for this band was Charlie, Gerard Dott (clt), David 'Eed' Smith (tbn), Alex Marshall (gtr), Norrie Bell (bs) and Pete Drummond (drms). Eed Smith also sometimes played feature numbers on banjo. Gerard Dott recalls that Charlie formed this band after he had had a year or so out of jazz, although Irene McNair does not remember Charlie ever having such a break. I have never really discovered why the trombonist and banjo player David Smith was called Eed. The nearest to a consensus amongst those who knew him is that it may have derived from the second syllable of David. Apparently Charlie and Eed planned to turn the band into a cabaret act complete with carefully rehearsed comedy spots featuring the two of them. Gerard Dott says that they did actually get as far as rehearsing material and even bought some slapstick-type effects, such as custard pies, for the act! It seems that these plans eventually came to nothing and the band settled down as a traditional jazz band again.

Charlie had an amazing, natural gift for fronting a band and for communicating with the punters. He had an original and very rapid wit and could extemporise convoluted and very funny announcements, about tunes and band members, like no one else I ever heard. He had a highly inventive way of introducing members of his band and Irene McNair remembers how he would introduce the guitar player Al McPake as Pete McPoke! Gerard Dott, who played clarinet with him some years later and was of a quiet and retiring disposition, would be introduced as *'Leader of The Morningside Tongs'* or on occasion, *'...mild mannered Clarke Kent',* the alter ego of Superman. He had a sharp eye for personal characteristics and facial expressions and quickly would pick out something that enabled him to put a label on people. I suspect that, in the same way that cartoonists work, Charlie would work on the image of an individual until the punters thought that they too, could see what Charlie could see. Thus, over the years, Johnnie Harper became Biffo the Bear, Pete Ritchie was Doris Day, George Howden was Ethel and Colin Archbold, who came in later on bass guitar, was Corporal Smegma!.

Gerard Dott remembers Charlie, when the band had two simultaneous residencies, one in an up-market hotel and the other in a shabby, run-down pub where incredibly, the drinks were dearer than they were in the posh hotel, telling the punters in the run-down place to remember that they were *'...paying for the surroundings'!.* Gerard also speculates that the band may well have lost the residency in the end, because of Charlie's frequent reference to the price of the beer! It was at this pub too, that Charlie would refer to its location in his best Bronx accent, saying that they were situated at the *'...carner of Bread and Spittal',* meaning on the corner between Bread Street and Spittal Street.

Trombonist George Howden told me about an evening when the McNair band was booked to play in one of those rather bleak village halls, somewhere north of the Highland line. As the band was getting ready to play, George noticed that there were only four or five punters in the hall and no sign that there were to be any more. George mentioned this to Charlie, saying that this looked like their lot for the evening. Apparently the four or five punters were sitting in a solemn line along one of the walls and, after the first number, Charlie announced through the PA system *'The doctor will see you soon'!* George also tells the tale of another time when a punter approached Charlie asking the clarinettist's name, as he would like to have a word with him. The clarinettist was Gerard Dott, not one of the world's most loquacious individuals and someone who, very sensibly, tended only to speak when absolutely necessary. Charlie pointed at Gerard and told the enquiring punter *'That's him over there but don't get talking to him or you'll never get away'!*

Whenever I saw him at one of his many pub residencies, I was struck by how much at home he always looked; the jazz pub was Charlie's natural habitat. Charlie had a genius for involving his audience and absolutely revelled in the camaraderie and rapport that he was able to establish so readily. He would get so involved in the whole business that he would be most reluctant to stop playing when the end time came. Gerard Dott remembers that, when the pub licensing hours were changed in Scotland and pubs could stay open until 11.00 pm instead of 10.00 pm, Charlie expected the band to be delighted, in spite of the fact that they had to play an extra hour for no increase in the already miserable money! At one pub residency, the band was officially supposed to stop at 11.00pm and playing on after this was liable to incur the wrath of sundry neighbours. Gerard also remembers that sometimes, following mysterious negotiations, the endlessly enthusiastic Charlie would announce in triumphant tones *'We can play until 11.30 (or 12.00 or 12.30) tonight!'*

Most Charlie gigs had a tendency to start a bit late and finish quite a bit late. This was particularly galling for the more indolent amongst Charlie's bandsmen, such as Jack Graham, whose ideal would have been to start a quite bit late and finish quite a bit early. When the band had started late, Charlie would genially assure any concerned punters that all would be well – the band would play everything a bit faster until they had caught up! Charlie continued successfully to lead his band in his own inimitable fashion for many years and we shall meet them again later in this book, when we have a look at the next few decades.

In December 1959, Mike Hart and **Archie Sinclair (trombone)** got together with a view to setting up a new band. Archie Sinclair was born in Leith on 8th June 1933 and educated at George Heriot's School. He started his working life with the Bank of Scotland, before emigrating to Canada in 1953. While working for a Toronto bank in 1954, he met and married Betty, also from Leith and also like Archie, of Shetland ancestry. Then in 1955 and still in Canada, he took up the trombone. When a group of fellow Scots exiles decided to form a band and found themselves short of a trombone player, Archie knew exactly what he had to do. He walked into a second hand shop and bought a trombone, not in the least deterred by the fact that he had no idea how to play it. As John Gibson of the Edinburgh Evening News was to say *'Cursed with a landlady who had no ear for jazz in its embryonic state, Archie was forced to practise at night in the bank – until the police were called to investigate the strange noises which someone thought were part of some devilish plot to rob the bank'*[116].

Another ex-pat Scot, Stu Eaton, relates[117] that he played trumpet with the Imperial Jazz Band in Toronto in about 1955/56. This band included Ian 'Daz' Arnott on clarinet, and Stu Eaton has said that they were later joined by Archie Sinclair on trombone. By the time Archie returned to Edinburgh in 1956, he was getting a better sound from the trombone, found a job in advertising and soon made his way around the jazz spots, sitting in whenever he had the opportunity.

The story goes that Mike Hart and Archie, having brought together the personnel for a band, as yet unnamed, were walking through the business part of town when they spotted a brass nameplate outside an impressive doorway. This plate bore the name of some respected, legal gentleman together with the word Advocate. They immediately adopted the name Jazz Advocates for the new band and then later, added the name Old Bailey. One tale is that Archie added this bit after reading about the Lady Chatterley's Lover book trial at the Old Bailey in London. However, Archie himself

---

[116] Gibson J, programme for 'Tribute to Archie Sinclair Concert', 27 February 1970.
[117] SBS Newsletter No. 163, July 2010

liked to tell people that *'I had a habit of standing at the bar, so why not 'Old Bailey?'* The band therefore, became known as **Old Bailey and his Jazz Advocates** and, whatever the truth about the origin of the name, it was to go on to be one of Edinburgh's most successful and best loved bands. Although Archie was to be the key figure in the success of the band, tribute must again be paid to Mike Hart who, as was so often the case, was again a part of a new development in Edinburgh jazz.

The original line up of the new band included Ian 'Tello' Telford (tpt), Jack St Clair (clt), Archie Sinclair (tbn), Mike Hart (bjo and gtr), Donald Macdonald (bs) and Bobby Stewart (drms). Archie, like Charlie McNair, had a genius for communicating with people. As the journalist and drummer George Crockett was to say in an article published in 1966 *'What I have always respected about Archie, or 'Old Bailey', as he has become known to us all, is the fact he combines a musical integrity with a sense of humour. And in a jazz scene that has all too often been dour and humourless, this commendable combination has somehow got through to all who have enjoyed listening or dancing to his band for the past six years.'*[118]

Of course, the time was ripe for jazz bands fronted by great communicators like Archie Sinclair and Charlie McNair. The 'Trad Boom' was well established with the general public and traditional jazz bands were flavour of the month as far as bookings for local gigs were concerned. In addition, the local and national press were running regular weekly jazz columns and other articles, often written by knowledgeable and supportive journalists like John Gibson (Edinburgh Evening News), Alastair Clark (The Scotsman), Dougie Middleton (Edinburgh Evening News) and George Crockett (Edinburgh Weekly).

One report in the Evening News[119] said *'The Eighty Eight Club, situated in Henderson Place (off Henderson Row) is probably Edinburgh's nearest approach to a typical London*

---

[118] Crockett G, Edinburgh Weekly, December 1966, all efforts to trace the copyright holder of this article have failed but the author wishes to acknowledge the valuable record that this article represents.

[119] Edinburgh Evening News, 'Jazzman this is for you', undated, probably 1960

jazz haunt, with its discreet lighting and decor, slick seating, and generally intimate atmosphere. Local groups provide the music – modern on Fridays and Saturdays from 9.30pm to 2am, and traditional on Sundays from 8 to 11.30pm.....Pulling in the crowds on Sundays are 'Old Bailey and his Jazz Advocates', who, although only two months 'old', are finding plenty of work with their brand of 'trad' which is going down particularly well with Bilk fans. The Edinburgh based Advocates play at Hawick Town Hall every second Saturday and are due at the Haddington Corn Exchange to-morrow'.

Another undated article[120] from about the same time reported *'The Eighty Eight Club, Edinburgh jazz haunt gutted by fire three weeks ago, is to be re-built. Work will begin soon on the Pitt Street site and the club, which is run by Londoners Paul and Brian Waldman, should be ready by the end of April. Meanwhile, Old Bailey and his Jazz Advocates, who were the resident Sunday evening band at the 'Eighty Eight', have switched to the Tempo Club in the High Street for Wednesday evening sessions. The Tempo is also owned by the Waldman brothers'.* As the above articles had been kept by Carol Telford, it seems likely that they date from the time Tello was with the Old Bailey band in 1960. Around the same time, the Old Bailey band was proving to be a popular draw at the Premier Club in Dunbar, and in Coldstream and Hawick in the Border country.

The Old Bailey Band, as it came to be called, had rapidly established itself as one of the most able and entertaining of the local jazz bands, not only in Edinburgh but also in Scotland generally. The personnel of the band did not remain stable and, as is often the case with new bands, there were several changes before the band settled down. However, thanks to Archie Sinclair and Mike Hart, the band's policy and presentation remained steady and successful. The diary was well filled with local and more distant gigs and residencies were fixed up. At the time that the McNair band was in the Jazz Gallery, the Old Bailey Band was resident in the Tempo Club in the High Street and The Place Jazz Club at 4 India Buildings, Victoria

---

[120] Edinburgh Evening News, '88 Club will be rebuilt', undated, probably 1960

Street and run by the Waldman brothers. India Buildings, the former home of the Edinburgh Jazz Club, seems to have had an affinity with jazz.

Tello did not stay for long and, by as early as March 1961, he had left to be replaced by Andrew Lauder. Andrew joined on a 'temporary trial basis' which he claims, with the Old Bailey band still getting together for re-union gigs in 2011, has still not been ratified by either the band or himself after 50 years! Andrew was to stay for the remainder of the band's first existence, which lasted until 1970, and then throughout its various reincarnations in the 1970s and 80s. Other early changes saw Charlie Welch come in on drums, Graeme Robertson, Gerry Rossi and Forbes Laing had spells on bass and Jack St Clair was replaced by Jack Graham on clarinet. Unfortunately, the band made few recordings, just a single[121] with 'Teddy Bear's Picnic' on one side and 'Beale Street Blues' on the other, made in the Place Jazz Club in about 1963 and a single track, 'Hey Look Me Over', on the Student Charities record in about 1966[122].

The departure from the Old Bailey band in 1962 of **Jack St Clair (clarinet)**, resulted in Jack setting up his own band, firstly as a four piece then a full six piece, the **Jack St Clair Jazz Band**. This more or less coincided with the breakup of the Fred Terry band and Jack recruited me and John Yuille, on bass and banjo, from the Fred band. Later, Johnnie Harper came in on banjo and Donald 'Chick' Murray on drums. Jack also recruited Bill Munro on trombone and two trumpet players in succession, firstly Alec Fleming in June 1962 then, when Alec went abroad in 1963, an Irishman called Mervyn Morrison. In early 1964, there were disagreements in the Jack St Clair band and Mervyn, Gerard Dott, Bill Munro, Johnnie Harper, me and Chick Murray all left to set up a short lived band called the **New Savoy Jazz Band**. At first, we intended to call the band the New Savoy Jump Band, because the name sounded different, until someone asked if we were actually

---

[121] See Discography appendix
[122] Ibid

211

going to play jump style jazz. On reflection, we decided that we were not and hastily changed to Jazz Band.

The New Savoy band entered for the National Jazz Federation Jazz Band Contest in July 1964 and succeeded in getting through the local heat to take part in the 12 band Scottish finals in Ayr. It was at the Edinburgh heat of this competition that the band was complimented by one of the judges who said that it was *'Honestly the best amateur traditional band we have come across in Scotland and one of the best in the whole contest'*. Chick Murray says it was Max Jones of the Melody Maker, while I remember him as being called John Gee, but it does not really matter who it was, it was just nice to be complimented. Unfortunately, we played badly at the Scottish finals and were unplaced. Bill Munro decided to stop playing for a while in September 1964 and no sooner had Dave Margaroni (tbn) been lined up to replace him, than the short history of the New Savoy Jazz Band came to an end. This was because three of us had been invited to join the Old Bailey band, and once again it was all change. Jack St Clair meanwhile kept his band running by bringing in Jim Petrie on trumpet and Alan Quinn on trombone among others, but eventually, Jack departed for the south where he soon established himself and once more got a band together, somewhere in Oxford area.

The Old Bailey band had been enjoying a reasonably stable period but, in Autumn 1964, Jack Graham, Forbes Laing and Charlie Welch all departed for reasons that varied depending on who was telling the story. One version was that it was a row about punctuality (certainly believable in Jack Graham's case!), another was that the three of them were not happy about a new late night residency that the band had taken on. Whatever the cause, there were vacancies on clarinet, bass and drums and these were filled by Gerard Dott, me and Donald 'Chick' Murray respectively.

The Old Bailey band had remained very popular and, in addition to plenty of local work, was also playing gigs all over Scotland. In my view, there is little doubt about why the band was such a popular success. The band had always been musically capable and played very much in the currently popular manner, however, it was Archie's personality that was the key. Archie was good looking, good natured, friendly and gregarious and, like Charlie McNair, he had a ready wit. He was always willing to chat to the punters in a friendly way and, again like Charlie, he spoke to them from the bandstand in a way that made them feel involved. He was a natural showman with a warm personality that drew people to him and made them like him and, liking him, they tended also to like the band.

Archie lived in the Trinity area of Edinburgh but considered himself to be a passionate 'Leither', that is a native of Leith, with a formidable loyalty to the port. He was also an enthusiast for the Hibernian Football Club, an institution also identified with Leith, and had a certain pride in his own ability as a footballer. On at least one occasion, he allowed himself to be persuaded to turn out for a 'show biz XI'. This was a popular gimmick of the time, when sundry hopefuls, with sometimes fairly sketchy connections to show business, would turn out against other celebrity opposition, usually in the name of some charity. Andrew Lauder used to say that Archie could have been a reasonable footballer, if only he had been able to run. Certainly, when I once went along to watch, he seemed to spend most of the game falling over, especially when the ball came anywhere near him. He was very keen though, although I have to say he is the only footballer I ever saw who habitually dribbled the ball without actually moving in any direction. Archie's great football heroes were the 'Famous Five', the legendary Hibs forward line of Eddie Turnbull, Willie Ormond, Lawrie Reilly, Bobby Johnstone and Gordon Smith. Of these, it was Gordon Smith he particularly worshipped and I fancy that, in the midst of his static dribbles, in his mind's eye he was acting out his vision of the great Hibs winger.

Gordon Smith was, of course, one of the great names in Scottish football in the late 1940s and 1950s, perhaps the most loved and admired of the 'Famous Five'. He remains to this day something of a legend who, although winning only eighteen caps for Scotland, played for all of eighteen years with Hibs, before enjoying further success late in his career with Heart of Midlothian and Dundee Football Clubs. A player of great skill and grace of movement, Gordon Smith played his part in three Scottish League titles with Hibs, another League title and the League Cup with Hearts and, in a final flourish, yet another League title with Dundee. Even I, a rugby playing product of a rugby playing school, was aware that this was a special footballer who inspired, not just admiration but reverence, in a whole generation of football followers. Indeed, after I became a member of the Old Bailey Band, I could hardly have failed to be aware of the prowess of Gordon Smith. In his cups, often in the bandwagon, when Archie was waxing lyrical about his enthusiasms, it could sometimes be hard to keep track of when we had left New Orleans and entered the Easter Road stadium. Sometimes it sounded as if the Famous Five had included Jack Teagarden or that Willie Ormond had made his finest recordings as a member of the Ellington band. In fact, if Archie had only known it, there seems to have been a valid connection between Gordon Smith and jazz.

In 2011, there was an article by Paul Forsyth in the sports section of 'Scotland on Sunday'[123] celebrating the publication of a book[124] about Gordon Smith by his son, Tony, a professional pianist. The book was called 'Gordon Smith: Prince of Wingers'. The article picked out a number of interesting facts from the book, including Gordon Smith's liking for the music of Fats Waller and Leadbelly and indeed *'...all things jazz and blues'*. Gordon Smith's interest in jazz is further confirmed by trombonist and drummer Ken Ramage, another HIbs follower, who told me that Gordon would often turn up at the Barnton Hotel in the 1970s, when the Festival City Jazz Band was playing. In his book, Tony Smith goes on to relate how, when on a holiday in France, Gordon Smith had discovered that Sydney Bechet was a guest at the same hotel. Apparently, the Scottish footballer and the great New Orleans clarinet and soprano sax player quickly became firm friends. So much so, that Bechet was soon providing Smith with tickets to some of his performances and they shared a number of early morning swims in the blue waters of the Mediterranean, before settling down to relax in the sun. It was reported that

---

[123] Forsyth P, 'Star among the Stars', Scotland on Sunday, 4 September 2011
[124] Smith Tony, 'Gordon Smith: Prince of Wingers', Black and White Publishing 2011

Bechet had said *'I can hear music in the sound of those waves, Gordon. The waves are talkin' to me man. You must be able to hear it.'* What a shame that Archie never knew about this friendship, he would have been ecstatic and the bandwagon tales would have become still more confusing.

The late night residency, which may well have caused the departure of Jack Graham, Forbes Laing and Charlie Welch, was up on the Calton Hill, at the east end of Princes Street. This was basically an Italian restaurant, the Candlelight Rooms, which had opened a jazz club on its top floor and called it the Manhattan Club. This was something of a departure for Edinburgh jazz. Most of the jazz venues had been in pubs, which closed at 10.00pm at that time, or other, non-licensed premises, which were available in the evening. This new jazz venue did not open until 10.00pm and ran on into the early hours of the morning, 2.00 am as I recall. Although slow to begin with (Mario, the manager, bought us a drink the first night he made a profit!), the club eventually caught on and attracted a good sized crowd.

Quite often, the Old Bailey band played as support band at functions involving touring jazz bands and sometimes members of the visiting bands were persuaded to come on to the Manhattan Club for a late night blow. An extraordinary night took place on 3rd September 1965, when there were an astonishing number of jazz musicians present. This was because it was the Edinburgh Festival time and a couple of famous bands were in town. The Bruce Turner Jump Band, with Sandy Brown guesting, was at Bungy's Night Spot in the High Street and the Chris Barber Band with Ottilie Patterson was doing a late night Fringe Show at the Playhouse. Elsewhere, Danny Moss was playing in a band with Ron Mathewson on bass. Something of a jazz geek even then, I took a note of who was there and who played. The list, with those that played marked*, was :

Trumpets: Pat Halcox*, Ray Crane*, Tommy Lister*, Johnny Smith, Pete Martin, George Roy, Charlie McNair, Pete Davenport
Trombones: Archie Sinclair*, Graeme Robertson*, Harry Cadger

215

Reeds: Gerard Dott*, Jack Graham*, Hamish McGregor, Sandy Brown*, Bruce Turner

Piano: Alex Shaw*, Ronnie Gleaves*, Jack Finlay, Ian Scott*

Guitar/banjo: Ruan O'Loughlan*, Johnnie Harper*, Mike Hart*, Stu Morrison, John Slaughter, Lachlan McColl

Bass: Ron Mathewson*, Ronnie Rae*, Malcolm Rees*, Graham Blamire*, Dave Buchan*, Jimmy Luke

Vibes: Bill Stronach

Drums: Graham Burbidge*, Laurie Chescoe*, Chick Murray*, Eddie Smith*, Duncan Docherty*, Mike Travis*

Archie and Mike had, of course, made sure that all the visiting jazzers knew that the Manhattan session was on and that they were all invited. It certainly was an incredible night, perhaps unprecedented in the history of Edinburgh traditional jazz. Archie had also made sure that the event was announced in the press. He was quoted as saying *'They are going to have the biggest rave of all time in Edinburgh. After midnight, all these musicians will be joining me at my resident club, the Manhattan, at Calton Hill. I can only forecast that Edinburgh will never have experienced anything like it. It is a celebration of my first anniversary at the club. At any time during night, the boys will be arriving and taking the stand as they feel like it. There could be something like 20 top musicians having a blow together.'*[125]
Another reason for the big turnout of local jazzers was probably because the club was supposed to be closing and this had been billed as the last night. In fact, the club re-opened exactly one week later, with not a Saturday missed! The Manhattan Club continued to run successfully until 21st September 1966, when it mysteriously burned down in the middle of the night. My bass and Chick Murray's drums were burned in the fire, causing complicated insurance claims. It had been a great venue and had

---

[125] Edinburgh Evening News, September 3rd, 1965

become a regular late night drop-in spot for many visiting jazzers, although seldom to the extent of the famous event described above. Earl Hines, Al Fairweather, Sandy Brown, Ray Kart, Dickie Kart and Bob van Oven of the Dutch Swing College band, George Chisholm and others had all dropped in and played at one time or another. The Manhattan Club, with its late night policy, had been a welcome innovation in Edinburgh, giving the jazz scene something it had never had before, but it was gone and nothing like it was to come along until the still distant days of the Edinburgh Jazz Festival.

The Old Bailey band, however, continued, keeping very busy, many times playing in support of famous, professional bands, such as those of Acker Bilk, Kenny Ball, Alex Welsh and the Dutch Swing College. Other gigs were in venues such as the Cephas Club, which was in the vaults beneath St George's Church in Shandwick Place, and numerous other gigs both in and out of town. A particularly memorable gig was a concert in the Usher Hall on 1st April 1966, when the band played second to the Alex Welsh band with the great Earl 'Fatha' Hines on piano.

In 1965, Mike Hart had gone abroad for a while and Johnnie Harper took over on banjo and guitar. Gerard Dott had dropped out in October 1965, after a year with the band, and had been succeeded by Hamish McGregor. Hamish tells the story of one gig when the band was making heavy weather of it, probably just one of those times when things were not going as smoothly as usual. Archie, with his advertising executive's instinct for style and presentation, turned to Hamish and said out of the corner of his mouth 'Smile – or you're fired!'. Then, in August 1966, Hamish left to form a band of his own, allowing the return of Jack Graham, presumably now forgiven for any transgressions in the past! Another change in 1967 was the temporary departure of Andrew Lauder who went off to play a dance residency at the Cavendish Ballroom and was replaced for time by Jim Petrie. Jim stayed for a number of months and then Andrew came back into the fold.

Old Bailey and his Jazz Advocates c 1969
L-R Graham Blamire, Chick Murray, Archie Sinclair,
Johnnie Harper, Jack Graham, Andrew Lauder
(from the collection of the author, photographer
unknown)

In January 1969, it seemed as though the days of Archie leading the Old Bailey band were over. I was studying in Glasgow as this time and, although I was home most nights and still a member of the band, I was not around the Edinburgh jazz scene to the extent I had been. However, there had been pressure from Archie's employers about his high jazz profile and an increasing need for him to put more time into his work activities. Whatever was at the back of it, an article in the 'Evening News' announced that *'Old Bailey (off the stand he's Archie Sinclair, 35 year old director of an advertising firm in the West End) has blown his last note as trombonist-leader of the Jazz Advocates'*[126].

The article went on to explain that the band had been founded by Archie and Mike Hart in 1960 and that, over the

---

[126] 'Edinburgh Evening News', 'Fond ta-ta to Old Bailey', January 1969

years, they had been one of Scotland's busiest semi-pro bands, saying *'Now OB is quitting because of business commitments'*. Archie was quoted as saying *'I'm handling over leadership to another Edinburgh trombonist, Kenny Ramage, who's got professional experience and who, I am sure, will do a grand job. The band is otherwise carrying on as before'*. Archie's final blow with the band was to be at Johnnie Harper's wedding in January 1969. I missed most of this period with the band, being away in Glasgow a lot of the time, tied up with my final professional exams, with Dave Margaroni depping for me on bass. However, the new arrangement was to have a fairly short life as Ken Ramage, a professional musician who naturally needed more than the Old Bailey band could provide to make a living, returned to work on the boats a few months later. As it turned out, clearly missing playing and unable to keep away, Archie by then felt able to return and, by the late Summer of 1969, he was back playing his trombone and leading the Old Bailey band as before. Now clear of exams, I too was able to return to the band that summer. Sadly, this was to be a tragically short come-back for Archie because, on Saturday 29th October 1969, things came to a horrible and shocking halt.

The band had played at the YMCA in South St Andrew's Street, which had succeeded the Manhattan Club as a residency. Afterwards, Archie Sinclair and several others had gone out to Andrew Lauder's house in Ratho Station for a bit of a party. On the way back into town, their car hit a stationary lorry on the Glasgow Road, near the City boundary. All four in the car were killed. Archie left a widow, Betty, and two young children, a host of grieving friends and colleagues, and a shocked and numbed jazz band. In retrospect, it was a tragedy that he had ever started to play again.

With Betty Sinclair's full support, the band played a gig to which it was committed the next night, with Dave Margaroni coming in on trombone. After much discussion and again with Betty's support and encouragement, the band decided to continue, changing the name slightly to **Old Bailey's Jazz Advocates** (instead of Old Bailey and his Jazz Advocates), but after a year or so, disbanded in 1970.

There had been a benefit night in memory of Archie in Eaglesham, run by the Glasgow promoter Andy Daisley with strong support from the George Penman Jazzmen, and a concert in the Odeon Cinema in Edinburgh, which featured the Chris Barber band, the Old Bailey band, the New Society Syncopators and the McCalmans Folk group. In the end, for the members of the band, Archie was irreplaceable and, although the band was to get together again in the future, it was right to stop when we did.

Of the others in the Old Bailey band of the early 1960s, **Bobby Stewart (drums)** was born on 17th January 1938 and educated at James Gillespie's and Tynecastle schools in Edinburgh. After school, he made his living as an electronics and radar engineer. He had followed in the footsteps of his father who was also a drummer. His father, Bobby senior, who was clearly something of a character, mostly played drums in dance music and became quite well-known for his method of playing the last tune at each session. His habit, as the final number got going, was to steadily dismantle his drum kit while continuing to play until, by the end of the tune, everything was neatly packed up but for the snare drum and perhaps one cymbal on which he had continued! Bobby senior, at one time, played for dancing in the Star Cafe in Leith Street and their music was relayed by some mysterious means to dancers in another venue some considerable distance away. Whether or not they were paid double for this extraordinary arrangement, is not known.

Bobby junior, in spite of having a drummer for a father, was self-taught and never received any drum tuition from his Dad. While most of his contemporaries did their couple of years National Service, Bobby signed up as a Regular and was in the RAF for three years, during which he played in both military and dance bands. It was during this period that Bobby learned to read music and he played side drum in the military band and a full drum kit in the dance band. He got a lucky break when he was stationed in Baghdad, the established drummer in the station band, which played a mixture of jazz and dance music, departing on the plane on which Bobby had just arrived. Bobby was immediately drafted into the band for the Christmas Concert and remembers that the first tune he was required to play was 'Intermission Riff'.

On his return in 1959 to Edinburgh after his service in the RAF, Bobby joined the band of Charlie McNair. Bobby recalls an appearance in the Usher Hall when the McNair band was playing as support band to the Clyde Valley Stompers. When the interval ended and the McNair band was due to start the second half of the show, half of the band were still in the Shakespeare Bar and the remainder took the stage with only the banjo, bass and Bobby on drums. Not in the least thrown by finding themselves reduced to a trio, they extemporised on Bob Haggart's 'Big Noise from Winnetka', a tune which is economical in its instrumental needs, until their missing comrades eventually slunk onto the stage. Bobby remained with the McNair band for a year or two then moved on to the newly formed Old Bailey and his Jazz Advocates, with which band he remained for about a year, before giving way to Charlie Welch.

For a time, Bobby had shared a flat with another drummer, Sandy Malcolm, and they shared out gigs too, when necessary. By this time, he had developed a liking for more modern forms of jazz and Swing and increasingly played with others of a similar persuasion, including Ron Gilbertson (reeds and flute), Bill Stronach (vibes), Dougie Campbell (guitar) and Dizzy Jackson (bass). With these musicians, and others including Joe Capaldi (reeds) and Eric Rinaldi (trumpet), he played many small group sessions in the Royal Mile Cafe, which belonged to the Rinaldi family. He also put in some time playing regular gigs with the Alex Shaw Trio, in which he and Alex were joined by the excellent bass player, Jimmy Luke. Bobby's interest in the more modern forms of jazz is reflected in the drummers whom he considers have influenced his style. These include Joe Hodge, who played with the Dave Brubeck combo and was his main influence, Joe Morello, Jo Jones and Buddy Rich, although he also adds '... and all the drummers of the Swing era'. Between 1965 and 1967, Bobby went off to play music full-time, playing on cruise liners which sailed between South Africa and Australia, when his ability to read music came in more than handy.

221

The boat gigs came Bobby's way through the good offices of the Edinburgh piano player, Ronnie Bates, whom, it will surprise nobody to learn, was known as Master Bates.

Bobby's later career in Edinburgh jazz was to include work, in venues including the Athenian and the Laughing Duck, with a group fronted by trombonist Ken Ramage and which included Jack Finlay (pno), Dave Margaroni (bs) and vocalist Kenny Charleston. This group later led to the formation of the Jack Finlay Trio, in which Bobby played with bassists Ken Macdonald and, later, Kenny Ellis. This top class trio became a regular backing group, for more than a decade, for many of the mainstream jazzers who came to play at the Edinburgh International Jazz Festival. He also made a further contribution to local and Scottish jazz when he served for a while as secretary of Platform, the jazz promoting organisation, replacing the southwards-heading Charlie Alexander and working with treasurer Jack Finlay. However, although he was much involved in the more contemporary forms of jazz, not all of Bobby's playing was to be with mainstream and modern jazz musicians. On many occasions he returned to the more traditional style, playing quite regularly with Mike Hart's Society Syncopators and a variety of other Edinburgh jazz bands over the years. His long career in Edinburgh jazz (which he describes as his *'chequered career'*) also included spells with the award winning 'Musician's Union Big Band', Pete Seaton's Band and Fat Sam's Band. In the 2000s, he was a member of the 'Mellotones', a group specialising in the music of the great singer Mel Torme, with Alan Anderson on piano and Jimmy Taylor on vocals and bass, playing weekly sessions in the Jazz Bar, a venue in Chambers Street. In 2011, at the time of writing, although complaining of a number of *'aches and pains'*, Bobby Stewart remains one of Edinburgh's best drummers, as comfortable and competent in the role of traditional jazz drummer as he is in the more rarefied atmosphere of mainstream and modern forms of jazz.

Donald Macdonald (bass, reeds), the original bass player in the Old Bailey band, was born in 1939 and educated at George Heriot's School but was not involved in jazz while at school. Donald was to become an architect, a profession that seems to have contributed more than its fair

share of Edinburgh jazzers. After school, he found him
playing a 'home built' bass and says that he was pr
ganged into playing in a band with Fraser Gauld (tpt), Ja
McMahon (clt) and Alan Ritchie (bjo). He was a found
member of the Old Bailey band but soon left to concentra
on his final year of architectural studies at Edinbur;
College of Art. Later, in the 1970s, he was to play bass wi
an outstanding band, the New Society Syncopators, pι
together by Mike Hart and about which we will hear in th
next chapter. In the early 1970s, Donald gave up playin
bass for a while and took up saxophone, mostly playing alt
sax but later played the seldom heard bass sax. Later stil
he made a return to his original instrument to play bas
with a top class band put together by Hamish McGregor ir
the 1980s, Fat Sam's Band. Donald played with this band
from 1981 to 1988, playing at many festivals and touring
extensively.

Donald Macdonald was the first of what was to become a
bass playing dynasty, one brother Ken also playing bass,
another brother Angus playing brass bass for a time and
Ken's son Owen, was to be yet another bass player. Donald
senior, father of Donald, Ken and Angus, was a long-term
loyal follower of the jazz scene and skilled artist who drew
many memorable cartoons which featured in jazz
publications and Edinburgh Jazz Festival programmes.

Donald 'Chick' Murray (drums), born in 1943, was a
school contemporary of Gerard Dott and me at George
Heriot's School but, although interested in drumming, was
never a member of the school pipe band. He was unusual
in the Edinburgh traditional jazz world as his inspiration
was neither classic nor purist jazz, but the music of the
Swing era, especially that of Benny Goodman and his star
drummer, Gene Krupa. He had been captivated by the bio-
pic of Krupa's life, the 'Gene Krupa Story' and had been to
see it five times in a single week! He then attended
Keating's School of Music in 1960/61 and, after some work
in dance bands, first appeared around the jazz scene in
1962, encouraged by his links with me and Gerard Dott.
His interest in Swing made his style quite a bit different
from most of the local traditional jazz drummers, who were
more concerned to sound like Baby Dodds or Zutty

Singleton, and this had a major impact on every band with whom he played. His playing was rock steady and, although quite a powerful player, the tight, crisp sound he got, gave any rhythm section in which he played a controlled, well organised feel.

He had come up by way of Jack St Clair's Jazz Band and then the New Savoy Jazz Band, before joining the Old Bailey band at the same time as me in 1964. He was to stay with the Old Bailey band until it broke up in 1970 but was again with the band when it reformed in the mid-1970s. The interim period remained busy for Chick, who played with both four-piece and six-piece bands led by Ken Ramage at the White Cockade (the Ken Ramage Jazz Advocates), before moving on to Seven Up, a band put together by Hamish McGregor. Chick later played at the Old Smiddy Inn in Pencaitland with Edwin Holland, whom he rates as one of the best arranger/musicians of the time, and this experience enabled him to become established on the dance band circuit. In 1974 he returned to the jazz scene when he joined the Charlie McNair band, becoming part of a strong line-up with Charlie, Jack Graham or Gerard Dott (rds), Ian McCauley (tbn), Johnnie Harper (bjo and mouthorgan), Johnnie Phillips (gtr) and Colin Archbold (bs).

Chick has fond memories of periods when this band was augmented by two guest musicians, Ally Dawson, a professional guitarist from Edinburgh who had been working in South Africa, and the one and only Sandy Brown, who was back in town on alternate weeks while working on the acoustics of the Festival Theatre. Sadly, this would be almost the last that Edinburgh would see and hear of Sandy, who was to die in March 1975. We will pick up Chick's 1970/80s jazz career in later chapters, when we follow the adventures of the re-formed Old Bailey Band, its metamorphosis into the Scottish Jazz Advocates and his playing with a new band, the Jazz Masters. He eventually retired from playing in the early 1990s, although he continued to make occasional appearances with various dance bands and at Old Bailey re-union gigs.

Chick was, however, to make another, and important, contribution to Edinburgh jazz when, in the mid-2000s, he became part of a small group of veteran jazzers who met

regularly in town to chew the fat and reminisce about the old days. It was not long before this group came up with a notable project. Their plan was to organise an exhibition celebrating Edinburgh jazz and to pursue both the setting up of an archive and the writing of a history of Edinburgh jazz. As their plans became increasingly focused, this group became known as the Edinburgh Jazz Archive group (EJAG) and we will hear much more about them later in this book[127].

The **clarinet and piano player Gerard Dott**, born on 14th February 1943 and educated at George Heriot's School, had started in skiffle in the late 1950s, first of all playing guitar and then saving up to buy a clarinet. At first he listened to the playing of Monty Sunshine of the Chris Barber band, before moving on to an appreciation of the music of the Duke Ellington Orchestra, particularly the playing of the great clarinettist, Barney Bigard. Like Chick Murray, Gerard's style developed in a way that was markedly different from most of his fellow clarinet players, many of whom had been inspired by Johnny Dodds, George Lewis or the British 'trad' clarinettists, such as Acker Bilk. Gerard had started with the schoolboy band, the Mound City Jazz Band and then graduated by way of the New Savoy Jazz Band to the Old Bailey band in 1964. He also had a spell when he played piano with the Climax band in the early 1960s, when they had residencies in the Crown Bar, the Imperial Hotel at the top of Leith Street and in the North Merchiston Boy's Club, in Watson Crescent.

Gerard was also drawn into a band led by a young trumpeter, not long out of school, called Pete Martin, whom we will meet shortly. Both Gerard and Chick Murray were to become long term Edinburgh jazzers, with both later putting in substantial spells with the Charlie McNair band, in Gerard's case joining Charlie's band in 1966. It was at the end of this period in 1972, after six years with the McNair band, that Gerard caused a minor sensation when he suddenly went off to play full time with a remarkable folk-rock band, the Incredible String Band. They included Mike Heron, who had been at school with me, Gerard and

[127] See Chapter XVII

Chick, and Robin Williamson, who had been the banjo player in the schoolboy Mound City Jazz Band. In time, Robin Williamson, who was born on 24th November 1943, was to make a big name for himself in the world of traditional Scottish and Irish culture as a multi-instrumentalist, musician, singer, song writer and storyteller.

In the String Band, Gerard played several instruments, including the clarinet, tenor sax, keyboard, bass guitar and the five-string or Bluegrass banjo. Gerard stayed with them, touring in the USA and elsewhere, for about a year, before he returned to the Edinburgh jazz scene. On his return, he played for a while in a Folk Group called Carterbar with which I was also involved, again playing several instruments, as well as with a short-lived band called The Granton Jass Works, in a residency at the White Cockade in Rose Street. Later, in the 1970s, he was to play with the Nova Scotia Jazz Band at the Hailes House Hotel and then in a four piece off-shoot of this band with Gus Ferguson (tpt), Johnnie Harper (bjo and gtr) and me, before re-joining the Charlie McNair band. After his second stint with the McNair band, he took a break from playing for a while in the early 1980s, then returned to play a band led by Jim Petrie at the Glenelg Hotel and also a pub in Elm Row. This was a fairly short term engagement and was followed by Gerard becoming a member of a band initially led by Donald Macdonald at Basin Street. Later, after Donald left, Bob Craig took over the running of the band and, when Al Fairweather returned to Edinburgh, Bob brought his old colleague into the band. However, in about 1987, disillusioned with the jazz scene, Gerard stopped playing, a break from music that was to last for all of eighteen years, before he made a belated but welcome return in 2006.

In the interest of completeness, I had better give some information about myself, **Graham Blamire (bass),** born in Edinburgh on 10th March 1943 and educated at George Heriot's School. I became involved in music by way of skiffle in about 1957, mostly through being in the Scouts, and my first tentative efforts were on the washboard. The skiffling crowd with whom I was involved included Colin

Oswald, Mike Travis and Gerard Dott, the latter two, like me, going on the develop their musical interests into jazz. A short-lived effort to play guitar went nowhere but, when the first attempt to put a jazz band together came along, it was clear that there was a vacancy for a double bass player. I managed to cajole my parents into buying me a double bass from Methven Simpson's music shop. This first instrument was a Selmer bassette which, although it had a normal finger board and strings, had a considerably reduced body or sound box. This, while making it easier to transport, did tend to make it look as if a normal bass has shrunk.

I followed much the same path as Gerard Dott, moving on from the school-boy Mound City Jazz Band to play, in succession, with Fred Terry's Jazz Band, Jack St Clair's Jazz Band and the New Savoy Jazz Band, before joining the Old Bailey band in September 1964. This was the occasion of the great upheaval in the Old Bailey band, when Jack Graham (clt), Forbes Laing (bs) and Charlie Welsh (drms) all departed, their places taken by Gerard Dott, me and Chick Murray respectively. The membership of the Old Bailey band at this time thus included, in addition to us three newcomers, Andrew Lauder (tpt), Archie Sinclair (tbn) and Mike Hart (bjo). This was a time of great popularity for this band and it was an extremely busy period, with gigs all over Scotland as well as occasional forays into the north of England.

After the break-up of the Old Bailey band in 1970, I went on to play folk music with the Caiystane and Carterbar folk groups, while simultaneously playing jazz with the Granton Jass Works. There was also a particularly rewarding year or so with the Society Syncopators, then still in their early format, with Ian Telford, Dave Paxton, Bob Craig and Mike Hart still in the band. The resurrection of the Old Bailey band, arranged by Hamish McGregor in 1975, brought me back into the Old Bailey fold and I was to remain with the band for the rest of its history, including its re-birth as the Scottish Jazz Advocates in 1981. This brought opportunities to play with many famous visiting jazzers, particularly concerts with Bud Freeman and Wild Bill Davison in the Dominion Cinema 1976, and a host of others in the early years of the EIJF.

A disappointment was missing out on trips with the band to the Sacramento Jazz Festival, caused by my college teaching commitments of the time, although I did manage the trip to play at the Eindhoven Jazz Dagen in 1983. In the late 1970s, I took over organising the Nova Scotia Jazz Band, an off shoot of the Old Bailey band with a residency at the Hailes House Hotel in the Kingsknowe area of town, and then the four-piece version of this band which played at the Original Hotel in Roslin. Later, I was to play a lengthy spell with Bill Salmond's Louisiana Ragtime Band and be instrumental in forming the Jazz Masters and Maid of the Forth Stompers, bands which we will meet later.

When he was nine years old, finding a broken banjo in his grandmother's attic (could she have been a banjo player? Perhaps an old banjo should be called a granjo?) was the unlikely start for another Edinburgh jazzer who was to make a career in jazz. **Johnnie Harper (guitar, banjo, bass guitar)** was born in Edinburgh on 4th December 1944 and attended Daniel Stewart's College. Johnnie's interest in jazz was awakened by listening to jazz records belonging to school pals, the first that he remembers being a recording by Louis Armstrong of St Louis Blues, which was on both sides of a 78 rpm record. After this, he moved on to the recordings of Bix Beiderbecke and the Eddie Condon bands, thus following a 'Chicago' route, rather than one oriented towards New Orleans bands. After repairing the attic banjo, he set about learning to play it, receiving some assistance with a few chords from Fraser Gauld, who was to become a prominent local trumpeter. Like many of us of this generation, Johnnie first got into skiffle, at the early age of about eleven. This was followed, when he was about fifteen or sixteen, by the formation of his first 'band', which included, in addition to his own banjo playing, a trumpeter, a clarinet player, a guitarist and someone playing a tea chest bass[128].

---

[128] For those too young to remember or so old that they have forgotten, a tea chest bass consisted of a large plywood box (the tea chest) stood open side down, with a string leading from the centre of the upper side to the top of a pole (which was usually a brush handle). The lower end of the pole was set on corner of the upper surface of the tea chest and, by plucking the string while tightening or loosening

Johnnie's first experience of live jazz came in about 1958/59, when he went along to the West End Cafe, where he heard Charlie McNair's Confederate Jazz Band. Although it was a long time ago, he thinks that the band was made up of Charlie (tpt), Jack Graham (clt), Archie Sinclair (tbn), Mike Hart (bjo), Dizzy Jackson (bs) and Sandy Malcolm (drms). His second exposure to live jazz, also in the late 1950s, was at the Royal Mile Cafe in the High Street, where it was the Royal Mile Jazz Band that played, with Eric Rinaldi on trumpet and, again, Archie Sinclair on trombone. The others in the band he cannot now recall but he does remember that Bill Marshall sat in with the band, playing a mandolin.

Later, Johnnie went along to a 'Bring Your Instrument' event at the Place Jazz Club where he was heard by Chick Murray. Chick, clearly impressed, invited him to a practice of the Jack St Clair band which, being short of a banjo player at just the right time, soon recruited him. This was followed by the formation of the New Savoy Jazz Band and then, when Mike Hart went abroad in 1965, Johnnie rejoined Chick Murray and me, this time making up the Old Bailey rhythm section. Johnnie remained with the Old Bailey band until its breakup in 1970, after which he played in a rock band with his guitar playing brother Mike. Too good a player to be long without a jazz gig, he was soon recruited by trombonist Ken Ramage and later became a member of the Charlie McNair band, with which he remained until the Old Bailey band was reformed in the mid-1970s, of which we will hear more later. Other Edinburgh bands that Johnnie played with, before beginning his professional career, included the Charleston Trio (latc 1960s) which consisted of Johnnie, Mike Hart and singer Liz Stewart, Seven Up led by Hamish McGregor (early 1970s), Johnny Horne and the Hornets (early 1970s), Tangerine (1970-72) which included his brother Mike on guitar, and the Nova Scotia jazz Band and Nova Scotia Quartet, both in thc mid to later 1970s.

---

the tension on the pole, different notes could be produced in imitation of a double bass. This 'instrument', though crude, could be surprisingly effective

Although the first period in the history of Old Bailey's Jazz Advocates came to an end when the band broke up in 1970, it was not to be long before the band name returned to the Edinburgh jazz scene. When Ken Ramage, who had already led the band for a spell in 1969, returned to town from his latest stint on the boats in the early 1970s, he brought the Jazz Advocates name back into use, putting together a band under the name of the **Ken Ramage Jazz Advocates**. The band he formed was a strong one and included Jim Petrie on trumpet, Ken himself on trombone, Johnnie Harper on banjo and Chick Murray on drums. As usual with local bands, there were to be a number of changes in the line-up as time went on, with Jack Graham, Hamish McGregor or Gerard Dott playing reeds at one time or another and similarly with Dave Margaroni, Norrie Bell or Jimmy Luke playing bass. The drum chair was later occupied by Pete Ritchie or Bill Weston, who was not a native of Edinburgh but a visitor and whom Ken remembers as a very good drummer. When Johnnie Harper went off to join the Charlie McNair band, Colin Warwick, a relative newcomer whom we shall meet more fully in a later chapter, was recruited on banjo. All of these changes maintained a strong line-up and the band did very well, with residencies at Lucky McLeucher's Howf, which was actually in the Doric Hotel, and at Jean Ferguson's long-established jazz spot, the White Cockade in Rose Street. Records kept by both Ken himself and Colin Warwick, who played with the band, indicate that the Ken Ramage Jazz Advocates came to an end sometime in 1971. In any case, once again the lure of full time playing beckoned for Ken Ramage and, by 1973, he was back on the road.

The clarinettist Gerard Dott, who had put in about a year with the Old Bailey band in the 1960s, also played with an enterprising band which played in a mainstream style and was led by **trumpeter Pete Martin**. Pete Martin was born in Edinburgh on 25 June 1947 and attended George Watson's College before going on to Edinburgh University. He recalls that the late 1950s and early 1960s was the time of the 'trad boom' and, because of this, it was relatively easy to hear 'jazz type' sounds, giving as an example the fact that the girl next door had a Chris Barber EP! Pete started playing trumpet when he was aged nine, although he did not come from a musical family, and was shown how to play scales by the school janitor. Later, he was to have some lessons on reading music from reed player Jack Duff but was otherwise self taught and very much influenced by jazz recordings in all styles.

Looking back almost fifty years later, Pete remembers that there were positive reasons for his early interest in mainstream jazz. His thinking was (and to some extent still is) that both Dixieland and bebop relied heavily on conventions, which placed considerable limitations on what a soloist could do. In contrast, Pete considered that middle period jazz was of a relatively uncluttered nature, which allowed plenty of space for a soloist to express himself. He also felt that it encouraged a melodic way of playing. Speaking with Pete in 2010 while writing this book, he said that he believed that this approach had allowed him to remain open to a wide range of jazz styles and he emphasised that he still takes genuine pleasure from hearing players from all styles and periods of jazz. Pete's open approach was fairly unusual amongst aspiring jazzers around 1960, when most of us were Hell bent on aping the 'trad' sound we were hearing on the radio and television. However, he was far from alone in his jazz tastes and, even at school, he was associating with a group of young jazz musicians who shared his views.

They included a couple of fine guitarists, Lachlan McColl and Charles Alexander who would continue in mainstream jazz throughout their playing careers, and Allen Skinner who played drums. Pete began sitting in with local bands in the early 1960s and Gerard Dott remembers when the young Pete, clutching a trumpet and looking about twelve years old, turned up at a gig and was allowed to sit in. Apparently, even then he was well advanced and he astounded the band with his already accomplished and rapid technique. After this, Pete played some gigs with the equally young Hamish McGregor and continued to look for sit-in opportunities

By 1964, Pete had formed a band of his own, the **Pete Martin All Stars** which he continued to run until about 1968. This was a good, enthusiastic band, willing to go its own way when everyone else was playing 'trad', playing broadly in the tradition of the Duke Ellington small groups. In addition to Pete and Gerard Dott, the All Stars included Lachlan McColl (gtr), Alan Skinner (drms), Brian Keddie then Dave Margaroni and later, George Howden, (tbn), Dave Buchan (bs) and, occasionally, Jack Finlay (pno). Looking back, in 2010, Pete felt that the name of the band was not quite as cringe making then as it is now! He explained that they had settled on the name because everybody in the band had played in other bands already.

At various times between 1964 and 1968, the band had residencies at the Crown Bar, Rutherford's Bar, which was in the High Street on the other side and just uphill from John Knox's house, the Woolpack opposite the McEwan Hall and at The Athenian in Howe Street. Latterly, frequent guests with Pete's band included Gordon Cruikshank on tenor and Howard Copland on alto sax. Around about the winter of 1964/65, Pete was playing the interval spot at the Manhattan Club, where the Old Bailey band was resident, with a quartet, which, if memory serves me right, was a cut down version of his All Stars band. Pete also played with Hamish McGregor's band The Memphis Road Show around 1967 to 1969 and with a band put together by pianist Jack Finlay, the Jack Finlay Quintet. Unfortunately, Pete was then lost to Edinburgh jazz, his career taking him of south of the border in 1969, where he became a Senior Lecturer at the University of Manchester.

He continued to be very active in jazz and, over the years, played with some great names including Jimmy Witherspoon, Eddie 'Cleanhead' Vinson, Roy Williams, Danny Moss, Bobby Wellins, Don Weller, Eddie Thompson, Henry Lowther, Gary Boyle, and Nikki Iles, amongst others. He also made recordings with the Don Rendell/Joe Palin Trio and the Alan Hare Big Band. Pete lists his favourite jazz musicians as *'Louis Armstrong, Count Basie and Clark Terry then'* and *'Kenny Wheeler, Woody Shaw and Duke Ellington later'*. When he told me this, I was surprised that he put Duke Ellington in his 'later' list, as I had always associated Pete with a great regard for the music of Duke Ellington, even when he first appeared on the Edinburgh jazz scene in the early 1960s.

232

The Pete Martin band's **guitarist, Lachlan MacColl**, was born in 1946 and spent much of his early childhood in Shetland, Orkney and Lanarkshire, before coming to Edinburgh, where he attended George Watsons Boys College between 1959 and 1964. Thereafter, he went on to study sculpture at Edinburgh College of Art before starting a career in teaching art in 1970. His mother was musical and a good singer and Lachlan, always in interested in sound, found himself particularly attracted towards stringed instruments. His older brother too, exerted an influence on his developing interests, when he brought home some recordings of Django Reinhardt and Mile Davis. Looking back, Lachlan says that he made an immediate connection with this music. He considers that he must have been at just the right age to begin to absorb the rich expressiveness and emotion, in what he describes as *'this timeless, powerful music'*, although the Reinhardt and Davis recordings were made almost twenty years apart. He also comments that he was unable to find the same depth of communication in the then popular 'trad', nor was he able to embrace the Rock 'n Roll, or beat music as it was then called, that he heard on Radio Luxembourg.

Lachlan was given a guitar by an older friend, who was already playing in a 'Shadows' type of band (ie modelled on the backing group of the singer Cliff Richard, the Shadows). This does not seem to have been a particularly distinguished instrument as he notes that, at that time, cheap, mail order guitars were not for the faint hearted! However, he got stuck in, made some progress and was eventually rewarded with the acquisition of better instrument. Lachlan was fortunate to be at school just a year behind Charles Alexandcr, already an accomplished guitarist and bass guitarist who was to have distinguished career in jazz. Charles Alexander gave the young Lachlan some invaluable initial guidance and advice and then he just got on with it; listcning and learning and trying to pick out the sound of the acoustic guitar on jazz big band recordings. He also became aware of the solo guitarists, those whose guitars were electrically amplified, noting particularly the influential Charlie Christian, who made his name initially with Benny Goodman, and the wonderfully lyrical George Barnes, who was to make so much memorable music with the cornet player, Ruby Braff. Lachlan cites as his main influences, guitarists such as Jim Hall who could accompany sensitively on electric guitar and the excitement and percussive drive of Herb Ellis, particularly when Ellis was with the Oscar Peterson trio. The dynamic playing of Wes Montgomery, a highly influential guitarist especially in the 1960s, was also to leave its mark on Lachlan's own playing and he treasures memories of hearing Montgomery in 1965 and Jim Hall in 1966, both in Ronnie Scott's Club in London, trips that he made with Charles Alexander.

It will have become clear from the above, that Lachlan MacColl's jazz interests and playing really put him beyond the scope of this book. However, he was another of these versatile and able musicians, like Ronnie Rae and Tom Finlay, who were more than capable of straddling the line between the older forms of jazz and the later music coloured by the changes brought by bebop. His own playing certainly reflects what he says above about guitarists who could accompany sensitively and he was, and is, a quietly effective rhythm player and soloist who always seemed to me to enhance and bring out the best in the musicians around him. Back in the 1960s when I first heard and played with Lachlan and the Pete Martin band, I thought of them as very much in the 'modernist' camp and moving in a different direction, away from the traditions of jazz and the music I was trying to play. Now in 2011, it is perfectly clear that their music was right in the main stream of jazz development, informed by and reflecting the more complex harmonies and rhythms of post-bebop jazz. They were just as concerned with lyrical improvisation, the characteristic altered pitch and sounds of jazz, expressive communication and swing, as were any of the earlier jazz stylists. In 2011, Lachlan MacColl remains a stalwart of the wider Edinburgh jazz community, still the thoughtful, sensitive guitarist he has been for almost fifty years in local jazz.

Charles Alexander (guitar), who was also associated with the group around Pete Martin, was born in Edinburgh on 10th May 1946 and, like several of the others, attended George Watson's Boys College. He had access to a ukulele

234

when he was about eleven years old but had graduated to a guitar by the time he was thirteen. He was to be largely self taught and, like most youngsters, he was at first attracted by the pop music of the day, teaching himself to play tunes associated with the Shadows and the American guitarist, Duane Eddy. He then found himself recruited into a school beat group called Unit 1, in which he was to play bass guitar. This was just before the Beatles era and the music they played mostly took the form of 'covers' of the recordings of popular stars of the day, including the Everley Brothers and the Shadows. This brought him into contact with another bass guitar player, Alastair 'Atty' Watson and also Mike Heron, the guitarist and singer later to make his name as a founder member of the Incredible String Band. Then was to come a seminal experience. Atty Watson let him hear some recordings of Django Reinhardt and he experienced one of these eureka moments, the like of which will crop up many times in this book, and his musical world was changed forever. This first exposure to the music of Django Reinhardt he found an overwhelming experience and the impact was such that he '...almost slid off the sofa'. Jazz was henceforth to be the music for Charles and he did not take long to acquire some Django LPs of his own.

His interest in jazz established, he was soon in contact with Pete Martin and Lachlan MacColl, both a year behind him at school, and quickly became involved in their early jazz activities. Although he was not really a member of the band, he remembers playing with the Pete Martin band at their first resident spot, at Rutherford's Bar in the High Street. I am fairly sure that these would be the sessions that Gerard Dott has spoken about, when he recalled playing with Pete's band at pub gigs when he was the only one in the band who was over the legal age for drinking! It was with Pete Martin and the group around him, that Charles was to develop his knowledge and interest in jazz.

It was not long before Charles made contact with many other Edinburgh jazzers, amongst whom was the pianist Alan Anderson who recruited him to play in his quartet. Keen to advance his playing, Charles fixed up a number of lessons with Dougie Campbell and was greatly taken, not only with Dougie's skill as a guitar player and teacher, but also his pawky humour. Apparently, Charles had landed a gig with an accordion player with whom he had never played but, one lunchtime in Paddy's Bar in Rose Street, discovered that Dougie had played with him. When he asked Dougie what the accordion player was like, Dougie's response was that he had never got over the death of George Formby! Speaking with Charles when writing this account, I was struck by a very perceptive comment made by him. He said that, not only had Dougie Campbell given him great encouragement, but it was also from him that he 'had learned how to learn'.

By now becoming very keen on jazz, although he had no thoughts at the time of ever making a career of it, he also took other musical work that came along and played many commercial gigs with the drummer Duncan Lonie, who ran a dance band. Others with whom Charles became involved were, not surprisingly, jazzers who were interested in the more modern and contemporary forms including Jack Finlay, Ronnie Dunn and Bill Mulholland, another fine guitarist and very capable jazz musician, although he also played other forms of music. Mulholland played in a top local beat group, the Dean Hamilton Combo, and his expertise and playing was a major influence on Charles who sometimes depped for Alan Coventry, the Dean Hamilton Combo's bass guitarist. There was plenty of jazz around in the Edinburgh of the middle 1960s and others with whom Charles would play many gigs were the trombonists Ken Ramage and Brian Keddie, bass player Ronnie Rae, vocalists Jimmy Gilmour and Jimmy Leslie and drummer, George Crookes.

Charles had attended Edinburgh University, where he ran the University Jazz Club, before graduating with a law degree, although he was never to practise in this field. A module in this course of study was in forensic medicine which brought him into further contact with Dougie Campbell, who worked in this field. In fact Charles' career was to be in music and jazz and in 1973, he left Edinburgh for the south where, for nine years, he was to be Director of the Jazz Society in London. With this organisation he produced hundreds of jazz events, from weekly jazz club meetings to major jazz festivals, including the Camden Jazz

Week. After his stint with the Jazz Society, he concentrated on his own playing career and was soon one of the leading jazz guitarists in London. His other major interest was in jazz education and he was to become jazz guitar tutor at the Richmond Adult Community College. In 1984, he was to found Jazzwise Publications, which markets instructional books on jazz, software and DVDs and which, later, was to publish the monthly Jazzwise Magazine and organise the annual Jazzwise Summer school.

Broadcasting was also to open its doors to this versatile and extremely able proselytiser on behalf of jazz and he presented seven series of BBC Radio 2's Six Silver Strings programmes and was to write and present the 12-part series The Guitar in Jazz for BBC Radio 3. His many and varied talents far from exhausted, Charles also ventured into the world of writing and in 1999 his book Masters of the Jazz Guitar was published by Balafon Books and, in addition, he was to co-author two books with Nick Freeth, The Acoustic Guitar and The Electric Guitar. A player of his calibre was bound to make many recordings and amongst his more recent have been the CDs When Lights Are Low (Deep River Records) and A Handful of Stars, on both of which he played with the saxophonist, Jeffrey Benson and Comparing Notes (33 Records) featuring his jazz guitar duo with Andy Robinson.

It may that some readers will see Charles Alexander's jazz activities as outwith the main subject of this book but, to my mind, like others we have heard about, he belongs right in the centre of the broad spectrum of jazz. His early inspiration came from Django Reinhardt and, partly through the influence of Brian Keddie and Pete Martin, he was soon captured by the wonderful music of the Basie and Ellington orchestras. The iconic jazz series broadcast by the BBC, Jazz 625, was another fertile source of inspiration and opened up the world of international jazz for Charles, as it did for so many of us in the 1960s. His contribution to jazz was immense, embracing jazz administration, publishing, writing and broadcasting, all in addition to his own fine playing and recording career. At the time of writing in 2011, Charles Alexander remains as active and busy as ever, thirty eight years on from leaving his home city and still London based. The attractions and opportunities of London were so often to act as a magnet, pulling south so many of Edinburgh's finest jazz talents but, when their influence and impact on a wider world of jazz is considered, it would be small-minded to be too parochial about it.

For a very long time, Edinburgh saw nothing of Pete Martin or the band then, as a result of an invitation from Roger Spence who was working with the Edinburgh International Jazz Festival, he got his All Stars band together for a re-union concert at the 2010 Festival. The re-union band with Pete (tpt), Gerard Dott (clt), George Howden (tbn), Lachlan McColl (gtr), Tim Pharoah (bs) and Allen Skinner (drms), was very close to the 1960s line-up. Jack Finlay was there too and played a few numbers with the band. They played extremely well, the concert was a sell-out and, for a little while at least, it was the 1960s again for some of us. Apart from anything else and unlike the rest of us, Pete still managed to look much as he had in the 1960s, if no longer quite 'about twelve'! With a bit of luck the Pete Martin All Stars will be back for more Festival appearances in the near future.

The 1960s was a mad time for most of us, the years of Pop Art and Carnaby Street, Flower Power and hippies smoking pot, love-ins and 'Ban the Bomb', but a good time too. There was plenty of traditional jazz around and a big following to go with it, even if most of them had little interest in or knowledge of jazz history. The 'Trad Boom' did not last all that long and was more or less over at a national level by 1962 and the advent of the Beatles. However, at a local level, 'Trad' remained popular and, whatever else it had done to the music, it had brought in a good number of new players. The excesses of some UK bands at the height of the craze, with daft uniforms and funny hats, tunes with little scope for jazz interpretation and little regard for what jazz really was, was sad and a bit depressing, but there was a good side as well. There was nothing to be lost and everything to be gained by a good humoured, lively presentation and the encouragement of the participation of the jazz punters who came along to listen. These two unforgettable Edinburgh band leaders excelled at this – Charlie McNair and Archie Sinclair, the great communicators - and the great entertainers.

Chapter IX

Return of a 'Gangster'

As the sixties rumbled on, the established Edinburgh bands rumbled on too then, in 1966, there came welcome news of the impending return of one of the great Edinburgh Revivalist pioneers. **Dave Paxton**, one of the original RHS Gang, had been working in the middle-east for about fifteen years, based variously in Bahrain, Italy and Lebanon, mostly in the oil industry. His main job had apparently been as a Stillman which, although it sounds as if he might have been making whisky, actually meant he was engaged in commissioning new refineries and training local personnel to operate them. There was a great sense of anticipation in the Edinburgh jazz scene when news of his imminent return spread, especially amongst those who remembered his playing in the 1940s. Those of us who were too young to remember these early days were left in no doubt that this was the return of very high class jazzer.

If my memory serves me right, preparations were made in advance to have a band ready assembled for him when he eventually arrived. It seems likely that Mike Hart and Bob Craig, fellow RHS Gangsters, and Ian Telford, would have been involved in this, and had agreed with Dave to have a band assembled, ready for his return. Whatever was going on in preparation, I remember being aware that a **Dave Paxton Jazz Band** was about to appear. Sure enough, the band duly appeared and I know that I depped on bass with them in the Crown Bar in June 1966. As I recall, the band was Ian 'Tello' Telford (tpt), Dave Paxton (clt), Bob Craig (tbn), Mike Hart (bjo/gtr), Donald Macdonald (bs – for whom I was depping) and Iain Forde (drms). I had been an established member of the Old Bailey band for a couple of years by this time and was well accustomed to playing with good players, but this was some band. Dave must have felt almost as if he had never been away.

The front line was outstanding, built around **Ian 'Tello' Telford's (trumpet)** fiery, early Armstrong inspired lead, with both Dave, playing wonderfully well, and Bob Craig integrating with the trumpet lead as to the manner born. Tello was the hottest trumpet player of my time in the Edinburgh jazz scene. Having said that, I have to acknowledge that I never heard Al Fairweather during his early days in Edinburgh and, by the time Al returned in the late 1980s, his health had deteriorated and he was a more subdued trumpeter than the glories of his playing on the 'McJazz' and other recordings. Tello was born in Glasgow in 1933 and came to live in Edinburgh at the age of eleven, after his father had died. He had a cousin called Norrie Sinclair for whom Tello's uncle had fixed up piano lessons. The cousin was not all that keen and sometimes, when he was supposed to be practicing tunes, Tello would take over on the piano and play the tune by ear, better than his cousin could manage from the written music. This was reassuring for the uncle until he came through one day and discovered that it not his son but his nephew who was playing. Clearly a kindly man, the uncle offered to pay for piano lessons for Tello who, however, turned down this musical opportunity.

Later, clearly of a musical bent and with a good ear and after completing his National Service in the RAF in 1954/55, Tello took up the cornet, teaching himself how to play. Shortly after this, he started to play in a band that Bob Craig was running and also with Mike Hart's Blueblowers, in the Shoestring Cafe. Speaking in 2010 with Tello's widow, Carol, she recalled that he had been keen to try a flugelhorn, and when his daughter Karen was offered a chance to play in her school band, Tello persuaded her to ask to try out a flugelhorn. He then appropriated the instrument for a try-out of his own! Later, liking the mellow sound of the bigger instrument, he bought one for himself.

Tello was clearly a player of considerable open-mindedness, interested in trying new things, and keen to explore the ins and outs of how jazz worked. Peter Davenport remembers hearing Tello and fellow trumpeter Kenny Jack experimenting with a two trumpet partnership, of the type used by Joe 'King' Oliver and the young Louis Armstrong in the Creole Jazz Band, and arguing furiously about who should play which notes.

Tello's confidence in the late 1950s was now sufficient to allow him to set up a band of his own and he put together an outfit with himself on trumpet, Karl Eckeval on clarinet, Clive Hamilton on guitar, Donald Macdonald on bass and Colin Cant on drums. Then, in 1960, came the formation of the Old Bailey band, of which Tello was the first choice and original trumpet player, as described in Chapter VIII. He left this band after about a year and again put together a band of his own, again including Karl Eckeval, Donald Macdonald and Colin Cant. This band played at monthly dances which took place in the common room of the Edinburgh College of Art. Iain Forde recalls that Karl Eckeval was replaced in this band by Al Clark, now playing sax, the reason being that Karl did not have a phone and could not be contacted about gigs! Quite understandably, he was not very happy about this and complained about it quite bitterly for some time!

In the meantime, Tello had met Dave Paxton on his occasional visits home from his work in the Middle East. Dave had complained of being starved of jazz records out East, and Tello had been sending a selection out to him. An article in the Edinburgh Evening News[129], unfortunately not dated, refers to Dave Paxton sitting in with the Charlie McNair band and playing a farewell to Rhythm Club members at a session where he was '...*backed by trumpeter Iain Telfer* (sic), *Mike Hart and the nucleus of the resident group'*. The article goes on *'Dave, who works in the Bahrain oil refineries, has come to the end of his three-month vacation during which time he has played with Old Bailey and the Climax band. Dave and Ian Telfer* (sic) *were renewing an old partnership at the club on Wednesday, as the last time Dave*

---

[129] 'Edinburgh Evening News', 'Jazz about Town', undated

was on leave – two years ago – they formed a very successful group'. It sounds very much as if the seeds of the future Dave Paxton Jazz Band, which was to become the New Society Syncopators, had been sown during Dave Paxton's spells of home leave.

The secret of the integrated togetherness of the Tello, Dave Paxton and Bob Craig front line, I am certain, was their complete familiarity with the style in which they were playing. Many years later in 2010, when I was a member of an Edinburgh Jazz Festival discussion panel on Edinburgh traditional jazz, someone from the floor contributed a comment that, in the early days, enthusiasts listened very intently to jazz records, until they knew every nuance and detail of the recordings. I am sure this was true and I can remember being astonished at the detailed knowledge that people like Tello, Dave and Bob had of the early Armstrong records. They knew every note played, every inflection, every subtlety, and were able to apply this, in arranged and improvised passages, to their own playing. Alastair Clark, in his obituary on Bob Craig in 1998, said about Bob and Dave that their playing partnership *'...was a particularly symbiotic and fruitful one, for Paxton, like Bob, felt that the creative apogee of 'traditional jazz' had been reached by the Armstrong Hot Five and Hot Seven groups'*[130]. This perceptive comment also applied, exactly in my view, to the equally symbiotic and fruitful partnership of Bob, Dave and Tello in this band of the late 1960s and early 1970s. The three of them had listened to and loved the same style of jazz all their lives, their knowledge of it was profound, and consequently they gelled completely as a playing unit. There was not much wrong with the rhythm section either, which also played as a proper unit, and romped along in good style.

Just what happened after this is lost in the mists of time. Dave Paxton was a magnificent player but never, to my knowledge, had any sort of hankering after a band leader's role, with all its trials and tribulations.

---

[130] Clark A, 'The Scotsman', 5th August 1998

**Dave Paxton – master clarinettist
(photo by permission of Jim Walker)**

Playing was his thing and I think that it would have been his playing on which he would have wanted to concentrate. Mike Hart, as so often, was really the driving force behind the organisation of the band and Bob Craig, not Dave Paxton, led the band on the bandstand. Eventually, the band changed its name and became known as the New Society Syncopators and it was under this name that they really established themselves in Edinburgh. They rightly became very popular and had a big following, with a number of pub based residencies and plenty of away gigs. The band was to become known affectionately as The Syncs.

In the early 1970s and after the breakup of the 1960s version of the Old Bailey band, I was fortunate enough to have a spell of about a year playing with the Syncs in their early form. The bass player, Donald Macdonald, had decided to take up saxophone and had gone off to concentrate on this, and I took his place. By this time, there were changes in respect of the drummer as well and Chick Murray came in for a while. However, great drummer though he was, his Swing style was not really right for this band and after a while, Billy Alison replaced him, and then a drummer called Vic Reynolds. These two were both fine drummers, in Billy Alison's case an exceptional one, but again their more modern styles were not really right for the band. In the end, Iain Forde, whose style was just right, came back into the band. He had only left in the first place because, for a while, he was unable to play all the gigs because of work and family commitments. Apparently Iain's welcome return came about at the behest of Alastair Clark, who was about to present the band on Radio Scotland from the BBC studios in Queen Street. Alastair was in a position to stipulate that Iain and Donald Macdonald, both of whom had not long left the band, should return for the broadcast, so that the band was as it had been when the broadcast was first arranged. This took place in late 1969 and 1970 and, although I had just replaced Donald, it was absolutely right that he returned for the radio show. The broadcast resulted in some recordings which are still around and which, I believe, were simply made by someone recording from their radio. It is a great shame that these recordings have never been made available more generally, as the music is terrific. Donald Macdonald played, not me, so I have no stake in saying this; in my view they are among the best recordings made by an Edinburgh band in my time. They only exist, as far as I know, on the private copies made of the radio programme and it is unlikely that they will have survived in the BBC archives. Iain Forde gave me a copy of a few of the tracks, and the whole band, but Dave Paxton in particular, is in top form.

Drummer Billy Alison, who was born in 1933, was another of the Edinburgh jazzers who had a broad interest in jazz and was able to play in both traditional and more modern forms of the music. He had learned pipe band drumming when in the Scouts, when he was ten years old. In 1947, at age only fourteen, he had toured in Holland with his Scout band, the 148th Troop St Cuthbert's, and had recorded at Radio Hilversun. After leaving the Scouts, Billy bought a drum kit, put in some serious practice, then went along to a 'come as you please' session at the Palais de Dance in Fountainbridge. Here he sat in with the Jimmy Walker Quintet, on Kenny Duff's drum kit. Kenny Duff, impressed with Bill's playing, soon handed on a gig at St Cuthbert's Hall, near the Art College, at which Billy made his debut. After this, Bill teamed up for a while with an accordion player called Johnny Robertson.

By 1951, he was playing at a modern jazz club in India Buildings with Ron Carruthers and Alex Tait but was then called up for National Service and posted to Germany. Here he formed what he called 'a camp trio' (the mind boggles - just how camp were they?!) which played at mess dances and other gigs outside the camp. Back home again after demob, Billy joined Tony Fusco's dance band, which played in the Picardy Place Hall, and was involved in other dance gigs with Fred Murray (bs) and Fred Duligal (ten sax), who later went to Canada. He also played at American bases both with and for, keyboard player Bert Valentine. In 1956 Billy joined Pete Seaton and bass player Gerry Rossi at the Berkeley Restaurant in Lothian Road and then moved to the Pallais de Dance, with the Hal Collins Quartet, again with Seaton and Rossi and leader Hal Collins on guitar. Later he was with Pete Seaton again, this time at the George Hotel, where he remained for the next thirteen years.

It was during this time that Billy had some time off for various sessions with the BBC including, in 1962, programmes such as 'Variety Ahoy!', which went out from the naval dockyard at Rosyth, and 'Piano Provided', which went out from the Queens Street studios. There was a four month break in 1963 from the George Hotel when Billy, together with Edinburgh jazzers Tom Finlay (pno) and Ronnie Dunn (bs), went cruising to the West Indies, playing as a Latin American Trio, teamed up with an orchestra as part of what many musicians on the boats were to call 'Geraldo's Navy'. In 1965, Billy recorded the programme 'For Your Entertainment', again from the BBC studios in Queens Street. Much later, in the 1970s, Billy was joined at the George Hotel by pianist Alex Shaw and bassist Ronnie Rae, in what was obviously a high class jazz trio. By 1973, this trio had moved to Henry Spurway's hotel, the Elm Tree, in West Calder and, during this period, recorded at the STV Gateway studios in Leith Walk for Bill Tennant's 'Come Tuesdays' programme. In addition, there were a number of University lunch time sessions when Billy accompanied some of the British modern jazz aristocracy, including Tubby Hayes and Joe Harriot. There was also work with various small groups between 1983 and 1986, during the Edinburgh International Jazz Festivals.

Never really a traditional jazz musician, Billy was, like the guitarist Dougie Campbell, one of the Edinburgh musicians who were flexible enough to play in many styles. He was to demonstrate this flexibility much later when, at the turn of the 1980s, he played with Al Fairweather, Dave Paxton, trombonist Bill Smith and pianist Ian Scott, at the Ritz Hotel in Grosvenor Street at Haymarket. Technically excellent, Billy Alison was much admired by fellow drummers and was a tower of strength in any band with whom he played.

Geraldo's Navy
Tom Finlay, Billy Alison, Ronnie Dunn
(from the collection of Billy Alison, photographer unknown)

As well as their various residencies in venues such as The Wee Windies in the High Street and the Lochewe Hotel in Royal Terrace, the Syncs played many away gigs and, on one of a series of gigs at Ledlannet House in Fife, the band shared the bill with the American mouth organ maestro, Larry Adler. Sometimes the indefatigable Jackie MacFarlane was added to the band as vocalist and there was one memorable night when the band, with Jackie, played at Stirling University. This was while I was a member of the band and we shared the bill with a very good but exceptionally loud rock band called, if memory serves me right, Tear Gas. The event was absolutely packed but even the students wilted in the face of the rock band's volume and they all hastily retreated to the bar in the next room. When we went on, by comparison with the rock band's awesome stage presence, we must have looked really feeble and pathetic. The six of us standing there, with just one microphone and a tiny combo amplifier for Jackie's vocals, and surrounded by several acres of rock band gear.

Alastair Clark wrote it up in the Scotsman the next weekend and said *'There were four staccato foot stomps and the New Society Syncopators, fired by the hot coals of Ian Telford's trumpet, were surging forward like a steam engine that shows no sign of ever stopping'*. To the amazement of the band, the students came pouring back into the hall, packed themselves about twelve deep around the bandstand, cheering and yelling their approval. As Alastair Clark reported[131], the students roared appreciation *'...and finally hoisted Jackie MacFarlane shoulder-high and carried him out of the hall like the conquering hero he was'*. Clark then described the band's Thursday night residency in the Royal Mile Centre saying *'There's a curious quality of incipient decadence rather than revival about this setting, but the jazz is as rich and meaty as any you can find in these islands'*. He then continued *'The Syncopators take Jelly Roll Morton, the King Oliver Band and the Armstrong Hot Five and Hot Seven as favoured prototypes and the reproduction is uncannily accurate and vibrantly alive in numbers like 'Snake Rag' and 'Wild Man Blues''*. Alastair also compared

---

[131] Clark A, 'Trad crosses the sound barrier', 'Scotsman' September 1972

the vigorous heat of the Syncs performance to some recordings of British trad bands during the 'Trad Boom', commenting on how 'namby-pamby' the latter had become.

It is hard now to track just what happened within the ranks of the New Society Syncopators after this, not helped by the fact that I had dropped out of the band at the end of 1972, to be replaced by Norrie Bell. Gradually the original personnel left the band, beginning with Tello, and the sound of the original band was lost forever. Mike Hart was running the band and, as the originals left, he was able to bring in top class replacements but, being jazz musicians, each had his own style and sound and inevitably, with every change in personnel, the band sound changed. The band, in spite of the changes, was to continue very successfully through the 1970s until they amalgamated with the re-born Old Bailey band, but that is story for another chapter.

Later, Tello played in a band at the White Cockade in Rose Street, a band which included Donald Macdonald, now on sax, and Ken Macdonald, Donald's brother, on bass. Carol Telford recalls that this band 'went modern'! After this, Tello joined the Charlie McNair Jazz Band, playing second trumpet to Charlie. I remember hearing the band at this time and noticing how well Tello understood the role of the second trumpet, no doubt the outcome of his much earlier experiments in a two trumpet line-up with Kenny Jack. Other Edinburgh bands tried two trumpets, but none in my view managed to use the system as convincingly as when Tello was involved. Ian 'Tello' Telford died on 5th April 2002 at the age of 68, following a lengthy period of ill health and after being inactive in jazz for a number of years.

Bill Salmond (banjo and guitar), who was born in Edinburgh in May 1941, had attended the Royal High School but was not influenced at all by the notable jazz heritage of the school. In the mid-1950s, in common with so many of his generation, he became interested in skiffle music and Lonnie Donegan, and this led to him forming a skiffle group in about 1957. In 1958, a friend took him to the Moir Hall in the Pleasance, where he heard the early Climax Jazz Band. Then, a year later, he went through to Glasgow to hear the George Lewis band, then on tour in the UK, and this was to be the major influence on his playing and playing career. Bill was to remain loyal to the purist style for the rest of his career and, as a banjo player, he took for his main models, George Lewis' banjoist Lawrence Marrero and two other Americans, George Guesnon and Emanuel Sayles.

As the 1950s came to an end and the 1960s began, Bill played with several bands, including one run by the trombone player Bill Munro, and another led by the clarinet player, Jack St Clair. Later, he had a shot at running a band under his own name. I remember playing with one of his bands in 1961, under the name **The Savoy New Orleans Jazz Band**, in Rutherford's Bar in the High Street and at the Lotus Club in Musselburgh. This band included a fine trumpet player called Brian Smith who had put in a spell with the Climax band and who, unfortunately, soon departed for London. In addition, there was Grant Liddell who played clarinet, a drummer called Gordon Thompson and a trombone player called Alan Quinn who, like Bill, was still an important Edinburgh jazzer several decades later, although in Alan's case with a lengthy break in the middle. I can remember going to a practice session with this band of Bill's. Rather oddly, it took place in the basement of the Edinburgh Stock Exchange, entry to which, if I remember rightly, had been arranged by Grant Liddell. I also remember this band of Bill's playing alongside the Climax band at the Mardi Gras Club, which was located in the North Merchiston Boy's Club in Watson Crescent and, I think, run by the Climax band bass player, Jim Young.

The Climax band had a residency at that time in the cellar of Jim Young's house and, not surprisingly Bill, with his interest in purist jazz, used to go along to listen. When the banjo player Alan Ritchie left the Climax to go to London, Bill was the obvious replacement and he joined the band in late 1961, joining Jim Petrie (tpt), Jack Weddell (tbn), Jake McMahon (clt), Jim Young (bs) and Pete Ritchie (drms). This was a strong line-up and the Climax remained a formidable band in the purist tradition. When speaking of this time in his jazz career, Bill, like others, made the point that there had been constant changes in the local bands, as National Service interrupted the playing lives of the older band members. However, it was now the early 1960s and

National Service had become a thing of the past, allowing the Climax band to settle down. Bill was to remain with the band until 1968 when he finally moved on, his departure from the band triggered by one of those typical squabbles that can break out even in the most settled of bands. On this occasion, it was something to do with the band being asked to play over the agreed time at a gig and one band member refusing, because he had to get home to allow the baby sitter to go off duty! Bill was not involved directly in this particular uproar but I suspect that, with his earlier experience of band leading, he was already beginning to think it was time once more to put together a band of his own.

It was then, in early 1969, that Bill put together the first of his bands under the name **The Louisiana Ragtime Band**, the band which he was still running 40 years later. The first version of the band had Fraser Gauld (tpt), Gerard Dott (clt), George Howden (tbn), Willie Mack (bs) and Chick Davis (drms) in addition to Bill himself on banjo. The new band's first gig was in the Cephas Club in February 1969, practices took place during the next month and they started on their first residency on 17th March 1969, in the Lothian Bar in Lothian Road. Chick Davies dropped out after just a few months and was replaced by Iain Forde and then Pete Ritchie, before John Nicholson (later known as John McGlynn) took over. Clarinettist Gerard Dott left in about July 1970, to be replaced by George Gilmour. Other residences held by the band around this time were at Merryman's Cellar in Hanover Street, between March and July 1970, after which they moved on to the Haymarket Bar. Many other gigs were played, including the Cephas Club, which was a regular every month for a while, the YMCA and the Kirkcaldy Jazz Club. Later, while holding down a gig at the Carlton Hotel, a trumpeter from Dundee, Robin 'Gus' Ferguson, came into the band for a while. Later still, Bill featured his first 'trumpetless' front line, a formula that he was to use many times in the future, when the clarinettist George Duncan and trombonist Jack Weddell fronted the band and shared the lead duties.

It is much to Bill's credit that, if he was unable to find a player who suited the style he was pursuing, he would often do without, rather than compromise the band sound. Bill also had an unusual strategy he occasionally used to recruit new band members. If there was no one around that seemed a good fit, he was perfectly prepared to create a suitable candidate, by persuading someone interested in the music to take up an instrument. It was by this method that Bill acquired his bass player, Willie Mack and drummer, Eric Jamieson and in both cases, he even put them in touch with appropriate local assistance while they were starting. In 1972, Bill also had the initiative to place an advert in the Evening News for a piano player. He had two applicants, both with the surname Scott and both came for an audition. As a result of this, Graham Scott, then still a schoolboy, got the job.

Bill Salmond's Louisiana Ragtime Band or the LRB as it became known, became a fixture on the Edinburgh jazz scene and, although there were quite a number of changes in the band over the years, it was always a good, driving band, firmly committed to early New Orleans jazz. It would be impossible now to list in chronological order, all the various changes in personnel, especially as some musicians had several separate spells with the band. However, a listing of those who played with the band gives an idea of Bill's success in keeping his band going for so long:

Trumpet: Fraser Gauld, Gus Ferguson, Dave Strutt, Kenny Milne, Brian Robertson
Reeds: Gerard Dott, George Duncan, Dave Paxton, George Gilmore, Ian Boyter
Trombone: George Howden, Jack Weddell, Alan Quinn, Simon Carlyle, Bob Craig, Martin Bennett
Piano: Graham Scott
Banjo/gtr: Bill Salmond (leader)
Bass: Jim Young, Adrian Bull, Willie Mack, Robin Galloway, Graham Blamire, Bill Brydon
Drums: Chick Davis, Iain Forde, Pete Ritchie, John Nicolson (McGlynn), Jimmy Elliott, Kenny Orr, Roy Dunnett, Eric Jamieson, Kenny Milne

I played with the band between 1985 and 1991 and was fortunate to be with the band when it reached several high spots in its history. Dave Paxton, who had left the Society Syncopators, had come in on clarinet and was to stay with the LRB for eighteen years, still playing wonderfully well. Bob Craig was on trombone for quite a lengthy period and then he was replaced by Martin Bennett, a vastly experienced English trombone player, who was also a good singer. Bill had recruited a young, inexperienced trumpet player who was to be with the band for some years, before going on to lead bands of his own. He was Brian Robertson and, with Martin Bennett directing the front line, Dave, Martin and Brian made a good and compatible unit.

In 1987, Bill took the band to the Enkhuisen Jazz Festival in Holland, and I never heard the band play better than on this occasion. We also made several trips to play at the new Bute Jazz Festival, on the Isle of Bute in the Firth of Clyde, where the band helped to launch this new venture and establish it on the Scottish jazz festival rota. This came about largely because Phil Mason, a red-hot New Orleans trumpet player from the south, had moved up to live on the Isle of Bute. Phil had been at University in Dublin with Martin Bennett and had played for years with the famous Max Colllie Rhythm Aces and then the Pete Allen Band, before basing himself in Scotland, from where he toured with his own band. Phil made many trips to play with the LRB, mostly at their residency in the Navaar House Hotel in Newington. This was always a well-attended gig and Phil's presence did us no harm at all and, I feel sure, was a positive factor in Brian Robertson's rapid progress on trumpet. Phil had founded the Bute Jazz Festival, a very popular festival that was to be a fixture in the Scottish jazz calendar for many years.

Over the years, the LRB played at festivals on the Continent (Enkhuisen, Gothenburg, Celerina, Davos) and toured in both Holland and Sweden. They were to be stalwarts of the Edinburgh International Jazz Festival and also featured at other UK jazz festivals including Orkney, Bute, Keswick, Largs and Kirkcudbright. They were selected to back a number of visiting stars, including pianist Alton Purnell, drummer Barry Martyn, trumpeter Kid Shiek Colar and sax players Sam Lee and Benny Watters. The famous American pianist Johnny Guarnieri played with the band on one occasion and, at the Navaar House Hotel, the drummer Barrett Deems and bass player Arvel Shaw, both former members of the Louis Armstrong All Stars, turned up one evening and sat in with the band. After over forty years, Bill Salmond's Louisiana Ragtime Band remains a Scottish jazz institution and shows no signs of stopping.

In finding **Graham Scott (piano)** through a newspaper advert, Bill Salmond introduced a jazzer who was to make a solid impact and who, almost as much as Bill himself, was to be a constant presence in the LRB. Graham was born in Australia on 27th March 1954 and was educated at Edinburgh's Daniel Stewart's College. He had piano lessons from age seven until he was fourteen and, at school, played bass drum in the pipe band. He was only seventeen when he was taken on by Bill and had responded to the newspaper advert which had asked for a 'bluesy piano player', which, naturally, we used to pretend to believe was actually for a 'boozy piano player'. In fact, Graham's playing was very much influenced by the blues and he had played a selection of 'Boogie Woogie' tunes at his audition. He had clearly listened to Boogie Woogie piano players such as Meade Lux Lewis and played a strong, two handed style which always reminded me of the playing of the American, Art Hodes. In addition to playing piano, Graham's experience of playing the bass drum made him a valuable addition to the various parade bands that often featured at outdoor events. These were marching brass bands in the New Orleans tradition, and usually organised by Jim Young (The Auld Reekie Parade Band) or the drummer, Kenny Milne (The Criterion Parade Band).

As well as his long term loyalty to the LRB, Graham also played with an excellent band put together in the 1980s by the returning Al Fairweather and then, in the 1990s, with Mike Hart's Edinburgh Ragtimers. As well as making all the festival gigs with the LRB, he also toured in the 1980s in Germany, Holland, Belgium and Switzerland with the band of Colin 'Kid' Dawson, a well known New Orleans styled trumpeter from Newcastle and did the annual Ascona Festival in Switzerland with the Criterion Parade Band. He joined the LRB in 1971 and forty years later in 2011, he was still there.

Bill Salmond's Louisiana Ragtime Band in Basin Street in 1987
L-R Graham Scott (pno), Dave Paxton (clt), the author (bs), Bill Salmond (bjo), Roy Dunnett (drms), Brian Robertson (tpt), Martin Bennett (tbn)
(from the collection of the author, photographer unknown)

Willie Mack (bass) was born in Douglas in Lanarkshire on 10th November 1943 and had a grandfather and father who both played pedal organ. His early interest in jazz came about through hearing the music of the British traditional bands during the 'trad boom' of the late 1950s and it led to a particular interest in the music of George Lewis, one of the great figures of the New Orleans Revival. Long before he ever played bass, Willie was approached by Bill Salmond's father, Bill Salmond senior, who enquired if he might be interested in playing bass in the Climax band, in which Bill junior was playing. I suspect that this was an example of Bill junior's laudable willingness to seek recruit's to the music he loved by encouraging individuals to take up an instrument. Take up the bass Willie did and, before long, he made his debut with the Climax band in 1965 and also played with a folk dance band called the Reivers, led by Adrian Bull. Adrian Bull was also to make an appearance on the Edinburgh jazz scene as a bass player but played mandolin in the Reivers.

Willie Mack then became a founder member of Bill Salmond's Louisiana Ragtime Band in the late 1960s and from 1980 to 1985 was also to be a member of the Spirits of Rhythm, splitting the bass playing duties with Robin Galloway. With these established purist styled bands, he had welcome opportunities to play with New Orleans greats Alton Purnell (pno), Kid Shiek Colar (tpt), Sammy Lee and Capt. John Handy (sax) and Teddy Riley (tpt). Willie visited New Orleans in 1970 and sat in with a band of veteran jazzers in Preservation Hall, including Kid Thomas Valentine (tpt), Andrew Morgan (ten sax), Orange Kellin (clt), Earl Humphrey (tbn), Las Edegran (pno) and the English ex-pat Barry Martyn (drms). Willie recorded with both the LRB and the Spirits[132] and was on the Spirits' LP 'Sam Lee meets the Spirits of Rhythm' in 1974. A banker in his day job, Willie Mack retired from playing, although not from listening to jazz, in 1985 and remains an active supporter of the local jazz scene.

George Gilmour (clarinet) was born in Edinburgh in March 1947, took up clarinet at the age of eighteen and later added both soprano and alto saxophones to his musical armoury. His playing was inspired and influenced by the playing of Sydney Bechet and later by the playing of George Lewis. He was recruited into the Climax band in the mid-1960s, replacing the London bound Jake McMahon, before joining Bill Salmond's Louisiana Ragtime Band. George had been invited for an audition with Bill Salmond before being offered a place in the band and recalls that, after playing some clarinet pieces, he began to open up his soprano sax case. Bill, at that time a strict New Orleans man to whom saxophones were anathema, said quietly but

---

[132] See discography Appendix

firmly *'You won't be needing that '* and George, just as quietly, shut the soprano back in its case again!

His style was ideal for both bands and he was a worthy successor to Jake McMahon in the Climax band. He was also active in the parade band scene and, being a very strong player with a big sound, he always sounded marvellous soaring over the typical hot, brassy ensemble of the parade bands. Powerful though his playing was, George was also able to play with great tenderness and feeling and I have always felt that he was an extremely soulful player. From the age of about thirty, George worked as a light house keeper and spells of two years in the west of Scotland and six years in the Orkney Islands, kept him out of jazz for about twelve years. However, a posting to the St Abb's Head light in East Lothian followed by a spell on the relief rota allowed him to begin playing in Edinburgh again around 1990. He re-joined the Climax band and, with them, made three trips to play at the Ascona Jazz Festival in Switzerland. He also played with Violet Milne's Spirits of Rhythm and, at one point, was playing with them on Sundays between 1.00pm and 4.00pm at the Stair Arms Hotel near Pathhead, before driving into Edinburgh to play with the Climax band, at a venue in Royal Circus, in the evening. In 1991, he replaced Dave Paxton in Bill Salmond's Louisiana Ragtime Band, with whom he played at the Gothenburg Jazz Festival in Germany in 1994. George stayed with this band for about seventeen years, eventually leaving in 2008. Since then, he has mostly played occasional gigs with a variety of bands but still, at the time of writing in 2011, plays regularly with Kenny Milne's Criterion Brass Band.

One of the drummers who played with the Louisiana Ragtime Band was **John Nicolson (drums)**. He was born on 8th September 1953 and was yet another in the long line of Royal High School jazzers, John recalling that was he at school with *'...a scary number of other musos'*. It was at school that he began his career as a drummer, becoming a member of the school pipe band, although, reflecting on this in 2011, he remarked that he had no idea why he had joined, adding *'...it wasn't for the clothes...'*. As far as jazz was concerned, his first drum influence was Joe Morello, the partially blind drummer who made his name with the Dave Brubeck quartet. In spite of this decidedly modern model, John's first Edinburgh jazz gig was with the Louisiana Ragtime Band in 1969, in the Lothian Bar, Lothian Road. This gig was a regular Monday evening spot for the band and John remembers the reward for his weekly contribution as '...*ten bob* (50p)*, a pint and a pie'*. Other Louisiana gigs were in the Cephas Club, under St George's West Church in Shandwick Place, and an appearance at the Usher Hall, where they played in front of two thousand Girl Guides!

Rapidly establishing his reputation as an able drummer, John soon began to expand his playing activities and it was not long before he started in the more general run of gigs, playing for weddings, dance bands, the infamous miners' clubs and what he describes as *'cocktail stuff'* in various Edinburgh hotels. His spell with the Louisiana band was followed by work with the Charlie McNair band, Ken Ramage's band and, in a more modern jazz setting, gigs with the fine sax player, Gordon Cruikshank. In addition, he played with piano player Jimmy Hendry in a swinging trio that included Ronnie Rae on bass, this gig being in what was then the Dragonara Hotel, at Belford Bridge. Further jazz gigs were with the Society Syncopators and the Jazz Advocates, both in their Old Bailey format and their later manifestation, the Scottish Jazz Advocates. It was with this latter band that John made trips to the Sacramento Jazz Jubilee in 1983 and 1984, depping for Chick Murray, and also appearing on the Scottish Jazz Advocates 1984 recording, 'All in Perfect Working Order'[133], on which he plays on two tracks along with Ronnie Rae, who also made the trip, covering for me on bass. In the 1980s, John was a regular in the programme of the Edinburgh International Jazz Festival (see chapter XII), in which he had some great jazz experiences, playing with famous names including reeds man Benny Waters, trombone legend George Chisholm, the great piano player Teddy Wilson, bebop trumpeter Red Rodney and the inimitable Humphrey Lyttelton. He Canada he played with

---

[133] See discography appendix

clarinetist Peanuts Hucko and, in Sacramento, played briefly with Bob Haggard, one time bass player with Bob Crosby's Bobcats, famous for his bass and drums feature with Ray Baduk, 'Big Noise from Winnetka'.

Although a highly capable and well-regarded jazz drummer, John had few other chances to record in jazz settings but his versatility enabled him to make many recordings in a wide range of other styles including Country and Western, rock and pop and radio commercials. Having embarked on an acting career in 1975, John also performed in musical theatre with Young Lyceum, Wildcat and 7:84. He later changed his name to **John McGlynn**, for professional purposes, and appeared in a range of TV series including 'Taggart', 'Soldier Soldier', 'Silent Witness' and 'All Creatures Great and Small'. John eventually left Edinburgh, basing himself in the London area, his departure a considerable loss to the Edinburgh jazz scene. After more than twenty five years in the south, he turned up again on a visit to Edinburgh in 2011, when he came along to the Jazz and Jive Club (see chapter XVII). He sat in with my band, the Maid of the Forth Stompers, demonstrating that he had lost none of his ability to swing or his energetic ability to drive a band along.

We have just met someone who moved away from Edinburgh but our next jazzer moved in the opposite direction. **Simon Carlyle (trombone, sousaphone)** was born in Cambridge on 10th September 1945 and moved with his family to Bristol when he was about four years old. He attended Bristol Grammar School before embarking on a six year course in Veterinary Medicine at Cambridge University, followed by a further three years completing a PhD. He then became a lecturer in veterinary pharmacology at the Royal Dick Veterinary College in Edinburgh from 1973 to 2006. His musical activities began when, as Simon puts it, his parents '...*inflicted piano lessons on him...*' at the age of about six. However, he had managed to escape from this to the Sea Mills Junior School Brass Band, when he was in about primary five. Here he became one of two cornet players under the enthusiastic direction and tuition of a Mr Ellison. Later, at Grammar school, he was to find sitting counting innumerable silent bars waiting for the next trumpet entry to be less than stimulating and, after a while, gave up on his budding orchestral career.

However, he was not to be lost to music for long and soon began to listen to some jazz and blues around Bristol, including the Acker Bilk band, in addition to which he also picked up on recorded jazz on the radio. One recording that particularly made an impression was the King Oliver band recording of 'Riverside Blues', which he heard on a history of jazz programme, and he lost little time in purchasing some jazz records of his own. A Chris Barber recording of 'Brownskin Mama' was one of the first, to be followed by EPs[134] featuring Bunk Johnson and Louis Armstrong. Shortly after this, an English teacher at his school started up a school jazz band as an evening club, and Simon, hastily recalling his brass playing skills, joined on cornet. This was clearly a fairly eclectic outfit, as Simon recalls them attempting written arrangements of material ranging from Fats Waller's 'Shortnin' Bread' to Thelonious Monk's 'Blue Monk'. However, it was to be at University where his career in traditional jazz kicked off in earnest.

Someone put up a notice asking for volunteers to form a band for the College's Rag Day float and Simon, discovering that one Dick Wharton was ahead of him with his trumpet, volunteered to get his father to send up an ancient trombone that had been liberated from the Bristol University's lumber room. He has little recall of the Rag Day event, apart from the grief they had to endure from the music shop from which they had hired the tuba. Apparently they were less than delighted about the large number of dents that it had acquired from pennies thrown into it by the crowd. Clearly undaunted by this unfortunate experience, the band decided to continue as the South Side Jazz Band and they struggled on with a late 1920s repertoire that Simon describes as 'both eclectic and

---

[134] It has just occurred to me that some readers made be flummoxed by this term. While 78 rpm records played at 78 rpm and had one track on each side, EPs were 'extended play' records that played at 45 rpm and usually had 4 tracks, 2 on each side. LPs, or long play records, were even more impressive, playing at $33^1/_3$ rpm and having anything up to 6 or 7 tracks on each side. My English teacher at school, 'Kipper' Heron, was greatly taken by EPs, referring to them enthusiastically as '4 sided records'!

esoteric', including such immortal gems as 'Barataria', 'Bring it on Home to Grandma' and 'Root Hog, or Die', as well as better known stuff like 'Sobbin' Blues' and 'Diga Diga Doo'. Later, when Dick left, he switched back to cornet and the band did several May Balls and other gigs, during which they warmed up for Lulu, played as support to the Chris Barber band and even spotted a young Prince Charles in the audience at one point.

Simon was eventually the only one left of the University band, his nine years being an unusually lengthy student career, and he began playing gigs with some of the town bands. As all of these were well supplied with trumpet and trombone players, he borrowed a double bass and re-launched his playing career with the Savoy Jazz Band. This does not seem to have gone all that well, as he lasted only the one session. However, a man of considerable tenacity and fortitude, he found that a month's practice '...*increased his mean survival time dramatically...*' and was soon playing quite regularly again. On completion of his PhD, he departed for his lecturing career in Edinburgh.

Simon says that he did not really model his playing on anyone in particular, which is not all that surprising as he would have needed a whole list of models to cover all the instruments he had tried. However, he did listen to a lot of recordings of the early recording bands including those of King Oliver, Armstrong, Jelly Roll Morton, Armand Piron, Fletcher Henderson, Jabbo Smith and many others. When pushed, he selected the great trombonist J C Higginbotham, whose huge sounding, shouting playing was such a wonderful feature of the Luis Russell band of the late 1920s and early 1930s, and believes that he developed his own tendency towards declamatory phrasing from him.

Now in Edinburgh, it was not long before he found his way into the local jazz scene, tracking down a band playing in the upstairs room of a pub on the Royal Mile, which seemed to be run by Mke Hart and included Jim Petrie (tpt) and Jack Weddell (tbn). Simon's first Edinburgh gig was in the famous White Cockade in Rose Street and was a jam session in which he found himself playing trumpet alongside Charlie McNair. This experience persuaded him into beating a hasty and prudent retreat to the trombone and it was on this instrument that he found himself sitting in with Bill Salmond's Louisiana Ragtime Band, at their sessions in the Minto Hotel. What became quite regular sittings in clearly went well and it was not long before he was invited to join the band. This was during one of the LRB's periods when they did not use a trumpeter and Simon was required to play lead on trombone. At first George Duncan played beside him on clarinet and then he was replaced by Dave Paxton. Simon described sitting next to Dave Paxton as a period he looks back to as both a pleasure and a privilege. The band played about twice a week and moved around a number of venues over the next few years. Eventually, Kenny Milne came into the band on trumpet and, after a brief period of experimentation with the expanded front-line, Simon found himself surplus to requirements allowing him, as he says, '...to spend more time with my family...'

The next opening for Simon came when Jim Young assembled his Auld Reekie Parade Band, in which Simon played trombone, but when Kenny Milne started up his Criterion Brass Band, it was time to dust off the old sousaphone he had picked up for next to nothing in Cambridge and had had in the attic ever since. This seems to have been around the time that the French band, L'Orpheon Celeste was making a big impression in the Edinburgh Jazz Festival (which puts it around 1979/80) and Simon believes that it was their example that inspired the the first version of the Diplomats of Jazz. This new four-piece echoed the format of the French band, with Jim Petrie (tpt, vocs), Andy Hampton (clt), Jock Westwater (bjo) and Simon on sousaphone. Rehearsals in Jock's print shop in Juniper Green gave Simon a chance to work out what he should be doing on his brass bass before they launched themselves on the Edinburgh public. Simon spent a couple of years with the Diplomats before being replaced by Bill Brydon. From that point on, his playing became less, except for a couple of years around 2000, when he played with Mike Westwater's Tweed Valley band. Currently, in 2011, his most regular gigs are with the Criterion Brass Band, although he adds wryly that he does occasional depping jobs with other bands, especially if it is an outside gig with a chance of rain.

Arriving from the south, Simon Carlyle had soon established himself on the Edinburgh jazz scene and, although he was really a multi-instrumentalist, it was on the scarce sousaphone that he really made his mark. However, it was on trombone that he played on the LRB's 1976 recording, which has become something of a New Orleans collector's item. He was also on a number of recordings made by the Criterion Brass Band, which will be found in the discography, and on some jazz festival recordings made by the Tweed Valley band. He has also played in other forms of music and has recorded Early Music CDs with the Edinburgh Renaissance Band and, in 2005, played with a klezmer band called She'koyokh, on Czech radio. Happily, in 2011, he is still around and recently filled in for me with the Maid of the Forth Stompers. Soon, I hope to persuade him along to a session or two to sit in, although on which instrument that will be must remain a mystery until he actually turns up.

Chapter X

How to eat Stovies While Singing 'Georgia on my Mind'

Before leaving the 1960s, a look at the career of **Alan Anderson (piano)** will give a very good insight into the Edinburgh jazz world, particularly the University jazz scene, of that time and beyond. It also gives a good indication of the wider jazz context in which Edinburgh traditional jazz existed, both in terms of the more modern forms of the music and geographically, in the neighbouring Border counties. Although Alan himself was to play mostly in the more modern styles, he did play in traditional bands and he was yet another of that versatile, able group of jazzers who were equipped to play in a broad range of styles. Alan was born in Ilfracombe in Devon on 22nd June 1943 but, by the time he was three months old, the family had moved to Scotland. His early schooling was at a variety of junior schools in the south of the country, before he settled in at Berwickshire High School in Duns. From there, he was to advance to Edinburgh University, from which he would eventually graduate with a law degree. Both the Anderson parents were interested in music, Alan's mother playing piano and church organ and his father keen on the dance band music of his era.

Alan can remember hearing jazz on the radio, later realising that this would have been BBC Jazz Club which, in those days, followed the football results on a Saturday afternoon. He had piano lessons between the ages of seven and thirteen, which he loathed, and never sat any exams or got any grade passes. However, his future as a piano player was saved by his 'ear', which enabled him to play some of the pop songs he heard on the radio, and he even started to write some little arrangements in a manuscript book provided by one of his despairing piano teachers. One of these arrangements recently came to light and its date is nicely indicated, the tune being the 'Ballad of Davy Crockett', a song that was an enormous success in the mid-1950s. By then, Alan's reading was good enough for him to attempt some of the simpler classics, as well as ragtime and boogie-woogie pieces popularised by Winnie Atwell. His blossoming talents on the piano came to the notice of his school music teacher who soon had him involved with the school orchestra, an experience from which Alan feels he gained a lot. Later, a school jazz band was formed and, dressed like the Acker Bilk band, they were included in the end of term concert. It looks as if the Border schools were a bit more tolerant of jazz than those in Edinburgh, where so many school jazz activities had rapidly hit the buffers of scholastic disapproval.

At University, Alan went along to the Fresher's Conference where he soon discovered one Roger Craik, sitting behind a desk labelled Rhythm Club. When he discovered that Alan could play piano, Roger invited him to a Fresher's audition at the SRC hall in Chambers Street. He must have done alright because, just a week or two later, he found himself in the same venue at the Fresher's Concert, playing Honky-tonk Train Blues and, as an encore, Bad Penny Blues, accompanied by Roger on drums and Ronnie Dunn on bass. Rather poignantly, Alan reports that, having played his own first gig with Ronnie, they were again playing together nearly fifty years later, on 16th October 2010, the day before Ronnie's sudden and unexpected death at the age of sixty nine.

Then came what Alan calls a 'sudden lurch' in his jazz appreciation when, having only managed to take in shows by Humphrey Lyttelton and the Chris Barber bands while at school, he discovered that the University Rhythm Club was running a bus to Glasgow. Ever the enthusiast, he rapidly made sure he was included, without having much of a clue as to who he was going to hear. It turned out to be a stellar bill featuring the Dizzy Gillespie Quintet, with Lalo Schifrin on piano, and the show was opened by the John Coltrane Quintet, including Eric Dolphy, McCoy Tyner and Elvin Jones. Alan remembers the Coltrane group's playing of My Favourite Things, which lasted for half an hour, with Coltrane's solo accounting for at least half of that!

Back in Edinburgh, he quickly made contact with local jazzers through the Rhythm Club and soon began to pick up gigs with bands run by Jim Baikie and Duncan Lonie, although this was mostly dance work. This type of experience, as it did for many musicians, resulted in him learning a vast repertoire of material in a very short space of time. The norm was to play a lot of medleys and the horn players in these bands, people like saxist Ron Gilbertson and trumpeter Derek Lawton, would simply signal the key of the next tune and Alan would have to follow, whatever the key and whatever the tune. He also played a lot of University gigs and was a frequent sitter-in at local jazz spots. After a year or so, Alan became first choice piano player with Roger Craik's Swing Six, a band which often included Eric Rinaldi (tpt), Jack Graham (rds), Dizzy Jackson (bs) and Roger himself on drums and which made at least one LP recording. He also became involved in the Rhythm Club administration as treasurer and helped book some of the big names including Tubby Hayes, for lunch-time University gigs, when they were in town for other bookings. The Rhythm Club also featured regular record sessions, as well as live presentations.

Late night parties and jam sessions at drummer Sandy Malcolm's flat, at the corner of George Street and Hanover Street, were a feature of this time, with the result that Hanover Street, with good reason, was soon re-christened Hangover Street. There were many clubs featuring jazz in town at this time and among those that Alan visited were: The Roost (Leith Street), The Manhattan Club (Calton Hill), The Place later to become Nicky Tam's and The Gamp Club (both Victoria Street), Rutherford's Bar and Bungy's (both the High Street), the Coda Club, The New Yorker (Shandwick Place), The Athenian later to become The Laughing Duck (Howe Street), The Rainbow Rooms, the Royal Chimes Club and Moby Dick's. One great gig that remains bright in Alan's memory was at the Gamp Club, when Tubby Hayes was backed by Dougie Campbell (gtr), Ronnie Rae (bs) and Billy Alison (drms), all of course Edinburgh jazzers. The Manhattan was the home of Old Bailey's Jazz Advocates, with Archie Sinclair (tbn), Andrew Lauder (tpt), Mike Hart (bjo), Graham Blamire (bs) and Chick Murray (drms) and Alan recalls how the band's sense of humour, particularly that of band leader Archie Sinclair, made these sessions memorable, as well as Andrew Lauder's renowned collection of wild life photographs.

Alan later became secretary of the University Rhythm Club, a post he was to hand over, two years later, to guitarist Charles Alexander. It is clear that, in the 1960s and onwards, University jazz was fairly heavily dominated by the more modern forms of the music, while the rest of Edinburgh jazz remained largely in the hands of the traditionalists. This rather emphasises the point made earlier by Roger Craik, that these sub-divisions of the local jazz scenes tended to operate quite separately, without a lot of mixing. However modern in its leanings or not, guest jazzers who were featured by the Rhythm Club demonstrate a more eclectic choice as they included Ronnie Ross (bari sax), Sandy Brown (clt), Al Fairweather (tpt), Joe Harriott (alto sax) and, would you believe it, The Temperance Seven! Alan himself played quite a bit with a quartet which included, at various time, Johnny Hope (bs gtr), Dave Margaroni (bs), Brooke Coventry (drms) and Ivor Shalovsky (drms). After graduating in 1965, Alan remained in Edinburgh for a time and continued his jazz activities, including much socialising and the late night parties and jam sessions which continued to thrive, often in the company of others interested in contemporary jazz, such as Jack and Tom Finlay and Bobby Stewart. Also around much of the time was Duncan Lonie, then best known as a dance band leader and drummer and now, in 2011, a director of the Edinburgh International Jazz festival, about which we shortly will hear much more. In those days too, Paddy's Bar, run by Paddy Crossan in Rose Street, was the meeting place greatly favoured by the jazz fraternity every Saturday lunch time. Alan reports that, in the mid-2000s and almost fifty years on, Paddy was still around, frequently turning up at Saturday afternoon jazz sessions at 80 Queen Street.

Although Alan Anderson joined his father's legal practice in Coldstream, he continued to spend a lot of his time, especially at weekends, in Edinburgh. However, by about the mid-1070s, a jazz scene began to come together in the Border country, starting with jam sessions in Berwick and Kelso, and Alan, a party and jam session animal if ever there was one, was soon involved. In time, a Borders Big Band was formed and Alan was to dep with them on a number of occasions. There was also a band, which included Francis Cowan on bass as well as Alan, which was called Border Crossing and which played the then fashionable 'crossover' music, combining jazz with rock and also including standards and Latin-based material.

Alan was also to become involved with the jazz promotion organisation Platform and soon set up a Borders branch, which promoted many jazz events over the years, featuring some high class jazz names such as Martin Taylor, Tommy Whittle, Benny Waters, Danny Moss and his wife singer Jeanie Lamb, Joe Temperley, Jimmy Deuchar, Alex Welsh and his Band and Blues Night with Alexis Korner. A Platform jazz weekend at Melrose featured local jazzers, together with the Gateway Jazz Band from Carlisle, accompanying George Chisholm (tbn), and the Dave Shepherd Quartet. Sadly, after putting on their most ambitious project, a concert show-casing the great vibes player Red Norvo with guitarist Tal Farlow and bassist Ronnie Rae, funding became a problem and the Borders Branch of Platform had to be wound up.

Alan Anderson was to make many more contributions to Edinburgh jazz, traditional and modern, over the coming decades, frequently playing at the Edinburgh International Jazz Festival in the 1980s and '90s, playing with the Old Bailey band and with the Wooltown Re-visited Jazz Band, a reincarnation of Hawick's famous Wooltown Jazz Band. His Edinburgh jazz festival gigs also included backing work with a trio including bassist Ronnie Dunn and drummer Ken Mathieson, when he had the opportunity to play with visiting alumni such as Jim Galloway, Roy Williams, Jim Douglas and, from the USA, Benny Waters and Dick Carey.

In the 1990s, after moving to live in North Berwick, he even managed a regular Edinburgh gig at, successively, Preservation Hall in Victoria Street, Morrison's Bar in Morrison Street and Harry's Bar in Randolph Place, with a band put together by drummer Toto McNaughton. This was clearly a good band and included at times Alex Gentleman (ten), Dougie Campbell (gtr), trumpeters Donald Corbett and Colin Steele and bass players Roy Percy and Lindsay Cooper. This band attracted many quality sitters-in, including Tommy Smith and Gordon Cruikshank (both ten sax) and singer Danny Street, the gig eventually coming to an end for Alan around the year 2000.

Later he was to play keyboard with the Royal British Legion Big Band, rehearsing with them at the Lady Haig Poppy factory at Canonmills every week. At the time of writing in 2011, Alan remains with this band, which underwent a couple of name changes, firstly to the slightly less daunting moniker, RBLS Big Band and then to The Sound of Seventeen Big Band. He now serves as its treasurer, and has played with the band at the famous North Sea Jazz Festival at the Hague in 2002 and at the even more prestigious Montreux Jazz Festival the following year, followed by other Festival appearances at Derry and Cork, the Edinburgh International Jazz Festival and on the Fringe. Alan Anderson remains an extremely active jazz musician, playing regularly in Edinburgh at good venues like the Tron Bar, Henry's Jazz Cellar, The Bridge and The Jazz Bar, the latter two run by the fine Edinburgh modern jazz drummer, Bill Kyle, although sadly The Bridge was destroyed by a disastrous fire in 2002. He also plays and arranges in a trio with bass player and vocalist Jimmy Taylor and Bobby Stewart or Dave Swanson on drums. They are called the Mellotones and focus mainly on the music of Mel Torme. With this trio, Alan has played long residencies at the Caledonian Hotel, 80 Queen Street and the Jazz Bar and says that, in 2011, he considers Edinburgh one of the best places in the UK for jazz.

Alan Anderson's jazz career exemplifies an issue which has surfaced again and again as I have been writing this book and which, I have to admit, has now become less clear than it seemed when I started off – just where do the fault lines, if they exist at all, occur in jazz? Musicians like Alan may have a preference for the more modern and contemporary sounds but, looking back at the time of writing, the music they play does not seem to me to be anything like as different from 'traditional jazz', as once seemed the case. Even within what is more clearly the traditional jazz bag, there are so many subdivisions and categories, that it is really much easier to see all of it as a continuum of jazz, in which you just have to find the bit you like best. Perhaps Alan Anderson would feel, like me, that he loves and respects all of jazz but likes some forms of the music more than others. Live and let live seems a reasonable philosophy!

The 1970s started with Edinburgh jazz in good shape. Although the Old Bailey band had disbanded in 1970 and the Pete Martin All Stars had broken up when Pete left town in about 1969, Mike Hart's Society Syncopators, the Climax Jazz Band, the Louisiana Ragtime Band and Charlie McNair's Jazz Band, played on as strongly as ever. Some of the Climax boys were back in town after their various sojourns in London, although that did not include Jake McMahon or Kenny Milne, both of whom unfortunately remained in the south. The Climax band had several residencies in the 1970s including one at the Bruntsfield Links Hotel, run by publican Ian Whyte in Whitehouse Loan, and another at the White Cockade, a long term jazz venue in Rose Street.

Johnnie Harper, who was to join the Charlie McNair band in the early 1970s, and Gerard Dott who was on clarinet at that time, recall that Charlie's band played residencies at quite a few pubs, clubs and hotels in the 1970s. These included The Place, a large establishment on several floors, going down from the top of Victoria Street to the level of the Cowgate far below. The Place had been a mainstay of jazz in the 1960s and later, re-named Nicky Tams, was to become a popular venue for folk music. There was also Bungy's, located in a close off the Royal Mile, run by the Waldman brothers, and another long term jazz venue. The Cephas Club, which functioned as a sort of youth club in the crypt of St George's church in Shandwick Place, was presumably run by the church and sometimes featured jazz. The Gallery Club in Hanover Street was another hang-over from the 1960s, and there was also the Lochewe Hotel and the Festival Tavern in Lothian Road.

Charlie also played in two other pubs and it was at these that I remember Charlie building a very large and devoted following, almost a cult following, particularly amongst the student population. These were the White Cockade in Rose Street and the Yellow Carvel, a pub with a sea-faring theme, situated in Hunter's Square, behind the Tron Church. To drop into one of these sessions when Charlie was in full cry, was a lesson in how to establish a rapport with the crowd, as Charlie exchanged banter and a great deal of almost surreal wit with the punters, bar staff and band.

In the late 1960s and into the 1970s, the McNair band still had Eed Smith on trombone, although he occasionally reverted to banjo for special comedy features such as 'Out of the Dawn There Came a Moonbeam'. There was also a strong rhythm section of Alex Marshall (gtr), Jimmy Luke (bs) and Pete Ritchie (drms), in which the vastly experienced Jimmy Luke would constantly shout instructions to Pete Ritchie about what he should be playing, such as when he should move on to the high hat cymbal and when he should hit a back beat. Pete, placid and long suffering soul that he was, did not seem to mind. By now the Purple Eyes Jazz Noise image, cultivated by Charlie at an earlier point, was in abeyance and the band was becoming again a tight little Dixieland band, kicked along by its excellent rhythm section.

Around this time too, the McNair band took on a regular spot at the Kirkcaldy Jazz Club, which was held in the Rose Bowl in Anthony's Hotel. This was an impressive circular ballroom and the gig became famous for the stovies, which were served free to everyone at the interval. Once, when the stovies were late to appear, Charlie was inspired to offer a demonstration of how to eat a bowl of stovies while singing 'Georgia on my Mind', which he did although none too successfully! It was here too, that Charlie's limerick habit started. An earnest young man approached Charlie one evening and asked if the band ever did any 'Jazz and Poetry', at that time the height of fashion in serious jazz circles. Charlie, equally earnestly, assured him that just such an event was planned for the second half. When the moment came, the band struck up an impressive twelve bar riff and Charlie marched up to the microphone to declaim *'There was a young man from Winnukta.....'!* The bass player, Tim Pharoah, was often with the band on these Kirkcaldy gigs and apparently Tim, too, developed a taste for Limericks, he and Charlie often spending the journey home swapping their favourites.

By the time the McNair band were established in their residencies at the Yellow Carvel and the White Cockade, the band had Charlie (tpt), Gerard Dott (clt), George Howden (tbn), Johnnie Harper (bjo), Colin Archbold (bs gtr) and Pete Ritchie (drms). Johnnie Harper had replaced Jock Westwater who had himself replaced Alec Marshall, after the latter went off to London to become a band manager/impresario. Gerard remembers this as a particularly good period for the McNair band and believes that the healthy following built up amongst students and young people in general, may have owed something to George Howden's involvement with the rock group, Mama Flyer. In addition, the band's repertoire at that time included several numbers with a rock flavour, including 'Revival' and the Beatles song, 'Norwegian Wood'. A particularly popular feature of the White Cockade sessions were Charlie's regular slanging matches with the formidable female publican, who had an awesome command of invective. She was the redoubtable Jean Ferguson, whom Charlie routinely referred to as *'our resident madam'!*

I remember once depping with Charlie's band in the Yellow Carvel and being faced with a request from a punter for 'Big Noise from Winetka'. This tune is a feature for bass and drums only and was made famous by its creators, Bob Haggart and Ray Bauduc of the 'Bob Crosby Bobcats'. Charlie knew I had sometimes played the tune with the Old Bailey band and suggested I played it with his drummer, Pete Ritchie. Pete indicated that he was only vaguely familiar with the tune but off we went nonetheless. I should have known better. 'Big Noise' is usually started by the drummer playing a sort of sprightly rattle on the rim of a drum. Unfortunately Pete brought it in at a tempo that would have been suitable for a fairly melancholy blues. It

272

was my fault, I should have set the tempo for Pete and our rendering of the tune (that is rendering as in 'to tear apart') was a total disaster. The tune never got off the ground and was greeted with a stony silence by the punters. Charlie offered comfort by suggesting that the world was not yet sufficiently artistically advanced for such a novel and musically challenging departure from tradition. He asked for a round of applause for our courage and, of course, being Charlie, got it.

Alastair Clark, in an article in the 'Scotsman' in 1972[135] said of the McNair band *The band are* (sic) *tough, rumbustious, versatile – capable of leapfrogging the years from trad to groovy, riff-borne rock-and-soul without apparently causing any bewilderment among the audience or themselves. They're at their best in a throbbing version of Herbie Hancock's "Blind Man" which takes them well out of the traditional bag'.* He went on to comment on Charlie himself saying *'Charlie McNair, on trumpet, typifies the eclecticism of the band, blowing in a breezy hotch-potch of styles that somehow manages to accommodate comfortably New Orleans, Dixieland, main-stream, bop and Blood Sweat and Tears. His singing covers an equally broad area, from Big Bill Broonzy to Frank Sinatra. It all hangs together'.* The photo accompanying this article shows Charlie's band of the time, with Jack Graham (clt), Charlie, George Howden (tbn) and Johnny Phillips (bs gtr), all in action in the Yellow Carvel.

During the 1970s, Charlie made many changes to the line-up of his band. He snapped up Johnnie Harper and Chick Murray when they became available and there were many other changes, which are too many to chronicle accurately. Johnnie Harper remembers the main changes and compiled the following list, noting that some of the musicians left the band for a while but made a comeback at a later date:

Trumpet: Charlie McNair

---

[135] Clark A, 'Trad crosses the sound barrier', 'The Scotsman', September 1972

Reeds:	Gerard Dott, Jack Graham, someone called Stewart who had 'big hair'!, George Duncan, Sandy Brown
Trombone:	George Howden, Ian 'Olly' McAulay, Bill Munro, John Arthur
Banjo:	Jock Westwater, Johnnie Harper, Harald Vox
Bass:	Jimmy Luke, Johnnie Harper (on bass guitar), Norrie Bell, Tim Pharoah, Colin Archbold
Drums:	Pete Ritchie, Chick Murray, Tom 'Toto' McNaughton

Around 1971, Charlie began featuring a solo guitarist in the band and took on in turn Johnnie Fitzsimmons, Ally Dawson, Mike Harper and Johnnie Phillips. The solo guitar was dropped at the end of the seventies. Another innovation was the use of bass guitar instead of the more traditional double bass. A surprising name in the above list is that of Sandy Brown. Sandy had returned to the Edinburgh area for a while in the early seventies, while he was establishing a business base in South Queensferry, and played with the McNair band whenever he could.

A regular in the McNair band towards the end of the 1960s and into the early 1970s was **George Howden (trombone)**, who was born in Edinburgh in 1948. George had learned to play trombone with the Salvation Army when he was about 12 years old. Whilst at school, he played with the Leith Silver band, his school orchestra and the Edinburgh Youth Orchestra. In the mid-1960s, George formed his own band before, in the late 1960s, joining the Pete Martin All Stars, the young and progressive Edinburgh mainstream band. Next came his years in the Charlie McNair band, George crediting Charlie with being a big influence on his subsequent career in jazz. Towards the end of the decade, he also joined the jazz/rock band, Mama Flyer.

Charlie McNair's Jazz Band
L-R Harald Vox, Bill Munro, Toto McNaughton, Colin
Archbold, George Duncan, Charlie McNair
(from the collection of Harald Vox, photographer
unknown)

In 1974, he left Edinburgh for the bright lights of London where he again formed a band of his own, Howden's Hotshots, with the help of his great friend and former colleague in the McNair band, the guitar player Alex Marshall. The Hotshots played at venues all over the UK and on one occasion, supported the Alex Welsh band at the 100 Club in Oxford Street. A regular gig was at the Kensington Hilton where, over a seven year period, George played with many famous jazzers including Stan Greig and Mike Cotton. Later in the mid-1970s George and his band put in a couple of months playing at a venue in Cadaques, Spain and, during this run, they were invited to play for the surrealist painter Salvador Dali and his wife. They also found time to record a single of 'Ice Cream' and to record some jazz sessions for BBC Radio 2. During his years based in the south, George played and recorded with many of the best known British jazzers of the day including Alan Elsdon, Tony Pitt, Brian Lemon, Keith Smith, Laurie Chescoe, Al Gay, Jim Douglas and, not long before he died, Edinburgh's Alex Welsh. It was to be all of 35 years and

2009 before George Howden returned to Scotland, when he and his wife based themselves in the Scottish Borders. Happily, this enabled him to make the 50 mile journey to Edinburgh for gigs and he was soon back in action in the Edinburgh jazz scene as if he had never been away.

Another who was to be long-term stalwart of the Charlie McNair band was **Colin Archbold (bs gtr)**, who joined the band after an extensive career in rock music. Colin was born on 14th November 1944 and educated at the Edinburgh Academy and his first job on leaving school was to train as a window dresser with St Cuthbert's Co-operative Store in Bread Street. He started his musical career as a bass guitarist with a band called the Sabres, for whom he auditioned successfully in 1961, and with them he toured US army bases all over Scotland and played the Star Club in Germany, as well as gaining a considerable local reputation. 1965 saw him a member of the Roadsters and, by 1968 he had made a move into jazz oriented music, playing in Hamish McGregor's Memphis Road Show. More time in rock music followed with Brody, a band which was on the verge of signing up to an important recording contract which sadly fizzled out at the last moment. Time with other rock groups, including Gasoline Alez and Chaktra, followed before he joined the McNair band in the early 1970s, a band with which he would remain for nearly thirty years. Colin Archbold was a man with a considerable zest for life and, in addition to his musical activities, he ran a building firm, had an enormous enthusiasm for fast cars and was a extremely enthusiastic cricketer, turning out for the Woodcutter's Club, who played at Bangholm Sports Ground, near Goldenacre.

Particularly memorable was Colin's ready ability to play up to the inventive wit and general anarchy that flowed from the irrepressible Charlie McNair and it was no surprise that his stint with the McNair band was to be a long one. He was to share in many of the best years of the McNair band's lengthy service in Edinburgh jazz, including the years when Charlie flirted with a rock influence and became something of an Icon of Anarchy for the Student population. Unfortunately, by 2001, Colin Archbold was experiencing serious health problems which brought an end to his playing and, on 4ᵗʰ June 2005, he died in Edinburgh at the early age of just sixty. His obituary by Alasdair Steven appeared in the Scotsman of 10ᵗʰ August 2005[136].

A new but short-lived band started up in the early 1970s, with Fraser Gauld (tpt), Gerard Dott (clt), Paul Munro (tbn), Jock Westwater (Bjo), Iain Forde (drms) and me on bass. Paul Munro's wife, Jacqui, sang with the band which, like Charlie McNair's band, had a residency in the White Cockade in Rose Street. The band adopted the name of **The Granton Jass Works**, a name which makes me cringe to this day. Iain Forde recalls that this band later 'morphed' into a slightly different form, with Donald Macdonald, now playing sax, and Ovin Helseth (bs) coming in. Iain also reports that they practiced in Donald Macdonald's house behind a wall of instrument cases, as a defence against Donald's Dalmatian dog, which had developed a strong desire to eat Jock Westwater!

Jock Westwater (banjo), a member at times of both the McNair band and the 'Granton Jass Works', had been around the scene for a number of years. Jock was born in Edinburgh in 1949 and educated at Daniel Stewart's College. He was lucky enough to have an uncle who was a regular at the West End Cafe and Jock developed an interest in jazz through listening to his uncle's collection of 78 rpm records. His interest in playing banjo came a bit later, after he got out into the local scene and heard the local bands, in particular, the playing of Mike Hart. Jock claims to have been bullied into *'bashing out chords'* for his brother Mike, when he took up clarinet in 1962, although I find it hard to believe that Jock was ever being bullied into anything by anyone!. He had played with a succession of bands in the 1960s, including some involving his brother, and a variety of small combos led by the trombonist, Ken Ramage. Jock also had a spell with the long established Climax band on his CV.

One of the bands, involving his brother and clarinettist George Duncan, was given the name **Jock Strap and his Two Swingers**, another was the **Bash Street Kids** and yet

136 Steven A, 'Colin Archbold', The Scotsman, 10ᵗʰ August 2005, by permission of Alasdair Steven

another was the only jazz band whose name began with an apostrophe, the **....'king Great Band**. There seems to me to be a common thread running through this sequence of band names and it makes me strongly suspect that Jock Westwater was responsible for the 'Granton Jass Works' moniker as well. Jock also played with a band called **The Great Northern Jook Band**. This was a jug and washboard band that played 1920s jug and country blues material and songs associated with Jim Kweskin, the American jug band leader. In the later 1970s, Jock again played with a fair number of bands including the **Jack Graham Jazz Band**, the **Criterion Jazz Band** led by drummer Kenny Milne and **Jim Petrie's Jazz Band**. All of these bands had comparatively short lives but the association with Jim Petrie was to lead to the formation of a top class and long lasting band, the **Diplomats of Jazz**, some years later in the 1980s. The 1980s would also bring Jock the opportunity to play in two very good bands put together by two returned Edinburgh veterans - Al Fairweather and Dave Keir, but the story of these bands is for a later chapter. Jock Westwater was a man of many bands. Why he moved about so much I do not know but it seemed to suit him. His expertise on the banjo and his experience of so many bands, gave him a huge repertoire of material which made him a particularly versatile and able player to have as a dep.

After a year or two in the early 1970s away playing on the boats, the trombonist, Ken Ramage returned to the Edinburgh jazz scene and it was not long before he was back in action. A band had been put together by a piano player called Ian Scott, which he called the **Festival City Jazz Band**. Ken Ramage not only joined this band but 'fronted' it - that is led the band on the bandstand. The full line-up of the band was Charlie Malley (tpt), Jimmy Shortreed (clt and alto), Ken Ramage (tbn), Colin Warwick (bjo), Kenny Burns (bs) and Russ Cessford (drms). This band commenced on a very successful and well supported residency at the Barnton Hotel. Ken Ramage stayed with the band for the next eight and half years and then his trombone playing came to an unfortunate and sudden stop. It was understandably a sad and traumatic business for

Ken, so much so that he can recall in detail exactly what happened. He had been having increasing dental problems for some time and, on Easter Sunday 1983, while playing 'Tishomingo Blues' in the Barnton Hotel, his teeth gave way altogether, and that was the end of his trombone career. He was obviously distressed by this and his accomplished playing was a sad loss to the Edinburgh scene. However, he had another string to his bow and, in time, he was able to develop this and, some years later after a spell living in the USA, he was able to return to active playing in Edinburgh as a drummer.

The Festival City Jazz Band had meanwhile moved to a new residency in the Crest Hotel on the Queensferry Road, near Blackhall. They also, for some reason, changed their name and became the **Capital Jazz Band**, although this was often given as the **Capital City Jazz Band**. It seems likely that the name change came about when the band leader, Ian Scott, dropped out of the band. Ken Ramage had continued to play and front the band but, after he was forced to stop playing, Graham Robertson came in on trombone and Kenny Burns, the bass player, took over running the band. Others who played with the 'Capital Jazz Band' around this time included a top class **reeds player, Jock Graham** who was from Fife. Jock Graham was a vastly experienced player who not only played all the reed instruments but was also an accomplished flute and violin player, and he had played for years with the big band led by Fife's famous band leader and arranger, Tommy Sampson. Jock Graham's son, Dave Graham, also played piano with the Capital band for a while and a very good former professional jazz drummer, Billy Law, came in on drums. This was another successful and well supported gig and there were often other Edinburgh jazzers dropping in for a sit-in with the band.

The **banjo player Colin Warwick**, who played with both the Festval City and Capital Jazz Bands, was a late starter in jazz. Colin was born in Edinburgh on 20th July 1942 and attended Bruntsfield Primary and Boroughmuir Senior Secondary Schools. He went on to have a long career with the Royal (Dick) School of Veterinary Education, where he was on the technical staff, providing a photographic and graphic service. On his retirement in 2005, he was awarded an MBE for services to veterinary education and, in 2011, was continuing his involvement with the 'Dick Vet', now as an Honorary Fellow of the University of Edinburgh, working on veterinary history. Colin's first exposure to jazz came about through hearing LP recordings of the Stan Kenton band, back in the 1950s. This was followed by his first purchase of a 78 rpm record when, as he puts it '*...not knowing any better, I bought 'Truckin'' by the showman and drummer, Eric Delaney*'! Happily he seems to have soon recovered from this unpromising start and went along to hear the Ken Colyer band at the Tollcross Central Hall in early 1954, when the band still included Chris Barber and Lonnie Donegan, a session which also included some skiffle music. Later, at the same venue, he was to hear the Mick Mulligan band with singer George Melly. Now well and truly hooked on traditional jazz and with the Trad Boom in full swing, Colin soon found his way to the various Jazz Band Balls held at the Fountainbridge Palais where, as well as the local jazz bands, he heard the bands of Sandy Brown, Terry Lightfoot and Acker Bilk. Another source of memorable jazz experiences was the Usher Hall, where he heard George Lewis, Big Bill Broonzy, Earl Hines, Oscar Peterson and Sister Rosetta Tharpe, who was touring with the Chris Barber band.

At that time, Colin had never imagined that he would actually play in a jazz band but eventually, he purchased a second hand zither banjo, disposed of the unwanted fifth string and learned a few chords. Soon he was playing at impromptu sessions in his flat in East Preston Street, sessions which included friends and work colleagues with an interest in music. It was through one of these that Colin met the banjo player Jock Westwater who, as Colin remembers it, was playing at the time with Jim Petrie's Quartet. By then getting more and more into his playing, Colin spotted a newspaper advert for a 'Bacon and Day' 1930 vintage banjo and bought it for the princely sum of £25. In spite of his scant experience of playing, it was not long before he landed his first gig which was in 1970 with the Climax Jazz Band, in the Haymarket Station Bar. Colin remembers the line-up of this edition of the Climax band as

Jim Petrie (tpt), Jack Weddell (tbn), George Gilmour (clt), Jim Young (bs) and firstly Iain Forde then John Nicholson (drms), with Colin himself on banjo. He then became a member of the Ken Ramage Jazz Advocates, which was resident in the White Cockade pub in Rose Street. The line-up of this band when Colin became a member, was Jim Petrie (tpt), Ken Ramage (tbn), Hamish McGregor (rds), Colin Warwick (bjo), Jimmy Luke then Norrie Bell (bs) and Donald 'Chick' Murray (drms). As Colin remembers it, Ken Ramage led this band during the period around late summer and autumn 1971, which was probably squeezed in between Ken's various spells away playing on the transatlantic liners.

When his spell with the Ken Ramage band came to an end, Colin joined the newly formed West End Jazz Band, of which we will hear more later, and was with them at their resident spot in the Ailsa Craig Hotel in Royal Terrace. The line-up of the band at this time was Alec McIntosh (tpt), Angus Macdonald (tbn), Eddie Hamilton (clt), Tom Bryce (pno and ldr), Colin Warwick (bjo), Charlie McCourt (bs) and Roy Dunnett (drms). During his spell with the West End band came the move, in 1978, to the band with which Colin was to spend many years: the Festival City Jazz Band, later to be re-named the Capital Jazz Band. This band played in the Dixieland style and was resident at the Barnton Hotel, on the outskirts of town on the Queensferry Road and had an experienced line-up, with Charlie Malley (tpt), Ken Ramage (tbn), Jimmy Shortreed (rds), Ian Scott (pno), Colin on banjo, Ken Burns (bs gtr) and Russ Cessford (drms). This was a very well supported gig and the band regularly played to packed houses each Sunday afternoon. In 1982, after a personnel shuffle, the band, as we have heard, changed its name to the Capital Jazz Band. By that time, Graeme Robertson had replaced Ken Ramage, the excellent Jock Graham had arrived from Fife to play reeds, George Cavaye had taken over on piano, Ken Burns had added a tuba to his armoury and the fine drummer, Billy Law, had joined the band. In 1986, the band made their move to the Crest Hotel, further into town along the Queensferry Road, where they continued to draw good crowds. In addition to his banjo playing, Colin sometimes regaled the crowd with a vocal or two, sometimes 'Hello Central Give Me Dr Jazz' and sometimes a harmony version of 'Dapper Dan', in partnership with bass player Ken Burns.

I always felt that one of the reasons for the success of both the Barnton and the Crest Hotel sessions, lay in the policy of the band to welcome other jazzers and invite them to sit in. Often a pianist such as Danny Dorrian or George Bartleman would play during the band's break and, in the second half, great variety and interest would be added by some high class guests. These often included players of the calibre of Jack Duff (rds), Al Fairweather (tpt), Johnny McGuff (tbn), Ralph Laing and Stan Greig (pno) and, a future major star of more modern forms of jazz, the young Tommy Smith (ten). In addition to these distinguished names, even I sat in once or twice, the band's tolerance sufficient to allow one of my vocal efforts. They also welcomed proper singers and these included Blanche Calloway, the daughter of the famous American band leader and singer Cab Calloway, Jean Mundell, Liz McEwan, the blues singer Tam White and the indefatigable Jacky MacFarlane, now quite advanced in years but still teetotal and still travelling everywhere by bus.

Colin Warwick also played briefly with Angus Macdonald's Deep South band, John Arthur's Dr McJazz and the Dave Keir Quartet and depped with most of the Edinburgh jazz bands at one time or another. I remember an occasion in the 1990s when Colin depped on the Cruise boat, the Maid of the Forth and, when I arrived, it was to find him displaying a hither too unknown talent, playing bagpipes for the punters on the Hawes Pier! He counts amongst his best jazz memories playing with the Festival City band in support of George Chisholm with Keith Smith's Hefty Jazz at an evening session at the Barnton Hotel in 1986 and a number of gigs in far-flung parts of the country such as Dumfries, Bute, Peebles and Kintore. There was also a blustery weekend in 1989 at the Cork Jazz Festival with a band improbably called the BP Old Boilers, courtesy of trumpeter Charlie Malley who worked in the oil industry.

The advent of the Edinburgh International Jazz Festival in 1979 was to bring him many more gigs and the chance to play with top class visitors like Roy Williams (tbn) and the reeds men, John Barnes and Jim Galloway. It also brought him, like the rest of us, priceless opportunities to hear and sometimes to meet, some of the great names of jazz, in Colin's case including Sandy Brown, Benny Waters, Teddy Wilson, Dick Hyman, Stephane Grappelli and many more. His regrets include never hearing Louis Armstrong live, missing out on the Edinburgh jazz scene of the 1950s when some of the big names were still around and being unaware of the Stud Club when it was in St Peter's Buildings, just down the road from his parent's house. Colin Warwick stopped playing in 1996 after a local jazz career of twenty six years but still has his banjo. Who knows, we may not yet have seen and heard the last of a late starting but enthusiastic and popular jazzer.

We have already met the **trombone and bass player Graeme Robertson** back in chapter VII, when we heard that his interest in jazz had begun, when still at school, in the company of drummer Kenny Milne and clarinet player, Karl Ekeval. Graeme was born in the Granton area of Edinburgh on 26th November 1935 and attended Wardie Primary School and Broughton High School. He did his National Service in the RAF between 1954 and 1956, based at Uxbridge in North West London. Continuing to live in the London area after NS and now married, he undertook a course at Houndslow Teacher Training College, Middlesex, in 1956/57 before embarking on a varied career which included spells as an engineer, an insurance agent, a door to door salesman and a shop assistant in a legal forms firm. On his return to Edinburgh in 1961, he worked with the Ministry of Power and as a taxi driver. As a youngster, he had been interested in the radio and books and, the youngest of six, discovered an interest in music through listening to records, mostly of Swing music, which were brought home by his brothers on pay day.

His interest in music now awakened and his listening having expanded to take in Louis Armstrong's Hot Five, on which he heard the playing of trombonist Kid Ory, he proceeded to teach himself to play trombone. With Kenny Milne and Karl Ekeval, Graeme had started playing in a school boy jazz band, although it had a somewhat unorthodox line-up at first, including Karl Ekeval on accordion and Graeme himself on kazoo. His first public playing experience came while he was in the RAF, where he was fortunate enough to fall in with one Jack Potts, a multi-instrumentalist from Newcastle whose main instrument was cornet, who taught him a lot about jazz. Graeme later attended the famous Parker's Brass Studio in London, where he honed his developing playing skills. Early gigs included a regular spot in the Queen's Arms, Uxbridge and, after he had completed his spell in the RAF, with a band called the Apex Jazz Band at a club run by the band itself, in Penge, in South London. This band was attached to an agent who arranged gigs for the band in the Ken Colyer Club and other venues in London. Graeme's first professional work was with the Mike Peters Jazz Band in 1959 and, when he returned to Edinburgh in 1961, his replacement with the Peters band was none other than Roy Williams, later to make a great name of himself with the Alex Welsh and Humphrey Lyttelton bands and to become recognised as one of the finest trombonists in jazz.

Graeme lists his jazz and trombone influences as Kid Ory in the early days, followed by Jack Teagarden, then on to the modern playing of Charlie Parker and two of the giants of modern jazz trombone, J J Johnson and Kai Winding. However, a man with a broad appreciation of jazz, he told me his listening taste was very wide and he considers that his own playing, in the end, was *'influenced by just about everybody'*. Certainly, after I became aware of Graeme's playing in the early 1960s, it was clear that he had already abandoned the New Orleans tradition and was already firmly in the mainstream of jazz. In fact, his playing always struck me as cool in style, with a thoughtful, musicianly approach. He was to further expand his musical knowledge, as time went on, taking a course in trombone at Napier College of Music, from which he graduated in 1975 with a diploma in both playing and teaching. He also became interested in writing and arranging music and this was to play a larger and larger part of his musical activities.

Graeme's return to Edinburgh saw him, in 1962, form a band under his own leadership, a band to which he gave the unlikely name of **Sam Pig and his Trotters**. Besides Graeme on trombone, the line-up included Al Clark (tpt), old school pal Karl Ekeval (clt), Frank Gifford (bjo) and Sandy Malcolm (drms). His next move came about through fairly unusual circumstances, involving a sudden and unplanned switch of instrument. Graeme had been at an 'after gig' party one night, a party which was also attended by some of members of the recently formed Old Bailey and his Jazz Advocates. At some point the Old Bailey bass player departed, leaving his bass to be collected the next day. Graeme, who had 'fooled about' on someone's bass when he was very young, picked up the bass and played as best he could in a jam session with some of the remaining Old Bailey crowd. To his astonishment, this led to a visit a day or two later from Archie Sinclair and Mike Hart, who invited him to join OB on a regular basis! Nothing loath, he bought himself a bass, fixed up some help from bass player Ian Brown, accepted the invitation and found himself a member of what was fast becoming Edinburgh's busiest jazz band, doubling his future potential for gigs into the bargain.

In the mid-1960s, Graeme joined the Charlie McNair band before, as he put it, *'going commercial'*. By this, he meant moving out into the wider gig world and taking on work with various dance bands, including that of Jimmy Mitchell in the Cavendish Ballroom and work in Tiffany's, a night club with cabaret, which was part of the Mecca empire. He also put in almost ten years playing in the band at the Plaza, a famous Edinburgh dance hall. He clearly built a successful career in this more commercial world, mostly playing bass. Answering an advertisement in the Melody Maker led to six months in the Gulf Hotel in Bahrain, and other work included a cruise on a P & O liner and a summer season with Jack Duff in Jersey. He also picked up commercial gigs recording radio jingles for Radio Edinburgh and other work involving composing and arranging music. The late 1960s and early 1970s saw him move into the field of folk music, when he played and recorded, again on bass, with such groups as The Cairn, The Islanders, The Humble Bums and Bread, Love and Dreams.

Other regular work included playing in Working Men's Clubs, a setting renowned as a fertile source of muso's anecdotes and Graeme Robertson was no exception. He told me of gig at one of these clubs when the evening was begun by the resident Social Convenor who, after much tapping and blowing into the microphone to make sure it was working, set the tone for the evening's entertainment. *'As some o' youse a'ready ken, last week saw the sad death of auld Wullie, a regular attender o'the Club for many years, who always sat in that chair over there. We will now have a minute's silence in memory of auld Wullie'.* There followed a respectful silence until the Social Convenor felt time was up: *'Now, movin' on tae a more serious subject, it has came to the Committee's attention that some o' youse are pissin' on the back wall o' the car park.........'.*

Graeme's trombone and jazz playing was not neglected over the years either and included jazz gigs with Jack Duff and bass player Lindsay Cooper, work with the Finlay-Gentleman Quintet and playing time with a rehearsal band that played weekly sessions in Nicky Tams, formerly known as the 1960s jazz spot, The Place. He would also become a member of the Capital Jazz Band, taking over the trombone chair from Ken Ramage and playing and singing with the band for many years, when they were resident in the Esso Hotel, on the Queensferry Road. The years 1972 to 1980 saw him heavily involved as an instrumental teacher with the Education Dept of Edinburgh City Council and this led to the formation of several youth bands, playing in the Swing style, including, in the early 1980s, the first youth band to be featured at the Edinburgh International Jazz Festival. There were also appearances for the youth band at the King's Theatre, with the Gang Show. The mid-1980s saw him become a member of Hamish McGregor's fledgling Fat Sam's Band, in which Graeme's son Nick, another talented musician, was also to appear, as vocalist. With Fat Sam's Band, Graeme played at jazz festivals in Cork, Lille, Bruges and Sacramento, further expanding his impressive and varied CV. He made a number of jazz recordings with the Fat Sam and Capital bands, which will be found in the discography appendix.

Graeme Robertson was one of the most versatile and busy jazzers throughout his long career as both trombonist and bass player in Edinburgh jazz, before finally bringing his active gig playing to a halt around 2003. At the time of writing in 2011, he and his wife are living in retirement in Bo'ness in West Lothian, while Graeme keeps up his musical interest by running a rehearsal band in the Corstorphine area of Edinburgh, for which he writes, arranges and directs. A serious and hard-working musician, Graeme Robertson brought to Edinburgh jazz a trombone style that was outwith the usual traditional jazz style and, as a teacher, he leaves a legacy of well-tutored young musicians who will help keep up Edinburgh's strong reputation as a musical centre well into the 21st Century.

Billy Law (drums) was born in Edinburgh on 1st August 1940, educated at Sciennes and Darroch schools and began pipe band drumming in the Boys Brigade when he was twelve years old. An avid listener to radio and records, Billy soon developed an interest in jazz, although he recalls that there was very little jazz on the radio in the early 1950s. He began going along to the Condon Club in India Buildings almost every Sunday evening and it was there that he heard the Alex Welsh band for the first time. Now competent on a drum kit, Billy began playing jazz and dance music with like-minded, local youngsters in the mid-1950s, although he did not become a member of a jazz band until later. The guitarist Jim Baikie gave him his start in playing with good musicians around 1957 and he remembers these times as being surrounded by people who helped him make progress. In 1960, the trombone player Ken Ramage recommended Billy to a Danish band, the Jazz Cardinals, and he started his career as a professional jazz drummer with them, touring in West Berlin, Denmark and Sweden. After returning to Scotland, he became a member of the Clyde Valley Stompers, then under the leadership of clarinettist Pete Kerr. He stayed on with Pete Kerr, when the clarinettist returned to Scotland after his spell leading the Stompers, and became a member of his new band, Pete Kerr's All Stars. With this band, in the early 1960s, Billy made two extended play records at the Waverley Studios in Edinburgh. In March 1964, he joined the band of another clarinet player, Terry Lightfoot, and in the same year, played with blues singer Long John Baldry. He was also to play with the jazz bands of Bob Wallis, Max Collie and Charlie Galbraith, Billy recalling that it was all very enjoyable but work was scarce. He did, however, manage to buy a houseboat, in which he lived at the famous Eel Pie Island on the Thames.

A short period co-leading a band with a star of the future, the famous rock singer Rod Stewart, was followed by him joining Alec Harvey's Big Soul Band in 1965. Apparently, time with this band was extremely entertaining, the chief mirth-maker being one Bob Nimmo, who is said to have almost made Billy ill with laughter. This was followed by a spell gigging with bands such as pianist Lennie Felix's trio, Colin Smith's Sextet and the Alex Welsh Band. Billy greatly admired the Welsh band, especially its drummer Lennie Hastings, who was his favourite drummer in the Dixieland idiom. He then became a member of another fine band, the band led by trumpeter Alan Elsdon. Although the Alex Welsh band was the usual choice to back visiting American jazzers, the Elsdon band got a look in too. Billy missed their tour with trumpeter Wingy Manone but was with them for a tour with clarinettist Albert Nicholas. Unfortunately, this was an unhappy tour but the next was clearly a knock out.

The guest this time was none other than Ed Hall, one of the greatest of jazz clarinettists, who in his time had played in the clubs owned by gangsters, put in five years with the Louis Armstrong All Stars without a single rehearsal, and who, in Billy's words *'had seen it all'*. For the three weeks of the tour, Billy had the pleasure of driving a car with Ed Hall sitting beside him and listening to all Ed's stories. The whole Elsdon band loved Ed for his kindness and generosity to all of them and he once called Billy *'a Goddamn life saver'*, when the drummer saved a particularly messy ending. An especially appreciated habit of Ed Hall's was always to make a point of praising the band to the audience. Although the band was not aware of it at the time, they were recorded at one of the concerts with Ed Hall and two CDs were issued. This had been a happy time for the Alan Elsdon band, which was in good form and feeling refreshed. Billy considers that the CDs are a great reminder of that good time and, in his words, are *'not too bad'*, although like all jazzers he *'would like a re-take'*!

After leaving the Elsdon band in 1969, Billy returned to Edinburgh, where he played for a number of years in the pit band at the King's Theatre. In addition, he played many gigs with Edinburgh jazz and dance bands, including the spell with the Capital Jazz Band described above, and he took part in a Clyde Valley Stompers re-union tour in 1982. In the 1980s and 1990s, Billy was to play with bands organised by Al Fairweather and Ralph Laing, after these two veterans had returned to Scotland. Billy's father, Willie Law, was a 'weel kent' face around the Edinburgh jazz scene for many years, always welcome when he made one of his regular appearances at jazz gigs all round the town, a loyal supporter of the local bands and not only those in which his son was playing. Writing this in 2011, it is sad to relate that Billy Law has not played for many years, a loss to the Edinburgh jazz scene of one of its best ever drummers.

Another with several bands to his name was **Hamish McGregor (reeds, trombone, Hammond organ, vocals)**, who was born in 1946 and educated at Merchiston Castle School. He had developed an interest in traditional jazz, which was at the height of its 'Trad Boom' popularity at the time, while still at school. As a school boy, Hamish was already getting bands together to make recordings and getting to know the local Edinburgh jazz scene. It was soon clear that he was an enterprising and determined individual with a flair for presentation and there was little doubt that he would go on to be a successful band leader and a major force in the local scene. He came from a musical family and had started out playing clarinet, with trombone as his second instrument. There are some privately made recordings of a band put together for the recording session and featuring his trombone playing and singing. Hamish recruited a trumpet player from Dunfermline, Tommy Lister, together with Jack Graham (clt), Johnnie Harper (bjo), me (bs) and Charlie Welch, the Old Bailey drummer, for this recording session. The recording, it has to be said, is very much of its time, most of the material being the sort of novelty tunes associated with the 'Trad Boom' years. Hamish seemed to give up trombone after this and concentrated on clarinet although, in time, he played all the various saxes, tending to favour the alto sax.

After his year with the Old Bailey band, of which we have already heard, Hamish had led several bands of his own in the later 1960s, each lasting about two years, including a band he called **Hamish McGregor and his Clansmen**, which played in the style of the famous Alex Welsh Band. This band included trumpet player Tommy Lister, Dave Margaroni on trombone and the excellent Jack Finlay on piano. The Clansmen band was followed by what Hamish describes as a ten piece soul band, the **Memphis Road Show**, which included Tommy Lister plus Pete Martin on trumpets and bringing in a high class tenor saxophonist, Gordon Cruikshank. In turn, this was followed by a band called **Seven Up** which Hamish put together in 1969, just about the time the Old Bailey band broke up. This enabled him to recruit Andrew Lauder, Dave Margaroni, Johnnie Harper and Chick Murray from the Old Bailey band along with Johnnie Harper's brother, Mike, on solo guitar. In spite of the past histories of the musicians involved, the band played as an R and B combo, rather than as a traditional jazz band. This band broke up in 1971 and, for a few years, Hamish ran a series of combos featuring many of the above jazzers and, sometimes, Hamish on the Hammond organ.

In 1975, Hamish McGregor, now resident in South Queensferry, assembled a band to play a residency in the Forth Bridge Hotel in the village. The band he finally assembled included Andrew Lauder (tpt), Johnnie Harper (bjo and gtr), Chick Murray (drms) and me on bass. This band, it was clear, was going to have a strong flavour of the Old Bailey band as it had been when Archie Sinclair died. In addition, Hamish had signed up Sam Smith, a newcomer to the Edinburgh scene, to play trombone. **Sam Smith (trombone, vocals)**, whose full name, we discovered later, was actually Alastair Salmond-Smith, had been born in Edinburgh on the 15th of September 1940. He had been born with a kyphosis of the spine, an abnormality that had resulted in a hunched posture and short stature. He had started playing trombone when at the Royal College of Art in London, where he became a graphic designer, and his first band, while still at college, had been Colin Whale's Jazz Band. He had played with Dick Charlesworth and his City

Gents when he was about twenty five and many other bands, before making his way to Cumbria where he gigged with the well known Mick Potts Jazz Band around Carlisle. Eventually he had returned to Edinburgh, where Hamish got to hear of him and invited him to join the new band. In addition to being a good trombone player with a nice mellow sound and a particularly effective way of playing in the ensemble, Sam was a good singer rather in the style of Acker Bilk. He was also something of a character, with a remarkable capacity for gin, was soon popular with the crowds and fitted into the new band very well.

Since the break-up of the Old Bailey band in 1970, Andrew Lauder had done most of his playing in the dance band world, playing with the bands of Jim Baikie and Cam Robbie, and had also been involved with the George Hotel house band. This was run by Alec Walker who, in fact, no longer played himself but held the contract with the hotel to provide a band for dinner dances six nights a week. Andrew did these events on Wednesdays, Fridays and Saturdays for about five years. However, when the chance came to get together with most of the Old Bailey crowd, Andrew was up for it. The residency in Queensferry was not to last long and soon the band, by now once more calling itself **Old Bailey's Jazz Advocates**, had moved to the Fountain Inn, situated behind the Barnton Hotel in Whitehouse Road.

This gig became remarkably popular and at one stage, punters were arriving a full hour before the band was due to start, simply to secure a good seat. The 'Jazz News' pamphlet for the Edinburgh International Jazz Festival for 1979 referred to the Fountain Inn as '..a veritable Mecca for Scots (nay, international) jazz freaks'. What was also remarkable was the number of followers of the band from the 1960s who turned up and became regulars again. This residency continued very successfully and then, in March 1976, the Old Bailey band was selected by promoter Ed Baxter to back Bud Freeman, the famous Chicagoan tenor sax star, in concerts at the Dominion Cinema in Morningside. These were followed by further concerts with Freeman and then a couple more with the great American trumpeter Wild Bill Davison, also in the Dominion, in

August and September 1976. The band was augmented by Tom Finlay on piano for these concerts and his playing greatly impressed the visitors, both of whom would have liked to take Tom with them for the rest of their solo tours.

The Freeman concert in August was reviewed by Alastair Clark in the Scotsman where he said *'A dapper, likable little man,* (Bud Freeman) *was on stage for something like three hours and was still blowing hot choruses round about 2 a.m. He was, of course, in canny fettle, rarely extending his improvisations beyond familiar territory and enthusiastically seeing to it that ever member of the supporting Old Bailey's Jazz Advocates had an abundance of solo space.....Tom Finlay played some super piano... notably when backing Freeman in a swingy quartet setting'.*

The Old Bailey band also took on a second residency in March 1977 at the Hailes House Hotel, in the Kingsknowe area of town but, when Hamish McGregor, Andrew Lauder and Chick Murray decided they did not want to take this on and dropped out, the band took on the name **The Nova Scotia Jazz Band**. The spaces were filled by bringing in Gus Ferguson on trumpet, Gerard Dott on clarinet and Dave Rae on drums. The choice of name was in a way unfortunate, as there was no real connection with the much better known band of the same name from the 1950s. After a while, banjoist Johnnie Harper also dropped out and his place was taken by first, Jock Westwater and then the banjo player originally from Germany, Harald Vox. This became another well attended residency and it lasted until June 1979.

Another off-shoot of the Old Bailey/Nova Scotia bands was a four piece band, the **Nova Scotia Quartet**, that took on a residency at the Original Hotel, Roslin. This was my doing and it came about because I had been greatly taken by two sets of recordings of American jazz quartets. These were the well known 'Big Four' recordings by a four piece including Muggsy Spannier and Sydney Bechet and a wonderful set of only four tracks made by Rex Stewart, Barney Bigard and Billy Taylor of the Duke Ellington band together with Django Reinhardt, when Ellington was on tour in France. The early membership of the Nova Scotia Quartet briefly included Andrew Lauder and John McGregor on clarinet but soon settled down with Gus Ferguson (trumpet), Gerard Dott (clarinet, Johnnie Harper (guitar and banjo) and Graham Blamire (bass).

Harald Vox (banjo) was born in Berlin on 25th November 1938 and began playing piano at age seventeen and then banjo at nineteen. His first band was Old Bucket's Jazz Band, which was based at Lake Constance, followed by several other bands, one of which he describes as *'an oompah band'*, in Southern Germany around Ravensburg, Ull, Stuttgart and Hanover. Harald then moved to the UK to attend teacher training college, where he played in a local non-jazz quartet. He then moved to Edinburgh in 1970, where he was introduced to the local jazz scene through hearing the Old Bailey band, becoming friendly with the Old Bailey banjo player Johnnie Harper, and picking up a few gigs. When Johnnie Harper left the Old Bailey off-shoot, the Nova Scotia Jazz Band, Harald was on hand to take over and, around the same time, he put in spells with the West End Jazz Band and the Spirits of Rhythm.

Harald had established himself around the Edinburgh scene at just the right time, as Johnnie Harper had left town in the late 1970s to make a full-time career for himself in jazz, and Harald was there to fill the gap. In 1978, he joined the Charlie McNair band, with whom he was to stay until the mid-1990s, and also played with a band called Dr McJazz. Clearly very busy, Harald was also playing with Frank Birnie's East Coast Jazz band at the Blue Lagoon on Monday evenings, where he was to stay for many years. Between 1992 and 1997, Harald played with the Maid of the Forth Stompers and then started playing through in Glasgow with Muldoon's Jazz and Blues Band.

By this time, there was much more cross-over between the Edinburgh and Glasgow jazzers, mainly because of the diminishing number of traditional jazz musicians around, and quite a number of Edinburgh musicians were involved with Glasgow bands, including Dave Strutt, Gus Ferguson, Andrew Lauder and the bass player, Dick Walink. Harald Vox then became a member of the well known George Penman Jazzmen with whom he was to stay until George Penman's death in 2009, after which he was to play a major part in keeping the band together as Penman's Jazzmen, with whom he continues to play at the time of writing in 2011.

Meanwhile, picking up our story where we left it in the late 1970s, the Old Bailey band itself was still pulling in good crowds at the Fountain in Barnton. The guitar and banjo player, Johnnie Harper had been with the band between 1965 and 1970 and then again from 1975, when the band reformed. In mid-summer 1978, Johnnie took the step we have already heard about, which was one that he had been contemplating for a while; the decision to try to make a living as a full time jazz musician. He left the Old Bailey band, in which he had made a big reputation for himself, and pursued a professional career which saw him play with the bands of Steve Mason, Jumbo Richford and Colin Dawson. Later, he was to be a member of the French four piece band which had been a great success in Edinburgh in 1978, L'Orpheon Celesta and then the band of the outstanding English clarinet player, Sammy Rimmington.

A move to Norway in 1984 led to work with the Magnolia Jazz Band, the Ophelia Ragtime Orchestra, Jazzade and the Roshnes Jazz Band. On several occasions, he made return visits to play in Edinburgh, particularly during the Edinburgh International Jazz Festivals of which we will hear much more in the next chapter. This included the Festival of 1979, when he returned to play the whole of the Festival with the Old Bailey band. When Johnnie left the Old Bailey band in 1978, his replacement was the man he himself had replaced in 1965, band founder member Mike Hart. Mike was still running his own band, now called Mike Hart's Society Syncopators, and this new arrangement was bound to lead to times when gigs clashed and indeed, this was the reason that Johnnie Harper had played the 1979 Festival with the Old Bailey band.

Then, in October 1979, the Old Bailey band acquired a second musician whom they were sharing with the Syncs, pianist Tom Finlay. This, in turn, led to Tom's piano playing brother Jack covering the 1980 Edinburgh Jazz Festival with the Old Bailey band, with an American banjo player, Ed Turner, covering for Mike Hart. This was clearly not an ideal situation as, just when the band needed to be at its best, things were disrupted by having to get deps up to speed with arrangements and routines, excellent though the deps were. This was a real issue as the band had been building more and more arrangements and new material into its repertoire, under the enthusiastic leadership of Hamish McGregor. This can be appreciated by a listen to an LP recorded by the band in 1980 and called 'Complete with Bum Notes'. This recording was eventually reviewed by Ray Coleman in the Melody Maker who noted that *'Scotland has always had a strong reputation for fiery traditional jazz bands'*. The review also picked out Andrew Lauder's trumpet playing for its *'outstanding tone and authority'* and referred to Sam Smith's trombone contribution as a *'rasping joy'*[137]. Meanwhile, the residency at the Fountain Inn came to an end, when the place was sold, and the band took on a succession of other residencies including the Maybury Road House and The George Hotel in George Street, with others coming along as they moved into 1980s. In 1980, they worked with George Melly on an STV film about the Edinburgh Jazz Festival, made some radio broadcasts and went to the Dunkirk Jazz Festival. Here they became European Amateur Jazz Champions for 1980, succeeding the Syncs who had won the title in 1979. However, the problem of sharing musicians with another band remained. It was not to be resolved until January 1981.

The **Society Syncopators** had continued under the leadership of Mike Hart but inevitably the band sound had altered a great deal, as the band line-up changed. Tello was the first of the Old Guard to leave, followed by Dave Paxton and Bob Craig. The replacements were Gus Ferguson, a trumpeter from Dundee, Jack Graham on reeds and Johnny McGuff on trombone, all of whom were with the band by the mid to late 1970s and the piano player, Tom Finlay, had been added around the same time. These were top class jazz musicians and the band was to continue on its successful course throughout the seventies.

Robin 'Gus' Ferguson (trumpet, flugelhorn) was born in Dundee on 26th September 1942 and educated at the Harris Academy. After starting with piano lessons at the

---

[137] Coleman R, 'Melody Maker', December 5, 1981

age of seven, he switched to trumpet when he was eleven years old and had a half hour formal lesson every school-day lunch time until he was sixteen. The formal teaching of a legitimate method presumably accounts for the technical assurance with which he handles the trumpet and his ability to read music, a relatively rare craft amongst the traditional jazz fraternity. He played in the Dundee Schools Brass Band and Dundee Schools Orchestra. Gus also put in some time with the Tay Division Royal Naval Reserve Band, the Bobby Hayes Sextet and the Domino Dance Band. The Domino Dance Band featured a combination of Scottish country dance music and current popular hits. Each week the Dominoes would buy the sheet music of the latest Top Twenty hit and practice it in the car on the way to their next gig. Their gigs were in village halls and hotels all over Perthshire and Angus.

An early influence on Gus was the show trumpeter Eddie Calvert. Gus then began to listen to recordings of Louis Armstrong and the bands of Kenny Ball, Chris Barber and Acker Bilk, who were all getting a fair amount of air time on radio and TV, and this prompted him into starting to play that kind of music. Gus was particularly impressed by Kenny Ball's technical excellence on the trumpet and also admired the Ball band, which he considered had a bright, new sound and was more up-to-date in its approach than other bands. When he was about nineteen, he started playing in a Dixieland band on Saturday lunch times in the Top Hat pub in Princes Street, Dundee. The band later became known as the Top Hat Seven, a band of which Gus became the leader.

In December 1968, Gus's day job moved him to Edinburgh, where he soon made an impact on the local jazz scene, and formed a band which included Jimmy Shortreed on clarinet, Johnnie Harper on banjo and John Nicholson on drums. When talking about his early days in Edinburgh, Gus made the point that many local jazz musicians were active in several bands simultaneously and did not confine their playing to a single band. The Gus Ferguson Jazz Band eventually developed into a band which Gus named the **Rhythm Method**[138] and they had a Saturday lunch time residency in a hotel in Princes Street. Jackie MacFarlane would often drop in for a song or two and it is likely that Bill Smith was on trombone in this band.

Shortly after this, jazz enthusiast Dave Mylne persuaded Gus to disband his own outfit and join Mike Hart's Society Syncopators. The Syncs, who were later to adopt the name **The Scottish Society Syncopators**, had just lost the services of trumpeter Ian 'Tello' Telford and Gus was the replacement. At first, Gus played in the front line with Dave Paxton and Bob Craig but, by the late 1970s, both Dave and Bob had moved on to be replaced by Jack Graham and Johnny McGuff. The line up of the band was completed by Tom Finlay on piano, Mike Hart who led the band on banjo and guitar, Ken Macdonald on bass and Bobby Stewart on drums. This was the line up when the band made its first LP, recording 'Jazz Tattoo', in March 1980. The LP included a couple of Scottish tunes, 'My Ain Folk' and 'Loch Lomond', both sung by Jack Graham, and in his sleeve note, Dave Mylne said *'It is courageous that they include such traditional Scottish items as 'Loch Lomond' and 'My Ain Folk'. There are pitfalls in such a policy, but the band treat their folk music with such good taste and good humour that it is completely successful'*[139].

Mylne also pointed out that this was not the only notable activity of the band around this time and says *'In 1978 the band entered the Dunkirk jazz contest and came second in the traditional section. In 1979 they carried off the first prize with trombonist Johnny McGuff winning the "individual musician of the competition" award. Fired with enthusiasm from these successes in France, Mike landed an invitation to take the band, with all expenses paid, to the Sacramento Jubilee in 1979. They were a resounding success and were there again in 1980 to join the sixty other bands that make the festival so unique'*. Mylne went on to report *'As one fan from Reno wrote to an English friend, after hearing the*

---

[138] A band called 'Bill Jones' Rhythm Method', led by trombonist Bill Jones, is listed in the 1980 EIJF programme apparently having chosen a similar name.

[139] Mylne D, sleeve note on 'Jazz Tattoo', 'Mike Hart's Scottish Society Syncopators', Parsnip Records PR1001 (See discography appendix)

Syncopators in California – "You would do yourself well to go out of your way to hear these guys. They stole the show, as it were. The way these boys in their kilts played Dixieland, you would think they invented the stuff". High praise indeed, but well deserved. A hearing of the 'Jazz Tattoo' LP confirms that this was a very good band playing a wide choice of material with considerable fire and feeling.

Others who played with the Syncs during this period included Charlie Malley, the trumpeter from Falkirk who had been with the Climax band for a spell in the 1950s, and Dave Strutt, a top class trumpeter, who came originally from Colchester. Gus Ferguson reckons that, as he was unable to make the trips to Dunkirk in 1978/79, due to business commitments, it must have been one of these two who were with the Syncs when they competed. Gus Ferguson was to remain a major player on the Edinburgh jazz scene for years to come and we will catch up with him again in the 1980/90s, when he was an original member of another important group, Fat Sam's Band.

Mike Hart's Society Syncopators

EUROPEAN JAZZ CHAMPIONS · DUNKIRK 1979

For Bookings:
MIKE HART
1 St Stephen Place
Edinburgh 6
Scotland, UK
Tel: 031-226-3736

Ken Macdonald, Johnny McGuff, Charlie Malley, Jack Graham, Frank Birnie, Mike Hart, Tom Finlay (by permission of Mike Hart)

The piano player with both the Syncs and the re-formed Old Bailey band, **Tom Finlay (piano)**, was born in Fife in 1939 and came to Edinburgh to study accountancy in 1959. He had already been taking piano lessons in Fife, where he ran a band but in Edinburgh, he enrolled at Johnny Keating's School of Music in 1961, to further develop his playing. He soon formed a band in Edinburgh which included Colin Terris (French horn), Jimmy Gilmore (tenor sax), Kenny Wheatley (guitar) and Robin Kelso (bass). They played one gig in the Papingo Club but, perhaps because it was at the height of the 'Trad Boom', their more modern style was not successful. At Keating's School, Tom met Alec Gentleman, a jazzer from Falkirk who was studying tenor sax, and this led to him joining a band run by Ken Ramage (trombone) which had Alec Gentleman on tenor sax and Ronnie Dunn on bass. When Ken Ramage went abroad, the band continued but took a new name, the 'Finlay Gentleman Quartet'.

This band soon established itself and was popular with the 'non-trad' section of the Edinburgh jazz public. It was frequently the support band for London based mainstream and modern jazzers visiting Edinburgh and, in September 1963, Tom Finlay together with Ronnie Rae on bass and Billy Alison on drums, were included in an Edinburgh group that backed the West Indian sax player Joe Harriot in the Student's Union. At that time, young jazz musicians tended to get together at the Tempo Club, which was in the High Street behind John Knox's house, and the 369 Club which was also in the High Street. The band, which was playing in the jazz funk idiom, found some work through the Art College and Edinburgh University, where there were lunch time sessions. In addition to his work in the more modern forms of jazz, Tom had, of course, also played with the Chicagoan styled Royal Mile Jazzmen, with the likes of reeds man Jack Duff and drummer Sandy Malcolm, as we heard in Chapter VI. Then, in 1964, Tom went off to play on the transatlantic liners and a couple of years later in 1966, went on a world cruise with Graeme Robertson, now playing bass, and Bobby Stewart on drums. This brought them the chance to hear many great American musicians in

New York, musicians that up until then they had only heard on record.

The constant playing required on these trips had another benefit too; having started as enthusiastic amateurs, the ceaseless practice made polished professional musicians of them. This stood them in good stead and they found plenty work, in both dance and jazz combos, when they returned to Edinburgh. Tom Finlay was to become one of the most versatile and respected of all of Edinburgh's jazzers, a man who could play as easily with top flight visiting musicians as he could with local jazz bands of any type. The list of top-flight jazz musicians with whom Tom played is a very lengthy one, too long to give here, but amongst them were reeds men Peanuts Hucko, Bob Wilber, Scott Hamilton and Bud Freeman, and trumpeters Doc Cheatham, Harry 'Sweets' Edison and Red Rodney, who had played with the Charlie Parker Quintet between 1949 and 1951 – a distinguished list from the main stream of jazz, some of whom did not appear in Edinburgh until the advent of the Edinburgh International Jazz Festival in late 1970s. It was in the 1970s too, that Tom was persuaded by Mike Hart to join the New Society Syncopators and he was with the band on their successful trips to Dunkirk. He was to remain an important Edinburgh jazzer for many years and at the time of writing in 2010, is as active and admired, both as a band pianist and solo, as ever.

Chapter XI

New Orleans Jazz in the 1970s

Things were happening in the Edinburgh purist jazz world in the 1970s as well, although by then, this form of the music was usually called New Orleans jazz. **Violet Milne (piano, vocals)**, wife of drummer Kenny Milne and mother of trumpeter Finlay, had been born in Glasgow in 1936. She had started singing with the Vintage Jazz Band in Glasgow in 1958, a band that included Farrie Forsyth on drums. After moving to Edinburgh, she sang with the Climax band and then, after moving to London, sang with the Kid Martyn Ragtime Band. There followed a period living in Essex, when she was not active in jazz while raising her family and then, in 1971, she took up piano. This led to gigs with various bands before she became a member of the Essex based Criterion Jazz Band in about 1975. In 1977, Violet and Kenny returned to Edinburgh. Back on home territory, in December 1979, Kenny was instrumental in forming a band for a one-off gig supporting the touring Freddy Kohlman Band from New Orleans, and they played alongside the Kohlman band at the Adam Rooms.

The new band, which they christened the **Spirits of Rhythm**, sounded so good and had played so well that, after the gig, they decided to keep the band together. The original line-up was Fraser Gauld (tpt), George Duncan (ct), probably Bill Jones (tbn), Violet (pno), Willie Mack (bs) and Kenny on drums. There was also a banjo player whose pony tail hair style has proved more memorable than his name! Kenny had taken up trumpet around 1970, about the same time as his son Finlay began on the same instrument. At the time the Spirits of Rhythm were formed, Kenny was already heavily committed playing trumpet with Bill Salmond's Louisiana Ragtime Band and, with Kenny unable to spare the time, Violet took over the running of the new band. The Spirits, as the band was to become known, was to become an Edinburgh institution and would be the band with whose name Violet would always be associated.

The band was immediately successful and was included in the second Edinburgh International Jazz Festival in 1980. Over the next couple of years, there were a few changes in the band but by 1984, the line up had stabilised, with Ian Boyter replacing George Duncan, Jack Weddell coming in on trombone, Brian Weld on banjo and Robin Galloway on bass, a line up that was to last. The Spirits had several very successful residencies and amongst them was La Grenouille in the New Town, Sorbonne in the Cowgate, Nobles Bar in Constitution Street in Leith, the Stair Arms out beyond Dalkeith near Pathhead and the Haymarket Bar and Basin Street, both of which were near Haymarket Station. Basin Street is of particularly fond memory for many local jazzers as it was, for years, a major venue for local jazz with jazz bands featured almost every evening of the week. It was located in the upstairs bar of the Haymarket Station Bar and had reproduction posters of old time jazz bands and musicians on the walls of the stairway. At one time the Spirits following was such that it allowed them to feature at Basin Street on two consecutive evenings each week.

The Spirits, throughout their long (and continuing) history, played in the New Orleans style and played a major part in keeping this type of traditional jazz alive and well in Edinburgh. The band's reputation, coupled with that of Kenny Milne who had a well-deserved reputation as a drummer in New Orleans circles, enabled them to play at many jazz festivals, both in the UK and on the Continent. Included in these were the Ascona and Arosa Jazz Festivals in Switzerland and, in the UK, jazz festivals at Glasgow, Peebles, Dundee, Kirkcudbright, Girvan, Bute, Orkney, Keswick and Bude, in addition to the Edinburgh International Jazz Festival (EIJF). In the latter, they became an essential component of the programme and, at the time of writing in 2010, the Spirits can claim with pride, that they have featured in the EIJF every year since their debut in 1980. This makes a still growing total of thirty one consecutive appearances at the EIJF, the only one they missed being the very first in 1979, hardly their fault as it took place four months before the band was formed. The Spirits also made several tours in Switzerland, mostly playing in hotels, and a particularly memorable event in their history was an invitation to play at the World Economic Forum at Davos, also in Switzerland, where they shared the lime light with US President Bill Clinton.

The band also made several recordings, the first being an LP which featured them with guest tenor saxophonist Sam Lee, who had been born in Napoleonville in Louisiana in 1911 and moved to New Orleans in 1926. This LP was recorded in April 1984 at the Hart Street Studios in Edinburgh and the band line-up was the stabilised one given above, but with the bass playing duties shared between Robin Galloway and Willie Mack. The Spirits also appeared on a compilation tape recorded at the Keswick Jazz Festival, issued by Lake Records, and appeared on another compilation recording, called 'Jazz Around the World', issued by Jazz Crusade. In addition, Kenny's investment in some high class recording gear has enabled the issue of several other CDs, produced by the band themselves[140].

In the nature of bands, the passing years brought some changes in personnel. After Fraser Gauld stopped playing, Violet often used just a two-piece front line, with Ian Boyter on reeds and Jack Weddell on trombone sharing the lead role, although the fine trumpeter Dave Strutt played with them for an extended period in the 1990s. The obvious choice on trumpet would, of course, have been Violet's and Kenny's son Finlay, who became a very good player, but unfortunately, Finlay's work in television took him away from Edinburgh. Jack Weddell was in and out of the band at least three times before he eventually retired from playing. Brian Weld also left, to be succeeded by Nigel

---

[140] See Discography Appendix

Porteous, but later made a return to the band. On bass, after Robin Galloway left Edinburgh, Fred Murray, Roy Percy, Dizzy Jackson and Graham Blamire all played with the Spirits for spells. At the end of the first decade of the twenty first century, the Spirits of Rhythm continue to play in their mellow, warm and relaxed New Orleans style, with a line-up that is remarkably similar to that of the early 1980s – Violet and Kenny Milne, Ian Boyter, Alan Quinn on trombone (who sadly was to die in early 2011), Brian Weld and the veteran bass player, Dizzy Jackson.

Fraser Gauld (trumpet), the Spirits' original trumpeter, was born on 10th May 1940, educated at Daniel Stewart's College and was to become a computer programmer in his 'day job'. He had violin lessons at school and played in the school orchestra but soon decided that the violin did not suit him. His older brother, Alastair 'Shorty' Gauld, was already involved in jazz and played banjo in Mike Hart's Blue Blowers, playing alongside Mike and Ian Telford on trumpet, at the Shoestring Cafe in the Royal Mile. Apparently, the older Gauld had a recording of Bunk Johnson playing 'Tishomingo Blues' and when Fraser heard this he was hooked. He decided that he wanted to play clarinet but, as no clarinet was available at school, he managed to borrow a school trumpet from someone in the school orchestra. Like so many of us of that generation, he then proceeded to teach himself to play his instrument. Bunk Johnson was to remain Fraser's model throughout his jazz career.

The next step was obviously to start a band and Fraser soon got together with others at school to begin their playing careers in one of the junior school classrooms, which happened to have a piano. The original little group had Fraser, who knew enough to play a little piano, Sandy Gracie on clarinet and one or two others. Another pupil at the school was Iain Forde, already playing trombone, who looked in and intimated that he was interested in joining them. According to Iain Forde, Fraser was musically the key member of this group. This was because he was the only one who knew anything about chords and was able to demonstrate on piano and, because his brother owned a banjo, on that instrument as well. However, the jazz pioneers of Daniel Stewart's College were to go the way of so many similar attempts in those unenlightened times. The Headmaster, Dr Robbie, got to hear of their efforts and proclaimed that it must stop forthwith, and of course it did. However, salvation was at hand in the person of the school chaplain, a Mr Chisholm, who took pity on them and arranged for them to practice in a church storage hall, next to John Knox's house in the High Street.

Fraser and the others practiced like mad and soon organised a jazz concert, inviting all their friends from school and even one of the teachers. They obviously used their limited manpower with great skill and versatility and were able to present, not only the jazz band, but a skiffle group and a jug band as well. The cost of a ticket was kept down to one penny and all unsold tickets were put in the bell of the school tuba, from where they made regular but unscheduled appearances for years afterwards, to the general mystification of successive generations of Daniel Stewarts College tuba players. The invited teacher duly attended and wrote a report on the concert, which stated that the music had been terrible and, in a critique of the jug band's performance, added that '...for some reason Stuart McGregor spat into a jug'. Nothing daunted, two of the intrepid band, Fraser himself and Willie Cairns, set themselves to making a full-size, plywood replica of the school's double bass. Fraser proudly reports that this was accomplished, 'complete with the curly bit on top', presumably meaning the scroll. Unfortunately, although the result 'looked perfect', it turned out to sound like a tea chest. Even this did not deter them, and they began to practice in Iain Forde's mother's house in Ann Street.

After leaving school, enthusiasm intact in spite of Headmasterly opposition, instrument manufacturing setbacks and typical jazz critic negativity, Fraser and Iain Forde met up with others with jazz playing aspirations. These were Jake McMahon and two brothers, Alan and Peter Ritchie, whom they met at the Stud Club, then functioning in St John's Hill, and they soon formed a band. Willie Cairns dropped out and, having found a replacement in the person of Donald Macdonald, they turned their carpentry skills towards manufacturing a trolley on which to transport the bass to his house in Portobello. (It does not surprise me in the slightest that a trolley was required for the home made double bass. When I was in the Scouts at about the same time, lack of any real instruments inspired us to make a guitar from a kit. It too, looked alright but turned out to be of incredible weight, as well as having a feeble sound which was inaudible at a distance of about three feet. It came in useful at camp to stop things blowing away in a strong wind.) Fraser and company meanwhile started holding practices in India Buildings.

There followed a bit of a gap in Fraser's jazz career as, while he was at Edinburgh University, he did little playing. However, by 1964 he was free from studies and joined Bill Salmond's band, with whom he played residences at the Woolpack, the Lothian Bar and at the Cephas Club, situated in the crypt of St Georges West church in Shandwick Place. Although a church establishment, this latter venue turned out to be a dangerous place. One night, a mob of aggressive young yobs turned up and invaded the band room. At the time, this room was being shared with a group of Gillespie's school girls who were getting changed into dancing outfits for a dance demonstration. The girls ignored the yobs and continued changing. This impressive display of coolness under fire and stiff upper lip was too much for the yobs who, according to Fraser, were 'dumbstruck'. However, their yobbishness soon reasserted itself and shortly afterwards, they switched off all the lights and began to throw bottles at the band stand, before making off into the night with the till.

In the 1970s, Fraser played with a succession of bands with peculiar names including the Granton Jass Works and the 'king Great Band, which had Jock Westwater (bjo), Walt Smith (clt), Paul Munro (tbn) and Dave Rae (drms). He also played with a band called Deep South, which played in the Nelson Hotel and included Angus MacDonald (tbn), Andy Hampton (clt), Colin Warwick (bjo), Robin Galloway (bs) and again, Dave Rae (drms). None of these bands lasted for very long and, at the end of the 1970s, Fraser became a member of Violet Milne's new band, The Spirits of Rhythm, and this one did last.

**The Spirits of Rhythm in Basin Street at Haymarket
Back row: Kenny Milne (drms), Violet Milne (pno), Brian
Weld (bjo), Fred Murray (bs),
Front row: Ian Boyter (rds), Fraser Gauld (tpt), Jack
Weddell (tbn)
(by permission of Ian Boyter)**

With the Spirits, Fraser played at their residency in La
Grenouille and he remembers that Brian Weld, who had
played the banjo with the Climax Jazz Band back in the
1950s, happened to be passing the venue one evening,
heard the band, came in into the pub and was more or less
immediately recruited to play banjo. Although Brian had
not played for twenty five years, he soon rediscovered his
previous skills and was quickly back in the swing of things.
Fraser was on the recording that the Spirits made with
Sammy Lee and whoever wrote the sleeve notes paid Fraser
a well-deserved compliment, saying that he was *'nicknamed
'Phraser' because of his electrifying runs'*. While playing
with the Spirits Fraser also played with a band put together
by the trombonist, Alan Quinn. This band was based at the
Temple Hall, a hotel in the Portobello area, and adopted the
name of the hotel, calling themselves the Temple Hall

Stompers. The band, in addition to Fraser and Alan Quinn, had Eddie Hamilton (clt), Beverly Knight (bjo), Jimmy Tunnah (bs) and Roger Hanley (drms).

Meanwhile, Fraser went with the Spirits to play at a couple of Ascona Jazz Festivals but, just before a third visit in 1987, his playing came to a sad and premature end. There was a history of the ear trouble, tinnitus, in Fraser's family and unfortunately, he found himself afflicted with this debilitating condition. The medical advice was to keep away from loud noises and it was soon apparent that the sound of a New Orleans band in full cry came well within the medical concept of loud noises. Fraser had no option but to stop playing. He made an attempt some twenty years later to play again, but the tinnitus quickly returned and the attempt came to nothing. The loss of Fraser's trumpet playing was a major blow to Edinburgh jazz and especially to the Spirits of Rhythm. He was an assured, hot player with a delicious sense of timing and swing, in both his lead work and his soloing. The extent of the loss is well illustrated by the difficulty the Spirits had in replacing him, often choosing to play without trumpet than to settle for less than the standard that Fraser Gauld had set.

George Duncan (clarinet, alto sax) was born in Edinburgh 9th September 1945 and, after early schooling at Flora Stevenson's School near the foot of Orchard Brae, transferred to George Watsons College when he was twelve. His family was not a particularly musical one, although his father liked the singing of Bing Crosby, and it was his Crosby records that first attracted the young George to music. His older brother Billy had some jazz records, including some by the George Lewis band and the Louis Armstrong All Stars, and these soon attracted George's interest. The Lewis recordings, from around 1952, included Burgundy Street Blues, a tune that George was later to play many times, together with Mamma Don't Allow and Yaka Hula Hickey Dula. His interest in jazz now established, George, at the age of thirteen, decided to take up clarinet and, after a few introductory lessons, taught himself how to play.

His first venture into active playing came about because his mother, convinced she had a musical prodigy on her hands, responded to an advert and arranged an audition for him. This was in the Spring of 1962 and, at the age of about sixteen, George duly attended his audition in a church hall in Constitution Street in Leith. It turned out that this was an attempt to form a jazz band to be called the 'Stories Alley Jazz Band', after a lane off the Kirkgate in Leith. This was because one of the band had managed to filch the street sign bearing the words Stories Alley and had set it up on the bass drum. The only one of the band, most of whom were in their mid-twenties, whose name George was able to remember was the drummer, George Hutchison, known as Hutch. George's audition was successful and, although it was really just a practice band, he also played a couple of gigs with them. However, his mother, who had arranged it in the first place, now got cold feet. Mindful of his approaching school higher exams, she put pressure on him and George resigned. George's mother probably felt she had been right, as his school results were good enough to allow him to go off to study pharmacy at Robert Gordon's College (now University) in Aberdeen, a period when he did little playing.

Before going to Aberdeen, George had made further contacts within the Edinburgh jazz scene and had played at the Woolpack pub, near the McEwan Hall, with one of Bill Salmond's early bands, a band which included Alan Quinn on trombone. On his return to Edinburgh in 1969, he soon got back in touch with Bill and, in 1970, began playing regularly with Bill's band which also included Dave Strutt (tpt), George Howden (tbn), Willie Mack (bs) and Kenny Orr (drms). This was in a residency in the Haymarket Station Bar (later to become Basin Street) which lasted until 1971 after which the band, now with Gus Ferguson on trumpet and Graham Scott on piano, moved to a new spot in the Carlton Hotel on the North Bridge. The Carlton gig came to an end in 1972 but by then the band had taken on another spot, at the Canmore Lounge. This pub stood at the crossroads between the Grange and Causewayside, and the residency was to continue until 1974. This gig was followed by a move to the St Clair Hotel in Minto Street, by which time Bill had dropped the trumpet and was using a two piece front line, with George often playing the lead on alto sax.   George's Edinburgh jazz career then came to a temporary halt as he moved to London, where he teamed up with two other Edinburgh exiles, Kenny Milne and Dougie Boyter, in Kenny's Criterion Jazz Band.   George also played with a band run by a drummer called John Petters and, with the latter band, George played with two fine trumpeters, Ken Sims and Freddie Randall.

George's return to Edinburgh in 1979 put him in the right place at the right time. Kenny and Violet Milne had also returned to town and George joined the new band put together by Violet, the Spirits of Rhythm, with whom he would stay until 1982.   After the three years with the Spirits, George was to join the band with whom he was to stay for the next seventeen years, the band of Charlie McNair.

Ian Boyter (reeds), was born in 1943 in St Andrews but later moved to Edinburgh, where he attended Boroughmuir Senior Secondary School.   Ian was to become a graphic designer.   He was self taught on alto sax and, at the age of sixteen, started playing in rock bands including The Outlaws and Ricky and the Eagles.   However, when he was twenty two, he stopped playing altogether and was not to resume until he was thirty five.   This time, it was the jazz scene that attracted him and his first band was to be the Spirits of Rhythm, replacing George Duncan in time for the 1983 Edinburgh Jazz Festival.   In addition, Ian soon started his own band, the Gumbo Jazz Band, which bore a strong family likeness to the Spirits of Rhythm, with a line-up of Finlay Milne and later, Donald Corbett (tpt), Bill Jones (tbn), Violet Milne (pno), Tony Sergent (bs), Kenny Henderson (bjo) and Roger Hanley (drms).   The Gumbo band had a residency in the Spider's Web, in Morrison Street.

Ian, by this time, had added clarinet to his armoury, although he always regarded sax as his main instrument. He soon proved his worth in a jazz context, being a natural improviser with a strong, muscular sound on tenor sax and a warm, woody tone on clarinet.   He was ideally suited to the New Orleans style and, after starting with them in 1983, was to remain loyal to the Spirits for almost thirty years at the time of writing in 2011.   Ian also frequently played as a dep around town, but was also to become a member of

310

other bands at various times, an example being Jim Petrie's Diplomats of Jazz. The Spirits, however, always had first call on his services. In the 2000s, he played for a time with the Maid of the Forth Stompers and also became a member of Bill Salmond's Louisiana Ragtime Band.

Over the years, Ian broadened his experience and style and was always keen to take every playing opportunity. In 2010, he set up his own jazz band website and is able and willing to put together bands from duos up to full seven-piece New Orleans bands. He also plays in a singer-led Swing band, 'Swing Supreme'. He has tried his hand at writing tunes and constantly works on extending his musical knowledge. However, the New Orleans style always seemed to me to be Ian's natural jazz habitat, with his preference for a free improvising setting, whether demonstrating his ability to play the orthodox role of the reeds as secondary to a trumpet lead or taking the lead role himself.

No account of Edinburgh traditional jazz would be complete without a look at another aspect of the New Orleans influence – the bands which were sometimes called **Parade Bands**, sometimes Marching Bands and, especially in the USA, Brass Bands. These bands generally played at outdoor events and were very much part of the New Orleans jazz tradition. William J Schafer's book, 'Brass Bands and New Orleans Jazz'[141] explains that *'The brass band in nineteenth century America was as ubiquitous in its time as juke boxes and electric music systems in ours'*. What he is referring to here is, of course, not the brass band in a jazz context but the fact that *'When even large cities could not raise a symphony orchestra, every village had its silver cornet band and bandstand in the square'*. Shafer goes on to explain that the brass band was a major contributor amongst the many and varied sources that went to create jazz in the late nineteenth and early twentieth century. He goes on to say *'If we look carefully at early New Orleans music in milieu and time, the brass band emerges as a major source, a gene pool, for jazz'*. Thus, along with sundry other

---

[141] Schafer W J, 'Brass Bands and New Orleans Jazz', pages 8 and 9, ISBN 0-8071-0282-2 pbk, by permission of Louisiana State University Press, 1977

sources such as complex African rhythms and 'blue' tonality, European notions of harmony and form, Ragtime, French and Spanish rhythms and American folk traditions, the music and even the actual form of the nineteenth century American town and city brass bands, must be seen as a significant component in the heady mix that went into the making of jazz. Schafer, quoting an observer of the black music milieu after the civil war, also tells us that, as early as 1878, *'New Orleans has several fine brass bands among its coloured population'*. It seems unlikely that these bands would sound like the New Orleans Parade Bands of today. It is probable that they were marching bands, using principally brass instruments, modelled on the military bands of the time, and designed to provide suitably rousing music, when municipal pride demanded it.

However, it seems that, as time went by, the tide of influence turned, and the New Orleans Parade Bands became more and more influenced by jazz music. From then on, it seems, the parade bands of New Orleans increasingly adopted the mores of jazz: improvisation, particularly simultaneous improvisation, a tendency to bend or 'blue' the pitch of notes and, above all, the sensuous rhythmic nuances that came to be called swing. This latter factor is perhaps the most telling of all, providing what Schafer calls *'...a tension between the march's strong, striding 1-and-3 beat emphasis with the Afro-American penchant for 2-and-4 accents'*. Part of this development seems to have been a move away from the formality of the nineteenth century brass bands, with their use of written parts, towards a looser, much more informal and extemporised performance, albeit with a clear discipline that determined the role of each instrument in producing a coherent, integrated ensemble. Rex Harris, writing in his book 'Jazz' in the 1950s, says *'..."jazzing" of marches was achieved partly by the trick of shifting the accent from the strong to the weak beat and partly by allowing solo players to "decorate" the melody they were playing – solo improvisation; or several players to indulge in their extemporisation simultaneously – collective improvisation'*[142].

---

[142] Harris R, 'Jazz', 4th edition, page 57, Penguin Books, 1956

In other words, the New Orleans parade bands became less like military bands in character and more like a New Orleans jazz band, but on the move rather than static.

Schafer points out that the brass bands provided a training ground for many great jazzmen such as King Oliver, Bunk Johnson, Kid Ory and Louis Armstrong. However, he also says that brass band playing in New Orleans, in addition, produced a cadre of men who persisted with the brass band tradition after 1920 and regarded themselves as different from jazz musicians, still playing from written scores and not 'ear men' like the jazzers. The names of some of the famous New Orleans Parade Bands have come down the years to us: the Allen Brass Band (1907-1950) led by the father of the great trumpeter, Henry 'Red' Allen, the Eureka Brass Band which started in 1920, the Excelsior Brass Band active between 1880 and 1931, Kid Howard's Brass Band of 1945-1950 and, more recently, the Olympia Brass Band and the revived Onward Brass Band of about 1960. The personnel listed by Schafer for these bands and many others, are scattered with the names of famous New Orleans jazz musicians.

The first key figure in the development of Parade Bands in Edinburgh was the double bass player Jim Young of the Climax band who, thanks to his military band training, also played both tuba and sousaphone. We have already heard, in Chapter VII, the story of the first marching band in Edinburgh, when the combined Climax and Kid Martyn bands took themselves from the Tempo Club in the High Street to play for Hogmanay revellers at the Tron Church. This is the first record of which I am aware of a marching jazz band in Edinburgh, although it was really just two existing jazz bands getting together to play out of doors. The venture was so successful that the Climax band repeated it at Hogmanay for several years. As for the marching aspect, Jim says that a better description might be that they shuffled along!

Jim Young then spent some time, between 1963 and 1967, based in London, where the strong New Orleans jazz movement had already led to the formation of a number of Parade Bands. Jim's ability to play brass bass ensured that

313

his services were much in demand and he was soon involved, playing many Parade Band gigs in London and on the Continent. He also recorded with several of these bands, one of which was Casimir's Paragon Brass Band, which also included Edinburgh's Jake McMahon on E-flat clarinet. Jim made a second LP with the Paragon band, recorded live on the streets of Rouen in France, on November 22nd 1970. He was also on the LP 'Dejan's Olympia Brass Band in Europe', which was recorded in Berlin on 4th August 1868, the cover of which has a photo of the band including Jim, on the steps of St Paul's Cathedral. Jim was also present on some tracks on a second LP made by this band, which was recorded in London at St Martin's in the Field and St Paul's Cathedral, on 26th July 1968. Chris Barber too, called on Jim's services, when he made a double LP of Parade Band jazz. This was issued as 'Chris Barber Special' on Black Lion Special recordings (BLP 20108/9), in 1975 and features the Beatles tune, 'All My Loving'.

On his return to Edinburgh, Jim Young was soon into action forming a proper marching band in the New Orleans tradition, which he called the **Auld Reekie Parade Band**. This band proved very popular and played at the Edinburgh Students' Charities Processions, where it was heard by the very large crowd that used to turn out for this annual event. At that time, in the late 1970s, the Edinburgh New Orleans bands had an annual Hogmanay Jazz Band Ball and it became the tradition that the bands would exit just before midnight, before making a grand entry as a marching band, bringing in the New Year with suitable flourish. The Auld Reekie band was also involved in the early Edinburgh Jazz Festivals and, indeed, featured at the opening event of the very first Festival, in Tiffany's Ballroom, in St Stephen Street, in 1979. The Auld Reekie Parade Band of that year can be heard playing 'St Louis Blues' on the special compilation LP that was issued to celebrate the 1980 Festival. Playing with them were two visitors from New Orleans, drummer Andrew Hall and tenor saxist Teddy Johnson.

Jim Young describes the classical line-up for a Parade band as: two trumpets, two trombones, one brass bass (tuba or sousaphone), an E-flat clarinet, one or two saxophones, a snare drum and a bass drum. It was traditional to have someone in a sort of drum major role at the head of the band where, instead of a drum major's mace, he was equipped with a brolly and a whistle. Apparently this was more for show than any real musical function, although he would use the whistle to call the band to attention before moving off. Kenny Milne, like Jim Young much involved with Parade Bands, claims that it was the function of the brolly man to draw the attention of the band to potential hazards in their path, such as holes in the road or piles of horse or dog poo lying about! A parade band was, in fact, governed by the snare drummer and the senior trumpeter. When the band was on the move but not playing, the snare drummer's job was to tap out the beat on the snare, so the band could march (or shuffle!) along in time. At the point when the band was to begin to play again, the trumpeter would play a short phrase that told the band the tune they were to play and its key. It was then the function of the snare drummer to play an introductory pattern of ratta-tat-tats, after which the band would burst into action. The usual marching formation had the trombones at the front, followed by the two trumpets with the brass bass between them, then the reeds, and finally the two drummers. The tradition, started in New Orleans, was for a 'second line' of people to march along behind the band, some with brollys, all moving in time with the beat of the band and making a colourful and lively display.

Jim recruited for the 'Auld Reekie' band among the Edinburgh traditional jazzers, most of whom played in the band at one time or another. They included Jim himself (brass bs), Jim Petrie, Fraser Gauld and Kenny Milne (tpts), Jack Weddell, Bob Craig and Sam Smith (tbns) and George Gilmour and George Duncan (rds). Sometimes Kenny Milne, Pete Ritchie or Bill Warden would play the snare and sometimes others had to be dragooned into the band at short notice when they were short. Kenny Milne remembers being back in Edinburgh on holiday and being hastily recruited by Jim Young to play the bass drum. On that occasion, the Auld Reekie band was augmented by a group of Musicians Union members, which Kenny Milne

315

remembers as including Jimmy Shortreed (clt), George Roy (tpt) and Russ Cessford (drms). Apparently this came about because the M.U. had been asked to put together a Parade Band, probably for the Charities procession, and they had turned to Jim Young for help. Kenny's unexpected stint on bass drum ended with him *completely knackered and covered with blood from where he had knocked his knuckles off against the bass drum*! On another occasion, an alarmed Kenny Macdonald was hauled out of the crowd at the start of a parade to play the bass drum.

Kenny Milne says that Parade Bands generally had become much less dependent on written music, *'less dots oriented'* was his description, as time went on and by about the 1970/80s, they played as almost totally improvising bands. However, it was by no means a musical free for all. The role of each instrument within the eight to ten piece band was clearly understood, so that the whole made an integrated sound, much in the same way as in the traditional New Orleans bands' ensemble playing. Kenny himself founded Edinburgh's second parade band, which he called the **Criterion New Orleans Brass Band**, in time for the second Edinburgh Jazz Festival in 1980. He drew on much the same pool of musicians as had Jim Young, and Jim himself sometimes played bass drum with them when Graham Scott, the regular bass drummer, was unavailable.

Kenny recalls that they sometimes greatly increased the size of the band for especially demanding jobs, when extra power was needed, such as the annual Jazz Festival parade along Princes Street, when they would sometimes have a band of sixteen to twenty, including five trumpeters. A former next door neighbour of the Milne family when they lived in Essex, Edwin Adcock, often came up take on the role of the drum major brolly man, more correctly called the Grand Marshall. In New Orleans, parade bands were often accompanied by dancers and Kenny and Violet Milne's daughter Jennifer, her pal Cathy McInally and Margaret Cut, a long time supporter of Edinburgh jazz, often took on this job. Jennifer and Cathy in particular, became quite well known as dancers, dressing for the part and strutting their stuff with considerable flair and enthusiasm, which always took a trick at parade time.

The Criterion Brass Band became successful in the long term, the longest serving of Edinburgh's parade bands. They played at many Edinburgh Jazz Festivals, as well as jazz festivals on the Continent at Ascona, Davos, and Celerina, usually travelling as an eight or nine piece band, including the two dancers. They also became regulars at other jazz festivals in Scotland, including those at Peebles and Glasgow, as well as frequent gigs at gala days at South Queensferry and Loanhead and even played at a few funerals. The band's publicity pamphlet listed their gigs as including Galas, openings, barbecues, concerts, product launches, sports events, car rallies, fund-raising events and corporate entertainments, all of which in the past had been enlivened by the band's infectious beat and raunchy music. The repertoire is described as including rags, stomps, spirituals, dirges, blues, popular melodies and traditional jazz marches. Typical tunes played are given as When the Saints Go Marching In, Doctor Jazz, Panama Rag, The Old Rugged Cross, Down in Honky Tonk Town and Basin Street Blues. At the time of writing in 2010, the Criterion Brass Band have issued three CDs of their music. Musicians who played with the Criterion Brass Band included:

Trumpets:	Kenny Milne, Finlay Milne, Fraser Gauld, Jim Petrie, Adam Latto and Colin Dawson
Trombones:	Jack Weddell, Bob Craig and Sam Smith
Reeds:	Ian Boyter, George Gilmour, George Duncan and Cameron Greig
Brass bass:	Symon Carlyle, Jim Young and Dick Staughan (from Newcastle)
Snare drum:	Kenny Milne, Eric Jamieson, Mac Rae (from Newcastle)
Bass drum:	Graham Scott, Bill Salmond, Bill Martin, Jim Young and Beverly Knight

Adam Latto also sometimes played bass drum, sousaphone or euphonium. Sometimes, a Parade Band would be improvised on the spot, when the occasion demanded it. I can remember members of the Spirits of Rhythm and the Louisiana Ragtime Band forming up as a Parade Band to lead us all from the ferry to the Stromness

Hotel, at the start of the Orkney Jazz Festival in the late 1990s.

The Criterion Brass Band in full cry
Graham Scott (bass drum), George Gilmour (clt), Alan
Quinn (tbn), Simon Carlyle (sousa)
(photo courtesy of Peter Davenport)

A third Edinburgh Parade band, which was to be called the **Honestas Brass Band**, was formed in 1987 by Adam Latto. **Adam Latto (cornet, trumpet, tuba, euphonium, sousaphone and bass drum)** was born in Fisherrow on 22 November 1937 and educated at Mussellburgh Grammar School, where a class mate was the bass player, Ronnie Rae. Adam was very much a Musselburgh man, indeed something of an authority on the history of the town, and the band's name came from Musselburgh's reputation as the 'Honest Toun'. Adam by day was an antiquarian book seller and for many years, he traded from his book shop, by the side of the River Esk, in Musselburgh. He returned from National Service around 1958, at the age of twenty one, and started cornet lessons with the local brass band, Musselburgh and Fisherrow Trades Prize Band. He had always had an interest in jazz but it was not until he heard Kenny Milne's Criterion Brass Band that he decided to get actively involved. The Honestas Brass Band first got together to practice in March 1987 and this was followed by a marching rehearsal along at the Old Grange Mining Museum at Prestongrange, just to the east of Musselburgh. Over the years, Adam used many musicians in the Honestas band and the stalwarts who were the mainstay of the band, are shown below:

Trumpet: Adam Latto, Graham McArthur, Jimmy Welsh, Gus Ferguson

Trombone: Andrew Mulhern, Alan Quinn, Sandy Barclay, Gavin Dawson

Reeds: Eddie Hamilton, Bob Busby, Bob McDowell, Alex Munro, George Mitchell

Snare drum: Roy Dunnett, Eddie Hamilton, Roger Hanley, Ian Forrest

Bass drum: Bill Salmond, Beverly Knight, Brian Weld, Adam Latto

Brass bass: Bill Brydon, Lindsay Cooper, Fred Freyling-Kelly, Adam Latto

In addition, long-serving Edinburgh jazz followers Gerry and Cathie Brennan were recruited to act as Grand Marshalls in the New Orleans tradition, always leading the way with great flair and panache.

The Honestas band played its first gig at Wallyford Miner's Gala on 6th June 1987 and remained in action until 1989, when there was a two year break in its history, largely because several key members became unavailable. However, Adam got the band together again in 1992 and over the next fourteen years, the band was never short of gigs. They played at many Edinburgh Jazz Festival events, taking part in the Mardi Gras in the Grassmarket on numerous occasions and in the Festival opening parade. In seven consecutive years, 1996 to 2002, they played at the Hawick Jazz Festival. Other gigs were at the Danderhall Gala, the Leith pageant, the Leith Jazz Festival from 1992 to 2002, the St Stephen Street Festival and, on one occasion, a funeral at the Corstorphine Hill cemetery.

Caricature of Adam Latto by trumpeter Jimmy Welsh (from the collection of Adam Latto, by permission of Jimmy Welsh)

They even played at a Chinese Dragon Boat Race at Leith Docks and a Hibs v Hearts match at Easter Road, although which was the more bizarre event, I cannot say! As time went by, of course, there were times when Adam had to fill gaps in the band and many of the well known Edinburgh jazzers made appearances, including the leaders of Edinburgh's other two parade bands, Jim Young and Kenny Milne. Adam himself had to play both snare and bass drum at times when availability was a problem. Adam Latto retired to live in the Border country in 1993, living just over the border near Berwick upon Tweed, but kept the Honestas Brass Band going until 2006, when their final gig was the Edinburgh International Jazz Festival Mardi Gras. While living near Berwick, Adam played sousaphone in the Tweed River Jazz band for twelve years.

The purist or New Orleans tradition was and is a very strong part of Edinburgh jazz. Starting in the 1950s, when the Climax Jazz Band made its first appearance, right through the 1960s and 70s with the Louisiana Ragtime Band and the Spirits of Rhythm and on into the 1980s and

90s when, in addition to the jazz bands, there was the strong marching band presence with the Auld Reekie, Criterion and Honestas Brass bands, New Orleans jazz was an integral part of the Edinburgh jazz scene. At the time of writing in 2011, the New Orleans tradition remains the strongest part of Edinburgh traditional jazz, with the Edinburgh Jazz and Jive Club featuring the Spirits, the Louisiana Ragtime Band, Brian Robertson's Forth River Ragtimers, Jim Petrie's Diplomats of Jazz and the Criterion Brass Band, all still around and all with their roots firmly in the New Orleans tradition. There is even a latter day revival of the spirit of the Climax band itself, styling themselves the Anti-Climax Jazz Band!

Chapter XII

The Edinburgh International Jazz Festival

Not for the first time, Mike Hart had an idea in his head and it concerned the setting up of some sort of notable and regular jazz event in Edinburgh. He had heard that there was a festival of traditional jazz held in Sacramento in California and, interested to find out more, made a special visit, flying out there in 1978. The Sacramento event had been founded in 1973 and was called the Sacramento Jazz Jubilee, later to become the Sacramento Jazz Festival. The founder was a trumpeter called Bill Borcher, who led a band called the Oregon Jazz Band. Clearly a man of wide interests, Bill Borcher also had connections with one of the bigger breweries and was a basketball coach. The original plan which Borcher had contrived, had been to get hold of all the traditional jazz band leaders that he knew who owned or ran their own jazz clubs, and ask them if they would be interested in playing at the Jazz Jubilee for nothing! Borcher then arranged for the brewers to provide beer, also for nothing, for the entire weekend of the event. His next move was to arrange for members of his basketball association to serve in the local bars, where they sold the beer, and used the proceeds to fund the event and pay the invited foreign bands. While this scheme may seem wildly unlikely, Bill Borcher had brought it off and the Jazz Jubilee had run very successfully, since its inception in 1973. In addition to the American bands which appeared for nothing, guest bands from all over the world were also featured, although they were paid.

Mike met with Bill Borcher, picked his brains, had a good look at the Jazz Jubilee, and returned home Hell-bent of starting something similar in Edinburgh. Mike was not one to let the grass grow under his feet and, later that same year, he was already able to launch his first mini-festival. This first attempt to get something going was really a small-scale trial run and can be seen now as just the forerunner of what was to become a major event in the world jazz festival programme – The Edinburgh International Jazz Festival (EIJF).

This initial event took place in Stewart's Ballroom on Abbeyhill, off Regent Road and not far from Holyrood Palace. Mike had managed to persuade the owner to put up £500 to fund a jazz event that was to run over a Friday, Saturday and Sunday in the summer of 1978. The bands that Mike booked were all local and were his own New Society Syncopators, Jim Petrie's Jazz Band and Bill Salmond's Louisiana Ragtime Band. In addition, guest artistes were booked to appear with the Syncs and they were the fine tenor sax player from London, Al Gay and Edinburgh's own RHS Gangster, pianist and drummer, Stan Greig. Assessing it afterwards, Mike considered that the event had been reasonably successful. He had certainly learned a lot and was sufficiently encouraged to start planning immediately for a much more ambitious project in the following year. It was from 1979 rather than 1978 that the history of the Edinburgh Jazz Festival really began and certainly, when the Silver Jubilee celebrations for the first twenty five years took place in 2003, the twenty five began with the 1979 Festival.

For **1979**, Mike approached local brewers Drybroughs, who agreed to sponsor a 'pub trail', and christened the whole event **The Edinburgh Jazz Festival**. An organising committee, or board of directors, was formed. This included Ian Nelson, representing Drybroughs, and a good number of the local jazzers, including both musicians and non-musicians. Sam Smith, the Old Bailey band trombone player, for example, was recruited to handle much of the programme design and text, on the basis of his experience in graphic design work, and Donald McDonald, the bass and sax player, took on the job of organising the running order at gigs. A printed programme was produced, for which advertisers were attracted, and an ambitious programme it proved to be. The 1979 Jazz Festival was to run from Sunday 26th to Thursday 30th August and it started with a Festival Jazz Ball in Tiffany's Ballroom in St Stephen's Street, the programme for which included the local Russ Moore's Big Band, Old Bailey's Jazz Advocates and the Auld Reekie Parade Band. There were also three guest bands: L'Orpheon Celesta from France, the Onward Jazz Band from Newcastle and the special guests, the Oregon Jazz Band, led by Bill Borcher. The pub trail sponsored by Drybourghs was an especially ambitious part of the programme, as it was mostly free and featured a frequent, indeed frenetic, change-over of bands.

The 12 venues for the Festival were the George Hotel (Bar I and Bar II) in George Street, the Claremont Hotel in Claremont Crescent, Calton Studios in Calton Road, La Grenouille in Abercromby Place, The Northern bar at Canonmills, the Hopetoun Bar in Morrison Street, the Tankard Lounge in Rose Street, the Abercorn Inn in Piershill, Tramps near Tollcross, the St Vincent Bar in St Vincent Street and the Broughton Bar in Broughton Street. As far as I remember, the two venues in the George Hotel and Calton Studios were paying venues, but the rest were free. All of the venues operated throughout the five days of the Festival and, while some of the venues featured evenings only programmes, many also had lunchtime sessions. It was later announced that over 20,000 people took part[143]. To give a flavour of the programme, here are a couple of extracts:

George Hotel - 'Bar I' - Tuesday 28th August

3.30-4.15	Savannah Syncopators
4.15-4.45	L'Orpheon Celesta
4.45-5.30	Savannah Syncopators
7.30-8.45	Savannah Syncopators
8.45-9.45	Onward Jazz band
9.45-10.45	Mike Hart's Society Syncopators

---

[143] Edinburgh International Jazz Festival 1980 programme

10.45-11.30   L'Orpheon Celesta

Tankard Lounge – Monday 27th August

6.30-7.30   Old Bailey's Jazz Advocates
7.30-8.45   Deep South
9.00-10.00   Charlie McNair's Jazz Band
11.00-12.00   The Rhythm Method

The Northern Bar – Thursday 30th August

12.30-2.00   Onward Jazz Band
7.30-8.30   Louisiana Ragtime Band
9.30-11.30   Old Bailey's Jazz Advocates

The above extracts demonstrate an ambitious and quite intricate piece of planning, with the bands involved in short sets. However, what the above extracts do not show, is the fact that the bands were appearing at several venues each evening. As an example, I was playing with the Old Bailey band and our programme for Wednesday 29th August was:

6.30-7.30   Tramps
8.15-9.30   Abercorn Inn
10.15-11.30   George Hotel (Bar One)

Those familiar with the geography of Edinburgh will appreciate that these three venues are a long way apart, involving much travelling between spots. In addition, there was a lot of gear to shift, including amplifiers, large instruments such as double basses and drums, as well as all the musicians. I can testify to the fact that this type of programme was extremely hard work, however there was a great pioneering spirit and it was also great fun – even if I would not like to undertake anything this strenuous now-a-days! We probably would not have managed at all if it had not been for the heroic efforts of the couriers and drivers, volunteers who were there to help with moving gear, finding parking spaces and even calming down over-stressed and temperamental bandsmen. The full line-up of bands for this first Edinburgh Jazz Festival numbered 18 (ten

Edinburgh bands and 8 from elsewhere) and the 1979 Roll of Honour was as follows:

Guest bands -	Edinburgh bands –
L'Orpheon Celesta (France)	Russ Moore Big Band
Onward Jazz Band (Newcastle)	Old Bailey's Jazz Advocates
Oregon Jazz Band USA)	Auld Reekie Parade Band
Savannah Syncopators (England)	Bill Salmond's Louisiana Ragtime Band
Cooper/Hayton Duo	Mike Hart's Society Syncopators
George Penman Jazzmen (Glasgow)	Climax Jazz Band
Gateway Jazz Band (Carlisle)	Charlie McNair's Jazz Band
Deep South	Rhythm Method
	West End Jazz Band
	Djangology

One of the bands listed above is **Djangology**, a new band which grew, completely unintentionally, out of guitarists Neil Munro and Johnny Harper and reeds man Gerard Dott getting together for practice sessions at Neil Munro's house. Apparently, the Jazz Festival organizers had heard of this activity and, without consulting any of them, included them in the Jazz Festival programme. They also bestowed on them the name Djangology, in recognition of the Reinhardt influence in Neil's playing. Johnny Harper was unable to make the Festival gigs because of other playing commitments and they became a four piece band with a membership of Gerard Dott, Neil Munro on solo guitar, Ian Aitken, who was to go on to play with the pop star Shakin' Stevens, on rhythm guitar, and Johnny Phillips on bass guitar. Later, they had a residency at Le Grenouille and made a brief TV appearance during the Festival playing 'Fascinating Rhythm'. Sadly, the band only lasted a couple of years, disbanding in 1980. Neil Munro had never been happy with the imposed name, apparently considering it to be too type casting in character and, by its nature, unnecessarily restricting their musical freedom. In protest, when the time came for their final gig, Neil had them billed as The Norman Hitler Big Band!

There is no intention in this book of attempting a detailed account of the Edinburgh Jazz Festival and its developments over the many years to come. Rather, I will give an outline account of the early years, the main developments and the increasingly impressive list of great jazz names who took part, as the Festival established itself, becoming, in a surprisingly sort time, a premier event on the international jazz stage.

In **1980**, the Jazz Festival was to run from 24th to 28th August and was now styled **The Edinburgh International Jazz Festival** (EIJF). It was again in association with Drybroughs and the programme stated that '...*the festival broadens its wings geographically and stylistically but still retains an emphasis on hot traditional jazz and undiscovered musicians. Twenty-one bands and five soloists from six different countries, playing at sixteen venues and performing over 200 sessions'.* It was also announced that '*the programme's character has developed considerably to include some of the creators of the music alongside a number of exciting new discoveries. There are more events, more spontaneous guests, a much bigger marching parade – and no electric pianos!'*[144] Other innovations were that the BBC was to broadcast some sessions from the George Hotel and that a Jazz Bus would provide free transport between venues. Festival T-shirts were available, as was an All Venues Badge. A 1980 Jazz Festival LP was available at £4.50 which featured eleven different bands including Edinburgh's Auld Reekie Parade Band, the Storyville Five, the Louisiana Ragtime Band, the Charlie McNair Jazz Band, Mike Hart's Society Syncopators and Old Bailey's Jazz Advocates. Guest bands featured on the LP were L'Orpheon Celesta, WASO, George Penman's Jazz Band with Fionna Duncan, the Savannah Syncopators and the Sammy Rimmington Jazz Band.

Star visitors for 1980 included the remarkable reeds player Benny Waters, who had been born on 23 January 1902, had played and recorded with 'King' Oliver and Fletcher Henderson, and who was still playing as dynamically as ever. Benny was to continue his amazing playing career until after his 95th birthday in 1997, on which occasion he recorded an album called 'Live at Ninety Five' for Bluenote, and finally died on 11 August 1998. Other notable visitors included drummer Andrew Hall and trumpeter Teddy Riley from New Orleans, blues singer Jan Sutherland from Merseyside, trombonist Roy Williams from

---

[144] Edinburgh International Jazz Festival 1980 programme

Luton, the Bourbon Street Jazz Band from Denmark, the New Black Eagle Jazz Band from the USA,, Sammy Rimmington's Jazz Band from London, a gypsy band called WASO from Belgium, who played in the Django tradition, and a banjo virtuoso from the USA, Ed Turner. In addition, there were several returners from 1979 including L'Orpheon Celesta, the Savannah Syncopators and Kid Dawson's Onward Jazz Band. All of the 1979 local bands appeared but, in addition, there were Bill Jones' Rhythm Method, the Corstorphine Jazz Youth Orchestra, the Storyville Five and Violet Milne's Spirits of Rhythm.

A welcome inclusion was that of Edinburgh's own piano maestro, Alex Shaw with his trio, said to be '...*as far as the Festival goes towards "modern" jazz*'! There was again an extensive free pub trail, featuring an increased number of venues. The bands had extremely demanding schedules once again, with three gigs in a day commonplace. However, a great compensation for several of the local bands was a number of sessions where they backed one of the guest solo stars. Below is a day's programme for one of the George Hotel venues, as an example of how the Festival had grown in all ways:

George Hotel I – Tuesday 26th August 1980

12.30-2.00pm	Alex Shaw Trio with Benny Waters
12.15-3.00pm	L'Orpheon Celesta
3.00-4.00pm	WASO
4.15-5.00pm	New Era Jazz Band
5.30-6.30pm	Corstorphine Jazz Youth Orchestra
7.00-8.00pm	George Penman's Jazz Band with Fionna Duncan
10.15-11.30pm	Festival All Stars – Teddy Riley, Benny Waters, Roy Williams, Stan Greig, Billy Law, Ronnie Rae

Once again, there was a great atmosphere and a sense of supporting something very worthwhile. There were really enormous crowds turning out, right through from the opening Parade along Princes Street to the closing sessions on Thursday 28th August.   Things were looking and sounding good.

The **1981 EIJF** ran from 23rd to 27th August 1981 and was again sponsored by Drybroughs.   Iain Nelson, Drybrough's Sales and Marketing Director, said in the printed programme *'We at Drybroughs are delighted with the continued growth, both physically and conceptually of the Edinburgh International Jazz Festival....Through the use of Drybroughs pubs and hotels in Edinburgh as mainly free entry venues, we feel that the original concept of live jazz at grass roots level is being maintained. The Drybroughs Youth Jazz Band Trophy will be awarded for the first time this year following a competition involving nine youth bands. It is vital that young talent is recognized and encouraged in order to assure the future of Jazz in Scotland."*[145] Mike Hart, also in the programme, said *'This year looks as if it will be the most exciting yet, with four great bands from the USA, one from Denmark, one from France, one from Belgium and a whole host of bands and top class solo musicians from the UK'.*

The Youth Jazz competition, to be held in the Queen's Hall, was a particularly welcome innovation, with several prizes on offer. In addition to the Drybourgh's Trophy for the most promising band, there were to be prizes for individual merit, including the Pete Seaton Shield for the best young musician and other prizes donated by Gordon Simpson's Music Shop and the Musician's Union. The youthful competitors included the Tommy Smith Quintet, the Midnight Blues Band, Twang, the Wester Hailes Education Centre Syncopators and the Corstorphine Youth Jazz Orchestra. No one knew then, of course, that the young tenor saxist, Tommy Smith, was to become a world famous jazz musician within a few short years. Tribute was paid to Platform, the Scottish jazz promotion organisation who had organised jazz groups and classes under the guidance of Gordon Cruikshank, for generating *'...a whole new youth jazz scene with all sorts of different aspects of jazz music finding its way into the curriculum'.*

There were again many returning, successful bands from previous years, with new guests including The Jazz Society

---

[145] Official Programme, 1981 EIJF

from the north of England, the Batchelors of Jazz from Glasgow, the Watergate 7 + 1 from France, and the Golden West Syncopators and the High Sierra Jazz Band and the Tarnished Six from the USA. New solo visitors included clarinetist Ian Arnott, whom we last met as a young associate of the RHS Gang in the early 1950s, banjo player Johnny Harper briefly home from his travels, pianist Fred Hunt and trumpeter Digby Fairweather. The established favourites Benny Waters and Roy Williams were back again. There were several new local bands making a first appearance as well, including Swing 81, the Apothecaries of Jazz who were a composite band from all over the UK, the Festival City Jazz Band and the Scottish Jazz Advocates. A number of unattached local jazzers were featured as soloists guesting with various bands, including vocalist Jackie MacFarlane, drummer Dave Swanson, Gus Ferguson, Donald McDonald and Alex Shaw. The Festival again kicked off with a parade along Princes Street and two major Jazz Band Balls were held, one on the opening night and the other, billed as a Grand Farewell Ball, on final night in the Big Top Marquee at Prestonfield House Hotel. The latter was to culminate with a Great Breakfast Jam Session, timed to finish at 4.30am! Ian Nelson of Drybourghs, writing in the next year's programme, said of the 1981 Festival *'The response from bands and enthusiasts alike was staggering – venues throughout the town were bulging at the seams and the overall atmosphere was absolutely fantastic'.*

The **fourth EIJF** took place between Sunday 29th August and Thursday 2nd September **1982** and was billed as the **Drybourghs Edinburgh International Jazz Festival**. Mike Hart, in his Message from the Director said of the Festival to come *'We are unique, because 60% of our venues are free, we are taking jazz to the people. We are unique because, unlike many other festivals, we do not require "name" artistes to "put bums on seats", we invite performers for their excellence, enthusiasm and good humour. Lastly, we are unique because our setting is Edinburgh – need I say more!'*[146] Mike also paid a particular tribute to Donald

[146] Edinburgh International Jazz Festival 1982 programme

McDonald saying that his '...*effort and dedication has been beyond the call of duty.*'

Once again, the programme had been expanded, with bands from the USA, Canada, Poland, Austria, West Germany, France, Denmark, England and Scotland. Again, many old favourites were back but with many new comers, including the Carol Kidd Trio, the Ralph Laing All Stars, the Royal Society Jazz Orchestra, the Ness River Rhythm Kings, the Hot Antic Jazz Band, the Merseysippi Jazz Band, the Seatown Seven, the South Frisco Jazz Band, the Traditional Jazz Four, the Trevor Richards Trio, the Bluenote Seven and the Dave Donohoe Band. The programme listed a total of 32 bands, with one new Edinburgh band making its first appearance. This was the **Gumbo Jazz Band** which featured Finlay Milne, trumpet playing son of Kenny and Violet, Ian Boyter (rds), Dave Bradford (tbn), Tony Sergent (bs) and Mac Rae (drms). Although this was to be quite a short lived band, with a couple of musicians who were not Edinburgh based and presumably brought in for the Festival, it marked the first appearance of Ian Boyter who was to become a long serving Edinburgh jazzer. Unfortunately, the talented Finlay Milne was not to become an Edinburgh fixture. His work in TV took him to the south, although happily he was to make fairly regular return visits in the future.

However, impressive though the list of bands was, it was the number and quality of the solo guests that demonstrated just how far the EIJF had come in four short years. Old favourites like Benny Waters, Al Gay and Roy Williams were there again, as were Fred Hunt and Digby Fairweather, but added to them was a positive feast of great names. The new comers were headed by the great Teddy Wilson, surely one of the finest jazz pianists in all of jazz and the versatile Dick Carey, the original pianist with the Louis Armstrong All Stars, who was equally adept on trumpet and alto horn. From Canada were singer Jodie Drake and sax man Jim Galloway, an ex-pat Scot from Ayrshire. From the UK there was the one and only Humphrey Lyttelton, pianist Eddie Thompson, guitarist Jim Douglas once of Gifford in East Lothian, the reeds maestros Johnny Barnes and Dave Shepherd, bass player Paul Sealey

331

and Roy Crimmins, trombone player in one of the late Alex Welsh's best bands. In addition, there was a host of Scottish based musicians who were making guest appearances with many of the bands. It was some programme and it was some Festival. The pub trail was as big as ever, and there was an increase in the pay-to-get-in venues. Ian Nelson, in the programme for the next year said of the 1982 EIJF *'I asked if 1982's Jazz Festival could possibly follow the success of the previous one. The answer was resounding, pulsating, exciting and definite. The Festival really took off, and for four days, Edinburgh rang out to hot sounds played by musicians from countries as far apart as Poland and the USA, but sharing a common bond, a love for jazz'*[147].

However, it did not come without cost. The work done and the problems faced by the organizers can be gauged from Mike Hart's comments in EIJF 1983 programme: *'We have made it to our fifth year! It never ceases to amaze me how it all comes together, after battling through what seemed to be insurmountable odds. This year we had to overcome the cancellation of our biggest attraction, which was to be held at Murrayfield Stadium – The Jazz Pavilion, four weeks prior to the Festival. This meant a frantic search for a site, ranging from farmer's fields to ice rinks! We are extremely fortunate in acquiring the Sports hall at Meadow Bank Stadium thanks to the kind assistance of the Director of Recreation and Leisure'.* The Festival was once again sponsored by Drybroughs although, sadly, this was to be their final year.

The **1983 EIJF** started, as had become the tradition, with the jazz parade along Princes Street followed by the Youth Jazz Band competition, which continued to attract a good number of quality entries. There were eight entries this year and the prizes made up an impressive list:

The Drybrough Cup for the best Youth Band
The Pete Seaton Shield for the best Young Musician
The Musician's Union Prize for the best Young Drummer

---

[147] Edinburgh International Jazz Festival 1983 programme

The Gordon Simpson Prize for the Most Promising Young Musician
The Alex Welsh Trophy for the Most Promising Young Trumpeter.

The Festival dates this year were Sunday 28th August to Friday 2nd September 1983. Yet again, there had been expansion, with nineteen guest bands from across the world and fifteen from Scotland. Again, the list of solo performers was quite remarkable. Newcomers from the USA included trumpeter Adolphus 'Doc' Cheatham who had worked with Chick Webb, Teddy Wilson, Cab Calloway and Benny Goodman, Count Basie's lead alto saxophonist Earle Warren and Al Casey, who had made his name as guitarist with Fats Waller and his Rhythm. From the UK came the fine piano players Brian Lemmon and Dill Jones and clarinetist Acker Bilk. Given that the likes of Benny Waters, Roy Williams, Jim Galloway, Fred Hunt, and Dave Shepherd were back again, together with a host of Scottish jazzers, it meant that, yet again, the organizers had put together an appetising array of talent. Newcomers amongst the visiting bands were the Natural Gas Jazz Band, the Rosie O'Grady Band, the Climax Band from Canada, the Pete Allen Jazz Band, the Hot Club of London, Kid Boyd's New Orleans Jazz Band and Tommy Burton's Sporting House Four. In addition, Humph was back but with his full band this time, as usual packed with star names, and there was the band of a terrific trumpeter from Australia, Bob Barnard, the first band from Oz to appear at the EIJF.

BBC Radio Scotland had presented an engraved bowl to be awarded to the band chosen by a panel of judges as the best in the festival, with bands of four or more members and with no professional musicians eligible to compete. The 1983 winners were to be the Hot Antic Jazz Band from France. Among the Edinburgh bands new to the Festival were the Jack Finlay Trio and the East Coast Jazz Band led by drummer, Frank Birnie. The band included some illustrious local names including Jimmy Shortreed on reeds (what else?!) and trombonist Johnny McGuff, whose main band was now the Scottish Jazz Advocates. The 1983 EIJF programme totaled twenty eight listed as solo guests and an incredible thirty three bands.

A band, although not one from Edinburgh, that should be mentioned is the **Apothecaries of Jazz**. This band was made up of jazz-playing pharmacists from across the UK and was an advertising venture sponsored by the pharmaceutical companies, the Winpharm Group and Hobbypharm. They played in the New Orleans style and described themselves a 'Dispensers of Fine Jazz'. The band was led by banjoist Bernard Hardisty and varied from seven to as much as thirteen-piece, including a couple of vocalists and a Grand Marshall. Two Edinburgh pharmaceutical jazzers, Kenny Milne (tpt) and George Duncan (rds), were involved and had played with the Apothecaries at the EIJF in 1981/82/83 and were to do so again in 1986. This band travelled widely on behalf of their sponsors and, in addition to many jazz events in the UK, appeared in Hong Kong, Malta and Hawaii as well as making a number of appearances on TV.

There were many local benefits from the EIJF and not least among them, was the fact that so many ordinary followers, with perhaps, only a casual liking for the noise that traditional jazz bands make, had become familiar, not only with some of the biggest names in jazz, but also saw that some of the top local musicians were no slouches either. In addition, there were some people, visitors and locals alike, attracted to the EIJF, who had no previous interest in jazz whatsoever but rapidly became converts.

It was sad that Drybroughs, who had given such terrific support over the first five years, felt it was time to drop out. Without their support there would have been no EIJF, or at best, a very much less ambitious one, and their withdrawal could have spelt the end of a great project. As Mike Hart was to say in the 1984 programme *'After the withdrawal of our previous sponsors, in February of this year, I did not know if we were in a position to continue. At the eleventh hour, however, Edinburgh's foremost suppliers of 80/- ale came to the rescue'*. It had been a near thing but the sixth EIJF show was to go on.

The new sponsors for 1984 were to be another famous name in Scottish brewing, **Scottish Brewers** and their sponsorship of the EIJF was to be under the banner of their famous brand name, **McEwens**.   Like their predecessors, McEwens were to put their weight behind the pub trail which, in the eyes of many including a lot of the local musicians, had been one of the great successes of the early Festivals.   Mike said *'I would also like to thank the owners and managers of our new free trade venues for their enthusiastic support.   Without them the jazz festival would have been but a shadow of its former self'*.   This meant, of course, a whole new list of pub venues which were part of the McEwens empire and, although some good venues were lost, it was exciting to be playing in new places and attracting people local to the pubs.   The Scottish Brewers Chairman himself, Alastair Mowat, was involved and on the Board of Directors of the EIJF, which seemed an encouraging sign of the new sponsors commitment, and he said *'As a company, Scottish Brewers strongly believe that we should support those who support us and we are therefore equally delighted to have been able to save this now well established and very popular event which has become such a prominent supporting feature of the Edinburgh Festival'*.   It should also be mentioned that Alastair Mowat was to be a consistent and generous supporter of the EIJF over many years.   A jazz enthusiast himself, his contributions to the festival went far beyond his business involvement and were to include a sizeable personal donation to the EIJF funds.   With friends of that calibre, the future of the EIJF looked to be secure for a long time to come.

The programme for the **1984 McEwen's EIJF (19th to 24th August)** was, as had become usual, to start with the Youth Jazz Band Competition on the morning of the opening Sunday.   The Sunday afternoon saw the now traditional closing of Princes Street for the Jazz Parade, this year featuring no less than nineteen floats, which continued to attract thousands of spectators.   The Sunday night and small hours of Monday morning were devoted to the traditional Opening Jazz Band Ball at the Jazz Pavilion in Meadowbank Stadium.   The same venue was to host other special events including a Salute to Humphrey Lyttelton, a Tribute to Count Basie, a Midnight Folly, a Take me Back to

New Orleans Carnival and the Grand Farewell Ball. There was also another innovation, a Jazz Tap and Jive competition. In addition to the main venues at the Meadowbank Stadium and the George Hotel, there were fifteen pubs and hotels on the still mostly free pub trail.

This year the programme listed thirty-three bands, an impressive array of solo stars and an even longer list of Scottish jazzers, making guest appearances. Once again, there were many familiar and welcome faces, who had appeared in earlier festivals, and the list of new comers featured some resounding jazz names. Amongst them was Count Basie's great tenor sax star Buddy Tate, pianist Red Richards, tap dancer Will Gaines and cornetist Warren Vache, all from the USA. From the UK there was Kenny Baker, one of the country's finest ever trumpeters, the inimitable trombonist George Chisholm, one of Europe's best ever jazz musicians, and singer Beryl Bryden. New comers amongst the bands included Monty Sunshine's Jazz Band, the Frog Island Jazz Band with clarinetist Cy Laurie, Bob Kerr's Whoopee Band and the Midnight Follies Orchestra, all from south of the border, Sweden's Sveriges Jazz Band, the Hot Cotton Jazz Band from the USA, the Jazz Classics from West Germany and the Sensation Band from Canada. From the Continent came Italy's Milano Jazz Gang and Leonardo Pedersen's Jazz Kadel from Denmark. There could be no doubt that the EIJF was living up with a vengeance to the International part of its title.

More locally, there were a couple of new bands, the **Jack Graham Jazz Band**, a new departure for the perennial side-man Jack Graham, and the **Alan Anderson Band**, from their base in the Border country and playing in a mainstream style. A band specially put together for the festival was **The Rising Sons**, a band of youngsters, some of whom were offspring of well known jazzers, including trumpeter Finlay Milne, son of Kenny and Violet, Sammy Rimmington junior, a clarinetist like his Dad and Emile Martyn, drummer son of the well-known Barry. Carol Kidd, a great singer with a growing international reputation, and Dave Batchelor were over from Glasgow and, of course, there were all the usual suspects from Edinburgh. The

EIJF continued to go from strength to strength and the new sponsors had settled in comfortably.

So the first six years, from 1979 to 1984, of the EIJF had been and gone. So far, it was clear that each year had been better than the last, the choice greater, the number and quality of the guests becoming more and more impressive. In the Programme for the 1986 McEwen's EIJF, the Scotsman jazz writer and critic, Tony Troon, wrote *'...it was in 1980 that the EIJF began to operate a policy which transformed the event over succeeding years, giving it breadth and serious purpose to stand alongside its other quality of providing foot-tapping entertainment. This policy was the hiring of individual jazz stars to mix into the broth, giving jazz patrons some evidence of creative origins to counterbalance the derivative hordes. (A few of these derivative bands, however, were undeniably good)'*[148]. There may be a hint of an 'art for art's sake' stance in Tony's comments (although as one undoubtedly numbering amongst the derivative hordes, I am glad he added the last bit), none the less, in essence, he was quite right. He was also correct, later in his article, when he hailed the EIJF policy of inviting jazz musicians who were *'...below the level of mega-stardom that dominates the popular arts'* but were musicians of *'...great ability and individuality who should not be overlooked'*. He gave as examples of this, the not obvious choices of Teddy Riley and Benny Waters, the first such guests of the EIJF.

However, it must be pointed out that, if it had not been for the efforts of the foot-tapping entertainers, a vast number of the people who turned out to support the early Festivals would not have turned out, the Festival could well have shriveled and died and the followers would never have had the chance to hear the distinguished visitors. Tony Troon also paid tribute to what he called 'The Second Chorus Factor' – the fact that many musicians who had spent years buried in the sections of bands were musicians who, as Tony said, had huge quantities of bottled up creative talent. He gave, as examples of this factor,

---

[148] Troon A, 'The Second Chorus Factor', McEwen's Edinburgh International Jazz Festival programme, 1986

musicians such as Fats Waller's guitarist Al Casey and trumpeter Doc Cheatham, both wonderful players who made an enormous impact in their performances at the EIJF.

The EIJF was now in the midst of what, for many, were to be especially memorable years. With hindsight, it is fairly clear why this should be so. The EIJF had been created, in the first place, to be a festival of traditional jazz. This meant, of course, traditional jazz in its broadest sense, embracing any of the many strands of jazz in its pre-bebop form. Later, as the years went by, the spectrum was to widen and increasingly, more modern forms of jazz were to be presented (Edinburgh's Tommy Smith was to be prominent amongst them), as were jazz influenced performers with a more general public appeal, such as Georgie Fame and Van Morrison. However, in the mid-1980s, that trend was only just beginning and the EIJF was still very much oriented to the earlier forms of jazz. What was clear from the history of jazz, of course, was that, from the late 1940s on, by far the greater number of new, young, cutting-edge jazz musicians, especially amongst the Afro-Americans, was playing in the bebop and post-bebop style. By the mid-1980s, this shift had been going on for about forty years and, inevitably, the great names from the pre-bebop world who were still around and active, were getting fewer and fewer.

The first generation of post-bebop jazzers were, by the 1980s, themselves becoming veterans, so it was hardly surprising that the surviving pre-bop greats were well into the twilight of their careers. There were also many great players who had come into jazz post-bebop, who were not really revivalists, but had been content to stay more or less within the mainstream, pre-bebop style. These included players such as Ruby Braff, Scott Hamilton, Ken Peplowski, Kenny Davern, and others, but the pool of the older players was inevitably contracting. In the mid-1980s, however, there were still some of these pre-bebop veterans to invite to the EIJF, still playing wonderfully well and providing a late but privileged opportunity to hear them. It would be true, I think, to say that the 1980s represented the last flowering of the middle period of jazz; the playing of jazzers who had themselves been inspired by and had built on, the earlier forms of the music and who had added greater technical and musical knowledge and skill. As a measure of the quality of the EIJFs of the mid-1980s, it is worth running the eye down those who featured as solo guests, some real veterans others much younger, in the years 1983-1987. The years in which they appeared are shown:

Buddy Tate 1984/85/86/87
Al Casey 1983
Red Richards 1984
Warren Vache 1984/85
Doc Cheatham 1983/84
Earle Warren 1983
Benny Waters 1983/84/85/86
Jim Galloway 1983/84/85/86/87
Henri Chaix 1983
Acker Bilk 1983
Fred Hunt 1983
Len Skeat 1983
Dave Shepherd 1983/84/85/86
Kenny Baker 1984
George Chisholm 1984
Roy Williams 1983/84/85/86/87
Will Gaines 1984
Brian Lemon 1983/84/85/86
Paul Sealley 1983/84
Al Casey 1985/87
Al Fairweather 1985/86
Carl Fontana 1985
Gus Johnson 1985/86
Jane Jarvis 1985
Milt Hinton 1985/86
Ray Bryant 1985/86
Spanky Davis 1985/86
Tommy Smith 1985/87
Bruce Adams 1986/87
Bill Aldred 1986/87
John Barnes 1986/87
Harry Edison 1986/87

Jack Fallon 1986
Stan Greig 1986/87
Al Grey 1986
Dick Hyman 1986
Humphrey Lyttelton 1986/87
Fapy Lafertin 1986
Johnny Parker 1986/87
Dave Newton 1986
Jack Parnell 1986/87
Lillian Boutte 1987
Janusz Carmello 1987
Wally Fawkes 1987
Ray Foxley 1987
Al Gay 1987
Dave Green 1987
Reggie Johnson 1987
Oliver Jackson 1987
Brain Kellock 1987
Thomas L'Etienne 1987
Johnny Letman 1987
Jay McShann 1987
Grover Mitchell 1987
Danny Moss 1987
Mike Peters 1987
Antti Sarpila 1987
Mark Shane 1987
Ralph Sutton 1987
Bruce Turner 1987
Martin Taylor 1987
Al Cohn 1987
Bob Wilber 1987

Of course, the above list is by no means the end of the story of these vintage years. Some listed as guests in the above were there in other years but featured, not as solo guests, but as band leaders, for example Humphrey Lyttelton. Also not shown above is the host of bands, some of them very notable, which appeared in the same years. Nor does the list include the talented array of local bands and soloists who played their usual crucial role, particularly on the vastly popular pub trail. It would be tedious to try to list everyone who played and every special session that took place, but perhaps the above does demonstrate the quality, as well as the sheer quantity, of jazz on offer in the mid-1980s. This is not to imply that the earlier Festivals were any less memorable or that there were not terrific Festivals to come but for many, and I believe this includes Mike Hart himself, these years were the peak.

But it was not only the increasingly impressive list of solo stars and bands that made the mid-1980s EIJFs so memorable. There were also some new developments that demonstrated the increasing ambition and confidence of the event and its organisers. In **1985 (18th to 23rd August)**, the special tribute events continued, in this case celebrating the centenaries of both Joe 'King' Oliver and Jelly Roll Morton. In addition, there were more sessions featuring all-star groups brought together from among the guest list, usually under the leadership of one of the great names, and international groups, bringing together jazzers from all over the world. The line-up of the Festival All Stars at the Opening Ball in 1985 of Buddy Tate (ten sax), Spanky Davis (tpt), Carl Fontana (tbn), Ray Bryant (pno), Al Casey (gtr), Milt Hinton (bs) and Gus Johnson (drms), would have enhanced and added lustre to any jazz event in the world.

Other All–star sessions were led by Buddy Tate, Warren Vache, Al Fairweather, Carl Fontana and Roy Williams. Top Scottish jazzers, including Ronnie Rae (bs), Tony McLennan (drms), Jack Finlay (pno), Kenny Ellis (bs) Dave Swanson (drms) and Francis Cowan (bs), were fittingly included in some of the All-Star bands. For the first time, there was a collaborative venture with the Scottish National Orchestra, arranged jointly by the McEwen's EIJF and the Edinburgh International Festival, including the premier of a new work specially commissioned by the EIJF. This was described in the programme as the climax of the Festival and took place in the Usher Hall under the baton of Russell Gloyd. The new work, entitled 'Hot and Suite', had been written by Jim Galloway and was described as '...*a fantasia for orchestra and jazz ensemble with the concept being a loose chronological look at some of the major signposts on the journey that jazz has made since its beginnings'*[149]. The performers and signposts were introduced throughout the evening by Humphrey Lyttelton.

Thirty three bands were listed in 1985, and there were twenty venues which, happily, still included fourteen free venues on the pub trail, although a couple of them were only free for lunch time sessions, tickets being required in the evening. Locally, 1985 was marked by the first EIJF appearance of Hamish McGregor's new band, Fat Sam's Band, playing in a jump jive, R 'n B and Swing style, a band which was to become a long-term fixture on the Edinburgh jazz scene and which was to build for itself, an international reputation. Another local new comer was the Gordon Cruikshank Quartet, playing in a modern style, with Gordon fronting on tenor sax, backed by Dave Newton (pno), Brian Shields (bs) and Mike Travis (drms).

In **1986 (17th to 23rd August)**, again sponsored by McEwens, the EIJF was to host a total of thirty seven bands, not including the various star-studded bands put together for special sessions. It also featured an increase in the number of paying venues, with seven of these dubbed Gold Star Venues, for which tickets were required. The free pub trail remained in good health, with thirteen venues well scattered across the town. Important events included another major Usher Hall concert. Mike Hart introduced this in the Programme by saying '*I am delighted to announce that, due to the great success of our joint concert with Edinburgh Festival last year, our closing production will be held again in the Usher Hall, titled 'the Golden Age of Jazz' presented by Dick Hyman'*[150].

---

[149] Introduction, McEwen's Edinburgh International Jazz Festival programme, 1985.
[150] Edinburgh International Jazz Festival programme 1986

The Opening Ball at Meadowbank was graced by one of the put-together bands and again, it was like one of those bands we used to put together in our imaginations when we were young. This one had a real flavor of the old Count Basie band with a line-up of Harry Edison (tpt), Al Grey (tbn), Buddy Tate (ten sax) and the same wonderful rhythm section that had enthralled everybody the previous year, Ray Bryant (pno), Milt Hinton (bs) and Gus Johnson (drms). It was billed as Harry Edison's Harlem Stampede and throughout the seven days, it made several appearances with one or other of the legends nominated as leader. There was also a 1986 Festival All Stars which had Spanky Davis (tpt), Roy Williams (tbn), Jim Galloway (rds), Johnny Parker (pno), Jack Fallon (bs) and Jack Parnell (drms).

Milt Hinton was a revelation on bass. I remember standing with a group of other bass players, which from memory included Ronnie Rae, Roy Percy and Jerry Forde, by the side of the band stand at Meadowbank, listening to him play with the other legends. Without exception, we were utterly captivated by his playing. In the case of one of us, I believe that the experience of listening to Milt Hinton radically altered his whole concept of what the double bass was capable of and changed his whole approach to his instrument from then on. Apart from his outstanding solo work, I was struck by Milt Hinton's seemingly effortless power and swing. Every note was so well centred, so well placed and moved so seamlessly through the structure of each tune, that the rest of the extremely distinguished band seemed simply to lie back on his beat and be carried along with it.

The **1987 McEwen's EIJF** ran for eight days, from 15th to 22nd August. Mike Hart, writing his customary introduction in the official programme[151], said *'This year's Festival has taken another stride towards being one of the most exciting events in the World's Jazz Calendar. I have included some interesting new faces along with some of the old favourites, plus some of the American Jazz Giants who deserve more recognition in Europe'*. It had seemed clear that there had been some broadening of scope over several

---

[151] Edinburgh International Jazz Festival programme 1987

years, but there was a definite and conscious acceleration of the process in 1987. This was high-lighted by the journalist Kenny Mathieson, then of WIRE magazine, who headed his article in the 1987 official Programme *'So What Happened to Edinburgh's Trad Bash?'* He answered his own question by saying *'Simple, it has moved with the times – Mike Hart hasn't been letting the grass grow under his feet. From its humble origins in an Edinburgh Ballroom, with a full two guests from the international jazz scene – well, okay , from England – the Festival has not only grown in size, reputation and merit, it has also steadily diversified in the process, if never quite to the extent evident as this year.'* [152]

The heading for Kenny Mathieson's article sounded, as was probably intended, a bit provocative. 'Trad Bash' is hardly a complimentary term and there seemed to be a hint that, to achieve artistic and critical respectability, the EIJF had seen a need to embrace a wider spectrum of jazz. With hindsight, although not at the time, I think he was correct. As the great veteran originals of the middle period of jazz faded away, there would have to be an increasing reliance on the reproduction by others of earlier forms of jazz. There would soon be much less scope to present originals, even if some were well past their prime. I think this is partly the point that Tony Troon was making in the 1986 Programme when he spoke of *'...giving jazz patrons some evidence of creative origins to counterbalance the derivative hordes'*[153]. The ability to present evidence of creative origins in the future was going to require an opening of the door to more modern and contemporary jazz musicians. The message from both Tony Troon and Kenny Mathieson to the EIJF seemed to me to be something like – by all means celebrate the jazz glories of the past but jazz is not just the past, it has a present and a future as well. It is only fair to add that both Kenny Mathieson and Tony Troon had a great many good things to say about the EIJF, to the extent that Tony headed his 1987 Programme article *'The Ninth in an Increasingly Impressive Series'*.

---

[152] Mathieson K, Edinburgh International Jazz Festival programme, 1987
[153] Troon A, Edinburgh International Jazz Festival Programme, 1986

Of course, as years went by, the tendency to look backwards was to continue with a policy of laying on tribute packages, where musicians were expected to represent the styles of past masters. However, generally it was the bands and band arrangements that represented the style being celebrated, with soloists free to play as they pleased. In addition, although the concept was by definition derivative in nature, the tributes did sometimes feature musicians who had been involved with the originals. A notable example of this was the presence of Buddy Tate in the Tribute to Count Basie in 1984. The big event for 1987 was The King of Swing, a tribute to Benny Goodman, which featured some of the original Goodman big band scores and was presented by the great clarinetist, Bob Wilber. These were, of course, notable anniversaries and well worth marking in this way and, backward looking or not, they were of a very high standard.

Equally sincere and welcome were events dedicated to the memory of jazz musicians who had recently died, including Alex Welsh, Fred Hunt and Gordon Dillon, trumpeter with the George Penman Jazzmen from Glasgow. Perhaps ringing slightly less true and with a more obvious commercial slant, were presentations in years to come under titles such as 'Joe Bloggs plays the music of Louis Armstrong'. On a personal note, it always seemed to me that, in a jazz context, Joe Bloggs should play the music of Joe Bloggs. However, I am well aware that it is easy for me to say that, when I did not have to worry about selling tickets and filling venues. Speaking of venues, 1987 saw the advent of two new major ones, a 1000 capacity Jazz Big Top on the Meadows and the Jazz Amphitheatre in Lothian Road. In total, there were eight Gold Star venues and fourteen free venues on the pub trail.

There really can be little doubt that there was a clear case, and probably a need, to open up the EIJF to contemporary and more modern forms of jazz and, in 1987, the EIJF board had taken decisive action to widen the range of jazz on offer. The programme included the Tommy Chase Quartet, described as *'selling hard-driving bop to the youthful club goers of London'*, the Dave Newton Band, the Clark Tracey Quintet who *'delivered melodic jazz in the modern style'* and the Stan Tracey Trio, all of whom were firmly in the modern camp. It was also good to see local representatives of the more modern approach, with the inclusion of the John Burgess Band, fronted by John Burgess on tenor sax, who had been a winner in a previous Youth Jazz Competition. The EIJF had come a long way since the early years and the coy comment in the 1980 programme that Alex Shaw and his trio were *'...as far as the Festival goes towards "modern" jazz'.*

Also featuring as a name in an EIJF programme for the first time, was **Brian Kellock**, then aged around twenty-five and having just finished his Bachelor of Music degree at Edinburgh University. Brian was to go on to become one of the finest jazz musicians Edinburgh had ever produced, a world renowned piano player, with the interest and capability to play wonderfully well in virtually any form of jazz. His career is really beyond the scope of this book and his many recordings will be found listed in the major catalogues. However, in 1987, due presumably to a typo, it was not as Brian <u>Kellock</u> that he appeared in the Programme but Brian <u>Kellog</u>. What an opportunity he had, had he been so inclined; he could have formed a band in the Spike Jones tradition and had a major career as Brian Kellog and the Corn Flakes!

In the **1988 McEwen's EIJF** Programme, Mike Hart said *'For our tenth anniversary year we have over 400 musicians from all over the world performing in 23 venues sponsored by Scotland's leading brewer'*[154]. There were now twelve Gold Star venues, two concert venues but the free venues had dropped to just nine and, for the first time, the pay-to-get-in venues were outnumbering the free venues. Mike also stressed the fact that he was featuring great artistes who had been brought in for their excellence and not necessarily for what he called their show biz appeal. A fascinating Hall of Fame was included in the Programme, which listed all the individual performers and bands who had been featured over the ten years. The Hall of Fame came to the remarkable total of 294 bands and individuals who had appeared in the Programmes. Heaven knows what the total

---

[154] Edinburgh International Jazz Festival programme 1988

number of individual musicians would have been, taking into account that many of those listed were bands of anything up to twelve or fourteen piece.

1988 saw the return of many established favourites but also a good number of distinguished newcomers from the pre-Bebop end of the spectrum, including Scott Hamilton (ten sax), Art Hodes (pno), Jake Hanna (drms), Howard Alden (gtr), Dan Barrett (tbn), Dave McKenna (pno), Jack Lesberg (bs), Bob Barnard (tpt) and Tommy Whittle (ten sax). There were around forty seven bands listed in the Programme, of which some twenty one were new comers to the EIJF. New bands included seven from England, three from the USA, one each from Holland, Australia, Canada, Portugal and Germany and, encouragingly, half a dozen from Scotland. It was good to see amongst the English contingent, a band called Dix Six Plays Bix, not because of the fairly excruciating name, but because the tradition associated with Bix Biederbecke always seemed to be a bit under-represented in jazz generally. It was also good to see Fionna Duncan, who had sung in many EIJFs as a band singer, featuring with a band under her own name. Fionna's band was notable too as it included not only her musical partner, Ronnie Rae, on bass but Ronnie's sons, Ronnie junior on piano and John on drums. The trend towards more modern artistes continued with the Courtney Pine Quintet, Peter King (alto sax) and the John Rae Collective. This last was a real pointer towards things to come, featuring not only John Rae himself but Brian Kellock (pno), Kenny Ellis (bs), Kevin McKenzie (gtr), Colin Steele (tpt) and Phil Bancroft (ten sax), every one of them representing the future of Scottish contemporary jazz, and every one a name to note.

An innovation that was to be a significant pointer to future festivals was the inclusion of a number of blues specialists including Louisiana Red (gtr/vocs), the Beaker Blues Band, the Johnny Mars Blues Band and, featuring Edinburgh's own remarkable blues singer, the Tam White Band. There was also a special blues event called Really the Blues.

A concert in the Queen's Hall was given the title Djangology and focused on the musical tradition of Django

Reinhardt, with Fapy Lafertin, the remarkable gypsy band WASO and a special expansion of Edinburgh's Swing 88 into the Swing 88 Big Band. The 10th Anniversary Concert in the Usher Hall was A Tribute to Woody Herman and starred the NY Jazz Orchestra and the Concord All Stars, with Warren Vache, Scott Hamilton, Dan Barrett (tbn), Dave McKenna, Jack Lesberg, Jake Hanna and Howard Alden. The show also featured Doc Cheatham and the Harlem Blues and Jazz Band. It was said of this band in the Programme *'This band brings together, under the leadership of maestro Doc Cheatham, a selection of veteran jazz and blues musicians whose careers reach back to the flowering of classic jazz in the 20s and 30s'*. The line-up was terrific and included old EIJF favourite, guitarist Al Casey. Some band, some Programme and some Festival. Things continued to look good.

And that is as far as this book will track the EIJF year by year. We have looked at the developments over the first ten years and noted the remarkable growth from small beginnings to a place in the international jazz calendar. We leave it with its future, at least in the meantime, assured. The future, however, would bring many changes. The amount of more modern forms of jazz would increase gradually and the introduction of specialist blues artistes would lead, in 1997, to a change in the name to the Edinburgh International Jazz and Blues Festival (EIJBF). Gradually too, the free pub trail, an immensely popular part of the early Festivals, would diminish and disappear and with that would come a gradual decline in the part played by the local Edinburgh traditional bands. This was a great pity and was greatly mourned by many supporters but, in the end, they had had the solution in their own hands. The free pub trail fell by the wayside because, although the punters turned out in droves in the pubs, there was a tendency for them to sit and enjoy the music but a lack of a tendency to buy many drinks. Both the major sponsors dropped out because, in the end, their pubs just did not do enough business.

The Festival had started as an event simply celebrating traditional jazz and, while it was that and that alone, its success was plain to see. However, it was always inevitable that its character would change as time went on and it grew bigger. Mike Hart had started with quite a small, hard-working committee, drawn mostly from people already involved in the local traditional jazz scene. As the Festival grew, the numbers required to plan and run the event had to get bigger. As the Festival grew, more sponsors were required and the Edinburgh City Council took a stake in it. It was necessary to find ways to attract more people, sell more tickets and find ways for the Festival itself to generate more in the way of funds. Names with more clout with the general public began to appear, less pure in jazz terms perhaps, but always with a jazz orientation. New and still more ambitious venues came along, including the Festival Theatre and even St Giles Cathedral. Major changes like these did not exist in a vacuum, they brought their own changes. New people, new sponsors and new interests brought new ideas and influences and changes in policy and direction. Change was inevitable but there is no doubt that the early Festivals, those from 1979 and through the 1980s into the 1990s, are looked back upon with a great deal of affection by an awful lot of people, musos and punters alike.

However, the involvement of local bands in the EIJBF did not stop by any means. Some like Bill Salmond's Louisiana Ragtime Band, Violet Milne's Spirits of Rhythm, Jim Petrie's Diplomats of Jazz, Hamish McGregor's Fat Sam's Band and Mike Hart's Scottish Society Syncopators continued to appear in the Programme virtually every year. As the pub trail diminished, new free events appeared including the Mardi Gras, a spectacular outdoor celebration of jazz, held on the first Saturday to launch the Festival and staged in the historic Grassmarket. Jazz on a Summer's Day, another free open air event, took place in Princes Street Gardens, in the heart of the City and nestled below Edinburgh Castle. This latter event particularly, was an enormous success and reputably drew the biggest crowds of any jazz event in the UK. These were major events within the Festival, with big name bands involved, and with the accent still on traditional jazz.

Jumping forward many years, a glance at the Programme for the 2009 EIJBF demonstrates just how far the Festival

348

had come over its first 31 years, especially if compared with the examples, given earlier, of the Programmes in the first few years. In 2009, the Festival Chairman, Brian Fallon, introduced things by saying that the Programme included '...all the styles of jazz and blues, from every era of the music. You can hear the most exciting contemporary jazz groups, and the world's leading exponents of the earliest jazz piano styles, and all the stages in between'[155]. What was described as straight ahead jazz highlights included American trumpeter Roy Hargrove, Courtney Pine presenting his new project based on the music of Sydney Bechet and trumpeter Ryan Kisor, blowing up a storm with a special quintet. Atomic, The Thing and Konrad Wiszniewski represented the modern jazz zone and there was a new funk programme, featuring New Orleans drummer Stanton Moore, Elephant and Ibrahim Electric. Jack Bruce, Eric Burden and Maggie Bell were welcomed back. Singer Sinne Eeg made her Scottish debut, while Carol Kidd and Barabra Morrison returned to the Festival. A series of concerts was to take place featuring Dwayne Dopsie and the Zydeco Hellraisers, Colin Steele's Stramash and Paris Washboard.

There was a strong Scottish element too, with blues singer Tam White, Borderer David Milligan, a composer and pianist who was to write scores for the first ever Edinburgh Jazz Festival Orchestra, and baritone saxist Joe Temperley, now in his eightieth year and late of the Ellington Orchestra. Dick Hyman, now Hon President of the EIJBF, was returning as were tenor saxists Phil Bancroft and Tommy Smith, Colin Steele, Graeme Stephen, Konrad Wisziewski and Kenny Mathieson's Classic Jazz Orchestra. Several bands were described as defining the Edinburgh music scene including Fat Sam's Band, Melting Pot and Moishe's Bagel. There were shows dedicated to the music or influence of Duke Ellington, Robert Burns and Chet Baker.

Traditional jazz was featured at the Heriots Rugby Club Pavilion, courtesy of the 'Edinburgh Jazz 'n Jive Club', whose home it was throughout the year. There was also

---

[155] Edinburgh International Jazz and Blues Festival 2009

traditional jazz elsewhere with Phil Mason's New Orleans All Stars, Tricia Boutte, Edith Budge, the Batchelors of Jazz, Bill Salmond's Louisiana Ragtime Band, Swing 2009 and the Spirits of Rhythm with Thomas L'Etienne, all appearing. However, there was no doubt that by 2009, the main component of the programme was contemporary and modern forms of jazz. There were eighteen pay-to-get-in venues, for many of which booking in advance was essential, the pub trail was long gone and the only free outlets were Jazz on a Summer's Day in Princes Street Gardens and the Mardi Gras, in the Grassmarket.

Another interesting trend had been started in the 1999 EIJBF, when there was a re-union presentation of Old Bailey's Jazz Advocates. This was not a celebration of famous Edinburgh jazzers who had made their name on the National or International stage, but simply of a local band that had, in its day, been popular on a local level. The concert took place in the Hub, up on the Royal Mile near the Castle and, in addition to the Old Bailey band, featured Fionna Duncan, the George Penman Jazzmen and The Wolverines from Sweden. The response was gratifyingly enthusiastic and the show was a sell-out. This successful venture was to be developed much further in 2003, with a Silver Jubilee of Edinburgh Traditional Jazz in the Queen's Hall. This was a celebration of, not only the first twenty five years of the EIJBF, but also of the important part that the local bands had played and we will explore it in more detail later in this book. The re-union policy apropos local bands was to continue and, in the 2010 EIJBF, there were successful re-union concerts featuring the Old Bailey band, the Climax band and Pete Martin's All Stars. It was as if 1965 was alive and well and living in Edinburgh.

By the 1990s, a Board of Directors had long ago replaced the committee of local jazz enthusiasts and included several Edinburgh Councillors and figures from the world of business. By 2010, Mike Hart was styled Founding Director and there were two professional producers, Fiona Alexander and Roger Spence. Changed days indeed, but the EIJBF was clearly in good shape and was still up there with the best of European jazz events. There were regrets of course. Many mourned the early Festivals with their great atmosphere, accent on entertainment and amateur enthusiasm. Many mourned the loss of the free pub trail venues – even if they had seldom bought more than a half pint of beer all evening! But the EIJBF was still a vibrant event with an International reputation, great musicians still came to play at it, local jazz was still there in greater strength than ever, if different in character. I wonder what Sandy Brown would have made of it? Would he have approved, or at least accepted it, in its 2010 form? I think he would have recognized that any art form, or festival celebrating an art form, that was to remain properly alive, had to change, had to recognize change and allow the new generations to take the lead.

But none of it, early days or later, would have happened at all without a lot of effort and goodwill from a lot of people. Particularly in the early days, scores of local jazz people gave their time and effort freely, as planners, organizers, couriers, designers and musicians - and even more of them as the essential 'bums on seats' too. Even in the first EIJF in 1979, Dryboroughs, although the principle sponsor, were not the only ones who contributed. The 1979 Festival Committee's thanks to the good number of local businesses and friends who had donated equipment, assistance, and finance were recorded in the Official Programme. Trophies were donated by the Musicians Union and the local music shops and suppliers. Even after Dryboroughs dropped out and McEwens became the major sponsor, there were many others whose contributions were crucial, including companies, both local and national, and individuals who took advertising space in the printed programmes.

There were also those at the heart of it all, the Committee and later, the Board, members whose responsibility it was to plan, organise, promote and run the EIJBF. By 1986, there had to be a special page of Acknowledgements in the Programme, to record all those who had played a part, with a special mention for what was called '*a vast volunteer army*'. However, this is not the place to attempt to pay tribute to the all those whose input and hard work made the EIJBF possible. Nor am I going to attempt to acknowledge all those, both individual and corporate, who donated funds and equipment or helped in so many other ways. For those who wish to find out about all this, it is all recorded in the Official Programmes, many copies of which are still around. It is hoped that a full set of these will eventually be lodged in the Edinburgh Central Library Jazz Archive, launched in 2010[156] by the Edinburgh Jazz Archive Group[157].

However there is, of course, one person whose contribution underpins that of everyone else. Without Mike Hart's vision, energy and sheer bloody-mindedness, it is probable that nothing would have happened at all and there would have been no EIJBF. Mike's involvement in Edinburgh jazz began in the early post-WWII days, when Sandy, Al, Stan, Bob Craig, Dave Paxton, Archie and John Semple, Alex Welsh and all the rest of the pioneers, were laying the foundations of what was to become Edinburgh's reputation as a major jazz centre. Later, Mike was to be a factor, sometimes the crucial factor, in many of the key events in Edinburgh jazz developments - a founder member of the Climax Jazz Band, joint founder of the Old Bailey band and involved in the creation of the band that was formed for Dave Paxton's return from the Middle East. In addition, Mike was to be a key figure in the Scottish Jazz Advocates and leader of the Scottish Society Syncopators. He was an early pioneer of Edinburgh bands traveling abroad to play at festivals and to tour, and an extremely effective proselytizer on behalf of Edinburgh jazz. In addition to all of which he was, for over half a century, one of the most active musicians on the Edinburgh jazz scene.

It was Mike who created the Edinburgh International Jazz and Blues Festival. Without the EIJBF, few of us would have heard great players like Benny Waters, Doc Cheatham, Harry Edison, Buddy Tate, Milt Hinton, Carl Fontana and many more, certainly not on our own doorstep. Fewer still would ever have had the chance to actually play with these visiting stars. I still find it hard to believe that I played with a musician, Benny Waters, who

---

[156] Central Library Jazz Archive, Edinburgh Central Library, www.edinburgh.gov.uk/greenpencilaward
[157] Edinburgh Jazz Archive Group 2010 - Jim Keppie, Bill Strachan, Donald 'Chick' Murray and Drew Landles

had played and recorded with Joe 'King' Oliver. In terms of the EIJBF, Mike began as simply Director of a small jazz event in 1979 and continued in this role as the EIJBF grew and developed and, sometime around 1989, became a charitable limited company. For years, Mike worked in a voluntary capacity and it was a long time before he was employed by E.I.J.F Ltd and paid a salary as Artistic Director. His sterling efforts on behalf of jazz in Scotland were recognized in 1995, when he was awarded an MBE in the Queen's Birthday Honours List. The citation said *'Michael Warner Hart, for services to jazz in Scotland'*. Mike said in response *'I am extremely flattered by this honour and accept it on behalf of all the musicians and volunteers who have helped me to achieve a high profile for Scottish jazz'*. It was appropriate that the citation said Scottish jazz, because the success and fame of the Edinburgh event spurred many others across Scotland into action and jazz festivals have sprung up all over the country.

A further recognition of Mike's achievement in founding and driving the EIJBF was a citation from the City of Sacramento in 2008, in celebration of the thirtieth anniversary of the EIJBF. Headed 'Resolution by the City Council', as well as congratulating both Mike and the City of Edinburgh itself, the document concluded by saying:

'Now, therefore, be it resolved, by the Mayor and Council of the City of Sacramento, that we do hereby recognize the Edinburgh Jazz and Blues Festival on the occasion of its 30th Anniversary and do hereby extend our best wishes for a wonderful, fun-filled music celebration.'

Later, as others took stakes in the EIJBF, Mike was able to hand over responsibility for parts of the event to others and, as he moved into his seventies, his direct influence necessarily lessened. By 2010, now styled Founding Director, he remained on the Board and continued to exert a positive force on behalf of jazz, in an economic climate where the whole world seemed to be obsessed with commercial issues.

11 newmarket rd . edinburgh . eh14 1rj
tel +44 (0) 131 477 3500 . fax +44 (0) 131 477 7303
accounts +44 (0) 131 443 2437
www.ece.uk.com . info@ece.uk.com

Mike Hart MBE
Founding Director of the EIJF
(cartoon by Neil Kempsill[158] 2003, from the collection of
Mike Hart)

Mike at times, like many effective people, could be controversial, confrontational, short-fused and infuriating but he also had vision, energy, tenacity, utter determination and, when he wanted to, a great deal of charm. Without him, Edinburgh jazz would have been greatly the poorer.

---

[158] All efforts to trace Neil Kempsill have failed but his original work in producing this excellent caricature is acknowledged

Chapter XIII

The Boom Years Begin

The 1980s, invigorated by the success of the EIJF, was to be a busy and productive decade for the Edinburgh jazz scene. So healthy was the local scene, that many bands were able to run more than one residency a week and few bands in those days were sharing musicians with another band. The jazz following was numerous and enthusiastic enough to support, at least for a while, the publication of a local jazz magazine. This was called simply **Jazz Magazine** and the first edition appeared in November 1983. In charge of advertising was Jan Hill, whose idea the magazine was, and the editor was Andrew Pattison. The front cover was graced by a caricature of Bill Salmond, hair awry, strumming his banjo, stomping his foot and filling the air with noxious fumes from a large cigar. There was an editorial that explained the magazine's purpose and future plans, which were to include space for reader's letters. A selection of beautifully drawn jazz cartoons, produced by Donald Macdonald senior, father of the Macdonald bass playing dynasty, brightened up the pages. There were many adverts, some of which advertised local bands, jazz venues and jazz associated businesses.

Regular features included a Pub Survey which gave a critical review of a selected jazz venue, the one featured in this first edition being the amazing Basin Street at Haymarket, where there was jazz every night except Friday. A Hot Club News feature gave an update on the Hot Club, a non-profit making venture which existed '...*to promote New*

Orleans jazz in Edinburgh'. Platform News was written by Roger Spence and explained that Platform was *'..a grouping of seven non-profit making jazz promoting clubs with a base in Edinburgh'* and gave a comprehensive account of their activities and promotions to come. Gordon Cruikshank had contributed Jazz Train, an article describing how schismatic jazz was and focusing mostly on post-Bebop jazz. There was the first of what was to be a series on Legends of Jazz, the first subject being Bix Beiderbecke. Another regular feature was to be a Jazz Horoscope, written by Violet Milne, setting out our predicted fortunes under the signs of the Zodiac and indicating the best dates for recording, buying hi-fi equipment, socialising, creativity, looking for work, using your initiative, putting a band together, new projects and new gigs. There was even a Speakeasy News which seemed to be a slot in which new talent was described, this first one being about an eleven year old drummer, David Stewart, who had been sitting in at various jazz gigs. Most interesting of all in retrospect are the two pages headed Edinburgh Scene[159] and listing the regular jazz gigs around town. This gives such a clear account of the venues of the time and the sheer number of jazz gigs, that it is well worth showing in full.

Edinburgh jazz gigs in November 1983:

Monday

East Coast Jazz Band	Blue Lagoon Lounge	9.00 to 12.00
St Stephen Street Stompers	Raffels Bar	8.30 to 11.00
Grange Band	Grange Hotel	8.30 to 11.00
Bob Craig Jazz Band	Preservation Hall	8.30 to 11.00
Guitar Duo	Basin Street	8.30 to 11.00

Tuesday

Louisiana Ragtime Band	Navaar Hotel	8.30 to 11.00
East Coast Jazz Band	Sovereign Bar	8.30 to 11.00
George Roy Jazz Band	Oliver's bar	8.30 to 11.00
Jazz Machine	Preservation Hall	9.00 to 11.30
West End Jazz Band	Basin Street	8.30 to 11.00

Wednesday

Cottontoes	Argyll Bar	9.00 to 11.00
Louisiana Ragtime Band	Basin Street	8.30 to 11.00
'Band'	Northern Bar	8.30 to 11.00

---

[159] 'Jazz Magazine', Issue 1, November 1983, by kind permission of Jan Hill.

Charlie McNair Jazz band	Goblet Bar	9.00 to 12.00
Capital City Jazz band	Magna Carta	8.30 to 11.00
Bill Waugh Jazz Band	Preservation Hall	8.30 to 11.00

Thursday
West End Jazz Band	Ailsa Craig Hotel	8.30 to 11.00
Spirits of Rhythm	Basin Street	8.30 to 11.00
Scottish Jazz Advocates	Platform 1	8.30 to 11.00
Blue Swing	Calton Studios	8.30 to 11.00
Afton Trio	Afton Hotel	8.30 to 11.00
Bob Craig Jazz Band	Glenelg Hotel	9.00 to 12.00
Nite Life	Royal British Hotel	8.30 to 11.00

Friday
3 D	Calton Studios	8.30 to 11.00
Spirits of Rhythm	La Sorbonne	8.30 to 11.00
Jazz Machine	Eglinton Hotel	8.30 to 11.00
Phil Bancroft Trio	Clarinda's Wine bar	8.30 to 11.00
Neil Munro Trio	Basin Street	8.30 to 11.00
Edinburgh Jazz Quartet	Magna Carta	8.30 to 11.00
Blue Swing	Traverse Theatre	8.30 to 11.00

Saturday
Swing 83	Calton Studios	9.00 to 11.00
George Roy Jazz Band	Oliver's Bar	1.00 to 3.00
St Stephen Street Stompers	Raffles Bar	2.00 to 5.00
Alex Shaw Trio	Platform 1	12.00 to 2.00
Jack Graham	Eglinton Hotel	8.15 to 11.15
Blue Swing	La Sorbonne	8.30 to 11.00
See note*	Basin Street	8.30 to 11.00
Border Crossing	Nicky Tams	2.00 to 5.00

Sunday
Alex Shaw Trio	Platform 1	12.00 to 2.30
Capital City Band	Barnton Hotel	1.00 to 4.00
Festival City	Westfield Function Suite	1.00 to 3.00
Jazz Machine	Eglinton Hotel	2.15 to 5.15
Scottish Jazz Advocates	Platform 1	8.30 to 11.00
Old Reekie Footwarmers	Glenburn Hotel	8.30 to 11.00
Charlie McNair Jazz band	Granary Bar	8.30 to 11.00
Blue Swing	Black Hart Bar	8.30 to 11.00
Jack Graham	Basin Street	8.30 to 11.00
Royal Jazz Band	Royal Hotel, Portobello	8.30 to 11.00

The above listing reveals a total of forty nine regular, weekly jazz gigs. Added to that, the same magazine carries an advert placed by Platform, which shows that they were running weekly, late night jazz events at the Queens Hall. It is hard to credit now that there were so many venues, so many regular gigs, so many bands and enough followers to go round. In addition, of course, a large number of bands require a large number of jazz musicians to fill them. In fact, the Edinburgh jazz scene had again received a timely injection of new blood – or to be strictly accurate, fairly old blood. We have already seen the reasons for the first two expansions in the local jazz scene – firstly the Revival in the 1940s and secondly, the 'trad boom' in the late 1950s and early 1960s. Both of these stemmed from quite sudden and unexpected increases in the popularity of jazz but this time the reason was very different: it arose primarily because, of all things, the discotheque.

The late 1960s and the 1970s had seen the rise of the disco and the subsequent drop in the employment of live dance bands. This mainly affected the all-purpose dance bands which offered a menu of traditional dances such as fox trots and quicksteps and waltzes, spiced up a bit with versions of tunes from the current Top Twenty. The more specialised dance bands, such as those playing Scottish Country Dance music, were less affected but it was becoming clear that the old style dance bands by no means suited the generations that had been raised on the Beatles and the Rolling Stones. The youngsters wanted something that sounded like the music they heard on the radio, television and juke boxes. They did not want to dance to somebody playing Beatles tunes on a violin or accordion, they wanted to dance to the music of Beatles themselves, or something very like it. There were two ways to achieve this. One was to book local rock bands imitating the music of their heroes and the other was to dance to the recordings of the heroes themselves.

Recording and playback technology had, of course, been developing at a furious pace and, by the 1960s, was well able to deal with the demands of playing records for dancing, even in quite a major way and in sizable venues. The days of dinner-jacketed musicians solemnly playing formal programmes of traditional dance music would never be the same again and the days of the manic, fast talking disc jockey had arrived. Locally, dozens of dance band musicians - piano and accordion players, trumpeters and reeds players, drummers and double bass players - accustomed to plenty of regular work, began to find themselves confronted by increasingly empty booking diaries. Many of them were enthusiastic musicians who wanted to keep playing and some of them turned to the jazz scene.

Jazz and dance music were historically closely related and there were many who considered jazz, particularly the traditional variety, primarily to be dance music. As late as the 1930s Swing era, band leaders like Benny Goodman considered their bands to be dance bands. Goodman's huge popularity had been, at least partly, founded on his band's appearance on a regular radio broadcast call 'Let's Dance' and his signature tune at that time had the same name. Goodman, expressing his admiration for piano player Teddy Wilson, called him the finest dance band musician in the USA. Even if, at a local level, some dance band music was 'light music' of the kind abhorred by Sandy Brown, even if some of it was churned out on autopilot in an artless, soulless and swingless manner, it was certainly not all like that. Nor was it all po-faced, some of the dance bands being just as good at falling about as were the jazz bands. There is an authentic story of one Edinburgh dance band that arrived to play at a quite high-powered gig. On being directed to where they were to play, they were delighted to be told that there was a drink for the band on the bandstand. When they clambered onto the bandstand, they were even more delighted to find a crate of beer and six assorted bottles of spirits, including a rather nice malt. Being the band they were, they naturally ignored the beer and got laced in amongst the spirits. They were sent home in disgrace after the spot dance for having drunk all the prizes.

There were plenty local musicians playing in dance bands whose first love was jazz. There were many local jazzers who took as much dance band work as was offered, simply to be playing, including musicians of the calibre of Andrew Lauder, Tom Finlay, Johnny McGuff and Jim Baikie. Jim Baikie was, in fact, at that time, much more active on the dance scene than on the jazz one and ran one of the busiest and most popular dance bands around. There were others too, such as trumpeter George Roy and reeds man Jimmy Shortreed who, although most of their playing had been in dance work, were more than capable jazzers. One result of the collapse of the dance band scene was an influx of musicians to the local jazz scene, even if some made the transition with more success than others, just when the local jazz scene, spurred on by the success of the EIJF, was burgeoning.

Meanwhile, Issue 2 of the Jazz Magazine was published, covering December 1983 and January 1984. The regular feature Pub Survey this time was about the Westfield Function Suite, where the Festival City Jazz Band, led by pianist Ian Scott, had a regular spot. Hot Club News reported a successful Speakeasy event at the Magna Carta Lounge which congratulated those attending on their 1930s gear, for which prizes had been awarded. The Hot Club Hogmany Jazz Party was to be held in the Minto Hotel Function Room on 31st December and tickets were available from the secretary, Terry Jamieson. Platform News told us that *'On January 16th, the young Edinburgh saxophonist Tommy Smith should fly of to the USA, taking up his scholarship to Berklee College in Boston'*. There was to be a benefit concert, featuring Tommy, Martin Taylor and George Chisholm, on 12th January to raise funds towards the £6000 that Tommy required to pay for his studies. Warren Vache was appearing at the 'Platform' gig at the Queen's Hall on 20th January and it was noted *'...it's still rare to have a major new artist who takes his inspiration from the style which pre-date Parker and Gillespie's be-bop revolution'*. Gordon Cruikshank's article spoke of the Edinburgh based Hep, which he reported was Scotland's only jazz specialist jazz label, and which had issued a recording called 'Songs for Sandy', recorded live at the Queen's Hall by trumpeter Digby Fairweather. The recording *'...portrayed the life and musical personality of clarinettist the late Sandy Brown...and shows why he, along with Bruce Turner, is* (sic – presumably Gordon meant 'was') *about the best pre-bop clarinettist/saxophonist in Britain today'*. The Record Review feature told how the Louisiana Ragtime Band had issued their first LP, 'Louisiana Ragtime', which was now a recognised collector's item, about seven years previously, and reviewed their new recording which was called 'Linger Awhile'. The new LP was recommended as a Christmas gift.

Issue 3 of Jazz Magazine, in March 1984, included a Pub Survey of the Blue Lagoon where drummer Frank Birnie led the East Coast Jazz Band every Monday evening. Hot Club News announced their first 'do' for 1984, a night at the Sorbonne. Those attending were invited to wear a costume portraying a song title and there were to be prizes for guessing what the title was. A Hot Club invitation to the French band, the Hot Antic, had been withdrawn because of the ridiculous fee demanded. The Edinburgh Scene gig guide showed that regular weekly gigs had dropped slightly, to thirty nine per week. Platform was putting on concerts at the Queen's Hall on 2nd March (Jimmy Feighan Quartet), 9th March (Al Cohn), 16th March (Stewart Forbes Quartet), 19th March (Eddie Prevost Quartet), 23rd March (Joe Temperley with the Bruce Adams Quartet) and 30th March (George Keiller Quartet and Festival City Jazz Band). The coming EIJF was previewed and Humphrey Lyttelton was profiled.

The Speakeasy feature contained a perceptive review, written by a visiting Australian sax player called Lew Smith, of one of Platform's shows in the Queen's Hall. This, in fact, was the benefit concert in aid of Tommy Smith's educational venture to the USA, which had been advertised in Issue 2. Lew Smith, after telling of his long wait in a draughty corridor for tickets, had been impressed by the young Tommy and wrote *'As a saxophonist, I had never heard anyone with the control, range and fluency displayed at such a tender age. As a jazz player I was amazed at his maturity and constant flow of ideas. Sure, he's derivative, but the prospect in five to fifteen years of a major performer in the world of jazz is a very bright one indeed. His demeanour was modest, and he thoughtfully thanked all his backers and the audience for their support for his campaign'.* Prophetic words indeed. Although Tommy's style puts him beyond the reach of this book, he had been taken by his father, Tommy Smith senior, to jazz gigs all over Edinburgh where he was encouraged by the musicians and allowed to sit in, when at his earliest stage of development. Later, when there was a television documentary about Tommy, Jimmy Shortreed, who played clarinet with the Festival City Jazz Band, appeared and spoke of the young Tommy who, in turn, confirmed that Jimmy had been one of his early inspirations. Tommy came from the Wester Hailes area of the city and the story of the support given to him by the local community and the Edinburgh jazzers, is a heart warming one.

And that is where the Jazz Magazine seems to end. The March 1984 issue is the last that I have and I am sure I would have bought and kept any further issues. It was an ambitious project and very well produced but, perhaps, too ambitious to survive, even in the healthy jazz climate of 1980s Edinburgh. However, it has left a detailed record of what the Edinburgh jazz scene was like in the early 1980s, when the EIJF was young and the town pulsed every week to the sound of forty nine jazz gigs.

Jazz Magazine may have come to an abrupt end but the Edinburgh jazz scene had never been healthier, at least in terms of the sheer volume of jazz being played. The renewed energy deriving from the EIJF not only gave the established bands a welcome boost, it also fuelled the formation of several new bands. One of the established bands had in fact been around since the early 1970s when it had been put together by Falkirk trombonist John Arthur, but at first had played mostly in the Falkirk area. He gave the band the name **Dr McJazz** and, as the 1970s moved towards the 1980s, they increasingly became a feature of the Edinburgh pub jazz scene. The original line-up included Des Monaghan (tpt), Bob Busby (rds), John Arthur himself (tbn), Gus McKay (bs gtr) and his wife Helen McKay on vocals. The other rhythm players varied but included Harald Vox on banjo and Roger Hanley or Johnny Johnson on drums. Later changes brought in George Duncan on clarinet, when Bob Busby went overseas, and a photograph of the time shows a young Martin Foster playing clarinet with the band. A band flyer from the 1970s has the foot note *'The total height of the band is 38 feet and 2 inches'*!

The Dr McJazz Band played in a number of the established Edinburgh jazz pubs, including the Glenelg Hotel, later to be called Young's Hotel, in Leamington Terrace. It was when this hotel changed hands and became a Chinese restaurant that their residency there came to a halt. As Norrie Thomson was to say on a Dr McJazz CD sleeve note *'The new owners didn't want any Cornet Chop*

362

Suey on the menu! The band was also to hold a very successful resident spot for about four years on Saturday evenings at Basin Street, in the Haymarket Station Bar, in the 1980s. The band also played at many jazz festivals over the years, including those in Edinburgh and Leith.

As we have already heard, the Edinburgh traditional jazz scene had been extremely active in the 1970s and **John Arthur (trombone)** was as busy as anyone. John was born on 27th October 1930 and played piano during his teens, with local small dance bands around Falkirk. Later he completed his National Service but continued to be involved in music of one kind or another. He taught at the Falkirk College, in the electrical engineering department, and, after attending Edinburgh University for three years during which he stopped playing, he returned to the Falkirk College to teach in the English and Communication Studies Department. He retired from the college in 1993. John had taken up trombone in the 1950s and, in the 1960s, joined Andy Lothian's Dundee based jazz band, before joining the Vernon Jazz Band in Glasgow. John travelled widely with this band and also took part in a number of Radio broadcasts from Glasgow on the 'Come Thursday' programme. It was when the Vernon Jazz Band folded, around 1969/70, that John formed the Dr McJazz Band, at first playing mostly around Falkirk but later becoming established in Edinburgh.

John's trombone heroes were the great Jack Teagarden and, in the UK, Chris Barber, and it was on the Barber band that the Dr McJazz Band was to model its style. That style can be heard on a couple of recordings, retrospectively issued on CD, 'The Incredible McJazz', recorded in 1992 but issued in 2003, and 'Doctor McJazz – A Miscellany', issued in 2009, many years after the band had ceased to be active[160]. In addition to playing with the McJazz band, John also put in time with Jim Petrie's band in the Glenelg Hotel, with the West End Band in the Ailsa Craig Hotel and, for a time, played in the Blue Lagoon (later to become the Caley Sample Room) on Thursdays with pianist Ian Scott's band. John also played with Charlie McNair's Jazz Band

---

[160] See discography Appendix

during their Wednesday evening residency in Preservation Hall in Victoria Street. He was also to undertake a week-long tour in the south of England with a band led by Dumfries based trumpeter, John Cowan, during which they had the famous Kenny Ball as guest trumpeter. At the time of writing, John Arthur, now just into his eighties, continues to play trombone, at the Edinburgh Jazz and Jive Club, with Brian Robertson's Forth River Ragtimers and Fred Murray's Club House Seven.

The clarinet player who played an important part in the formation of the Dr McJazz band was **Bob Busby (reeds),** who was born on 17th December 1935 in Edinburgh. Early in Bob's life, his family moved to Falkirk, where he received his schooling and where he also received classical training on piano up to Grade 8. His introduction to jazz came in 1952 when a friend Max Murray, later to play centre forward for the Glasgow Rangers, played him a recording of the Humphrey Lyttelton band playing 'Get Out of Here and go on Home'. A year later, now switched on to jazz, Bob gave up piano and bought a clarinet. By 1957 he was proficient enough to form a Falkirk based jazz band which included Charlie Malley on trumpet and Arthur Ferguson on drums, to which they gave the name the Memphis Jazz Band. Later, when Bob was studying chemistry in Glasgow, he met up with Graham Stark at jam sessions at the Glasgow Tech, where they formed the Tech Jazz Band. Graham Stark was then playing piano and was later to become a well-known Glasgow based piano and trumpet player, for many years associated with the Kit Carey Jazz Band. Bob remained with the Tech Jazz Band until 1961, when Graham Stark left. After this, Bob played only occasional gigs, mostly with Stark or trombonist John Arthur, another Falkirk based jazzer. Then, in 1969, Bob joined Dr McJazz, the band which had been formed by John Arthur.

At first, in the early 1970s, the new Dr McJazz band played mostly in the Falkirk area but then, in about 1975, Charlie Malley, the Falkirk based trumpet player then playing with Mike Hart's band in Edinburgh, invited both Bob and John Arthur through to Edinburgh and they began to be offered gigs in the city. They both played in the

Glenelg Hotel with Jim Petrie's band, which also included Jock Westwater, Dizzy Jackson and Iain Forde, in the latter part of 1977 and made a CD. However, for Bob this came to an end when, in September 1978, he left for Oman where he remained until his return to the UK in 1982.

After his return, he joined the West End Jazz Band, which we will hear more about shortly, and remained with them through 1982 to 1984 when he again went abroad, this time to Saudi Arabia, where he stayed until 1986. His return this time saw him play from 1986 to 1988 with the Yelly Dug Jazz Band, apparently named after a dog at the cafe where they played, the Ca Va in the High Street. The proprietress of the pub had heard Bob play at Basin Street and asked him to put a band together like the one she had heard. The Yelly Dug band, in addition to Bob on reeds, included Jim Petrie (trumpet), Bob Craig (trombone), Jock Westwater (banjo), Dizzy Jackson (bass) and Iain Forde (drums). They remained at the Ca Va on a weekly basis for a few months and then lost the spot when the cafe changed hands. Shortly after this, the Saturday evening spot at Basin Street became available and Bob was invited to put a band in. This he was happy to do and he was to hold the Basin Street residency until about March 1988. The band continued to use the name the Yelly Dug Jazz Band but there had been changes in the line-up by this time, with Beverley Knight taking over on banjo and Roger Hanley replacing Forde on drums. Two CDs were made by the Yelly Dug Jazz Band around this time. Bob was then abroad again between 1988 and 1997, when he managed to play occasional gigs in Africa and Abu Dhabi, before again returning to the UK. 1997 saw him join Dave Keir's Hot Five, with which band he remained until 2002, after which he joined Jim Petrie's Diplomats of Jazz in 2003.

To my ears, Bob's style on clarinet has always seemed to have a discernable Sandy Brown influence, hot phrasing and a sharp edge to his tone giving him an attack in the Sandy manner. Alongside the equally hot trumpets of Dave Keir and Jim Petrie in the late 1990s and 2000s, Bob's playing provided a very compatible counterpoint, enhancing their lead on trumpet and matching them in his commitment to hot jazz. Bob made a couple of recordings with the Dave Keir band, 'Stomp Stomp Stomp' in 1999 and 'Redman Blues' in 2002, details of which can be found in the Discography and both of which nicely demonstrate his playing[161].

Tom Bryce (piano) was born in Maddiston, a village just outside Falkirk, in 1940 and attended the local primary school and Falkirk Technical School. After leaving school, he began an apprenticeship at Bonnybridge Power Station and became an electrical power engineer, studying at a number of technical colleges, including the Paisley Tech, through in the west of Scotland. His father was an accomplished piano player with certificates to his name and he saw to it that Tom began piano lessons at the age of eight years which continued until he was twelve. His father was clearly a man of good sense and he told Tom not to bother about certificates but to play piano with the object of enjoying himself. Tom was also fortunate in having a piano teacher who was as open minded as his father and who encouraged him to play a wide variety of music from light classics to pop. By the early 1950s, Tom was listening to the Light Programme on a crystal set and found himself attracted to the music of the big bands and jazz bands of the day. After this, he began to find himself automatically trying to put some swing into his piano playing (he says he still is) and it was not long before he latched onto the fact that there was a something of a jazz revival in the offing. At first, he listened to the British traditional bands, including those of Chris Barber and Ken Colyer, but it was not to be long before he found himself greatly taken by the music of the George Lewis band. He also bought many music books that included the works of W C Handy, Jelly Roll Morton, Duke Ellington and the ragtime pianists. A bit out of this particular jazz bag, he also had and has, a fondness for the piano playing of George Shearing, who was in the process of becoming one of the great names of modern jazz.

Tom moved to Edinburgh in the mid-1960s and, with a friend who also worked with him at the Cockenzie Power Station, he began to find his way into the Edinburgh jazz scene, listening to the Climax band at the White Cockade in

---

[161] See Discography Appendix

Rose Street and Bill Salmond's band at the Hopetoun Lounge, in Morrison Street. Later, in the 1970s, he added to his rota the Hailes House Hotel in the Kingsknowe area, where he heard the Nova Scotia Jazz Band. At the White Cockade, Tom met Alec McIntosh who, like Tom himself, worked for the Electricity Board and, discovering that Toshy played trumpet, they began to get together to play some music. A notice in the Evening News brought to Tom's attention that the YWCA had a small modern piano, which they considered underused, and were looking for people interested in playing it. On the back of this, he went to along to a meeting, arranged by one Amie Jamieson of the YWCA, and soon declared his interest in jazz and the piano. This led to a group of interested individuals getting together at the YWCA, which they were all required to join (I don't know about anyone else but I have never thought of Tom as a young Christian woman), and it soon became clear that they had the makings of a jazz band.

In addition to Tom and Alec McIntosh, there was Dave Galloway who played trombone and Dave's bass playing son Robin Galloway, who had learned on a bass which he had made himself. A banjo player, who was a pupil at the Rudolf Steiner school, also came along but did not stay long. However, before he disappeared, he had arranged for another banjo player to take his place, who turned out to be Harald Vox, then a teacher at the same school. Soon, the gradually expanding group was joined by Bill Martin on drums and then Eddie Hamilton came along, acting on a tip off from Dave Paxton, who had heard that there was a new band looking for a clarinet player. In fact, the YWCA sessions, which were originally intended to be just people getting together for a blow, attracted rather more than was needed for a single band and there quite a few others who also came along as well, including some women folk. The YWCA was located in Randolf Place in the West End of Edinburgh and, after each session, the whole gang would hasten across to the nearby West End Bar to revive themselves. It was therefore natural that, when the time came to decide on a name, they chose to call themselves the **West End Jazz Band**. The name West End, of course, also had a resonance with New Orleans, as a place name on the nearby Lake Pontchartrain, and appeared famously in the title of the Joe 'King' Oliver tune, made famous by Louis Armstrong, West End Blues.

The band's first residency was at the Loch Ewe Hotel in Royal Terrace and they started there on 17th August 1978 with a line-up that had now settled down as Alec McIntosh (tpt), Eddie Hamilton (clt), Angus Macdonald (tbn), Tom Bryce (pno), Bill Somerville or Colin Warwick (bjo), Charlie McCourt (bs) and Roy Dunnett (drms). They then moved to another hotel under the same ownership, the Ailsa Craig also in Royal Terrace, where they were to play on Thursdays for about three years, before taking on a second weekly spot on Tuesdays, at the famous Basin Street at Haymarket, where they were to stay until 1989. It was while at the Ailsa Craig that they arrived one Thursday to find the place full of Welshmen, up for the rugby international at Murrayfield. Late in the evening, a Welshman asked to borrow the microphone and proceeded to make an emotional announcement about a colleague, the highlight of whose life had been the biennial visit to Edinburgh for the rugby. Apparently this chap had died, leaving instructions that his ashes were to be scattered on the Murrayfield turf after a Welsh win, and his pals had a casket containing his ashes with them. Unfortunately for their plans, Scotland beat Wales on the Saturday and when the band arrived the following Thursday, there was the casket of ashes, returned to the hotel bar, on a shelf with the many bottles of whisky, ('resting with the spirits', as the Evening News put it), and there it remained until the next Welsh victory several years later.

In between the longer residencies, there were a number of other, briefer residencies for the West End band in venues including the Northern Bar at Canonmills, the Grange Hotel in Grange Loan and the Dell Inn at Slateford. In addition to their successful and well supported gigs, the West End band became a regular feature of the EIJF, making their debut in 1979 and remaining in the programme for many years. In one EIJF programme, it was said of the band: *'Under the eagle eye of Tom Bryce, part-time custodian of the nation's power supply, this bizarre collection of painters (Hitler type), whisky samplers, post oafish officials, aviators,, etc have a common desire to play unpretentious, good time, sing along interpretations of the jazz standards'*

Tom Bryce looks back on the 1980s as a great time for Edinburgh jazz and so it was, with jazz sounds bursting out of pubs all over the City and more bands than you could count. As well as his own West End band, he was to put in a little time with other bands too, playing for a while with the Climax band, during their residency at the Black Bull in the Grassmarket. Of course, in the nature of bands, there were changes in personnel along the way in the West End band and both Bill Smith and John Arthur played trombone at various times, Dennis Morton played drums, Gus Mckay came in on banjo, Des Monaghan from Polmont on trumpet and, in 1982, Bob McDowell replaced Eddie Hamilton. Although Bob did not stay all that long before going off to the West Indies to work, this was to be a significant change in the future of the band. In the meantime, Bob Busby followed by George Duncan replaced Bob McDowell and the band played on until 1989 when, with the Ailsa Craig gig long gone, Basin Street stopping its jazz policy and Tom Bryce involved in the complexities of a change of job, a new marriage and building a new house, the West End Jazz Band came to a halt.

It was not until 1998 that the band got together again, this renaissance being triggered off by the return of Bob McDowell to live in Linlithgow, County town of West Lothian. Bob contacted Tom Bryce to suggest that they reform and it was agreed that Bob would take on the running of the band, which from then on was to be Linlithgow based. They also agreed a policy of trying to involve West Lothian based jazzers and, already having Bob from Linlithgow and Tom from Faucheldean, they were able to recruit Andrew Lauder from Threemiletown (tpt), Bill Smith (Livingston) or John Arthur (Falkirk) for trombone, Dick Walink from Broxburn (bs) and, West Lothian apparently being a banjo free zone (which should help the local housing market), Kenny Henderson from Dunfermline, on banjo.

THE WEST END NEW ORLEANS JAZZ BAND

"THE BAND HAS JUST PLAYED THE BASIN STREET BLUES EXCEPT FOR
EDDIE WHO WAS UP BEALE STREET FOR A WHILE."

Cartoon of West End Jazz Band by Donald Macdonald snr
Charlie McCourt (bs), Eddie Hamilton (clt), Roy Dunnett (drms), Alec McIntosh (tpt), Colin Warwick (bjo), Tom Bryce (pno), Angus Macdonald (tbn)
(by permission of Ken Macdonald)

There was to be a succession of drummers, including Malcolm Brown, Roy Dunnett and Kenny Milne, before a very promising local youngster called Jack Wilson was also recruited.

Bob McDowell had definite ideas about promoting jazz and he soon set up the Linlithgow Jazz club, whose first home was the Masonic Hall next to the Burgh Hall, right in the heart of the town. Later the Club moved into the Burgh Hall itself, where they enjoyed a long and successful run. Unfortunately, this was to come to an end after a lengthy refurbishment programme, when it was decided that the premises were likely to be required for the like of wedding receptions and the Jazz Club found itself homeless. Bob McDowell made strenuous efforts to find a new venue and at various times, the Club functioned in the Linlithgow Rugby Club and the West Lothian Golf Club premises but with many trials and tribulations along the way. At the time of writing, they seem to have settled in the Queen Margaret Hall, at the east end of the town, and it is hoped that this lively and well-supported jazz club continues to flourish, as it deserves. The Linlithgow Jazz Club has featured many famous guests over the years, including the likes of Warren Vache, Bob Barnard, Roy Williams, Johnny Barnes, Jeff Barnhart and Martin Litton and the West End band itself has featured at the Keswick Jazz Festival, in Cumbria.

Tom Bryce, thinking back over his playing career, said that his real interest was in creating a platform for the front line players and that he was never really all that much concerned with the piano's solo potential. He felt that the West End Jazz Band had, in the main, lived up to his hopes that its members could play as long as they wished, could leave when they wished and remain friends, so that they could return in the future when the opportunity arose. Tom said that he had felt it to have been a great privilege to be a part of the Edinburgh jazz scene, to have known and played with so many great people and to have been part of the West End Jazz Band that he founded, a band that has already lasted for over thirty years.

Bob McDowell (reeds) was born on 16th March 1956 in Belfast and educated at Belfast Royal Academy and Queen's University, Belfast, becoming a chemical engineer and, latterly, a wine merchant. A visit to hear a live jazz band at the Glenmachen Hotel, just outside Holywood, County Down, when he was seventeen, resulted in him becoming 'totally hooked' on jazz – and how often have we heard similar stories in this book already? Bob had learned to play clarinet at school but says that it only 'became alive' for him after hearing jazz. He reckons that he listened to just about everybody he could but, if pushed, he would have to name Sydney Bechet as a special favourite. When he moved to Edinburgh in the course of his work, he got a lucky break, arriving to listen to a West End Jazz Band session and having a sit in with the band, on the very night their clarinet player was leaving. This was in 1982 and he was soon a member of the band with which he was to stay until 1988, his tenure only coming to an end because he moved away to work in the West Indies.

When he returned to live in Linlithgow in 1998, it was not long before the West End Jazz Band, which had ceased to play in the early 1990s, was re-born with Bob taking on the leadership of the band. Under Bob's hard working lead, not only did the West Lothian based band thrive but so did the Linlithgow Jazz Club, which he founded. As always with new ventures, there were problems to be solved and developments that took time. For example, at first there was no drummer in the reformed band, as there was no room in the Masonic Hall in Linlithgow, the club's first home, but there was more room when they moved to the Burgh Hall in 2001. In addition to the long list of solo stars already given above, the Club played host to an impressive array of visiting bands which included three from Australia, two each from Norway and Sweden, and four each from France and the USA. However, there were other important aspects to Bob's jazz endeavors. Certainly not the least of his many contributions to local jazz, and to jazz in general, was his securing of an Art's Council grant which was used to pay for *'half the piano'* for the jazz club and to fund educational visits to eighteen primary schools. These visits, providing youngsters with what would often be their first experience of jazz and its history, were a great success and Bob has said that the youngsters were *'the best audience ever'*.

The bass player with the West End Jazz Band, after they became West Lothian based, was **Dick Walinck (bass)**. Dick was born on 3rd December 1955 and, after attending George Heriot's School, went on to study at the Kirkcaldy Technical College, Edinburgh's Stevenson College and Napier University, before going on to become a senior software engineer in the computer industry. Dick was self-taught on guitar and first got involved in playing in public in 1974 when, with some of his pals from university, he formed a band called Jasper Morgan and The Chams, which played Latin American music. This band had a fairly short career but was the cause of Dick changing instruments when, finding that the Chams had too many guitarists, Dick found himself forced to buy and play a bass guitar. His involvement in jazz came about after he had gone along to hear the Festival City Jazz Band in a hotel in Princes Street and, finding himself as relaxed as a newt, allowed himself to be persuaded into having a sit-in with the band. In spite of, by his own account, *'making a mess of it'*, the experience awoke in him a determination to learn about jazz chord sequences. When, just a week or so later he sat in again, the bass player with the band, Kenny Burns, invited him to provide holiday cover at the band's regular gig at the Barnton Hotel.

In spite of his conversion to jazz, Dick continued to play bass guitar until, one night at a party, the drummer Frank Birnie discovered that Dick had a double bass at home. This soon resulted in not very subtle pressure to switch to double bass, which he did, and it was not long before he established himself as a bass player on the Edinburgh jazz scene. However, he was to remain interested in other forms of music and, over the years, he played many gigs with bands playing folk and Celtic music, including Norfolk, Callenish and Drombeg. In the Edinburgh jazz world, he soon became a member of Frank Birnie's East Coast Jazz Band, playing between 1980 and 1995 at their popular and well-supported Monday evening residency at the Blue Lagoon (later to be called the Sample Room), in Angle Park Terrace. A particularly memorable night at the Blue Lagoon was when the exceptional guitarist Martin Taylor, who had played with the great violinist Stephane Grappelli between 1979 and 1990 and later led the famous Spirit of Django band, sat in with the East Coast Jazz Band.

It was in 1998, when the West End Jazz Band was re-formed by Bob McDowell as a West Lothian based band, that Dick became a member and he has remained with the band ever since. This band, driven along by Bob's organizing energy from their Linlithgow Jazz Club base, brought Dick the chance to play with a number of the famous guests that Bob managed to attract to the club, including trombone maestro Roy Williams, American cornetist Warren Vache, reeds man John Barnes and the great Australian trumpeter, Bob Barnard. Later, from 2002, Dick was to be one of a number of Edinburgh jazzers who made regular trips across country to play with the Glasgow jazz bands, in his case trombonist Hugh Muldoon's Jazz and Blues Band, then playing in Laurie's Bar in the Candleriggs. In 2005, when this band spilt in two, Dick was to stay with the part of the band that stayed on in

Laurie's Bar to become banjo player Davie Wilson's Uptown Shufflers. He was also to play with another Glasgow jazz band, the Witnesses, which included the well-known Glasgow trombone player and vocalist Jackie Murray, in a fortnightly residence at the Three Judges pub at Partick Cross. Dick Walinck, to whom I was often grateful for his willingness to cover for my holidays, made a number of recordings including 'Scotsounds' in 1979 and 'Thingummygig' on STV in 1978, both with Norfolk and in the jazz field, with the Uptown Shufflers in 2008, on a CD called 'Live at Glasgow River Festival'. In 2011, as well as providing a bit of Edinburgh culture in the Glasgow jazz scene, he continues to help keep the jazz flame alive in West Lothian, with the West End Jazz Band.

Eddie Hamilton (clarinet) was born on 8th July 1937 and educated at Craiglockhart and Tynecastle schools. To trade, he was a painter and decorator and later became a postman. His musical background he describes as 'mostly classical' but he became switched on to jazz through going to see Chris Barber and George Lewis, when he was twenty. Inspired by this experience, he made his way to Mev Taylor's music shop, in Clifton Terrace near Haymarket, where he purchased his first clarinet. When he was asked if he wanted a case to go with the instrument, he said that he did but was astonished when he saw that the case was *'square and not long'*! However, undaunted, he took instrument and case home and, when he opened it, was dismayed to discover that the musical instrument inside was in four pieces. Believing that a clarinet was supposed to be all in one piece, he went back to Mev Taylor's a couple of days later to seek elucidation. The people in the shop were amazed that anyone who had bought a clarinet did not know how to assemble it, let alone play it. However, they showed Eddie what to do to turn the four pieces into a clarinet and gave him a book on how to play it. This had pictures showing black for closed and white for open holes and, after that, it was simply a matter of practice.

Eddie then bought some George Lewis records and set about learning the Lewis style, becoming in the process a devoted fan of the New Orleans clarinetist. His active playing of jazz began when he started going round jazz gigs in town and met Dave Paxton, then playing with the Louisiana Ragtime Band, who told him about a group who were looking for a clarinet player, in the hope of forming a jazz band. Eddie discovered that this group held rehearsals in a café in Randolph Place, near the West End of Princes Street. He went along on a cold dismal night and arrived to find himself in the company of a piano player called Tom Bryce, a trumpeter called Alex McIntosh and a few others. He was welcomed with open arms and became a regular member of the group. This group was to become the West End Band and their first gig was in 1978, at the Lochewe Hotel in Royal Terrace, with a line-up of Eddie, Alex McIntosh, Tom Bryce, Dave Galloway (tbn), Harald Vox (bjo), Robin Galloway (bs) and Bill Martin (drms). Eddie stayed with them until 1982, when he left the band.

Later that same year, he was asked to play with what he calls a 'makeshift band', at the Stockbridge Festival in St Stephen Street. However, foul weather put a stop to this gig and the band retired, as bands do, to the nearest hostelry, the Baillie on the corner of the street. There they met the owner of Raffles Bar, a pub near the other end of St Stephen's Street. This gentleman asked them to play the rest of the afternoon in his pub, an invitation which they accepted with alacrity. They got a great reception and, to their delight, found themselves with a regular Saturday spot. They quickly decided to call themselves the **St Stephen Street Stompers** and the band that day was Eddie, Alex McIntosh, Angus Macdonald (tbn), Colin Warwick (bjo) and Frank Birnie (drms). The gig went well, lasting for about a year and half, although the personnel of the band was to change as time went on. Dave Strutt, Brian Robertson and Andrew Lauder all played trumpet at one time or another, Kenny Henderson and Beverley Knight had a spells on banjo, Jimmy Tunnah and Roy Percy played bass, Bill Brydon sousaphone and Roger Hanley drums, with Hugh Smith playing washboard at other times. Sometimes special guests were persuaded along and these included Mac Rae from Newcastle, who played both drums and trumpet, the well-known clarinetist Brian Carrick also from Newcastle, the trumpet and trombone team of Pam and Llew Hird and, more locally, Jim Petrie.

After the demise of the Raffles sessions, Eddie fixed up a regular spot for a couple of years at the Cavern in Leith, where he reduced the band to a quartet to suit the cramped space, with a line-up that was for the most part Eddie, Dave Strutt, Beverley Knight and Bill Brydon. The highlight of the St Stephen Street Stompers career was their appearance in August 1985, on a live broadcast of the Radio 2 show, Brian Matthews Round Midnight. This show went out from the Caledonia hotel during the EIJF for several years and often featured bands appearing at the festival. Eddie still treasures a taped copy of the show, the band at the time having, in addition to Eddie, Brian Robertson (tpt), Kenny Henderson (bjo), Angus Macdonald (tba) and Hugh Smith (washboard). Eddie remembers the occasion as very enjoyable and never to be forgotten. Eddie seemed to have an affinity with bands called 'Stompers' and he was to go on to play with Alan Quinn's Templehall Stompers, followed by ten years when he was with Brain Robertson's Ellwyn Stompers. At the time of writing in 2011, he is still in regular action, still playing and singing in his inimitable and sincere fashion, with Brian Robertson's Forth River Ragtimers.

November 1980 saw the first gig for a major new Edinburgh band, which was not only almost unique in drawing its main influence from a European model, but would go on to establish itself with a reputation that extended far beyond Edinburgh. This band was formed jointly by guitarist John Russell and trumpeter Dave Strutt and was inspired by the gypsy band WASO, which had made the first of several appearances at the EIJF in summer 1980. John Russell had been a long term admirer of the music of Django Reinhardt and had, as he puts it, *'been living for years'* on a diet of the recorded output of the great Belgian gypsy guitarist. He confesses to being thunderstruck by the experience of hearing the Django style live, in the form of WASO. John and Dave Strutt lost no time in searching out local musicians who would be able to play in this style and, in a few short months, had their new band ready.

Their choice of a name was an inspired one, christening the band **Swing 1980** but with the plan of updating the name incrementally with each passing year. Of course, a regularly changing band name poses a problem for a writer concerned with tracing the band over time but, for the purposes of this book, I will refer to the band simply as Swing 1980-2011. The original line-up was John Russell (rhythm gtr), Dave Strutt (tpt), Dick Lee (rds), Neil Munro (solo gtr) and Fergus Currie (bs). John Russell says that the band policy was democratic decision making (which he qualifies by adding the word Machiavellian!) and always having a regular residency, which serves to keep everyone focused and reminds them of their first band choice. Wise words these, especially the latter part and, I am sure, a sensible way of building band loyalty in a world where even jazz musicians in established bands are sometimes tempted to take the first gig that comes along.

A quality outfit from the start, Swing 1980-2011 were never short of gigs and, over the years, held residencies in a number of good venues including La Grenouille, the Cygnet Lounge, Bannerman's in the Cowgate and the Malt Shovel in Cockburn Street. This last residency was to become established as the longest running of any held by an Edinburgh jazz band and, in 2011, Swing 1980-2011 had completed, with only the shortest of breaks, an incredible total of twenty seven years at the Malt Shovel. Their success was well deserved, the whole band always committed to the best playing they could produce and, when required, always recruiting high class musicians. This is, in many ways, a tribute to John Russell who, together with Dick Lee has been with the band throughout its thirty year history. One of the finest ever rhythm guitarists from Scotland, John, in addition to his own fine playing, has been a sort of guardian of the band's quality throughout.

There were changes of course, but always with good players replaced by other good players. On bass, after short spells from Fergus Currie, who now lives and plays classical music in Athens, and Ian Hope, Jerry Forde played from 1982 to mid-1987 before handing over to Roy Percy, who remains with the band in 2011. Neil Munro played from 1980 to 1984 and was succeeded in turn by three other fine solo guitarists, Martin Leys from 1984 to 1990, Phil Adams from 1992 to 2002 and Stephen Coutts, from the west of Scotland, who joined the band in 2002 and remains in place in 2011. Stephen's early musical career was spent studying classical violin and it is perfectly clear that classical music's loss was very much a major gain for jazz. He is an exceptional guitarist with many gigs with great jazz musicians on his CV, both in Europe and in Canada. With his background in violin playing and his skill as a guitarist, it is not surprising that, when the chance came along, he struck up a friendship with the great French jazz violinist, the late Stephane Grappelli. Stephen Coutts is described by his colleagues, with every justification, as a 'musician's musician'. I once played a gig with Stephen, in a trio led by Ayrshire's outstanding trumpeter Mike Daly and, once I had come to terms with feeling more than a bit out-classed, I was considerably knocked out by Stephen's apparently effortless ability to play any tune suggested and his endlessly creative and beautiful improvisations.

Swing 1980-2011 have made a number of recordings issued on CD, their first being 'Live at the Cygnet' from 1984, with others issued in 1986, 1998, 1999, 2002, 2005 and 2009[162]. These recordings give a good account of a remarkable band which, in addition to jazz standards and pieces associated with the Django Reinhardt tradition, always included a great deal of unusual material in their repertoire. Dick Lee, who was a highly active musician involved in all sorts of jazz and Scottish musical traditions, including many interesting fusions of styles, was always a highly original player and a fertile source of compositions and arrangements. The band also made a number of radio broadcasts over the years, amongst which were Round Midnight in 1985, a number of 'arts programmes' on radio Scotland in the 1990s and Stephen Duffy's 'Jazz Train', which went out live, in 2008.

Edinburgh jazz folk lore includes a number of versions of a story involving Swing 1980-2011 and a fabled trip to China. Here, at last, is the true version, provided by John Russell. Dick Lee had come up with the idea of the band going to play in China and, the band being supportive, in

---

[162] See discography Appendix

1986 they started raising money to fund the trip. Money was raised by various means including the band's own efforts, sponsorship from private business and Edinburgh Council, who were supportive because of twinning arrangements with Xian and seeing it as a cultural trip. After a great deal of difficult and shambolic communication, the band, which at the time had John, Dick Lee, Martin Leys and Jerry Forde, set off for China in July 1987. It should be mentioned that Roy Percy had by this time taken over from Jerry Forde on bass but, because the planning had been going on while Jerry was in the band, Roy stood aside for the trip.

Swing 2011 outside their long-term residency, The Malt Shovel
Roy Percy (bs), John Russell (gtr/ldr), Stephen Coutts (solo-gtr), Dick Lee (rds)
(by permission of John Russell)

They arrived and had been in Beijing for a week after which they were to fly to Xian to give what John called a *'huge concert'*. There was also a plan to get the band to

Shanghai before returning to Beijing, presumably so that they could play in all three cities, although this was not clear to the band. Wherever the band went in their extensive travels round the tourist itinerary in Beijing, they found themselves accompanied by a team of three - a translator, a guide and a driver - who took them around in an air-conditioned mini-bus. They then discovered, after a few days, that they were picking up the tab, not only for their own expenses, but also those of their Chinese team. Hasty calculations revealed that this was going to put them well beyond their planned expenditure. Protests directed at their translator got them nowhere as he indicated that he was not in a position to change anything until several committees had approved any changes to the programme. At this point, the band became convinced that the Chinese, a notably inventive people, must have invented bureaucracy.

A contingency plan of simply heading for Xian and their concert came to naught when bad weather closed in and all flights were cancelled. A series of hair-tearing meetings resolved nothing and the band decided to get themselves off the hook and get an early flight home. With a great deal of hard work on the part of the band and a certain amount of luck, they managed to get an Air France flight and fled after ten days of mind-boggling frustration. John confesses having his hitherto positive and democratic feelings towards the People's Republic somewhat diminished by the experience and says that it had been like being on another planet. So there we have the true story from the horse's mouth and, as John says, if anyone asks *'Did Swing 1980-2010 play jazz in China?'* the answer is no, except in their hotel room. And I thought that it was a right hassle depping in Glasgow pubs. Born in 1980, Swing 1980-2011 shows no sign of ever stopping; let us hope that there will be many more annual increments added to the name of this remarkable Edinburgh jazz band.

John Russell (guitar), the heart beat of Swing 1980-2011, was born in Edinburgh on 28th April 1945, attended St Ignatius and St Anthony's schools and became a college lecturer. His early exposure to jazz came from hearing British trad bands on the radio but it was when he heard a recording of the great Django Reinhardt that he was struck by his personal musical thunderbolt. This was his music and it has remained so over the half century plus that has passed since. Not surprisingly, he took up guitar, on which he was self taught. It is equally unsurprising that, although he numbers all the jazz greats amongst those he regards as his jazz heroes, it is the great guitarists which interest him most. John's early playing experience was with various dance bands in the early 1960s. He also had a band of his own, Jason and the Argonauts, which he led between 1961 and 1966 and with whom he *did the Beatles and Rhythm and Blues thing'*.

His early ventures into the Edinburgh jazz scene were in the 1970s, when he sat in with the bands of Charlie McNair and Hamish McGregor. Later, of course, his playing was dominated by his work with Swing 1980-2011 but he also managed to fit in work with a number of other bands, all of them of considerable quality. These included the Ralph Laing All Stars in 1995, the Alex Yellowlees Hot Club around 1999/2000 and the Scottish Jazz All Stars between 2006 and 2008. The latter was a band put together by Glasgow trombone player Dave Batchelor, mostly to work at jazz festivals, and which included some stellar Scottish jazz names in its membership, including Lennie Herd (tpt), Forrie Cairns (clt), Brian Kellock (pno) and Ronnie Rae (bs). Forrie Cairns had, of course, initially made his name with the Clyde Valley Stompers and had the distinction of being the only clarinettist whom Sandy Brown, in 'The McJazz Manuscripts', acknowledged as a possible challenger. I made a trip to play on the Isle of Arran with both Lennie Herd and Forrie Cairns in 2007 and, although Forrie was by then in his seventies, he was still playing wonderfully well, as indeed was Lennie.

With Swing 1980-2011, John Russell made many recordings which show to great advantage his sterling rhythm guitar work, providing a clean, crisp chordal sound of impeccable tempo, worthy of the Basie band's Freddie Green himself. The Swing 1980-2011 recordings can be found in the discography Appendix but John made a couple of other recordings with the Alex Yellowlees Hot Club, 'Hot Club Live' in 1999 and 'Hot Club Style' in 2000. His work with Swing 1980-2011 brought him opportunities to play with many renowned jazzers, amongst them reeds man Benny Waters, trumpeters Warren Vache and Digby Fairweather, trombonist Roy Williams, guitarists Howard Alden, Marty Grosz and Diz Disley and piano player Brian Kellock who has also recorded with Swing 1980-2011. It must have pleased John a great deal also to play, on many occasions, with the guitarist that he considers to be Django Reinhardt's true successor – Fapy Lafertin.

The reeds player with Swing 1980/2011 throughout its entire existence to date, has been **Dick Lee (clarinet, bass clarinet, recorder, soprano sax)**. Dick was born in Kenilworth, Warwickshire, on 20th April 1951 and was educated at Leamington College for Boys. Dick occasionally worked on building sites, on the oil rigs, as a groundsman and, in what he says must be the worst job in the world, checking for pressing faults on LP records, hot off the presses at the Polydor factory in Walthamstow. This task may seem straightforward but it had its hidden perils. It involved sampling the record surface by lifting the needle every sixty seconds or so but also entailed, to save time, having to play the 33 rpm records at 45 rpm – sheer torture for a musician of any sensitivity. In this job, he did 8 hour shifts, changing all the time, and with a mind-numbing preponderance of James Last and Herb Alpert, it's a wonder that he survived. However, it seems that the oilrig work had notable compensation, his clarinet sounding amazing when played in the leg of an oil rig which, according to Dick, had a reverb like the Taj Mahal! However, he was to be and was to remain, a full time musician. I say musician rather than jazzer advisedly, fine jazzer although he is, as Dick was to be an astonishingly wide ranging player, embracing an impressive spectrum of different forms of music.

Dick's parents always loved music, including classical, jazz and an array of other forms, and he feels fortunate that, from an early age, they surrounded him with music. Not only did his parents take him to City of Birmingham Symphony Orchestra concerts from the age of six but they also bought him a clarinet and sent him to the Birmingham School of Music, for clarinet lessons with the CBSO principal clarinettist, John Fuest. However, in the end, it was jazz that was to enthral him, although he never had any jazz lessons. He did, however, manage to pack in a lot of listening, every week for many years his mother sending him cassettes of Jazz Record Requests and Sounds of Jazz, recorded from the radio. All this listening soon enabled Dick to distinguish jazzers whom he particularly liked, his main influences forming an eclectic line-up of Joe Venuti, Adrian Rollini, Django Reinhardt, Lester Young, Benny Goodman, Don Ellis, Charlie Parker and Johnny Dodds.

The first encounter of the young Dick Lee with Edinburgh jazz took place, not in Edinburgh, but in Ardfern in Argyll in about 1978, when he heard and sat in with the New Society Syncopators (later, of course, to be known as Mike Hart's Scottish Society Syncopators). This was the first time he had ever played with a real jazz band. He cannot remember the full line-up of the band on this memorable occasion but does remember the inimitable Jackie MacFarlane in top form. He also remains grateful to Mike Hart for allowing *'an unknown chancer'* to get up and play with the band, something he considers to have been a life-changing experience. In 1980, Dick moved to live in Edinburgh where he joined a band called the Southside Strutters, which included one Robin Harper, later to be well-known as a Green MSP in the Scottish Parliament, on rhythm guitar. Then he joined Swing 1980.

To an extent, Dick's jazz career, from then on, was to be that of Swing 1980/2011 but there were many other ventures along the way. He formed a couple of bands under his own leadership, Dick Lee's Chamber Jazz between 1989 and 1997, No No Nonet from 1990 to 1996 and Dick Lee's Septet, from 1999 to 2005. However, he continued throughout to play with Swing 1980/2011, as they established themselves as one of Edinburgh's and the UK's finest small jazz combos. A busy man, Dick Lee, but that was far from all. He also managed to fit in a great deal of playing with other musical combinations, including some ground-breaking fusions of jazz with Celtic music, playing and recording with bagpiper Hamish Moore, ex-Pentangle guitarist John Renbourn, the approximately thirty-six piece La Banda Europa and the innovative folk styled quintet, Bag o' Cats. His other jazz outings kept him busy too and, in addition to appearing on all the Swing 1980/2011 recordings, he also played and recorded with drummer Kenny Mathieson's Classic Jazz Orchestra, a terrific band playing Kenny's arrangements of classic jazz of the 1920s and '30s, with whom he appeared on the albums 'Jelly's New Clothes' and 'The Classic Jazz Orchestra Salutes the Kings of Jazz'. In 2011, Dick was working and recording with accordionist David Vernon, with whom he has toured and produced the recordings 'Reeds United' and, their most recent album, 'Airlocked'.

When asked about the great players with whom he had played, he listed tenor sax players Benny Waters and Konrad Wyzniewski and Edinburgh's own trumpeter Jim Petrie, for whose playing Dick has a great deal of respect and a warm admiration. In 2011, Dick Lee is still as busy as ever, his latest venture his band Dr Lee's Prescription, his playing still agile and quirky, one of the most refreshingly original of all Scotland's jazz musicians.

The third bass player with Swing 1980/2011, was **Jerry Forde (bass)**, who was born in Edinburgh on 27th November 1961. Jerry had a proper Edinburgh jazz pedigree, his father being Iain Forde, who had made a notable contribution to Edinburgh jazz over several decades, mainly as a drummer. Jerry attended Bruntsfield Primary School, before completing his education at James Gillespie's High School, and later graduated as a civil and structural engineer, having studied at Napier and Edinburgh Universities. With a father already heavily involved in jazz, it was inevitable that the young Forde would have an early exposure to the music, Jerry claiming that his first personal response to jazz came at an Anita O'Day and Johnny Dankworth concert in London in 1961 when, still in the foetal state, he gave his mother a good kicking during the performance! Jerry shared with me membership of the 38th Edinburgh scout troop, although quite a number of years apart, and his earliest musical efforts included playing banjo-ukelele and 'a bit of trumpet' at scout camps.

Jerry reports that *'other than pre-natal foot tapping and dancing'*, his earliest memories of jazz were of his father playing the music of the great names of jazz at a generous volume, on 78 rpm and vinyl LP records and a Ferrograph reel to reel tape recorder. Oddly, Jerry has no memory of Iain playing drums in the house, although he is sure this must have taken place, but he does recall a number of band practices in their basement, in Warrender Park Road. His Dad also played a lot of jazz piano in the house and they had a pianola, complete with a selection of piano rolls, most of which were of music hall tunes. Jerry discovered that these could be 'jazzed up' by pedalling like mad and playing them very fast. Apparently the pianola was actually owned by the clarinet player George Gilmour who, at that time earning his living as a light house keeper, had found that there was no room for it in the light house! Many of the piano rolls belonged to the bass player Jim Young. Jerry's early memories of life at home include hearing the records and admiring the album covers, of the likes of Fats Waller, Louis Armstrong, Bunk Johnson, Johnny Dodds and many others. Yet another early exposure to jazz was Jerry's attendance, on his twelfth birthday in 1973, at the last appearance in Scotland of Duke Ellington with his orchestra.

Jerry had piano lessons from the age of 7 and slowly worked his way through the various grades. His final tutor, Stan Banigan, was keen to encourage him to try some fairly unusual material, including less well known Scott Joplin rags, Erik Satie and Debussy, plus what Jerry calls some *'very quirky material from a variety of sources'*. Obviously a go-getting sort of character, Jerry managed to purloin an acoustic guitar which had been bought for his sister Emily and then managed to purchase steel and a twelve string guitars, on which he learned both chord and line playing. By about 1976, he had begun swapping pop guitar chords and had made a number of musical connections and friendships, still in the 1980s pop music idiom. Other early musical activity during school days was playing *'reluctant tuba'* and using his guitar playing skills, on both rhythm and bass guitar in teenage bands, playing a strange mixture of *'progressive rock, punk and new wave'*, whatever that might be.

However, the latent family interest in jazz was about to make itself felt. He started to have a go at jazz bass, still on the bass guitar, and his first *'very tentative'* gig was with

Jim Petrie's band in the Glenelg Hotel. He reports that he *'got through, just about'*. Having made a start and probably with encouragement from his Dad and other jazzers, he then bought a double bass from Ken Macdonald, who also provided a few lessons. He was soon reached a decent level of competence and found that his ability to read music from his piano playing days helped him a great deal, although when he reads bass music he has to mentally transcribe it from the piano, commenting that it is just as well that it is light on crochets! From then on, Jerry's progress was down to practice and playing gigs, finding plenty of motivation from increasingly taking on work with several of the Edinburgh bands. Some early experience was with Bill Salmond's Louisiana Ragtime Band, with which he gradually built up his volume and stamina. However, in spite of experience in the New Orleans style, he decided against attempting to learn the slap style, partly because he preferred to use steel, rather than gut, strings.

Joining Swing 1982 in March of that year, brought a whole load of new challenges, with Jerry having to learn a lot of new material, new techniques and quite tricky key and tempo changes, plus having to brush up his sight reading. He was with the band when they were awarded the 'Best Band Award' at the EIJF in 1983 and made the famous, if ultimately abortive, trip to China in 1987, described above. He also owed a lot to his friend and mentor, the late Francis Cowan, whom Jerry describes rightly as *'a formidably real musician'*, with whom Jerry did a lot of rehearsing and playing. Playing with Francis brought him huge gains in bass technique, helping him cope with difficult rhythmic patterns and sight reading and extend his range on the instrument, including some arco (bow) work. Recently, at about the time of writing in 2011, he has made a partial return to his roots, digging out his bass guitar in response to the demanding writing of Dick Lee for a new band, Dr Lee's Prescription with Dick himself, Phil Adams and Marcus Ford, having to learn some fairly fiendish parts. This includes some very fast, very high playing with a range of shifting time signatures, although still *'just about'* within the jazz tradition. And to think that I used to find Muskrat Ramble and Basin Street Blues quite hard enough.

Jerry now plays his third double bass, his first having been returned to Ken Macdonald in about 1985, for the use of Owen Macdonald in his early bass playing years. His second had belonged to the late Tony Sargent and this instrument, although Tony played left-handed, was actually strung for right-handed playing, with Tony standing on the 'wrong' side of the bass. Talk about making things difficult for yourself! Apparently Tony's bass, although made by an amateur, had a really good carved front and an ebony fingerboard. Jerry eventually bought a top-class instrument in 1999, had it set up by Ken Macdonald, and is still playing it in 2011.

When asked about his bass playing models, Jerry points to a whole line of great players - Ray Brown, Walter Page from the Basie band, a number of fine bassists who played with the band of Duke Ellington, Niels-Henning Orsted Pederson, Percy Heath, Gary Karr (a virtuoso classical double bass player), the one and only Milt Hinton and Jaco Pastorius. You would be hard pushed to improve on that list. A bass player with a serious and conscientious attitude to his music, Jerry Forde's Edinburgh jazz CV embraces spells with the Louisiana Ragtime Band 1980 to '81, Swing 1982 to '87 (and on-going deps for Roy Percy), the Bill Jones Quartet, the Alan Yellowlees trio/Quartet, Mike Hart's Scottish Society Syncopators, Le Jazz Hot, duos, trios, quartets, quintets and big band jazz with Francis Cowan from 1984 to '96 and the Marcus Ford trio from 1996 to the present. With the Syncopators, he toured in the USA and Poland in 1986, in the company of Dave Strutt and Andrew Lauder (tpts), Johnny McGuff (tbn), Tom Finlay (pno), Frank Birnie (drms) and band leader Mike Hart himself, on banjo and guitar.

His career has also brought him into the recording studios and he has made recordings with Swing 1984, the Society Syncopators (1986) and Le Jazz Hot (2001)[163]. Asked about great players he has played with, he lists Milt Hinton in the sessions at the Edinburgh International Jazz

---

[163] See discography appendix

Festival called 'The Judge Meets the Section', when 9 bassists played together and he recalls that he had to 'detune' his bass to play the lowest part required. There was also an occasion when he claims he *'played for Ray Brown'*. This turning out to be a gig in 1999, when Jerry played in Suruchi's Indian Restaurant, and Ray Brown came in for a meal! There were also gigs involving Fapy Lafertin, with Swing 1985 and sits-in with Al Fairweather's band with Jerry's Dad, Iain, on drums. One of the few second generation Edinburgh jazzers, Jerry Forde remains a fine player and one of the younger musicians (ie under the age of fifty!) who are involved in Edinburgh traditional jazz. On such as he, depends the future of the music. In fact, he may be a link to a third generation from the same family, his youngest daughter Lauren playing alto sax and, according to Jerry, having a *'good jazzy/bluesy ear'* and his brother Miles having two sons, Robbie and Jamie, who are keen piano players with a wide musical interest, including jazz. I liked Jerry's final comment on bass playing – *'Ah, contra-basso, eso se toca contrabajo!'* (a Spanish word play on the similarity of double bass and hard-work). He never spoke a truer word.

Roy Percy (bass) was to be, not only a very good bass player, but also a man of many bands, all of them of a high calibre, often being a member of several of them at the same time. He first began to make a name for himself in the mid-1980s, particularly when, in November 1986, he took over from Jerry Forde in Swing1986. He joined the band when they were already well established and with a burgeoning reputation for swinging and extremely well-played jazz. The takeover was gradual, as we have already heard, with Jerry Forde playing out a number of gigs already in his diary before he departed for the south, where his day job had taken him. Roy was remain with the band in the long term and is still there at the time of writing in 2011, when the band is, of course, known as Swing 2011.

When vocalist Craig McMurdo broke up his first band, the Gooseberries, and formed a new outfit to be called That Swing Thang in 1986, Roy jumped at the chance of playing with the new band. Initially playing in the jump jive style of Louis Prima and Louis Jordan, with some jazz standards and Nat 'King' Cole material in the mix as well, the band swiftly grew from its original vocalist, two guitars and double bass format to become a 'full sized' band with vocalist, trumpet, sax, trombone, guitar, piano, bass and drums. With That Swing Thang, Roy made many appearances on television, including Blue Peter, Pebble Mill at One and This Morning, in addition to countless Grampian TV's Art Sutter Shows and a good number of Hogmany shows. He stayed with the band until around 2004/04 but still makes occasional appearances with Craig McMurdo when the singer resurrects his smaller combo to perform the jump jive and Nat Cole material. In 1988, Roy also became a member of the trio put together by reeds man Martin Foster, Le Jazz Hot. This was a peppy little band, originally with Raymond Gillespie on guitar, capable of playing with considerable fire, although in fact playing a wide spectrum of material, embracing everything from ragtime to lounge music. With them, Roy appeared on a televised TV show called 'The Big Break' and remained with the band until 1992, although he has continued to make occasional appearances with the band right up to the present time in 2011. Another band with its roots in jump jive, Hamish McGregor's nine-piece Fat Sam's Band, also recruited Roy's services in 1998. With them, he travelled twice to play at the Sacramento Jazz Jubilee, in 1998 and 2000, to the Los Angeles Sweet and Hot Festival in 2001, a Middle East tour in 1999 and a number of forays to Scandinavia, before eventually leaving the band in 2005.

A highly versatile player, as befits a bass player with a living to make from the music, Roy also ventured into the purist style, joining the famous Climax Jazz Band in the late 1980s and remaining with them until around 1992. With them, he played at the Ascona Jazz Festival in 1990 and made a number of trips to play with the band in Holland. Still in purist mode, Roy also put in a number of spells with the Spirits of Rhythm, playing with them more or less continuously from 1990 to 2000. Still in the realm of New Orleans jazz but in the classic style, Roy played for a time with Al Fairweather's Sundowners in the early 1990s, where he found himself alongside Al's fellow veterans Bob Craig and Dave Paxton. Not surprisingly, Roy's skill and versatility brought him many depping gigs with other Edinburgh bands, including Mike Hart's Society Syncopators, Bill Salmond's Louisiana Ragtime Band and the Maid of the Forth Stompers. At the time of writing, Roy has been playing and recording with a tidy four-piece band led by the outstanding trumpet player from Ayrshire, Mike Daly, a band which includes John Burgess on clarinet and Duncan Findlay on banjo. Many other recorded examples of Roy's playing, with a variety of bands, can be found in the discography appendix.

As a fellow bass player, I naturally never played in a band with Roy, but I was interested to watch his development from his early days until the present, when he is one of the most sought after bass players in the country. It has always seemed to me that he was very much influenced by the playing of the great Milt Hinton when he made his appearances at the EIJF in 1985 and 1986. Hinton was a wonderful player, not only a rock solid powerhouse in the rhythm section but a terrific and melodic soloist as well. Roy was already a good player but, after hearing Hinton, he seemed to me to make major strides forward, even managing to master some of the tricky double and triple slap techniques that were such an appealing feature of the American's style. No one worked harder than Roy Percy in developing his technique and style and he has become deservedly successful as a professional musician. It is gratifying to see top class younger jazzers, such as Roy, Mike Daly and John Burgess, although more than capable players of more modern forms of jazz, clearly valuing the older styles and helping to keep the main stream of the music alive and well in the twenty-first century.

Chapter XIV

Advocates, Syncopators and Fat Sam

The re-formed **Old Bailey's Jazz Advocates** had enjoyed a remarkable run of success since getting together again in 1975 and they entered the 1980s in good shape, with a line-up of Andrew Lauder (tpt), Hamish McGregor (rds), Sam Smith (tbn), Tom Finlay (pno), Mike Hart (bjo), Graham Blamire (bs) and Donald 'Chick' Murray (drms). A residency at Waterman's Bar in the Grassmarket between June and November 1980 was followed by a move in January 1981 to the Garrick Bar, in Spittal Street, near the Usher Hall. However, the band was still sharing both Mike Hart and Tom Finlay with Mike's band, the Scottish Society Syncpators, and the time had come to resolve the situation. At the start of 1981, the two bands in effect merged. The new line-up was an eight piece band with Andrew Lauder, Hamish McGregor and Sam Smith being joined in the front line by Jack Graham and a rhythm section of Tom Finlay, Mike Hart, Graham Blamire and Chick Murray. In addition, the famous jazz singer from Glasgow, Fionna Duncan, joined the band and a new recording was planned.

After some debate, the new band was given the title the **Scottish Jazz Advocates**. Alastair Clark, in his Sounds Around column in the Scotsman, announced the new band by writing *'Happily, Edinburgh's home-based trad musicians never die – they just reshuffle themselves into a different permutation. The latest chapter in a long and complex history involves Old Bailey's Jazz Advocates and Mike Hart's Scottish Society Syncopators, formerly the New Society*

Syncopators. Are you with me so far? Well, they've merged under the title of the Scottish Jazz Advocates and the new eight piece band can be heard tomorrow at the first of a series of free sessions at the Caledonian Hotel, Edinburgh'[164]. Alastair was quite right and on 25th January 1981, the new band took up a residency in the Caledonian Hotel, at the West End of Princes Street. John Gibson also announced the merging of the two bands and his article in the Evening News provides an interesting comment on the times, giving the price of a pint of beer as fifty nine pence, lager at sixty two pence and whisky at fifty nine pence[165].

The Caledonian Hotel, one of the great nineteenth century railway hotels, was a prestigious venue and the new band's residency was to be for a four week trial in the first place, with success promising a permanent gig. In fact, by May, John Gibson was able to write in the Evening News, *'Business has been so brisk for the Scottish Jazz Advocates at the Caledonian Hotel on Sunday night since they took their trad music there in March that the sessions have been extended to Thursdays'[166].* John Gibson also announced that the Caledonian Hotel, or the Caley as it was known, was to be added to the list of venues for that year's EIJF. He also wrote that the Advocates were to fly to California the next week for concerts, radio and TV spots and to plug their new album which was called Live at the Caley, which featured Fionna Duncan on several numbers. The recording was made in March 1981, live in the Caley, as the name said. Unfortunately, it was recorded the day after a Scottish rugby international against Ireland and the well-oiled Irish rugby supporters packed into the bar tended to make their presence felt throughout the entire proceedings! There followed a trip to play at the Sacramento Jazz Festival, where the band made a good impression with strong prospects of an invite for the next year. 1982 brought a BBC Radio 1 Jazz Club broadcast, when the band

---

[164] Clark A, 'Sounds Around', The Scotsman, 24th January 1981

[165] Gibson J, 'Joining up for the sound of jazz', Edinburgh Evening News, 24 January 1981

[166] Gibson J, 'More gigs for the Advocates', Edinburgh Evening News, 7th May 1981

played as support band to the Clyde Valley Stompers, who were on a re-union tour with Fionna Duncan. Fionna sang with both bands on the broadcast.

The jazz **vocalist, Fionna Duncan**, was born at Garelochhead, Dunbartonshire, on 5 November 1939. In 1950, she joined the school Ballad and Blues Club, while she was attending Rutherglen Academy, and from second year at school, she sang the soprano lead in several Gilbert and Sullivan operas run by the very go-ahead music department. These included 'The Dukes Dilemma' and 'Country Girl' and she further extended her activities by joining 'The Bankhead Players', a well known amateur drama group, with whom she appeared around Glasgow and the surrounding area. All this experience was to be of great value to Fionna in her career in music, gaining her not only a solid foundation in music but also in stage presentation and, in addition, she was to leave school with a pass in Higher Music. Her brother Ian was a piano player and, at only seventeen years old, Fionna sang with his modern jazz group, the Lindsay McDonald Quartet, at the Glasgow University Student's Union and became resident singer in the Glasgow University Snug Bar, singing every Saturday evening. In 1956, while on a business trip to the USA, she sang on TV, did several radio programmes and turned down a prestigious recording contract with Riverside Records. The contract would have required her to move to live in the USA permanently, and she turned it down because of this.

On returning to Scotland, Fionna auditioned for the BBC in Glasgow and, for the following two years, she had a regular Saturday morning radio broadcast with the Joe Gordon Folk Four on a show called 'Skiffle Club'. Next came another Saturday morning radio show, 'Saturday Club'. Around this time, she also became vocalist with Glasgow's Steadfast Jazz Band and then, after winning a talent contest, joined Forrie Cairns' All Stars. This was followed by Fionna signing up to sing with the famous Clyde Valley Stompers, which also included Forrie Cairns on clarinet, and she was with them when the band played long summer residencies on the Isle of Arran, great times which were to become something of a legend. I did a gig on Arran on 2007, in a quartet featuring Forrie Cairns, Lennie Herd (tpt) and Alastair McDonald (bjo/vocs), and was amazed by the endless number of punters who came up to speak with Forrie and reminisce about the great days of the Stompers on Arran, almost fifty years after the events. After her time with the Stompers, Fionna returned to a band led by Forrie Cairns, and was to be a member of his Clansmen, until 1964. This was followed by a tour in Germany as a solo singer and then she took up a residency at the Georgian Club in London, a gig which lasted from about 1964 to 1970 (the Who's Who of British Jazz says 1966 until 1971). This night club gig, which entailed a show of ninety minutes every evening during which she sang with the Georgian Dixielanders, provided Fionna with a terrific opportunity to extend her repertoire and style and she has said that it was a great learning experience. The evening sessions were a draw for many of the leading 'Show Biz' personalities of the time and, although the show was directed by Billy Petch and Bobby Chandler from Talk of the Town, it afforded Fionna more invaluable show experience, as she organised the rehearsals, sorted out the lighting and was involved in auditioning new acts. All this added up to a performer right on top of her game, with a thorough understanding of how to project and with formidable stamina.

Fionna returned to Scotland around 1970 as a full time vocalist, touring in Europe and the USA. By 1977, she was singing with the Glasgow based George Penman's Jazzmen, an arrangement which continued until 1981, when she began singing with the Scottish Jazz Advocates. Later, she was to make guest appearances with the Eggy Ley band between 1984 and 1986. In 1985, she formed her own trio, with musical partner Ronnie Rae on bass, Ronnie's son John on drums and Brian Kellock on piano, a top class group featuring the finest players in Scotland. With this stellar Trio, Fionna made many international festival appearances and toured in Canada and Switzerland. Fionna was to continue to work successfully with the trio and as a solo singer throughout the 1990s, starred at the EIJF and other festivals and, from 1995, ran many successful jazz vocal workshops. The workshops developed rapidly over the next few years and became an important fixture on the Scottish jazz calendar, providing an invaluable training ground for aspiring young vocalists. This part of her career must have given Fionna, and her team of professional tutors and musicians, a vast amount of satisfaction. Her career was dotted with recordings, many of which are still available today, all of them demonstrating her consummate ability as a jazz singer with style, energy and a remarkable sense of timing. Fionna Duncan, with a jazz career now in excess of forty five years, remains a major Scottish jazz name and, in the 2000s, was as popular as ever and continued to be one of the biggest draws on the Scottish jazz scene.

The Scottish Jazz Advocates c 1984
L-R Hamish McGregor, Johnny McGuff, Graham Blamire,
Chick Murray, Andrew Lauder, Tom Finlay, Mike Hart
(from the collection of the author, photographer
unknown)

Meanwhile, the Jazz Advocates Caledonian Hotel gig, in spite of being located in a very large lounge, continued to draw packed crowds on both the Thursday and Sunday evenings. Early in 1983, Jack Graham left the band and was not replaced, reducing the band to seven piece plus Fionna Duncan. Also in 1983, the Jazz Advocates made a trip to London where they played at a wonderful jazz pub, the Prince of Orange in Rotherhythe, and the famous 100

Oxford Street, a jazz club since the 1950s. May and June of that year saw another trip to Sacramento followed by a tour in California at the end of which, the trombone player Sam Smith, decided to stay on and the band came home without him. The replacement for Sam was Johnny McGuff, who fitted in immediately and added a formidable soloist to the band's line-up. The Caledonian Hotel, impressed with the success of the two jazz nights they hosted each week, then developed part of their premises into a special live music lounge. The Caley had originally been a railway hotel in the great days of rail travel, and the area they developed had once been the left luggage department of the Caledonian Station. They called the new lounge Platform 1 and it was up and running in time for the 1983 EIJF. Platform 1 became the venue for the Jazz Advocates sessions and was also added to the EIJF venues. The EIJF that year attracted BBC Radio and Brian Matthew, a well known DJ and broadcaster, presented his nightly show Round Midnight from the Caledonian Hotel. The Jazz Advocates took part in several of these radio shows and, as in previous EIJFs, the band played host to a number of distinguished guests including Jim Galloway, Acker Bilk and Count Basie's famous lead alto sax player, Earle Warren. Later that year, the band went to Holland to play at the Jazz Dagen in Eindhoven, a three day jazz festival where they again met and played with Earle Warren.

In March 1984, the band recorded yet another album, this one given the title 'All in Perfect Working Order'. As this was again targeted at the American market, it was given a Scottish flavour and included Johnny McGuff's remarkably agile playing of the Scottish march 'The Black Bear', complete with a chorus on bagpipes! August 1984 brought the usual packed EIJF programme for the band and then, shortly after this, the Scottish Jazz Advocates came to an end. Hamish McGregor had plans to put together a different kind of band and he left the Jazz Advocates in September 1984. There was a brief period when plans were discussed to keep the band together but, in November 1984, the Scottish Jazz Advocates were wound up. The demise of the Jazz Advocates brought the opportunity for Mike Hart to get the **Scottish Society**

Syncopators together again, which he did, including Andrew Lauder, Johnny McGuff, Tom Finlay and Mike himself from the Jazz Advocates and bringing in Jack Graham, Francis Cowan (bass) and Frank Birnie (drums).

Francis Cowan (bass, guitar, cello, lute, composer, arranger, teacher), who was born in Duns in 1940, was a remarkable musician who made his mark across a wide spectrum of Scottish music. Perhaps best known for his work as a jazz guitarist, he also performed in the classical and folk fields and was a well-known and respected instrumental teacher. In addition to his excellent work on guitar and bass, he also played cello and lute and had made a name for himself as a writer and arranger. During his brief stay on bass with the Syncs in the early 1980s, he contributed a number of excellent arrangements and recorded with the band on their 1985 album "Huntin', Shootin' and Jazz'n", a recording which includes a rarity in traditional jazz, a bowed bass solo. His many other involvements in Edinburgh music included a lengthy spell in a duo with the singer Melanie O'Reilly, as well as performing solo and leading a number of bands from trios up to eight-piece. A technically accomplished and extremely versatile musician, Francis was much respected for his unfailing musicality, enthusiasm and likeable personality. Tragically, Francis was to die in a road accident on 20th September 1996 at the age of only fifty six, leaving a huge gap in Scottish music generally, as well as in Edinburgh jazz. As another bass player, I never played a gig with Francis and did not know him well but knew enough to like him and hold him in great regard as a musician. I wish to acknowledge the excellent obituary contributed to the Scotsman by Kenny Mathieson, from which some of the details in this brief account have been taken[167].

Mike Hart soon found a Sunday lunchtime venue for the reconstituted Syncs in the Learmonth Hotel, just over the Dean Bridge, and this was soon established as another successful jazz gig. The hotel ran this session as a jazz brunch and one of the local newspapers was able to say

---

[167] Mathieson K, 'Francis Cowan', The Scotsman, September 1996

that it was a success from day one. The article reported that the music was right, the room was right and so were the encouragingly big crowd and the food and drink prices. The final stamp of approval had been provided by the indestructible Jackie MacFarlane who was there, impromptu and unpaid as ever! By the early days of 1985, Mike had expanded the band to include a second trumpeter, this being the excellent Dave Strutt. The Scottish Society Syncopators, with many changes in personnel along the way, were to continue as one of Edinburgh's top bands, playing at jazz festivals in the UK, North America and Europe, recording and broadcasting right through the 1990s and into the new century. Among those who later played with the reformed Syncs were Jake McMahon, Jack Duff and Martin Foster (reeds), Bruce Adams (trumpet) and Ken Macdonald, Gerry Forde and Ricky Steele (bass).

Both the Scottish Jazz Advocates and the Scottish Society Syncopators were graced by the playing of Johnny McGuff on trombone. **Johnny McGuff (trombone)**, who was born in Edinburgh on 13th February 1932, was one of the most remarkable of all Edinburgh jazzers. He came from a musical family and, at age twelve, he started lessons on trombone with a tutor called Bill Tabener. He made rapid progress and, after some early experience playing with the Arniston Brass Band from Gorebridge and the Newtongrange Brass Band, he was playing with local dance bands within a year of beginning lessons. One of his very first appearances in public was when he sat in with a dance band in which his father, Gordon McGuff, was playing drums. When he was just thirteen, he featured in a concert at Newbattle Abbey, for troops stationed in the area. After leaving school, Johnny completed an apprenticeship as a bricklayer before serving his National Service in the Royal Artillery, when he played with army bands and at any dance band gigs he was offered. After discharge from the army, he was soon in action with some of the leading Scottish dance bands of the time, including bands led by Edwin Holland, Tommy Sampson, Johnny Kildare, Pete Seaton and Cam Robbie. Later there was to be a spell at the Locarno Ballroom in Liverpool, regular broadcasts with the BBC, the teaching of music in schools in Dalkeith and Gorebridge and a stint with Ken McIntosh's band.

Johnny McGuff drew his inspiration from three sources: Jack Teagarden, Don Lusher and George Chisholm. The trad boom of the late 1950s and early 1960s put his technically accomplished and inventive playing very much in demand and he found himself playing with the Clyde Valley Stompers, during the period when they were led by clarinettist Pete Kerr. With this band, he made many TV appearances, including the famous Morecambe and Wise Show. Later, Johnny played with Terry Lightfoot's Jazz Band before returning to Edinburgh. Back on home ground, he was soon snapped up by Mike Hart to play with the Society Syncpators, with whom he travelled to the Dunkirk Jazz Festival in 1979. There, in addition to the band's success, Johnny won the award for best soloist in the competition. He then became one of the Scottish Jazz Advocates, replacing Sam Smith when he decided not to return from California, after the Sacramento Jazz Festival in 1983. Johnny stayed with the Jazz Advocates for the remainder of the band's existence and then, when Mike Hart reformed his Scottish Society Syncopators in November 1984, he became a member of that band.

Over the years, Johnny made many trips with these bands to play at jazz festivals in the UK, Europe and the USA. He was always a major draw at these events, his blistering attack, agile technique and inventiveness catching the ear of jazz fans wherever he played. His reputation led to him being invited to the USA to take part in a specially assembled international all-star band. He also won the best trombonist award in Radio Two's 1991 Big Band competition. It must have pleased him that he was presented with this award by one of his own heroes, the great Don Lusher. Johnny was always a terrific all-round musician, and he was as comfortable playing with a brass band, a theatre pit band, a ballroom orchestra and the Scottish country dance bands of Jim Mcleod and Bobby Colgan, as he was in a jazz setting. He was endlessly versatile and, as Ken Mathieson was to point out in his obituary on Johnny in 2005 '...*he was even able to combine the two styles* (ie jazz and Scottish country dance music) *in* his feature number, *"The Black Bear"*, *which went down equally well at jazz concerts and jazz gigs. No mean feat.'*[168] When top jazz musicians toured Scotland as soloists, Johnny was always first on their list when a band was being assembled to play with them and, in this context, he played with jazzers such as Acker Bilk, Alex Welsh, Kenny Ball, Humphrey Lyttelton, Yank Lawson, Wild Bill Davison and Jim Galloway. He was always one of the select group of local jazzers who were picked, and were good enough, to play in the genuine all-star bands that were assembled during the EIJFs.

It is impossible to write about Johnny McGuff without mentioning his sense of humour, as he was consistently one of the funniest raconteurs around the Edinburgh jazz scene, his stories told with great good humour and enthusiasm. Ken Mathieson gave a couple of examples and they are too good to leave out now. As Ken wrote in Johnny's obituary *'John's habit of taking an afternoon snooze on tour meant he sometimes missed band meals, so when the merits of French cuisine were being discussed in the tour bus, John said "I much preferred the meal I didn't get in France to the one I missed in Germany".* The other came about when Johnny was on tour in the USA and, as Ken reports, *"He once emerged blinking into the California sunshine and observed "Newtongrange has a great day for the Gala".'*

In the course of his long career, Johnny amassed a fund of wonderful tales of bands and gigs and his telling of these tales, in his own inimitable fashion, brightened many a weary journey. He claimed that, at the end of one gig when the crowd had been less than ecstatic about the band, one trusting member of the band had enthusiastically told the rest of them that they would have a return booking the following winter. This seeming unlikely, he was queried about the source of his information and, according to Johnny, reported that he had heard one of the punters say *'It'll be a cauld day before we have that band back again'!* Another tale, my favourite amongst the McGuff collection of anecdotes, concerned one of his innumerable appearances

---

[168] Mathieson K, 'John McGuff' obituary, The Scotsman, 14 July 2005

in the 'clubs', the Working Men's and Miner's Welfare institutes that once peppered the southern half of Scotland. Johnny was playing in a band, as part of an evening of entertainment, and the interval act was a young female singer, who was struggling to make herself heard or appreciated. Accompanied by a keyboard player, she was rapidly losing the attention of the crowd, from which arose a mounting hubbub of conversation. In the middle of her spot, the club social convener suddenly leapt up on stage and started banging a tin tray to get attention. In mid-song, the hapless singer's voice faltered and faded away. *"Now then ladies and gen'lemen,"* said the social convener firmly *"In this club we have a great tradition of showing the same respect for the bad acts as we do for the good yins, so let's have a bit of order if you please'.* Then, turning to the singer with an encouraging wave of his hand *'On you go hen'*'!

Johnny's career continued until December 2004, when his playing came to an end because of cancer. He died on 11th July 2005 and Mike Hart, with whom he had played so often, said *'He was the most outstanding musician in the band. He was the man who made the band sound the way it did. He was of huge importance. Johnny was an amazing comedian and kept us laughing all the time. He was one of those guys who didn't have a enemy in the world. He will be sorely missed.'* For myself, I never played with anyone whose playing and company gave me more pleasure and it was a great privilege to have known him. Johnny McGuff featured on a number of recordings made by the Scottish Jazz Advocates and the Scottish Society Syncopators, which remain to remind us of one of the best jazz musicians that Edinburgh ever produced.

Dave Strutt (trumpet, mellophone, vocals), who was to play with the Syncs throughout most of the 1980s and well into the 1990s, was born in 1942 at Colchester in Essex. This was a part of the country under heavy attack from German bombers at the time but, hard as Hitler tried, he failed to wipe out the young Strutt.

**Mike Hart's Scottish Society Syncopators
Tom Finlay, Jack Duff, Murray Smith, Dave Strutt,
Ricky Steele, Johnny McGuff, Mike Hart
(from the collection of Mike Hart, photographer
unknown)**

In fact, Dave not only survived but can still recall the street party that greeted the end of the war in 1945, describing it as potentially a great gig, if only the war had lasted another fifteen years! Dave was educated at Colchester Royal Grammar School where, with a group of like-minded friends, he tried to start a school jazz society, only to be thwarted by an obstructive headmaster (and how often have we heard similar stories throughout this book?) Dave had already joined the local town band with a view to getting his hands on an instrument and in this he was successful, being allocated a trombone. However, this project too came to a sad end because of an official abhorrence of jazz, when one day the bandmaster stood up and announced '*I hope none of you young lads is going to go off and play this jazz stuff*'. Recognising a less than sympathetic environment, Dave abandoned this attempt but was rather more encouraged by an enlightened examination board which set him an essay on Louis Armstrong, when he sat his 'O' level English!

Dave traces his interest in jazz to his older brother Ray, who thwarted his attempts to listen to Children's Hour on the radio, insisting instead on tuning in to the American Forces Network, which broadcast from Germany. Apparently, this station featured an announcer who introduced each record in a dead-pan voice and included in his selection some recordings of the great Sarah Vaughan. Dave claims that his brother was in love with Sarah Vaughan, which he says surprised him, as he himself was unable to distinguish between one singer and the next. He does however acknowledge that all this unwilling exposure to jazz oriented broadcasts may have helped him to develop an ear for sounds, something he considers the absolute essential for appreciating jazz.

Looking back now, Dave regrets that he never had the benefit of any proper training. He had bought himself a battered trumpet in Soho when on a day trip to London and, as he says wryly, being aware that there were ample opportunities to play for even the fairly incompetent in the 1950s, he simply relied on his ear and taught himself. By this time, Dave too had fallen in love, not with Sarah Vaughan but with the playing of Louis Armstrong, which he henceforth took as his model. In those days, the art colleges tended to be hotbeds of jazz enthusiasm, as we have already witnessed in Edinburgh, and Dave discovered that, at the Colchester Art School, there was a pianist called John Addyman and a clarinet player called Bernard Watson. He had the good fortune to become involved with these two, who were the first adults he had come across who were prepared to be encouraging and help him to acquire some playing experience. Dave soon widened his interest in jazz, next discovering the magic of Bix Beiderbecke and then, with his pal Dick Mayhew, spending a great deal of time searching out records by Jelly Roll Morton. They knew that Morton was important in jazz history but found that his recordings were very hard to track down. This will ring bells for many who sought jazz recordings in the 1940s and 50s, when nearly all the early recordings had been deleted from the catalogues. The days of endless re-issues and compilations were still years ahead and collectors still grubbed about in dusty junk shops, searching out the precious (and incredibly fragile) 78 rpm relics of the twenties and thirties.

Dave, for some reason no longer clear to him, did not become caught up in the burgeoning, Ken Colyer inspired, enthusiasm for the purist music of Bunk Johnson and George Lewis and his interest remained with the music of the 1920s. Reminiscing recently, he recalled with great pleasure the happy hours, crouched over a tiny gramophone in Dick Mayhew's front room, trying to distinguish the playing of Louis Armstrong from that of King Oliver, on one of the re-issue London label ten inch LPs.

Dave's next move was to Leeds University, at which he says he was a *'tragically incompetent student'*, but where he discovered one saving grace – there was plenty of jazz! He found himself playing with a student band called Casey's Hot Seven, with whom he played at the Moorside Working Men's Club to what he describes as *'...a capacity audience of pissed students'*. However, alleged academic incompetence and pissed students apart, University life was to bring him into contact with what he describes as *'...a lot of intense and varied jazz influences'*. Dave has been known to say in retrospect that going to University was the biggest mistake of his life but he also recognises that it had a deeply defining influence on him. Looking back now, he says that he *'...discovered the wider horizons of jazz - saw some really great players and wasted an awful lot of time (possibly) in dank cellars filled with fragrant vapours from the cigarettes of bleary eyed hipsters'* which, the great players excepted, sounds to me a bit like Easter Road on a bad day.

After he escaped from Leeds academia in 1969, Dave hitched a lift up to Scotland with his girlfriend, who had managed to get a job at Edinburgh University. At that point, his plan was to stay for an indeterminate but limited time. The 'indeterminate but limited time' turned out to be thirty five years, a period which included one marriage and two children. After that length of time and with two children born and raised in Scotland, it is hardly surprising that he considers himself to be an adopted Scot. Scotland in general and the Edinburgh jazz scene in particular was, in my view, extremely lucky to have him. Dave was an integral part of the Edinburgh jazz scene for most of my jazz career, he was and is a very fine trumpet player and an extremely likeable bloke. If he was on trumpet, it was likely to be a good gig and he was easy to get along with. Yet, in spite of all that, there was one occasion when he found himself excluded from a gig at which he would have loved to have played. The reason given for his omission was, of all ludicrous things, that Dave was not a Scot! The gig was a Sandy Brown memorial event, and Dave was told that it was absolutely essential to recruit a Scottish trumpet player and he was therefore, unsuitable. Dave was undoubtedly hurt by this exclusion and I wonder what Sandy Brown would have had to say? According to George Melly in 'Owning Up', Sandy was a *'convinced nationalist'*[169], by which I guess he means a Scot with a great regard and loyalty towards all things Scottish, perhaps even with a belief that Scotland should be independent in the political sense, probably even very nationalist when Scottish and English teams are tearing lumps off each other at Murrayfield or Hampden Park. I can certainly believe all of that of Sandy but so what? Sandy was a jazzer who played international music, loved the blues of the Afro-Americans beyond any other music, lived and played much of his music in the south and sought out and revered others for what they could play, not for where they came from. I really do not think Sandy would have cared a damn if the trumpet player at the memorial concert had come from Mars, as long as he could really play.

Dave found the Edinburgh of the 1970s full of opportunities to play traditional jazz and one of his first associations was with a band called the Doon By Jazz Band. This band included Jock Westwater on banjo, Gerard Dott on clarinet, George Howden on trombone and, apparently, me on bass, although I have absolutely no memory of the band. I do, however, remember the ramifications of Dave's difficulty with the local accents. He claims that his untutored English ears had great difficulty with my rather awkward name, as spoken by Jock Westwater, and that he heard it as Grimble Mire, which he continued to believe was

[169] 'Owning Up' by George Melly, (Copyright © George Melly, 1965) Reprinted by permission of A. M. Heath & Co Ltd

my name for some considerable time. I was quite puzzled to find myself addressed as Grimble, although in an entirely friendly way, and remember wondering what part of the world he came from. It had quite a vogue for a while and I even thought of adopting it as a nom de plume, if I ever actually managed to start writing about jazz. Even now it occasionally turns up, usually when Bill Salmond is around, when he not infrequently greets me with a dignified and welcoming 'Ah, Grimble'. In spite of finding myself renamed Grimble, I was much impressed by the playing of this newly arrived trumpeter but I was rather put out by his then current habit of holding his trumpet so that it pointed to the floor when he played. At that time, I liked my trumpet players to point their trumpets skywards, in the best Hollywood manner, like Danny Kaye in the Five Pennies film. Later on, he not only continued to play beautifully but also took to holding his trumpet in the approved way. I wonder now if I ever said anything but I hope not.

In 1980, during the EIJF and in the company of John Russell, Dave heard the wonderful guitar playing of Fapy Lafertin with gypsy band WASO. This had a profound influence on the two of them and they made an almost on-the-spot decision to attempt something along the same lines. Showing remarkable energy and speed-off the-mark for jazzers, it was no time at all before the band that was to be Swing 1980 was born, the history of which we have already explored. Of course, the EIJF had given an enormous boost to Edinburgh jazz and, in paying tribute to the sterling work of Mike Hart in this context, Dave picks out in particular the opportunities that the Festival brought, not only to hear but actually to play with some great players. Like me, he finds it almost incredible that we played with Benny Waters, a man who had played with King Oliver in the 1920s and whose career marched with that of jazz itself. Like many others, Dave considers that the EIJF was no ordinary festival, it was something unique and within it were some never to be repeated experiences.

After leaving Swing 1985 in that year, Dave joined Mike Hart's Scottish Society Syncopators, at first in a two trumpet team with Andrew Lauder and later in partnership with the outstanding trumpeter from Glasgow, Bruce Adams. His move from Swing 1985 to the bigger band was partly to build up his experience of playing in a traditional line-up, deciding that after five years he needed more freedom and less pressure than he was finding in the smaller band. His tongue in the cheek explanation now is that, inside the cultured small group man, there was a brash, extrovert Dixieland horn player struggling to get out! The other reason for his move was the chance that the Syncs offered to get to jazz festivals elsewhere and he went on to play with the band in Sacramento, Vancouver, Dresden and in the South of France. The Syncs also brought him the opportunity to record with the great Wild Bill Davison. This was on an LP that is now considered something of a collector's item, as it turned out to be just about Wild Bill's final recording session. This recording was to produce a particularly satisfying moment when, years later in France, someone played him a track from this album and he was able to say 'Oh yes! That's me!', to general stupefaction.

After his stint with the Syncs, Dave was one of the first Edinburgh based jazzers to make regular trips across the country to play with Glasgow based bands, in his case, George Penman's Jazzmen. The Penman band, then as always, was a sturdy band very much in the mould of the successful British trad bands but it brought Dave a chance that he particularly savoured – playing alongside George Kidd, one of the finest trombone players that Scotland ever produced. The Penman experience also introduced Dave to what he describes as the surreal world of West of Scotland bowling clubs, a sort of lost world of archaic social mores, replete with such carefully preserved customs as 'Gentlemen, you may now remove your jackets'! Other enjoyable west coast gigs were those with George Hewitt's New Orleans Joymakers, at their monthly gigs at the Harbour Arts Centre in Irvine, and the Glasgow City Centre pub gigs with the band of trombonist, Hugh Muldoon. He particularly enjoyed the totally relaxed and unrehearsed approach of these bands, something I would endorse, having also played many times with both of these bands.

When he finally departed the Penman band Dave, given his complete lack of any Bunk Johnson pedigree, was surprised to find himself offered the trumpet chair in Violet Milne's Spirits of Rhythm. I, too, was with the Spirits around this time and, while it could be said that there was a certain stylistic anomaly between the band's asserted style and Dave's Bixian trumpet playing, I thought the band sounded great. Like me, Dave thoroughly appreciated the drive and swing of Kenny Milne's work on the drums and, looking back now, he picks out the playing of Ian Boyter, hailing him rightly as *'...a man with an amazing innate sense of swing and a listening ear'*. With the Spirits, Dave made regular trips to Switzerland and a couple of expeditions to the Orkney Jazz Festival.

Dave's long Edinburgh sojourn was at last to come to an end when, in 2004, he departed to live in rural France. There, at the time of writing and in spite of a dearth of local jazzers, he still manages to play in what he describes as *'...some great little venues'*. These include the Jazz Cafe at Reveillon, run by British trumpeter Bob Tinker, the Cafe de Routes at Alencon, where the delightful and generous host Dominique Destombes plays bass, and even a jazz club in Caen which is held on the back of a lorry! An unexpected meeting, which also led to some gigs, was with a pianist whom Dave discovered playing outside a cafe at the national Fete de Musique. This turned out to be one Cal Finnegan, whom Dave had last met forty five years previously at university! Dave Strutt's move to France deprived Edinburgh of one of its best and most versatile trumpet players, but our loss was France's gain and it is good to know that he is still in regular action and keeping his chops in trim.

Bruce Adams (trumpet) was a professional jazz trumpeter who played with the Syncs for a while after Andrew Lauder dropped out. This preserved for a time the two trumpet format, with Bruce in partnership with Dave Strutt, and Dave has said what an inspiration it was to play alongside him. According to John Chilton's 'Who's Who of

British Jazz'[170], Bruce Adams was born in Birkenhead on 3rd July 1951 and came from a show biz family which had been involved in the music hall world, before setting up home in Glasgow a year or two after Bruce was born. Bruce's father was a comedian, guitarist and vocalist and his mother a dancer. He made an early start on trumpet and won the TV talent series Opportunity Knocks when he was fourteen years old. After leaving school, he toured in variety with his father and played at Expo '67 in Montreal. He also completed a tour in Aden with the great comedian, Tony Hancock, which must have been a memorable experience. Later work included spells on the liners QE2 and Canberra before he returned to his Glasgow base from where he undertook freelance work and worked with saxophonist Bill Fanning. By the early 1980s, Bruce had picked up a number of jazz awards and, by 1984, was featuring as a solo artiste in the EIJF programmes. He was included in the Syncs line-up for the EIJF in 1987, '88, '89 and '91. An international jazz name with a big reputation, Bruce Adams has toured and played extensively and appeared at many festivals across the world. Among the many notable names with whom he has played are Dick Hyman, Benny Carter, Bob Wilber, Bill Aldred, Alan Barnes, and Pascal Michaux, as well as frequently leading bands of his own.

As an extra attraction, the Society Syncopators sometimes featured the excellent singing of **Wendy Weatherby (vocals, cello, composer).** Wendy was and is something of an all-rounder in music, as capable of swinging along with a traditional jazz band as in exploring the haunting folksongs of Scotland or the glorious works of Robert Burns. With rather more of an academic background in music than the average traditional jazzer, she graduated from the Royal Scottish Academy of Music and Drama in 1983. Her wide musical interests have taken her all round the world to sing and play at festivals in the UK, the continent of Europe, the USA and the former Soviet Union. She has worked, both as a cellist and a singer, with some of

[170] Chilton J, 'Who's Who of British Jazz', 2004 edition, reproduced by permission of Continuum International Publishing Group

the most notable names in Scottish music including Hamish Moore, Billy Jackson, The Pearlfishers, Michael Marra and Phil Cunningham. Her theatre credits include 'The Ship' and 'The Big Picnic' (Bill Bryden), John Bett's adaptation of Robert Burns' 'The Jolly Beggars' for Wildcat, Catherine Wheels 'The Story of the Little Gentleman' and Wee Stories' 'Arthur' and 'Tam O' Shanter', Wendy composing the music for this latter production. She also composed the music for the film scores of 'A Thief in the Night', 'Tickets for the Zoo' and 'Saved', which appeared on Channel 4 and BBC-2. In 2001, Wendy landed a commission from Celtic Connections which led to the creation of 'Daybreak at the World's Edge', the poems of William Soutar set for four cellos and three male voices. A further major achievement was another larger scale work in 2004, based on Lewis Grassic Gibbons 'Sunset Song'. With 'Cloud Howe' and 'Grey Granite' in 2005, Wendy completed the famous Gibbons trilogy 'The Scots Quair', which was performed at the 2007 Celtic Connnections festival, in the Glasgow City Halls. In 2010, Wendy was nominated as Scots Traditional Singer of the Year and, although she did not win the title, she would have got my vote if I had had one.

In addition to her performing activities, Wendy is also active in the teaching field and has hosted many workshops in both cello and singing. She teaches cello at RSMAD, the School of Excellence in Plockton, Newcastle University and the Adult Learning Scots Music Group in Edinburgh. She also features regularly with Dr Fred Freeman's illustrated lectures on Robert Burns, when she has performed alongside Marc Duff (ex-Capercaillie), John Morran (Deaf Shepherd), and Sandy Brechin (Jimmy Shandrix Experience). Wendy continues to be in demand all over the world, as both cellist and singer, and has a host of recordings to her name, some solo and some with others. Her website[171] is packed with information about her career, recordings and all her other music and drama activities and is commended to all jazzers who remember her singing with the Society Syncopators and other Edinburgh jazz bands.

---

[171] http://wendyweatherby.co.uk

With all these multifarious calls on her time, it is surprising that she ever managed to find time to sing with jazz bands but, when she did, she brought a cheery, joyful personality, great musicality and no mean ability to swing.

The Sync's long-serving **drummer, Frank Birnie**, was a relatively late arrival on the Edinburgh traditional jazz scene. Frank was born in Edinburgh on 31st March 1936 and educated at Balgreen Primary and then Saughton (later to be called Carrickvale) Secondary School. After leaving school, he began an apprenticeship in marine engineering, at Robb's Shipyard in Leith, just a few years after Stan Greig had followed the same route. After completing his apprenticeship, he went into the merchant navy and his first trip abroad, which paid £46 a month, was to last for all of two years! He loved the life at sea and appreciated the opportunities it brought to see the world, visiting far flung places such as Japan, Singapore and Hong Kong, among many others. His interest in music had begun early when he played 'drums' on a kitchen chair, accompanying his Uncle Jock who played a five-row button accordion. He acquired his first real drum kit, which consisted of a snare drum and bass drum and cost £15, when he was fifteen. Frank had another musical uncle, Uncle Bertie, who was lead drummer in the Granton Gas Works Pipe Band, and it was he who taught Frank the rudiments of drumming. When he started to play in public, it was with his Uncle Jock and another accordion player called Alec McKenzie, playing Scottish Country dance music, performing at weddings and similar functions, and Frank remembers having to transport his drums by bus to these gigs.

Later, he was to expand his playing into the club scene, often backing cabaret acts in the company of Clive Greathead who played organ. Once, playing in Billy's Bar, a large establishment in Prestonpans, they were accompanying a singer who was in full cry when they were approached by what Frank describes as a 'wee wuman'. This lady turned out to be the treasurer who had come to hand over the band's wages, which she insisted on doing, including having Clive sign a receipt, while he continued to back the somewhat bemused singer! As it turned out, this eccentric behaviour was considered the normal procedure and it continued throughout their tenure at the venue. Around this time, Frank found other playing opportunities in dance work, including a couple of years at the Heart's Supporter's Club in Craigmillar.

Sometime in the 1970s, Frank ventured into the jazz scene and became a regular at the Yellow Carvel pub, where he listened to the Charlie McNair band and had the occasional sit in. It was not long before he decided that he fancied playing more of their kind of music. Eventually, sometime around 1977, he was offered a jazz gig. This was at the New Liston Arms in Kirkliston and it came about through the trombonist, Sam Smith. Sam was playing there in a band that included Andrew Lauder (tpt), Jack Graham (rds), Tom Finlay (pno) and Mike Hart (bjo) and, when he arrived, Frank realised that he knew none of them, except Sam himself. After several numbers, the little trombonist turned to him and said *'You're spoiling us!'* Thinking that he was making a mess of things, Frank began apologising when Sam interrupted saying *'No, no, I mean you are swinging'*. This led to Frank becoming a permanent part of the band and his jazz career had begun.

Things moved rapidly and by 1978 he had visited the Dunkirk Jazz Festival with Mike Hart's Society Syncopators, where they came second in the traditional jazz category of the band championship. In 1979 the band, including Frank, returned to Dunkirk and this was the year they were crowned European Champions in the same category and, later that same year, he went with the band to play at the Sacramento Jazz Jubilee in California. However, his involvement with the band was to come to an abrupt halt in 1980, when the Society Syncopators amalgamated with Old Bailey's Jazz Advocates, thus creating the Scottish Jazz Advocates. Nothing daunted, Frank kept playing with other bands and when, only a year or two later, the Jazz Advocates broke up, Frank was again included in Mike's re-formed band, now to be called the Scottish Society Syncopators. This time, his stay was to be a prolonged one and was to include several more visits to Sacramento, tours in France, Germany and Poland (they were there when the Chernobyl nuclear disaster occurred) and a number of recordings. It was on one of these trips that the band, and

Mike Hart in particular, began to invent pseudo-Germanic names, in the German style of combining nouns. A duck became known as a 'quackinpecker', a handkerchief a 'snotterviper', a friendly dog was a 'barkinschnuffler' and a savage one a 'barkinschnapper'. The game apparently became less popular with the banjo section when Dave Strutt decided that a banjo player was an 'arschenclanger'! A cherished memory from the trip to California came when Frank was introduced to the well-known American drummer, Nick Fatool. When Fatool realised who Frank was he exclaimed *'Shit man! You're in the Scottish band. They tell me you kick a mean set of skins!'* The records that Frank made with the Syncs included their excellent 'Huntin', Shootin' and Jazz'n' album and also the particularly memorable LP that included as guests, the ex-patriot Scot Jim Galloway (rds) and the great American trumpeter, Wild Bill Davison[172].

A big, strongly built man who was a powerful drummer, Frank later formed the East Coast Jazz Band which played an extremely successful ten-year residency at the Blue Lagoon, continuing well through the 1990s. This was a gig at which sitters-in were always made welcome by the amiable drummer and which was to become a popular Monday night drop-in spot for many of the Edinburgh jazz musicians. Frank Birnie played on well into the 2000s, finishing his playing career in mid-decade when playing with Jim Baikie's Jimjammers at the Sheraton Hotel.

Ken Macdonald (bass), was born in 1948 and attended George Heriot's School but was not involved in any jazz activity at school. There was marked musical interest in his family, with elder brother Donald already active as a bass player on the Edinburgh jazz scene, and Ken first tried his hand as a guitar player in a folk group. Ken's interest in jazz was ignited when he went along to the Loch Ewe Hotel in Royal Terrace, where he heard the Society Syncopators. This was the Syncs in their original form, with the Telford/Paxton/Craig front line and Ken's brother Donald on bass, with Mike Hart and Iain Forde completing the rhythm section. A bit later, when he was attending

---

[172] See discography appendix

Aberdeen School of Architecture, Ken followed in Donald's footsteps and set about learning to play double bass. At first he played an old bass of Donald's on which he had fitted a new plywood front, already showing an aptitude for the instrument repair work by which he would eventually make his living. However, when Ken returned to Edinburgh in 1975, he found that Donald's bass was available. Donald had, for the time being at least, abandoned bass in favour of playing sax, and Ken switched to using Donald's instrument. Donald then persuaded Ken to play a couple of numbers with the Syncs, who were playing at a party in Iain Forde's house, and there he was heard by Jim Petrie. Jim was looking for a bass player for the Climax band at the time and invited Ken along to play with the band.

Ken's first Climax gig was in 1975 in the Yellow Carvel and he was clearly a success. He was promptly taken on permanently and was to remain with the band for three years. In 1978 he joined Mike Hart's Society Syncopators and recorded with them on their album 'Jazz Tattoo', recorded on 9th March 1980. He was also with the band when they made their triumphant visits to the Dunkirk Jazz Festival, coming second in the traditional jazz section in 1978 and taking first place in 1979. Ken was to stay with the Syncs until 1983, when the band merged with the Old Bailey band to become the Scottish Jazz Advocates. Shortly after this, Ken left Edinburgh to undertake a violin making course at the Violin Making School in Newark, in Nottinghamshire. After completing the course, he made his living for a year or so in musical instrument work but then joined a local architectural firm part time, dividing his time between the two very different occupations. Ken was to remain in the south, playing gigs around the Midlands with many professional musicians, until his return to Edinburgh in 1989. Back home, he at first combined free lance architecture with instrument repair work but later, was able to concentrate fully on the latter, mostly specialising in the double bass.

After his return to Edinburgh, Ken was also soon in demand as a bass player, playing many gigs with a wide variety of bands over the years. He played about six years with Jim Petrie's Diplomats of Jazz, when they were resident in Leslie's Bar, a beautifully preserved Victorian bar in Causewayside. He was also very active backing visiting musicians at jazz festival time and in small group work, often with guitarist Dougie Campbell, and Tom or Jack Finlay. A spell of several years in the 1990s with a band led by Alan Quinn at the Templehall Hotel in Portobello, was followed by playing with a quintet, led by trumpeter Brian Robertson, in the Elwyn Hotel in Portobello Road, a residency that continued for about ten years, before ending in 2009. This in turn paved the way for Ken to remain with Brian Robertson when he formed his seven piece band, the Forth River Ragtimers in 2000, a band with which he was still playing in 2011. Ken would also make a brief return to the Climax band when they got together for a re-union concert, alongside the similarly re-formed Old Bailey band, during the 2010 EIJBF. Ken's son Owen is now continuing the family tradition of producing high quality bass players. Owen, like Ken himself, is a creative and flexible bass player, well able to play in traditional jazz bands, although his preference is naturally for more contemporary jazz, and he is much involved in work with trios and quartets, often backing singers.

The bass player who succeeded Ken Macdonald with the Syncs was **Ricky Steele (bass)**, who was born in Edinburgh on 8th January 1960 and attended Perth High School, before qualifying as an accountant. While still at primary school, Ricky's attempts to teach himself to play his older sister's trumpet came to an abrupt halt when he was caught and taken up to the 'big school', to which the trumpet belonged. Expecting to be in trouble, he was instead asked to play something for the trumpet tutor who, clearly quite impressed, provided him with some early lessons. After moving to secondary school in Perth, he continued with his trumpet tuition and played for the school band, before graduating to the county orchestra. This was followed by some gigs with the Perth Theatre pit orchestra, before moving on to play cornet with the Perth Silver Band. Clearly a promising and enterprising musician, he also taught himself to play guitar, which opened up the opportunity for him to play in a rock band while still at school. In addition, he played both guitar and trumpet in a dance band and then, when he was in his late teens and early twenties, he switched to playing bass guitar with both the rock band and the dance band.

Going along to listen to a local jazz band brought Ricky his first chance to hear a double bass up close. It did not take him long to decide that this was the instrument for him and, hastily swapping a Gibson 175 guitar for a double bass, he proceeded to teach himself to play it. He was soon a member of the local jazz band, staying with them for a year or two, before becoming part of a new band which started a regular Sunday gig in Perth. This was clearly a band of some quality, as their regular trombonist was the excellent George Kidd and another two famous jazzers from Glasgow, Carol Kidd and Fionna Duncan, appeared as guest vocalists. Carol Kidd was obviously impressed by Ricky's playing and, after the death of her regular bass player Alec Moore, she booked Ricky to play in her own three piece backing group. Ricky, whose jazz heroes have included bass players Scott la Faro and Ray Brown, then came down to Edinburgh to play a gig with a Scottish jazz legend, Edinburgh's Alex Shaw. This was to be the start of his long involvement with the Edinburgh jazz scene and the beginning of a twenty five year run at the EIJF. In 1986, he moved to live in Edinburgh and, after depping with many of the local bands, he became a member of Mike Hart's Society Syncopators, with whom he remained until the early 2000s. Ricky recorded with the Syncs and also made a number of recordings with the Tom Finlay Trio, including three CDs made in Cuba which included a number of Cuban musicians. An extremely able and versatile bass player, Ricky Steele worked with too many top jazzers to list in total but noting just Al Cohn, Warren Vache, Milt Hinton, Bob Barnard, Doc Cheatham, Roy Williams and Red Rodney as examples, gives some idea of the quality of jazz with which he was involved.

Another jazz musician who, like Ricky Steele, arrived from Perth and was to be a notable addition to the Edinburgh jazz resources, was **Campbell Normand (piano)**. Campbell was born in Perth in 1962 and educated at Perth High School. He had formal piano lessons up to grade five from the age of seven and lessons in playing the organ from age twelve. A talented musician, Campbell also played tenor horn in the Perth Silver Band and, briefly, the French horn in the Tayside Schools Orchestra. By the age of fourteen, he had made a start on his keyboard career and was playing organ in club bands around Perth. His interest in jazz was triggered by visits to Sunday jazz sessions at the Murrayshall House Hotel, near Perth, where he was eventually given the chance to sit in with the resident jazz band and, in no time at all, he was hooked on the music, citing his favourite jazz pianists as Oscar Peterson and Monty Alexander.

In 1980, Campbell moved to Edinburgh where he attended Edinburgh University before graduating as a lawyer, specialising in civil litigation. Not surprisingly, he was attracted to the playing of Alec Shaw, attending many of the great Edinburgh pianist's trio sessions at Platform One, the entertainment lounge in the Caledonian Hotel. Campbell's first experience of playing in the EIJF came in 1988, when he made up a fine rhythm section with Ricky Steele (bs) and Kenny Mathieson (drms)[173], backing the well known trumpeter Bob Wallis and Glasgow's Forrie Cairns on clarinet. It was also around this time that he joined a band of which we will hear more very shortly, Hamish McGregor's Fat Sam's Band, staying for about three years and with which band he has continued to dep ever since. After his spell with Fat Sam's Band, most of Campbell's playing has been with small bands and trios, as well as working with various vocalists. He has, of course, remained busy, as befits a player of his quality and versatility, playing several times a month, another of the group of able Edinburgh musicians who are able to play across a wide spectrum of jazz styles.

1982 saw a winter jazz event which was billed as 'Mardi Gras – Grand Carnival Masquerade - Jazz Band Ball'. This seems to have been a one-off venture and it took place on Tuesday 23 February 1982 in the Astoria Ballroom in Abbeymount.   The programme stated that the intention was to '...brighten up the dull month of February and get

---

[173] This is Kenny Mathieson, the well known drummer and band leader from the west of Scotland and not the journalist of the same name.

people back to life after recovering from the New Year period'. The event was to feature six bands playing continuously for five and a half hours in two ballrooms, plus guest stars and musicians. There was to be something for everyone from *'...hot dance music to pure Dixieland'* to *'Ory's Creole Eating House'* for meals and snacks and patrons were invited to wear Carnival costume or fancy dress and masks. The guest bands were the eleven piece Savannah Syncopators from the north-east of England, the Severnside Jazz Band who were normally resident at the Shrewsbury Jazz Club and the Bourbon Jazzmen from the west of Scotland, led by Glasgow based trumpeter, Dave Mathews. The local bands on the bill were the Festival City Jazz Band, Jim Petrie's Jazz band and the West End Jazz Band. Solo attractions were Fionna Duncan and Edinburgh's own Mr Five by Five, the inimitable Jackie MacFarlane, who were to sing with several of the bands.

Drummer Frank Birnie, then leading the East Coast Jazz Band, also made a guest appearance and both Frank and bass player Dick Walink were thanked for lending instruments. As well as giving details about the Mardi Gras, the programme gives an interesting snapshot of Edinburgh jazz in the winter of 1982, carrying advertisements for some of the venues then supporting jazz, including the Grange Hotel, the Ailsa Craig Hotel (both the West End Jazz Band), the Black Bull (the Climax Jazz Band), the Caledonian Hotel (the Scottish Jazz Advocates), the Hopetoun Bar (the Louisiana Ragtime Band), the Barnton Hotel (the Festival City Jazz Band), the Bonnington Bridge Bar (Frank Birnie's Jazz Band), the Glenelg Hotel (Jim Petrie's Jazz Band), the Garrick Bar featuring both the Charlie McNair Jazz Band and Swing '81 (sic), who according to this publication, appeared to have forgotten to update their name. There was also a full page advert for the Goblet in Rose Street, which styled its sessions featuring the Charlie McNair Jazz Band, the Goblet Jazz Club. This latter advert included a wonderful picture of a debonair Charlie McNair in a DJ, complete with buttonhole carnation, cigar and trumpet, and looking like one of those pictures of jazzers like Bix Beiderbecke and Frankie Trumbauer in the early 1920s. There was also a photograph of an extremely relaxed looking Mike Hart clutching pint and grinning like a Cheshire cat, the caption of which said *'Happiness is a Jazz Festival Director on the last night!'*

When Hamish McGregor left the Scottish Jazz Advocates in October 1984, he was soon into action forming his new band. What he had planned, was a band that would play in the 'jump-jive' tradition of Louis Jordan. He recruited Gus Ferguson on trumpet, Graeme Robertson on trombone, Bill Simpson on tenor and soprano saxes, Tom Finlay on piano, Tony Howard on guitar, Bobby Miller on bass guitar, Kenny Mathieson on drums and Nick Robertson (son of Graeme) on vocals. Hamish set himself to think up a name for the new band and came up with the moniker **Fat Sam's Band**. The name came from a song title, 'Fat Sam from Birmingham', which had been recorded by Louis Jordan and was, in fact, the only song Jordan ever recorded with a big band. After rehearsing, the band played its first gig on St Valentine's Day, the 14th of February 1985. The venue, formerly known as the Capercaillie, was to re-open on that date as The Elephant and Castle.

Fat Sam's Band was to go on to be extremely successful, playing all over the world from its Edinburgh base and, in addition to all the foreign gigs, was to be just as busy in Edinburgh. About a year and a half after the band was formed, Hamish negotiated a residency with Edinburgh businessman John Edmonds, which was to be in a new venue just opening. This was an American styled restaurant located in the old Edinburgh Meat Market building, on the corner of Fountainbridge and Semple Street, and the venue adopted both the band's name and logo. Fat Sam's Downtown Diner became a fashionable and very popular eatery, famous not only for its food and music, but also for Percy the Piranha, a large and ferocious looking fish, which swam about in a tank just inside the door. The band celebrated the 9th anniversary of its launch in 1995 in Fat Sam' eatery' on 16th February 1994, and the programme included a re-union of Old Bailey's Jazz Advocates and another Edinburgh band we will meet shortly, the Jazz Masters. The restaurant, which at its peak was especially popular as a venue for youngster's birthday celebrations, eventually closed in 2000. In 1990, the band appeared on the television programme Opportunity Knocks, hosted by the comedian, Les Dawson. They sounded and looked very good on the programme (I still have a video recording of their spot) and were placed third out of the seven competing acts. There is little doubt that, on talent alone, they should have been placed higher than this, perhaps even first, but jazz was not riding high in general popularity at that time.

Fat Sam's Band
(by permission of Hamish McGregor)

Over the years, the membership of the nine-piece Fat Sam's Band inevitably changed from time to time and, at one time or another, the following were members of the band:

Trumpet:	Gus Ferguson, Tom McNiven, Bill Hunter
Trombone:	Graeme Robertson, Jimmy Mann
Clarinet/Alto sax:	Hamish McGregor
Ten sax:	Bill Simpson, Tom Chalmers, Jack Duff, Steve Meeker, John Burgess, Iestyn Evans, Gordon McNeill
Baritone sax:	Martin Foster, Jack Duff
Keyboard:	Tom Finlay, Campbell Normand
Guitar:	Tony Howard, Phil Adams
Bass:	Donald McDonald, Lindsay Cooper, Roy Percy
Drums:	Kenny Mathieson
Vocals:	Nick Robertson, Hamish McGregor

The list of festivals alone at which they played, never mind all the other gigs, gives an idea of their popularity and their ability to attract bookings from all over the world. On the band website[174] in 2010, the list of festivals at which the band had played included fourteen in the UK, two in Ireland, nineteen in Europe, one in the Middle East, one in Canada and four in the USA. Bearing in mind that quite a few of these were visited many times, some indeed on an annual basis, this is some list. In addition, by the end of 2011, they had made six recordings, issued on CD as 'Fat Sam's Band' and packaged as volumes I to VI, and it is likely that there will be many more to come. On the website, the versatility of the band is emphasised, with three speciality programmes on offer for different occasions:

- *'A Tribute to Louis Jordan'*, the King of Jump Jive
- *'A Night at the Cotton Club'*, featuring the music of early Ellington and Calloway – 1920's and 30's
- *'An Evening of Jump-Jive – Boogie – Swing – Jazz – Blues – R and B'*, from Glenn Miller and Duke Ellington to Fats Domino and the 'Blues Brothers'

The website declares that *'Versatility and variety is the band's bye-line and is such that it offers a wide variety of*

---

[174] www.fatsamsband.com

musical sounds and styles in its performance. Allied to a strong presentation, the band is both a highly polished jazz-based Showband and a serious interpreter of mainstream jazz'. Fat Sam's Band was always a highly professional outfit, always well rehearsed and exciting and without doubt, the most commercially successful of the Edinburgh bands within the traditional jazz style. Hamish McGregor was, right from the start, a talented, natural showman with a real flair for presentation and he was the key factor in the band's success. Fat Sam's Band celebrated its Silver Jubilee on February 14th 2010 with a show in the Queen's Hall, as high-octane and dynamic as ever and, at twenty five years old, showed no signs of ever stopping.

Chapter XV

Bands Old and New and Returning Veterans

The early 1980s had already seen the continuation of several of the established bands and the formation of a number of new ones. The **Climax Jazz Band** was still going as strongly as ever and had found a good new residency. The Queen's Hall had opened in about 1979, as a major new concert venue, and Jim Young's firm had fitted out their kitchen. Jim had casually talked about the band to someone at the Hall when the work was going on and the happy result of this was that the Climax band landed a residency, playing every Friday evening, not in the main hall, but in the bar. The residency lasted about a year but another happy outcome of the gig was that they were able to celebrate the band's twenty-fifth anniversary in 1981, by staging a Silver Jubilee concert in the Queen's Hall. Another band in the purist traditional, the **Spirits of Rhythm**, had been formed in the dying days of 1979, as we have already heard. As the new decade began, they had quickly established themselves as a major new attraction and were to go on to become another of Edinburgh's long serving bands.

The **Charlie McNair Jazz Band** had stormed into the 1980s with Charlie in his usual ebullient form. Early in the decade, Charlie had residencies at the Goblet Lounge in Rose Street and the prestigious Granary Bar, part of the Dragonara Hotel, beside the Dean Bridge. The band by this time had, in addition to Charlie himself, Bill Munro (tbn), Gerard Dott (clt), Harald Vox (bjo), Johnny Fitzsimmons (bs gtr) and Kenny Milne (drms). At other times, it was Dizzy Jackson, Johnny Phillips or Peter Gordon–Smith on bass. At some point, Gerard Dott dropped out of the Goblet gig and George Duncan came in on clarinet and, by late 1982, George was playing all of Charlie's gigs. Gerard Dott moved on to play with a band at the Haymarket Station Bar. At first this band was led by Donald MacDonald, now playing a variety of saxes, with Bob Craig (tbn) and a rhythm section of Graham Scott (piano) together with two original RHS Gangsters, Dizzy Jackson (bss) and Bill Strachan (drums). Gerard joined the band after sitting in one evening and recalls that Bob was amazed that he wanted to join on clarinet as Gerard had been doing a lot of piano playing at this time, mostly depping in the Louisiana Ragtime band, when Graham Scott was unavailable. Over time, Bob gradually became the band leader and then, in the late 1980s, Al Fairweather returned to Edinburgh and joined the band, a move that was later to lead to a residency at the Glenelg Hotel in Leamington Terrace, off Gilmore Place.

Meanwhile, Charlie McNair also moved residencies and had taken on what was to become his main gig from 1983 to 1994, Preservation Hall in Victoria Street. Preservation Hall, a venue clearly named with jazz in mind, provided several other bands with a residency as well, including George Roy and his Jazzmen and the East Coast Jazz Band. In his various residencies, perhaps especially at Preservation Hall, Charlie's usual ability to charm his audience ensured him a packed house on most nights and the devoted following of a large group of regulars, again largely composed of students. Other 1980s residencies for the McNair band were in Harry's Bar, near the West End, Bentley's in Rose Street (which he played using only a quartet) and Pierre Victoire in Dock Place, Leith.

Gerard Dott tells the story of the time when Charlie had a new banjo player who, although he would become a good player, at the time was lacking in both experience and confidence. Because of this, he had developed the alarming habit of sometimes panicking if he was unexpectedly thrown a banjo solo and simply stopping dead in his tracks, leaving the rest of the band to thunder on. Never one to miss an opportunity for a good laugh, Charlie hatched a plot with the rest of band. They picked a fairly complicated tune, with which they knew the banjo player was already struggling and on which, if he was signalled to take a solo, they knew he would go into sudden stop mode. At the pre-arranged moment, Charlie suddenly and dramatically signalled for the banjo solo and as expected, the banjo player stopped dead. At the same moment, the entire band also stopped dead. They then solemnly counted the bars of a completely silent banjo chorus before coming in a right place, as if nothing had happened, which indeed had been the case! Charlie McNair, already the great survivor across four decades of Edinburgh jazz, was in fine fettle as the 1980s wore on.

The McNair band trombonist of the 1980s was **Bill Munro (trombone)**, who was born in Ayrshire on 4th February 1936 and attended Ayr Academy. His family was musical and Bill has described his mother as playing piano *'like an angel'* and his father as a having a fine baritone voice. Early piano playing lessons came to nothing because of *'lack of both interest and manual dexterity'*, Bill much preferring rugby and cricket. Sometime around 1951, he remembers being knocked out by some music he heard on a radio station called A.F.N. This stood for American Forces Network and the music broadcast was by the likes of the bands of Paul Whiteman, Benny Goodman, Glenn Miller, Artie Shaw and Tommy Dorsey. Shortly after this, a friend let him hear some scratchy old 78 rpm recordings of the Louis Armstrong Hot Five and Seven and King Oliver's Creole Jazz Band. Brought up on classical music, Bill had no idea that such exciting music existed and from that point on, he was hooked on jazz. Around the same time, he heard the Humphrey Lyttelton band with Wally Fawkes on clarinet and Johnny Parker on piano and thought they were wonderful.

His introduction to live jazz came around 1954 when the Clyde Valley Stompers played a gig at Ayr Pavilion. The Stompers were extremely popular in the west of Scotland at that time and Bill was impressed by their trumpeter, Charlie Gall, and the leader and trombonist, Ian Menzies. The Stompers had a singer with them, a *'real belter of a red hot mama'* according to Bill, and she was called Mary

MacGowan. He also remembers that, good though they were, the Stompers were sometimes referred to disparagingly as 'white dixielanders' by the more purist inclined jazz followers. This I find an interesting comment from such an informed source, as it has always been my impression that, while very strong in Edinburgh, the purist movement never seemed to have had as much influence in Glasgow and the west of Scotland. Bill's next exposure to live jazz came when the Chris Barber band played Ayr Town Hall when as Bill says, *'the joint nearly erupted'*. The Barber band was then the top British traditional jazz band and the crowd would not let them leave the stage until they had played umpteen encores. They certainly had a major impact on Bill Munro who, from then on, set his heart on learning to play jazz trombone.

In 1956, Bill moved to Edinburgh where he worked as an apprentice engineer with McTaggart Scott and Company and pursued his professional studies at the Bristo Tech and Heriot Watt Colleges. An opportunity came up to listen in to a rehearsal of the works silver band, at which Bill discovered that they had a spare trombone. He was quick to express an interest and was duly invited to become what they called a 'learner'. Things went quite well for a while and then he was promoted to play in the real band. The band was under the direction of a Yorkshire army band master who took exception to Bill's habit of tapping his foot while playing. Bill received a severe Yorkshire-type bollocking from this worthy along the lines of *'I'm the fooking conductor here tha' knows. Tha' sits to attention in my fooking band'*. This led to a sad parting of the ways, although ameliorated by Bill sneakily managing to hang on to the trombone. Valiant efforts to progress on the instrument led to skirmishes with a less than thrilled land lady, who objected to dying cow noises from the bedroom, forcing Bill to drive his vintage Riley to the Pentland Hills on wet Sundays, where he serenaded the bemused sheep with the trombone slide sticking out of the car window.

By 1957, Bill had begun to find his way into the Edinburgh jazz scene. At India Buildings on Sunday evenings he heard Archie Sinclair and Johnny Winters while, at another regular Sunday gig at the West End Cafe, he came across Charlie McNair, Jim Young and Mike Hart. He also made his way to the jazz club then running in Jim Young's basement in St Peters Place, where the great George Lewis and Jim Robertson put in an appearance, and to the Stud Club during its sojourn in the Pleasance, where he met Jim Petrie, amongst others. Another jazz haven was at the Royal Mile Cafe where trumpeter Eric Rinaldi, son of the cafe owner, had a regular Saturday night gig. Clearly making his way successfully into the local jazz scene, disaster then struck the budding jazz trombonist. An untimely audit was conducted within the ranks of the silver band which revealed the absence of the trombone which Bill had neglected to return and he had no option but to hand it over. Fruitless attempts to purchase a second hand horn led eventually to the purchase of a new trombone, courtesy of the generosity and support of Pete Seaton, of which we have already heard. Disaster circumnavigated, Bill was back in action.

Sometime around 1959, he was approached by a young trumpeter, Fred Terry, who informed him that a pal was trying to put a band together and was short of a trombone player. The pal turned out to be the clarinet player Jack St Clair, and Bill went along for an audition at the Pooles Synod Hall. The audition clearly worked out well and the band began regular practices before Jack announced their first public engagement. This was the interval spot at the West End Cafe, where they supported the resident band. This did not work out quite as intended. Although trombone player Bob Craig congratulated them on their playing of Chimes Blues, which he said was the best he had heard from an amateur band, the acclaim they had received from the punters offended the resident band to the extent that they were not permitted to play the second interval! Nothing daunted, the Jack St Clair band soon had a number of gigs in the back room of the Crown Bar of fond memory but again, not without unforeseen problems. One gig there in 1959 culminated in woeful humiliation, with the band having to organise a whip round to raise 5/- (25 pence in today's money) towards the hall rental. This was all of thirty bob (£1.50) and, as they had charged 1/- (5 pence) entrance money, it would seem that they had attracted only twenty five punters. Bill had recently married and his wife, Chris, was less than impressed by this financial embarrassment, especially as she had had to shell out to get in, commenting *'Huh, I thought you guys were supposed to be a big draw'*.

Bill reports that the band was improving by this time and sometimes even managed to play almost in tune, this technical breakthrough no doubt assisting them in securing a weekly gig at the Place Jazz Club in Victoria Street. By now it was the early 1960s and I had joined Bill in the Jack St Clair Band. Around this time, there was one away booking that both Bill and I both recall with a certain affection, if not with great clarity. This was at the Inchnacardoch Hotel on the banks of Loch Ness. The band had been booked to play at the local village hall on the Friday evening and then, for the entertainment of owner's guests, at the hotel itself on the Saturday night. We had a horrendous journey up from Edinburgh in foul weather and arrived very late for the Friday gig, something that seemed to bother the Highland punters not one whit. They merely waited patiently until we had arrived, made a commensurate adjustment in the finishing time and on we went. Saturday was spent sleeping and drinking in about equal proportions and then we played all evening and all night, until about six in the morning. We did not play continuously, of course, and there were hazy interludes during which a barman, who was a confusing mixture of black Barbadian and Highland teuchter, sang incomprehensible Gaelic songs with the local Ghillie. An accordion player also appeared at some point and in an excess of enthusiasm, I tried to play bass along with him. I think I got sworn at for my efforts although, as this was in Gaelic, it is just possible, although unlikely, that it was complimentary. At six in the morning it was broad daylight and at least half the band, reeling from lack of sleep and Highland hospitality, took advantage of our host's generosity to go splashing about on Loch Ness in the hotel rowing boat, to our extreme peril. The other half, I believe, went out on the ponies from the hotel's pony trekking stable but as none of them would ever speak about this experience, I have no idea what happened. Everything else about the weekend is a blank.

Bill stayed with the Jack St Clair band for a while and then stayed on when it became, sans Jack, the New Savoy Jazz Band. However, by 1964, pressures of family and work responsibilities led to him stopping playing and he sold his trombone, not resuming playing, with a new trombone, until 1980. His services were soon snapped up and he was to spend most of the 1980s with the Charlie McNair band, during one of its best periods as already described above, before finally retiring from music in 1990 and later moving back to live in Girvan in Ayrshire. Bill lists as his favourites and influences many of the great Americans including Armstrong, Ory, Ellington, Oliver, Bechet and Morton and amongst, the UK jazzers, Lyttelton, Sandy Brown and Chris Barber. His own playing was much in the Barber style, itself founded on Ory, and he was a particularly fine ensemble player. I played quite a bit with Bill in the early 1960s and what stays in the memory is his enthusiastic attack, which never failed to drive the band along in good style. He had a nice mellow tone and a sure musical ear, both of which were a sad loss to the Edinburgh jazz scene during the years when he was inactive.

Although there must be a large number of punter-made private recordings featuring Bill, especially during his 1980s time with the McNair band, there seems to be a lack of any professional recordings to remind us of his playing. Bill himself remembers the recording of a session with Jim Petrie's band in the Crown Bar in about 1960 but I have not been able to trace this. There was also a BBC recording made at the Queen's Hall in about 1983 with the Charlie McNair band. This included the tunes *Buddy's Habit, Weary Blues, Apex Blues, If You's a Viper*, and *Yes, Yes in Your Eyes*, but it seems likely that this was a broadcast recording and not made for general release. Bill has a taped copy and, although he says that he did not think much of it at the time, on hearing it more recently, he felt that the band had generated a lot of atmosphere. He once played this recording for his daughter Claire, who expressed herself as most impressed, saying *'Bloody magic Dad, I had no idea you guys were as good as that'*. Bill suspects that she was after a loan at the time.

Bill Salmond's Louisiana Ragtime Band had long ago demonstrated their ability to keep a residency going in the long term, keeping the Hopetoun Lounge in Morrison Street busy from June 1976 until April 1983. The band, which by now had the major attraction of Dave Paxton in the clarinet chair, then moved on to the Navaar House Hotel, on the south side of town, in June 1983. This was a gig that was to become something of an institution and it was to continue until February 1999. In fact, so successful was the Navaar gig, that it became another of these residencies where loyal and regular followers would arrive long before the band, determined to ensure they got a seat. It actually went a bit further than that, as many of them were anxious to secure, not just a seat, but their <u>usual</u> seat, and would look a bit miffed if it was already taken. There was also a sensibly supportive landlord who not only supplied a decent piano, but made sure that it was kept in tune. The bar was invariably packed each Tuesday evening, with many spilling out into the hallway and listening through the doorway behind the piano. Bill had many contacts throughout the world of New Orleans jazz and he was often able to invite visiting players to join the band at their Tuesday evening sessions. In the early 1980s, Kenny Milne was Bill's trumpeter and when Kenny left, Bill replaced him with a new comer, Brian Robertson.

Brian Robertson (trumpet), who was born in Edinburgh on 31st December 1955 and educated at Portobello High School, had been a regular follower at the Hailes House Hotel sessions, where the Nova Scotia Jazz Band of the late 1970s played. These sessions stimulated Brian into taking up the trumpet and he took lessons for a couple of years from trombonist and brass teacher, Graeme Robertson. He soon got fed up playing scales and arpeggios and set out to learn the rest of what he needed on his own, keen to start playing jazz as soon as possible. A common story this – conscientious music teachers must shudder when their pupils start to show an interest in jazz. Brian says that Graeme Robertson was a very able teacher but had soon realised that Brian was *'not very good at dots'* and just wanted to play jazz! Brain's original inspiration had been Gus Ferguson, then of the Nova Scotia band, and Brian's first sortie in public, in a highly nervous condition, was a sit in with that band at the Hailes House Hotel. Shortly after this, he teamed up with trombonist Andy Mulhern and formed the **Darktown Jazz Band**, whose first gig was at the Parkside Bowling Club in Edinburgh. After this, they soon found themselves making headway in the Edinburgh jazz scene but the Darktown Jazz Band came to an end when Brian joined Bill Salmond's Louisiana Ragtime Band in early 1986.

In spite of his early liking for the Dixieland style of the Nova Scotia Jazz Band, Brian soon transferred his allegiance to the purist form of jazz, forming a lasting admiration for the music of the Ken Colyer band. In particular, he cites as his ideal the Colyer rhythm section when it consisted of John Bastable (banjo), Ray Foxley (piano), Ron Ward (bass) and Colin Bowden (drums), asking *'How could a front line fail with a rhythm section like that?'*. He also admires the trumpet playing of Bix Beiderbecke and the American west coast revivalist, Lu Waters. In addition, he cites Louis Armstrong, Tommy Ladnier, Red Allen and Muggsy Spannier as favourites but says that Ken Colyer was the main influence on his own style. Speaking with Brian Robertson in 2010, he said what a privilege it had been to have played with local musicians, the 'local greats' he called them, such as Dave Paxton, Al Fairweather, Johnny McGuff, Jimmy Shortreed, Bob Craig, Andrew Lauder, George Gilmour and Kenny Milne. He also expressed his fears for the future of the music, pointing out that these great players, many of them already gone, were not being replaced, raising the possibility that Edinburgh traditional jazz, so strong for more than half a century, would just fizzle out. However, Brian himself was to do what he could to bolster the local jazz scene, going on later to form and run a band of his own and to remain a force on the local scene for decades to come.

Brian, in my view, probably learned quite a bit in his early days from the fiery, New Orleans styled trumpeter, Phil Mason. Phil, a professional jazz musician with Max Collie's Rhythm Aces, had taken up residence on the Isle of

Bute and later formed a touring band of his own. In addition to touring from his Isle of Bute base, Phil quite frequently made the trip over to Edinburgh, where he was a regular visitor at Bill Salmond's Navaar House gig. A colleague of Phil's, the trombonist Martin Bennett, also moved up to Scotland for a while in the 1980s, living on his hundred year old sailing ship, berthed at Irvine. Martin became a member of Bill's band and his authoritative playing and ability to direct a front line were also useful pointers for Brian. Martin stayed with the Louisiana Ragtime Band for more than two years between 1985 and 1987, when the line-up was Brian Robertson (trumpet), Martin Bennett (trombone), Dave Paxton (clarinet), Graham Scott (piano), Bill Salmond (banjo), Graham Blamire (bass) and either Roy Dunnett or Eric Jamieson (drums). In this form, the band made annual trips in the later 1980s to play at the Bute Jazz Festival, which had been founded by Phil Mason and which was to become an important event in the Scottish Jazz calendar.

In May 1987, Bill took his band over to Holland to play at the Enkhuizen Jazz Festival. By then, the band had been blessed with a stable line-up for some considerable time, enabling it to play in the well-integrated manner that is so essential to the New Orleans style. When Martin Bennett left to return south, the replacement was Bob Craig who, several years later, gave way to Alan Quinn. The Louisiana Ragtime Band ended the 1980s as it had entered the decade, with a strong line-up and in great demand.

One of the Louisiana Ragtime Band's regulars was **Roy Dunnett (drums).** Roy was born in Edinburgh on 22nd August 1941 and made his start on playing drums with a Boys Brigade pipe band. In his teens in the 1950s, like so many of us of that generation, he was attracted to skiffle music and soon found himself playing washboard in a skiffle group. Later, he played drums in a variety of dance bands before moving on to rock music, in which style he played with a group with the glorious name of the Screaming Citizens and another rock band, the Rapiers. The bass guitarist in the latter was Scott Murray, brother of jazz and dance band bass player Fred Murray, and with this band Roy was to play in the Locarno Ballroom in Slateford Road and the Palais de Dance, in Fountainbridge.

Roy's debut in jazz came in the 1970s when he joined Bill Salmond's Louisiana Ragtime Band, with whom he played at their residency in the Hopetoun Lounge in Morrison Street. Roy was later to be replaced in the LRB by Eric Jamieson but had returned to the band by 1986 and played with the band at its residencies at the Navaar House Hotel, the Sands Hotel in Joppa and at Basin Street, in the Haymarket Station Bar. He also made the trips to play at the Enkhuizen Jazz Festival in Holland and the Isle of Bute Jazz Festival, both in 1987, as well as playing with the band at several EIJFs. A spell out of jazz followed but by the late 1990s, Roy had reappeared on the Edinburgh jazz scene and in the 2000s was playing regularly with Brian Robertson's Forth River Ragtimers and a band led by the bass player, Fred Murray, Fred's Clubhouse Seven. Roy was something of a character and I have to say, I liked him a lot. I remember a phone call from him which came right out of the blue. He had a habit of beginning new conversations as if you were in the middle of an on-going verbal interaction. *'Oh, by the way'* he said, when I answered the phone *'I've just phoned you for a chat. I'm bored with the speaking clock and I've fallen out with the Samaritans, so I thought I'd give you a ring'.* An indefatigable conversationalist, Roy Dunnett's presence in the car to or from a gig ensured that there would be no awkward silences.

Eric Jamieson (drums), born in Edinburgh on 19th September 1940 and educated at Tynecastle School, had become interested in jazz by his mid-teens, through listening to records and the radio. In particular, he became interested in the music of the George Lewis band and, when he was about fifteen years old in the middle 1950s, he began to venture out into the Edinburgh jazz scene. He soon found his way to the Condon Club, which was located in India Buildings in Victoria Street, and amongst the bands he remembers from around that time was the Climax Jazz Band, with Jim Petrie on trumpet. Eric remained a regular listener and jazz supporter around the Edinburgh jazz scene for many years, with no thought of becoming a musician, and then, in the 1970s, he began going to the Hopetoun Lounge in Morrison Street, where the attraction was Bill Salmond's Louisiana Ragtime Band. At that time, Kenny Milne was playing trumpet with the band but there was frequently no drummer. Knowing Bill Salmond's commitment to the pure New Orleans style, I am sure that this was because there was no one around and available at the time who played drums in the style that would have suited the band. Bill, with a clear view of how he wanted his band to sound, would certainly have chosen to do without a drummer, rather than compromise the band's style. Kenny Milne would have been ideal of course, but, as he was already playing trumpet in the band, he could hardly play drums as well. However, Kenny was to come up with a solution and it was he who approached Eric Jamieson and asked him if he had ever considered having a go at drums. Although this had never crossed Eric's mind, it was not to be long before Kenny had persuaded him into going along to the Milne house on Liberton Brae, where Kenny took him under his wing and they began a series of drum lessons. In addition to working on the rudiments of drumming and probably to help him develop a proper feel for jazz drumming, Kenny soon encouraged Eric to start playing in a band setting and, with the young Finlay Milne already developing his skills on trumpet plus Kenny Henderson on banjo, there was soon a practice band in full cry at Liberton Brae.

Eric's first real gig was with the LRB at the Hopetoun Lounge, when the band included Bill, Kenny, Dave Paxton, Symon Carlyle then playing trombone, Graham Scott and Willie Mack on bass, and later he made the move with the band to their new residency at the Navaar House Hotel. As we have already heard, Eric was to alternate with Roy Dunnett a number of times but he was with the LRB when they made their recording 'Way Down Yonder in New Orleans'[175]. He was also to play with the band at a number of jazz festivals, among them Edinburgh, Bute, Keswick, Dumfries and Orkney. Speaking with Eric now, he remembers with particular affection the early EIJFs and the

---

[175] See discography appendix

opportunities they brought play with visiting players of the calibre of trumpeter Teddy Riley from New Orleans and the great veteran reeds man, Benny Waters. He also has fond memories of playing with another New Orleans legend, the sax player Sammy Lee. Eric played on for a number of years, mostly with the LRB but also putting in a lengthy spell with Alan Quinn's Templehall Stompers, at the Templehall Hotel in Portobello but sadly, his playing came to a stop in the late 1990s, because of health problems. However, his interest in jazz continues at the time of writing in the second decade of the twenty-first century and it would not surprise me in the least if we have not seen the last of Eric Jamieson, jazz drummer.

When Kenny Milne left his trumpet playing slot with the Louisiana Ragtime Band in 1986, he had no intention of allowing his trumpet playing to come to an end. Of course, he continued to be very busy as drummer with the Spirits of Rhythm but it was not long before he put together a new band, built around his trumpet lead. This he called the **Criterion Jazz Band**[176] and the original membership included Jack Weddell (tbn), Ian Boyter (rds), Jock Westwater (bjo) and, a newcomer to the Edinburgh jazz scene, Bill Brydon on sousaphone. Later on, Bill Smith would replace Jack Weddell on trombone while reeds man Jimmy Shortreed and banjo players Brian Weld and Beverley Knight would also put in time with the band. In the bustling jazz climate of the mid-1980s, it was not long before the Criterion band was filling its bookings diary. They landed a plumb gig at the prestigious golfing centre of Gleneagles, where they played a 'Sunday Jazz Brunch' engagement in the Gleneagles Hotel for about three years. Closer to home, there was another run of gigs associated with the serving of food, at Fat Sam's Eatery in Fountainbridge, where for a couple of years the band played two evenings a week. All this playing at restaurants was not without its side effects and Kenny Milne, recalling that the Fat Sam's Eatery gigs included a meal as part of the deal, reckoned he had put on about a stone in weight

---

[176] Not to be confused with the Criterion Brass Band, a parade or marching band, also led by Kenny Milne

during this period! The Criterion Jazz Band played on, regularly and successfully, well into the 1990s and, even at the time of writing in 2010, still occasionally gets together when suitable gigs come up.

Another two new bands, with a close relationship to each other, appeared on the local scene in the later 1980s. In 1986, a five piece band was formed with the intention of playing in the so-called 'mainstream' style. At first there was no name for this band but with its first gig imminent, a temporary name had to be found and it appeared in the Merlin, a pub in Morningside Road, as the Rhythm Aces. Not only was this name inappropriate to the style of music played but it was also the established name of a full time touring band, Max Collie's Rhythm Aces, so the name was hastily dropped. The Merlin gig did not last long, and by March 1987 the band had moved to a slot at Basin Street. Basin Street was the upstairs lounge of the Haymarket Station Bar, next door to Haymarket Station, and was one of the best jazz pubs that Edinburgh ever had. The upstairs bar had been designed for jazz sessions, with old jazz posters and photographs on display in the stairway and the lounge walls decorated with murals depicting New Orleans scenes. For years, Basin Street hosted jazz six, or even seven, nights a week and was an important venue during the EIJF. The new band appeared at the 1987 EIJF as 'Graham Blamire's Jazz Band', as a permanent name had still not been chosen, but at last and after what seemed endless discussions, the somewhat immodest sounding title of **The Jazz Masters** was agreed. The membership of the band was Andrew Lauder (tpt and flugelhorn), Jimmy Shortreed (rds), Jack Finlay (pno), Graham Blamire (bs) and Donald 'Chick' Murray (drms). The material played was, in the main, a combination of small band Swing tunes, many of them associated with the Benny Goodman small groups, and tunes from the Duke Ellington repertoire. There was also some original material, with Andrew Lauder writing a couple of tunes and Graeme Robertson and Al Fairweather contributing both original tunes and arrangements.

Jack Finlay (piano), brother of fellow pianist Tom, was born in Fife in 1944 and was to become a Chartered Accountant. Jack and Tom were born into a musical family which encouraged interest in playing musical instruments but, in spite of this, Jack only received one piano lesson, which took place when he was seven years old. This is hard to believe considering how proficient a piano payer he was to be but, apparently, the experience was so off putting, that he did not return to the piano keyboard until he was thirteen years old, when he set out to teach himself! There was plenty of music in the house to influence him, including recordings of Benny Goodman, Ruby Braff, Vic Dickenson and other jazz greats. Jack was to move to Edinburgh where his first gig was with the Pete Martin All-Stars in Rutherford's Bar. He also played with vibes player Bill Stronach and then was with the Charlie McNair band when it had, in addition to Jack and Charlie, Graeme Robertson (tbn), Robbie Robertson (rds), Dougie Campbell (gtr), Kenny Wheatley (bs) and Bobby Stewart (drms). This was the period when the McNair band was pursuing something of a mainstream policy, and it was already clear that Jack's interest was towards the more modern end of the jazz spectrum. Spells with Hamish McGregor's bands, the Clansmen and the Memphis Road Show, followed and then Jack moved to Jersey, where he played two summer seasons with Edinburgh's Jack Duff who was then resident in Jersey. A return to Edinburgh in 1970 saw him join the Ken Ramage Quartet and later, another quartet with Brian Keddie (tbn), Ian Croal (bs) and Bill Kyle (drms).

Jack, along with Kyle, Croal and guitarist Charlie Alexander, became a founding member of the jazz organisation Platform, which started in Edinburgh but later had branches in Glasgow, Aberdeen and Dundee. Platform did an enormous amount of good work in the jazz field, including bringing the Duke Ellington Orchestra to the Usher Hall in 1973. Jack had become a highly capable jazz piano player, well up to the demanding roles he took on during the EIJFs, when he accompanied the likes of Benny Waters, Harry Edison, Art Farmer, Joe Temperley and various other big jazz names. Benny Waters in particular, was greatly impressed by Jack's playing and regularly requested that Jack backed him on his many visits. As well as a sparkling solo player, Jack was always a particularly sensitive accompanist when backing horn players and

437

singers. He playing was also much appreciated by bass players because of his incisive attack and sparing, open, left hand work that kept the rhythm sound light and airy, leaving plenty of space for everyone to be heard.

Jack claims that he was *'corrupted by the traddies'* in the guise of the present writer and Chick Murray when, in 1986, he was a founder member of the new Jazz Masters. In our defence, it has to be pointed out that this band was not all that 'traddy' and soon built up a repertoire of material associated with Goodman, Ellington and even some fairly modern jazzers, including Gerry Mulligan and Benny Golson. After the Jazz Masters finished in the early 1990s, Jack returned to work in trios and duos of his own, often in the company of like-minded musicians such as Kenny Ellis and Kenny McDonald (bs) and Bobby Stewart (drms). A piano player whose style was influenced by Teddy Wilson, Bill Evans and Oscar Peterson, in 2011 Jack Finlay was as busy as ever, a versatile and much respected pillar of the Edinburgh jazz scene.

In April 1987, the Jazz Masters became a six piece band for a while when the fine trombone player, Brain Keddie, came in. Brian also contributed a number of tight, swingy arrangements but, unfortunately, his stay was a short one, as he moved off to work in Paris in June of the same year. There was quite a bit of interest in the band from other musicians and many came along as invited guests or just to sit in at the Basin Street gig, amongst them trumpeters Al Fairweather and Dave Strutt, pianist Ralph Laing, singers Liz McEwen and Fionna Duncan, reeds man Dick Lee, trombonists Dave Keir and Graeme Robertson and tenor saxists Gordon Cruikshank and Dave Roberts. As the band was only five piece, in contrast to most of the others which were six or seven piece, it had been possible to negotiate a small amount of extra money to allow guests to be invited on a paid basis, every week or two. Later, after Brian Keddie had disappeared to France, the Jazz Masters again became six piece for a spell, this time the addition being John Bancroft who, when his medical duties allowed it, played vibes with the band. John was a medical consultant, who played both vibes and piano, and was the father of three youngsters, all of whom were to make their considerable mark on jazz. Sophie was a fine singer and the twins, Tom and Phil, who were born in 1967, were to become important jazz musicians at the highest level in contemporary jazz, going on to make international names for themselves. Tom played drums and Phil tenor sax but both were talented writers and arrangers as well, and both came along to sit in with the Jazz Masters, Tom in addition once depping for Chick Murray at one of the regular gigs.

A guest who made a number of appearances with the Jazz Masters, both at Basin Street and during the EIJF, was **singer Liz MacEwan**. The presence of Jack Finlay on piano, who had often worked with Liz and was familiar with her material, meant that we could find common ground with the greatest of ease and I remember us wishing that she could sing with us all the time. Liz was already established as one of Scotland's best jazz singers, with a great personality and a fine, adaptable voice. She had started in Tiffany's Nightclub in Edinburgh away back in the 1970s, with The Band of Gold, and had sung all types of music, all over the world. This included a tour with Demis Roussos and singing in US Army bases in West Germany, her wide musical experience enabling her to build up a formidable repertoire of songs from all genres. In addition to her free lance career, Liz also sang for four years in the 1980s alongside Edinburgh's blues legend, Tam White, with his band, the Dexters, and worked with them on a number of albums and BBC broadcasts. Liz also worked as a backing singer with the well-known Scottish band, Runrig and toured with another legend, Van Morrison. Her appearances at the EIJF were many and in particular, included sell-out success with her 'Tribute to Peggy Lee' shows. Liz also worked for a time on the luxury liner the QE2 before returning to Edinburgh in 1990 and, a thoroughly experienced professional, she has continued to be in demand across the country ever since. Accompanied by her pianist, she has performed at well-known Edinburgh venues such as the Dome, Centotre and Cafe Grande and the Balmoral Hotel. Her success continued with appearances at Aberdeen's The Albyn and the Jamhouse in Edinburgh, where she was often accompanied by the Jack Finlay Trio. She also notched up successes in company with the Frank Holden Experience, an eighteen piece Swing band featuring the best of Glasgow's horn players. A class act and as well-liked and respected by musicians as she is popular with her audiences, Liz MacEwan, in the 2000s, remains one of the countries' best and most sensitive singers.

The Jazz Masters' Basin Street gig lasted until December 1988, after which residencies were tried at the Postillion pub, near the St Andrew's Square bus station, where Fionna Duncan, Sophie Bancroft and Edith Budge all sang with the band, and at the Westbury Hotel in Corstorphine, but neither of these lasted long. After this, the Jazz Masters survived mostly on one-off gigs into the 1990s, when there was a spell when they played regularly at Fat Sam's Downtown Diner. The band played in the EIJFs in 1995 and 1996 but, by late 1996, the band had ceased to play. There were several reasons for this. Although there had been encouragement and even some enthusiasm for their mainstream style from many of the local jazz musicians, especially Al Fairweather, Gordon Cruikshank and Graeme Robertson, this was not matched by support from the jazz followers. The local jazz crowds preferred a more New Orleans or Dixieland oriented sound and found the music of the Jazz Masters less familiar and less to their taste. On one notable but depressing occasion, a regular jazz follower approached one of the band (me) at Basin Street and said quite aggressively *'I thought this was supposed to be a jazz band?'* On being assured that that was so and asked what his problem was, he replied with some heat *'There's no banjo and no trombone'!* In the face of this character's apparent belief that he had a divine right to define jazz, there did not seem much point in arguing with him. The other reason for the band's demise lay in the other commitments of the band members and in particular, the increasing activity of another band, formed at around the same time, and drawing three-quarters of its members from the Jazz Masters.

A cruise boat sailed every summer from the Hawes Pier in South Queensferry, taking passengers around the picturesque islands of the Firth of Forth, where they could enjoy the scenery and wildlife, as well as admire the great

Forth Bridge from water level. This was the Maid of the Forth and its owner had added jazz cruises to his programme in 1986. In summer 1987, the owner, John Watson, contacted me to offer the gig on a regular basis. A band was put together which included three of the Jazz Masters, Andrew Lauder (trumpet), Jimmy Shortreed (reeds) and Graham Blamire (bass), who, with the addition of Bill Salmond (banjo), were to be the band which would eventually play under the name of the boat as **The Maid of the Forth Stompers**. This was to become one of Edinburgh's longest running resident gigs and by 2011, the band were in its twenty-fifth consecutive season. Early in the band's history, they began taking gigs ashore, in addition to the boat work, sometimes expanding for special occasions to five or six piece.

Jimmy Shortreed (reeds), the reeds player with both the Jazz Masters and the Maid of the Forth Stompers, was born in Hawick on 22nd November 1922. Jimmy bought his first clarinet, for which he had saved for three years, when he was twelve years old in 1934, and later added alto sax to his repertoire. His impressionable teenage years were, of course, in the 1930s when the great Swing era was in full cry and the bands of Benny Goodman, Artie Shaw and the Dorseys were at the peak of their popularity. In particular, the Swing era had been dominated to a large extent by the virtuoso clarinet playing of Goodman and Shaw and it was Benny Goodman who was to be Jimmy's inspiration. This brought about a strange anomaly many years later, when Jimmy became fully involved in the Edinburgh traditional jazz scene. Jimmy was about half a generation older than the Revivalists of the 1940s and his clarinet style and tastes in jazz, had already been formed by the time the 1940s came along. Because of this, and unlike clarinettists such as Sandy Brown, Dave Paxton, Ian Arnott and Jake McMahon, his playing was not influenced by either of the two dominant styles of the Revival. The anomaly was that, although Jimmy was older than the Revivalist clarinet players, he was actually playing a style that, in terms of jazz history, was younger and more recent than that of the Revivalists. The roots of Jimmy's style lay in the second half of the 1930s, rather than in the period between 1920 and 1935.

**Jimmy Shortreed in 1996
(photo by the author)**

During his war service between 1941 and 1945, Jimmy played in RAF dance bands and, after the war, most of his playing was in local small dance bands and in the reeds sections of various big bands, which also played for dancing. Although his main musical love was jazz and Swing, he would see no contradictions in playing dance music. The big band Swing craze of the 1930s was primarily seen as jazz based dance music and, throughout his career, in addition to his dance band work, Jimmy quite often helped out with the Edinburgh jazz bands. As with so many of the dance band regulars, Jimmy found himself short of playing, when the discos decimated the dance bands in the 1960s and '70s, and it was then that he became increasingly directly involved in the Edinburgh jazz scene. He was one of the dance band regulars who made the switch to jazz playing with a natural ease, where some of the others struggled. He was drawn into the Festival City Jazz Band through his pal, the piano player Ian Scott, who had also found himself short of dance work, and he played with them in the Barnton Hotel from about 1975. Later, Jimmy was a regular for many years at drummer Frank Birnie's East Coast Jazz Band sessions, on Monday evenings at The Blue Lagoon. Then in 1986, he was invited to join the new band just being put together, the Jazz Masters. This was my doing and it was because, as well as very much liking Jimmy's playing, I reckoned that he would make an ideal partnership with the trumpet playing of Andrew Lauder. That partnership worked out very well and was continued when the Maid of the Forth Stompers band came along. Jimmy played out the rest of his career with the latter band, starting on the cruise boat in 1987 and eventually retiring from playing after the cruising season ended in autumn 2001, just a week or two before his seventy ninth birthday.

Jimmy was a gentle, courteous man, universally liked among the Edinburgh jazzers, both musicians and followers. His playing, its roots in the playing of Benny Goodman always obvious, featured a lovely, singing tone and a fluent, lyrical way of improvising. After Jimmy died, I wrote an appreciation of him for the Scotsman[177] and, referring to the Blue Lagoon sessions in particular, said *'His melodic and very accessible playing made him a great favourite with the loyal and sizable crowds that turned out every week and his feature numbers were a weekly highlight...He brought to his music a friendly and open joyfulness that touched everyone who listened'.* That last point was well illustrated by a regular at the Blue Lagoon who, when explaining why he liked Jimmy's clarinet playing so much, said *'...there always seems to be a smile in his playing'.* The only commercial recordings of his playing are a set made by the Maid of the Forth Stompers in 1995. However, there is another set of studio quality recordings, unfortunately never yet issued, with the Jazz Masters. These show Jimmy in the type of small band Swing setting

[177] Blamire G, 'Jimmy Shortreed – an appreciation', The Scotsman, 12th January 2006

which suited him very well and several tracks show very good examples of his playing. The excellent Gordon Cruikshank also guests on tenor sax on some of the tracks and even now, more than twenty years after they were recorded, it would be good to see them made available. Jimmy Shortreed died at the age of eighty three, on December 11 2005 and Artie Shaw's beautiful recording of Stardust, one of Jimmy's all time favourites, was played at his funeral.

A jazzer mentioned above and whom few would classify in the traditional category nonetheless deserves his place in this book, because of his staunch support for all forms of jazz and the time he put in with at least a couple of the more traditional jazz bands, including the Jazz Masters with whom he made the recordings[178] spoken of above. He was **Gordon Cruikshank (reeds)**, who was born on 12th September 1949. Gordon had been encouraged in his interest in jazz by a neighbour, the fine piano player Alex Shaw, and had played flute at school, before taking up the various saxophones. He had been active in the Edinburgh modern jazz and rock scenes in the late 1960s, as well as playing with Hamish McGregor's Memphis Road Show. He also worked with the blues singer Tam White and, in the 1970s, was to collaborate with many jazz musicians interested in the more modern forms of jazz, including Lachlan McColl, Brian Keddie, Dave Newton, Kenny Ellis, Bill Kyle and Tony McLennan. Gordon made a big reputation for himself in his chosen style and accompanied many visiting jazz musicians from south of the border and the USA as well as becoming a member of Head, the leading Scottish 'jazz fusion' band. He also made a career for himself as a broadcaster, presenting 'Take the Jazz Train' and 'Jazz Junction' on Radio Scotland and 'Sound of Jazz' on Radio 2, when it was broadcast from Scotland. In addition, he founded and directed a jazz school which flourished principally at Broughton High School in Edinburgh. This organisation was attended by many up and coming jazz musicians and was active in introducing to

---

[178] Studio quality recordings made in 1988 in Finger's Piano Bar, Edinburgh, these at 2010 had not yet been made available on general release

jazz and helping to develop many later prominent jazz musicians including Tommy Smith, Phil and Tom Bancroft and John Rae.

Although as a player, Gordon belonged with the mainstream/modern end of jazz, he was, in fact, interested in the whole of jazz and knew a great deal about the music and its history. He showed an eclectic taste in his record selections on the 'Jazz Train' and took an interest in the whole Edinburgh jazz scene, modern and traditional. He frequently would remind his listeners about jazz gigs, of all schools, and made a habit of dropping in for a blow at the Jazz Masters sessions at Basin Street. I had many a chin wag with him in his favourite Morningside boozer, Bennetts Bar in Maxwell Place, where we would chew the fat about jazz in general and the Edinburgh scene in particular. He once told me how nervous he felt when he was included in one of the specially assembled big bands during an EIJF and found himself sitting between Buddy Tate and Benny Waters in the reeds section. What always came over was his love for all of jazz and his genuine admiration for great local players such as Sandy Brown, Al Fairweather, Alex Shaw and Dave Paxton. Gordon Cruikshank made a great contribution to jazz in Edinburgh and Scotland in several fields and it was a tragedy when, after moving to York in the 1990s, his health broke down and he died in 2002 at the age of only 52.

There were two highly significant returns to the Edinburgh jazz scene in the 1980s, both concerned jazzers who had been big Edinburgh names in the early post-war years, both had made careers for themselves as jazz musicians in the south and both were to make their mark all over again in Edinburgh jazz. They were Dave Keir and Al Fairweather. **Dave Keir** was the first to return. After his career as a professional jazz musician, Dave had become a school teacher, making use of his degree and teaching mathematics and physics, and had remained in this profession for more than twenty years. In all that time, he had played almost no music, only once playing with a school band at one of the schools. He had played no jazz whatsoever and he did not resume his jazz career until after he had taken early retirement from teaching and returned to Edinburgh. His return to playing came as a result of a chance meeting with Mike Hart in 1980. Mike was of course, by then running the Edinburgh International Jazz Festival, and he invited Dave to sit in with his band. This signalled a return to regular playing and during the early 1980s he played in Edinburgh with Charlie McNair's Jazz Band, Frank Birnie's East Coast Jazz Band, The Capital Jazz Band and Mike Hart's Edinburgh Ragtimers. He was also a welcome sitter-in at other sessions and, in the later 1980s, would quite frequently turn up at Basin Street at Haymarket to sit in with the mainstream styled Jazz Masters. At first Dave, a multi-instrumentalist, pursued his come-back on trombone, the instrument on which he had made his name but later, in the 1990s, he decided to make a change which I remember him telling me he had long intended, making the trumpet his main instrument.

The other veteran to return was **Al Fairweather** who, after about thirty five years in the south, came back to his home city in the late 1980s. He had started to think about returning in about 1982, when he had played in Edinburgh with a band organised by pianist Ralph Laing. The Bluenote Jazzmen from Bristol had made a late withdrawal from the EIJF that year and Mike Hart had asked Ralph, then living near Bristol, to arrange a replacement. He put together a band which was to play as the Ralph Laing All Stars and, with the inclusion of Al on trumpet, it was intended that the band would play some of the McJazz material, that is the music written and arranged by Al and Sandy Brown in the mid-1950s. The band was clearly a good one with some resounding names, including Micky Cooke (tbn), Nick Cooper (rds), Wayne Chandler (gtr), Harvey Weston (bs) and Tony Allen (drms), in addition to Al and Ralph himself. The band came north, opened with a gig in the Perth vicinity, then worked their way through two gigs a day at the EIJF. They also played a number of gigs on their way back south and Ralph Laing recalls how Al had enjoyed all this. He was in the midst of family troubles, the most serious of which was his wife's multiple sclerosis, and he was unhappy in his teaching post. However, the short tour north had been a success, the band had played well and Al had said to Ralph '...*we must keep doing this*'.

The band then did a few jobs in the south at venues such as London's 100 Club and, in the following Spring of 1983, they made a BBC Jazz Club broadcast and undertook another short Scottish tour. This time the band included two other Scottish jazzers, Johnny McGuff on trombone and Francis Cowan, an extremely able Edinburgh bass player. This time, the itinerary included a gig at the Queen's Hall and one south of the border, in Carlisle.

Unfortunately, Al suffered a serious heart attack later in 1983, which was to stop him playing for a year, and he required to be fitted with a heart pace maker. To add greatly to his troubles, his wife Judy then died after a long period of deteriorating health. Realising perhaps that there was little now to keep Al in the south, Ralph Laing pointed out to him that, as properties in Edinburgh were then selling at a much lower rate than in London, he should be able to sell up in Harrow, return to Edinburgh and have a decent nest egg into the bargain. Happily for Edinburgh jazz, Al was to take Ralph's advice and he returned permanently to Edinburgh in 1987.

Less happily, he was still not in the best of health and the heart attack in 1983 had clearly taken its toll of his energy and confidence. The journalist and trumpeter Alastair Clark was later to write that it had been a distinctly subdued Al who returned to Edinburgh[179]. However, while I am sure that this was true, it was not long before he was making his way back into active playing. I have already, in an earlier chapter, written of how modest Al was about his achievements in jazz, nevertheless, it bears repeating now when he soon showed himself more than willing to get involved around the local jazz scene, playing again, as in his early days, with Edinburgh bands in Edinburgh pubs. An early regular gig seems to have been organised by Al's old sparring partner, Bob Craig, who soon took the chance to bring Al into the band that was playing on Sunday evenings in Basin Street. The line-up of this band, in addition to Al and Bob, included Gerard Dott (clt), Graham Scott (pno) and two other veterans of the 1940/50s, Dizzy Jackson (bs) and Bill Strachan (drms).

---

[179] Clark A, ' Bob Craig', 'Scotsman' obituaries, 5 August 1998

After the Basin Street gig folded, there was a gap before Bob fixed up a replacement venue. When he did, he phoned Gerard Dott to invite him to play at the new venue, only to discover that he had decided to stop playing and Gerard has confirmed that this was in 1988. Gerard's decision to stop playing was, of course, a significant loss for the Edinburgh jazz scene that would not be reversed until 2006, but it does seem to have opened the door to bring together a notable front-line partnership - Al, Bob and their fellow RHS Gangster, Dave Paxton. The new gig that Bob had arranged was at Young's Hotel, formerly the Glenelg Hotel, in Leamington Terrace, and henceforth, the band was to play under Al Fairweather's name. There is a photograph dated 1989, shown on Dave Paxton's profile on the Sandy Brown Jazz website[180], which shows the band playing there with a line-up of Al, Bob and Dave with Graham Scott (pno), Jim Young (bs) and Kenny Milne (drms), clearly a formidable line-up, dominated by veterans from the 1940s and '50s. The caption below the photograph on the website suggests that the band may have played under the name of Fairweather Friends. However, Jim Walker has a number of privately made recordings of the band in Young's Hotel around this time on which the band is given as the Sundowners and are all dated 1989 and 1990.

I remember going to hear the band on a number of occasions and they sounded marvellous. Just like the Dave Paxton, Ian Telford and Bob Craig front line of the Society Syncopators in the early 1970s, this front line too benefitted from same extraordinary compatibility of the three horn players – Al, Dave and Bob gelling as to the manner born. It was a great privilege to hear this band and, although we were not to know it then, it was just about the last chance to hear three of the original RHS gang playing together regularly. It must have been a great gig musically for the whole band but it brought an added non-musical bonus for Bob and Jim Young, both of whom lived within about a hundred yards of the hotel!

---

[180] http://www.sandybrownjazz.co.uk/profiledavepaxton.html

**Al Fairweather's Sundowners – Young's Hotel 1989
Jim Young, Dave Paxton, Al Fairweather, Kenny Milne,
Bob Craig
(by permission of Jim Walker)**

Al was to also to take on a number of other gigs on a regular basis, among them Frank Birnie's Monday evening spot at the Blue Lagoon, and he played for a time at the Clarenden Hotel where Roger Craik, in August 1988, both played in the band and made a recording of a session. The journalist Tony Troon, writing in the Scotsman after the untimely deaths of both Dave Paxton and Al Fairweather in 1993[181], said how much the partnership of the two veterans was relished around the Edinburgh jazz scene, commenting that *'Fairweather-Paxton was an act to catch'*. He had previously sought information in his regular jazz column as to whether anyone had any recordings of the two of them playing together. He had received two positive responses, one jointly from Jim Walker and Bill Todd and the other from Roger Craik. Tony Troon says how much he was impressed by a recording that featured not only Al and Dave but also Bob Craig in a band that also included Jock Westwater on banjo. Tony picked out a *'...very fine version of 2.19 Blues and a typically intricate Paxton reading of*

---

[181] Troon A, 'Fairweather and friends', The Scotsman, 1993

Black and Blue with simple and telling muted trumpet by Fairweather'. Of the session recorded by Roger Craik, Tony said *'You could hardly remain unaffected by the ideal pairing – a trumpeter who deals in powerful, clear statements and a clarinettist supplying intricate embellishment'.*

Jim Walker who recorded the other set, had pointed out that *'Al constructed his phrases in coherent paragraphs while Dave set off Al's directness with wonderful embroideries and confidently taken breaks'.* Tony summarises his thoughts by saying *'... each understands his role perfectly and never runs short of an original statement. Made for each other'.* These are eloquent tributes to two great players and it was Edinburgh's extraordinary good fortune to have them playing together, often in the company of Bob Craig, as their distinguished careers drew to a close. Unfortunately, these were simply private recordings made by punters at regular pub sessions and they were not intended, nor of a suitable recording quality, for general release.

Al Fairweather - 1989
(by permission of Jim Walker)

450

We all knew, of course, that Al had been in poor health for some years when he returned to Edinburgh in 1987, but it was still a real shock when he died suddenly in 1993, following a second heart attack. He had been commissioned to paint a portrait of the wife of a fellow local musician, the drummer Billy Law, and she had gone round to collect it. Al had gone into the next room to fetch the painting and she heard him fall. In his will, Al left most of his written band arrangements to Ralph Laing who has handed them on to the British Jazz Archive, which is based in Loutham in Essex. Steve Voce, a distinguished jazz critic, wrote Al's obituary in the 'Independent'[182] and said that Humphrey Lyttelton had gone to some trouble to point out that Al had been an influence on his own playing. Humph had said *'When I first heard him he scared me to death. He had a wonderful tone derived from Armstrong's playing which was unique to Al'.* That was quite a compliment coming from another of the UK's top trumpeters.

Another trumpeter and journalist, Alastair Clark, wrote[183] that it had been a subdued Al who had returned from the south and, while this was undoubtedly true, he was a still a very fine player and it was a great privilege and pleasure to get to know him and to play with him back in his home town. Dave Paxton was only sixty seven when he died and Al only sixty six. We could have hoped for many more years from them but, sadly, it was not to be. But what a joy and privilege it was hear Al, Dave and Bob playing together, during those precious six years between Al's return in 1987 and 1993.

Al's friend and musical collaborator, **Ralph Laing (piano)**, was born in Sanquhar in Dumfriesshire in 1936 and was educated at Kilmarnock Academy, before going on to St Andrew's University. Ralph believes that his interest in jazz must have begun at a very early age as, when he was only just able to walk, his party trick was to go over to the stack of 78 rpm records at home, pick out Duke Ellington's recording of 'Ring Dem Bells' and insist on it being played.

---

[182] Steve Voce, obituary 'Al Fairweather', 'The Independent', 24 June 1993
[183] Clark A, 'Obituaries – Bob Craig', 'Scotsman', 5 August 1998

He also remembers hearing a recording of Fats Waller's 'Alligator Crawl' when he was about eight or nine years old and considers that it was this that got him hooked on jazz. He was later to meet up with the Edinburgh born trombonist and RHS gangster, George Hewitt, who shared Ralph's interest in jazz and was living in Irvine in Ayrshire. Ralph had received piano lessons while he was at school but later took up trumpet and got involved with the local Burgh Band, with which he had some trumpet lessons. His heart however, was in jazz rather than the Burgh Band. A Glasgow jazz band with the wonderful name of St Mungo's Disciples then came to play in Kilmarnock on the Saturday of a student rag week. This band included trumpeter George Ogilvie, trombonist Bob Nummey and reeds player Maurice Rose, the first two of whom are still playing regularly in Glasgow at the time of writing in 2011. Ralph went along to hear them and, having taken along his trumpet, he asked for a sit in, as did George Hewitt, who had appeared with a trombone.

Together Ralph and George formed a couple of jazz bands, firstly the Ayrshire Jazz Band and then the Eagle Jazzmen. However, Ralph's career on trumpet was to be short and he was soon to return to the piano, on which he was to make his reputation in jazz. He was also to become well known as an erudite and knowledgeable jazz critic and a frequent writer of sleeve notes. In addition, he wrote quite a number of jazz related articles and features, the most significant of which was perhaps the two volume 'Jazz Records – the Specialist Labels', which he and Chris Sheridan published in 1979/80 and which, thirty years on, remains in print today. Ralph, who held a high ranking post with Rolls Royce, retired to Edinburgh in February 1991 and soon established himself as a highly respected contributor to the local jazz scene.

He kept his Groove Juice band going until 1993, with Al Fairweather contributing many arrangements, and continued to do some work with the band on the Continent, although Al only took part in a few of these trips. Ralph also put together bands to play at the EIJF, all high quality outfits, one of them having a line-up of Al, Jack Duff (rds), Bob Wilson from Nottingham (tbn), Lindsay Cooper (bs) and

Richie Bryant (drms), with Ralph himself on piano. He also took responsibility for the rhythm section that hosted the EIJF jam sessions, using the same line-up as above. Another joint project between Ralph Laing and Al Fairweather was the writing of a musical version of Kingsley Amis's Lucky Jim. When Al died, the musical score was complete but there was no script. However, this has now been written although the work has yet to be performed. In 2011, Ralph Laing continues to live in Edinburgh and plays whatever gigs come along, a fine player with a long and distinguished jazz pedigree.

A new development in 1987 was the starting up of a new, independent, local jazz festival. This was a 'single venue' festival set up and run by **Ken Ramage**, the former trombone player now playing drums, and it was run on the basis of no charge to the punters. David Stewart, of the company D M Stewart, had negotiated sponsorship with one of the breweries and then fixed up an agreement with Ken to put on a week long programme of evening jazz events in the Guildford Arms, in West Register Street, close to the east end of Princes Street. This was one of the pubs run by the Stewart family and not only was it in a central and prestigious location, it was also one of Edinburgh's finest surviving Victorian pubs. Believed to date back to about 1890, it featured enormous sand blasted windows, wood panelling on the walls, a complex and beautifully decorated ceiling and a lounge bar perched on a balcony. It says much for the quality of the Guildford Arms decor that it managed to exist literally next door to the sumptuous Cafe Royal, another marvel of Victorian pub design, without being in any way diminished by its neighbour's splendid marble floors, ceramic murals and sculptured ceilings. Sponsorship in the early years, without which the event could not have taken place, came from the Harviestoun and Atlas Breweries.

Ken's jazz festival, which became known as the **Guildford Arms Jazz Festival**, was to present jazz of the traditional to mainstream type and was to become a successful annual event. The programme originally ran for a week, taking place each evening from 9.00pm to 12.00 midnight and generally the first two nights coincided with the last two nights of the EIJF. Each evening featured a band built around Ken's own drumming, filled out with invited jazz musicians, mostly local but also including an impressive list of guests from further afield. Typically, there would be a piano, bass and drums rhythm section fronted either by a team of horn players carefully selected to blend well together or a guest soloist.

It is not possible to list all the many local jazzers who played a part but a random selection of names will give some idea of the quality and style of jazz that graced the Guildford over the years. The Edinburgh scene contributed the likes of pianists Tom and Jack Finlay, Ron Carruthers and George Cavaye, trumpeters Al Fairweather, who played all the Guildford Arms festivals between 1988 and 1992, Andrew Lauder, Gus Ferguson and Jim Petrie, bass players Ken Macdonald, Kenny Ellis, Ronnie Dunn and Dizzy Jackson, guitarist Lachlan MacColl, reeds men Jimmy Shortreed, Jack Graham, Bill Simpson, Jimmy Woods and Phil Bancroft, trombonist Graeme Robertson, vocalists Wendy Weatherby and Jean Mundell and many others. Guests from elsewhere in Scotland included pianists Frank Tinson and Jimmy Martin, bass player John Hartley from Aberdeen, tenor sax player Dave Roberts from Inverurie, another tenor man, Robbie Richardson, from the Borders and trumpeter Al Gibson from West Lothian. Glasgow provided trumpeter George Ogilvie and the major attraction of vocalist Fionna Duncan.

The guest list from further afield was just as impressive and must be headed by the great trombonist Roy Williams, a star of both the Alex Welsh and Humphrey Lyttelton bands, who was to be an ever-present attraction over a span of twenty four years (and still counting). The London jazz scene was further represented by trumpeter Terry Meechan, clarinettist Ian Christie who was the guest star at the very first Guildford Jazz Festival in 1987, another Welsh and Lyttelton alumnus in reeds player John Barnes, guitarist Jim Douglas and the fine alto sax and clarinet player Bruce Turner, who made many appearances. Ken Ramage also sometimes arranged additional gigs or even little tours for his guests from the south, when he would take them, along with his backing trio, to venues in the north of Scotland.

Speaking with Ken in 2011, he recalled one such trip when the guest soloist was Bruce Turner who asked him to make a detour on the way home to visit Pitreavie Castle, where Bruce had been stationed during the war.

In addition to the Guildford event and the north of Scotland gigs, Ken was also active in arranging jazz weekends and charity jazz band balls through the year, some of which took place in the Masonic Club at Shrubhill, a very large venue which he was able to fill for a number of years. Al Fairweather, a great supporter of local jazz since his return from the south, played at all the early Jazz Band Ball events run by Ken as did pianist Alex Shaw, although Alex never managed to play the Guildford Arms Festivals. Sadly, Al Fairweather, who had been a constant support for Ken's various projects between 1988 and 1992, died just before a Jazz Band Ball run by Ken in the Leith Ex-serviceman's Club in June 1993. In a well-deserved gesture, Ken then ran the event as a tribute to Al, with Roy Williams on trombone, Jack Duff on reeds and Andrew Lauder coming in on trumpet in Al's place. Another trumpeter, George Ogilvie, sometimes brought his whole band over from Glasgow to play at the Jazz Band Balls. As a further contribution to the success of his various ventures, Ken and his wife Viv (who sadly died in 2010) would often provide accommodation for visiting jazzers, thus cutting costs in a budget that none-the-less usually ended up over-stretched. What should certainly be mentioned is that there was always a collection in aid of children with cancer at the Guildford events and the proceeds from the various jazz band balls went towards the annual Edinburgh Taxi Trade Handicapped Kiddies Outing. It was small wonder that Ken was able to count on the support of so many jazzers from Edinburgh and elsewhere for these events.

The first run of Guildford Jazz Festivals continued until 1992 but this sequence of seven years actually included nine festivals, as Ken ran two festivals in both 1990 and 1991. However, that brought the Guildford Jazz Festval to an end for the time being as Ken made a return to the USA, where he was to stay for the next nine years. Happily, his return to Edinburgh saw the resumption of his partnership with David Stewart and the Guildford Arms, with the first of a new series of festivals taking place in 2003. Since then, the Guildford Jazz Festival has again been an annual event, with sponsorship provided by the excellent Orkney Brewery, which brought the name 'Orkney Jazz at the Guildford Arms'. Many well-known jazzers from Edinburgh and elsewhere have taken part in the series of festivals beginning in 2003, their number including many who had already played a part in the first series, together with others such as reed players Gerard Dott, George Duncan, and Martin Foster, trombonists Alan Quinn and Dave Batchelor and many others. Guests from further afield have included reeds man Jim Galloway from Toronto and, in 2010, Frank Perowsky, a top tenor sax man who had played with the likes of Woody Herman, Peggy Lee, Sarah Vaughan and Billy Eckstine.

In the year of writing of 2011, the Guildford Jazz Festival continues to flourish, still attracting good crowds and still delivered without cost to the punters. It now takes place over no fewer than thirteen evenings and is advertised as part of a package: The Guildford Arms Free Fringe Music, the jazz festival being followed by Caledonian Folk and Blues at the Guildford. Like the rest of Edinburgh jazz, the Guildford Arms Jazz Festivals continued to be affected by losses among its regular contributors, with both Ronnie Dunn and Alan Quinn dying in the months following the 2011 event. However, others filled the gaps and the 2011 Guildford Arms jazz programme went ahead from 5th to 17th August and was, as usual, a well-attended success. It featured various combinations under the names the Ken Ramage Trio and the Ken Ramage Dixie Six and was again headed by the ever loyal and popular Roy Williams. The singer Freddie King also appeared, as did Jim Petrie's Diplomats of Jazz. The 'cast' for 2011 was billed as Keyboard: Jack Finlay, Campbell Normand, Dave Graham, Graham Scott and Steve Grossart; Trumpet: Jim Petrie, Andrew Lauder and Brian Robertson; Trombone: George Howden; Reeds: Dick Lee, Bob Busby, Bill Marshall and Andy Hampton; Bass: Ken Macdonald, Kenny Ellis, Owen Macdonald and Graham Blamire; Banjo: Bev Knight; Vocalist: Patsy Hindley and Drums: Ken Ramage. The

Guildford Jazz Festival, after twenty four years, albeit with a break of about ten years, showed no signs of stopping for as long as the now seventy-four year old Ken Ramage, who had worked so hard to organise the festivals as well as annually knocking his pan in at the drum kit, wanted to keep it going.

The 1980s had certainly been a busy decade. Traditional jazz in the pubs and elsewhere and the EIJF were thriving and there were plenty of punters willing to turn out and support both. As a demonstration of just how vigorous the jazz scene was in the later 1980s, a list published in April 1987 shows the following:

Jazz in Edinburgh – 8.30-11.00 unless stated – April 1987

Monday	Starbank, Newhaven	Jim Petrie J.B.	9-12
	Blue Lagoon, Angle Park Tce	East Coast J.B.	
	Fingers Bar	Jazz pianist	
	Malt Shovel	Sophie Bancroft and trio	
Tuesday	Basin Street	West End J.B.	
	Navaar House Hotel	Louisiana Ragtime Band	
	Handsel, Stafford St.	Lachlan McColls trio	
	L'Attache	Liz McEwan, Brian Keddie	
	Struan Hotel (Zoo)	Darktown J.B.	
	Malt Shovel	Swing 1987	
	Fingers Bar	Jazz pianist	
Wednesday	Basin Street	Louisiana Ragtime Band	
	Preservation Hall, Victoria St.	Charlie McNair J.B.	9-12
	Scotty, Piershill	Darktown J.B.	
	Fingers Bar	Jazz pianist	
	Maxie's Bistro	'Take Three'	
	Fat Sam's	Fat Sam's Band	
	Royal Hotel, Roslin	Martin Leys Quartet	
Thursday	Basin Street	Graham Blamire J.B.	
	Templehall, Esplanade, Portobello	Templehall Stompers	
	Fingers Bar	Jazz pianist	
	Cassis, Abercromby Place	The Jazz Machine (Joe Capaldi)	9-12
Friday	Basin Street	Spirits of Rhythm	
	L'Attcahe, Rutland Hotel	Fionna Duncan with Ronnie Rae Trio and Bruce Adams	
	Fingers Bar	Jazz pianist	
	Ellersley House Hotel	Frank Tinson Trio	
Saturday	Preservation Hall	Toto McNaughton J.B.	2-4
	Platform 1 (Caledonia Hotel)	Alec Shaw Trio	12-3
	The Shore Bar, Leith	Geoff Byrne trio (Lunchtime)	
	Basin Street	Yelly Dug J.B.	

	L'Attache	Fionna Duncan and Trio
	Clarendon Hotel, Grosvenor St.	Festival City J.B.
	Fingers Bar	Jazz pianist
Sunday	Learmonth Hotel	Society Syncopators 1-4
	Sheraton Hotel	Mike Hart J.B (brunch)1-3
	Crest Hotel, Blackhall	Capital City J.B. 2-5
	Platform 1	Ronnie Rae Trio
	L'Attache	Fionna Duncan Trio
	Haymarket	Jean Mundell and the Embers
	Grosvenor Hotel	Alexander's Big Band (dancing)(£2)
	Fingers Bar	Jazz Band

The above list shows that there were forty-two regular jazz spots each week, with a remarkably wide choice of styles on offer. Almost all were free, with only the Grosvenor Hotel charging at the door, although you were supposed to buy 'brunch' at the Sheraton. The total of forty-two regular weekly gigs is not far off the total of forty nine shown in Chapter XII in respect of November 1983. As Edinburgh traditional jazz ended the 1980s, it was clearly still in robust good health.

Chapter XVI

Millennium Done Been Here and Gone

The 1990s began with a good number of established bands still in vigorous action including the Louisiana Ragtime Band, the Spirits of Rhythm, Mike Hart's Scottish Society Syncopators, Fat Sam's Band, the Climax Jazz Band, the Criterion Brass Band (now billed in the EIJF programme as the Criterion New Orleans Parade Band), Dr McJazz, the Templehall Stompers, the Jazz Masters, Swing 1980-2010, Charlie McNair's Jazz Band, the Maid of the Forth Stompers and the Alex Shaw Trio. Although the Jazz Masters stopped playing early in the decade, most of these long serving bands were to continue for many years to come, although inevitably with some changes in their ranks. The West End Band too, after disappearing for a year or two, got together again later in the decade under reeds player Bob McDowell's leadership, the band playing from a Linlithgow base, with many of its members living in West Lothian.

Trumpeter and vocalist Jim Petrie had continued to be extremely active in Edinburgh jazz since his debut in the 1950s and he had remained involved with the Climax Jazz Band throughout most of the 1960s. In the early 1970s, Jim played in the White Cockade pub in Rose Street with a band led by trombonist Kenny Ramage, a residency that lasted for a couple of years. This band was the successor to the short-lived Ken Ramage's Jazz Advocates that Kenny had led in 1969. Jim also played for over two years in another band involving Kenny, this being the Festival City

Jazz Band. This band was based in the Barnton Hotel and included Jim, Kenny, Jimmy Shortreed (rds), the nominal leader of the band Ian Scott (pno), Colin Warwick (bjo), Ken Burns on (bs) and Russ Cessford (drms). When the Ramage band finished at the White Cockade, Jim continued with the Tuesday evening spot for a further five years or so, fronting the Climax Jazz Band, which had Jack Weddell (tbn), George Gilmour (clt), Colin Warwick (bjo), Ken Macdonald (bs) and Roy Dunnett (drms).

Through the later 1970s and early 1980s, Jim led a succession of bands which appeared under a variety of names. Most of these bands were built around a core of players, drawing on Edinburgh's now large population of experienced jazzers. Jim was in the Black Bull pub in the Grassmarket for five years with a band that included Bob Craig (tbn), George Duncan (clt), Tom Bryce (pno), Harald Vox (bjo) and Jim Young (bs). Other successful residencies were at the Golden Rule in Yeaman Place, off Fountainbridge, and at the Glenelg Hotel, where he played with a band that included Bob Craig or John Arthur (tbn), Andy Hampton (rds), Jock Westwater (bjo), Dizzy Jackson (bs) and Iain Forde (drms). Jim's band had appeared as the Jim Petrie Jazz Band in the very first Edinburgh Jazz Festival in 1978 and again in 1980. In 1983 they appeared as the Jim Petrie Quartet, with a line-up of Jim on (tpt), Andy Hampton (rds), Jock Westwater (bjo) and Simon Carlyle (sousa). By 1986 they had become the Vindaloo Stompers (I detect the hand of Jock Westwater in this name), with the same personnel as 1983 but with the addition of Gerard Dott also on reeds and Iain Forde on drums. By 1987 they had become Jim Petrie's Chinese Jazz Band (Jock again, I'll bet) with Jim, Andy Hampton and Bob Busby (rds), Jock Westwater (bjo) as before and Simon Carlyle (sousa). In the late 1980s and into the early 1990s, Jim continued to be involved with the Climax band, which played at the Claret Jug in Great King Street and another venue in Drumsheugh Gardens, the band at this point in its long history, having Jim, Jack Weddell, George Gilmour, Jock Westwater and a young Roy Percy making his debut on bass. Unusually, the band did without a drummer at this time.

However, in 1988, the band which Jim was to lead for the next twenty years and more was formed, growing out of the bands Jim had led in the earlier 1980s. The original line-up of the new band, which was to be called the **Diplomats of Jazz** and which would become a major and long term Edinburgh band, was Jim Petrie (tpt and vocs), Andy Hampton (rds), Jock Westwater (bjo) and Simon Carlyle (sousa). Jim had, of course, started in the 1950s as a strong adherent of the purist/New Orleans school of traditional jazz. Originally with a style based on early New Orleans trumpet players such as Bunk Johnson and Avery Kid Howard, later in his career Jim was to make a deliberate change in his style, unconvinced that his existing style really suited the new quartet setting. He had listened to the playing of great trumpeters belonging to the classic jazz tradition and, in particular, took on board the influences of early Louis Armstrong and Jabbo Smith. Jim himself came to describe his playing from then on as belonging to the classic tradition and, in my view, he made a great success of the re-modelling of his style. Jazz orthodoxy has it that jazz musicians will have set their style and reached their creative peak early in their careers, as early as in their twenties or thirties. In my view, Jim Petrie was able, very successfully, to reinvent his style as he grew older and, always a fiery player, was still extending his expressive range in middle age. His playing was greatly admired by many, in particular one American visitor. This jazz enthusiast had toured around the Edinburgh jazz pubs and was intrigued to find Jim playing in many of them with different bands. He told Jim *'Man, you sure wear a lotta hats!'* and declared him to be *'A National Treasure'*, a notable and well deserved tribute to a long serving and sincere jazzer.

The Diplomats of Jazz had their first gig at the Palmerston Hotel and then moved on to play Sunday afternoons at the Ettrick Hotel in the Polwarth area for all of eight years. They also had successful residencies at various times at the Glencairn Hotel in Royal Circus on Sunday evenings, a spell at the Bank Hotel opposite the Tron Church and four and a half years in the Golden Rule in Yeaman Place. There were changes in the Diplomats in the

461

early 1990s with Jack Graham taking over on reeds from Andy Hampton, Bill Brydon replacing Symon Carlyle on sousaphone and Beverley Knight coming in on banjo to replace Jock Westwater, eventually leaving Jim as the only original member.

Another adventure for Jim was a re-forming of the early Climax Jazz Band from the 1950s, for a long distance tour. This came about through the efforts of Tom Wood, who had played piano with the early Climax band in the Stud Club in 1959, and had subsequently emigrated to Australia, where the tour was to take place. The band that made the trip in 1992 as the Climax Re-union Jazz Band was as close to the original line-up as possible with Jim Petrie (tpt and vocs), Jack Weddell (tbn and vocs), Jake McMahon (clt), Mike Hart (bjo), Jim Young (bs) and Kenny Milne (drms). Their old colleague from the 1950s, Tom Wood, who was then playing with the New Zenith Jazz Band, joined up with them in Australia. The tour was a great success and was celebrated by a recording, made after their return home, with Tom Finlay deputising on piano for Tom Wood[184].

A clear signal of the way things were to go appeared in the mid-1990s. Traditionally, there had been a jazz scene in Edinburgh and another, almost completely separate one, in Glasgow. However, in the mid-1990s came the first indications of a decline in the number of active jazz musicians and the Edinburgh and Glasgow jazzers began to be more involved with each other. Jim Petrie was one of the first, joining the Glasgow based George Penman Jazzmen in 1995 after depping with them on many occasions, succeeding Alec Dalgleish as Penman's trumpeter, an arrangement that was to last for seven years. Later, other Edinburgh jazzers would follow Jim into the Penman band, including trombonist Johnny McGuff, trumpeter Gus Ferguson, who eventually replaced Jim Petrie, and the banjo player, Harald Vox. Indeed, Harald Vox was to take over the running on the Penman band after George Penman died in 2009.

---

[184] See discography Appendix

The Diplomats of Jazz in the late 2000s
Bill Brydon (sousa), Jim Petrie (tpt), Bev Knight (bjo),
Bob Busby (rds)
(from the collection of Jim Petrie, photographer
unknown)

The Penman band in fact had gone a stage further even than using cross-City musicians; they actually had a band residency in Edinburgh, at the Fairmile Inn, once called the Ski Lodge, at Fairmilehead. At the time, clearly suffering an attack of acute parochialism, I remember feeling astounded by their brass neck and thinking that it was like having aliens from outer space living in your street.

Eventually other west coast based jazzers started to appear playing Edinburgh gigs, alhough this tended to be small bands made up mainly of jazzers from the west, rather than Glasgow jazzers making up the numbers in Edinburgh bands. Those who later played regularly in the capital included the exceptional trumpeter from Ayr, Mike Daly, who both ran and played at regular resident spots at the Sheraton Hotel and the Dome, a large pub occupying a magnificent former bank building in George Street. Banjo player Kit Carey, trumpeter Graham Stark and clarinetist Duncan Nairn were three west based jazzers who made frequent appearances at these city centre gigs. Jim Petrie, after his stint with the Penman band, even set up a band that was called the Two Cities Jazz Band. This band was jointly led by Jim and the Glasgow clarinet player Ivan Henderson, who had played with the Penman band for many years. Jim and Ivan, together with the Glasgow banjo player and entertainer Alastair McDonald, made many weekend trips to play in Denmark. Here they were joined by a Danish bass player and drummer to make up a five piece band which was highly rated in Denmark. The movement west to east of Glasgow jazzers to play with Edinburgh bands was much less marked, which seems to indicate that, by then, Edinburgh had a greater number of available, active jazz musicians than Glasgow.

Meanwhile, the Diplomats had gone from strength to strength in their various resident spots through the 1990s and on into the new century. Jack Graham would eventually leave the band when he moved away to live in Spain and his replacement was the experienced clarinet player from Falkirk, Bob Busby, still playing in his hot, spikey style. Jim Petrie and Bob made an exciting combination and, with the by now long established rhythm team of Bev Knight and Bill Brydon, the Diplomats were to remain a popular and feisty band, punching well above their four-piece weight. Over the years, the Diplomats played at many jazz festivals and Bob Busby tells the tale of a gig at the Leith Jazz Festival when a lady approached the band to say how much she had enjoyed their performance and asked Bob his name. When he told her, she said 'Bob who?' causing Bill Brydon to invent a mythical jazz publication 'Bob Who's Who's Who of Jazz'!

Later, the Diplomats were to move to a two year spot in Leslie's Bar, one of the finest of Edinburgh's historic pubs with a wonderful Victorian interior, and later to the Reverie, formerly the Wine Glass, on Newington Road. The Diplomats of Jazz made several CDs[185] over the years, two of them featuring Jack Graham's agile and sympathetic

---

[185] See discography Appendix

clarinet weaving its spells round Jim Petrie's peppy trumpet line, wonderful reminders of one of Edinburgh's long line of great clarinettists.

The Diplomats long-serving **banjo player, Beverley Knight**, was born in Dundee on 20th August 1959 and attended the city's Craigie High School, before coming to Edinburgh to study at Napier University and Moray House College of Education. There had always been music playing in the house when she was young, her father keen on classical music, her mother singing at concert parties, and it was as a teacher of music and brass instruments that Bev was to make her living. Bev's interest in music had begun early, learning to sing harmonies along with her mother, and she was to begin guitar lessons when she was still at primary school. Later, at secondary school, she moved on to euphonium and spent a lot of time while at school taking part in concerts and shows, something she would continue while studying in Edinburgh. In the early 1980s, Bev had a friend who owned a banjo and she became fascinated by the instrument. She managed to buy herself a cheap, 5-string banjo and a book on how to play Bluegrass style but in retrospect describes her attempts as a 'total failure'! However, salvation was at hand when a friendly barman scribbled down some G banjo chord shapes for her and she was away. Her earlier experience on guitar meant that she had an understanding of how chords worked and she was quickly able to pick up the basic chords on the banjo.

As a youngster, Bev had listened to all sorts of music, including jazz, and had developed a wide musical taste which remains to this day. However, about the time of the early banjo experiments, Bev's interest in jazz increased and she began to expand her knowledge of chords, greatly helped by getting out around the Edinburgh jazz scene to listen to the local bands. She also found that listening to recordings of bands from the 1920s and 1930s helped her to form her style of playing. In jazz terms, her particular liking is for the classic jazz of the twenties and thirties. However, when asked about her favourites, it is bands rather than individuals she quotes, naming the famous bands of Louis Armstrong, Jimmy Noone and Fletcher Henderson but also citing less well-known names such as

McKinney's Cotton Pickers and Charlie Johnstone's Paradise Orchestra.

Bev's jazz career in Edinburgh was kick-started by a lucky chance. She was walking to her school teaching job one morning, when a supply teacher asked her if anyone in the music department played banjo. I shudder to think what response such a question would have received if it had been directed to the music department when I was at school but happily, times had changed. It turned out that the supply teacher's husband, John Keenan, played double bass in a band and they were short of a banjo player. It did not take long for Bev to offer her services, together with what she describes as her 'few chords', and she found herself a member of the St Stephen Street Stompers. This was in the 1980s and the Edinburgh pubs were alive with jazz bands. Before long, Bev had established herself in the usual way, by depping with as many bands as she could, and soon built up her experience and her repertoire of chords. She also made a point of getting round the pubs to hear the variety of styles on offer and eagerly took the chance offered by the 1980s EIJFs to listen to the fabulous mix of jazz available, finding this a wonderful way to add to her jazz experience.

It was not long before the jazz scene cottoned on to the fact that there was a new and able banjo player about and a musically educated female one at that, which made a nice change. In the 1980s, Bev was to play with many of the local bands including the Templehall Stompers, Charlie McNair's Jazz Band, the Centurion Jazz Band, the Spirits of Rhythm, Kenny Ramage's band and Al Fairweather's Sundowners, sometimes in depping arrangements which could go on for months. Her reputation as a good player soon reached Glasgow and she was also to play with the George Penman Jazzmen and the band led by clarinet player Ivan Henderson, through in the west.

In 1993, Bev joined the band with which she would remain for many years, replacing Jock Westwater in Jim Petrie's Diplomats of Jazz. This was to be the band with which Bev would be most identified and, with them, she made her debut on record. She was on the Diplomats 'Body and Soul' recording in 1995 with Jim Petrie, Jack Graham and Bill Brydon and, over the next fifteen years or so, made many other recordings with the band, all of which will be found in the discography appendix. She also recorded with the Ivan Henderson band, which included Jim Petrie on trumpet, appearing on their CDs 'Midnight with Scotland's Two Cities Jazz Band' in 2000 and 'Ivan Henderson's All Stars Play at Goldenacre' in 2007. Bev's jazz career also brought her the opportunity to play with some well known jazzers from elsewhere, including Martin Litton, Norman Field, Annie Hawkins, Colin Bowden, Phil Mason, Roy Williams and Fionna Duncan. She considers herself to have been very fortunate to have started when Edinburgh was buzzing with jazz every night and having so many opportunities to play with so many bands, some of them of a very high calibre. After nearly twenty years with the band, Bev Knight remains an indispensible stalwart of the Diplomats of Jazz and of the Edinburgh jazz scene.

In 1990, another jazz festival had sprung up within the City boundaries and, as in the case of the EIJF, we will explore it in outline, looking only at the major developments over its years of existence. Leith, although incorporated with Edinburgh in 1929 and sometimes called Edinburgh's port, quite rightly prides itself in being an independently minded, lively and forward looking town in its own right. Famous for its waterside pubs, eateries and extensive docks, Leith also made its mark as a jazz town when it ran its own **Leith Jazz Festival** in the 1990s.

In **1990**, the annual Leith Festival, Pageant and Gala included, for the first time, a jazz event which featured sixteen bands in nine venues, every one of which offered free entrance. The jazz schedule was featured as a special section in the Leith Festival printed programme. It was headed Leith Jazz, and was to take place over three days, from Friday 15th to Sunday 17th June. The programme announced that Leith jazz was organised by the Leith Visitor Development Group with the help of Mike Hart of the EIJF. The jazz event was funded by the pubs involved and an impressive list of around twelve sponsors. The nine venues were The Tattler in Commercial Street, the Waterfront in Dock Place, the Trading Post and The Shore Bar both on the Shore, Todd's Tap and the Cavern Bar both in Bernard Street, the Chequers and Port o' Leith both in Constitution Street and McKirdy's in Assembly Street. The list of sixteen bands included some familiar local names in the Wendy Weatherby Trio, the Diplomats of Jazz, Charlie McNair's Jazz Band, the Fionna Duncan Trio, the Ken Ellis Trio, Dr McJazz, the Jazz Masters, the Spirits of Rhythm, Hip Replacement, Swing 1990 and newcomers Le Jazz Hot. From Glasgow came the George Penman Jazzmen and from south of the Border, Brian Carrick's Heritage Hall Stompers. The biggest name was that of the exceptional trumpeter from the USA, Warren Vache, who was to appear with the Brian Kellock Trio at McKirdy's on the Friday and the Trading Post on the Saturday. The Saturday programme included a parade in the Shore area which featured The Criterion Parade Band, the Auld Reekie Parade Band and the Falkirk Foot Tappers.

For **1991**, the event was billed as the Leith Jazz Festival (LJF) in its own right, rather than merely as a part of the wider Leith festival, and had expanded to include over fifteen venues in bars and restaurants. There were twenty performers, with Mike Hart's St Louis Ragtimers, Jack Duff's Band, the Louisiana Ragtime Band, Le Jazz Hot, Swing '91 and Ralph Laing's Jazzmen with Wendy Weatherby among the local additions. Some bands with a more contemporary style were also included, with Mike Travis' EH15, the Jan Swanson Quartet and the Sylvia Rae Quartet all appearing. There was no big international name for 1991 but visitors from elsewhere included the West Jesmond Rhythm Kings from Newcastle. An expanded list of over thirty sponsors had contributed and the LJF issued its own printed programme, instead of relying on a section within that of the Leith Festival.

A similar pattern was in place for the **1992 LJF** but it was announced that, this time round, the event was in association with Burton Ale. Although there was a drop in venues to ten, it was a full and ambitious programme, with events on the Friday evening, lunchtime, early evening and late evening gigs on the Saturday and Sunday, and an afternoon street parade each day. Newcomers included John Burgess Jazz, Jeanie Maxwell and the Jazzwegians, Making Waves, the Jelly Roll Band, Swing Palace, Annie

McNichol and Jazz Therapy and the well known singer, Danny Street.

During one of these early LJFs, I remember playing on an outdoors bandstand on the Shore, perched above the Water of Leith just at the point where the river enters the waters of Leith Docks. I was speaking through the microphone, which means that it must have been with the Jazz Masters, when Mike Hart drew up driving his tiny three wheeled vintage car. He was dressed very stylishly in period gear with a leather helmet and goggles and when I greeted him over the PA as Biggles and commented that I thought people usually had two roller skates, he shook his fist at me.

The association with Burton Ale continued in **1993** and **1994**, when the new acts in 1993 included the Sophie Bancroft Trio, Freddie King, the Tees Valley Jazz Men, the Two Step Ticklers, The Goodbye Look (this sounds a defeatist sort of name to me – I wonder if they got any more bookings?), the Eddie Severn Duo, Edith Budge and Friends, and the Martin Foster Quartet, with an expanded Le Jazz Hot, styling itself a jazz orchestra. There were also to be 'Strolling Players and Street Performers' each afternoon and a notable new venue was the Cruise Ship Edinburgh, a large vessel permanently moored at The Shore. The 1993 street parade was to include, in addition to the Criterion and Auld Reekie Parade Bands, the George Heriot's Swing Band, Picante, the Jackson Five (not <u>that</u> one surely?) and the popular and decorative Brolly Dollies. Additional attractions were an Antique and Craft Fair, a Kite Spectacular and Kite Flying Display and a Street Party, which featured some of the parade bands plus Dr McJazz, the Louisiana Ragtime Band and Jazz Company. The 1994 programme had a slightly increased number of venues and brought in the Kevin Dorrian Quartet, Jim Baikie's Jim Jammers and Carol Clegg and Speakeasy and the Honestas Parade Band made its first appearance.

By **1996**, the LJF was in association with Caledonian 80/- Ale and introduced itself proudly as the '...*only entirely free Jazz Festival in Scotland'*. There were eleven venues and top of the bill was a guest from Canada, Mose Scarlett, described as a crooner and raconteur whose '...*musical* *cache includes countless gems of Jazz, Blues, Ragtime and Swing'.* Most of the old favourites returned and included for the first time, amongst many others, were the local Broughton High School Big Band, the Porky Boys, the Dave Keir Quartet, the Jean Mundell Trio and the Edinburgh University Big Band with Fionna Duncan. Other newcomers were the Jazz Ecosse All Stars and the Duck Fat Jazz Band with both the Lochwinnoch Carnival Orchestra and the New Orleans Wanderers joining the parade bands out on the streets.

The LJFs for **1997**, **1998** and **1999** continued the association with the Caledonian Brewery and kept faith with many of the stalwarts from previous years. Welcome additions were the Dougie Campbell Trio, the Liz MacEwan Quartet and the Portobello High School Jazz Band, with Brian Carrick's Heritage Hall Stompers making a return after an absence of several years. 1998 saw the debut of the local Yelly Dug Jazz Band, Eddie Hamilton's St Stephen Street Stompers, the Jack Duff Band and the Jack Finlay Trio. Other debutants included Blues Incorporated, the Dana Dixon Blues Band, Dr Chicago, Some Days are Diamonds and another band with a slightly discouraging sort of name, Mud in Your Ear! This reminds me of Eddie Condon's famous question when contrasting some of the less harmonious of the bebop sounds with older jazz. Condon asked *'Does it enter the ear like broken glass or like honey?'* but I wonder what would he have made of jazz entering the ear like mud?! In addition, the 1998 street events were augmented by a Big Band Extravaganza and the Edinburgh Samba School, both scheduled for Tower Place. Local first timers for 1999 were the Gus Ferguson Fast Five, the Rootsie Tootsie Blues Band, the West End Jazz Band, the Roy Percy Trio and a band simply billed as Mike Hart's Jazz Band. Other newcomers included the Arhoolies, the Chilli Dogs, Jazz Incident, Quintet East, Sugar House, Swing Bridge and Le Vieux Jazz Men.

The 1999 LJF was followed by two blank years when there was no festival but happily **2002** saw a resumption of activities. Caledonian Brewery seemed to have dropped out as sponsors but the printed programme had an introductory spiel by Lord Provost of Edinburgh, Lord

Lieutenant and Admiral of the Forth Eric Milligan who said that the Council was '...*delighted to be supporting the Festival along with a number of commercial sponsors*'[186]. In fact, the organisation of the LJF seemed to be in slightly different hands, a statement in the programme announcing that the 'Leith Jazz Festival is a Mike Hart Festival Production' with an organising committee chaired by Paul Nolan, Councillors Tom Ponton and Brian Fallon in the role of organising secretaries with Mike Hart himself and his colleague Jim Thomson as treasurer, representing 'Mike Hart Festival Productions'. Tribute was paid to Lord Provost Eric Milligan, Councillors Steve Cardownie and Phil Attridge, Sir Tom Farmer and Norrie Thomson's volunteers, '...*without whom the festival could not have taken place*'. There was a new spread of venues this year as well, which included Ocean Blue, Mariachi, the Cameo Bar, Club Java, the Persevere Bar, the Waterline, Nobles, the Central Bar, the Waterfront, Ocean Terminal and Next Generation, with a street parade and another outdoor event at Commercial Quay. A free jazz bus, supplied by Lothian Buses and featuring 'some fine music' was to tour the venues at thirty minute intervals. The programme continued to feature many of the bands which had played over the first ten years of the LJF while a number of new faces included Delta Croft Review, the Louisiana Shakers, the Pat Quin Four, Rev Doc, the Standard Bearers, the Todd Gordon Quartet, Vent D'est, Joe Gordon's Banjos and the local Roger Hanley's Jazz Hounds.

Sadly, the 2002 Leith Jazz Festival was to be the last of what had been a very worthwhile and innovative project. The lack of major sponsorship from a brewer meant that there was no longer a list of the brewer's pubs as convenient venues and for 2002, there had been a scramble to secure a suitable scatter of suitable premises. In spite of strenuous efforts to attract new sponsors and supporters, it became clear that the Leith Jazz Festival was no longer financially viable. Reluctantly, the organisers accepted the inevitable and Scotland's only completely free jazz festival came to an end. It had been a brave and highly successful

---

[186] Milligan Rt Hon Eric, Leith Jazz Festival programme for 2002

venture in spite of being cursed by several years of foul weather and, given that it was free to the punters, it had done extraordinarily well to run for a total of eleven years. In my view, a view I know was shared by many jazzers, Leith, with its historic waterfront, old pubs of character and picturesque streets, was a highly atmospheric and conveniently compact location for a jazz festival. Perhaps it would not be too fanciful to say that it was possible to feel something of the romance and waterside image of New Orleans. Its demise was a sad loss and it was to be greatly missed by musicians and punters alike for whom it felt like a gaping hole in the annual jazz panorama, as we moved on into the first decade of the new century.

The trio **Le Jazz Hot** had turned up in the inaugural Leith jazz event in 1990 and was led by **reeds player Martin Foster**. Martin had been born in Edinburgh in 1962 and his early interest in jazz had been sparked by listening to some of his Dad's records, which featured the likes of the Chris Barber and Sid Phillips bands. He took up the clarinet when he was still at school, after hearing the American clarinetist Peanuts Hucko playing with the Syd Lawrence Orchestra in the Usher Hall. Hucko was, of course, a very fine reeds player who had played with many great bands, including those of Glenn Millar, Benny Goodman and Eddie Condon. He had also been a member of the Louis Armstrong All Stars for a couple of years in the late 1950s. I remember once hearing him described as a sort of 'Dixieland Benny Goodman', which I considered unfairly dismissive of a very good player, although he certainly processed some of the smooth technical ease of Goodman. It is perhaps not surprising then, to hear that Martin found himself attracted to the playing of Goodman himself and that of his fellow great Swing stylist, Artie Shaw. Very much in the same stylistic pattern, Martin told me that, once he had started sitting in with some of the Edinburgh bands in the late 1970s, he reckoned that he had picked up some useful tips from Jimmy Shortreed, another clarinetist firmly in the Swing tradition, whom he considered an early and encouraging influence.

Martin also took up the alto saxophone and developed his playing by becoming a member of the Edinburgh Youth

Jazz Orchestra, run by Jimmy Grossart, before moving onto soprano and later baritone sax. Not content with playing these instruments, he was to go on adding new ones, finally playing all the members of the sax family, from the tiny sopranino right through to the enormous bass sax, as well as bass clarinet and flute. With an impressive array of instruments at his command, he was well able to take on the demanding role of the only horn fronting a trio and, in 1989, he formed Le Jazz Hot, together with Raymond Gillespie on guitar and Roy Percy on bass, making their mark at the LJF in 1990 as we have heard. This same band was included in the EIJF in 1991, when the official Programme hailed **Raymond Gillespie (guitar)** as a player who '...*in spite of his tender years has already graduated from being a Reinhardt clone to develop his own unique style*'.

The combination of a large range of instruments as well as the ability and flexibility of his co-conspirators in the rhythm section to respond to changes in style and dynamics, meant that even within the apparent limitations of a trio, Le Jazz Hot was particularly known for its wide-ranging repertoire and versatility. Inspired by the approach of the small groups of the twenties led by the likes of Joe Venuti, Le Jazz Hot featured a truly eclectic repertoire, influenced by the sounds of Bechet, Gerry Mulligan, Goodman, Adrian Rollini, Ellington, and Mozart, along with occasional flurries of Klezmer and Tango. As Roy Percy once said, the music of Le Jazz Hot featured '...*everything from Ragtime to lounge music*' - often within a single number. It was once described as the biggest three-piece band in the country. The 1991 EIJF Programme also alerted readers to look out for the expanded Le Jazz Hot Orchestra at the Cotton Club. This was a line-up which occasionally augmented the trio with trumpet, trombone, tenor sax and drums. It played a variety of music from the early Ellington repertoire through to touches of Spike Jones and his City Slickers.

It would be sometime in the early 1990s that I first heard Martin and what struck me, as it did everyone who heard him play, was his fleet-fingered ability to play his instruments at great speed. This was to be further demonstrated years later when, at a concert in the Queen's Hall in 2003, he astonished everyone by playing the traditional clarinet chorus from High Society, a renowned test piece for clarinet, on the bass sax!

As well as keeping various versions of le Jazz Hot going, Martin moved into other jazz settings and, over the years, featured with Francis Cowan, Fat Sam's Band, the Tommy Samson Big Band, the Dick Lee Septet and Ken Mathieson's Classic jazz Orchestra. Although he describes himself as a clarinetist at heart, Martin Foster has continued to play all the saxes but with a penchant for the baritone and bass, as it is his contention that '...with sax, size really does matter'!

Bill Salmond's Louisiana Ragtime Band entered the 1990s seven years into their long Navaar House residency, which was to continue for many years yet. The line-up of the band at the start of the decade was Brian Robertson (tpt), Dave Paxton (clt), Graham Scott (pno), Bill himself (bjo), Graham Blamire (bs), Roy Dunnett (drms) with Bob Craig (tbn) being replaced in 1990 by Alan Quinn. **Alan Quinn (trombone, piano)** had been born in Leith on 9th May 1943 and always considered himself to be a 'Leither'. He attended Holy Cross Academy and was to become a structural engineer. Alan had two elder brothers, Tommy who was some fifteen years older and Jimmy about twelve years older, who were both musicians. Tommy played saxophone and Jimmy piano and, while both of them played a lot of dance music, both were interested in and played early Be-bop jazz, frequently with Johnny Smith, another Leither, on trumpet. The two elder Quinns also played in resident dance bands at the Maybury Roadhouse out on the Glasgow Road, Tommy playing with Danny Dorrian's band in one hall while Jimmy played a couple of evenings each week, in another hall in the same building.

When he was five years old, Alan's father made him a model tin sax and this, plus his brothers' playing, stimulated an early interest in music. His first real instrument was piano and he had some piano lessons from both brother Jimmy and Danny Dorrian.

Bill Salmond, Alan Quinn and Ian Boyter
When Kit Carey sent this photo to Ian Boyter he said *'I*
noticed the notice behind you and noticed that you had
taken no notice of the notice'!
(by permission of Kit Carey)

However, an accident which left him with tendon damage in an arm put an end to his career as a pianist and, at about seventeen, after hearing Acker Bilk's Paramount Jazz Band on the radio, he bought himself a trombone. As a budding trombonist, Alan was taken under the wing of the famous Leith Silver Band, which provided him with some tuition and with whom he played alongside a trumpeter called Donald Bremner. Donald Bremner, like Alan, would also become involved in the Edinburgh jazz scene when he played, albeit for only a short time in 1961, with the schoolboy Mound City Jazz Band, which included the clarinettist Gerard Dott, drummer Mike Travis and the present writer on double bass.

It was not long before Alan made his debut in Edinburgh jazz, joining an early Bill Salmond band called the Savoy Jazz band, followed by Jack St Clair's band and also playing with the Climax Jazz band, in which he replaced Jack Weddell during his time away in London. Alan was to find himself drawn into the purist New Orleans style of jazz, although he says that this was not really through any conscious choice on his part. He reports that it came about as *'almost an accident'* through playing with Bill Salmond's band and the Climax band, both bands in the New Orleans tradition. However, an allegiance to New Orleans jazz suited him very well as it introduced him to the Deep South sound of George Lewis's trombone player, Jim Robinson, who was to remain Alan's model for the rest of his playing career. Alan was to remain associated with the New Orleans style of jazz throughout his long, although interrupted, career in Edinburgh jazz. He reckons that his Bebop inclined brothers must have been fairly taken aback by his adherence to an early form of jazz but, if they were, they put no obstacles in his path. However, another force was soon to put a stop to his jazz playing.

Keen to play, Alan soon discovered that there was an active dance band scene in Edinburgh in which he saw the potential for more playing opportunities. Clearly feeling that the trombone was not all that much in demand in the dance bands, in 1967 Alan bought himself a bass guitar, taught himself how to play it and, for the next sixteen years, confined his playing to dance band gigs. It was not to be until 1983 that he was to return to jazz. It came about through going to listen to clarinettist Eddie Hamilton's band, the St Stephen Street Stompers, where he jumped at the chance of a sit-in with the band and found himself hooked again. In the mid-1980s, he formed a band of his own, the Templehall Stompers, named after their residency in the Portobello area of town, the Templehall Hotel. This was clearly again to be a band in the New Orleans tradition, the original line-up including Fraser Gauld (tpt), Eddie Hamilton (clt), Beverley Knight (bjo), Jimmy Tunnah (bs) and Eric Jamieson (drms). Later, after the sad death of Jimmy Tunnah, Lindsay Cooper played bass for a while before Ken Macdonald came in. Further changes would bring in Brian Robertson on trumpet and Bill Salmond on banjo, while Jim Petrie also did some sessions with them on trumpet.

While continuing to play with his own band at the Templehall Hotel, Alan was to join Bill Salmond's Louisiana

Ragtime Band in 1990 in which, as we have heard, he replaced the veteran RHS gangster, Bob Craig. The LRB line-up that Alan joined was Brian Robertson (tpt), Dave Paxton (clt), Graham Scott (pno), Bill Salmond (bjo), Graham Blamire (bs) and Roy Dunnett (drms). A few years later, when Brian Robertson left the LRB, Alan played on in a two man front-line, first of all in partnership with Dave Paxton, then, when Dave left, with George Gilmour. The LRB two man front-line, sharing the lead between clarinet and trombone, would continue for most of the next two decades, right through to the end of the long-running Navaar House Hotel gig in 1999 and beyond, well through the first decade of the new century.

Later, when the Templehall Hotel changed hands and the gig came to an end and the successful replacement gig at Miller's Foundry Bowling Club also ended, Alan gave up band leading, feeling that he simply needed a break. As the 2000s moved on and the number of active jazzers around the Edinburgh jazz scene became fewer, Alan was to find himself in ever greater demand, eventually playing simultaneously with the LRB, the Spirits of Rhythm, the Anti-Climax Jazz Band and also playing some jazz in a mainstream style with the reeds player, Ian Boyter. Always a player with a great sense of swing and a vigorous, full sound, Alan was also a good singer and an entertaining band leader with a particularly nice line in humour. His sixteen year sabbatical between 1967 and 1983 was a major loss to Edinburgh jazz but it was good in 1983 to welcome back to the fold a player who always seemed to me to have a natural affinity for jazz. An endlessly good humoured and very likeable personality and a gifted communicator, Alan's comeback to Edinburgh jazz was highly successful and, for almost another thirty years, his playing and singing was something to be sought for on the Edinburgh jazz scene, always adding great drive and swing to all the bands with which he played. Sadly, Alan Quinn, one of the best liked of all Edinburgh jazzers, died of cancer on 4th February 2011, at the age of only sixty seven.

I had played bass with the Louisiana Ragtime Band, in addition to the Jazz Masters, between 1985 and 1992 and, when I left, it was Bill Brydon who took over. **Bill Brydon**

(sousaphone, double bass) was born in Edinburgh on 30th December 1963 but was to attend school in the Border country, at Galashiels Academy, and go on to have career as a Director of Human Resources. His conversion to jazz came about through a friend at University who let him hear a recording of Jelly Roll Morton's 'The Chant' and Bill reports that he was *'hooked instantly'*. It is extraordinary how frequently descriptions of a 'Eureka Moment' have cropped up when gathering data for this book. Many jazzers have reported similar immediate turnings on to jazz through a single exposure to the music. Both bass player Jim Young and drummer Kenny Milne have spoken of how they had felt the hairs on the back their necks rise, when they first heard certain jazz recordings and it was the same in my case. It happened for me at school when, late one summer term, our English teacher, 'Kipper' Heron, invited the class to bring in favourite records to play and explain to the class why we liked them. I remember taking a skiffle record but it was the playing of someone else's choice, a recording of the Kid Ory band playing Swanee River, that was my instant turn-on to jazz. I lost no time in buying a copy of the LP for myself and I still have it which, even after more than fifty years, still has the power to remind me of that first magical realization that this was the music for me. In common with Jim Young, it was the rhythm that affected me and, to this day, I consider swing to be the one really indispensible ingredient of jazz.

Bill Brydon had started in music by learning to play cornet in his school band before eventually switching to the tuba. In time, he transferred his brass bass expertise to the tuba's bigger brother, the sousaphone. It was on this enormous instrument that Bill made his first appearances on the Edinburgh jazz scene, playing in Kenny Milne's Criterion Jazz Band from 1986 until 1993. The sousaphone that Bill played had an interesting history, having been played in an Edinburgh professional band called Leslie Jeffries' Rialto Orchestra, which had made a number of recordings in the 1920s. Bill joined Jim Petrie's four-piece band, the Diplomats of Jazz, in 1990 and remains a member of this band more than twenty years on, in 2011. Later, with the encouragement of Bill Salmond, Bill added the double bass to his musical weaponry and opened up a second and parallel jazz career for himself, continuing to play sousaphone with the Diplomats and joining Bill Salmond's Louisiana Ragtime band on string bass. Bill replaced me with the LRB when I left in the early 1990s and he has managed to accommodate the demands of both these successful bands over many years, appearing on a number of recordings with each[187].

Like Bev Knight, Bill quotes bands rather than individuals when he talks about his jazz influences, listing amongst them McKinney's Cotton Pickers, the Fletcher Henderson Orchestra and King Oliver's Dixie Syncopators. When asked about great names he had played with, he said that there were none, although he had stood in an Edinburgh pub queue once with the great bass player, Milt Hinton! Bill had taken the chance to ask him about Tiny Parham's Bluesicians, a band with whom Hinton had recorded in the 1930s. On another occasion, he had got close enough to Benny Waters to ask him about arrangements he had written for the Charlie Johnson Paradise Orchestra in the mid-1920s. Asked about memorable gigs he had played, he cited an occasion when, with Bill Salmond's band, he had played in a beautiful, wooden-built, 17th century church in Sweden, recalling that, when the audience got to their feet, the ancient wooden balconies had started to bounce up and down, causing a certain amount of consternation in the band.

In playing both brass and string bass, Bill Brydon reflects what was once the norm in jazz, when early players with a responsibility for the bass line, like Pops Foster and John Kirby, routinely played whichever was required by the band's musical arrangements. The important difference in Bill's case was that he played the two instruments in separate bands and very wise too, in my opinion. Even with modern transport, the thought of carrying both a sousaphone and a double bass to every gig is a daunting one, fraught with the risks of prolapsed inter-vertebral discs and worse, and how they managed in the early days is beyond me.

---

[187] See discography Appendix

479

The trumpeter Brian Robertson, who had been with Bill Salmond's Louisiana Ragtime Band since 1986, left the band sometime in 1994. However, while still playing with the LRB, in 1987 he had begun playing with Alan Quinn's Templehall Stompers, at their residency in the Templehall Hotel. This was another well supported gig and they usually packed the place on Thursday evenings. When the Templehall gig finally folded and the band moved to a new regular spot at the Millers Foundry Bowling Club in Parker Terrace, off Portobello Road, Brian went with them. The new place was just as successful as the Templehall had been, as the crowd moved with the band, and the tradition of packed Thursday evenings continued until 2000, when this residency too came to an end. Anxious to keep a regular spot going, Brian Robertson went to the nearby Ellwyn Hotel in Portobello Road and asked if there was any possibility of playing there. Perhaps aware that the band had been bringing in good business at the bowling club, the answer was yes. However, as Alan Quinn had decided to take a break, Brian found himself putting a band into the Ellwyn Hotel himself, thus beginning his career as a band leader.

Initially, he put in a four piece band with himself, Eddie Hamilton, Brian Weld on banjo and Bill Brydon on bass. When the veteran Brian Weld took a break from playing for a while, his temporary replacement was Andrew Mulhern, who had by then added banjo playing to his skills on trombone. Brian Robertson later decided to expand the bands scope and expanded it into a five-piece by adding Graham Scott on piano. The Ellwyn gig attracted a very loyal following, including some who came along for a sit in with the band, regulars being Jimmy Welsh with his trumpet, and Bill Brown on banjo, each of whom seldom missed a night over the all the years the gig lasted. They always got a sit in, this adding greatly to the atmosphere of a friendly and welcoming gig. Drummer Frank Birnie, at his long-running gig at the Blue Lagoon, followed the same policy, actively looking for sitters in, and there is no doubt at all that it added to the popularity of the gig, as well as encouraging jazzers who seldom played. At the Ellwyn, other regulars to play with the band were Alan Quinn and the afore-mentioned Andrew Mulhern, on trombone this time, who would often arrive with their horns and usually end up playing the whole night. After a while, the bass player Bill Brydon left the band and Owen Macdonald, son of Ken and the latest in the seemingly endless line of bass playing Macdonalds, came in. Owen was a student at the time and Brian remembers that he would sometimes set up a music stand with his University notes on it and get on with his studies, while Owen himself and the rest of the band were playing! The punters apparently just assumed that he was reading the music. After Owen left, his dad, Ken, took over on bass.

Brian had called the band the **Ellwyn Stompers** and they made a CD in 2002 to which he gave the name 'The Ellwyn Stompers (almost) Live at the Ellwyn Hotel'[188]. The Ellwyn residency ran for a good ten years or so, only ending in May 2010, to the lasting regret of its many regulars, or as Brian says, those who had not already gone to the great Preservation Hall in the Sky! In fact, Brian had put his finger on a serious and increasing problem. Just as the average age of the bands tended to increase by one for every year that passed, so did that of the punters. Just as there were very few young musicians coming into traditional jazz, so there was a sad lack of young punters coming along. I think we all knew it, although nobody had any answer for it and, as far as the pub residencies were concerned, the writing was beginning to appear all too clearly on the wall.

Brian Robertson was to form a second band in 2000, this one for the purposes of making recordings and playing club gigs and festivals, rather than with any intention of seeking a residency. Regular gigs included Pete Davenport's jazz nights at Tullbannocher in Comrie and also evenings at Mugdock, a country park north of Milnegavie near Glasgow, which put on jazz nights several times a year. I did several of these latter nights with the band and thoroughly enjoyed the tiny and always well-filled theatre, which had good acoustics and a great atmosphere. The new seven-piece band Brian called the **Forth River Ragtimers** and its membership was Brian himself on trumpet and vocals,

---

[188] See discography Appendix

481

Sandy Barclay from the Borders who played trombone until about 2007 when he was replaced by John Arthur, Eddie Hamilton (clt), Graham Scott (pno), Brian Weld (bjo), Ken Macdonald (bs) and, persuaded out of retirement, Roy Dunnett (drms). Between 2000 and 2009, the Forth River Ragtimers produced four CDs[189], with a fifth due to be recorded in early 2011.

A sad but inevitable effect of the passing years became all too clear in 1993, which saw the deaths of three Edinburgh jazz stalwarts. **Dave Paxton**, who had been playing latterly with Jim Petrie's band, became ill and died on 19th April 1993, just a few days after his sixty seventh birthday. A band was put together to play at Dave's funeral and it included Al Fairweather, Jim Petrie and Dave Strutt (tpts), Bob Craig and Dave Keir (tbns), Jack Graham and Jack Duff (rds), Mike Hart (bjo) and Dizzy Jackson (bs). An obituary by Tony Troon appeared in the Scotsman in which he, rightly, called Dave a *'rare talent'*[190]. I also contributed an appreciation in which I hailed him a *'master of the classic jazz clarinet'*, remarking on the great enthusiasm he brought to his music and emphasising his ability to play *'...originally and personally within a long established idiom, allowing it to continue as a living tradition rather than mere reproduction of a past era'*[191].

Al Fairweather, as well as playing in the band, had also spoken eloquently at Dave's funeral and it was a considerable shock when Al himself died, just a few weeks later, on 21st June 1993, at the age of sixty six. Tony Troon again contributed an obituary in the Scotsman and commented on Al's recorded output, noting that his performances stood out as *'...adventurous and unusual in the catalogue of traditional-mainstream jazz'*. Tony also remarked on Al's talent as an arranger, particularly noting his work with the Brown-Fairweather band of the 1950s, when his skill at *'...placing new ideas in a context which had to win over a basically conservative audience, managed to*

---

[189] See discography Appendix
[190] Troon A, 'Dave Paxton: Jazz Clarinettist', The Scotsman, April 1993
[191] Blamire G, 'A master of the classic jazz clarinet', The Scotsman', 26th April 1993

assert itself against the odds'[192]. John Gibson also paid tribute, linking Al's name with that of Sandy Brown, and pointing out that *'A stack of recordings, many of which do not sound dated today, is their legacy, along with memories galore to be cherished by jazz fans and friends here and countless musicians down south, who held their music in the highest esteem'[193].*

The third blow of a sad year came in December when **Jackie MacFarlane** died at the age of seventy three. Again there were tributes in the Scotsman and the Evening News and there were letters to the newspapers too, which spoke of him as a natural charmer and said how much he would be missed. One letter said that Jackie had been one of the nicest and kindest people that the writer had ever known. We have already heard how, in the early days, Jackie and Sean Connery were fellow bouncers at the Jazz Band Balls in the Oddfellows Hall in Forrest Road. I understand that, after Jackie died, a newspaper reported that the former Lord Provost, Eleanor MacLaughlin, who had supervised Connery's investiture as a Freeman of the City, had got in touch with the film star's agents to tell them of the loss. To her surprise, she shortly afterwards received a phone call and a voice said *'Hello Eleanor, its Sean here....'.* Connery explained that film contracts prevented him from getting back for the funeral but he subsequently sent a sympathetic letter which was passed on to Jackie's family. John Gibson, in an article in the Evening News, said *'A man who brought much pleasure to music lovers is to get his own memorial in the city'[194].* This was a reference to the setting up of a bench in Nicholson Square with a plaque which, it was planned, would say *'In memory of Edinburgh's Mister Jazz, from his fellow artists, friends and music lovers'.* Charlie McNair, Dave Strutt, Bob Craig, Dave Keir, Mike Hart and Dizzy Jackson all played in the band at Jackie's funeral. Years later, in 1998, I was asked to write an article about Jackie for a south side local magazine and I ended it

---

[192] Troon A, 'Al Fairweather: jazz trumpeter', The Scotsman', 22nd June 1993

[193] Gibson John, 'City loses top jazzman Al', The Edinburgh Evening News, 22nd June 1993

[194] Gibson John, 'Jackie's melodies linger on', Edinburgh evening News, December 1993

by saying *'...he was unique and, whatever else, a lot of people thought well of him'*.

**Plaque on Jackie MacFarlane's memorial seat in
Nicholson Square
(photograph by the author)**

As the years passed, the losses continued with the death of **Bob Craig** at the age of seventy on 4th August 1998. Towards the end of his life, Bob had tended to confine his playing to the Criterion Brass Band, the Edinburgh marching band run by Kenny Milne. Bob had played with that band at the EIJF Mardi Gras in the Grassmarket just a couple of days previously and had seemed well and in good form. However, sadly, he collapsed after suffering a stroke at home the next day and died in the Royal Infirmary just a day later. Bob had been an integral part of the Edinburgh jazz scene for fifty years and, with his death, we lost a real character. John Gibson paid tribute in the Evening News and quoted Bob's long time friend and colleague, Dizzy Jackson, as saying *'At his peak, Bob was well-rated and was ever ready to blow. He never had a bad word to say about anybody and nobody had a bad word for him. He* *plunged into the Mardi Gras with typical enthusiasm'.* John also quoted Charlie McNair as saying *'Bob played in my band off and on for five years. He was just a lovely bloke'[195].* The Criterion Brass band played at Bob's funeral, which was a simple grave side ceremony, Bob having not been a religious man. It was strange to see the band without Bob at the front with his trombone. Members of his family paid tribute to him as did his former classmate Bill Strachan, and a recording of Bob playing the tune 'Ory's Creole Trombone' with an early Sandy Brown band, was played. He was a huge miss on the local jazz scene, not only because of his playing, but also because of his cheery, good-natured and endlessly optimistic personality. As Alastair Clark put it, *'A truly lovely man'[196].*

The importance of the jazz followers, the punters, should never be underestimated. Without them there would be no scene at all or, at best, sad and lonely musicians playing for their own amusement behind closed doors. In fact, in the case of quite a number of the punters, their contribution went far beyond simply turning up to support bands. Many were willing helpers at the EIJF, taking on all manner of responsibilities, acting as couriers, drivers, venue organisers and, minders (especially for some of the more elderly visiting jazzers), and generally making sure that all the unseen and sometimes thankless tasks were covered. However, there were several loyal and hard-working punters whose efforts went still further. In March 1989, Bill Bruce and Elliott Davies launched a publication called The Scottish Jazz News. This was to be a regular free production, sent out to all EIJF volunteers and with supplies of copies available at all the regular jazz venues. In addition, for only £2 a year, you could have a copy mailed to you. The venture was, at least in part, subsidised by advertising, but I suspect that Bill and Elliott carried some of the costs themselves, particularly at the start. The main content at first was a comprehensive gig listing, covering all the many weekly jazz gigs in Edinburgh, with

---

[195] Gibson John, 'Sadness as jazz legend dies', Edinburgh Evening News, August 1998

[196] Clark A, 'Obituaries – Bob Craig', 'Scotsman', 5 August 1998

additional information about one-off gigs. Listings and one-off information were also given for Glasgow, Saltcoats, Kilmarnock, Ayr, Greenock, Inverness, Dumfries, Perth, even Belfast and Tyne and Wear and many more areas would be added later. There was a letters page, a couple of articles, news about jazz festivals in the offing and even a competition, which offered EIJF tapes as prizes.

The intended circulation dates were unclear but it was hoped at the start to have the next edition out in May of that year. In fact, the organizers beat that date with an edition in April which included all the previous features and appealed for contributors such as writers, cartoonists and cross word puzzle compilers. There was a leading article on the forthcoming Glasgow Jazz Festival and a review of the Bude Jazz Festival. With some trepidation I also ventured into print in this issue, albeit anonymously. I had written sleeve notes for the Scottish Jazz Advocates LP 'All in Perfect Working Order', which had a tartan theme designed for the American market. In the sleeve notes, I had developed the tartan theme, lampooning the band, writing each member up under a pseudo-Scottish Mickey-taking name which purported to caricature their personalities. The drummer Chick Murray, of a mildly grumbly and critical disposition, was given the name Crabbit McGrump and pianist Tom Finlay, supposedly a hard headed businessman, was Graspin McCash. For the Jazz News, I invented an environment called the Edinburgh Jazz Jungle and populated it with a whole range of strange, musical, animal inhabitants under the tile 'The Bestiary of Jazz'. The series was prefaced with the statement *This exciting, fascinating, serialised account will take you, for the first time, into real contact with the inhabitants of a unique and highly specialized habitat – the Edinburgh Jazz Jungle'.*

I dug out these writings recently and I have to say they are fairly cringe-making in retrospect. Trombone playing Bob Craig with his trademark moustache appeared under the genus 'Glissinfartinsliders', with his specific name of 'Raspinroarin Raftache', and poor old Mike Hart, banjo player and antique dealer, came out as 'Djanglemikehart Junkenhustler'. Looking at these 'portraits' now, I was lucky not to be lynched although, in my defence, I did clear them with each victim before they went to print. In addition to my efforts, the second edition of Jazz News also reported that the graffiti on the Basin Street ladies' loo wall included the announcement *'I love Kenny Milne – he plays a mean drum'*. The perpetrator of this public declaration of affection is unfortunately not known but it does remind me of my favourite bit of pub graffiti. Sometime in the 1960s, one of the Rose Street pubs, clearly fed up with graffiti all over the loo walls, invested in a blackboard. This was put up on the wall in the men's loo, handily placed above the urinals, and complete with a little wooden ledge for the chalk. It was a sad failure. The next time I went in, the blackboard was completely blank and beside it, scored about an inch deep into the wall, were the words 'Where is the f- -king chalk?'

Jazz News did very well, each edition containing more and more information about the Scottish jazz scene and attracting plenty of letters of encouragement, some of them even from remote and barely civilised places like Australia and Glasgow. Issue number three came out in June and number four appeared in August 1989, in good time to include a EIJF flyer outlining that year's programme. The magazine was also a very useful means of communication amongst the jazz crowd, helping ambitious punter-trips to be organized to as far-flung a jazz festival as the Sacramento Jazz Jubilee. The magazine itself became more ambitious too, arranging reviewers for all the Scottish jazz festivals and making sure that new jazz ventures were given maximum publicity, often assuring a good turnout even on opening nights. Letters poured in, many of them reminiscing about days gone by, and giving news of jazz elsewhere. Articles appeared about great historical jazz figures such as Jelly Roll Morton and Pee Wee Russell. An interesting slant on the times can be gleaned from the listings, which were headed 'Regular Free Venues'. Jazz News issue number four, dated August 1989, shows an almost incredible fifty-two free weekly gigs in Edinburgh, with ten gigs each Saturday, which I think probably represents the highest point of jazz activity that the City ever reached. By October that year the total had dropped to fifty but on Wednesday evenings, there was a choice of no fewer than twelve venues offering jazz, including Fat Sam's Band at Fat Sam's eatery, Fairweather Friends at Young's Hotel, and Fionna Duncan with the Jack Finlay Trio at the Fairmile Inn, out on the Biggar Road. I have come across no records that show a greater concentration of jazz in Edinburgh than at this time, and almost all of it was free!

Unfortunately, it proved impossible to maintain the Jazz News production rate. In 1990, which saw the commencement of Volume Two of the magazine, with issue numbers one to five appearing in consecutive months between March and July. However, the sixth issue seems not to have appeared until well on in the year and contained an apology from the editors citing pressure of work (ie day job type work) as the reason for the delay. Around this time, the issues also stopped carrying a date, which I think was probably a sign that the editors could not be certain when they would be able to issue it. Number seven of that Volume was also delayed and seems not to have appeared until after April 1991, judging by the reports of events included. The new Volume Three started sometime in 1991 but probably not much before the EIJF in August, instead of March when it should have begun, and it appears that only three more issues came out. The last I have, issue three of Volume Three, seems to have been issued sometime between April and August 1992 and, as I am sure I would have kept any others that appeared, that seems to have been the last one.

It was a pity that the venture came to a halt. It was great while it lasted, full of useful information about regular gigs, one-off events, jazz festivals and a forum where jazzers could express their views and reminisce about old times. It even began to print quite prickly letters, indicative of ruffled feathers, the first issue of Volume Three including a letter complaining bitterly about upheavals in the membership of Glasgow's George Penman band. Both George and the apparent victims of the upheaval went into print with explanations designed to calm the multitudes, but it was good to see a bit of spice amongst the more common epistles of praise and fond memories; more of such spice would have been very welcome, in my view. The Scottish Jazz News was a noble effort and was to be much missed but I think it probably came to an end for an all too common reason. Nearly all good ideas of this sort are driven by the selfless dedication of a very small number of people, in this case hardly more than two or three. Energies are bound to run down, work and family concerns are bound to exert pressure and enthusiasms can become eroded. There needs to be recognition of the real pressures of driving an ambitious project like this and some sort of 'succession planning' put in place. Bill Bruce and Elliott Davies, both alas now gone, did the Edinburgh jazz scene proud, and were to do so again, but what a pity some of us did not read the clear warning signs that they were feeling the pressure. Some of us could have pitched in with a bit of help or even an offer to take over the show for a while, allowing them to ease out, at least temporarily. However, Jazz News came to an end, as all good things do, and it has to be said, there would soon be other signs that the boom years were passing too.

There was another jazz punter driven initiative in the late 1990s. Again it involved Elliott Davies but this time in partnership with another loyal and long-term supporter of the Edinburgh jazz scene, Roy MacGregor. By 1997, the EIJF had been around for about eighteen years and, not unnaturally, there had been a number of changes in both direction and format. Mike Hart was still at the helm but it had been necessary to add a number of others to the festival board, including Assembly Direct as co-promoters, and there was no doubt that the proportion of more modern and contemporary jazz had increased. It was in 1997 too that the jazz festival was to restyle itself the Edinburgh International Jazz and Blues Festival (EIJBF), although a separate Blues Festival had run in tandem with the EIJF for year or two prior to this. In addition to new influences on policy and programming, the part played by the local traditional jazz bands was now less prominent and there seems to have been a fear that, with the withdrawal of the McEwan's sponsorship in the mid-1990s, the free pub trail would be very much diminished or even disappear completely. This seems to have been a realistic fear as the 1995 EIJF had included a McEwan's Pub Trail with seven venues all offering free admission and both lunch time and

489

evening sessions whereas, by 1997, the EIJF had replaced the free pub trail with two free outdoor events, the Commonwealth Mardi Gras in the Grassmarket and the Commonwealth Jazz on a Summer's Day, set around the Ross Theatre in Princes Street Gardens.

Concerned and unhappy about these changes, the energetic Davies and MacGregor set out to demonstrate that there was still a large number of faithful supporters who wanted to listen to the local bands in free venues and that they would turn up in sufficient numbers to keep the publicans happy. Accordingly, a mini-festival was set up to run concurrently with the EIJBF, offering a programme of ten bands playing in a couple of venues, both free of charge. The two venues were the Caley Sample Room, formerly the Blue Lagoon and a year-round jazz pub, and the Royal Ettrick Hotel, only a short walk from the Sample Room and another regular jazz venue. The programme was quite ambitious in that it was to run over eight days from the 4th to the 10th of August, and the organisers managed to book most of the local traditional bands. Those who played in the mini-festival that year were the Spirits of Rhythm, Bill Salmond's Louisiana Ragtime Band, Jim Baikie's Jim-jammers, Dr McJazz, the St Stephen Street Stompers, Le Jazz Hot, the Dave Keir Jazztet, Charlie McNair's Jazz Band, the Diplomats of Jazz, Bill Marshall's Dixie Elastic Band and a twelve-piece band put together by bass player Fred Murray. In addition, there was the Tweed Valley Jazz Band from the Borders and a special guest appearance of a group of Sengalese Drummers.

The Caledonian Brewery had been approached and chipped in with a form of sponsorship which took the shape of kegs of their beer provided free to the venues, the sale of which which helped pay for the bands. Further support without charge came from reeds man Ian Boyter, a graphic designer to trade, who provided the art work for the programme free, as a gesture of support. The printed programme stated that *'Our aim is to offer traditional jazz free, during the official Edinburgh Jazz Festival'* and was headed up the 'Sizzling Summer Festival of Jazz'. There was also a further statement which said *'Jazz in Edinburgh owes a large debt to Sandy Brown and Al Fairweather in particular. Many of their contemporaries are playing in the bands listed here and our hope is that the music will inspire future musicians'.* Although there were only evening sessions, the venture was popular and very well supported and was a definite success.

Encouraged by their first venture, the organisers put on a second program in 1998, this time billed as the Edinburgh Jazzcrawl, and again supported by the Caledonian Brewery. In the programme blurb, the previous year was justifiably celebrated by the organisers who said *'Last year we were delighted by the support the venture received. You seemed very happy and filled the venues'.* There was a change in the venues with the Gillsland Hotel replacing the Royal Ettrick and the addition of a third venue, this being W J Christie's, a pub in the West Port, near the Grassmarket. The Jazzcrawl ran over nine days between 31st July and 8th August and featured seventeen bands, including many of the previous year's participants. Newcomers included Alan Quinn's Templehall Stompers, the Yelly Dug Jazz Band, Fay Levey and her Quartet and the Maid of the Forth All Stars. The new venue W J Christie's apparently did not attract quite the support of the other two, perhaps because it was not within walking distance of the others and also because it featured pay-at-the-door events on the first two evenings. In spite of the odd hiccup, the Jazzcrawl was a success, just like its predecessor of 1997, and was again well supported. However, that was to be the end of the experiment and, indeed, it seems very clear that there was never any intention of establishing a long-term rival to the EIJF. The principle objective had been to demonstrate that traditional jazz played in pubs, mostly by the local bands, remained a major draw and, satisfied that they had achieved this, Elliott Davies and Roy MacGregor left it at that.

There is no doubt at all that the free pub trail had been a very popular part of the EIJF but it has to be remembered that it was only free as far as the punters were concerned; the bands still had to be paid. It only existed because of the support and sponsorship of major brewers and it appears that, from the brewer's point of view, it ran at a loss. As we have already noted, a large turnout and a packed lounge does not necessarily mean that there is an equivalent increase in the bar sales. However, Elliot Davies and Roy MacGregor were happy that a point had been made and, even if there would be no return to the heady days of a free pub trail with a generous scattering of venues all over the City, traditional jazz and the local bands would continue to play their part in the future EIJFs, although it was to be the early 2000s before there was much evidence of this. Elliot Davies, endlessly supportive follower of Edinburgh traditional jazz, whose characteristic laugh could so often be heard ringing out even over the sound of a jazz band in full cry, died in the summer of 2010 and a band organized by Bob McDowell played at his funeral.

The name of the Ayrshire trumpeter Mike Daly has already appeared in this chapter, as has that of reeds player John Burgess. These two would eventually get together in a band set up by John Burgess in 2009, the Nova Scotia Jazz Band, the third Edinburgh based band of that name after the 1950s band started by George Crockett and the 1970s version, which had been an off-shoot of the Old Bailey band and played in the Hailes House Hotel. **John Burgess (reeds)** was born in Haddington on the 25th of August 1967 and attended James Gillespie's High School in Edinburgh, between 1979 and '84. Although he was to make a relatively late start as a jazz musician, his interest in jazz had a solid background through his mother Frances, who had been Alex Welsh's girlfriend throughout his years in Edinburgh, the two of them having got together even before Alex met up with Archie Semple and joined Archie's band. Frances had been very much immersed in Edinburgh jazz, through her friendship with Alex, and had known all the 1950s jazz crowd and, although they had drifted apart, had remained friends with Alex right up to time of his death in 1982. She had kept what John calls *'a small but select'* LP collection which included recordings by the likes of Fats Waller, Louis Armstrong, Muggsy Spannier and Jelly Roll Morton, in addition to the recordings of the Alex Welsh band. John Burgess's interest in jazz stemmed from that of his mother and, by 1982 at the age of fifteen, he had volunteered as a helper at the Edinburgh International Jazz Festival.

This was during what many would consider to have been the apogee of the EIJF and gave John the chance to hear many great jazzers at close range. He was particularly taken by the playing of Buddy Tate, Warren Vache and Earle Warren but also recalls with great admiration bands such as Kusbandet, the Hot Antic, the New Black Eagle and the Swedish Jazz Kings, all of which had a major effect on him. He was also an eager listener to the recordings and stories of the Edinburgh jazz greats from the 1950s, which he describes as having been a huge thing for him and his future in jazz. In 1985, when he was seventeen, John managed to procure a clarinet, courtesy of Mike Hart, and from another source, a plastic alto saxophone. He had, in fact, intended to take up the cornet but the secondhand model on which he had his eye in Mev Taylor's shop had been sold when he went back and he was persuaded to buy the alto sax instead. John made the typical jazzer's self-taught start but also took a few lessons from Gordon Cruikshank and reinforced his early learning by transcribing solos from sheet music.

John made a start to his active music career after only a few weeks of playing, when he formed a band with Alex Poots, who now runs the Manchester Festival. I remember him turning up at the 1986 EIFJ young musician's competition in 1987, a year when I was on the judging panel. Once again demonstrating my nerdish tendencies, I still have my notes from that occasion from which I see that the nineteen year old John, by this time playing tenor sax, was leading a quartet called 'Jazz Monk'. I had also jotted down that he played '...*very measured, confident tenor*' and also displayed confidence in his presentation. There was stiff competition among the more modern youthful presentations that year in the form of the young trumpeter Colin Steele fronting another quartet, 'First Light'. Regarding Colin, I had noted '...*very good trumpet with a nice tone and little vibrato*' and his '...*good, fat tone and smooth execution on flugelhorn*'. Both John Burgess and Colin Steele were, of course, to go on to notable success in jazz and I cringe now to think that I once sat in judgement on them but, no matter how convenient it would be, none of us can really escape our past!

The programme for that youth jazz competition included the information that John was already gravitating between Edinburgh and London and, also in 1987, he was to move full time to London. There he played and recorded with many top notch jazz names, too many to list in full but including Alan Skidmore, Jim Mullen, Maggie Nichols, Roy Williams, Forrie Cairns and Brian Kellock. He also appeared at festivals and clubs in Spain, Germany, Finland, Sweden, Denmark, Norway, Italy, the Czech Republic, North Africa and the Middle East and, in 1989, his trio won the prestigious NFMS Special Concert Artist Award.

The boy from Haddington was certainly going places fast and, in 1994, he left London to study under George Garzone at the Berklee School of Music in Boston, USA and also took private tuition from Jerry Bergonzi. This was followed by a move across the USA to San Francisco, where he studied with Joe Henderson, before moving north to Seattle and then settling in Vancouver. A return to Edinburgh in the later 1990s saw John put in four years with Hamish McGregor's Fat Sam's Band, where he sat alongside another great Edinburgh reeds man, Jack Duff, and took part in a couple of recordings[197]. He also did some work with a band put together by pianist Ralph Laing which, as John has noted, '..happily included Al Fairweather'. John returned permanently to the UK and Edinburgh in 2005, where he became briefly a member of Bill Salmond's Louisiana Ragtime Band and free lanced with a number of well-established Edinburgh jazzers, including Gus Ferguson, Martin Foster, Tom Finlay and Hamish McGregor, as well as playing with Edinburgh's famous blues man, Tam White with whom he stayed until Tam's untimely death in 2010.

Talking with John Burgess in 2011 was to discover a man who had played in an impressive spectrum of musical styles. Apart from playing with his own groups and the bands mentioned above, he had also played improvised music with 'GIO', smooth jazz with 'Blue Soul Groove', modern classical music with 'Music from the Brewhouse' and post bop jazz with the 'Chris Wallace Quartet'. He had also collaborated with stellar names such as the New York

---

[197] See discography appendix

pianist and Hammond organ player Gary Valente and bassist John Webber. In addition to all of that, in 2009 he formed the afore-mentioned Nova Scotia Jazz Band which included Mike Daly on trumpet, Duncan Findlay on guitar and banjo and first Roy Percy and then Ken Macdonald on bass. With John Burgess's jazz history in mind, it may seem surprising that this band played in the classic jazz tradition but it was obvious from speaking with John that his regard for jazz was exceptionally wide in its range. He nominated, in chronological order, his jazz influences as Muggsy Spannier, Wild Bill Davison, Archie Semple, Ben Webster, Johnny Hodges and Zoot Sims, a solid and impressive set of milestone musicians in jazz history. He spoke of his admiration for the playing of Dave Paxton, as well as that of the other big names of 1940s/50s Edinburgh jazz. It was clear that he had retained a huge regard for the Alex Welsh band, in whose footsteps the Nova Scotia Jazz Band followed. Indeed, John confirmed that he had based his clarinet playing on that of Archie Semple, the great Edinburgh clarinetist who made his name with the early Alex Welsh band of fond memory. He also spoke of his pride in belonging to a town that had produced, not only the core of the Welsh band but *'...guys like Sandy Brown, Al Fairweather, Stan Greig, Dave Keir et al'* and, successful modern player though he most certainly is, there was not the slightest doubt about his sincerity. At the time of writing in 2011, John has recorded over seventy times as a 'side man' and has issued seven albums as a leader. With all this behind him and every sign of a long and promising career to come, John Burgess is a worthy name in the long list of high class jazz musicians from the Edinburgh area, a man with a deep knowledge of and respect for jazz of all eras.

Now we come to something of a rarity in Edinburgh traditional jazz; a jazz musician who was born as late as 1987! **Jack Wilson (drums)** must have got heartily sick of constantly being referred to as 'Young Jack Wilson', as if he had been baptized that way, but the truth was that, by the age standards of Edinburgh traditional jazz, he seemed virtually embryonic when he first appeared. Jack was born on 8th May 1987 and was educated at Woodlands High

School and then its replacement, Braes High School, both in Falkirk. There was little in the way of jazz to be heard around his home although his parents, who were young in the 1960s, provided him with plenty of exposure to 1960s music, such as that of the Beatles, the Hollies and Rod Stewart. In addition, his relatively rural environment also provided plenty of Ceilidh and Scottish Country Dance music, plus what Jack has called *'a liberal sprinkling of bits and pieces like Val Doonican and Kenneth McKellar'*. Not perhaps the most promising background for a future traditional jazzer but Jack believes that this eclectic musical hotch-potch may well have made him a bit more open minded about music than most of his contemporaries.

His opportunity to start playing drums came in his second year at high school but only because it was a part of the syllabus for S2 students in music, not because he had sought it out. In fact, Jack considers that, if the opportunity had not presented itself in this way, it is quite likely that he would never have played drums. As it was, he turned out to have something of a flair for the instrument and, with an offer of free tuition for Standard Grade students of music, he was able to continue through his third and fourth years and, for three years, he received tuition from Stewart Blackwood, who taught percussion around the Falkirk schools.

Jack's first contact with jazz came through, of all unlikely institutions, the Church of Scotland. Innes Duncan, a family friend and a member of Torphichen Kirk, had organized a band to give young people in the church a chance to play. Amongst them were Innes Duncan's two daughters, each of whom played an instrument and both of whom went with their father to Monday evening sessions in Linlithgow, run by Bob McDowell, to give youngsters the chance to try their hand at playing jazz. Jack soon found himself with an invitation to go along with the Duncan family to one of these sessions. This was the first time young Jack (there I go again) was to play this kind of music and he had no idea what to expect. As a result, he went along with only a pair of drumsticks and ended up battering away on a collection of instrument cases! In attendance at the session, were Tom Bryce, Andrew Lauder and banjo player Hans Koal, all giving up their time to encourage these fortunate youngsters to take an interest in traditional jazz. It was as a result of these sessions that Jack was given the chance to play at the Linlithgow Jazz Club's Christmas party, when he sat in with the West End band on Malcolm Brown's drum kit. Jack was fourteen years old at the time.

His first proper gig was when he was asked to dep for Kenny Milne with the West End band at Gardening Scotland, a horticultural show at the Royal Highland Show ground at Ingliston. He must have done well on his debut because he continued to dep for Kenny over the next year or so and was also given every chance to sit in on Kenny's kit at the Jazz Club. Later, when Kenny stood down from the West End band, Jack was taken on as their regular drummer. Asked about highlights of his years with the band, he picked out gigs when he played with star guests trumpeters Duke Hietger and Bob Barnard and pianist Jeff Barnhart, saying he would be glad to play with them every day, as indeed would most of us. Playing with another fine trumpeter, Enrico Tomasso, in a show at the Falkirk Town Hall was another special gig.

I was interested to hear what Jack had to say about his influences and was not all that surprised when he named, not contemporary rock or jazz drummers, but two jazz drummers representative of earlier styles and from very different environments. One was Gene Krupa, the great Chicagoan who made his name with the Benny Goodman band, picked out by Jack for his endlessly hard-working but not intrusive playing, especially when with the smaller combos, such as the Goodman trios and quartets or the famous McKenzie and Condon Chicagoans. Jack's other influence came from Edinburgh's own Kenny Milne, Dean of New Orleans drummers, to whose playing Jack had listened through his formative years. He could hardly have had a better model and, to this day, Kenny remains someone to whom Jack looks up and whose approval matters to him. Another influence, although not from a drummer, came from banjo player Harald Vox, who put in a number of years with the West End band. At a band rehearsal Harald, fairly unceremoniously, pointed out to Jack just how loudly he was playing and advised that he should cut down the volume pronto. Thereafter Harald, a kindly and considerate individual, continued to encourage Jack to play in a light manner, something for which Jack remains grateful, commenting that he regularly receives compliments from musicians and punters alike, on his ability play quietly. Quite rightly, Jack values such compliments, saying that he would much rather be perceived as a quiet, sensitive player than a portable Blitzkrieg!

Later in his career but still only in his late teens and early twenties, Jack was to join the throng of cross-country travellers, playing in Glasgow with Hugh Muldoon's Jazz and Blues Band in 2005/06 and Davie Wilson's Uptown Shufflers from 2006, while continuing to play with the West End Jazz Band in Linlithgow. Jack is one of the very few recruits from his generation to join the Edinburgh traditional jazz scene. He rapidly gained a deserved reputation as a fine drummer and, by the end of the first decade of the new century, this was reflected in invitations to dep with established Edinburgh bands such as Bill Salmond's Louisiana Ragtime Band, the Maid of the Forth Stompers, Swing Supreme, Mike Hart's Scottish All Stars and John Burgess' Nova Scotia Jazz Band. Jack's career and progress in jazz, with early encouragement at school, the opportunity provided through the church youth activities and then further chances arising via Bob McDowell's sterling work in West Lothian, demonstrate just what can be done to stimulate interest in jazz, even among youngsters in the early twenty first century. However, if traditional jazz is to thrive in the future, there is no doubt that we will need many more like Jack Wilson, not the least of whose contributions to the Edinburgh jazz scene has been to reduce the average age of any band in which he plays by a fair number of years!

Chapter XVII

I Can't Get Finished

The importance of the contributions to jazz of Sandy Brown and Al Fairweather, not just in Edinburgh but internationally, had long been recognised and was well documented in jazz literature. However, by the mid-1990s and with both Sandy and Al by then gone, there was still no formal mark of their achievements in their native city. It was to take the initiative and energy of a Swansea based clarinet player and long time admirer of Sandy's playing to get things moving. He was, of course, Dr John Latham and he wrote to The Scotsman newspaper on 12 June 1996. In his letter, he pointed out that Sandy was *'arguably the most original and innovative British post-war jazz musician'* and added that *'Together with Al Fairweather and Stan Grieg he revolutionised British jazz when he left Edinburgh for London in the mid-1950s'*. Latham then went on to make the case for some form of memorial saying *'...there is no memorial to him in his home town, no museum, no archive, statue, not even a plaque. Is it not time that the jazz fraternity in Scotland planned a suitable scheme in his memory?'*[198] It did not take long for others to express their support and, by the end on the month, Jack Duff, Janol Scott and Dickie Alexander had all written in to the paper.

Clearly not a man to let things slide, John Latham invited anyone interested in the proposal to meet with him

---

[198] SBS Newsletter No 1, July 1996, from letter of John Latham to 'The Scotsman', 12 June 1996

in the bar of the Royal Circus Hotel (previously the Glencairn Hotel) on Saturday 3 August 1996, when he was to be in Edinburgh. This meeting was a great success, with a good turnout including, amongst many others, Sandy's widow, Flo' Brown, and his old colleagues, Stan Grieg and Bob Craig. Dickie Alexander, a recently retired City Councillor, had persuaded the Lord Provost to take an interest and, after the 3rd of August meeting, a committee was formed with the resounding title of 'The Lord Provost's Sandy Brown Memorial Society'. Members who attended the first meeting of the committee were Dickie Alexander (appointed secretary and later, chairman), Bob Craig, Stuart Crockett, Sandy Currie, Mike Hart, Charles 'Dizzy' Jackson, Ralph Laing and Janol Scott, with apologies from Flo' Brown, D Kerr, A Rowan, and D Michie. Others who subsequently joined the committee were Dave Keir, Jack Duff and David Michie, the emeritus Professor of painting from the Edinburgh College of Art. Rightly and logically, it was agreed that the memorial would refer to both Sandy and Al Fairweather, and not Sandy alone. Further meetings followed and a bank account was set up for donations.

After considering several options, it was decided that a plaque would be the most fitting memorial. There were extensive discussions about where the plaque should be placed and various locations were discussed, including the frontage of the India Buildings, which had been the location of an early Edinburgh jazz club, the frontage of the Oddfellow's Hall, where so many jazz events had taken place, and the site of the long-gone West End Cafe in Shandwick Place, where the Brown band had held a lengthy residency. However, a near unanimous decision was taken that the Usher Hall, scene of the famous concert in 1953 when the Brown band shared the bill with Big Bill Broonzy, was where the plaque should be placed. Dickie Alexander's efforts ensured that this was approved by the town council, who were also prepared to rename one of the bars in the Usher Hall, 'The Sandy Brown Bar'. The design of the plaque was offered for tender and various designs were considered. Under the guidance of David Michie, a design submitted by the Edinburgh College of Art, the work of a talented Greek mature student called Stavroula Fylachtou, was selected.

Funds were raised by a group of jazzers, led by Jack Duff, who collected during the 1997 Edinburgh International Jazz Festival. Several generous individual donations were received, including one from David Binns on behalf of Sandy's former acoustic consultancy practice, Sandy Brown Associates. Stan Greig with Roger Horton, the owner of London's famous jazz venue The 100 Club, organised an evening at the club, when 16 members of Stan's London Jazz Big Band played, without payment, and the entire door takings were given to the fund. The Royal High School Former Pupils Association wished to make a donation but, after discussion, agreed to fund a replica plaque to be placed in the school. A large number of small donations were also received from the general public, demonstrating the wide-spread regard for and pride in, the work of Sandy and Al.

By February 1998, not only was the plaque ready but Paul Adams, of Lake Records in Workington, had issued a CD of the famous Usher Hall concert[199], the first time these recordings had been made available to the public. Furthermore, the fund raising efforts had been so successful that it was possible to have not two but three copies of the plaque made, one for the Usher Hall, one for the Royal High School and one for the '100 Club' in Oxford Street, London.

A problem arose in installing the Usher Hall plaque, as the building was effectively closed for three years for refurbishment, and, with this event delayed, the first plaque actually to be installed was the one at the Royal High School. This took place during the school musical concert in February 1998, when the plaque was unveiled by Flo' Brown. Stan Greig came up from London to attend and a band put together especially for the occasion played a programme that included many numbers associated with Sandy and Al. The band was organised by Ralph Laing, and included Charlie McNair (tpt), Dave Keir (tpt and tbn), Jack

---

[199] See discography Appendix, 'Sandy Brown – The Historic Usher Hall Concert 1952', Lake LACD94

Graham (clt), Jack Duff (rds), Mike Hart (bjo and gtr), Dizzy Jackson (bs) and Bill Strachan (drms). The 100 Club plaque was unveiled at a second session by Stan Grieg's London Jazz Big Band on 5th June of the same year and a large contingent from Scotland made the trip to London for the celebrations. After a lengthy delay, the Usher Hall plaque was finally put in place at a short unveiling ceremony on 1st August 2001. Since then, there has been a further closure of the Usher Hall for major refurbishment and, when I enquired about the plaque in April 2010 with a view to photographing it, it was to discover that this would not be possible as it was not there. However, I was assured that it was safely stored in the meantime at the City Arts Centre and would be re-installed in the Usher Hall in due course.

Sandy Brown 1929-1975, Al Fairweather 1927-1993
In memory of their contribution to music
(photograph by the author 2011)[200]

---

[200] This photograph was taken at the City Arts Centre, Edinburgh, in January 2012, by kind permission of David Patterson, Curator of Fine Art. It was expected that the plaque would be returned to the Usher Hall in the near future.

It is extremely satisfying that Sandy's and Al's music was recognised in this way. Satisfying too, that in celebrating their music with a memorial plaque in Scotland's premier concert hall, jazz itself was receiving notable recognition. It is to the great credit of all those who got involved, that the project came to such a successful conclusion. It is particularly to the credit of John Latham, without whose initiative nothing may have happened, and whose personal devotion to the music of Sandy and Al was to find further expression through his production of the Sandy Brown Society newsletters.

The cruise boat, Maid of the Forth, continued to feature jazz in its programme throughout the 1990s and on into the 2000s, the resident band, Maid of the Forth Stompers, playing for the general public rather than dedicated jazz followers. In the early 1990s, banjo player Harald Vox took Bill Salmond's place in the Stompers for a number of years and then he, in turn, gave way to Nigel Porteous. **Nigel Porteous (banjo, guitar, mandolin, bass guitar)** was born in Stirling on 24th July 1942 and, after primary school at Rumbling Bridge, attended Gordonstoun School near Aberdeen. From an early age, he had an ambition to be a jazz guitarist and, in pursuit of this, taught himself to play guitar and also mastered the mandolin. After leaving school, Nigel started work in the family business, a mill in Alva which manufactured Angora fine woollens. This led to him attending a two year full-time course at the Scottish Woollen Technical College in Galashiels, where he completed a City and Guilds certificate, but unfortunately, by the time he had finished his studies, the mill was on the point of closure. However, he was able to make use of his hard won certificate as it helped towards his acceptance into music school in Leeds, where he began a diploma course in jazz and light music.

Nigel had already made a start on playing in public while in the Stirling area, where he had played in local two-piece jazz groups in Bridge of Allan around 1970. While studying in Leeds, he soon found his way around the local music scene and was quickly into action, playing Irish music in the Leeds pubs, where his skills on guitar and mandolin brought him plenty of work. Also in Leeds, he played with a

503

band called the Big Four, which was modelled on the Sydney Bechet and Muggsy Spannier recording group of the same name, and did some broadcasting with this band. He also toured with a sixteen piece band, the Gene Mayo Band, on the Locarno circuit, a gig for which he hastily had to learn to play the bass guitar. Although things were clearly going well in Leeds, an offer in 1973 to play at the Speakeasy Club in Hong Kong, brought his studies to an end and he never completed his music diploma.

Attracted by this chance to play music for a living, he set off for Hong Kong as part of a trio, which included a reeds and piano player called Mike Greensill. His original intention was to stay in Hong Kong for six months but in fact it stretched out to about twelve years, with a break of five years from 1979 to 1985, which he spent in Spain. While in Hong Kong, Nigel was soon recruited by the wonderfully named Kowloon Honkers, a band which, although basically a Dixieland band, also included some show band material in their repertoire. The Honkers was a professional seven-piece band and with them, Nigel was to play at the Sacramento Jazz Jubilee in California, in 1985 and 1988. It was while living in Hong Kong, that Nigel was 'discovered' as a cartoonist, after someone saw him drawing cartoons on beer mats. This led to quite a bit of work as a free lance and eventually to a full time job, working as a creative cartoonist for an advertising company. This was just about the only nine to five job this most laid-back of characters ever had. As a cartoonist, an occupation which he shared with a number of other jazzers including Humphrey Lyttleton , Wally 'Trog' Fawkes, Diz Disley and Monty Sunshine, he adopted the pen name of 'Nurgle'.

Nigel's five year Spanish interlude was spent with a four-piece band, with which he played at many festivals. The band was called Hotstrings and was made up of a jazz violinist, two guitarists and a bass player. Unfortunately, Spain being outwith the European Common market at that time, the band was not allowed to be paid for any of their work and they found themselves playing numerous festival and pub gigs for nothing.

Nigel returned from Hong Kong to Scotland in 1989, settling in Edinburgh, where he soon established himself as a teacher of music, covering the various guitar styles, banjo and mandolin. A player of his calibre was never going to be without gigs for long and he soon picked up work with a band run by the trombonist Paul Munro. This band, which included Jack Graham on clarinet and Roy Percy on bass, had a residency at the Pilton Inn, out near Bonnyrigg and this was soon followed by work for Nigel with the Esk Valley Swing Band. In addition, Nigel himself formed the Bald Eagle Quartet, a band which had clarinet, guitar, bass and drums and played in the manner of the Benny Goodman small groups of the 1930s. The Bald Eagle band played at the Goblin Ha' Inn in Gifford and in the downstairs bar of the Haymarket Station Bar, where they were soon drawing in a respectable number of punters. The upstairs lounge of the Haymarket Station Bar, of course, had been the location of the renowned Basin Street, one of Edinburgh's best ever jazz venues. A change of ownership had brought the Basin Street jazz activity to an end, a move greatly regretted by many Edinburgh Jazzers. However, the success of the Bald Eagle Quartet in the downstairs bar soon persuaded the owners to think again. It was not long before they decided to re-open the jazz venue and were again in the market for jazz bands. Given that it was the success of the Bald Eagle band that had had sparked the re-birth of Basin Street, it was a shade unfortunate that they found themselves unemployed in the reshuffle, the owners deciding that there services were no longer required!

However, for Nigel at least, help was at hand. A near-by pub, the Haymarket Bar on the corner between West Maitland Street and Morrison Street, also featured jazz and their current attraction was Violet Milne's excellent New Orleans styled Spirits of Rhythm. Nigel went along to listen and was soon invited to sit in with band. This led to him depping when required and then, when Brian Weld dropped out, he became a member of the band. Nigel followed this same pattern with the Maid of the Forth Stompers, firstly depping with them on the cruise boat and then, in about 1996, joining the band on a permanent basis. For a number of years he continued, as had been agreed, to give the Spirits first preference when gigs clashed and this arrangement worked well but, in 2002, he left the Spirits and the Maid of the Forth Stompers became his main band.

Gradually he was persuaded to bring his guitar as well as his banjo to gigs and if at first he was a bit reluctant to do this, it was only because it involved him carrying much more gear around. However, his guitar playing vastly increased the band's scope and it soon became an essential ingredient of the band's style. Not one to push himself forward, he rather diffidently began to bring some of his original tunes along to band practices and these, together with some originals contributed by Andrew Lauder, were soon added to the repertoire, adding greatly to the individuality of the band. Nigel was a fertile source of entertainment for his fellow bandsmen. At one gig, his guitar suddenly ceased to function and, after a bit of investigation, it was discovered that it needed the battery in its pre-amp replaced. He briefly struggled to change the battery but, defeated by the technical intricacies of the task, he gave it up as a bad job, switched to banjo for the rest of the gig and put the new battery in his pocket. When we were clearing up at the end of the gig, there were sudden shrieks, indicative of pain, panic and consternation, from the banjo section. The battery had shorted out on the bunch of keys in his pocket, had become almost red hot and all but set him on fire. The clarinetist Ian Boyter tells the story of returning from a gig in the Sheraton Hotel with Nigel in the car. All the way home, Nigel grumbled that he was uncomfortable, his jacket felt very tight and he thought he must have put on weight. When Ian dropped him off at his house, there was a sudden outbreak of Nigel-type consternation and panic as he realized that the jacket he was wearing was not his. Not only was it not his, it was quite obviously a woman's garment, the sleeves finishing half was down his forearms. Ian had to take him back to the hotel where his furtive method of switching the jackets left him fortunate not to attract the attention of the security staff.

After Jimmy Shortreed stopped playing after the 2001 season, there were three or four years when the clarinet chair in the Maid of the Forth Stompers had no fixed incumbent. Mostly, it was Ian Boyter and George Duncan who played but, good players though they were, the band was unsettled. Used to a regular line-up, the band, after Jimmy Shortreed had retired, was unable to develop a new band sound because of the constant changes. Determined to do something about this, I discussed the situation with Andrew Lauder and came to the sad conclusion that there was no one currently available that we could approach. I then remembered Bill Salmond's ingenious method of recruiting – if there was no one around suitable or available, you had to invent someone! It was then that the name **Gerard Dott** came to mind. Gerard had not played since 1987 or thereabouts and had, in the meantime, moved away from Edinburgh, to Eddleston in the Scottish Borders. This seemed not all that far away and, in a spirit of optimism, I took myself off to Eddleston and broached with him the idea of a long-overdue return to active playing. I told him not to give me an answer right away but to think about it and I would phone him at the end of the week. When I phoned him, not at all sure what his response would be, I asked him if he had thought about my proposal. His response was *'I've been practicing all week!'* This was in March 2006 and, with the Maid of the Forth season getting under-weigh at the end of April and Easter holidays intervening, we had little time to get together in advance. In the end, we only managed a single run through and that was only possible because the first of the season's gigs on the boat was cancelled. This meant that Gerard was pitched into action with little chance to become familiar with our material or build up his playing stamina. However, he managed very well and, by the middle of May was back in full swing, as if he had never been away.

The band soon began to settle into a new sound and, over the next few years, developed a repertoire of less usual material, much of it dressed up a little with simple 'top and tail' arrangements. Gerard was responsible for coming up with some of the ideas for new numbers and arrangements and his arrival stimulated a much needed burst of energy in the rest of us, and not only in expanding the musical side. Previously content to have busy summers on the boat and quiet winters, Gerard's arrival had me scuttling about, busily seeking out winter gigs. The Maid of the Forth

Stompers joined the band rota at the Edinburgh Jazz and Jive Club, a new Edinburgh venture of which we will hear shortly, and eventually even found a pub residency, at the Grey Horse Inn in Balerno. This was a tiny place and was packed if we managed to attract more than about a dozen listeners. I reckoned that I had found the secret. Back in the early 1980s with the Scottish Jazz Advocates, on two evenings a week, we had regularly filled to capacity an enormous lounge in the Caledonian Hotel at the West End of Princes Street. Nearly thirty years later, I could still boast that we were playing to packed houses, it was just that the venue was a bit smaller. It was a cozy and enjoyable gig with a great atmosphere but it was perhaps a bit unfortunate that the band appeared on the pub website as the Maids of the Forth! The band was also expanded to a six-piece line-up for some on–shore gigs (there was no room for more than four on the boat), bringing in drums and on trombone, George Howden, a recent returner from the south. Winters, thanks to Gerard, were suddenly a lot less like a period of hibernation for the Maid of the Forth Stompers but it was gratifying to reverse the gradual loss of active jazzers and bring back a creatively original clarinet player who should never have been away.

Dave Keir had spent the years, since his return to Edinburgh in the 1980s, mostly playing the instrument on which he had made his name, the trombone. However, he had always considered himself to be a multi-instrumentalist and, sometime in the mid-1990s, he decided to concentrate on his cornet playing. The switch was highly successful and, in no time at all, he had established himself as a technically accomplished and very hot cornetist, making early appearances on this instrument with the Capital Jazz Band. Dave was of course, an extremely experienced jazz musician, in spite of a twenty year break while pursuing his career in teaching, and it soon became clear that he had definite ideas about the type of jazz he wanted to play. This he describes, in his profile on the Sandy Brown Jazzwebsite[201], as being the classic jazz of the 1895 to 1930 New Orleans period (which more or less accords with the

---

[201] http://sandybrownjazz.co.uk/profiledavekeir.html

definition of classic jazz used in this book) and, in 1998, he put together a band designed to play in that style.

In keeping with his chosen model, Dave called the band the **Dave Keir Hot Four** and its original membership was Dave on cornet, with Bob Busby (rds), Jock Westwater (bjo) and Dave's fellow veteran, Dizzy Jackson (bs). The band was immediately successful and was soon into action with residencies at pubs in Rose Street, one of which was Ma Scott's. They were also soon in recording action and, in the autumn of 1999, produced a CD called 'Stomp Stomp Stomp'. This was followed by a second CD, recorded in late 2000 and early 2001, which appeared as 'Redman Blues'. Both of these recordings[202] featured the original line-up and also a taste of Dave's instrumental versatility, with him playing cornet and trombone on the first and cornet, trombone and alto-sax on the second of the CDs. As an interesting side-line, Dave and Dizzy Jackson also got together with two jazzers who were in town for the EIJF. These were George Washingmachine (real name George Washington) from Sydney, who played violin, and a colleague from Dave's London days, the famous guitarist Diz Disley, and a private recording was made for posterity in Jock Westwater's flat. The recording took place the day after the dedication of the plaque in memory of Sandy Brown and Al Fairweather, which means that it was recorded on 2nd August 2001, and it was issued as 'Old Friends and New'[203].

Bob Busby left the Dave Keir band around 2004, when he was replaced on reeds by Jock Westwater's brother, Mike Westwater. Mike got a call from Jock (at one o'clock in the morning!) offering him the chance to join the band and Mike accepted. The band became the **Dave Keir Hot Five** when, at Mike Westwater's suggestion, the Borders based trombone player Gordon Melrose came in. With this line-up, the band continued well into the 2000s and they made appearances at various jazz festivals, including those at Peebles, Keswick, Hawick, Kirkcudbright and the EIJF. Mike Westwater recalls that when the multi-

---

[202] See discography appendix
[203] See discography appendix

instrumentalist, Keith Nicholls, perhaps best known for leading the Midnight Follies Orchestra, came as a soloist to play in Edinburgh, he specifically asked to be accompanied by the Dave Keir Hot Five. Sadly for the Edinburgh jazz scene, the playing of this hot and popular band was to be curtailed by Dave's decision, in about 2006, to move to the south west of England, to be near his family. Dave made a determined attempt to continue to run the band from the south and, although Mike Westwater dropped out to be replaced by Andy Hampton, for a number of years they continued to get together occasionally to play at the Jazz and Jive Club in Edinburgh.

Mike Westwater (reeds), brother of the banjo and guitar playing Jock, was born in Edinburgh on 16th November 1943, educated at Daniel Stewart's College and was to make his living as a civil and structural engineer. He became interested in skiffle and American folk music in his early teens and, after having made himself a guitar, someone gave him a banjo. His uncle had a vast collection of 78 rpm records and, while baby-sitting for his younger cousins, Mike heard his first jazz recordings. His uncle obviously had good taste in jazz, as some of the recordings Mike heard were by the Louis Armstrong Hot Five and Jelly Roll Morton. He then began listening to Acker Bilk's band, which he preferred to that of Chris Barber. However, he soon returned to earlier jazz, seeking out recordings from King Oliver to early Duke Ellington, quickly realizing that he preferred this type of jazz to that of the New Orleans Revival and the British trad bands. He also developed an interest in the music of the Quintet of the Hot Club of France, the wonderful continental band featuring the violin of Stephane Grapelli and the scintillating guitar of Django Reinhardt. Clearly inspired by the latter, Mike played rhythm guitar in a group that included a school friend, **Kenny Ramage (Guitar)**, whom Mike describes as a brilliant guitarist in the Django style. It should be pointed out that this was not the trombone playing Ken Ramage, whom we have already met earlier in this book. I, too, remember the guitar playing Kenny Ramage and he certainly was a very fine player, although I have no idea what became of him and have heard nothing of him for many years. Apart from his own playing experiences, the first live jazz that Mike remembers hearing locally was that of Old Bailey's Jazz Advocates at the Place in Victoria Street and Charlie McNair's band at the Crown Bar.

Mike asked his father for a clarinet for his sixteenth birthday and, his father duly obliging, he proceeded to teach himself to play by listening to 78 rpm recordings of Benny Goodman. He also developed his knowledge of chords from his earlier guitar playing and, aware of the importance of chord structure, cajoled brother Jock into playing the banjo as an accompaniment to his clarinet playing. Apparently, Jock was very reluctant at first but eventually became keen and, of course, went on to establish himself as a long term fixture on the Edinburgh jazz scene. Mike's father, acting on advice from an Edinburgh dance band trumpeter called Frankie Smith who styled himself 'Scotland's Louis Armstrong', arranged for him to have lessons from Harry Laidig. Laidig apparently at that time ran a local Dixieland/Swing band with his sons, which Mike says had been heard by an impressed Charlie McNair. Although fairly informal, the lessons were clearly effective and Mike became a competent reader of written music. Looking back on this, Mike thinks that it was perhaps a 'bum steer' because it drew him into a habit of transcribing solos played by others, rather than simply trying to play them as part of the learning process.

While still at school, Mike began playing clarinet with others of similar musical persuasion who lived nearby, including brother Jock, reeds man George Duncan and Jimmy Elliot, who would go on to play drums with several Edinburgh jazz bands. At University, Mike became friendly with Gerard Dott, who turned up in one of his classes and who invited him to sit in with the Mound City Jazz Band, by then mostly made up of students from the Royal Dick Veterinary College. Mike joined this band, playing both banjo and soprano sax. This was his first saxophone, which cost him £7 10/- (£7. 50 pence in today's money). After a brief flirtation with the Climax band, in which he replaced Gerard Dott but was himself replaced by George Gilmour, Mike left Edinburgh for Argyll, where he played with a multi-purpose band called the Callum Ross Band.

Later, by now based in the Border country, Mike again got involved in jazz and was a founder member of the Borders Big Band and, in 2011, was one of only four original members, after thirty three years with them. The prime mover in this band was the late Dave Young who many Edinburgh jazzers will remember as an excellent trumpeter with the Hawick based Wooltown Jazz Band. Mike had become interested in transcribing and arranging music for the Big Band but, opportunities to play jazz solos being few, he decided to put together a traditional jazz band, which he called the Tweed Valley Jazz Band. Several jazzers active in Edinburgh played with this band at various times, including Jock Westwater, Bill Brydon, Symon Carlyle, Jim Petrie and Bev Knight and it played at festivals in Peebles, Hawick, Kirkcudbright and Keswick, where they recorded in 1997. At the time of writing in 2011, Mike Westwater continues to play with the Borders Big Band and study jazz theory and arranging.

A sad reflection of the passage of time was the fact that, by the late 1990s, the traditional jazz scene in Edinburgh was no longer in its former healthy state. There were, inevitably, fewer traditional jazz musicians still active, fewer supporters around and a consequent decrease in the numbers of bands and jazz gigs, especially in the pubs. Concerned about the situation, the Spirits of Rhythm band leader Violet Milne and jazz enthusiast and record collector Norrie Thomson came up with the idea of setting up a proper jazz club in Edinburgh. This was an innovative step, as the Edinburgh jazz public had been accustomed to having their jazz provided free in the pubs. No one knew what the reaction would be to a pay-at-the-door venture, which the new club would have to be to raise funds to cover their overheads.

In September 2000, the **Edinburgh Jazz and Jive Club** was launched, with the stated purpose of promoting the enjoyment of live traditional jazz in all its forms, whilst at the same time providing a platform for local bands to play on a regular basis. The club was constituted as a non-profit making body and was to be run by a committee of three office bearers and four club members. It was to meet on a weekly basis on Friday evenings from 8.00 to 11.30pm and would feature two local bands each week with a visiting band, that is a band from elsewhere, about once a month. Non-members would be welcome at a slightly higher door price and the club opened its doors in the function suite of the Fairmile Inn, on the city boundary near Fairmilehead. This venue allowed the club to make an encouraging start although, with its long, narrow shape which tended to make the band feel a little separated from the punters, it was not ideal. However, the club met there very successfully until December 2006 when, suddenly and with no warning, the venue closed down, leaving the club without a home. However, the club committee was swiftly into action and, by late December 2006, Heriots FP Rugby Club had offered the use of their clubhouse facilities at Goldenacre. The loss of the Fairmile Inn venue, at first regarded as something of a catastrophe, soon came to seen as a blessing in disguise. The Goldenacre location offered a modern, well set-up clubhouse, which could seat up to a hundred and forty, with a good sized dance floor and was soon welcomed by the club members as excellent for both listening and dancing.

Bands which played in the local band rota included the Spirits of Rhythm, Bill Salmond's Louisiana Ragtime Band, Jim Petrie's Diplomats of Jazz, Brian Robertson's Forth River Ragtimers, Dave Keir's Hot Five and Roger Hanley's Jazz Hounds. Later, after Roger Hanley retired from playing, the veteran bass player Fred Murray took over the latter band and, after re-naming it Fred's Club House Seven, continued in the rota. Another change came when Dave Keir left Edinburgh and the Maid of the Forth Stompers filled the gap, although only during the winter months, when their seasonal cruise boat commitments were in abeyance. A further addition came when some former members of the Climax Jazz Band got together and joined the rota as the Anti-Climax Jazz Band!

It seems ridiculous to write in this final chapter about a musician who was born in 1931 and had been involved in music in Edinburgh, including jazz, in the 1950s, but in fact, it was in the 2000s that **Fred Murray (bass, bass guitar, vocals)**, was to become more involved in the jazz scene than at any other time in his lengthy career. Fred was born in Southampton on 22nd November 1931 and, with his family, moved to Edinburgh in 1940, after they had left Southampton because of war time bombing. Initially educated at the Dean Park School in Southampton, he attended Tynecastle School in Edinburgh before joining and later running, the family tool shop business. Fred did his National Service around 1950 and it was during this period that his interest in music really began to develop, after listening to Country and Western Music on the American Forces Network (AFN), broadcasting from Germany. When he was about seventeen, he had taken up guitar, having some lessons from Bill Oliver, who taught in Rae MacIntosh's music shop and played in the band at the Cavendish Ballroom. After this, when he was about twenty and after deciding that the *guitar did not make enough noise* (presumably it was unamplified), he bought a double bass from Mev Taylor's shop and again had lessons from Bill Oliver.

Although taking an interest in the 1950s skiffle craze, it was dance band work in which Fred became involved but he also made his first move into the Edinburgh jazz scene in about 1954, playing for a while at the Condon Club in India Buildings. There he played in a band, which he recalls as the Chicagoans, with the drummer George Crockett and, on saxophone at the time, Dougie Campbell. Apparently, Fred played with this band in a jazz band competition in Glasgow, in which they were placed second. It was also around this time that I, then a mid-teens schoolboy, first came into contact with Fred. I was interested in skiffle and, with a group of pals, decided that we wanted to play the music. One of them, Colin Oswald, who was the only one of us who actually owned an instrument, happened to live next door to the Murrays in Balgreen Avenue. Strange groaning noises heard through the wall were eventually identified as Fred practicing his double bass in the bathroom next door, a room to which his practicing had been banished on the grounds that it put him as far away from the rest of his family as possible! Although I never played in a skiffle band with Fred, he was approached for advice about annoying details like tuning, advice which, if my memory serves me right, he very graciously provided.

Later dance work included a four year spell with pianist Bert Valentine's band in the Miltonhouse Hotel, a band in which all the music was played from written scores, followed by about seven years playing in the Golden Circle, in Bathgate. The strength of the dance band scene at that time can be judged by the fact that each of these gigs provided Fred with three evenings playing a week. In the 1960s and '70s, Fred continued to play dance music with musicians such as Bill Sinclair (gtr), Ian Reid (drms) and Freddy Martin but, like all the others, found dance band work drying up as the discos started to dominate. He did, however, play at the last televised local heat of the TV show Come Dancing, which was broadcast from the Palais. The Murray family was permitted to stay up to watch Dad on TV and were rewarded with a brief glimpse of Fred's feet.

Fred also played at the Beach Ballroom in Dunoon with the Bert Valentine Band, where they were on a bill that included Kenneth McKellar and Andy Stewart. Top of the bill was the show trumpeter, Eddie Calvert. It was in Dunoon that Fred found himself recruited to play for a week with the visiting Laurie Gold and his Pieces of Eight, a band which played a sort of orchestrated jazz and did a lot of radio work. Laurie was the brother of the more famous Harry Gold and Fred's opportunity came about through a typical piece of band business, the resident bass player apparently having been fired for having a clandestine affair with the singer, who was supposed to be the band leader's girlfriend.

The years rolled by with a scatter of gigs at some of the big Edinburgh hotels, such as the North British, the Royal British and the George, but in his spare time, Fred began to go along to the Basin Street jazz bar to listen to the Spirits of Rhythm, placing this in about the late 1970s or early '80s. The Spirits' bass player at the time was Robin Galloway and, when he left, Fred took his place. Later, he moved with band to the Haymarket Bar and was to stay with them for four or five years, including a trip to the Ascona Jazz Festival in Switzerland. After this there was a gap in Fred's playing career, when the bass was consigned to the attic, which was to continue until about the year 2000, when he was persuaded out of retirement to play with a band assembled by drummer Roger Hanley, to play at the newly opened Jazz and Jive Club. A few years later, when Roger Hanley packed in, Norrie Thompson of the Jazz and Jive Club, anxious not to lose a band from the rota, asked Fred to take it on and Fred said that he would. When asked by Norrie what the band was to be called, Fred told him he hadn't a clue, with the result that the band was christened by Norrie and appeared on the Club rota as Fred's Clubhouse Seven. There it has remained ever since, with a line-up of Kenny Milne (tpt), Bob Busby (rds), John Arthur (tbn), Kenny Henderson (bjo), Gus Mackay (pno), Helen Mackay (vocs) and Fred himself on bass. The band has issued a CD which may be found in the discography appendix. Fred Murray, veteran bass player and vocalist, remains one of the most generous people I have ever met, instantly offering a drink to everyone he meets, endlessly cheerful and as universally popular as ever, after a career in local music that has already lasted almost sixty years.

The Jazz and Jive Club had turned out well, regularly bringing in a respectable if not enormous crowd, perhaps as much attracted by the chance to dance as by the chance to listen. Over the years, the policy of booking guest bands also worked very well and many distinguished visiting bands were featured, some of them almost on an annual basis. The visiting bands policy was a far-reaching one and the guests included bands from Denmark, Sweden, Norway, Germany, France, the Netherlands, the USA, Australia, England and Ireland, as well as from other parts of Scotland. Some guests came as solo artistes including the singer Lillian Boutte and the fine guitarist Marty Grosz. The club also did its bit in supporting the EIJF by featuring guest bands on the two Fridays of the jazz festival each year. The Jazz and Jive Club deserves great credit for its efforts in bringing quality guest bands and individuals to Edinburgh, and for providing a regular venue for the local bands, as pub jazz slowly melted away.

Violet Milne was elected club president, an office she held until the Autumn of 2010, when she decided it was time to step down. It is greatly to the credit of Violet, Norrie Thomson and those who served on the club committee that the Jazz and Jive Club has been such a success. It was a forward looking plan in the first place, without any certainty of support, but it paid off handsomely. Although another unwelcome sign of the times was the increasing need for bands to share musicians, after ten years the club is still going strong. Lang may its lum reek.

The year 2003 marked the twenty fifth anniversary of the EIJF, that is twenty five counting from the festival of 1979 and not including the 1978 mini-festival, which was really just a sort of trial run. Early in the year, Mike Hart contacted me to ask if I would be willing to get involved in organizing a celebration concert to take place during the EIJF that summer. I gave it some thought, met with Mike and agreed to take it on. The purpose of the event was not only to celebrate twenty five years of the EIJF but also to pay tribute to the important part that the local bands had played in the development and success of the Festival. From the start, it was clear that there were would be a number of difficulties. The diminishing number of active jazz musicians meant that several of the current bands, as mentioned above, were sharing musicians, meaning some inevitable duplication. In spite of this, there were a few individual musicians who should certainly have been included but who were not currently active with Edinburgh bands. In addition, two of the most prominent bands from the early days of the EIJF, the historically conjoined Old Bailey's Jazz Advocates/Scottish Jazz Advocates and the Scottish Society Syncopators, were no longer in existence as extant bands. In the case of the former, apart from a couple of re-unions, the band had not had any corporate existence for almost twenty years. The Syncs likewise were no longer really functioning as a regular unit and when Mike did accept bookings under that name, he would put together a band including as many of the former members as possible. In the end, it was decided that the programme would include five currently active and prominent bands: the Spirits of Rhythm; the Diplomats of Jazz; Swing 2003; Dave Keir's Hot Five and Bill Salmond's Louisiana Ragtime Band, plus 're-constructions' of the Jazz Advocates and the Syncopators. It was also decided, on Mike's strong advice, that the Jazz Advocates should appear under their Old Bailey moniker, as this would be likely to attract followers

517

from away back, even though the band had mostly appeared in the EIJF as the Scottish Jazz Advocates. Sadly, Charlie McNair, whose band had been a constant presence in the EIJF and which should most certainly have been included, was already suffering from the health problems that would finally end his jazz career and it was clearly unthinkable to have his band without Charlie himself.

In spite of the lack of the McNair band, it was beginning to look as though we had the ingredients of a good show. The seven bands between them covered a wide stylistic spectrum within traditional jazz, there was variety in the size and sound of the bands and the inclusion of the Jazz Advocates and the Syncs seemed likely to bring in a host of punters whose jazz loyalties stretched back as far as the 1960s. With hindsight, one mistake that I think we made during the planning, was not to give more thought than we did to a further reconstruction; that of the Climax Jazz Band, pioneers of the purist New Orleans tradition in Edinburgh and a band with a long and proud history. However, the majority of the band's longest serving members would be there in any case, scattered amongst the other bands, and the New Orleans style would be well represented by the Spirits and the LRB, while the Diplomats and Dave Keir's band nicely covered classic jazz. Both the Old Bailey band and the Syncs would represent a more arrangement oriented, populist style, with the Old Bailey band also associated with the Dixieland tradition. Providing a very welcome contrast to all the others would be Swing 2003, with their links to the European tradition, particularly to the Hot Club of France and the music of Django Reinhardt. The seven bands scheduled to play however, did not include two prominent and long-serving Edinburgh trumpeters, Gus Ferguson and Brian Robertson. This was soon resolved with Gus included in the Syncs, who would feature a two trumpet format, and Brian added for the occasion to the Spirits, who were currently without a trumpeter.

The title of the 'Silver Jubilee of Edinburgh Traditional Jazz' was adopted. This, of course, was not strictly accurate, it being the EIJF that was celebrating its silver jubilee rather than Edinburgh traditional jazz itself but, as it seemed to have the right ring about it, we settled for that. The running order was worked out by adopting a simple formula: there would be two halves separated by an interval, each half would start and finish with one of the larger (seven or eight piece) bands, with the smaller, mostly drumless bands occupying the in-between slots. This seemed a well balanced way to arrange things and it was further decided that each half would close with one of the reconstructed bands, simply in recognition of their novelty value, neither being active on the current Edinburgh jazz scene. We asked the band leaders to submit their proposed list of tunes, to try to avoid everybody playing Muskrat Ramble and Tin Roof Blues, and also to let us have a short history of their bands, to help introduce each band. Neither Mike nor I could come up with an obvious personality to present the show and we agreed that, in the event of us failing to find a more resounding name, I would be on standby as compere and, in the end, that is what happened and I was MC for the evening. Bill Marshall, who had undertaken similar duties in the EIJF before, was recruited as stage manager and we would be working with Assembly Direct's Steve Martin, as production manager, with Alan Martin in charge of sound. The date was to be 29th July 2003 and the venue, the prestigious Queen's Hall.

In the end it was a great success, with a full and enthusiastic house and a packed programme. In fact, it was really a bit too packed and overran its intended time by a fair bit, lasting for about three hours and forty minutes! In total, thirty five musicians played, with only seven of them playing in two bands on the night[204]. In my view, all the bands did themselves proud, with a good and varied selection of tunes, each band getting a rousing welcome and, no doubt, a special cheer from their own dedicated followers. The show was reviewed by Pat Napier in a write-up posted on the internet which said *'Should anyone ever have been tempted to relegate the trad jazz scene in Edinburgh to a backwater, the big Silver Jubilee celebration would have smashed that idea to smithereens'*. The review

---

[204] To give an idea of the state of Edinburgh traditional jazz in 2003, the full line-up for the 'Silver Jubilee' concert is given in Appendix I

noted that the second half had started with me reading out a list of the Edinburgh jazz musicians who were no longer around, and a depressingly long list it was. I read them out grouped by instrument and each group got an affectionate and, I am certain, sincere round of applause. I also offered a special welcome to Charlie McNair, no longer able to play but present as a special guest.

At the end, Mike Hart, who had managed to assemble an impressive nine of the Syncs former alumni for the show, spoke of how proud he was of Edinburgh's ability to produce so many talented jazz musicians and invited any of them who would like to, to join his band on stage for a final blast on the inevitable When the Saints go Marching In. A good few accepted and my final memory of the night was of a bemused Tom Finlay playing the piano surrounded by five banjo players, all strumming away merrily. Pat Napier was kind enough to call it *'...a glorious trip down memory lane'*. If memory serves me right, it was the best selling show of the 2003 EIJF.

By the end of the first decade of the new century, there could be little doubt that Edinburgh traditional jazz had made its mark, not only on the culture of Edinburgh and Scotland but also in the wider context of European and world jazz. The sterling efforts of John Latham, with his initiating role, and the many others who had become involved in 'The Lord Provost's Sandy Brown Memorial Society' in the 1990s had, as we have heard, ensured that the great work of Sandy Brown and Al Fairweather was properly commemorated in their native city and elsewhere. In addition, John had also, not only established the Sandy Brown Society in 1996, but had ensured that it was still continuing to thrive in 2012, issuing an informative Newsletter to a large membership every month.

At the end of 2006, Ian Maund had set up the Sandy Brown Jazz website on the internet[205], to make information widely available through the internet about Sandy, his music and his associates. In the way that Sandy Brown and his band developed a 'mainstream' bridge between 'traditional' and 'modern' jazz music, the website aims to

---

[205] **Sandy Brown website (http://sandybrownjazz.co.uk**

span all aspects of jazz through its free, monthly online magazine, *What's New*. In the magazine can be found news, album reviews, articles about new and established musicians, memories and photographs, quizzes, features and 'tasting' sessions for jazz music that you might not have heard before. Ian reports that the website regularly attracts readers and correspondents from around the world. Sandy Brown Jazz can be found at: http://www.sandybrownjazz.co.uk. The website is a marvellous source of information, not only about Sandy himself but also about many of his associates and related information and has been invaluable throughout the writing of this book.

The EIJBF had celebrated its 30th anniversary in 2008 and, however much it had changed and developed over the years, had become recognised as a major European jazz festival. The local traditional jazz bands and musicians had been celebrated in the 2003 Silver Jubilee Concert which recognised not only their considerable contribution to the EIJBF but also a local jazz scene which had burgeoned in the half century and more that had passed, since the Revival of the 1940s. Young and not-so-young Edinburgh musicians, some of them the sons and daughters of earlier Edinburgh jazzers, were highly active and were establishing names for themselves in the realm of modern and contemporary forms of jazz. Then, in the mid-2000s, came another initiative which would reinforce and put on record the reputation of Edinburgh as a major jazz centre.

We heard in earlier chapters[206] how a small group of veteran jazzers had got together on a regular basis in the mid-2000s to share memories and talk about their experiences of Edinburgh jazz since the 1940s. The group was small, with only four members: Jim Keppie, Bill Strachan, Donald 'Chick' Murray and Drew Landles but, between them, they represented a wide range of experience of local jazz. It was not long before informal chat and reminiscence started to crystalise into something with a definite purpose and, by the later 2000s, the idea of both an Edinburgh jazz archive and an exhibition was firmly in

---

[206] See chapters V and VIII

place and the previously informal group became the Edinburgh Jazz Archive Group (EJAG). Sadly, Drew Landles, who had been able to put on the record his memories of playing with the early Edinburgh jazz bands of the late 1940s and early 1950s, died in September 2010 but he did live long enough to see the first successes of the EJAG earlier that year.

There seems little doubt that Janol Scott, had he lived, would have been as enthusiastic and effective a member of the EJAG as he had been of the Sandy Brown and Al Fairweather memorial group, back in the 1990s. Janol and Jim Keppie had been classmates at the Royal High School back in the 1940s and had started attending weekly sessions of the Edinburgh Rhythm Club. This led to them making a start on collecting 78 rpm recordings which were not in great supply in these wartime years. Jim recalls that most were on the HMV label (including some by Jelly Roll Morton) or the Parlophone Rhythm series which included Bix Beiderbecke and, as British post-war jazz began to establish itself, Humphrey Lyttelton's band. These were purchased in Methven Simpson's shop, where they were served by a Miss Wood, or at Clifton's, in which case Betty saw to the transaction. The records apparently cost about 5/4d each and Jim and Janol always insisted on acceptable performances on both sides of the record and quite right too!

Janol Scott died on 2nd November 2007, too early to play a part in the EJAG, but his widow Winnie, later donated to the Archive many items from his sizeable collection, including LPs, CDs and books, and this constituted the Archive's first really significant contribution. In fact, it seems that this kindly donation was a major encouragement to the fledgling EJAG and came at just the right time to provide them with some real impetus and inspiration, so much so that the Edinburgh Jazz Archive was dedicated to the memory of Janol Scott, a life-long jazz enthusiast and collector.

The ideas behind the formation and aims of the EJAG are described by Jim Keppie, under the heading 'Edinburgh

Jazz Archive,' in the Sandy Brown Jazz website[207], to which readers may wish to refer. In pursuing the idea of an archive, it seems clear that there was a feeling that tribute should be paid to, not only Sandy Brown and Al Fairweather, who were now commemorated by plaques at three venues, but to the many others whose contributions to jazz were not so far short of theirs. There were certainly other fine players to remember, including such as the Semple brothers, Alex Welsh, Stan Greig and Dave Paxton from the early days and the many others who had followed in their footsteps. The EJAG deserves a great deal of credit for having the initiative and energy to do something which was crucial, if the story of Edinburgh jazz in the twentieth century was to be recorded before a vast amount of material was lost forever, as the ravages of time took their inevitable toll. The group's original ideas, in fact, were still more ambitious, as Jim explained on the Sandy Brown Jazz website in 2009, where he says:

'The possibility of a Scottish Jazz Archive, which would involve research facilities provision and the collation of material covering at least the major centres in Scotland, was originally mooted in my letter to the Sandy Brown Jazz website in April 2008. While this concept has (for practical reasons) had to be shelved, it is hoped that the arrival of one for Edinburgh alone (sizeable enough on its own) may spur jazz enthusiasts in Glasgow, Aberdeen, Dundee, Inverness and elsewhere to collect and record the evidence of jazz activities in their cities and towns'.

Amen to that, say I. In addition to setting out the idea of an Edinburgh jazz archive, it was through their hard work that agreement was reached with the Edinburgh Central Library to provide the necessary facilities for conserving and cataloguing collected material. The group also set out to gather this material and to encourage others to contribute. This was also explained on the Sandy Brown Jazz website where Jim set out what they were looking for, listing *'...recordings (78's, LP's, CD's), books, journals, photographs*

---

[207] Keppie J, http//www.sandybrownjazz.co.uk/forumarchive.html

523

and other ephemera relating to what was a particularly unique cultural development in the city, mainly from the 1940's onwards'. Significantly, because it was such a determined statement of purpose, he also added 'That said, it is important that we ensure and record the obvious evidence of local jazz provision through to the end of the 20th century and on to the present day and this we would endeavour to do'.

The EJAG also decided to launch the Archive by putting on the planned exhibition about Edinburgh jazz under the title 'Capital Jazz' and this took place in the Edinburgh Central Library on 31st July 2010, the opening day of the 2010 Edinburgh International Jazz and Blues Festival. It was a resounding success, hailed by a deservedly pleased Jim Keppie, who reported the event on the Sandy Brown Jazz website, saying:

'There was a goodly attendance of jazz enthusiasts and performers from yesteryear and today to view the assembled material on display covering the approximate period 1945-80. This consisted of explanatory texts, photographs, books, instruments and memorabilia as well as books containing memoirs and profile listings of local performers.

Musical support was provided by Ron Carruthers (piano), Tony Howard (guitar), Billy Allison (drums) and John Burgess (reeds) with speeches by Councillor Cairns (Edinburgh City Council), Jim Keppie (EJAG), and Hil Williamson (Edinburgh City Library).

Among those present were Ralph Laing, Mike Hart, Bill Strachan, Drew Landles, Andrew Gilmour, Jim Young, Mike Pollett, Graham Blamire, Jean Mundell, Roger Craik, Winnie Scott (widow of Janol Scott) and Ishbel Semple (widow of John Semple)'.

In his opening speech, Jim had recorded the sincere thanks of the EJAG to Liz McGettigan (Head of Libraries and Information Service) and also the Library officials, Hil Williamson and Garry Gale, for their enthusiasm towards the concept and their willingness to work with the EJAG in developing the whole Archive and exhibition project. The exhibition had launched the Archive very successfully and the hope and intention was that it would continue to grow and develop over the years, becoming a repository for written accounts, photos, posters, recordings and other memorabilia, a treasure house reflecting the quality and history of one the most significant of the UK's jazz centres. This certainly prompted me and probably many others, to encourage other jazz people to consider placing their jazz memorabilia in the Archive when the time comes, just as I intend to myself.

Back in 2009, Chick Murray had suggested that I might be interested in joining the EJAG, with a view to involving me in the writing part, and I went along to a couple of meetings. However, I was not at all sure that I could manage to write in partnership with a retired professional journalist, brought in from outside the group, which was what Chick proposed. In the end, I decided not to commit myself to becoming part of the group, aware that I usually worked better on my own. I was, nonetheless, fully in support of their plans and undertook to give them what help I could in putting together materials for both exhibition and archive. The work of the EJAG has been invaluable. Jim, Chick (in spite of serious health issues at the time), and Bill Strachan put an enormous amount of time and effort into the EJAG projects and, as an additional bonus for me (and, I hope, others!), it was to a large extent their initiative that spurred me into doing what I had always intended doing and getting on with writing this book.

And that is just about that. Deciding when and how to draw this account to a close has been something of a problem but a closing chapter describing the Sandy and Al memorial project, the triumphant Silver Jubilee concert and the advent of the Edinburgh Jazz Archive seems as good a way as any, even if the emphasis was now on the past. Edinburgh traditional jazz was to continue of course but the great years were over. In the hectic 1980s, there had been up to and beyond fifty traditional jazz gigs a week on offer in Edinburgh; at the end of the first decade of the new century, I was aware of only two or three regular spots (and they are fortnightly or monthly) plus the weekly programme laid on by the Jazz and Jive Club. Over the years, I built up a data base tabulating all the Edinburgh traditional jazz musicians and bands, in the period 1945 onwards, that I had been able to identify. The totals, which should be regarded only as minimum figures as there is no guarantee that they are complete, came to almost three hundred and fifty musicians and around a hundred bands. These are impressive figures, although it has to be remembered that they include a number of people and bands whose appearance was brief and transitory.

At the end of the first decade of the new century, the number of active Edinburgh traditional jazz musicians had declined to the point where most bands were sharing at least one and sometimes several musicians with other bands. The Edinburgh traditional jazz bands still in regular action were Bill Salmond's Louisiana Ragtime Band, the Spirits of Rhythm, Jim Petrie's Diplomats of Jazz, Brian Robertson's Forth Valley Ragtimers, Fred Murray's Club House Seven, the Maid of the Forth Stompers, Swing 2011 and, out in Linlithgow, the West End Jazz Band. In addition, there were still occasional appearances at the Jazz and Jive Club of a band under Mike Hart's leadership and a contemporary version of the old Climax Jazz band. Fat Sam's Band remained as professional and international in its appeal as ever. Many of us were crossing the country to fill out jazz bands through in the west, where the decline in numbers was just as pronounced. The diminishing numbers of followers was just as apparent everywhere, although Glasgow seemed to have managed to maintain its free pub gigs rather better than we had in Edinburgh.

What had happened to produce such a marked decline in such a relatively short space of time? The answer is simple. Three upsurges in interest had manned the Edinburgh traditional jazz bands since WWII – the original Revival in the forties and fifties, the trad boom in the late 1950s and early 1960s and, finally and less significantly, the recruitment that stemmed from the virtual demise of the dance bands in the late 1960s and 70s. At the beginning of the new century, the surviving Revivalists were in their seventies or even eighties, many trad boomers in their sixties or seventies and the dance band recruits had not, in the main, been young when they came over to jazz in the first place. The stark truth was that the generations that had driven traditional jazz for six decades were either retiring from active playing or shuffling off this mortal coil and there were next to no younger replacements coming into the music. When I started around 1960, the average age of a jazz band was probably around thirty, in 2000 it was around seventy. In 1964, at age twenty one, I was the youngest in the Old Bailey band, in 2011 I was the youngest in the Maid of the Forth Stompers at sixty eight! So the generations were moving on but the real problem was that there were virtually no youngsters taking their place. This, of course, raises the interesting question, can traditional jazz survive much longer?

It does not seem to me either logical or realistic to expect traditional jazz to ever again feature in the pop charts, that is, amongst the best selling records. With the possible exception of the trad boom years, traditional jazz in the second half of the twentieth century could never be defined as a part of pop culture proper. As George Melly said in his book 'Revolt into Style – the pop arts in Britain', Revivalist jazz differed from genuine Pop culture because it '...*looked back towards an earlier culture for its inspiration, thus admitting that it believed in a 'then' which was superior to 'now' – a very anti-pop concept'*[208]. Revivalist jazz and its various developments between the 1940s and the turn of the century existed alongside, first of all popular music (mostly 'crooners' such as Frank Sinatra, Guy Mitchell and Dickie Valentine) and then, after the mid-1950s, pop music (mostly beat music, Rock 'n' Roll and kiddie-pops). Even in the trad boom era, I do not think that the Acker Bilk, Chris Barber and Kenny Ball records that got into the charts could really be classed as genuine pop music. It seems to me that there were two factors that enabled records of this type to make it into the charts. First of all, the effects of the Revival were still in full swing and the large number of jazzers who were involved would have added up to quite a significant record buying group in their own right, particularly considering that the total record buying public then would have been much smaller then than it is now.

---

[208] 'Revolt into Style - the Pop Arts in Britain' by George Melly, (Copyright George © Melly 1970) Reprinted by permission of A. M. Heath & Co Ltd.

The bands of Bilk, Barber and Ball, and other British traditional jazz bands, had enormous followings at that time and there is no doubt that their records sold like hot cakes among their followers. However, these were basically jazz followers who would have been fairly unlikely to buy many of the other types of records that got into the charts.

The second factor, and this is a bit more like a genuine pop reason for buying records, was the influence of skiffle. Skiffle, and Lonnie Donegan in particular, was extremely popular in the later 1950s. Donegan's records were an almost constant feature of the pop charts at that time and they would certainly have to be considered a bona fide part of the pop culture of the time. However, the close relationship of skiffle with the British traditional jazz bands, remembering that Lonnie Donegan's first hit recording, Rock Island Line, was actually initially released as a track on a Chris Barber LP, brought many skiffle fans into contact with the music of the jazz bands. This was exactly the route by which I and many others first became aware of British traditional jazz and many of us were soon buying British jazz recordings for their own sake. What I am saying is that the appearance of traditional jazz recordings in the charts was simply a function of the sheer size of the jazz public at that time and they were not, nor should they be considered to be, a part of the genuine pop record buying public. It would need another Revival to fuel a similar upsurge in popularity, a highly unlikely scenario in respect of traditional jazz, the originals of which are now so far in the past. We may, in any case, have already witnessed a kind of second jazz revival, with a return to earlier forms of modern jazz like bebop, now that the excesses of free form have melted away and the angry sounds of civil rights jazz seem to have had their day.

A factor that may be missing today from the sort of sociological mix that sparked off the Revival, was the very nature of the troubled 1940s. It would take a sociologist rather than me to explore the part that WWII may have played in fostering the Revival but I have sometimes wondered if there was an element, at least in Europe, of harking back to the music of an earlier, safer and more stable time. I do not think that the trauma and upset of the war itself was a factor in initiating the Revival, as it seems to have been under way by the late 1930s before WWII had begun, but it may be that the unrest and uncertainty of the years leading up to the war played their part. It also seems unlikely to me that young musicians will be attracted to traditional jazz in any significant numbers. Why should they be? For a start, they hear very little of it in the broadcasting media. The few televised jazz programmes are usually scheduled for the middle of the night and the exiguous jazz ration on radio is broadcast mostly on stations that are unlikely to be routine listening for young people. If they are attracted to jazz at all, it would seem much more likely to be towards more modern and contemporary forms of the music, the music of jazz musicians closer to their own age.

It may seem contradictory but another factor that seems to me to militate against youngsters of today coming into traditional jazz is the fact that they have a vastly better chance of formal tuition in playing musical instruments than earlier generations. Today's youngsters, coming through the schools music departments, seem to me to be in a system that is designed to prepare musicians for orchestral music, for which it is no doubt important to produce virtually interchangeable technical experts. What training in jazz playing they receive, if any, will naturally be linked to the sort of jazz that most closely resembles the orchestral model, that is to the formal, music reading, big bands. Those among the young, aspiring jazz musicians with the talent and ambition to be jazz soloists are likewise much more likely to be attracted to the same context, the formally arranged, reading bands which also offer soloing opportunities. It would be asking an awful lot to expect many to break away from the very basis of their training into the informal, relatively unorganised, musical environment of a traditional jazz band. It is not that I have anything against formal training and I certainly would not go as far as to call it a 'clone factory', as did one Edinburgh jazzer with whom I was speaking recently. It is just that I think that formal training does not lead naturally to less formal music of an improvising nature and it is unlikely ever to be a ready source of aspiring traditional jazz musicians.

In fact, I am not at all sure that lack of formal training is such a bad thing in respect of playing jazz. I have already quoted Dave Strutt as emphasising the importance of sound in jazz. While there is no doubting the value of technical expertise, providing it is not used simply to show off technique, I wonder just how much of the individuality of jazz musicians is traceable to their being, at least to an extent, self-taught? Certainly, many great jazz musicians are readily identifiable by their individual, sometimes idiosyncratic, sound and this always seemed to me to be an essential component of their expressiveness, something that gives so much character to their playing. In contrast, well-trained, young musicians of today are a product of a system, the aim of which is, at least to an extent, to produce musicians who all sound the same. This seems to me to the antithesis of playing jazz, where individuality is paramount. There have been many technically more accomplished clarinet players than Johnny Dodds, George Lewis and Pee Wee Russell, many more technically brilliant trumpeters than Bubber Miley, Wild Bill Davison, and Muggsy Spannier, but not many who were more individualisitic. Even technical wizards, like the clarinettists Barney Bigard and Benny Goodman and the trumpeter Clark Terry, however much formal training they received, seem to have used their technical excellence as a basis from which to develop an individual jazz sound. I believe this was because they saw their formal training as preparatory to playing jazz, where they needed to establish themselves as individuals, as would be the norm in those days. It seems to me that these great players overcame the sameness that technical excellence could impose and became great individual jazz musicians almost in spite of it.

The above is, of course, far from being an original point of view. The French writer Jean Pierre Lion, when considering the 1920s career of Bix Biederbecke, made the same point in his extremely detailed book 'Bix – The

Definitive Biography of a Jazz Legend'[209]. Describing what happened when Bix sought formal trumpet tuition from Joseph Gustat, Lion wrote *'After listening to Bix's playing for a few minutes and observing his peculiar fingering technique, the professor advised him to give up any ideas of formal studies of the horn. He comforted Bix in his "faulty" playing – "erroneous" in regard to the playing taught in music schools – realising it permitted the young man to express himself in a unique and surprising manner'*. Lion went on to emphasise the point, writing that Gustat had the sense and finesse to avoid *'putting a wild animal in a cage'*.

So I cannot, in all honesty, pretend that I think traditional jazz has a great future. Although the regular UK publication 'Jazz Guide' still manages to pack up to sixty pages with news of traditional jazz bands playing all over the UK, I fear that the vast majority of them will be of a fairly advanced average age and I suspect the same holds true on the continent. Perhaps the type of traditional jazz that has the best chance of surviving the gradual disappearance of the current crop of active players is the purist or New Orleans style. This form of the music still has the underlying energy that comes from a 'cause', a sort of crusading spirit, and this might, just might, appeal to a future generation of stroppy teenagers. We, or rather our successors, will just have to wait and see.

This book has explored the course of Edinburgh traditional jazz and the people who played it, beginning away back in the 1920s, on through the pioneering years of the Revival, the excesses of the trad boom, the excitements of the Edinburgh International Jazz Festival and finally, up to and beyond the end of the twentieth century. We have met and got to know many of the principle personalities whose efforts and abilities were the building blocks of decades of marvelous music, most of it readily available at little cost. We may have to accept that traditional jazz has almost run its course and that the jazz flame will be carried

---

[209] Lion J P, 'Bix – The Definitive Biography of a Jazz Legend', Revised paperback edition 2007, reproduced by permission of the Continuum International Publishing Group,

on by musicians whose music may not sound much like the jazz we knew. But what a time it has been!

Looking back now, several things stand out. Through the decades there have been endless examples of Edinburgh jazz musicians whose careers were founded on their own, self-taught skills and their intrinsic ability to express themselves at their own level, great or humble as it may have been. Sandy Brown, Stan Greig, Alex Welsh and Archie Semple, who were to play at the top of the tree. Al Fairweather, whose talent and imagination produced, not only his own marvelous playing but some of the most original writing that ever lit up the British jazz scene and yet who said that it had all been a so hard, because of what he saw as his lack of technical skills. Tello who played the hottest jazz you could ever wish to hear and yet who told me that it was a constant battle against the limitations of his self-taught technique. Jazzers like Charlie McNair and Archie Sinclair, whose playing unlocked their talents as communicators and entertainers; great players like Johnny McGuff, Dave Paxton, Ronnie Rae, Kenny Milne and Alex Shaw, deserving of international reputations and yet content to play a great deal of their music on their home patch; and the legions of the rest of us whose DIY, rough-hewn techniques were all our own and yet were sufficient to release whatever creativity we possessed.

A local jazz scene so rich in talent and character that you would have had to go a long way to find the equal of the individuals listed above, when in their prime. The host of bands over the years - the early Sandy Brown and Archie Semple bands, the Climax Jazz Band, Charlie McNair's Jazz Band, the Nova Scotians, Old Bailey and his Jazz Advocates, the Society Syncopators, the Louisiana Ragtime Band, the Spirits of Rhythm, Swing 1980/2001, Fat Sam's Band, the Diplomats of Jazz and the Dave Keir Hot Five and so many more - many of which could hold their own against any local jazz bands, in their styles, in the UK. And the punters, as I have called them throughout this book and to whom it is dedicated, without whose enthusiasm and support there would have been next to nothing to write about. We have witnessed too, the sheer inspirational quality of jazz, the chance hearings that so often switched on individuals to a music that remained with them for the rest of their lives. The magic of a creative art form that could grip someone in an instant - regardless of obstacles of time, education, geography, race, colour or creed - leaving them with a life-long interest and the memory of their own, special, eureka moment.

In the end, what did Edinburgh traditional jazz add up to? George Melly wrote in 'Revolt into Style': *'It was inevitable that the spontaneous if mysterious enthusiasm which sprang up all over wartime Britain for an almost forgotten music, Negro jazz of the 20s, should lead eventually to an attempt to reconstruct the music and, by the end of the war, there was already one established band, the George Webb Dixielanders. Within a year or two the revivalist movement had spread to every major city in the British Isles....'*[210]. This seems to me to be rather a tunnel-visioned, simplistic view and more than a little London-centric. We have already heard from Jim Walker about what was going on in Edinburgh by that time and about the *'...group of rather older musicians who, around 1945, played at the Edinburgh Rhythm Club, located in the rehearsal room above Methven Simpson's music shop in Princes Street'*[211], the band that included Bob Fairley, Drew and Ma Bruce and Bill McGregor. In addition and perhaps even more significant, is the fact that Sandy Brown had formed his first band in about 1943, when he was still at school and Dave Paxton and George Crockett were certainly both already in action by that time.

Without wishing any disrespect to George Webb and the other early London pioneers, it seems perfectly clear that the Revival was spontaneously springing into life all over the place, and was most certainly not all triggered by what was going on in London. Nor can there be any doubt of the quality of what took place in Edinburgh in the 1940s. Sandy would be around the top of most people's list of the greatest British traditional jazz musicians and Al Fairweather, Alex Welsh, Archie Semple and Stan Greig

---

[210]'Revolt into Style - the Pop Arts in Britain' by George Melly, (Copyright George © Melly 1970) Reprinted by permission of A. M. Heath & Co Ltd.
[211] See Chapter III

would not be far away either, right up there with great contemporary jazzers from the south, like Humphrey Lyttleton, Wally Fawkes, Bruce Turner and Ken Colyer.

The succeeding generations too, proved a production line of many more wonderful players, some of whom played professionally, at least for parts of their careers in jazz. But it was not just the great players, although perhaps it was from them that the main strength came. The whole Edinburgh jazz scene was strong in so many ways: so many musicians, so many bands, so many venues, so many punters and over such a long time. We even have the biggest jazz event in Europe in the Edinburgh International Jazz and Blues Festival, thanks to the drive, enthusiasm and relentless hard work of Mike Hart and all the others who made it possible. Only in sheer numbers would London be ahead, because of the enormous scale of the place. However, it has to be remembered that a very significant number of jazz musicians associated with London were in fact not themselves Londoners but were attracted there by the opportunities offered. Putting sheer scale aside, by all other measures, in traditional jazz, Edinburgh has to be rated as one of the great jazz cities of the UK

It has been a pleasure and a privilege to be part of it and to write about it. For me at least, Edinburgh traditional jazz has been a constant factor that lit up my life and brought me many friends and great experiences. I just wish it was possible to go back to the beginning and start all over again.

Appendix I

'Silver Jubilee of Edinburgh Traditional Jazz'

This event was a concert in the Queen's Hall, Edinburgh, on 29th July 2003, celebrating both the 25th anniversary of the Edinburgh International Jazz Festival and the important part played in the success of the Festival by the local bands. The bands, in the running order in which they appeared, were:

1. 'The Spirits of Rhythm'

Brian Robertson (tpt), Ian Boyter (rds), Alan Quinn (tbn, voc), Violet Milne (pno, ldr), Nigel Porteous (bjo), Dizzy Jackson (bs), Kenny Milne (drms)

2. 'The Diplomats of Jazz'

Jim Petrie (tpt, voc, ldr), Bob Busby (rds), Beverley Knight (bjo), Bill Brydon (sousa)

3. 'Swing 2003'

Dick Lee (rds), Stephen Coutts (solo gtr, viol), John Russell (gtr), Roy Percy (bs)

4.   'Old Bailey's Jazz Advocates'

Andrew Lauder (tpt), Hamish McGregor (rds, voc, co-ldr), John McGuff (tbn), Tom Finlay (pno), Mike Hart (bjo, co-ldr), Graham Blamire (bs), Donald 'Chick' Murray (drms)

Interval

5.   'Dave Keir's Hot Five'

Dave Keir (tpt, ldr), Mike Westwater (rds), Gordon Melrose (tbn), Jock Westwater (bjo, voc), Dizzy Jackson (bs)

6.   Bill Salmond's Louisiana Ragtime Band'

George Gilmour (clt), Alan Quinn (tbn, voc), Graham Scott (pno), Bill Salmond (bjo, ldr), Bill Brydon (bs), Kenny Milne (drms)

7.   Mike Hart's Society Syncopators'

Dave Strutt (tpt, voc), Gus Ferguson (tpt), Jake McMahon (clt), Martin Foster (b-sax), John McGuff (tbn), Tom Finlay (pno), Mike Hart (bjo, ldr), Ricky Steele (bs), Bobby Stewart (drms)

Compere - Graham Blamire, **Stage Manager** - Bill Marshall, **Production Manager** - Steve Wilson (Assembly Direct), **Sound engineer** - Alan Martin.

Edinburgh Jazz Discography

This discography covers recordings made, issued and made available to supporters, by jazz musicians and bands associated with the Edinburgh jazz scene. Only recordings made whilst these musicians and bands were mainly domiciled in the Edinburgh area are included. Many of the musicians, bands and recordings are referred to in the preceding chapters.

A great many of the recordings included were funded by the bands or bandleaders and were only available at concerts and other gigs. Few were available through normal retail outlets. Some of the bands gave names to the labels under which recordings were made. Others did not bother and these are shown as 'band issue'. Where the recordings were titled this has been included.

Many of the well known Edinburgh jazz musicians travelled to London and turned professional. These included Sandy Brown Al Fairweather, Alex Welsh, Archie Semple, Stan Greig, Jim Douglas, Dave Keir and Ralph Laing. Recordings made by these musicians, whilst working in London, are well documented in discographies compiled and issued by the Dutch discographer, Gerard Bielderman and his associates.

With very few exceptions, the earlier recordings included have not been re-issued and are no longer available other than, from time to time, through specialised auctions or record sales. However, Paul Adams of Lake Records has undertaken some sterling work in re-issuing some of the early recordings by Sandy Brown, Archie Semple and Alex Welsh.

The entries relating to recordings made in the mid-1940s through to the early 1950s are, in many cases, tentative. As far as possible, the data shown have been confirmed against published discographies, including those published by Gerard Bielderman, John Latham and Norman Simpson. Other reliable authorities have also been consulted.

In recent years, the advances in recording technology have allowed bands and collectors to record both live and 'studio' sessions on portable recording equipment, without the need to hire professional recording companies. This has allowed bands to issue recordings without having to commit to specific numbers of discs. As a consequence of this, musicians and private collectors have recorded many sessions that have never been issued and remain in private collections. None of these have been included in this discography.

The discography does not pretend to be exhaustive. Very few discographies ever are. Should anyone reading this discography know of any recording(s) that should be included but are not, please contact the author (0131 312 8243). Similarly, please advise any errors of omission or commission.

I would like to acknowledge and thank the following people for the help they gave me in compiling this discography – Graham Blamire, Bob Busby, Peter Davenport, Pete Kerr, Kenny Milne, John Russell, Bill Salmond.

Abbreviations Used

alto	alto saxophone
audio-cas	audio cassette
bar	baritone saxophone
b-bs	brass bass (tuba or sousaphone)
b-gtr	bass guitar
bs	string bs
b-clt	bass clarinet
b-drm	bass drum
bjo	banjo
b-sax	bass saxophone
clt	clarinet
c-mel	c melody saxophone
cnt	cornet
cym	cymbal
drms	drums (full drum kit)
e-gtr	electric guitar
flt	flute
flug	flugelhorn
gtr	rhythm guitar
hca	harmonica
ldr	leader
melo	melophonium
org	organ
pno	piano
rec	recorder
s-drum	side or snare drum

solo-gtr	solo guitar
sop	soprano saxophone
sousa	sousaphone
tamb	tambourine
tbn	trombone
ten	tenor saxophone
tpt	trumpet
tba	tuba
voc	vocal
v-tbn	valve trombone
wsb	washboard

Anti-Climax Jazz Band

Jim Petrie (cnt), Alan Quinn (tbn), George Gilmour (clt), Brian Weld (bjo), Kenny McDonald (bs), Kenny Milne (drms)
Recorded: Edinburgh Jazz 'n' Jive Club, October 10, 2009

1. At a Georgia camp meeting	J'n'J CD002
2. Tishomingo blues	J'n'J CD002

Auld Reekie Parade Band

Colin Dawson, Kenny Milne (tpt), Bob Craig, Jack Weddell (tbn), George Duncan (?)(clt) or Dick Lee (?)(clt), Teddy Johnson (ten), Jim Young (sousa), Andrew Hall (s-drm)
Recorded: Edinburgh, 1980

1. St Louis blues	CPLP038

Boab And The Busbymen
Part 1

John Arthur on the 'Fawkirk' Piano and Left Foot; Bob Busby: (1st clt, voc): Track 14: 2nd clt, alto, ten over-dubbed,
Recorded:

1. Shake that jelly roll	private issue CD
2. Wolverine blues	private issue CD
3. In the gloaming	private issue CD
4. Eccentric rag	private issue CD
5. Out of the galleon	private issue CD
6. Chicago buzz	private issue CD
7. Shreveport stomp	private issue CD
8. Funny feather man	private issue CD
9. Every evening	private issue CD
10. Perdido Street blues	private issue CD
11. Love nest	private issue CD
12. A miner's dream of home	private issue CD
13. Gravier Street blues	private issue CD
14. Nothing blues	private issue CD

Sandy Brown's Jazz Band

Archie Semple (cnt), Stu Eaton (v-tbn), Sandy Brown (clt),
John Semple (pno), George Crockett (drms)

Yellow Dog blues	private acetate
Stomp, stomp, stomp	private acetate
Shoe shiner's drag	private acetate

Recorded: Edinburgh, 1946

Stu Eaton (tpt), Al Fairweather (tbn), Sandy Brown (clt), 'Ma'
Bruce (pno), George Crockett (drms), Dru Bruce (voc - 1)
Recorded: Edinburgh, October? 1946

1. Fidgety feet	private acetate
2. Careless love (1)	private acetate

Stu Eaton (tpt), Sandy Brown (clt), 'Ma' Bruce (pno), Billy Neill
(gtr), Bill McGregor (bjo), George Crockett (drms)
Recorded: Edinburgh 1946

1. Yellow Dog blues	private acetate
2. *Untitled number*	private acetate
3. Doctor Jazz	private acetate
4. Shoe shiner's drag	private acetate

Stu Eaton (tpt), Sandy Brown (clt), 'Ma' Bruce (pno), Billy Neill
(gtr), Bill McGregor (bjo), George Crockett (drms), Dru Bruce
(voc)
Recorded: Edinburgh, January 3, 1947

1. Careless love (DB-voc)	private acetate
2. Won't you come home, Bill Bailey?	private acetate

Stu Eaton (tpt), Bob Fairley (tpt-1), Sandy Brown (clt), 'Ma'
Bruce (pno), Billy Neill (gtr), Bill McGregor (bjo), George
Crockett (drms), Dru Bruce (voc)
Recorded: Edinburgh, 25 January, 1947

1. Buddy Bolden blues	private acetate
2. Jazz me blues	private acetate
3. Sad ole blues	private acetate
4. Royal Garden blues (1)	private acetate

5. Joe Turner blues (voc-DB)   private acetate

Stu Eaton (tpt), Sandy Brown (clt), 'Ma' Bruce (pno), Billy Neill (gtr), Bill McGregor (bjo), George Crockett (drms)
Recorded: Edinburgh, July 4, 1947

1. I ain't gonna give nobody none of my jelly roll
                                      private acetate
2. Careless love   private acetate

Sandy Brown's Smoky City Six
Stu Eaton, Bob Fairley (tpts), Sandy Brown (clt), 'Ma' Bruce (pno), Dave Mylne (drms), Dru Bruce (voc)
Recorded: February 20, 1947

1. Atlanta blues (Make me a pallet on the floor)
                                      private acetate
2. Baby, won't you please come home
                                      private acetate

Stu Eaton (tpt), Bob R Fairley (tpt), Sandy Brown (clt), 'Ma' Bruce (pno), Bill McGrgeor (bjo), Dru Bruce (voc)
Recorded: Edinburgh, 1948

1. Buddy Bolden blues   private LP
Further unknown titles   private LP

Sandy Brown's Jazz Band
Al Fairweather (tpt), Sandy Brown (clt), Stan Greig (pno), John Twiss (bjo), Will Redpath (bs), Willie Burns (drms)
Recorded: Edinburgh, October 29, 1949

1. Heebie jeebies   S&M unissued
2. Of all the wrongs you've done to me   S&M unissued
3. Of all the wrongs you've done to me   S&M unissued
4. Of all the wrongs you've done to me   S&M 1001
5. Melancholy blues   S&M unissued
6. Melancholy blucs   S&M1001
7. Irish black bottom   S&M Unissued
8. Irish black bottom   S&M1002
9. Alexander   S&M unissued

543

10. Alexander   S&M 1002

Al Fairweather (tpt), Bob Craig (tbn), Sandy Brown (clt), Stan Greig (pno, voc), Norrie Anderson (bjo), Bill Strachan (drms)
Recorded: Edinburgh, October 27, 1950

1. Chattanooga stomp	S&M LP-5
2. Georgia bo bo (voc-SG)	S&M LP-5
3. Snake rag	S&M LP-5

Al Fairweather (tpt), Bob Craig (tbn), Sandy Brown (clt), Stan Greig (pno), Norrie Anderson (bjo), Bill Strachan (drms)
Recorded: Edinburgh, November 11, 1950

1. Mandy Lee blues	S&M LP-1
2. Georgia grind	S&M LP-1
3. Willie the Weeper	S&M 1003
4. I'm going away to wear you off my mind	S&M 1003
5. Sobbin' blues	S&M LP-1
6. Buddy's habit	S&M unissued
7. Buddy's habit	S&M LP-1
8. Aunt Hagar's blues	S&M LP-1
9. Keyhole blues	S&M unissued
10. Canal Street blues	S&M Unissued
11. Wild man blues	S&M Unissued
12. Heebie jeebies	S&M LP-1

The Historic Usher Hall Concert, 1952

Al Fairweather (tpt), Bob Craig (tbn), Sandy Brown (clt), Stan Greig (pno, drms), Norrie Anderson (bjo), Dizzy Jackson or John Rae (bs), Jim 'Farrie' Forsyth or Bill Strachan (drms), Sandy Currie (announcer)
Recorded: Usher Hall, Edinburgh, February 23, 1952

1. I ain't gonna tell nobody	Lake LACD94
2. Room rent blues	Lake LACD94
3. Keyhole blues	Lake LACD94
4. If I had a talking picture of you	Lake LACD94
5. Squeeze me	Lake LACD94
6. High society	Lake LACD94

7. Buddy's habit	Lake LACD94
8. Gatemouth	Lake LACD94
9. The Entertainer	Lake LACD94
10. Ory's Creole trombone	Lake LACD94
11. Everybody loves my baby	Lake LACD94
12. Savoy blues	Lake LACD94
13. Just a closer walk with Thee	Lake LACD94

Note: the CD information regarding the identity of the bass player and drummer has been questioned

A Sandy Session

Al Fairweather (tpt), Bob Craig (tbn), Sandy Brown (clt), Stan Greig (pno-1, drms -2), Norrie Anderson (bjo), Jim 'Farrie' Forsyth (drms, wbd)
Recorded: Edinburgh, May 3, 1952

1. Lady love (1)	S&M unissued
2. Lady love (1)	S&M LP-3
3. Of all the wrongs you've done to me	S&M LP-3
4. Jazz lips (1)	S&M LP-3
5. Jazz lips	S&M unissued
6. Krooked blues	S&M LP-3
7. King of the Zulus	S&M LP-3
8. Margie	S&M LP-3
9. When you're smiling (1)	S&M unissued
10. When you're smiling (2)	S&M unissued
11. Jazzin' babies blues	S&M unissued

Sandy Brown (pno)
Recorded: Edinburgh, May 4, 1952

1. Maple leaf rag (take 1)	S&M unissued
2. Maple leaf rag (take 2)	S&M unissued
3. Weary Brown	S&M 1004
4. Untitled	S&M unissued
5. Little Rock getaway	S&M unissued
6. King Porter stomp	S&M unissued

Al Fairweather (tpt), Sandy Brown (clt), Norrie Anderson (bjo), Jim 'Farrie' Forsyth (wbd)
Recorded: Late May, 1952

The Lord will make a way somehow   S&M 1004

Al Fairweather (tpt), Bob Craig (tbn), Sandy Brown (clt, voc),
Stan Greig (pno), Norrie Anderson (bjo), Johnnie Rae (bs), Jim
'Farrie' Forsyth (drms), Mike Hart (drms), David Mylne
(narrator)
Recorded: BBC Scottish Home Service, Queen Street
Studios, Edinburgh, July 4, 1952

1. Dilly mama yeh (Everybody loves Saturday night)	
	Acetate
2. Gettysburg march	Acetate
3. Countin' the blues (Jelly Bean blues)	Acetate
4. Ory's Creole trombone	Acetate
5. Oh! didn't he ramble	Acetate
6. Tears	Acetate
7. Sandy's blues	Acetate
8. I'll see you in my dreams	Acetate

This recording has never been issued commercially
although it has had wide distribution on both acetate and
cassette among collectors.
The dates shown here are the correct broadcast dates and
have been verified by Tom Lowrie who has the original ticket
stubs from the concert, which show dates and times.

Al Fairweather (tpt), Bob Craig (tbn), Sandy Brown (clt), Drew
Paterson (pno), Norrie Anderson (bjo), Dizzy Jackson (bs), Jim
'Farrie' Forsyth (drms), Stan Greig (drms-1)
Recorded: London, July 11, 1953

1. Dr Jazz	Esquire 333, LakeLACD136
2. Dr Jazz	Esquire 10-310, 333, LakeLACD136
3. Four or five times	Esquire 20-022, 333, LakeLACD136
4. Four or five times	Esquire 10-310, 333, LakeLACD136
5. Wild man blues	Esquire 20-022, 333,LakeLACD136
6. King Porter stomp (take1)	Esquire 20-022, 333, LakeLACD136
7. King Porter stomp (take 2)	Esquire 333, Lake LACD136

Sandy Brown Blue Five

Alex Welsh (cnt) Sandy Brown (cl, voc - 1), Dizzy Jackson (bs), Alex Imrie (bjo), Stan Greig (drms)
Recorded: Glasgow Rhythm Club, West Nile St, December 11, 1953

1. Trouble in mind	S&M LP-2
2. Johnny is the boy for me	S&M LP-4
3. My man	S&M LP-4
4. Sweet Georgia Brown	S&M LP-4
5. Jenny's ball	S&M LP-4
6. Wolverine blues	S&M LP-4
7. Texas moaner	S&M LP-4
8. Careless love	S&M 10" LP unnumbered
9. Sweet Georgia Brown	S&M 10" LP unnumbered
10. Ole Miss'	S&M 10" LP unnumbered
11. Nobody's sweetheart	S&M issue details unknown
12. Ole Miss	S&M issue details unknown
13. My Monday date	S&M issue details unknown
14. Up above my head (1)	S&M issue details unknown
15. Limehouse blues	S&M issue details unknown
16. Heebie jeebies	S&M issue details unknown
17. Running Wild	S&M issue details unknown
18. High Society	S&M issue details unknown
19. My man	S&M issue details unknown

As far as is known, only one copy of each of LP-4 and LP-5 exist. Unfortunately, all attempts to get access to this recording and for information about it have been unsuccessful. Listening to what is available on taped copies of a few of these tracks, there are at least two sessions involved. One is 'live' and would be the Glasgow Rhythm Club recordings, the other tracks are studio recordings.

Capital Jazz Band

Charlie Malley (tpt), Graeme Robertson (tbn, voc - 1), Jackie Graham (clt, alto), George Cavaye (pno, voc-2), Colin Warwick (bjo), Ken Burns (bs, tba, voc - 3, ldr), Jimmy Henderson (drms)
Recorded: Edinburgh, March 3, 1990

1. Bugle boy march	band issue MC
2. Coney Island washboard (2)	band issue MC
3. Black and blue	band issue MC
4. Blaze away	band issue MC
5. I found a new baby	band issue MC
6. My gal Sal (1)	band issue MC
7. I'm crazy 'bout my baby (3)	band issue MC
8. Hiawatha rag	band issue MC
9. High society	band issue MC
10. Buddy Bolden blues (1)	band issue MC
11. Avalon	band issue MC
12. Yearning	band issue MC

Climax Jazz Band

Jim Petrie (cnt, voc), Jack Weddell (tbn), George Gilmour (clt), Mike Lunn (pno), Jock Westwater (bjo), Roy Percy (bs), Rinus Van De Peppel (drms)
Recorded: De Haagse Jazzclub, The Hague, November 25, 1990

1. Don't give up the ship	Jox 010
2. Tishimingo blues	Jox 010
3. Just a little while to stay here	Jox 010
4. Burgundy Street blues	Jox 010
5. My little girl	Jox 010
6. Old spinning wheel in the parlour	Jox 010
7. South	Jox 010
8. The curse of an aching heart	Jox 010
9. Climax rag	Jox 010
10. Till we meet again	Jox 010

Climax Re-Union Band

Jim Petrie (cnt, voc), Jack Weddell (tbn, voc), Jake McMahon (clt), Tom Finlay (pno), Mike Hart (bjo), Jim Young (bs), Kenny Milne (drms)
Recorded: Fingers Piano Bar, Edinburgh, June 13, 1992

1. Climax rag	band issue MC
2. Red man blues	band issue MC
3. Out in the cold again	band issue MC
4. East Coast trot	band issue MC

5. I'm forever blowing bubbles	band issue MC
6. Down in honky tonk town	band issue MC
7. Bright star blues	band issue MC
8. Girl of my dreams	band issue MC
9. Tea for two	band issue MC
10. Mama's gone goodbye	band issue MC
11. My blue heaven	band issue MC
12. There, I've said it again	band issue MC
13. Sweetie dear	band issue MC

Jim Petrie (cnt, voc), Jack Weddell (tbn, voc), Jake McMahon (clt), Tom Wood (pno), Mike Hart (bjo), Jim Young (bs), Kenny Milne (drms)
Recorded: Sydney, Australia, 1992

1. Somebody stole my gal	CRJB95
2. My little girl	CRJB95
3. All alone by the telephone	CRJB95
4. Baby, I want you tonight	CRJB95
5. Sensation rag	CRJB95
6. Big chief battle axe	CRJB95
7. At a Georgia camp meeting	CRJB95
8. Arkansas blues	CRJB95
9. That's a plenty	CRJB95

Criterion Brass Band
Everybody Loves Saturday Night

Kenny Milne (tpt, ldr), Dave Strut (tpt), Jack Weddell (tbn), George Gilmour (clt), Ian Boyter (ten), Simon Carlyle (sousa), Roy Dunnett (s-drm), Graham Scott (b-drm and cym)
Recorded: Edinburgh, 2001

1. Tell me your dreams	Hot Jazz
2. Everybody loves Saturday night	Hot Jazz
3. Just a little while to stay here	Hot Jazz
4. Ting-a-ling	Hot Jazz
5. Blue Monk	Hot Jazz
6. Down by the riverside	Hot Jazz
7. Mama Inez	Hot Jazz

8. Eh la bas	Hot Jazz
9. The laughing samba	Hot Jazz, J'nJ CD001
10. Ma, he's making eyes at me	Hot Jazz

Bourbon Street Parade
Finlay Milne, Jan Wouters (tpts), Alan Quinn (tbn), George Gilmour (clt), Ian Boyter (ten), Bill Bryden (sousa), Kenny Milne (s-drm), Graham Scott (b-drm), Jennifer Milne (tamb)
Recorded: Fairmile Inn, Edinburgh, 2004

1. Bourbon Street parade	Hot Jazz
2. St Louis blues	Hot Jazz
3. Precious Lord, take my hand	Hot Jazz
4. Jambalaya	Hot Jazz
5. High society	Hot Jazz
6. Beer barrel polka	Hot Jazz
7. St Thomas	Hot Jazz, J'n'J CD001
8. What a friend we have in Jesus	Hot Jazz
9. Over in the gloryland	Hot Jazz, J'n'J CD001
10. Li'l Liza Jane	Hot Jazz
11. Maryland, my Maryland	Hot Jazz
12. Bogalousa strut	Hot Jazz
13. Weary blues	Hot Jazz

Mardi Gras In New Orleans
Kenny Milne, Graham McArthur (tpts), Alan Quinn (tbn), George Gilmour (clt), Ian Boyter (ten), Simon Carlyle (sousa), Mac Rae (s-drm), Graham Scott (b-drm), Jennifer Milne (whistle, tamb)
Recorded: Fireman's Club, Edinburgh, 2006

1. Sing on	Hot Jazz
2. Just a closer walk with Thee	Hot Jazz
3. Does Jesus care?	Hot Jazz
4. Don't give up the ship	Hot Jazz
5. 'Tain't what you do	Hot Jazz
6. Sheik of Araby	Hot Jazz
7. Mardi Gras in New Orleans	Hot Jazz
8. Climax rag	Hot Jazz
9. Tuxedo Junction	Hot Jazz

10. Don't go 'way nobody	Hot Jazz
11. Down in honky tonk town	Hot Jazz
12. Scotland the brave	Hot Jazz
13. The Preacher	Hot Jazz
14. Red rides again	Hot Jazz
15. Four leaf clover	Hot Jazz
16. Chinatown, my Chinatown	Hot Jazz

Diplomats Of Jazz
Dreaming the Hours Away

Jim Petrie (cnt, voc)), Jack Graham (clt, alto), Jock Westwater (bjo), Bill Brydon (sousa)
Recorded: Bute Jazz Festival, date unknown

1. Oriental man	band issue MC
2. Trav'lin all alone	band issue MC
3. Shake it and break it	band issue MC
4. You'll long for me	band issue MC
5. Struttin' with some barbecue	band issue MC
6. Beaucoup de jazz	band issue MC
7. You made me love you	band issue MC
8. Melancholy blues	band issue MC
9. Anytime	band issue MC
10. Gravier Street blues	band issue MC
11. Blame it on the blues	band issue MC
12. Dreaming the hours away	band issue MC

Body And Soul
Jim Petrie (cnt, voc)), Jack Graham (clt, alto), Jock Westwater (bjo), Bill Brydon (sousa)
Recorded: Royal Ettrick Hotel, Edinburgh, February 20, 1995

1. Hey, hey baby	band issue MC
2. Sweet like this	band issue MC
3. I want a little girl	band issue MC
4. Shake it and break it	band issue MC
5. Supposin'	band issue MC
6. I'm not worrying	band issue MC
7. Marguerite	band issue MC

8. Body and soul	band issue MC
9. Snookum	band issue MC
10. What is this thing called love	band issue MC

Jim Petrie (cnt), Bob Busby (clt, alto), Beverley Knight (bjo), Bill Brydon (sousa)
Recorded: Edinburgh Jazz 'n' Jive Club, November 21, 2003

1. Wa wa wa	J'n'J CD001
2. Snag it	J'n'J CD001
3. I can't give you anything but love	J'n'J CD001

The Hut

Jim Petrie (cnt), Bob Busby (clt, alto), Norman Field (clt, c-mel-1), Beverley Knight (bjo), Bill Brydon (sousa)
Recorded: Fairmile Inn
(a) November 21, 2003
(b) April 26, 2004
(c) October 8, 2004
(d) December 12, 2004
(e) March 4, 2005
(f) June 10, 2005

1. Snag it (a)	band issue MC
2. Forty and tight (b)	band issue MC
3. Froggie Moore rag (b)	band issue MC
4. Mandy Lee blues (b)	band issue MC
5. Buddy Bolden blues (c)	band issue MC
6. Love nest (c)	band issue MC
7. Lost (c)	band issue MC
8. Bye and bye (d)	band issue MC
9. Marguerite (4)	band issue MC
10. You're a real sweetheart (1) (d)	band issue MC
11. I'm lonesome sweetheart (1) (e)	band issue MC
12. You're the one I care for (f)	band issue MC
13. Dreaming the hours away (f)	band issue MC
14. Irish black bottom (f)	band issue MC

Jim Petrie (cnt), Bob Busby (clt, alto), Beverley Knight (bjo), Bill Brydon (sousa) - with guest Norman Field (clt, alto, c-mel sax),
Recorded: Fairmile Inn, Edinburgh, March 4, 2005

My Monday Date

1. Martha	band issue CD
2. Keyhole blues	*unissued*
3. Lady love	band issue CD
4. Crying for the Carolines	band issue CD
5. Loveable	band issue CD
6. I can't give you anything but love, baby	band issue CD
7. East Coast trot	band issue CD
8. Blue and broken hearted	*unissued*
9. No moon at all	*unissued*
10. Until today	*unissued*
11. June night	*unissued*
12. What good am I without you	*unissued*
13. You're a real sweetheart	*unissued*
14. San	band issue CD
15. Sweet Ella May	band issue CD
16. Oriental strut	*unissued*
17. Try a little tenderness	*unissued*
18. My Monday date	band issue cd
19. I'm lonesome, Sweetheart	*unissued*
20. Once in a while	band issue CD
21. Sorry	band issue CD
22. Poor man blues	band issue CD
23. Swing that music	band issue CD

Jim Petrie (cnt), Bob Busby (clt, alto), Beverley Knight (bjo), Bill Brydon (sousa)
Recorded: Edinburgh Jazz 'n' Jive Club, June 25, 2010

1. New wang wang blues	J'n'J CD002
2. Cabin in the pines	J'n'J CD002
3. China boy	J'n'J CD002

Fiona Duncan And Her Jazz Friends
Fiona's Fellas

Fiona Duncan (voc), Gordon Dillon (tpt), George Kidd (tbn), Sam Smith (tbn-1), Dick Stroak (clt, saxes), Jack Finlay (pno), Johnny Harper (gtr), Johnny Phillips (gtr-2), Kenny McDonald (bs), Murray Smith (drms) Dave Swanson (drms-3)
Recorded: Craighall Studios, Edinburgh, March 1982

1. I ain't gonna play no second fiddle   FATT FH1000
2. You've changed   FATT FH1000
3. The eagle and me   FATT FH1000
4. Gimme a pigfoot and a bottle of beer (1)   FATT FH1000
5. I can't give you anything but love   FATT FH1000
6. Is you is, or is you ain't my baby?   FATT FH1000
7. Please don't talk about me when I'm gone   FATT FH1000
8. You've been a good old wagon   FATT FH1000
9. Gee baby, ain't I good to you?   FATT FH1000
10. Fine brown frame   FATT FH1000
11. I used to love you (2, 3)   FATT FH1000
12. If I could be with you   FATT FH1000
13. Someday sweetheart (3)   FATT FH1000
14. Dinah (3)   FATT FH1000

Al Fairweather Jazz Band

Al Fairweather (tpt), Bob Craig (tbn), Dave Paxton (clt), Christian Rosendal (clt-1 added), Jock Westwater (bjo), Jim Young (bs), Kenny Milne (drms)
Recorded: Glenelg Hotel, Edinburgh, January 31, 1990

1. Sunset Café stomp   limited issue CD
2. Black and blue   limited issue CD
3. I can't give you anything but love   limited issue CD
4. Rosetta (1)   limited issue CD
5. Canal Street blues   limited issue CD
6. Muskrat ramble   limited issue CD
7. Tin Roof blues   limited issue CD
8. Cakewalking babies   limited issue CD
9. Heebie jeebies   limited issue CD
10. Ole Miss rag   limited issue CD
11. Baby, won't you please come home
    limited issue CD
12. An apple for the teacher   limited issue CD

This was a privately recorded session and was made available on a limited basis to members of the Sandy Brown Society only.

Fat Sam's Band
Jive On Down
Gus Ferguson (tpt), Graeme Robertson (tbn), Hamish McGregor (clt, alto, bar, ldr), Nick Robertson (alto, voc), Bill Simpson (sop, ten), Donald Corbett (pno), Tony Howard (gtr), Bobby Millar (bs), Ken Mathieson (drms)
Recorded: Craighall Studios, Edinburgh, January 1986

1. Jumpin' jive *	Salmet 501
2. Jack you're dead	Salmet 501
3. Reet Petite and Gone	Salmet 501
4. Chartreuse *	Salmet 501
5. What's the use of getting sober	Salmet 501
6. That chick's too young to fry	Salmet 501
7. Choo-choo-ch-boogie	Salmet 501
8. Nobody here but us chickens	Salmet 501
9. You run your mouth	Salmet 501
10. Is you is or is you ain't my baby?	Salmet 501
11. Saturday night fish fry *	Salmet 501
12. San Francisco Fran	Salmet 501
13. Five guys named Mo	Salmet 501

Boogie On Down
Gus Ferguson (tpt), Graeme Robertson (tbn), Hamish McGregor (clt, alto, bar, ldr), Nick Robertson (alto, voc), Tom Chalmers (clt, ten, fl), Campbell Normand (pno), Tony Howard (gtr), Donald McDonald (bs), Ken Mathieson (drms)
Recorded: REL Studios, Edinburgh, March 15, 1988

1. Fat Sam boogie	FSC502
2. Flat foot floogie	FSC502
3. You're my meat	FSC502
4. Roll 'em *	FSC502
5. That cat is high	FSC502
6. Minnie the moocher	FSC502
7. Jumpin' with Symphony Sid *	FSC502
8. Caldonia *	FSC502
9. Echoes of Harlem	FSC502
10. Fat Sam from Birmingham	FSC502
11. Moten swing *	FSC502
12. Messy Bessy	FSC502

13. Alright   FSC502

Note: the above two recordings were issued as 'Fat Sam's Band, Volume 1, 1986 -88' on a double cassette and entitled as shown

Swing On Down

Gus Ferguson (tpt), Jimmy Mann (tbn), Hamish McGregor (clt, sop, alto, voc, ldr), Martin Foster (clt, sop, alto, bar), Tom Chalmers (clt, ten, flt), Campbell Normand (pno), Tony Howard (gtr), Donald McDonald (bs), Ken Mathieson (drms)
Recorded: Sonic Studios, Edinburgh, June 11, 1989

1. Miller Madness: Little brown Jug; Pennsylvania 6500; American patrol; String of pearls, Chattanooga choo-choo; In the mood *   FSB502
2. You know it too   FSB502
3. Basically blues   FSB502
4. Shape in a drape   FSB502
5. The Mooche *   FSB502
6. Meet me with your black drawers on *   FSB502
7. All of me   FSB502
8. Spain   FSB502
9. Tougher than tough   FSB502
10. Drop me off in Harlem *   FSB502
11. Night train   FSB502
12. That old devil called love *   FSB502
13. Sure had a wonderful time *   FSB502
14. Bugle call rag   FSB502

Ring Dem Bells
Gus Ferguson (tpt), Jimmy Mann (tb), Hamish McGregor (clt, sop, alto, voc, ldr), Martin Foster (clt, sop, alto, bar), Tom Chalmers (clt, ten, flt), Campbell Normand (pno), Tony Howard (gtr), Donald McDonald (bs), Ken Mathieson (drms)
Recorded: Sonic Studios, Edinburgh, 13 & 14 April 1991

1. Ring dem bells *   FSB503
2. All for the love of Lil   FSB503
3. Sweet Like This   FSB503

4. Stealin' apples	FSB503
5. Black butterfly	FSB503
6. Suey	FSB503
7. I want a roof over my head *	FSB503
8. Oui, c'est samba *	FSB503
9. I found a new baby *	FSB503
10. Lover man	FSB503
11. Everybody eats	FSB503
12. Mood indigo *	FSB503
13. Big 10 inch *	FSB503
14. On the sunny side of the street	FSB503
15. Let the good times roll	FSB503

*Note: * these recordings were issued as 'Fat Sam's Band, Volume 2, 1989 - 91' on a double cassette and entitled as shown*

Live at the Paisley Arts Centre

Gus Ferguson (tpt), Jimmy Mann (tbn), Hamish McGregor (clt, sop, alto, voc, ldr), Jack Duff (clt, sop, alto, ten, bar), Tom Chalmers (clt, ten), Tom Finlay (pno), Tony Howard (gtr), Donald McDonald (bs), Ken Mathieson (drms)
Recorded: The Arts Centre, Paisley, February 1994

1. Sweet Georgia Brown	FSB504
2. T'ain't what you do +	FSB504
3. Hay bab a rebop +	FSB504
4. In my solitude +	FSB504
5. Buddy Bolden's blues	FSB504
6. April in Paris +	FSB504
7. Down by the riverside +	FSB504
8. Davenport blues	FSB504
9. The drippy dripper +	FSB504
10. Mack the Knife +	FSB504
11. Rose of the Rio Grande	FSB504
12. Buona sera	FSB504
13. Embraceable you +	FSB504
14. Just a gigolo / I ain't got nobody +	FSB504

15. Fats Domino Medley: Be My Guest; Ain't That A Shame; I Want To Walk You Home; My Blue Heaven; Blueberry Hill + FSB504

Live At Fat Sam's Diner

Gus Ferguson (tpt),Eddie Severn (ten-1,), Jimmy Mann (tbn), Hamish McGregor (clt, sop, alto, voc, ldr), Jack Duff (clt, sop, alto, ten, bar), Tom Chalmers (clt, ten), Tom Finlay (pno), Tony Howard (gtr), Donald McDonald (bs), Ken Mathieson (drms)

Recorded: Fat Sam's Diner, Edinburgh, March 1994

1. Cotton Club stomp	FSB505
2. Meet Mr Rabbit	FSB505
3. Stranger on the shore +	FSB505
4. Jumpin' at the Woodside +	FSB505
5. Ain't got nothin' but the blues +	FSB505
6. China boy (1)	FSB505
7. Satin doll (1) +	FSB505
8. The kid from Redbank (1) +	FSB505
9. Shreveport stomp (1)	FSB505
10. Moulin a café (1) +	FSB505
11. Shiny stockings (1) +	FSB505

Note: these two recordings were issued as 'The Best of Fat Sam's Band, Volume 2' on a double cassette and entitled as shown

The Best Of Fat Sam's Band, Volume 1

This is the first CD issued by the band and is a 22 track compilation of SAL501, FSC502, FSB502 & FSB503, marked with an '*', with the following exceptions

20. Shape in a drape (recorded BBC London 'Opportunity Knocks' 1991

21. Ain't nobody here but us chickens (recorded BBC Scotland 1991)

22. Choo-choo-ch-boogie (recorded BBC Scotland 1991)

The Best Of Fat Sam's Band, Volume 2

This is the second CD issued by the band and is a 17 track compilation of, FSB 504 & 505, marked with '+'

Fat Sam's Band, Volume 3 – Live At Fat Sam's Downtown Diner

Tom McNiven (tpt), Dave Batchelor (tbn), Hamish McGregor (clt, sop, alto, ldr), John Burgess (ten, flt), Martin Foster (clt, alto, ten, bar), Andrew Barber (alto, bar – 1), Steve Meeker (ten – 1), Tom Finlay (pno, org), Tony Howard (gtr, voc), Roy Percy (bs, elb), Alistair Morrow (drms)
Recorded: April 15 & 22, 1998

1. Night train	band issue CD
2. It should have been me	band issue CD
3. Change my plan	band issue CD
4. Safronia (1)	band issue CD
5. Flight of the foo birds	band issue CD
6. Alright, OK, you win	band issue CD
7. I love the life I live	band issue CD
8. What's new?	band issue CD
9. Mr Blues is comin' to town	band issue CD
10. Splanky	band issue CD
11. You go to my head	band issue CD
12. Reet petite	band issue CD
13. Sweet home Chicago	band issue CD
14. Theme from Peter Gunn	band issue CD
15. Pink champagne	band issue CD
16. Sittin' on it all the time	band issue CD
17. 'Gators drag	band issue CD

Fat Sam's Band, Volume 4 – Live at Fat Sam's

Bill Hunter (tpt), Dave Batchelor (tbn), Hamish McGregor (clt, alto, voc, ldr), Martin Foster (alto, bar), Iestyn Evans (ten), Tom Finlay (pno), Eric Wales (gtr, voc), Roy Percy (bs), Alistair Morrow (drms)
Recorded: November 17 & 24, 1999

1. Up a lazy river	band issue CD
2. 9.20 Special	band issue CD
3. Big fat mammas	band issue CD
4. Jeeps blues	band issue CD
5. Minnie the Moocher	band issue CD
6. Skin deep	band issue CD
7. Is you is or is you ain't my baby?	band issue CD
8. Honeysuckle rose	band issue CD
9. Bad, bad Leroy Brown	band issue CD
10. Stardust	band issue CD

11. One sweet letter from you	band issue CD
12. Blue Lou	band issue CD
13. Jungle king	band issue CD
14. Fantail	band issue CD
15. Fat Sam from Birmingham	band issue CD
16. Basically blues	band issue CD
17. Buona sera	band issue CD
18. One O'clock jump	band issue CD
19. Flying home	band issue CD

Fat Sam's Band, Volume 5

Bill Hunter (tpt), Dave Batchelor (tbn), Hamish McGregor (clt, alto, voc, ldr), Allon Beauvoisin (alto, bar), Gordon McNeil (ten), Tom Finlay (pno), Eric Wales (gtr), Phil Adams (gtr-1) Mark Austin (bs) ,Roy Percy (bs-1) Alistair Morrow (drms)
Recorded: February 1, 2003

1. The Fat Sam boogie (1)	band issue CD
2. All of me (1)	band issue CD
3. Clementine (1)	band issue CD
4. Lester leaps in	band issue CD
5. Lover man	band issue CD
6. Let the good times roll (1)	band issue CD
7. Stompin' at The Savoy (1)	band issue CD
8. Swingin' the blues (1)	band issue CD
9. Hey now, hey now (1)	band issue CD
10. The angels sing	band issue CD
11. Mama do (1)	band issue CD
12. Opus 1	band issue CD
13. Guitar boogie	band issue CD
14. Have you met Miss Jones? (1)	band issue CD
15. Loch Lomond	band issue CD
16. On the sunny side of the street (1)	band issue CD

Fat Sam's Band, Volume 6 – Airmail Special

Bill Hunter (tpt), Dave Batchelor (tbn), Hamish McGregor (reeds, voc, ldr), Keith Edwards (reeds), Konrad Wiszniewski (reeds), Tom Finlay (pno), Campbell Normand (pno-2)Eric Wales (gtr), Ed Kelly (bs), Alistair Morrow (drms), Tom Gordon (drms-1)

Recorded:
(a) The Spiegeltent, Edinburgh, August 3, 2007
(b) The Jamhouse, Edinburgh, July 31, 2009
(c) The Jamhouse, Edinburgh, August 7, 2009

1. Airmail special (2) (c)	band issue CD
2. Old cow hand (1) (b)	band issue CD
3. Mercy, mercy, mercy (2) (c)	band issue CD
4. The summer wind (2) (c)	band issue CD
5. Salt peanuts (2) (c)	band issue CD
6. Benny's from heaven (2) (c)	band issue CD
7. Isfhan (1) (b)	band issue CD
8. East of the sun (a)	band issue CD
9. Keeping out of mischief now (b)	band issue CD
10. For once in my life (2) (c)	band issue CD
11. Old Fat Sam (a)	band issue CD
12. I'm getting sentimental over you (1) (b)	band issue CD
13. Old man river (a)	band issue CD
14. Harry James Medley: My silent love, You made me love you, I had the craziest dream (1) (b)	band issue CD
15. Cherokee (2) (c)	band issue CD
16. Jump (2) (c)	band issue CD
17. Satin doll (2) (c)	band issue CD
18. Walk between the raindrops (1) (b)	band issue CD

Jack Finlay Trio With Benny Waters
Edinburgh International Jazz Festival, 1986
Benny Waters (alto), Jack Finlay (pno), Kenny Ellis (bs), Bobby Stewart (drms)
Recorded: 1986?

1. Some of these days	1986 Edinburgh Jazz Festival LP

Fred's Clubhouse Seven
Kenny Milne (tpt), John Arthur (tbn), George Duncan (clt), Gus McKay (pno), Kenny Henderson (bjo), Fred Murray (bs, voc, ldr), Roy Dunnett (drms)
Recorded: Edinburgh Jazz 'n' Jive Club, October 10, 2007

1. Buddy's habit	J'n'J CD001
2. You are my sunshine	J'n'J CD001

3. You always hurt the one you love	J'n'J CD001
4. Savoy blues	J'n'J CD002
5. Goin' home	J'n'J CD002

Mike Hart With The Hot Antic Jazz Band
Concert du 10eme Anniversaire du Hot Antic Jazz Band
Michel Bastide (cnt, v-tbn, voc), Benny Waters (alto-1), Jean-Francois Bonnel (clt, alto, ten, cnt, voc), Stephane Matthey (pno), Jean-Pierre Dubois (bjo, gtr, clt), Mike Hart (bjo, voc-2), Bernard Antherieu (bjo-3), Christian Lefevre (bb, tbn), Stephen Joseph (drms, wbd), Jean- Francois Guyot (wbd-4), Dave Bennett (voc-5)
Recorded: Opera de Nimes, France, Friday, March 17, 1989

1. Shine (1,2)	HP-1
2. Nagasaki (1,5)	HP-1
3. I lost my gal from Memphis (1,4)	HP-1
4. Dans les rues D'Antibes (3)	HP-1
5. Petite fleur (3)	HP-1
6. Les oignons 3)	HP-1
7. China boy (1,3)	HP-1

Mike Hart is not featured on any other tracks
This recording was also released in DVD format

Mike Hart's International All Stars
Full House
Mike Daly (tpt), Bob Barnard (cnt-1), John Service (tbn), Hamish McGregor (clt, voc), Jonny Boston (ten, voc-2), Tom Finlay (pno), Mike Hart (bjo, gtr), Roy Percy (bs), Adam Sorenson (drms)
Recorded: The Famous Spiegeltent, Edinburgh International Jazz & Blues Festival, August 4, 2005

1. That's a plenty	Parsnip CD006
2. If you were the only girl in the world	Parsnip CD006
3. Savoy blues	Parsnip CD006
4. Cheek to cheek (2)	Parsnip CD006
5. Wild man blues (1)	Parsnip CD006
6. Keeping out of mischief (1,2)	Parsnip CD006
7. Way down yonder in New Orleans (1,2)	Parsnip CD006

8. I never knew (1,2)	Parsnip CD006
9. Avalon	Parsnip CD006
10. Shine	Parsnip CD006
11. If I had you	Parsnip CD006
12. Topsy	Parsnip CD006
13. After you've gone	Parsnip CD006
14. Sweet Lorraine	*unissued*
15. Strutting with some barbecue	*unissued*
16. Wild man blues	*unissued*
17. Nagasaki	*unissued*
18. Bourbon Street parade	*unissued*
19. My blue heaven	*unissued*
20. High society	*unissued*
21. Royal Garden blues	*unissued*
22. Everybody loves Saturday night	*unissued*

Mike Hart's (Scottish) Society Syncopators
Jazz Tattoo

Gus Ferguson (tpt, voc-1), Johnny McGuff (tbn), Jackie Graham (clt, alto, voc-2), Tom Finlay (pno), Mike Hart (bjo, gtr), Kenny McDonald (bs), Bobby Stewart (drms)
Recorded: REL Studios, Edinburgh, March 9, 1980

1. Go Ghana	Parsnip PR1001
2. My ain folk (2)	Parsnip PR1001
3. Willie The Weeper	Parsnip PR1001
4. New Orleans	Parsnip PR1001
5. Loch Lomond (2)	Parsnip PR1001
6. Rosetta (1)	Parsnip PR1001
7. Doin' the crazy walk	Parsnip PR1001
8. Buddy Bolden's blues	Parsnip PR1001
9. Muskrat ramble	Parsnip PR1001
10. Wolverine blues	Parsnip PR1001
11. T'ain't what you do (2)	Parsnip PR1001
12. Panama rag	Parsnip PR1001

Huntin' Shootin' And Jazzin'

Andrew Lauder (tpt),Dave Strutt (cnt ,tpt, mel) Johnny McGuff (tbn, v-tbn), Jackie Graham (clt, alto), Tom Finlay (pno), Mike Hart (bjo, gtr), Francis Cowan (bs), Frank Birnie (drms), Kenny Henderson (bagpipes-1)
Recorded: Craighall Studios, Edinburgh, March 3, 1984

1. Jubilee	Parsnip PR1002
2. New Orleans stomp	Parsnip PR1002
3. Aunt Hagar's blues	Parsnip PR1002
4. Goin' out the back way	Parsnip PR1002
5. Maple leaf rag	Parsnip PR1002
6. Sing, sing, sing	Parsnip PR1002
7. Trombone rag	Parsnip PR1002
8. Squeeze me	Parsnip PR1002
9. Maryland, my Maryland	Parsnip PR1002
10. Ostrich walk	Parsnip PR1002
11. Apple honey	Parsnip PR1002
12. Bagpipe haggis march (1)	Parsnip PR1002

With Wild Bill Davison and Jim Galloway

Wild Bill Davison (cnt-1), Jim Galloway (sop-2), Dave Strutt (cnt), Johnny McGuff (tbn), Hamish McGregor (clt, sop, alto, bar), Jackie Graham (clt, alto), Tom Finlay (pno), Mike Hart (bjo, gtr), Jerry Forde (bs-3), Francis Cowan (bs), Frank Birnie (drms), Wendy Weatherby (voc-4)
Recorded: Craighall Studios, Edinburgh, March 8, 1986

1. I never knew (1,2)	Parsnip 1003
2. Keeping out of mischief (1,2)	Parsnip 1003
3. Flying home (2)	Parsnip 1003
4. Hard hearted Hannah (4)	Parsnip 1003
5. B.M. rag (3)	Parsnip 1003
6. Save it pretty mama (1,2)	Parsnip 1003
7. Dans les rues D'Antibes (2,3)	Parsnip 1003
8. Big Bill (2,3)	Parsnip 1003
9. Our monday date (1,2)	Parsnip 1003
10. Creole belles (3)	Parsnip 1003
11. A kiss to build a dream on (2)	Parsnip 1003
12. Rockin' in rhythm (2)	Parsnip 1003

Happy Feet

Bruce Adams (tpt),Dave Strutt (cnt, voc), Johnny McGuff (tbn), Jackie Graham (clt, alto, voc), Tom Finlay (pno), Mike Hart (bjo, gtr), Ricky Steele (bs, bb), Frank Birnie (drms), Wendy Weatherby (voc)
Recorded: Fingers Bar, Edinburgh, March 6 & 7, 1987

1. Cakewalking babies	band issue MC
2. Ludo	band issue MC
3. Strutting with some barbecue	band issue MC
4. The right key but the wrong keyhole	band issue MC
5. Cheek to Cheek	band issue MC
6. Willie the Weeper	band issue MC
7. T'ain't what you do	band issue MC
8. Potato head blues	band issue MC
9. Mop mop	band issue MC
10. Sugar blues	band issue MC
11. Happy feet	band issue MC
12. Blues in the closet	band issue MC
13. Dippermouth blues	band issue MC

Rehearsing For A Nervous Breakdown

Bruce Adams (tpt), Johnny McGuff (tbn), Jake McMahon (clt, ten), Tom Finlay (pno), Mike Hart (bjo, gtr), Ricky Steele (bs) Murray Smith (drms), Wendy Weatherby (voc)
Recorded: Fingers Bar, Edinburgh, December 11, 1988

1. Black bottom stomp	band issue MC
2. Second hand Rose	band issue MC
3. I'm sorry I made you cry	band issue MC
4. Poor Butterfly	band issue MC
5. Liza	band issue MC
6. Strike up the band	band issue MC
7. Wild women don't have the blues	band issue MC
8. I found a new baby	band issue MC
9. Tin Roof blues	band issue MC
10. Rehearsing for a nervous breakdown	band issue MC

Rothesay 1993

Dave Strutt (tpt, voc), Dave Fimister (tpt), Johnny McGuff (tbn), Jack Duff (clt, alto, ten), Tom Finlay (pno), Mike Hart (bjo, gtr), Ricky Steele (bs), Murray Smith (drms), Wendy Weatherby (voc)
Recorded: Rothesay Jazz Festival, May 1. 1993

1. I never knew	*Raymer Sound unissued*
2. Maple leaf rag	*Raymer Sound unissued*
3. It ain't no sin	*Raymer Sound unissued*

4. I got what it takes   *Raymer Sound unissued*
5. Cakewalking babies   *Raymer Sound unissued*
6. Squeeze me   *Raymer Sound unissued*
7. Goin' out the back way   *Raymer Sound unissued*
8. Sister Kate   *Raymer Sound unissued*
9. Dinah   *Raymer Sound unissued*
10. Rehearsing for a nervous breakdown
                                Raymer Sound unissued
11. Putting on the Ritz   *Raymer Sound unissued*
12. Potato head blues   *Raymer Sound unissued*
13. Happy feet   *Raymer Sound unissued*
14. Baby, won't you please come home
                                Raymer Sound unissued
15. Just a gigolo   *Raymer Sound unissued*
16. Tea for two   *Raymer Sound unissued*
17. Rose of Washington Square *Raymer Sound unissued*
18. Sing, sing, sing   *Raymer Sound unissued*

Rothesay 1994
Dave Strutt (tpt, voc), Dave Keir (tbn), Jake McMahon (clt, ten), Brian Kellock (pno), Mike Hart (bjo, gtr), Ricky Steele (bs), Murray Smith (drms), Wendy Weatherby (voc)
Recorded: Rothesay Jazz Festival, April 28, 1994

1. Empty bed blues   *Raymer Sound unissued*
2. Them there eyes   *Raymer Sound unissued*
3. Maple leaf rag   *Raymer Sound unissued*
4. Lazy bones   *Raymer Sound unissued*
5. Too busy   *Raymer Sound unissued*
6. I've got what it takes   *Raymer Sound unissued*
7. Sister Kate   *Raymer Sound unissued*
8. Ory's Creole trombone   *Raymer Sound unissued*
9. Evil hearted blues   *Raymer Sound unissued*
10. 'Tain't no sin   *Raymer Sound unissued*
11. Cal'donia   *Raymer Sound unissued*
12. Keeping out of mischief   *Raymer Sound unissued*
13. Goody, goody   *Raymer Sound unissued*
14. Rehearsing for a nervous breakdown
                                Raymer Sound unissued

Jake's Melody Boys
Traditional Jazz Around The World
Jake McMahon (clt, ldr), Jack Weddell (tbn), Violet Milne (pno), Robin Galloway (bs), Kenny Milne (drms)
Recorded: 1996

1. All I do is dream of you	Jazz Crusade JCCD 3023
2. See See rider	Jazz Crusade JCCD 3023
3. Babyface	Jazz Crusade JCCD 3023
4. True	Jazz Crusade JCCD 3023
5. Underneath Hawaiian skies	Jazz Crusade JCCD 3023

Other tracks on this CD are by the Louisiana Shakers and Jesse's New Orleans Jazz Band

The Jazz Masters
Andrew Lauder (tpt), Jimmy Shortreed (clt, alto), Gordon Cruickshank (ten - 1), Jack Finlay (pno), Graham Blamire (bs, ldr), Donald 'Chick' Murray (drms)
Recorded: Fingers Piano Bar, Edinburgh, March, 1988

1. Chix at six	band issue MC
2. I'ts wonderful	band issue MC
3. How am I to know?	band issue MC
4. Nights at the turntable	band issue MC
5. Good Queen Bess	band issue MC
6. In the wee small hours	band issue MC
7. Shine	band issue MC
8. Black butterfly	band issue MC
9. Liza	band issue MC
10. Coquette	band issue MC
11. Pee Wee's blues	band issue MC
12. Perdido (1)	band issue MC
13. Blues march (1)	band issue MC
14. The Jeep is jumping (1)	band issue MC

Dave Keir's Hot Four
Stomp, Stomp, Stomp
Dave Keir (tpt, tbn), Bob Busby (clt, alto), Jock Westwater (bjo, voc - 1), Dizzy Jackson (bs)
Recorded: Edinburgh, Autumn, 1999

1. Come on and stomp, stomp, stomp	Jox unnumbered CD
2. Dallas blues	Jox unnumbered CD
3. Rhythm king	Jox unnumbered CD
4. Kansas City stomps	Jox unnumbered CD
5. Sobbin' blues	Jox unnumbered CD
6. Piggly Wiggly	Jox unnumbered CD
7. Sunset Café stomp	Jox unnumbered CD
8. Mandy Lee blues	Jox unnumbered CD
9. You're next	Jox unnumbered CD
10. Shake it and break it	Jox unnumbered CD
11. Lina blues (1)	Jox unnumbered CD
12 Ory's Creole trombone	Jox unnumbered CD
13. Angeline	Jox unnumbered CD
14. Weatherbird rag	Jox unnumbered CD
15. Riverside blues	Jox unnumbered CD
16. I'm goin' away to wear you off my mind	
	Jox unnumbered CD

Redman Blues

Dave Keir (tpt, tbn, alto), Bob Busby (clt, alto), Jock Westwater (bjo, voc-1), Dizzy Jackson (bs)
Recorded: Autumn 2000 / Spring 2001

1. Red man blues	Jox unnumbered CD
2. Tears	Jox unnumbered CD
3. Black and tan fantasy	Jox unnumbered CD
4. Love me or leave me (1)	Jox unnumbered CD
5. Chattanooga stomp	Jox unnumbered CD
6. Apex blues	Jox unnumbered CD
7. Walk that broad	Jox unnumbered CD
8. East St Louis toodle-oo	Jox unnumbered CD
9. Mandy make up your mind	Jox unnumbered CD
10. There ain't no sweet man worth the salt of my tears (1)	
	Jox unnumbered CD
11. East Coast trot	Jox unnumbered CD

12. Ole Miss rag	Jox unnumbered CD
13. Alligator blues	Jox unnumbered CD
14. Candy lips (1)	Jox unnumbered CD
15. Bouncing around	Jox unnumbered CD

Pete Kerr's Dixielanders
Al Clarke (tpt), Ken Ramage (tbn), Pete Kerr (clt), Bob McDonald (pno), Jim Douglas (bjo), Johnny Logan (bs), George Crockett (drms)
Recorded: Edinburgh, 1960

| 1. Stars and stripes forever | Waverley SLP505 |
| 2. Ice cream | Waverley SLP505 |

Al Clarke (tpt), Ken Ramage (tbn), Pete Kerr (clt), Bob McDonald (pno), Jim Douglas (bjo), Johnny Logan (bs), George Crockett (drms)
Recorded: Edinburgh, 1960

| 1. Coney Island washboard | Waverley SLP506 |
| 2. Waltzing Matilda | Waverley SLP506 |

Pete Kerr's Scottish All Stars
Jazz At The Capital
Mike Scott (tpt), Eddie Lorkin (tbn), Pete Kerr (clt), Mike Oliver (pno), Jim Douglas (bjo, gtr), Ron Mathewson (bs), Billy Law (drms)
Recorded: Craighall Studios, Edinburgh, 1963

1. Peter and the Wolf	Waverley ELP128
2. Night train	Waverley ELP128
3. The old spinning wheel	Waverley ELP128
4. Who's afraid of the big bad wolf	Waverley ELP128

More Jazz At The Capital
Pete Kerr (clt), Mike Scott (tpt), Eddie Lorkin (tbn), Mike Oliver, (pno), Jim Douglas (gtr/bjo), Ron Mathewson (bs), Billy Law (drms).
Recorded: Craighall Studios, Edinburgh, 1964

| 1. The ugly duckling | Waverley ELP135 |

2. Sonny Boy   Waverley ELP135
3. Davenport blues   Waverley ELP135
4. Drum break for Billy   Waverley ELP135

Maid Of The Forth Stompers

Andrew Lauder (cnt), Jimmy Shortreed (cl, alto), Harald Vox (bjo,gtr), Graham Blamire (b, ldr).
Recorded: Leapfrog, Edinburgh, March 21, 1995

1. Shine	band issue MC
2. Tishomingo blues	band issue MC
3. Mama's gone, goodbye	band issue MC
4. When somebody thinks you're wonderful	band issue MC
5. Summer set	band issue MC
6. Muskrat ramble	band issue MC
7. I found a new baby	band issue MC
8. Up a lazy river	band issue MC
9. Blues my naughtie sweetie gives to me	band issue MC
10. Wabash blues	band issue MC
11. 12th Street rag	band issue MC
12. Weary blues	band issue MC
13. Chinatown, my Chinatown	band issue MC

Andrew Lauder (cnt), Gerard Dott (clt), Nigel Porteous (bjo, gtr), Graham Blamire (bs, ldr)
Recorded: Edinburgh Jazz 'n' Jive Club, February 2, 2010

1. Always	J'n'J CD 002
2. Stevedore stomp	J'n'J CD 002

Ken Mathieson's Classic Jazz Band

Billy Hunter (tpt), Johnny McGuff (tbn), Dick Lee (clt, alto), Keith Edwards (ten), Martin Foster (clt, bar), Tom Finlay (pno), Ricky Steele (bs), Ken Mathieson (drms ,ldr)
Recorded: The Sound Café, Penicuik, September 19, 2004

1. Chicago breakdown	Demo
2. Shreveport stomp	Demo
3. The pearls	Demo
4. Sweet substitute	Demo
5. Buckini	Demo

Jelly's New Clothes
Billy Hunter (tpt), Ewan McAllan (tbn)), Dick Lee (clt, sop, alto), Keith Edwards (ten), Martin Foster (clt, alto, bar, bar), Tom Finlay (pno), Roy Percy (bs), Ken Mathieson (drms ,ldr)
Recorded: Castlesound Studios, Pentcaitland, 2006

1. Grandpa's spells	CJO-001
2. The pearls	CJO-001
3. Boogaboo	CJO-001
4. Froggie Moore	CJO-001
5. King Porter stomp	CJO-001
6. Jungle blues	CJO-001
7. Mamanita	CJO-001
8. Chicago breakdown	CJO-001
9. Dead man blues	CJO-001
10. Mister Joe	CJO-001
11. Shreveport stomp	CJO-001
12. Sweet substitute	CJO-001
13. Kansas City stomps	CJO-001

Salutes The Kings Of Jazz
Billy Hunter (tpt),Phil O'Malley (tbn), Dick Lee (clt, b-clt, sop, alto), Konrad Wiszniewski (ten), Martin Foster (clt,b-clt, alto, bar, b-sax), Tom Finlay (pno), Roy Percy (bs), Ken Mathieson (drms, ldr)
Recorded: Sound Café, Penicuik, 2007

1. Mahogany Hall stomp	Lake LACD 281
2. Mandy, make up your mind	Lake LACD 281
3. Blues for Kenny Davern	Lake LACD 281
4. Stompy Jones	Lake LACD 281
5. In a mist	Lake LACD 281
6. West End blues	Lake LACD 281
7. Sorry	Lake LACD 281
8. Morning glory	Lake LACD 281
9. Sweet like This	Lake LACD 281
10. Jitterbug waltz	Lake LACD 281
11. Buddy Bolden's blues	Lake LACD 281
12. Bojangles	Lake LACD 281
13. Georgia swing	Lake LACD 281
14. Singin' the blues	Lake LACD 281
15. Down South camp meeting	Lake LACD 281

Ken Mathieson's Classic Jazz Band With Duke Heitger
Celebrating Satchmo
Duke Heitger (tpt ,voc) with Billy Hunter(tpt), Phil O'Malley (tbn), Dick Lee (clt, sop, alto), Konrad Wiszniewski (ten), Martin Foster (clt, alto, bar), Paul Kirby (pno), Roy Percy (bs), Ken Mathieson (drms ,ldr)
Recorded: May 2008

1. Blues my naughtie sweetie gives to me	Lake LACD 286
2. Cornet chop suey	Lake LACD 286
3. When it's sleepy time down South	Lake LACD 286
4. Atlanta blues	Lake LACD 286
5. Song of the islands	Lake LACD 286
6. Wild man blues	Lake LACD 286
7. Down in honky tonk town	Lake LACD 286
8. Eventide	Lake LACD 286
9. Sweethearts on parade	Lake LACD 286
10. I got the right to sing the blues	Lake LACD 286
11. Among my souvenirs	Lake LACD 286
12. Coal cart blues	Lake LACD 286
13. Mahogany Hall stomp	Lake LACD 286
14. What a wonderful world	Lake LACD 286

Ken Mathieson's Classic Jazz Band With Alan Barnes
Alan Barnes (alto) with Billy Hunter (tpt), Phil O'Malley (tbn), Dick Lee (clt, sop, alto), Konrad Wiszniewski (ten), Martin Foster (clt, b-clt, bar), Paul Harrison (pno), Roy Percy (bs), Ken Mathieson (drms ,ldr)
Recorded: Sound Café, Penicuik, Midlothain, 2011

1. I can't believe that you're in love with me	
	Woodville WVCD133
2. Easy Money	Woodville WVCD133
3. A walkin' thing	Woodville WVCD133
4. The Glasgow Suite	Woodville WVCD133
A little at a time	
DN	
Waltz	
The Clyde	
8. Bright future	Woodville WVCD133

9. Stompin' at the Savoy	Woodville WVCD133
10. Honeysuckle rose	Woodville WVCD133
11. Malibu	Woodville WVCD133
12. Symphony in riffs	Woodville WVCD133
13. Doozy	Woodville WVCD133

Hamish Mcgregor's All Stars

Tommy Lister (tpt), Hamish McGregor (tbn, voc), Jackie Graham (clt), Johnny Harper (bjo), Graham Blamire (bs), Charlie Welsh (drms)
Recorded: Craighall Studios, Edinburgh, July 10, 1965

1. Molly Malone	private band recording
2. The Sheik of Araby	private band recording
3. Coney Island washboard	private band recording
4. Sit down you're rocking the boat	
	private band recording
5. I love my mother-in-law	
	private band recording

This recording was made for band members only

Charlie Mcnair's Jazz Band

Charlie McNair (tpt), Bob Craig (tbn), Jackie Graham (clt), Mike Hart (bjo), Dizzy Jackson (bs), Bobby Stewart (drms)
Recorded: Edinburgh, early 1960s

1. The fish man	Waverley Records SLP502
2. Big House blues	Waverley Records SLP502
3. Colonel Bogey march	Waverley Records SLP 504
4. My journey to the sky	Waverley Records SLP504

The Charlie Mcnair New Orleans Jazz Group

Charlie McNair (tpt), Jimmy Hilson (tbn), Joe Smith (clt), Dave Smith & Mike Hart (bjos), Sandy Malcolm (drms)
Recorded: St Andrew's Hall, Glasgow, June 30, 1956

1. Oh, didn't he ramble	Beltona ABL519 *

ABL519 other titles on this 10" LP are by the Clyde Valley Stompers and Alan Mason's Jazzmen

Charlie Mcnair's Jazz Band
Charlie McNair (tpt) Bill Munro (tbn), George Duncan(?) (clt ,alto), Harald Vox (bjo), Colin Archbold (bs), Toto McNaughton (drms)
Recorded: REL Studios, Edinburgh, 1980

Chimes blues   CPLP 038

Charlie Mcnair's Skiffle Group
Charlie McNair (tpt), Mike Pollett (tbn), Joe Smith (clt), Mike Hart (bjo), Sandy Malcolm (drms)

2. Hiawatha   Beltona BL2670
3. Meadow Lane Stomp   Beltona BL2670
Recorded: St Andrew's Hall, Glasgow, September,1955

Nova Scotia Jazz Band
Echoes Of The Mauve Decade
Mike Daly (cnt), John Burgess (clt, ten, ldr), Duncan Finlay (bjo, gtr), Roy Percy (bs)
Recorded: The Music Box, Edinburgh, September 14, 2009

1. At sundown   C-Side 007
2. Up a lazy river   C-Side 007
3. Chinatown, my Chinatown   C-Side 007
4. I want a little girl   C-Side 007
5. China boy   C-Side 007
6. 'Deed I do   C-Side 007
7. Please don't talk about me when i'm gone
                                        C-Side 007
8. Exactly like you   C-Side 007
9. Shine   C-Side 007
10. Do you know what it means to miss New Orleans
                                        C-Side 007
11. Dinah   C-Side 007

Chinatown My Chinatown

Mike Daly (cnt), John Burgess (clt, ten, ldr), Duncan Finlay (bjo, gtr). Kenny Mcdonald (bs)
Recorded: Carlisle, Gateshead & Reeth, June 2011

1. Chinatown, my Chinatown	C-side 029
2. I can't give you anything but love	C-side 029
3. At the jazz band ball	C-side 029
4. I want a little girl	C-side 029
5. Please don't talk about me	C-side 029
6. Way down yonder in New Orleans	C-side 029
7. Royal Garden blues	C-side 029
8. Wrap your troubles in dreams	C-side 029
9. All of me	C-side 029
10. Doctor Jazz	C-side 029
11. Up a lazy river	C-side 029
12. China boy	C-side 029
13. Do You Know what it means to miss New Orleans?	C-side 029
14. My blue heaven	C-side 029

Nova Scotia Jazz Band With Forrie Cairns

Mike Daly (cnt), John Burgess (clt, alto, ten, ldr), Duncan Finlay (bjo, gtr), Roy Percy (bs)
John Service (tbn 1, v -2), Forrie Cairns (clt - 3)
Recorded: Music Box, Edinburgh, September 6, 2010

1. Wabash blues (3)	C-Side 008
2. At the jazz band ball (1, 3)	C-Side 008
3. Sweet Lorraine (1)	C-Side 008
4. Five foot two, eyes of blue (1)	C-Side 008
5. Bye bye blackbird (3)	C-Side 008
6. Sweet Sue (3)	C-Side 008
7. When you're smiling (1,2)	C-Side 008
8. Wrap your troubles in dreams	C-Side 008
9. Chinatown, my Chinatown (1,3)	C-Side 008

Old Bailey And His Jazz Advocates

1. *Andrew Lauder (tpt), Archie Sinclair (tbn, voc, ldr), Jackie Graham (clt), Mike Hart (bjo), Forbes Laing (bs), Charlie Welsh (drms)*
Recorded: The Place Jazz Club, Edinburgh

Teddy bears picnic	not known
Beale Street blues	not known

2. *Andrew Lauder (tpt), Archie Sinclair (tbn, voc, ldr), Hamish McGregor (clt), Alex Shaw (pno), Mike Hart (bjo), Ronnie Rae (bs), Donald 'Chick' Murray (drms)*
Recorded: probably1966 as a track for the Edinburgh Students Charity Appeal

Hey, Look Me Over	not known

Old Bailey's Jazz Advocates
Complete With Bum Notes

Andrew Lauder (cnt, tpt), Sam Smith (tbn, voc-1), Hamish McGregor (clt, alto, bar, voc-2, ldr), Tom Finlay (pno), Mike Hart (bjo, gtr), Graham Blamire (bs), Donald 'Chick' Murray (drms)
Recorded: Craighall Studios, Edinburgh, February 10, 1980

1. When the midnight choo choo leaves for Alabam (2)	Salmet CS1094
2. Froggie Moore rag	Salmet CS1094
3. Carry me back to Old Virginia (1)	Salmet CS1094
4. Old man river	Salmet CS1094
5. Dapper Dan (2)	Salmet CS1094
6. Rent party blues	Salmet CS1094
7. Honeysuckle rose	Salmet CS1094
8. Teddy bears' picnic	Salmet CS1094
9. Yama Yama Man	Salmet CS1094
10. Sweet Georgia Brown	Salmet CS1094
11. Do you know what it means to miss New Orleans (1)	Salmet CS1094
12. Nobody's sweetheart (2)	Salmet CS1094

Dave Paxton

Dave Paxton (clt), others involved and recording date not known

1. Once in a while (?)	S&M?
2. Ole Miss (?)	S&M?

Whether or not this recording ever existed is open to debate. However, a reliable source has vouched for its existence. It is believed to be a 10" disc playing at either 45rpm or 33 1/3rpm.

Brian Robertson's Ellwyn Stompers
Almost Live at the Ellwyn
1. *Brian Robertson (cnt, voc), Eddie Hamilton (clt, voc-1), Graham Scott (pno), Andrew Mulhearn (bjo, tbn), Owen McDonald (bs) guests: Bob Busby (clt, alto), Brian Weld (bjo), Fred Murray (bs) Kenny McDonald (bs)*
Recorded: Ellwyn Hotel, Edinburgh, May 2002

1. Just a little while to stay here	band issue CD
2. A porter's love song to a chamber maid (1)	band issue CD
3. Love letters in the sand	band issue CD
4. Ole Miss rag	band issue CD
5. What a friend we have in Jesus	band issue CD
6. What the Lord has done for me	band issue CD
7. One sweet letter from you	band issue CD
8. Swannee River	band issue CD
9. Smiles	band issue CD
10. St Philips Street breakdown	band issue CD
11. Let me call you sweetheart	band issue CD
12. Frankie and Johnnie	band issue CD
13. Now is the hour	band issue CD

Brian Robertson's Forth River Ragtimers
Down In Honky Tonk Town
Brian Robertson (cnt) Alan Quinn (tbn), George Gilmour (clt), Graham Scott (pno), Brian Weld (bjo), Bill Brydon (bs), Kenny Milne (drms)
Recorded: Edinburgh, April 2000

1. Down in honky tonk town	band issue CD
2. South	band issue CD
3. Bye and bye	band issue CD
4. Exactly like you	band issue CD
5. Panama	band issue CD
6. Precious Lord, lead me on	band issue CD
7. Barefoot boy	band issue CD
8. Lord, Lord, Lord	band issue CD
9. Smiles	band issue CD
10. The old rugged cross	band issue CD
11. Dinah	band issue CD
12. Ballin' the jack	band issue CD
13. Play the blues for me	band issue CD
14. The curse of an aching heart	band issue CD
15. Now is the hour	band issue CD

Climax Rag

Brian Robertson (cnt) Alan Quinn (tbn), George Gilmour (clt), Graham Scott (pno), Brian Weld (bjo), Bill Brydon (bs), Kenny Milne (drms)
Recorded: Edinburgh, March 2002

1. Bourbon Street parade	band issue CD
2. Climax rag	band issue CD
3. Up a lazy river	band issue CD
4. When you wore a tulip	band issue CD
5. In the sweet bye and bye	band issue CD
6. You do something to me	band issue CD
7. June night	band issue CD
8. Only a look	band issue CD
9. Yes, yes in your eyes	band issue CD
10. Out of nowhere	band issue CD
11. Beale Street blues	band issue CD
12. Papa Dip	band issue CD
13. Put on your old grey bonnet	band issue CD

Thriller Rag

Brian Robertson (cnt) Alan Quinn (tbn), George Gilmour (clt), Graham Scott (pno), Brain Weld (bjo), Bill Brydon (bs), Kenny Milne (drms)
Recorded: Edinburgh, March 2003

1. Thriller rag	band issue CD
2. Ole Miss rag	band issue CD
3. When somebody thinks you're wonderful	band issue CD
4. Jealous	band issue CD
5. Dallas blues	band issue CD
6. Lead me Saviour	band issue CD
7. Moose march	band issue CD
8. Melancholy blues	band issue CD
9. In the upper garden	band issue CD
10. Gatemouth	band issue CD
11. Lonesome road	band issue CD
12. Underneath the sheltering palms	band issue CD
13. Oh! you beautiful doll	band issue CD

One Sweet Letter From You
4. *Brian Robertson (cnt), John Arthur (tbn), Eddie Hamilton (clt), Graham Scott (pno), Brian Weld (bjo), Kenny McDonald (bs), Roy Dunnett (drms)*
Recorded: Edinburgh, January 2009

1. Cakewalking babies	band issue CD
2. Buddy's habit	band issue CD
3. Samantha	band issue CD
4. Weary blues	band issue CD
5. Goin' home	band issue CD
6. One sweet letter from you	band issue CD
7. The postman's lament	band issue CD
8. Yaaka hula hickey dula	band issue CD
9. Somebody stole my gal	band issue CD
10. He touched me	band issue CD
11. At a Georgia camp meting	band issue CD
12. Sister Kate	band issue CD
13. It's nobody's fault but mine	band issue CD

Bill Salmond's Louisiana Ragtime Band
1976
Simon Carlyle (tbn), Dave Paxton (clt), Graham Scott (pno), Bill Salmond (bjo, ldr), Willie Mack (bs), Richard Lord (drms)
Recorded: Edinburgh, c1976

1. In the shade of the old apple tree	band issue MC

2. I'm putting all my eggs in one basket   band issue MC
3. Please don't talk about me when I'm gone

                                           band issue MC
4. Alexander's Ragtime Band   band issue MC
5. Marie   band issue MC
6. Tin Roof blues   band issue MC
7. Milneburg joys   band issue MC
8. At a Georgia camp meeting   band issue MC
9. Lady be good   band issue MC
10. Margie (faded out)   band issue MC

In The Shade Of The Old Apple Tree

Simon Carlyle (tbn), Dave Paxton (clt), Graham Scott (pno), Bill Salmond (bjo, ldr), Willie Mack (bs), Ian Forde (drms)
Recorded: Edinburgh, September 23, 1976
1. In the shade of the old apple tree   Dunedin DLP761
2. Sobbin' blues   Dunedin DLP761
3. Ciribiribin   Dunedin DLP761
4. See See rider blues   Dunedin DLP761
5. Ting a ling   Dunedin DLP761
6. Lucky me   Dunedin DLP761
7. Solitude   Dunedin DLP761
8. Buddy's habit   Dunedin DLP761
9. I double dare you   Dunedin DLP761

Way Down Yonder In New Orleans

Brian Robertson (cnt), Bob Craig (tbn), Dave Paxton (clt), Graham Scott (pno), Bill Salmond (bjo, ldr), Graham Blamire (bs), Mac Rae (drms)
Recorded: St James' Church, Portobello, date not known

1. Panama   band issue MC
2. Oh! You beautiful doll   band issue MC
3. Working man blues   band issue MC
4. Give me your telephone number   band issue MC
5. Big lip blues   band issue MC
6. Way down yonder in New Orleans   band issue MC
7. Together   band issue MC
8. Mabel's dream   band issue MC
9. Sweet Georgia Brown   band issue MC
10. Old fashioned love   band issue MC
11. C jam blues   band issue MC

Linger Awhile

Kenny Milne (tpt), Dave Paxton (clt), Graham Scott (pno), Bill Salmond (bjo, ldr), Tony Sargent (bs), Eric Jamieson (drms)
Recorded: Palladium Recording Studios, Edinburgh, 1980

1. Four leaf clover	Dunedin DLP801
2. Buddy's habit	Dunedin DLP801
3. St. James Infirmary	Dunedin DLP801
4. Lily of the valley	Dunedin DLP801
5. China boy	Dunedin DLP801
6. Untitled blues	Dunedin DLP801
7. Rebecca	Dunedin DLP801
8. Up jumped the devil	Dunedin DLP801
9. Linger awhile	Dunedin DLP801

Edinburgh International Jazz Festival, 1980

Kenny Milne (tpt), Dave Paxton (clt), Graham Scott (pno), Bill Salmond (bjo, ldr), Tony Sargent (bs), Eric Jamieson (drms)
Recorded: Edinburgh, 1980

1. Anytime	CPLP038

Other recordings on this LP by other bands

Live

Alan Quinn (tbn, voc), George Gilmour (clt), Graham Scott (pno), Bill Salmond (bjo, ldr), Graham Blamire (bs), Eric Jamieson (drms)
Recorded: New Orleans Express, Haymarket Bar, Edinburgh, December 18, 1993

1. On the road to home sweet home	band issue MC
2. Red Wing	band issue MC
3. Burgundy Street blues	band issue MC
4. Beautiful dreamer	band issue MC
5. Climax rag	band issue MC
6. Original Dixieland one-step	band issue MC
7. Big Chief Battle Axe	band issue MC
8. Mazie	band issue MC
9. St Philips Street breakdown	band issue MC
10. Wait 'till the sun shines Nellie	band issue MC
11. Ice cream	band issue MC

1995

Alan Quinn (tbn ,voc), George Gilmour (clt), Graham Scott (pno), Bill Salmond (bjo, ldr), Bill Brydon (bs), Eric Jamieson (drms)

Recorded: Craigmillar Arts Centre, Edinburgh, March 25, 1995

1.	Ting-a-ling	band issue MC
2.	Down by the old mill stream	band issue MC
3.	South	band issue MC
4.	When you and I were young Maggie	band issue MC
5.	Muskrat ramble	band issue MC
6.	High society	band issue MC
7.	In the sweet bye and bye	band issue MC
8.	I'll always be in love with you	band issue MC
9.	Savoy blues	band issue MC
10.	Clarinet marmalade	band issue MC
11.	Rambling Rose	band issue MC
12.	Willie the Weeper	band issue MC
13.	He touched me	*unissued*
14.	Exactly like you (take 1)	*unissued*
15.	Exactly like you (take 2)	*unissued*

All I Do Is Dream Of You

Alan Quinn (tbn, voc), George Gilmour (clt), Graham Scott (pno), Bill Salmond (bjo, ldr), Bill Brydon (bs), Eric Jamieson (drms)

Recorded: Queen's Hotel, Keswick, May 15, 1997

1.	Original Dixieland one-step	PEK Sound PKC-078
2.	Only a look	PEK Sound PKC-078
3.	High society	PEK Sound PKC-078
4.	I can't escape from you	PEK Sound PKC-078
5.	I'm alone because I love you	PEK Sound PKC-078
6.	When I leave this world behind	PEK Sound PKC-078
7.	All I do is dream of you	PEK Sound PKC-078
8.	Let me call you sweetheart	PEK Sound PKC-078
9.	Hold me	PEK Sound PKC-078
10.	Fidgety feet	PEK Sound PKC-078
11.	The first choice	PEK Sound PKC-078

Listen to the Mocking Bird

Alan Quinn (tbn, voc), George Gilmour (clt), Graham Scott (pno), Bill Salmond (bjo, ldr), Bill Brydon (bs), Taff Lloyd (drms)
Recorded: Labour Club, Keswick, May 17, 1998

1. Over the waves	PEK Sound PKCD-109
2. Clarinet marmalade	PEK Sound PKCD-109
3. He touched me	PEK Sound PKCD-109
4. What the Lord has done for me	PEK Sound PKCD-109
5. Franklin Street blues	PEK Sound PKCD-109
6. Don't go 'way nobody	PEK Sound PKCD-109
7. Listen to the mocking bird	PEK Sound PKCD-109
8. Cherry Blossom Lane	PEK Sound PKCD-109
9. Algiers strut	PEK Sound PKCD-109
10. June night	PEK Sound PKCD-109
11. Love	PEK Sound PKCD-109
12. Willie the Weeper	PEK Sound PKCD-109

Memories of George Lewis

Alan Quinn (tbn, voc), George Gilmour (clt), Graham Scott (pno), Bill Salmond (bjo, ldr), Bill Brydon (bs), Kenny Milne (drms)
Recorded: Keswick Jazz Festival, May 21, 2000

1. Collegiate	PEK Sound PKCD-153
2. My life will be sweeter some day	PEK Sound PKCD-153
3. 'Neath Hawaiian skies	PEK Sound PKCD-153
4. Burgundy Street blues	PEK Sound PKCD-153
5. The streets of the city	PEK Sound PKCD-153
6. Panama	PEK Sound PKCD-153
7. Mazie	PEK Sound PKCD-153
8. Rambling Rose	PEK Sound PKCD-153
9. There's yes, yes in your eyes	PEK Sound PKCD-153
10. Climax rag	PEK Sound PKCD-153
11. Ol' Miss rag	PEK Sound PKCD-153
12. Abide with me	PEK Sound PKCD-153
13. Ice cream	PEK Sound PKCD-153

Plays Hymns And Spirituals

Alan Quinn (tbn, voc), George Gilmour (clt), Graham Scott (pno), Bill Salmond (bjo, ldr), Bill Brydon (bs), Kenny Milne (drms)

Recorded: The Fairmile Inn, Edinburgh, March 22, 2002

1. Just a little while to stay here	Dunedin CD002
2. The old rugged cross	Dunedin CD002
3. Lord, Lord, Lord	Dunedin CD002
4. Lead me Saviour	Dunedin CD002
5. His eye is on the sparrow	Dunedin CD002
6. The streets of the city	Dunedin CD002
7. My life will be sweeter some day	Dunedin CD002
8. Nobody's fault but mine	Dunedin CD002
9. Only a Look	Dunedin CD002
10. Lily of the valley	Dunedin CD002
11. Abide with me	Dunedin CD002

Ballin' The Jack

Alan Quinn (tbn, voc), George Gilmour (clt), Graham Scott (pno), Bill Salmond (bjo, ldr), Bill Brydon (bs), Kenny Milne (drms)

Recorded: The Fairmile Inn, Edinburgh, April 8, 2003

1. Someday (you'll want me to want you)	
	Dunedin CD0403
2. The waltz you saved for me / Mobile stomp	
	Dunedin CD0403
3. You brought a new kind of love to me	
	Dunedin CD0403
4. When the swallows come back to Capistrano	
	Dunedin CD0403
5. A shanty in old shanty town	Dunedin CD0403
6. Moonglow	Dunedin CD0403
7. Roll along, prairie moon	Dunedin CD0403
8. Blue again	Dunedin CD0403
9. I can't believe that you're in love with me	
	Dunedin CD0403
10. Save your sorrow for tomorrow	Dunedin CD0403
11. I surrender dear	Dunedin CD0403
12. Ballin' the jack	Dunedin CD0403
13. Rose Room	Dunedin CD0403
14. Beautiful Ohio	Dunedin CD0403

Amazing Grace

Alan Quinn (tbn, voc), George Gilmour (clt), Graham Scott (pno), Bill Salmond (bjo, ldr), Bill Brydon (bs), Kenny Milne (drms)
Recorded: Edinburgh, March 31, 2004

1. Down by the riverside	Dunedin CD0304
2. This little light of mine	Dunedin CD0304
3. What a friend we have in Jesus	Dunedin CD0304
4. Lord, Lord, Lord	Dunedin CD0304
5. Silver Bells	Dunedin CD0304
6. Amazing Grace	Dunedin CD0304
7. Walking with the King	Dunedin CD0304
8. Precious Lord, lead me on	Dunedin CD0304
9. He touched me	Dunedin CD0304
10. In the sweet bye and bye	Dunedin CD0304
11. Do Lord	Dunedin CD0304

Let the Rest of the World Go By

Alan Quinn (tbn, voc), George Gilmour (clt), Graham Scott (pno), Bill Salmond (bjo, ldr), Bill Brydon (bs), Kenny Milne (drms)
Recorded: no details

1. Running wild	Dunedin CD0605
2. This love of mine	Dunedin CD0605
3. Let the rest of the world go by	Dunedin CD0605
4. When we danced at the Mardi Gras	
	Dunedin CD0605
5. Aura Lee	Dunedin CD0605
6. The very thought of you	Dunedin CD0605
7. Move the body over	Dunedin CD0605
8. When the blue of the night	Dunedin CD0605
9. Washington and Lee swing	Dunedin CD0605
10. Everybody loves somebody sometime	
	Dunedin CD0605
11. Sensation	Dunedin CD0605

Scottish Jazz Advocates
Live At The Caley

Andrew Lauder (cnt), Sam Smith (tbn, voc-2), Jack Graham (clt, alto), Hamish McGregor (clt, alto, bar, voc-3, co-ldr), Tom Finlay (pno), Mike Hart (bjo, gtr, co-ldr), Graham Blamire (bs), Donald 'Chick' Murray (drms), Fiona Duncan (voc –1)
Recorded: Caledonian Hotel, Edinburgh, c1980

1. Harlem bound	Sacramento Jazz SJS-17
2. Savoy blues	Sacramento Jazz SJS-17
3. Blues my naughtie sweetie gives to me (1)	
	Sacramento Jazz SJS-17
4. Big Bill	Sacramento Jazz SJS-17
5. Louisian-I-Ay (2)	Sacramento Jazz SJS-17
6. Cakewalking babies (1)	Sacramento Jazz SJS-17
7. Chimes blues	Sacramento Jazz SJS-17
8. Keeping out of mischief	Sacramento Jazz SJS-17
9. Cornet chop suey	Sacramento Jazz SJS-17
10. Hard Hearted Hannah (1)	Sacramento Jazz SJS-17
11. Basin Street blues (3)	Sacramento Jazz SJS-17

Transatlantic Stomp

Andrew Lauder (tpt, cnt), Sam Smith (tbn), Jackie Graham (clt, alto), Hamish McGregor (clt, alto, bar, co-ldr), Tom Finlay (pno), Mike Hart (bjo, gtr, co-ldr), Graham Blamire (bs), Ronnie Rae (bs-1), Donald 'Chick' Murray (drms), Dave Swanson (drms-2), Fiona Duncan (voc –3)
Recorded: Craighall Studios, Edinburgh, February 14, 1980

1. African Queen	Sacramento Jazz SJS-22
2. Sidewalk blues	Sacramento Jazz SJS-22
3. Fine brown frame (2,3)	Sacramento Jazz SJS-22
4. Memphis blues	Sacramento Jazz SJS-22
5. Russian rag (2)	Sacramento Jazz SJS-22
6. Mention my name in Sheboygen (3)	
	Sacramento Jazz SJS-22
7. Drop Me Off in Harlem	Sacramento Jazz SJS-22
8. Black bottom stomp	Sacramento Jazz SJS-22
9. I'm coming Virginia	Sacramento Jazz SJS-22
10. Some of these days (3)	Sacramento Jazz SJS-22
11. Snag it	Sacramento Jazz SJS-22
12. Papa Dip	Sacramento Jazz SJS-22

Andrew Lauder (tpt), Johnny McGuff (tbn), Hamish
McGregor (clt, alto, bagpipes), Tom Finlay (pno), Mike Hart
(bjo, gtr), Graham Blamire(bs), Donald Murray (drms), John
McGlynn (drms -1), Ronnie Rae (bs -1)
Recorded: Craighall Studios, Edinburgh, March 3, 1984

All in Perfect Working Order

1. Georgia swing	Teuchter Records
2. Between the devil and the deep blues sea (1)	
	Teuchter Records
3. Kansas City Man blues	Teuchter Records
4. If you were the only girl in the world	
	Teuchter Records
5. Get out of here	Teuchter Records
6. The Chant	Teuchter Records
7. I'm slappin' 7th avenue with the sole of my shoe	
	Teuchter Records
8. Yellow Dog blues	Teuchter Records
9. Moten swing	Teuchter Records
10. Ain't misbehavin'	Teuchter Records
11. Black Bear stomp (1)	Teuchter Records

Jazz at the Connecticut Traditional Jazz Club

*Andrew Lauder (cnt), Johnny McGuff (tbn), Hamish McGregor
(clt, alto, bar, co-ldr), Tom Finlay (pno), Mike Hart (bjo, co-ldr),
Ronnie Rae (bs), John McGlynn (drms)*
Recorded: Stamford, Connecticut, June 2, 1984

1. Ostrich walk	SLP20
2. Drop me off in Harlem	SLP20

Other material on this LP by other bands

Archie Semple And His Capitol Jazzmen

*Alex Welsh (cnt), Dave Keir (tbn), Archie Semple (clt, ldr),
Drew Landells (pno), Jimmy Mooney (gtr), Pat Malloy(?) (bs),
George Crockett (drms)*
Recorded: Edinburgh, May 4, 1952

1. New Orleans masquerade (take 1)	S&M LP unnumbered
2. New Orleans masquerade (take 2)	S&M unissued

3. Farewell blues	S&M LP unnumbered
4. South	S&M LP unnumbered
5. At a Georgia camp meeting	S&M LP unnumbered
6. Clark and Randolph blues	S&M LP unnumbered
7. Who's sorry now	S&M LP unnumbered
8. Jenny's Ball	S&M LP unnumbered
9. Singing the blues	S & M 1005
10. Who's sorry now	S & M 1005

Alex Welsh (cnt), Dave Keir (tbn), Archie Semple (clt, ldr), Drew Landells (pno), Jimmy Mooney (gtr), Pat Malloy(?) (bs), George Crockett (drms), David Mylne (narrator)
Broadcast: BBC Scottish Home Service, Queen Street Studios, Edinburgh, May 9, 1952

1. Chicago	acetate
2. Royal Garden blues	acetate
3. Mississippi mud	acetate
4. Farewell blues	acetate
5. Singing the blues	acetate
6. There'll be some changes made	acetate
7. Clarke and Randolph blues	acetate
8. After you've gone	acetate

This recording has never been issued commercially although it has had wide distribution on both acetate and cassette among collectors.
The dates shown here are the correct broadcast dates and have been verified by Tom Lowrie who has the original ticket stubs from the concert, which show dates and times

Spirits Of Rhythm
1. *Fraser Gauld (tpt), Jack Weddell (tbn, voc), Ian Boyter (clt, ten), Violet Milne (p, ldr), Brian Weld (bjo),), Willie Mack (bs), Kenny Milne (drms,)*
Recorded: Edinburgh, April 1,1984

3. Big Chief Battle Axe	Spirit LP
4. Let's get drunk and truck	Spirit LP
5. Darkness on the Delta	Spirit LP
6. Sweetheart of Sigma Chi	Spirit LP
7. Red Wing	Spirit LP

Sam Lee (ten, voc-1), Fraser Gauld (tpt), Jack Weddell (tbn, voc-2), Ian Boyter (clt, alto), Violet Milne (pno, ldr), Brian Weld (bjo), Robin Galloway (bs), Willie Mack (bs-3), Kenny Milne (drms, voc-4)
Recorded: Hart Street Studios, Edinburgh, April 7,1984

Everybody Happy?
1. St Louis blues (1)	Spirit LP/CD
2. Dinah (3)	Spirit LP/CD
3. Panama rag (take 1)	Spirit LP/CD
4. Rent party blues	Spirit LP/CD
5. Mr Sandman (2)	Spirit CD
6. Top hat (3)	Spirit CD
7. I love you so much it hurts (1)	Spirit LP/CD
8. My blue heaven (1)	Spirit LP/CD
9. The world is waiting for the sunrise	Spirit CD
10. Caledonia (1)	Spirit LP/CD, J'n'J CD001
11. Exactly like you (3)	Spirit LP/CD
12. Louisian-I-Ay (4)	Spirit CD
13. I can't give you anything but love baby (1)	
	Spirit LP/CD
14. Panama rag (take 2)	Spirit CD
15. Chinatown, my Chinatown	Spirit LP/CD

This recording was originally issued in LP format but was subsequently reissued as a CD with previously unreleased material included (Spirit CD)

Edinburgh Jazz Festival 1986
Fraser Gauld (tpt), Ian Boyter (ten), Violet Milne (pno, ldr), Brian Weld (bjo), Robin Galloway (bs), Kenny Milne (drms)
Recorded: Edinburgh 1986

1. If I had my life to live over   1986   Edinburgh   Jazz Festival tape

Other material on this tape features different bands

Ascona Jazz Festival
Fraser Gauld (tpt), Ian Boyter (ten), Violet Milne (pno, ldr),
Brian Weld (bjo), Robin Galloway (bs), Kenny Milne (drms)
Recorded: Ascona, July 1986

1. Red Wing   FNOM (It) 936

Other material on this LP features different bands

Jazz Hot and Groovy
*Dave Strutt (tpt, voc-1), Jack Weddell (tbn, voc-2), Ian Boyter
(clt, alto, ten), Violet Milne (pno, ldr), Brian Weld (bjo), Roy
Percy (bs), Kenny Milne (drms)*
Recorded: Southside Snooker hall, May 6, 1992

1. Dream man (1)	Spirit MC
2. Moose march	Spirit MC
3. West End blues	Spirit MC
4. When we danced at the Mardi Gras	Spirit MC
5. Lover (2)	Spirit MC
6. Bogalousa strut	Spirit MC
7. Just a little while to stay here	Spirit MC
8. Moppin' and boppin'	Spirit MC
9. When your hair has turned to silver (1)	Spirit MC
10. Whenever you're lonesome	Spirit MC
11. Bugle call rag	Spirit MC
12. Magic is the moonlight (2)	Spirit MC
13. June night (1)	Spirit MC
14. Mama's gone, goodbye	Spirit MC
15. Love nest (1)	Spirit MC
16. Boogie in C	Spirit MC
17. Rockin' (1)	Spirit MC

At Nobles Bar
*Jack Weddell (tbn, voc-1), Ian Boyter (clt, alto), Violet Milne
(pno, ldr), Beverley Knight (bjo), Roy Percy (bs), Kenny Milne
(drms, voc-2)*
Recorded: Nobles Bar, Leith during 1995

1. Oh, how I miss you tonight (2)	Spirit MC
2. Shine (1)	Spirit MC

3. Trust in me (1)	Spirit MC
4. If I had my life to live over (1)	Spirit MC
5. South of the Border (1)	Spirit MC
6. Chinatown, my Chinatown	Spirit MC
7. Once in a while	Spirit MC
8. Walking with the King (1)	Spirit MC
9. Georgia (1)	Spirit MC
10. Weary blues	Spirit MC
11. On the road to home sweet home	Spirit MC
12. Original Dixieland one-step	Spirit MC

Caledonia
Finlay Milne (tpt, voc-1), Ian Boyter (clt, alto, ten), Violet Milne (pno, ldr), Nigel Porteous (bjo), Roy Percy (bs), Kenny Milne (drms, voc-2)
Recorded: Borrowdale Inn, Keswick, May 19, 1996

1. I can't escape from you	PEK Sound PKC-056
2. Bogalousa strut	PEK Sound PKC-056
3. Darkness on the Delta	PEK Sound PKC-056
4. Panama	PEK Sound PKC-056
5. Blues for Borrowdale	PEK Sound PKC-056
6. Clarinet marmalade	PEK Sound PKC-056
7. Muskrat Ramble (1)	PEK Sound PKC-056
8. Cal'donia (1)	PEK Sound PKC-056
9. Crying my heart out for you	PEK Sound PKC-056
10. Dinah (2)	PEK Sound PKC-056
11. Tin Roof blues	PEK Sound PKC-056
12. The same old love	PEK Sound PKC-056
13. Moppin' And boppin'	PEK Sound PKC-056
14. Bugle boy march	PEK Sound PKC-056

Moppin' And Boppin'
Dave Strutt (tpt, voc-1), Ian Boyter (clt, alto, ten, hca), Violet Milne (pno, ldr), Nigel Porteous (bjo), Dizzy Jackson (bs), Kenny Milne (drms, voc-2)
Recorded: Edinburgh, May 1998 & January 1999

1. Mardi Gras in New Orleans (1)
Spirit CD005, J'nJ CD001

2. Absolutely, positively (1)	Spirit CD005

3. Cryin' my heart out for you	Spirit CD005
4. Just a little while to stay here (2)	Spirit CD005
5. My fate is in your hands (1)	Spirit CD005
6. The world is waiting for the sunrise	Spirit CD005
7. I owe it all to you (1)	Spirit CD005
8. Moppin' and boppin'	Spirit CD005, J'n'J CD 001
9. Someday you'll be sorry (1)	Spirit CD005
10. Travelling blues	Spirit CD005
11. See See rider (1)	Spirit CD005
12. I love you (1)	Spirit CD005
13. Indian Summer	Spirit CD005
14. Lonesome and sorry	Spirit CD005

Keswick Jazz Festival 2000

Clem Avery (tpt), Llew Hird (tbn, voc-1), Karl Hird (clt, ten), Ian Boyter (clt, ten), Violet Milne (pno, ldr), Dave Rae (bjo, voc-3), Dizzy Jackson (bs), Kenny Milne (drms)
Recorded: Calvert Trust, Keswick, May 19, 2000

1. Bugle boy march	*PEK Sound unissued*
2. Ole Miss rag	*PEK Sound unissued*
3. Old fashioned love	*PEK Sound unissued*
4. One sweet letter from you (2)	*PEK Sound unissued*
5. Big Chief Battle Axe	*PEK Sound unissued*
6. I want a little girl (1)	*PEK Sound unissued*
7. 2.19 blues (1)	*PEK Sound unissued*
8. Louisian-I-Ay	*PEK Sound unissued*
9. Moose march	*PEK Sound unissued*
10. South	*PEK Sound unissued*
11. Savoy blues	*PEK Sound unissued*
12. All the girls go crazy 'bout the way I walk (2)	
	PEK Sound unissued
13. Corrine, Corrina (1)	*PEK Sound unissued*
14. Swannee River	*PEK Sound unissued*
15. Canal Street blues	*PEK Sound unissued*
16. Bogalousa strut	*PEK Sound unissued*
17. Marie	*PEK Sound unissued*
18. Love songs of the Nile (1)	*PEK Sound unissued*
19. Running Wild	*PEK Sound unissued*
20. On the road to home sweet home	*PEK Sound unissued*
21. Royal Garden blues	*PEK Sound unissued*
22. Ice cream	*PEK Sound unissued*

*Alan Quinn (tbn), George Gilmour (clt), Violet Milne (pno, ldr),
Brian Weld (bjo), Fred Murray (bs), Kenny Milne (drms)*
Recorded: Edinburgh Jazz 'n' Jive Club, Edinburgh, August
14, 2009

1. Rose Room	J'n'J CD002
2. Hindustan	J'n'J CD002

Storyville Five
Edinburgh International Jazz Festival 1980
Donald McDonald (ten), Angus McDonald (tbn), Harald Vox
(bjo), Kenny McDonald (bs), Dennis Morton (drms)
Recorded: REL Studios, West Maitland Street, Edinburgh,
1980

1. Ice cream	CPLP 038

Other material on this recording by different bands

Swing 84
Live at the Cygnet
Dave Strutt (cnt, mel), Dick Lee (clt, saxes, rec), Martin Leys
(gtr, e-gtr), Johan Hoven (gtr), Jerry Forde (bs)
Recorded: Cygnet Jazz Cellar and Restaurant, Edinburgh,
July 31, 1984

1. Nuits de St. Germain des Pres	band issue MC
2. What is this thing called love?	band issue MC
3. Dream of you	band issue MC
4. Frans and Saskia	band issue MC
5. Nuages	band issue MC
6. Dinette	band issue MC
7. Rifftide	band issue MC
8. Crazy rhythm	band issue MC
9. Someday soon	band issue MC
10. Micro	band issue MC
11. Artillerie Lourde	band issue MC
12. Fleche d'or	band issue MC

Swing 86
Live at St John's
Dick Lee (rds), Martin Leys (gtr), John Russell (gtr), Jerry Forde (bs)
Recorded: 1986

1. Place de Bruckere	*band issue MC*
2. Jersey bounce	*band issue MC*
3. Port Carelle	*band issue MC*
4. September song	*band issue MC*
5. Brazil	*band issue MC*
6. Songe d'automne	*band issue MC*
7. I'll never smile again	*band issue MC*
8. I saw stars	*band issue MC*
9. Lentement Mademoiselle	*band issue MC*
10. Fleche d'or	*band issue MC*

Swing 98
Dick Lee (clt, saxes, rec), Phil Adams (e-gtr), John Russell (gtr, voc), Roy Percy (bs)
Recorded: 1998

1. Si tu me dis oui	Octavo Oct078
2. Jersey bounce	Octavo Oct078
3. Belleville	Octavo Oct078
4. Songe d'automne	Octavo Oct078
5. Caravan	Octavo Oct078
6. Minor swing	Octavo Oct078
7. Stompin' at Decca	Octavo Oct078
8. Fairweather	Octavo Oct078
9. Anniemation	Octavo Oct078
10. Mood indigo	Octavo Oct078

Swing 99
Get Happy
Dick Lee (clt, saxes, rec), Phil Adams (e-gtr), John Russell (gtr), Roy Percy (bs)
Recorded: 1999

1. Get happy	Octavo Oct CD009
2. Viper's dream	Octavo Oct CD009

3. Gee baby	Octavo Oct CD009
4. Meditation	Octavo Oct CD009
5. Troublant bolero	Octavo Oct CD009
6. Undecided	Octavo Oct CD009
7. Dream of you	Octavo Oct CD009
8. Linlithgow Suite	Octavo Oct CD009

      (a) Shank's pony
      (b) Bell I: Alma Maria
      (c) Equipoise
      (d) Bell II: Meg Duncan
      (e) Canal dream
      (f) Bell III: Saint Michael
      (g) The Loch
      (h) Train time

Swing 2002

Dick Lee (clt, b-clt, sop, rec), Brian Kellock (pno-1), Phil Adams (e-gtr), John Russell (gtr), Roy Percy (bs)
Recorded: 2002

1. Crazy rhythm	Octavo Oct CD2002
2. Cavalerie	Octavo Oct CD2002
3. Manor de mes reves	Octavo Oct CD2002
4. Del salle	Octavo Oct CD2002
5. China boy	Octavo Oct CD2002
6. Brazil	Octavo Oct CD2002
7. Nuages	Octavo Oct CD2002
8. Duke And Dukie	Octavo Oct CD2002
9. I'll see you in my dreams	Octavo Oct CD2002
10. Fleche d'or	Octavo Oct CD2002
11. West End blues (1)	Octavo Oct CD2002
12. Helensburgh Suite (1)	Octavo Oct CD2002

      Promenade
      Heavier than air
      Hill House
      Comet
      Hurricane

Swing 2005.

Dick Lee (clt, b-clt), Stephen Coutts (gtr), John Russell (gtr), Roy Percy (bs)
Recorded: Linlithgow Jazz Club, Burgh Halls, 2005

1. Limehouse blues	*band issue MC*
2. Moten swing	*band issue MC*
3. Minor swing	*band issue MC*
4. Nuages	*band issue MC*
5. One note samba	*band issue MC*
6. Jersey bounce	*band issue MC*
7. Honeysuckle rose	*band issue MC*
8. Melodie au crepuscule	*band issue MC*
9. Try a little tenderness	*band issue MC*
10. Moonglow	*band issue MC*
11. Troublant bolero	*band issue MC*
12. Stompin' At Decca	*band issue MC*
13. Paper moon	*band issue MC*
14. Caravan	*band issue MC*
15. Sweet Georgia Brown	*band issue MC*
16. Babik	*band issue MC*

Swing 2009

Dick Lee (clt, b-clt, sop, rec), Brian Kellock (pno), Stephen Coutts (gtr, e-gtr), John Russell (gtr), Roy Percy (bs)
Recorded: Dollar Academy Concert Hall, 2009

1. Crazy rhythm	Birnam LCR009
2. Moten swing	Birnam LCR009
3. Limehouse blues	Birnam LCR009
4. Body and soul	Birnam LCR009
5. Brazil	Birnam LCR009
6. Honeysuckle rose	Birnam LCR009
7. Seven come eleven	Birnam LCR009
8. Solitude	Birnam LCR009
9. Liza	Birnam LCR009
10. Caravan	Birnam LCR009
11. Try a little tenderness	Birnam LCR009
12. How high the moon	Birnam LCR009
13. Babik	Birnam LCR009